Contemporary
British Politics

Also by **Bill Coxall** *and* **Lynton Robins**
and published by Macmillan

BRITISH POLITICS SINCE THE WAR

3rd edition

Contemporary British Politics

Bill Coxall
and
Lynton Robins

First edition 1989
Reprinted four times
Second edition 1994
Reprinted twice
Third edition 1998

Published by
MACMILLAN PRESS LTD
Houndmills, Basingstoke, Hampshire RG21 6XS
and London
Companies and representatives
throughout the world

ISBN 0–333–73243–X

A catalogue record for this book is available from the British Library.

This book is printed on paper suitable for recycling and made from fully managed and sustained forest sources

10   9   8   7   6   5   4   3   2   1
07 06 05 04 03 02 01 00 99 98

Printed in Great Britain by
T. J. International Ltd

To **Hazel** and **Vivien**

Contents

List of figures, tables and boxes

Tables

Boxes

Preface to the third edition

The third edition of *Contemporary British Politics* retains the aims of preceding editions to discuss political institutions and political issues together and to locate the discussion within its historical, ideological, social, economic and cultural context. However, whilst retaining the approach and most of the structure of the second edition, the authors have taken the opportunity of a new edition to incorporate some significant changes. Firstly, as well as being comprehensively revised and updated, the third edition contains many new features. These include: brief descriptions of key political concepts throughout each chapter (indicated in bold type in the index); substantial bullet point summaries highlighting the main themes at the end of chapters; brief annotated reading lists; more extensive student assignments; and greater attention both to the impact of the European Union on British politics and to comparisons between the British and other leading democratic systems of government in line with the developing subject core.

Secondly, we have sought to sharpen the focus of the book by rearranging the contents. Thus, there is a new Part 2 entitled 'Political Participation and Communication' whilst the brief Part 4 of the second edition is dropped. Of the two chapters it contained, a shortened version of the material in 'From Thatcher to Major' appears in chapter 2 of the new edition whilst 'Power in Britain' becomes Chapter 4. Part 2 contains a new chapter on 'Political participation' which includes material discussed under political culture in the second edition. The former Part 2, 'Institutions and the Political Process', becomes Part 3 with a new chapter on territorial government and politics combining material on Northern Ireland, Scotland and Wales previously discussed separately. The new Part 3 loses the chapters on parties, elections and voting behaviour (now separated into two chapters), pressure groups and the mass media, which are relocated in Part 2. Finally, Part 3 of the second edition becomes Part 4, in which the material on the Unions and Industrial Relations and on Housing which formed separate chapters in the second edition is now included in the chapters on Management of the Economy and Health and Welfare respectively.

We hope that the third edition of this book will continue to be of use to A/AS level, university, college and other students of British government and politics.

We would like to record our thanks to our publisher Steven Kennedy (once again) for his efficient and enthusiastic guidance of the book, to Houri Alavi (also of Macmillan) for her hard work on the text, to our anonymous readers for their comments on the final draft and to all the teachers who made suggestions for the improvement of the second edition. Thanks also to Carole Shaw and General Services at the Scraptoft campus of De Montfort University.

BILL COXALL
LYNTON ROBINS

Acknowledgements

The authors and publishers are grateful to the following for permission to use copyright material.

Ashgate, for Table 6.2, data from Curtice and Jowell (1995), 'The Sceptical Electorate', in R. Jowell et al. (eds) *British Social Attitudes – 14th Report*, p. 154.

The Economist, for Figures 2.1, 3.1, 24.1 and 30.2 from various issues of *The Economist*.

Express Newspapers, for Box 11.1, front page of *The Express*.

Guardian News Service Ltd, for Figures. 7.2–7.3, 11.2, 23.2, 24.2, 26.2–26.4, 27.1, 31.1–31.3, Box 20.6, Chapter 18, Assignment 2 from various issues of The *Guardian*; and Figure 29.2, Tables 8.5, 30.1 and Box 26.1 from various editions of *The Observer*.

The Controller of Her Majesty's Stationery Office, for Figure 20.1, Tables 3.4–3.6, 3.9, 11.1, 15.1, 20.1, 31.1–31.2 and Box 23.1, data and graphics from Civil Services Statistics, Treasury Statistics and Annual Abstracts of Statistics and the Office for National Statistics.

Macmillan Press Ltd, for Table 19.4 from Stoker (1991), *The Politics of Local Government*, p.36; and Tables 4.3–4.4, data from Moran (1989), *Politics and Society in Britain*, 2nd edn, pp. 163, 166.

News International Newspapers Ltd, for Figures 9.5, 18.2, Tables 9.3 and 9.6 from various issues of *The Times* and *The Sunday Times*.

Newspaper Publishing PLC, for Box 17.3, from *The Independent*, 14 March 1995.

The New Statesman, for Table 9.9, data by Kirsty Milne from *New Statesman*, 30 August 1996.

Oxford University Press, for Table 11.3 from Rush (1990), 'Conclusion' from Rush, ed., *Parliament and Pressure Politics*, Clarendon Press, p. 272; Tables 7.5–7.6, 9.1, from Kellner (1997), 'Why the Tories Were Trounced', *Parliamentary Affairs*, 50:4, pp. 621, 619, 627; and Table 11.2, modified data from Seymour-Ure (1997), 'Editorial Opinion in the National Press', *Parliamentary Affairs*, 50:4, pp. 590–1.

The Politics Association, for Table 10.2 from Baggott (1992), 'The Measurement of Change in Pressure Groups Politics', *Talking Politics*, 5:1, p.20; Table 16.6 from Cowley (1996–7), 'Men (and women) behaving badly? The Conservative Party since 1992', *Talking Politics*, 9:2, p. 9; Figure 22.2 from Birch (1990), *Talking Politics*, 2:3, p. 103; and Table 9.2 from Tapper and Bowles (1982), 'Working Class Tories', in L. Robins, ed., *Topics in British Politics*, p. 175.

Rex Features, for Box 11.1 and Figure 11.1, front pages of *The Sun*.

Routledge, for Table 20.2 from Klug, Starmer and Wier (1996), *The Three Pillars of Liberty*, p. 55; Figure 30.1 from Clarke (1988), 'The Policy-Making Process', in M. Smith, S. Smith and B. White, *British Foreign Policy*, Unwin Hyman, p. 86; and Figure 25.1, adapted from Harrison, Hunter and Pollit (1990), *The Dynamics of British Health Policy*, Unwin Hyman.

Solo Syndication, for Box 11.1, front page of *Daily Mail*.

Photographs and cartoons:
Martin Argles p. 493; David Austin p. 450; Patrick Blower pp. 366, 382, 383; Steven Caroll p. 21; Central Office of Information p. 116, 252; Peter Clarke p. 444; Ted Dewan p. 435; Kevin Lamarque p. 156; Murdo MacLeod p. 354; PA News p. 488; Popperfotto p. 132; Lynton Robins p. 277; David Simonds pp. 341, 343, 487, 506.

Every effort has been made to trace all the copyright holders but if any have been inadvertently overlooked the publishers will be pleased to make the necessary arrangement at the first opportunity.

List of abbreviations

ACPO   Association of Chief Police Officers
ALF   Animal Liberation Front
ALRA   Abortion Law Reform Association
AMS   Additional Member System
ANL   Anti-Nazi League
ARA   Anti-Racist Alliance
ARM   Activity and Resource Management
ASI   Adam Smith Institute
AV   Alternative Vote
BBC   British Broadcasting Corporation
BCCI   Bank of Credit and Commerce International
BCS   British Crime Survey
BEUC   European Bureau of Consumer Associates
BMA   British Medical Association
BNP   British National Party
BP   British Petroleum
BPPS   British Political Participation Survey
BSA   British Social Attitudes
BSE   Bovine Spongiform Encephalopathy ('Mad Cow Disease')
BUF   British Union of Fascists
CAG   Controller and Auditor-General
CAP   Common Agricultural Policy
CBI   Confederation of British Industry
CCO   Conservative Central Office
CCT   Compulsory Competitive Tendering
CFCs   Chlorofluorocarbons
CIA   Central Intelligence Agency
CID   Criminal Investigation Department
CIS   Commonwealth of Independent States
CLEAR   Campaign for Lead-Free Air
CLP   Constituency Labour Party
CND   Campaign for Nuclear Disarmament
COPA   Committee of Professional Agricultural Associates

COREPER   Committee of Permanent Representatives (of the EU)
CPAG   Child Poverty Action Group
CPGB   Communist Party of Great Britain
CPRE   Council for the Protection of Rural England
CPRS   Central Policy Review Staff
CPS   Crown Prosecution Service
CPS   Centre for Policy Studies
CRE   Commission for Racial Equality
CSSB   Civil Service Selection Board
CTC   City Technology College
DEA   Department of Economic Affairs
DoE   Department of the Environment
DES   Department of Education and Science
DHA   District Health Authority
DMU   Directly Managed Unit
DPP   Director of Public Prosecutions
DSC   Departmental Select Committee
DSS   Department of Social Security
DTI   Department of Trade and Industry
DUP   Democratic Unionist Party
EC   European Community
ECHR   European Court of Human Rights
ECSC   European Coal and Steel Community
ECU   European Currency Unit
EDM   Early Day Motion
EEA   European Economic Area
EEB   European Environmental Bureau
EEC   European Economic Community
EFTA   European Free Trade Association
EGO   Extra-Governmental Organisation
EMS   European Monetary System
EMU   Economic and Monetary Union
EOC   Equal Opportunities Commission
EP   European Parliament

ERM	Exchange Rate Mechanism	MAFF	Ministry of Agriculture, Food and Fisheries
ESC	Economic and Social Committee	MEP	Member of the European Parliament
ETUC	European Trade Union Confederation	MINIS	Management Information System for Ministers
EU	European Union	MLR	Minimum Lending Rate
FCO	Foreign and Commonwealth Office	MP	Member of Parliament
FEFC	Further Education Funding Council	NATO	North Atlantic Treaty Organisation
FHSA	Family Health Services Authority	NDPB	Non-Departmental Body
FIMBRA	Financial Intermediaries, Managers and Brokers Regulatory Association	NEB	National Enterprise Board
		NEC	National Executive Committee
		NEDC	National Economic Development Council
FMI	Financial Management Initiative	NF	National Front
FO	Foreign Office	NFU	National Farmers' Union
FoE	Friends of the Earth	NHS	National Health Service
FPTP	First Past The Post	NUM	National Union of Mineworkers
FSA	Financial Services Authority	OECD	Organisation for Economic Cooperation and Development
FSB	Final Selection Board		
GATT	General Agreement on Tariffs and Trade	OFFER	Office of Electricity
GCHQ	Government Communications Headquarters	OFGAS	Office of Gas Supply
		OFSTED	Office of Standards in Education
GDP	Gross Domestic Product	OFTEL	Office of Telecommunications
GLC	Greater London Council	OFWAT	Office of Water
GMS	Grant Maintained School	OMOV	One Member One Vote
GNP	Gross National Product	OPD	Overseas and Defence Committee (of the Cabinet)
GP	General (medical) Practitioner		
GREA	Grant-Related Expenditure Assessment	OPEC	Organisation of Petroleum Exporting Countries
HAT	Housing Action Trust	PAC	Public Accounts Committee
HMIC	Her Majesty's Inspectors of Constabulary	PBSR	Public Sector Borrowing Requirement
ICI	Imperial Chemical Industries	PCA	Parliamentary Commissioner For Administration
IEA	Institute for Economic Affairs		
IGC	Inter-Governmental Conference	PCA	Police Complaints Authority
ILP	Independent Labour Party	PESC	Public Expenditure Survey Committee
IMF	International Monetary Fund		
IMRO	Investment Management Regulatory Organisation	PFI	Private Finance Initiative
		PLP	Parliamentary Labour Party
INLA	Irish National Liberation Army	PM	Prime Minister
IPPR	Institute for Public Policy Research	PMQT	Prime Minister's Question Time
IRA	Irish Republican Army	PNC	Police National Computer
ITA	Independent Television Authority	PPS	Parliamentary Private Secretary
JIC	Joint Intelligence Committee	PQs	Parliamentary Questions
LA	Local Authority	PR	Proportional Representation
LEA	Local Education Authority	PROP	Preservation of the Rights of Prisoners
LEC	Local Enterprise Companies		
LMS	Local Management of Schools	PSIS	Permanent Secretaries Committee on Intelligence Services
LSE	London School of Economics		

QMV	Qualified Majority Voting	SWP	Socialist Workers' Party
Quango	Quasi-autonomous non-governmental organisation	TEC	Training and Enterprise Council
		TGWU	Transport and General Workers' Union
RAF	Royal Air Force		
RAP	Radical Alternatives to Prison	TUC	Trades Union Congress
RSPCA	Royal Society for the Prevention of Cruelty to Animals	UDA	Ulster Defence Association
		UDC	Urban Development Corporation
RUC	Royal Ulster Constabulary	UDP	Ulster Democratic Party
SAS	Special Air Service	UK	United Kingdom
SATs	Standard Assessment Tests	UN	United Nations
SCS	Senior Civil Service	UNICE	Union of Industrial and Employers' Confederations of Europe
SDP	Social Democratic Party		
SDLP	Social Democratic and Labour Party	USA	United States of America
SEA	Single European Act	USSR	Union of Soviet Socialist Republics
SF	Sinn Fein	UUP	Ulster Unionist Party
SIB	Security and Investments Board	UVF	Ulster Volunteer Force
SNP	Scottish National Party	VAT	Value Added Tax
SPUC	Society for the Protection of the Unborn Child	WARA	Wing Airport Resistance Association
		WRP	Workers' Revolutionary Party
STV	Single Transferable Vote	WRVS	Women's Royal Voluntary Service

PART 1

THE CONTEXT OF BRITISH POLITICS

CHAPTER **1** | # What is politics?

In seeking an understanding of the nature of politics we consider three themes:

1. The features of human society out of which the need for politics arises. We ask 'How is the need for politics related to social conflict and cooperation?'
2. Whether certain areas of life are inherently non-political. We ask: 'Do all social groups have a political aspect?' and 'What makes a disagreement political?'
3. The role of violence in politics. We ask: 'Is politics a particularly non-violent way of resolving disagreements or does it comprehend all methods including force?'

Finally, we examine the main features of liberal democracy as a political regime, noting in particular its provision for institutionalised disagreement and the peaceful transfer of power.

Interests, viewpoints and conflicts

Politics arises out of a basic feature of human social life: the fact of differing interests and viewpoints. Differences of material interest develop because we live in a world of scarcity, and not abundance. In a utopia, where objects of need and desire are as freely available as the air we breathe, there would be no problems because we could all have everything we wanted. The real world, however, is one of limited resources, which are always more or less unevenly divided. And this is true wherever we look, equally true of states within the world community and of individuals and social groups within each national community.

Of course, logically, no disagreement, let alone conflict, *need* flow from this situation if, for example, each individual, social group and state were perfectly satisfied with the distribution of international and national resources and were prepared to put up with shortage and inequality. In reality, however, few *are* content and the world we actually inhabit is one of competition, often severe, for scarce resources. Each individual or group can only get a larger share at the expense of everyone else. And it is this that creates the political problem – that of settling competing claims upon a limited economic product. Politics, it has been said, crudely but not inaccurately, is concerned with 'who gets what, when and how'. It is the arena where conflicts arising from such disagreements are fought out and the process whereby groups make collective decisions about them. Its role is to aggregate, adjust and settle (although it can never finally resolve) these conflicts. It has been an important aspect of the life of all societies that have existed in history and is likely to be an important part of all societies that will or might exist. It is an ineliminable characteristic of human existence.

The disagreements that lead to the need for politics arise from differences of viewpoint as well as economic conflicts. There are disagreements because customs, moralities and ultimate goals differ. These differences, in turn, may reflect divisions of class, religion and race. They are expressed in membership of a variety of social institutions – such as clubs, trade unions, business and professional associations, political parties and churches. For modern societies are not monolithic structures, but present, on the contrary, a very considerable diversity. Pluralism – of beliefs and social groupings – is a fact, and it is by means of politics that the disagreements which flow from this fact are either reconciled or fail to be reconciled. Many of these differences stem from those systems of opposed beliefs which we call *ideologies* – for example nationalism, liberalism, anarchism, communism and fascism. These belief systems – or ideologies – shape a great deal of political action in the modern world. However, differences which call for political solution may, and often do, arise on less exalted grounds than ideology. Opinions may differ about the *truth* of a proposition (statement, theory, hypothesis) depending on its degree of elaboration and complexity, and about the *merits* of a thing (person, institution, decision, action). Controversy occurs because of the frequent need to make judgements of fact without conclusive evidence and judgements of value without conclusive reasons. Disagreements and conflicts which may call for political resolution are expressed schematically in Figure 1.1.

None of this is meant to imply that disagreement is more common or intrinsic a feature of human communities than is agreement. Politics does not necessarily involve conflict. In fact, we do have many things in common with other members of the community we inhabit and we often agree with them. A shared nationality is perhaps the most significant factor, overriding differences of class and religion to bind members of the same territorial state together. Often, as we shall see, a considerable degree of consensus exists on the decision-making procedure, even if this is rarely complete, and also on the norms and values (political culture) that underpin the political system. Again, material interdependence is another source of identity of interest: we may not be able to agree on the relative worth in terms of financial reward of various occupations – of doctors, nurses, teachers, solicitors, miners and dustmen – only that these jobs are essential and that the community as a whole is poorer if one or the other fails to carry out its tasks properly.

To summarise, agreement or consensus may derive from the following factors:

- Shared national identity (i.e. membership of same 'tribe');
- Agreement on decision-making procedure, or constitution (i.e. on method for resolving differences);

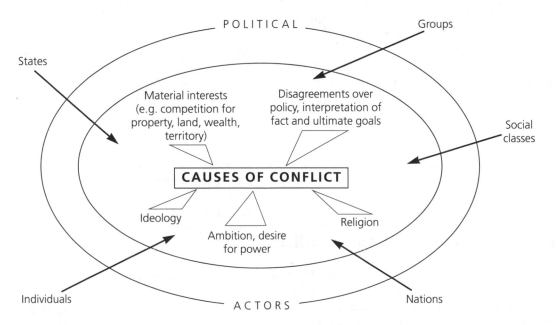

Figure 1.1 Causes of political conflict

- Sense of common interest and material interdependence (i.e. of being in the same 'boat' and needing to 'row together');
- Common political culture (i.e. shared political values and agreed ways of conducting political affairs).

To summarise the argument so far. **Politics** arises out of scarcity and diversity and the differences, disagreements and conflicts that emanate from these facts of human society. It is the arena in which such conflicts are expressed and the means by which they are resolved, resolution depending to a large extent on the possibility of agreement, cooperation and acting in concert, which are also features of human society. But this takes us only part of the way towards an understanding of the nature of politics. We now need to be more precise in specifying what is meant by such terms as 'groups', 'disagreement' and the 'expression' and 'settlement' of disagreements in this context. In particular, we need to ask three important questions. First, do all human social groupings have a political aspect and even if so do we nonetheless accord some groups a special status when we think about politics? Second, assuming that not all disagreements are political, by what criteria do we place a dispute in this category? What makes a controversy political'? Third, does politics involve a particular way of seeking to settle controversies – for example, by non-violent verbal persuasion – or can it include all methods of articulating and resolving conflicts?

Do all social groups possess politics?

In one sense, the answer to this question must be 'yes'. Politics affects all groups from the family to the world community. Thus, it is common practice to refer to subordinate groups in society as having a political element. As well as the politics of the family, we speak of the 'politics' of a school, of a company, of a civil service department. Equally, it is common practice to speak of international politics, to the politics of relations between states. Clearly, the well-established usage involved here goes beyond a mere manner of speaking. In fact, it has a twofold justification:

- Social groups at all levels contain structured patterns of relationships culminating in *decision-procedures*.
- These structures involve relationships of *authority, power* and *influence*, terms which are themselves pre-eminently political.

All social groups – from a trade union to the United Nations – possess a *decision-procedure* of some kind. Decision-procedure means a method of reaching collective decisions about what rules to have, how to change them once in existence, and how to apply them. This basic or fundamental rule which prescribes the form by which policy and executive decisions shall be taken is usually called the *constitution*. In a club, society or association, a constitution normally lays down such matters as the purposes of the organisation, the conditions of membership and, above all, the way in which its officials are to be selected. In other words, it will make provision for the government of the association. The need for *government* springs from the fact that in life decisions have constantly to be made and made now, not at some indefinite point in the future. Considerations of time and practicality have to be taken into account. Some matters are postponable; others, such as what action to take with regard to an unruly member, must be made quickly. Nor is it generally practicable to consult the entire membership on matters of urgency and routine. The constitution therefore designates who in an association may take such decisions and the procedures to be followed in reaching them. The 'politics' of the organisation may be said to consist in the attempts to influence the procedures and outcomes of its decision-making process.

All but the most random of social groupings are also political in another sense. There is *competition* to influence collective decisions. The phrase most commonly invoked to describe this feature of their existence is 'struggle for power'. The English political philosopher, Thomas Hobbes, writing in the seventeenth century, found the motive springs of this struggle in man's restlessness and ambition, in 'a

> **Politics:** the process by which issues affecting the collective existence of social groups are aggregated and settled (although not necessarily finally resolved).

general inclination of all mankind, a perpetual and restless desire of power after power, that ceaseth only in death'. There is competition both to achieve the positions of authority within a group or organisation and also among the ordinary members, employees and so on, to influence the possessors of authority. Indeed, the concept of power is so fundamental in the study of politics that it requires careful consideration at the outset. In particular, we need to distinguish three related terms which are often confused – 'authority', 'power' and 'influence'.

Authority, power and influence

Authority

The term **authority** is generally employed to designate the rightful use of power. It refers to power that is conferred by a rule and exercised in accordance with rules. This is pre-eminently the modern way of legitimating power. In contemporary advanced societies, the authority or *legitimacy* of governments derives from their being elected by a legal process (based on properly conducted elections) and exercising their rule according to law. Max Weber (1864–1920), the German sociologist, saw this kind of authority – *'legal-rational'* authority – as characterising the modern bureaucrat exercising power according to norms and laws, and contrasted it with *'traditional'* authority, which rests on an appeal to the ways and customs of the past, and *'charismatic'* authority, which derives from the compelling personal qualities of a single individual. A party secretary, a judge or a teacher, indeed anyone with an 'official' position within an organisation or society, may be said to be 'in authority' because a rule in a system of rules authorises each to give orders. So long as the authority continues to act within his legally defined sphere, those to whom he or she issues commands (however crudely or subtly) are required to obey. They may not, in fact, do so, but we should not regard their refusal to obey orders as justified unless the authority himself had abused or exceeded his jurisdiction. The word 'authority' in its legal sense refers not to any personal characteristics of its possessor but to the qualities of an *office.* When the term of office ends, the authority disappears. Of course, as already implied, a considerable part of the meaning of 'authority' is normative rather than descriptive. It refers to what should be, rather than what is, the case. A policeman who is overpowered by a criminal does not cease to be an authority. He simply lacks control over events. But it is at this point that we need a word other than 'authority' if we are to describe the realities of the situation adequately.

Power

The term **power**, to a much greater extent than 'authority', has an empirical and descriptive connotation. Power, in the words of Michael Oakeshott, is 'the ability to procure . . . a wished-for response in the conduct of another' although he adds that this effect can never be achieved with certainty because power as a social relationship must always contain an element of uncertainty and unpredictability. Indeed, against much in our common usage and ways of thought which suggests that power is a *possession* – as, for example, when we speak of the Chairman of ICI (Imperial Chemical Industries) as a powerful individual – it is worth emphasising the extent to which power is a *relationship*. Thus, whereas the concept of authority focuses upon the *entitlement* of an agent to issue commands, the word 'power' points to the way in which orders are received. It draws attention to whether they are actually obeyed. It constantly brings us back to the *consequences* of the competition for control which is always taking place.

Power and authority come together where commands can be described as not only rightful in the sense that the issuer is authorised to make them but also effective in the sense that they are carried out by those who receive them. But they move apart in cases where we say that although a group undoubtedly has *power* in the sense it can impose its

> **Authority**: the rightful use of power, the exercise of legitimate power.

> **Power**: the capacity to achieve desired goals by influencing the behaviour of others by means of peaceful persuasion, economic leverage or force or by a combination of these methods.

will on others even against opposition – as the Mafia, for example, can maim, kill and generally terrorise its enemies into submission – it has no *authority* to do so. This does not mean, of course, that the exercise of power necessarily involves force, although not infrequently it does. Equally, however, money, status, intelligence, education, knowledge, time, social connections and organisation can all influence group decisions and consequently may be identified as important political resources. Typically, in modern industrial societies, governments combine *authority* – the right to decide and act – and *power* – the capacity to compel obedience, if necessary by means of physical force.

Influence

To a very considerable extent in modern industrialised societies the exercise of power depends upon the ability to persuade people to behave in one way rather than another. The word **influence** is useful here because it directs attention to the *process* by which opinions are changed and behaviour altered. It points beyond a purely formal analysis of a structure of authority in terms of institutions and offices to the complex interplay between people within institutions and between institutions and groups outside. The politics of any institution appears rather like an iceberg even to those who try to follow it closely: nine-tenths of it lies beneath the surface, hidden from view. The term 'influence' directs attention to the ways in which collective decisions are moulded by a whole range of individuals and organisations other than – but of course not excluding – the formal authorities.

The concept of *pressure* entails the deliberate pursuit of influence by an individual or group. Attempts to influence the political process are often made by means of *pressure groups* which include a very wide range of economic, environmental, cultural and other organisations in Britain (see Chapter 10). In its broadest sense, *pressure* upon governments may come not only from pressure groups themselves but also from backbenchers in the government party, the opposition parties, the upper house, social institu-

| **Influence**: the ability to shape a decision or outcome often through the use of pressure. |

tions, old-established allies or partners within a treaty, and from 'events' (Figure 1.2).

It is now convenient to summarise these three terms. In the neat formulations of J. R. Lucas:

'Someone or some group has *authority* if it follows from his saying "Let X happen" that X ought to happen.'

'Someone or some group has *power* if it follows from his saying "Let X happen" that X does happen.'

'Someone or group has *influence* if the result of his saying "Let X happen" is that others say "Let X happen".' (Lucas, 1985; italics ours)

Politics, then, is about collective decision-making by groups, the political relationships of whose members are appropriately characterised by the terms 'authority', 'power' and 'influence'. But although this takes us some of the way towards an understanding of the subject, it does not take us far enough. Etymology enables us to complete the definition. 'Politics' derives from the Greek word *polis* meaning 'city-state'. This term had a broader significance than the modern word 'state': it meant state and church rolled into one. But the word has the merit in this context of directing attention to a dimension of meaning which has remained absolutely central to the word 'politics'. In its most fundamental sense, it relates to matters of state or the government of the state. Its concern, then, is not primarily with individuals in their private lives – as members of voluntary groups or in the family circle. As we have seen, these groups do have a political aspect as centres of power-relationships. But the major reference of politics is to individuals in their *public* relationships, as holding office in and seeking to influence affairs of *state*.

The state

The term 'state' refers to the supreme law-making authority within a particular geographical area. The concept first emerged in the sixteenth century to denote a novel form of association claiming sovereignty and exercising power within a given territory. Three characteristics of this new entity are of special importance here:

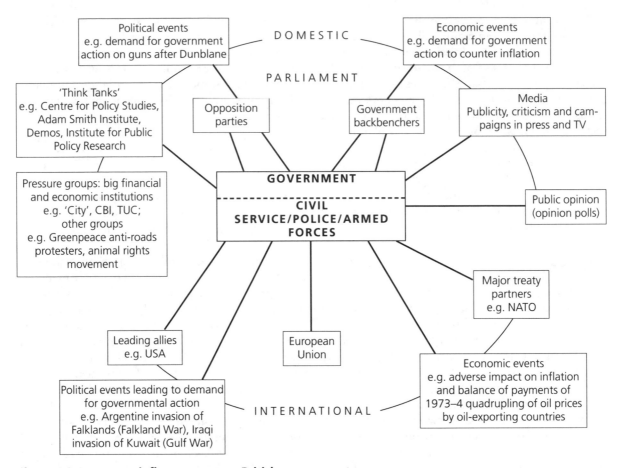

Figure 1.2 Important influences upon a British government

- The state is a *compulsory* form of association. Membership of a state, although not of a particular one, is obligatory. Indeed, although change of citizenship is normally possible, it is also difficult, and most people remain as citizens of the state in which they are born.
- It is *comprehensive*. It stands above and includes all partial associations and groups within its territory, giving or denying them rights of legal existence, regulating their powers over their members and helping to settle their disputes.
- The state is a *sovereign body* possessing supreme authority over its members. This authority includes extreme powers of coercion. Alone

among associations, the state may imprison us and, in the ultimate analysis, it may have the right to take our lives. Modern states conscript, punish and even put to death their citizens. Of course, the possession by the state of supreme sanctions over its members does not mean that it is the sole wielder of force in a particular community. It merely means that the state has the ultimate responsibility for deciding by whom force may be used (parents, schools, sportsmen) and to what degree, and for controlling and punishing the illegitimate users of violence (criminals, terrorists).

Quite clearly, these characteristics place the state in *a completely different category* from the other forms of association considered so far. Moreover, its possession of these characteristics transforms the significance of *those features which it shares* with voluntary and subordinate social groups and associations. To

---

Sovereignty: can mean both supreme legal authority and unchallengeable political power.

non-members, the decision-making procedures no less than the actual processes of the competition for authority, power and influence of a particular family, club, society, association, union or company are of no direct significance. But the constitution of the state and the struggle for power within it between individuals, groups and classes *must concern us all because we are all citizens.* Like it or not and whether we interest ourselves in public affairs or not, the nature of the regime and the outcome of the competition for power must affect us because of the non-voluntary, inclusive and sovereign nature of the state. We may choose whether or not to join a club; we cannot choose whether or not to be citizens of a state. In the modern world, there is no escaping it.

The comprehensive concept of the **state** needs to be distinguished from the more limited concept of **government**. The term 'government' refers to a specific set of individuals – ministry, administration or junta – which on a day-to-day basis directs the affairs of the state and exercises its authority. Whereas the term 'state' is comprehensive and embraces all law-making and law-enforcing agencies (government, legislature, judiciary, police, army), 'government' refers simply to the ruling body, whose power may be circumscribed by the legislature, judiciary, and so on.

The answer to our first question is now clear. Whereas partial associations have political aspects, such secondary, limited groupings are not usually our major concern when we think of 'politics'.

Rather, the term 'politics' normally centres upon decision-making within the only 'society' which touches us all – the community of communities – the state. In this central meaning, politics refers not just to those *actively involved* in public affairs on a day-to-day basis such as professional politicians and other full-time participants like pressure group

---

State: a compulsory, comprehensive association which is sovereign within a particular territorial boundary and has a monopoly of the legitimate use of force.

Government: the activity by which society is ruled on a day-to-day basis and the body responsible for such rule.

---

leaders, but also to all members of the state *as citizens.*

What makes a disagreement political?

The analysis to date – which has concentrated upon isolating a specifically 'political' element in the activities of social groups – also takes us far towards answering our second and third questions. Perhaps the best approach to the second problem – what makes a controversy political – is via a number of commonly expressed opinions. It is often said, for example, that religion, art, education or sport should either never become matters of political controversy or, in so far as they already are, should be taken out of political debate. The suggestion implicit in such remarks is that these spheres of human activity are inherently non-political. There is the further, pejorative, implication that they are sullied by being made 'political' since they naturally inhabit a finer, purer air than politics which is often stigmatised as 'dirty', an arena of unsavoury practices and lack of truth-telling, if not of downright lies, deceit and manipulation.

What should we make of this contention? Our principal comment must be that it appears to misunderstand the nature of politics. Politics has been defined as the process by which decisions affecting a society's collective existence are raised, discussed and settled, which means that, potentially, any matter at all may become a subject of public debate. Nothing exists in a watertight compartment sealed off from the political arena. Many people criticise sporting boycotts – for example, preventing cricketers from playing in South Africa before the ending of apartheid there – for (wrongly, in their view) bringing politics into sport. But politics is already in sport: athletes train with facilities provided by governments. The gesture of withdrawing from sporting contacts as a sign of disapproval of a country's policy (apartheid in South Africa) may be criticised for being unfair to athletes but not for politicising the inherently unpolitical.

This does not mean that it is not to be regretted when activities like athletics or cricket become the means of making political gestures, weapons in the international rivalry of states (although as instruments of persuasion not sending cricketers is infinitely preferably to sending gunboats). What is being argued is twofold.

First, the conditions under which a whole range of human social activities now considered as 'unpolitical' by nature (art, sport, religion, education) are practised depend ultimately upon political decision. The main reason for this is that the decision to establish and maintain a voluntary sphere of life for the free and unimpeded practice of these activities is itself a political decision and depends for its existence upon a continuing public commitment. In other words, it rests upon the particular system of moral values embodied in the liberal state, which has developed in Western societies over the past 200 years. This point that the rights of individuals and groups to practise these activities are inherently a matter for political decision can be simply illustrated. In the sixteenth century, the state imposed religious uniformity on its citizens, a practice which in succeeding centuries gradually gave way to toleration of a variety of religious denominations, which now possess the right to worship as they please. But the decision to tolerate – as formerly to prosecute and even persecute, for non-observance of a state-ordained creed – is a political one. It now becomes clear that those who maintain that politics should be kept out of a particular activity are expressing a (liberal) political preference, which itself reflects the conventional division between state – an area of compulsory activity, of public affairs – and society – the sphere of voluntary activity, of private affairs – that has grown up in the West since the eighteenth century. Equally, it is clear that the division itself depends upon a prior political guarantee (by the state) and that the boundaries of this division may from time to time shift.

Secondly, sometimes the desire to keep politics out of a particular activity arises out of a simple distaste for controversy and disagreement and a wish that it would stop (e.g. the resentment of businessmen, educationalists and the medical profession at political interference). But these demands are in themselves political. What they require by implication is that public discussion of these affairs in terms of preferences and priorities should cease in favour of administration by their practitioners. But there is no such thing as 'pure' administration unsullied by ideas and values. In practice, the 'experts' would have

to make 'political' decisions – allocate scarce resources between the various parts of their enterprises – and engage in political activities – lobby governments for a greater share of the public funds to be devoted to their concerns. A matter becomes political not because of the malign intent of politicians but because disagreement exists about it – e.g. how much 'private' medical practice to allow, and on what terms; or about a claim to a particular share of public expenditure. The differences of opinion and the clashes of interest which demand and generally receive public resolution in free societies do not cease if they are ignored or driven underground. The public saw little of it, but controversy over collective goals still took place in 'closed' societies like the former USSR (Union of Soviet Socialist Republics) (over the relative importance to be attached to defence, investment and current consumption, for example).

Because agreement in society can never be complete, politics will remain a permanent feature of human life. Agreement will never be complete for three fundamental reasons: first, because material resources are likely to remain scarce and their distribution at any given moment will be unacceptable to some; second, because our images of the 'good society', our 'Utopias', will almost certainly continue to diverge; and, finally, because, however much we eliminate irrelevant factors like wealth and status of birth from the struggle for positions of authority, these remain in their nature limited and, therefore, subject to competition. (The office of prime minister is a *positional* good – if I get it, you cannot have it, and vice versa.) For these reasons, disagreement, competition and the need for politics are likely to be with us for a long time yet. The idea that the world can be rid of politics and its practitioners reflects a secret desire for a kind of conflict-free, unchanging society that has never existed nor is ever likely to. Human societies will always require a process through which social conflicts can be resolved and an arena where such resolutions can take place; also, it might be added, advanced industrial societies will continue to need a special set of actors-professional politicians-who can broker settlements of such differences and act as midwives for new laws and sets of rules.

Politics, persuasion and force

'What words mean few can say, but with words we govern men', said Disraeli. Because politics is the art of persuasion, language is fundamental to it. How else could the expression of varying viewpoints and the search for common ground be conducted except through talk and writing, verbal and written communications?

Some writers have been so impressed with the centrality of words to politics that they have sought to define politics in terms of verbal communication. In other words, they have equated politics with *a particular (peaceful) method of* expressing and settling disagreements by compromise, conciliation and debate rather than by force. Thus, Bernard Crick writes:

> If the argument is, then, that politics is simply the activity by which government is made possible when differing interests in an area to be governed grow powerful enough to need to be conciliated, the obvious objection will be: 'why do certain interests have to be conciliated?' And the answer is, of course, that they do not have to be. Other paths are always open. *Politics is simply when they are conciliated – that solution to the problem of order which chooses conciliation rather than violence and coercion,* and chooses it as an effective way by which varying interests can discover that level of compromise best suited to their common interest in survival. (Crick, 1993, p. 30; italics ours)

This contention gains support, first from much in the European tradition of theorising about politics. *Political rule*, to Aristotle, was that method of ordering the affairs of a community which sought to draw all interests into government rather than a system in which one group overwhelmed all the others and ruled in its own interest alone. Indeed, the word 'politician', although increasingly signifying simply a person who engages in politics as a profession or career, does retain something of its earlier meaning as a kind of broker of interests, someone whose developed skills of articulacy were put to the service of expressing and mediating between the differing interests in a community.

Second, this understanding of politics gets some endorsement from contemporary usage. For example, on occasions when countries become bogged down in wars or in struggles against terrorists, like the British government with the Irish Republican Army (IRA) in Northern Ireland, it is often said that ultimately there will have to be a *political* solution. In the long run, the various parties to the dispute will have to sit down round a table and seek to resolve their differences by bandying words rather than by firing bullets. In both these well-established usages of the terms 'politics' and 'political', the contrast is with *force*. A political *solution* or *method* (discussion) is opposed to the use of violence (military means, repression, terrorism, war) in the settlement of conflicts.

However, this value-loaded understanding of politics is clearly at variance with the more neutral definition offered so far and, equally clearly, incompatible with it. Politics is here defined as the arena where social disagreements are expressed, and conflicts are reconciled or fail to be reconciled. This process may be peaceful or violent. In the real world, as is only too obvious, violence is everywhere. Just consider. The states which had experienced no political killing in the postwar period up to 1975 can be numbered on fewer than the fingers of one hand: New Zealand, Fiji and Iceland. At that date (1975) perhaps as many as half of the world's regimes owed their existence to a violent stroke within the previous generation. The collapse of communism in Eastern Europe and the USSR after 1989 was largely bloodless (except in Romania) but it was followed by an atrocious civil war in the former Yugoslavia and by nationalist armed struggles in parts of the former Soviet Union. Terrorism and counter-terrorism accounted for thousands of deaths throughout the 1970s and 1980s in Western Europe, the Middle East, South America, India and Sri Lanka. Between 1969 and 1992, political violence caused over 3,000 fatalities in Northern Ireland and between 1980 and 1988 over 11,000 deaths in Peru, where the 'Shining Path' (*Sendero Luminoso*) guerillas were active.

However, it is unnecessary to invoke such extreme – in some cases pathological – examples in order to realise the close relationship that exists between power and violence. Will, rather than force, may be the basis of the state in the sense that ultimately it rests on public opinion. But since survival is the primary requirement of any state and since its enemies, internal and external, may at any time deploy violence against it, clearly force – its possession of and readiness to deploy weapons – always backs up the state. This is not, of course, to equate violence with power. Indeed, all states, if they are wise, will seek to minimise the violence they use. Exccssive violence by the authorities may reduce their power by undermining public respect.

But this is by the way. The point is that to exclude violence from our definition of politics would be to rule out from consideration a very high proportion of actual behaviour in the real world. It would eliminate from our vocabulary a number of concepts – revolution, rebellion, *coup d'état*, terrorism, repression, war – vital to any understanding of recurrent social phenomena. It would also eliminate types of regime which (at least in the eyes of western liberals) relied excessively on force to control their populations – for example, military regimes such as Nigeria or authoritarian market stalinist regimes such as China. Violent means may be, and frequently are, used both in the maintenance and the overthrow of states and regimes. World history has largely been a story of war. We need to adopt a conception of 'politics' which recognises this fact. None of this is in any way to justify violence, of course. It is simply to say that no conception of politics which ignored it as a major means of social change and preservation would be realistic. And it is also to suggest that to equate politics in general with the non-violent resolution of conflicts is to identify it (narrowly, as well as somewhat misleadingly, since these states ultimately depend upon force, too) with a particular type of political system, the liberal democratic state.

The politics of liberal democracy

In the modern world, virtually all governments claim to be democratic including those described as autocratic. The reason for this apparently strange fact is not far to seek. The etymological origin of the word 'democracy' is the Greek word '*demos*' (people) and the modern meaning of the term reflects its Greek origin – 'rule by the people'. Since 1918 'democracy' has been the primary principle by which governments and governmental systems have sought to justify their existence. It is *the* contemporary method of legitimating power. Few political systems in the modern world do not claim to be operated by,

with the consent of or in the interests of the people. Thus, not only do the United States of America, France and the United Kingdom call themselves 'democracies', so also do contemporary communist regimes such as China and many other single-party states throughout the world and so too did former communist countries in Eastern Europe.

Such a widespread use of the term, however, is unjustifiable because it blurs important distinctions between genuinely democratic and authoritarian political systems. Thus, there was a democratic impulse behind former and existing single-party communist regimes and also, for example, in African single-party non-communist states. In communist systems, the ruling party aimed to channel public opinion from below and to mobilise it from above whilst in other single-party states the single party was intended to overcome ethnic divisions and reflect a national consensus (Beetham and Boyle, 1995, pp. 15–17). However, key aspects of a genuine democracy were absent. In particular, these states have lacked political opposition, press freedom, electoral choice and government accountability; in addition, they have been repressive, crushing political opposition by force, as the Chinese government did at Tiananmen Square (1989). Such regimes, along with many others in the world today, like traditional monarchies, fundamentalist Islamic theocracies and military dictatorships, are better designated by the term **authoritarian**. Such a term should not be confused with 'authority' (the rightful source of power, the legitimate issuer of commands) but is used to designate rulers who govern without regard for public opinion and individual rights and simply override opposition by the use of force (repression).

'Democracy' does remain a useful term of political classification, but is normally prefaced by the adjective 'liberal'; thus, *liberal democracy*. The term is thus used to characterise a form of government which institutionalises both political *choice,* even if limited, and universal *participation,* even if falling short of this ideal (see further, Chapter 6). It is the

---

Authoritarian government: a repressive form of government from above which rules without regard for popular consent, infringes individual rights and tolerates no opposition.

form of government associated with the Western world since the 1980s has become more widespread with the former East European communist regimes all moving towards this system as well as many Latin American, African and Asian countries(Hague, Harrop and Breslin, 1992, pp. 60–2, 378, 380; Heywood, 1997, pp. 32–4).

Joining the two terms enables us to express two basic features of this political system. It is *liberal* in two senses: first, because it is a *pluralist regime* in which there is open competition for power between individuals, groups and parties; and second, because it is a *limited system of government* in which the powers of rulers are curtailed by laws enforceable in the courts and the scope of government is restricted by a combination of convention, ideology and public opinion. It is *democratic* because government is both derived from and accountable to public opinion; derived from it in the sense that government owes its existence to regularly held elections based on universal franchise, and accountable to it in the sense that a legally guaranteed political opposition keeps government responsive to public opinion in the intervals between elections.

The term 'liberal democracy', then, expresses both a number of political values and a set of constitutional mechanisms for putting them into practice. This section explores further the values and institutions of liberal democratic systems of government.

Since 'democracy' must in a genuine way mean 'rule by the people', we begin by asking how popular government can be achieved in geographically extensive territories with large populations. Clearly, 'rule by the people' in its most fundamental meaning of direct democracy – that is, participation in decision-making by all citizens – is out of the question in any but the smallest and most primitive face-to-face communities. In large, populous modern states, democracy must be of the *representative* kind, in which popular participation in politics is largely indirect, through representatives whom 'the people', defined in terms of the universal franchise, elect to a representative institution such as an assembly or parliament. However, the fact that the only practicable system in the modern world is *representative democracy* does not mean that the idea of direct democracy is without influence. On the contrary, this concept has continued to infuse both the values and the institutions of representative democracies.

It is clear that the degree of popular influence upon governmental decision-making in this political system may vary greatly. The minimal conditions of democracy may reasonably be said to include regular uncoerced elections – from which corruption and intimidation have been removed – universal voting rights, a party system based on two or more competing parties, and free communications media.

States exceed these criteria to differing degrees. In the spectrum of democracy, the USA appears in many ways to be a more democratic country than the United Kingdom. It goes to the polls more often, at local, state and federal (i.e. national) levels, has an elective upper house and a more egalitarian culture. As well as being a major element in a liberal democratic political system, then, democracy is also an ideology. At the centre of democratic ideology is the doctrine that the more strongly the political system manages to incorporate popular influence, the better it is. This radical conception derives from the eighteenth-century European and American revolutions in general and from the theory of Jean Jacques Rousseau in particular. It is the doctrine of the sovereignty of the people.

To a very considerable extent, representative democracy as a whole rests on this political principle. What legitimates the activities of governments in this type of political system is *popular consent*. This does not mean that individuals, groups and parties may be taken to endorse every single decision a government may make. It simply means that because citizens possess the means to effect peaceful and genuine changes of government, their *support for the system in general* can be assumed.

Radical democrats, however, propound a strong version of the theory of popular sovereignty. They seek to make the promise of democracy into a reality. To close the gap between the public and its representatives, they favour a combination of constitutional devices, theories and institutions. In particular, they advocate frequent use of referendums and the delegate rather than the Burkean theory of the representative.

The model of **direct democracy** underlies radical theory. One example points up the contrast between what may be called the minimalist and maximalist versions of representative democracy. For the radical, the representative is an agent of the people, a mere instructed delegate; to the conservative, whilst the representative must at all times listen carefully to what his constituents say, his ultimate responsibility is to his own judgement.

In any case, it is clear that democracy in the modern world must be **representative**. But whom or what do the representatives represent? One obvious answer, implicit in the above discussion, is: their constituents, or more simply, their constituencies. The basis of representation in this sense is a particular unit of territory. Historically, in both the UK and the USA, this was the primary meaning of political representation, and, even after the right to vote became universal, it has remained of great importance. But territorial representation alone could not provide the basis of democratic government without the existence of another factor: that of *party*.

Party systems developed in the age of the universal franchise as the sole practicable method of enabling voters *to choose their rulers*. To understand the significance of party, it is enough simply to imagine a representative system without them. Voters could certainly decide which individual they wished to represent them in parliament, congress or assembly, but, without party, that is all that they would decide. And the assembly would be an unstructured grouping of individuals. The only way a government could emerge in such circumstances would be by the actions of the representatives themselves. Again, in the absence of party, this too would be a difficult task, even though informal groupings might well exist. So far as the electorate were concerned, government would be indirect, operating at one remove from popular influence, and also irresponsible. Modern representative democracy depends upon the existence of competing political parties.

In terms of the system as a whole, parties have two main functions:

Direct democracy: a form of democracy involving the direct, continuous participation of citizens in government; a system of face-to-face popular rule.

Representative democracy: a form of democracy in which the citizens rule through representatives they elect in periodic elections.

---

1. They enable voters to elect *governments*. This is because, in seeking election in particular constituencies, candidates stand as party men or women, not just as individuals; and are voted for (and against) as such, that is, as the representatives of party. Parties, therefore, group candidates coherently so that votes in one constituency can be related to votes in another. They narrow down the alternatives at elections in such a way as to enable the verdicts of constituencies to be aggregated into the selection of a government. Democratic government is, above all, *party* government. By deciding the party composition of parliament, voters in the United Kingdom also determine the party complexion of the government.

2. Party provides the primary source of political *opposition* to the government of the day. The role of the opposition parties is twofold: to criticise and to win concessions from the executive; and to provide an alternative government. Sometimes, the practice of institutionalising opposition by means of party causes irritation, even in well-established democracies: half the cleverest people in the country uniting to prevent the other half governing, was how one nineteenth-century writer, Sir Henry Maine, put it. In fact, however, effective party opposition is essential in liberal democratic theory because it makes governments accountable and provides genuine electoral choice as well as strengthening the system as a whole by enabling dissent to be openly expressed.

Indeed, it can even be argued that it is their legitimisation of the open expression of political dissent that constitutes the fundamental distinguishing mark between liberal democracies, on the one hand, and authoritarian regimes, on the other. It reflects a particular conception of the basic nature of political activity. Because disagreement is a basic feature of social life, it is considered wiser to make institutional provision for it – through free mass media and voluntary groups as well as through competing parties – than to attempt to suppress it. By these means, a minority may seek to transform itself into a majority and, above all, power may change hands peacefully.

That **liberal democracy** as a political system rests on rule by the ballot-box rather than by the bullet is undeniably a cliché yet one worth reiteration since it embodies an important truth. It does not mean, of course, that minorities *will* always 'play the political game' according to constitutional rules but it does put a high premium upon such behaviour. Nor is it intended to deny that force as an ultimate sanction lies behind the liberal democratic state as it does other types of regime. What it does suggest is

> **Liberal democracy**: a form of representative government in which majority rule based on competing parties, free elections and universal franchise is balanced by regard for individual and minority rights. The powers of government are limited by institutional checks and balances, a legitimate political opposition, a free media, a pluralistic tolerance of a wide range of groups and interests and an individualistic political culture

---

BOX 1.1
The liberal democratic political system

Major features

Open regime

High level of competition for power

Two-or-more party system

Variety of voluntary groups

Universal suffrage

Widespread popular political participation although for most people largely confined to elections

Free mass media

Legal and constitutional limitations on powers of office-holders

Political opposition is both permitted and legally provided for

System legitimated in terms of doctrine of popular sovereignty

Adherence to liberal ideas and norms of behaviour is widely diffused

Social and economic structure

Mainly advanced industrialised capitalist societies

Some poor market economies, such as India

Most market economies are now 'mixed economies' in that they contain – as a result of political decision – significant public enterprise sectors

Large and expanding middle classes

Geographical distribution

e.g. USA, UK, Australia, New Zealand, Canada, France, West Germany, Italy, The Netherlands, Belgium, Scandinavian countries, Israel, Japan, India, Sri Lanka that liberal democracies, in permitting a high degree of legitimate dissent, are also far more reluctant than other political systems to coerce recalcitrant minorities. Above all, it indicates that pluralist regimes regard compromise, conciliation and the willingness to negotiate as major political virtues and, in principle, consider political differences to be reconcilable.

Liberal democracy is by far the most difficult political system to operate successfully. This is because its complex pattern of institutions – which include a system of competing parties, free mass media, a diverse range of voluntary groups and an independent judiciary – are not only inherently hard to achieve but also themselves depend for their effective working upon favourable social and cultural conditions. These include a politically mature electorate and a political culture which is both tolerant of social diversity and respectful of legality. These circumstances have been virtually non-existent throughout the bulk of recorded history and remain comparatively uncommon at the present day. Only about forty countries – constituting less than one-third of the states of the world – can be described as liberal democracies (Box 1.1). It is no accident that this list contains most of the world's wealthy countries and is, in fact, largely composed of rich countries, the exceptions being India and Sri Lanka. Considered in social and economic terms, these liberal democratic states have three major characteristics. They are by world standards – with the exceptions we have noted – all rich or very rich; in most of them wealth tends to be – again, by world criteria – relatively evenly distributed; and they are all market economics. This argument does not imply economic determinism. Libya has a high level of income *per capita* but is a military political system.

The strongest correlation seems to be not between levels of wealth as such nor even between relatively even distribution of wealth and liberal democracy but between the market economy and a pluralist political regime. This is understandable since historically liberalism, as a political system, and capitalism have developed together over the past three hundred years, largely in the north-west corner of Europe and in North America. Indeed, in the present-day world, it is the liberalism rather than the 'democracy' of the liberal democracies that stands out. The features which most distinguish them from other types of regime are their constitutionalism, their social and political freedom and the fact that they permit political opposition, rather than the degree of participation they achieve.

Summary

- Disagreement is an inevitable feature of human groups and politics is the area of life in which such disagreements are expressed, modified and settled. Disagreements may arise out of differences of material interest and as a consequence of conflicts of belief and opinion. The existence of controversy and conflict in human groups does not preclude the existence of cooperation, solidarity and interdependence.

- Politics is concerned with the machinery, processes and outcomes of collective decision-making by social creatures whose common life is characterised by both by disagreement over the allocation of resources and values and by interdependence, cooperation and mutual need. People in societies therefore require an authoritative centre of decision and resource allocation, and this is provided by a compulsory, comprehensive, territorial association possessing a monopoly of the legitimate use of force known as a 'state'. States contain a pattern of offices (a constitution), a set of decision-makers (government) and an apparatus of power (army, police). But lower and higher-level human groups, from the family to the world order, possess decision-procedures and power-relations and therefore may be said to contain 'politics'.

- The intrinsically non-political area of life does not exist. All social activities are potential sources of disagreement and welfare and also potential contributors to the resolution of disagreements; hence, all possess a political aspect. Even the decision to create a private–public division of spheres, as in the liberal state, with a predisposition towards no government intervention in the 'private' sphere (art, religion, family life), is a political decision; as would be any decision to override it.

- Politics as a concept cannot be identified with a

non-violent struggle for authority, power and influence over the allocation of goods and the determination of collective goals. In the world as it is, violence is constantly used to maintain and overthrow states, regimes and governments, and much as we would prefer to resolve conflicts by persuasion rather than by force we need a concept of politics broad enough to recognise this fact. We may say, therefore, that politics includes all methods (violent and non-violent) of influencing the machinery, processes and outcomes of collective decision-making.

- Liberal democracy is a form of state which institutionalises disagreement and peaceful transfers of power. Liberal democratic regimes are open systems of government with competing parties, a variety of voluntary groups, widespread, unforced political participation, and an official opposition both permitted and formally provided for.

Questions

1. What is politics?
2. Is it appropriate to speak of politics existing within small groups or should the term 'politics' be limited to matters relating to the 'state'?
3. Analyse the main characteristics of liberal democracy. Is liberal democracy based on a more realistic understanding of the nature of politics than are other political systems? How far does it depend for its success on a society having reached a certain level of economic development?

Assignments

Assignment (1)
Examine the 'news' as presented in a daily newspaper (the newspaper can be either 'quality' or 'tabloid'). List the items which may be described as 'political' and state the criteria by which you have formed your conclusions.

Assignment (2)
Consider the following definitions of and statements about politics:

(a) 'Politics is a particular way of resolving conflict-peacefully, by conciliation and the search for compromise rather than the use of force.'
(b) 'The personal is the political.'
(c) 'Politics is at the heart of all collective social activity, formal and informal, public and private, in *all* human groups, institutions and societies.'
(d) 'Political power grows out of the barrel of a gun.'
(e) 'Politics is about who gets what, when and how.'
(f) 'Politics equates with affairs of state, government, the public realm; it is not concerned with the private sphere.'
   (i) Briefly explain the meaning of the propositions, and then
   (ii) State which one(s) you find convincing, and why.

Further reading

Leftwich, A. (ed.) (1984) *What is Politics?* (Oxford: Blackwell) is a valuable collection of essays on various concepts of politics; Crick, B. (1993) *In Defence of Politics*, 4th edn (London: Penguin) provides a stimulating defence of a particular (liberal) idea of the nature of politics; and Minogue, K. (1995) *Politics: A Very Short Introduction* (Oxford: Oxford University Press) offers a valuable brief commentary on the historical development of his theme as an activity and a subject of study.

Lucas, J. R. (1995) *The Principles of Politics* (Oxford: Oxford University Press, paperback edition) is a rigorous analysis of central political concepts. Hague, R., Harrop, M. and S. Breslin (1998) *Comparative Government and Politics*, 4th edn (London: Macmillan) and Heywood, A. (1997) *Politics* (London: Macmillan) are valuable comparative overviews of the main concerns of political science from a global perspective. Both contain very useful glossaries of concepts.

Finally, Dunn, J. (ed.) (1992) *Democracy: The Unfinished Journey 508 BC to AD 1993* (Oxford: Oxford University Press) provides a useful survey of changing views of democracy, and Beetham, D. and Boyle, K. (1995) *Introducing Democracy 80 Questions and Answers* (Paris and Cambridge: Unesco Publishing and Polity Press) provides a brief but incisive analysis of the concept.

Website
The Political Studies Association homepage has links to many politics websites:

http://www.lgu.ac.uk/psa/psa.html

British politics since the war

This chapter rests squarely on the assumption that British politics today cannot be properly grasped without an understanding of the country's postwar history. In the years between 1940 and 1955, a broad policy consensus emerged between the two major parties. It was a joint product of the Labour Government of 1945–51, which laid the foundations of postwar policies, and of the Conservative Government of 1951–5 which in broad terms accepted Labour's key legislation and policies. The dominant consensus, which lasted from the early 1950s to the mid-1970s, is variously described as 'Butskellite' (after successive Labour and Conservative Chancellors of the Exchequer, Hugh Gaitskell and R. A. Butler) and 'Keynesian' (after the economist, John Maynard Keynes). It covered all aspects of policy – foreign, social and economic. This chapter tells the story of its rise, its decline, its fall and the possible emergence of a new post-Thatcherite consensus.

The theory of the postwar consensus

Postwar British history may be conveniently divided into four distinct but overlapping phases: (1) 1940–55: The making of the consensus; (2) 1955–79: The consensus under strain; (3) 1979–97:

The ending of the consensus; and (4) After 1997: A new post-Thatcherite consensus under New Labour? (Boxes 2.1, 2.3, 2.4, 2.5).

The theory of the **postwar consensus** contains a large amount of truth but it should be remembered that broad consensus on fundamentals is compatible with significant differences in emphasis – as well as fierce rhetorical warfare – between the parties. Thus differences continued over nationalisation (Labour for modest increases, Conservatives in favour of denationalising to a small extent) and over welfare, where Labour's collectivist bias and enthusiasm for public spending, municipal housing and comprehensive schools contrasted with the Conservative Party's individualist bias and greater sympathy with private landlordism, private house-building, private schooling and the grammar school/secondary modern system in state education. Thus, the term 'consensus' as used here refers to broad agreement between governments and is not intended to denote or imply total agreement between the main parties on all aspects of policy, ideological agreement, rhetorical agreement, agreement on all policy details, agreement between front benches, or agreement between party activists (Seldon, 1994)

The postwar consensus involved a major world role for Britain (still the world's third economic and military power in 1945); a welfare state based on 'cradle to grave' provision of benefits and services for all citizens; and a mixed economy – four-fifths private sector, one-fifth public sector – run by governments on Keynesian lines in such a way as to maintain full employment.

1940–55: The making of the postwar consensus

BOX 2.1

The making of the postwar consensus, 1940–55

World role and welfare: the years of Attlee and Churchill
Governments: Coalition 1940–5 (Churchill); Caretaker (mainly Conservative) 1945 (Churchill); Labour 1945–50, 1950–1 (Attlee); Conservative 1951–5 Churchill.

The consensus involved:

- **Britain's 'world role':** Foreign policy was based on the view that Britain's 'special relationship' with the United States, leadership of a multiracial Commonwealth, possession of nuclear weapons and large conventional military capability gave the country a continuing leading status as a world power.
- **A welfare state:** The accepted basis of social policy was that a wide range of publicly provided benefits and 'universal' services should be available to all on demonstration of need and, in the case of the services, 'free' at the point of receipt. The keystones of the welfare state were a National Health Service providing health care to all regardless of income, a comprehensive system of social security and pensions based on national insurance contributions, and a state educational service compulsory to the age of 15 from which all fee-paying had been abolished.
- **A mixed economy:** The main elements of economic policy were: a largely private enterprise economy with a significant public sector of recently nationalised industries; governments' acceptance of the responsibility to manage the economy at a level of demand sufficient to maintain 'a high and stable' rate of employment; their adoption of Keynesian methods (i.e. the manipulation of fiscal and monetary mechanisms) in order to do so; and the operation of a 'corporatist' style partnership with the 'peak' organisation of business and labour in order to curb inflationary pressures and contain industrial conflict.

Framework of Britain's foreign, social and economic policy to 1970s established.

But Britain's claim to an independent world role suffered a severe setback at Suez (1956).

The resignation of Churchill as Conservative premier in April 1955 and of Attlee as Labour leader in December 1955 removed the two main architects of the postwar world in Britain from the political scene.

Britain's world role after 1945

Britain in 1945 saw itself and was perceived by others as a great world power. Although far out-matched in population, industrial production and military capacity by the new superpowers, the USA and USSR, it was far in advance of other potentially second-rank but heavily defeated countries such as Germany, Italy, France and Japan. The distinctive features of Britain's international position in 1945 were as follows:

- *One of the three major victorious powers in the Second World War:* Britain was one of the three major powers at the two conferences (Yalta and Potsdam) which, in default of a treaty, constituted the postwar settlement. Moreover, in Churchill, the country had a towering leader who, by a combination of personal magnetism and bluff, seemed able to treat on equal terms with the American and Soviet leaders, Roosevelt and Stalin.
- *Possessor of a huge empire:* At its peak in 1933, the British Empire covered nearly one-quarter of the world's land surface and contained almost one-quarter of its population. Although to some extent destabilised by the growth of nationalist movements in the non-white territories, the empire remained of considerable economic and military significance.
- *Having a 'special relationship' with the United States:* Strong historical, cultural and linguistic links between the two Anglo-Saxon powers underpinned their cooperation in both world wars. From 1942, Britain was a military ally of the United States in the war against Germany and Japan, but earlier the Lend-Lease Agreement (1941) provided a system of credits enabling Britain to obtain a continuous supply of American goods and materials in order to sustain its war effort.

Britain's postwar role in the world was powerfully shaped by Labour's Foreign Secretary, Ernest Bevin. A fervent patriot, Bevin based his policies on two principles – first, that a vigorous British foreign policy was vital to world peace; and second, that Britain was still a great power with important global interests to protect. To these ends, he presided over the development of a system of treaties for the global

Table 2.1 Postwar British prime ministers

1945–51	Clement Attlee	1970–4	Edward Heath
1951–55	Sir Winston Churchill	1974–6	Harold Wilson
1955–57	Sir Anthony Eden	1976–9	James Callaghan
1957–63	Harold Macmillan	1979–90	Margaret Thatcher
1963–4	Sir Alec Douglas-Home	1990–97	John Major
1964–70	Harold Wilson	1997–	Tony Blair

containment of communism (in alliance with the United States); the emergence of a complex imperial policy combining the development of the empire, the creation of the Commonwealth, and a system of global bases and strong points; and powerful defence forces backed by a British atomic bomb. The Conservative Government (1951–55) led by Winston Churchill with Anthony Eden as Foreign Secretary continued these policies.

The containment of communism

Bevin aimed at the close involvement of the United States in the defence of Western Europe against possible Soviet aggression. Hence he played a leading role in negotiating the formation of the *North Atlantic Treaty Organisation* (NATO) in 1949, which obliged the United States, Canada, Britain, France, the Netherlands, Belgium, Luxemburg and six other European countries to assist each other if attacked.

The Attlee Government also allowed American strategic bombers (with atomic capability from 1949) to be stationed in Britain (1946) and, when the Soviets blockaded Berlin (1948–9), participated with the US in an airlift of supplies to keep the city open.

Empire and Commonwealth

Britain saw its empire as an important asset in the postwar period and sought to maximise its value in a number of ways:

- Strategic withdrawal from untenable positions: e.g. the granting of independence to India and Pakistan (1947) and Burma and Ceylon (1948).
- Fostering the emergence of the Commonwealth as a method enabling it to continue to exercise informal influence as formal empire receded – a Commonwealth Premiers' Conference was held in 1949.
- Providing financial assistance for colonial and Commonwealth development, e.g. by participating in the Colombo Plan (1951) to help India and its neighbours.
- Using force to defend its interests: e.g. the long war fought against communist terrorism in Malaysia, suppression of revolts in Kenya and Cyprus and imprisonment of nationalist leaders such as Kwame Nkrumah (Gold Coast) and Dr Hastings Banda (Nyasaland).
- Preserving a worldwide system of naval and military bases, e.g. the Suez Canal Zone, Mombasa, Aden, Bahrein, Singapore and Hong Kong.

Defence and the British A-bomb

When the US brought atomic collaboration with Britain to an end (1946), a Cabinet Committee took the decision to develop a British A-bomb (successfully tested in 1952). The Churchill Cabinet later decided – in the wake of US and Soviet development of the more powerful H-bomb – that Britain should have this weapon too (1954).

Britain's extensive international security obligations and overseas commitments necessitated a large defence budget which rose to almost 8 per cent of GDP (Gross Domestic Product) in 1954, when Britain had a higher per capita burden of defence spending even than the United States.

European integration

Britain held back from taking part in talks about closer economic union with France (1948); the Schuman Plan for a European Coal and Steel Community (1952); and the Messina Conference (1955) which led to the creation of the European Economic Community (EEC) by the Treaty of Rome (1957). Several factors lay behind Britain's decision to hold aloof from membership of the Common Market at its foundation.

- Britain's conception of itself as a great power with a world role;
- Its unwillingness to compromise its national sovereignty and suspicion of the supranational, 'federalist' aspirations of the founders of the EEC.
- Its belief that its most important international relationships were with the United States and the Commonwealth and that closer economic ties with continental Europe were not in its long-term interest.

The welfare state

Wartime changes prepared the way for the development of the postwar welfare state.

- *The prominent role assumed by Labour* – the party of radical change – in the wartime Coalition Government: Labour held two posts in Churchill's War Cabinet and also key posts in home front Ministries.
- *A massive expansion in the role of government*: The government took on large-scale powers over the production and distribution of resources and over the labour force – e.g. its allocation of raw materials to priority purposes, manpower planning, price controls and rationing.
- *The development of blueprints for vast new government responsibilities in the provision of welfare and the maintenance of full employment*: The two main developments were the *Beveridge Report (1942)* and the *White Paper on Employment Policy (1944)*. The Beveridge Report called for a new social security system based on compulsory social insurance and fixed subsistence-level benefits in return for flat-rate contributions. In the White Paper, the Government accepted the maintenance of 'a high and stable level of employment' as one of the 'primary aims and responsibilities' of government after the war. The architects of these new policies were respectively W.H. Beveridge (1879–1963) and J.M. Keynes (1883–1946), both Liberals, both academics (Beveridge was a former Director of the London School of Economics (LSE) and Keynes a Cambridge don) and both temporary civil servants during the war. Beveridge assumed that in order to function properly his scheme would need to be accompanied by other sweeping

changes – family allowances, a comprehensive national health service and full employment. Keynes allocated government a central role in maintaining consumer demand for goods and services at a level sufficient to achieve and preserve full employment.

- *Government commitment to postwar social reconstruction*: This was signalled by actual legislation (e.g. the 1944 Education Act and the introduction of family allowances (1945)) and by the 1944 White Papers entitled *A National Health Service* (which envisaged a comprehensive health service with 'free' treatment financed by taxation) and *Social Insurance* (which accepted virtually the whole of the Beveridge Report and was quickly followed by the establishment of a new Ministry of National Insurance (1944)).
- *A leftward ideological shift in both elite opinion and public opinion*: Postwar social reconstruction enjoyed widespread support from reformist intellectuals, civil servants, the political parties, leading figures in the Churches, universities and media, and from public opinion, as indicated by the enthusiastic reception of the Beveridge Report, and the anti-Conservative trends in by-elections, the Mass Observation Survey, and opinion polls during the war.

The main welfare state measures introduced by the Labour Governments (1945–51) – and by the wartime Coalition – and broadly continued by the Conservative Governments in the 1950s are shown in Box 2.2.

The mixed economy

The major theme of postwar economic policy in Britain was closer government involvement in running the economy than at any previous period. This greater state involvement had three main aspects.

- *The creation of a mixed economy*: This was done by a series of important nationalisation measures introduced by the Attlee Government which, with the exceptions only of steel and road haulage, were retained by the Conservative Governments of 1951–64. Major industries moving into public ownership included coal, the railways, iron and steel, gas, electricity and civil aviation.

- *Government responsibility for economic management*: Chancellors of the Exchequer – both Labour and Conservative – used a combination of fiscal techniques (i.e. manipulation of tax rates) and monetary methods (i.e. interest rate changes) to manage the economy in order to ensure full employment, stable prices, economic growth, protection of the value of sterling, and avoidance of balance of payments crises.
- *'Corporate bias'*: This is a phrase coined by the historian Keith Middlemas to describe the close relationship between government and the 'peak' organisations of industry and the trade unions which was already embryonic in 1940, cemented during the war and continued after it. The rationale of corporate bias for government was the need to avoid the damaging industrial conflict that had occurred in the 1920s; the rationale of informal incorporation for business and the

unions was that it gave them a permanent voice in policy-making, thereby increasing their capacity to serve the interests of their members.

The tasks facing British governments immediately after the war were: to achieve the smoothest possible transition from a wartime to a peacetime economy; to negotiate foreign loans on the best terms available in order to cover the huge balance-of-payments deficits predicted for 1946 and 1947 (themselves the result of Britain's massive loss of foreign assets and exports during the war); and to encourage the recovery of Britain's export trade. By the mid-1950s, under Labour Chancellors Hugh Dalton, Stafford Cripps and Hugh Gaitskell, and Conservative Chancellor R. A. Butler, these goals had been largely achieved. But they were not achieved without crises, the worst year being 1947, when Britain faced both a severe fuel crisis (coal having failed to regain its prewar levels of output) and even more damaging massive balance of payments and sterling convertibility crises.

BOX 2.2
The welfare state: the main measures

- **Family Allowances Act** (1945). 5 shillings (25p) per week to every family for the second and every subsequent child. Indicated state adoption of the principle of contributing financially to the upkeep of children regardless of parental means.
- **National Insurance (Industrial Injuries) Act** (1946): established four types of benefit – injury benefit (payable for six months); disablement benefit (payable after that according to the degree of disability); supplementary benefit (e.g. hardship allowances); and death benefits for dependants.
- **National Insurance Act** (1946): in return for flat-rate contributions, the state provided seven types of benefit – sickness; unemployment; retirement pension; maternity; widow's; guardian's allowance for orphans; and a death grant for funeral expenses. The new pension, 26 shillings (130p), represented an increase of 16 shillings (80p) on existing pensions and was more generous than Beveridge had recommended. This Act began the extensive state responsibility for citizen welfare often referred to at the time and later as 'cradle to grave' provision.
- **National Assistance Act** (1948): supplementary allowances payable on a means-tested basis to bring National Insurance benefits up to subsistence level or to provide for people not entitled to those benefits.
- **National Health Service Act** (1946): provided a comprehensive service available free to all at the point of receipt and financed mainly by taxation. The NHS was managed

by three agencies: Regional Hospital Boards appointed by the Minister of Health to run the former local authority and voluntary hospitals; local executive councils (half lay members, half professional) to administer the general practitioner and dental, ophthalmic and pharmaceutical services; and the local authorities whose health and welfare services included maternity and child care, vaccination and immunisation, domestic help, home nursing and home visiting.
- **Education Act** (1944): introduced tripartite system of secondary education based on grammar, modern and technical schools, with selection by the 11+ examination; each type of school was intended to have 'parity of esteem'. Fee-paying in secondary schools was abolished and the school leaving age was to be raised to 15 in 1945, and to 16 as soon as possible after that (in fact, these intentions were not achieved until 1947 (15) and 1973 (16)). The Act created the office of Minister of Education to whom it gave the duty of providing a national education service. It gave more state aid to the voluntary (i.e. church) schools but subjected them to stronger public control.
- **Employment policy**: Government commitment to the maintenance after the war of 'a high and stable level of employment' (1944 White Paper) was seen by leading contemporaries such as Beveridge and Attlee to be as important as the measures described above in the attack on poverty and deprivation.

However, assisted by the recovery in world trade, by a financial injection through the US Marshall Aid programme for European Recovery (1948) and by a large fall in the cost of imports (1953), Britain's current account balance of payments came back into surplus in 1948 and more decisively in 1952–4. Moreover, by the mid-1950s, the removal of the wartime regime of physical controls over the economy was virtually complete and Keynesian methods of economic management effectively in place. The new fiscal and monetary methods of economic management had even acquired a name, – 'Butskellism'. Moreover, after a sharp increase in 1947 to over 1 million, unemployment fell to around 300,000 (1.5 per cent) for the next ten years.

1955–79: the consensus under strain

External Relations

The main themes of Britain's external relationships in this period were the collapse of the world role, the displacement of the Commonwealth by Europe, and the increasing reliance upon the United States. The major strand in Britain's domestic history was the continued reluctance to sacrifice its pursuit of national 'greatness' in order to dedicate itself to the goal of developing an efficient modern economy.

Decolonisation, which had slowed to a mere trickle in the 1950s, became a flood after 1960, with 17 colonial territories achieving their independence between 1960 and 1964. By 1979 the process was virtually complete, and little remained of the British Empire. Its dissolution was inevitable; only the factors underlying the timing of the process are in some dispute. Some historians attribute the post-1960 acceleration to the Suez affair (1956), when – in response to the nationalisation of the Suez Canal by the Egyptian leader, Gamal Abdel Nasser – Britain colluded with France and Israel to launch a joint military expedition against Egypt. However, the combination of a run on sterling and pressure from the USA and international opinion forced Britain to withdraw before its object had been achieved, thereby dealing a shattering and long-lasting blow to the country's self-image as a great power.

BOX 2.3

The consensus under strain, 1955–79

External reorientation and economic difficulties

Governments: Conservative 1955–64 (Eden, 1955–7; Macmillan, 1957–63; Douglas-Home, 1963–4); Labour 1964–70 (Wilson); Conservative 1970–4 (Heath); Labour 1974–9 (Wilson, 1974–6; Callaghan, 1976–9).

Decline in comparative position of the British economy and in Britain's international status. Main changes in Britain's external affairs:

- Rapid decolonisation (virtually complete by 1974);
- Erosion of Commonwealth as political entity and trading bloc;
- Weakening of 'special relationship' with USA (although Britain became totally dependent upon US for supply of nuclear weapons (1962));
- Reorientation of external policy towards Europe with a successful application to join the European Community (1972) following two unsuccessful ones (1961 and 1967).

In domestic affairs, governments faced unforeseen problems:

- Slow growth (compared with other advanced industrial economies) , mounting inflation and persistent balance of payments crises;
- Rising public expectations regarding welfare combined with increasing public disenchantment at the levels of taxation required to sustain the welfare state.

Incomes policies used to control inflation but usually ended in disarray despite some temporary successes.

1979 collapse of Government pay norm in public sector strikes ('Winter of Discontent') preceded Conservative election victory.

Consensus already under attack: in practice, by the Heath Government's non-interventionist experiment (1970–2) and the Labour Government's setting of monetary targets after 1976; and intellectually, in the emergence of alternatives to Keynesianism on the Right (monetarism) and Left (Alternative Economic Strategy – import controls) in the 1970s.

But Suez may well have been a less decisive influence on Prime Minister Macmillan's decision to speed up decolonisation in Africa after 1960 than President de Gaulle's decision to liquidate French colonial entanglements in North and West Africa after 1958 and the sudden decision of Belgium to withdraw from the Congo in mid-1960. Also, Britain was anxious to avoid further acute embarrassments such as the 1959 revelations of the Hola Camp 'massacres' in Kenya and of 'police state' conditions in Nyasaland (Holland, 1991, p. 298; Reynolds, 1991, p. 223; also, see Box 15.5 below).

Many historians argue that by the mid-1950s, Britain's overstretched global commitments and the huge burden of defence expenditure they necessitated were already damaging the country's economy. British governments were well aware of the problem. In 1956 Harold Macmillan as Chancellor of the Exchequer observed that

for every rifle our comrades in Europe carried we were carrying two. If we were to follow the European example, we could save £700 million a year. If only half of these resources were shifted into exports the picture of our foreign balances

would be transformed. If the other half were available for investment, there would be less critical comment about our low rate of investment compared to many other countries. (Chalmers, 1985, p. 65)

However, Macmillan as Prime Minister, even in the aftermath of Suez, remained committed to a world role for Britain, as signalled by the search for a genuinely independent British nuclear deterrent, the attempt to broker peace between the superpowers at Summit meetings and the adoption of a costly policing commitment 'East of Suez'.

By the end of the 1960s all these policies had collapsed. The British attempt at real nuclear independence ended in the cancellation of the surface-to-surface missile 'Blue Streak' in 1960 and the negotiation of an agreement to purchase a new generation of nuclear weapons launched from Polaris submarines from the United States (Nassau Agreement, 1962). Summitry collapsed spectacularly at Paris in the same year whilst Denis Healey as Defence Secretary finally managed to wind down military commitments 'East of Suez' with the 1967 promise to withdraw British forces from Singapore and

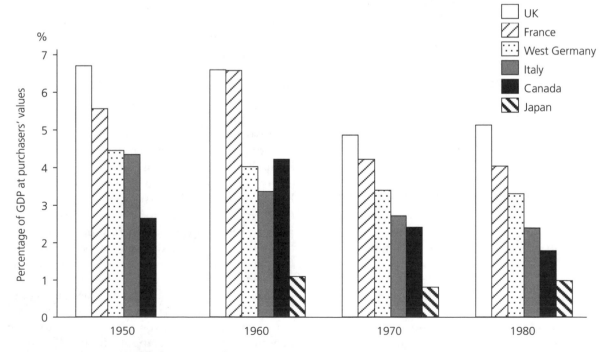

Figure 2.1 Comparative defence spending, 1950–80

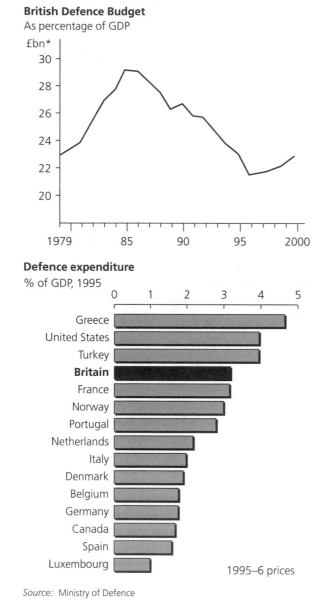

British Defence Budget
As percentage of GDP

Defence expenditure
% of GDP, 1995

1995–6 prices

Source: Ministry of Defence

Figure 2.2 Comparative defence spending, 1995

Malaysia in the mid-1970s. Figure 2.1 compares British defence spending 1950–80 with that of other advanced industrial countries whilst Figure 2.2 contains defence spending trends since 1979, together with an international comparison of defence spending in 1995.

By the mid–1960s, the notion of the Commonwealth as a world force was at an end, although the concept had succeeded in disguising the British retreat from empire. Britain's trade with the Commonwealth was also in decline, gradually in the 1950s, more quickly in the 1960s when exports to the EEC grew more rapidly than exports to the Commonwealth. Britain had responded to the formation of the EEC in 1957 by first attempting to block it and then by forming EFTA (the European Free Trade Association), the so-called 'Outer Seven'. It had banked on French political instability wrecking the EEC from within, but the emergence of de Gaulle as President (1958) turned this into a vain hope.

In 1960 Macmillan began a swift reorientation of Britain's external policy as it became evident that the EEC was succeeding. His motives were predominantly political – since the USA wanted Britain inside the Community as a counterpoise to Germany and France, membership was an important way to continuing the Atlantic partnership. But they were also economic. By the late 1950s it was already apparent that Britain's postwar rate of economic growth, although good by historical standards, was lagging well behind other European (and world) competitors (see below).

However, Britain's applications to join the EEC in 1961 and 1967 were both humiliatingly rejected by de Gaulle on the grounds that Britain was not truly European. The General's vetoes also owed much to wartime antagonisms and to French unwillingness to share European leadership with Britain. But he undoubtedly had a point about Britain's pro-American sympathies: in its final stage, Britain's 1961 application was overshadowed by Macmillan's negotiation of the Polaris deal with President Kennedy, whilst the 1967 application came in the wake of a secret deal by which the Americans agreed to support sterling, thus enabling the Wilson Government to stave off devaluation, in return for Britain's retaining its East of Suez commitment (Reynolds, 1991, p. 227).

When the Conservative Government led by the Europhile Edward Heath finally managed to secure entry to the EEC in 1973, it was on rather disadvantageous terms to Britain. By the end of the transitional period in 1978, Britain provided about one-fifth of Community income, which was reasonable, but in return, because the EEC's payments were skewed towards farm support in the Common Agricultural Policy, received back under one-tenth of EEC spending. However, a major change had occurred in the orientation of Britain's external politics which, from the early 1970s, became increasingly more European.

The welfare state

The bi-partisan consensus on the welfare state continued in this period, with government social spending rising ever more rapidly as a proportion of GNP. But broad overall consensus was compatible with differing policy priorities and emphases, especially in education and housing. Thus in education Labour began a rapid movement towards comprehensive schools which was continued by the Conservatives after 1970, even though their preference for selectivity (and the preservation of the grammar schools) would have made them unlikely initiators of such a policy.

In housing, Labour stressed the need for increasing the stock of council houses whilst the Conservatives encouraged owner occupation. Both parties moved increasingly towards means-testing in their social security policies but for Labour this was a regrettable departure from the principle of universality, whereas the Conservatives approved it as preserving work incentives and containing the growth of state welfare (Digby, 1989, pp. 65, 69).

The economy

There was little change in the sectoral balance of the 'mixed economy' before 1970 but rather more after that date. Road haulage and steel were both denationalised in the 1950s by the Conservatives, but Labour returned steel to public ownership in 1967. After 1970 Labour nationalised aerospace and shipbuilding (1977) and formed the British National Oil Corporation in order to influence the exploitation of North Sea oil. The nationalisation of Rolls-Royce (1971) by the Conservatives and the acquisition of a majority shareholding in British Leyland (1975) by Labour were prompted by the desires of governments to ensure the survival of major ailing companies.

However, the consensus on economic management came under increasing strain during the 1970s, with new directions in economic policy being proposed by the Conservative New Right and the Labour Left (Alternative Economic Strategy). The challenge to the consensus emerged against a background of accelerating economic decline, with Britain slipping ever more rapidly down the international 'league table' (see Chapter 3).

In addition, hitherto favourable economic indicators took a sharp downward turn. The inflation rate, which had been running at 2–3 per cent in the 1950s and 4–5 per cent in the late 1960s, rose to over 9 per cent in the early 1970s and thence, after the quadrupling of OPEC (Organisation of Petroleum Exporting Countries) oil prices in 1973–4, to over 24 per cent in 1975. Unemployment, which had averaged an annual 335 000 in the 1950s and 447 000 in the 1960s, also increased sharply after 1970, rising to an annual average of 1.25 million (1974–9). Economic growth, which had averaged 2.8 per cent per annum between 1948 and 1973 plummeted to a mere 1.4 per cent between 1973 and 1979. A new term – 'stagflation' – was coined to describe this unprecedented situation of slow growth combined with both rising unemployment and accelerating inflation.

The years 1972–9 were the heyday of 'corporatist' economic management between government, employers and unions, with interventionist governments using incomes policies including wage freezes in order to contain inflationary pressures. This approach was symbolised by Labour's 'social contract' with the unions (1974–5), in which the unions agreed to voluntary restraint on wages in return for favourable government social and industrial policies. Whatever the final judgement of historians on incomes policies (whether statutory, 1972–4, or compulsory non-statutory, 1976–9), they had the undoubted disadvantage of politicising industrial relations. The Heath Government's clash with the miners (1972–4) and the Callaghan Government's battle with the public sector unions (1978–9) helped to bring about their downfall (see also Chapter 23).

The welfare state was also under severe strain by the mid-1970s. In the 1950s, it had been expected that the rapid growth of the economy would enable welfare spending to rise without adding to the tax burden on households. But by the 1970s this expectation had been eroded. National income had failed to grow as rapidly as expected but government welfare commitments had increased dramatically.

The result was a steady rise in public expenditure which reached a postwar peak as a proportion of GDP of just under 46 per cent in 1975–6 (Table 2.2). The gap between public expenditure and revenue – which has to be filled by state borrowing (the Public Sector Borrowing Requirement) – increased dramatically even though the tax burden was at record levels. By 1975 even people officially classified as amongst the poorest in the community paid tax and the average wage-earner with two children paid one-quarter of his income in direct taxes compared with 3.3 per cent in 1955. By the mid-1970s public expectations of the welfare state were running well ahead of public willingness and national capacity to finance it.

Rapidly rising inflation and unemployment, slowing economic growth, and high and increasing levels of public expenditure and taxation led the Labour Government to move away to a certain extent from Keynesian methods and priorities of economic management in the late 1970s. First, Chancellor Denis Healey in his 1975 Budget refused to increase demand in the face of rising unemployment, thereby initiating a new emphasis on control of inflation as the major goal of government policy rather than the maintenance of a 'high and stable' level of employment. Dennis Kavanagh has called this policy shift 'a historic breach with one of the main planks of the postwar consensus' (Kavanagh 1990, p. 127).

Second, during the sterling crisis of 1976, the government adopted formal targets for the growth of the money supply (notes and coins in circulation plus sterling current accounts in the private sector and sterling deposit accounts held by British residents) as a way of reducing the rate of inflation. Finally, Labour also began the change from the

Public Expenditure Survey Committee (PESC) method of controlling public spending to the use of cash limits. Under PESC, public spending plans were not adjusted when growth turned out be lower or inflation higher than expected when the expenditure plans were drawn up. Under the cash limits methods, which began in 1976, each spending programme received a cash limit for the year and was expected to keep within its budget. However, although Labour initiated new priorities and methods in economic management, it was far from launching a new philosophy of government based on these new directions. That was the task the Thatcher Government, coming to power in 1979, set itself to carry out.

The ending of the consensus: 1979–90s

The erosion of the consensus in the 1970s paved the way for its overthrow by Margaret Thatcher. During this time, consensus ideas lost intellectual credibility and consensus governments lost political authority. The decline in the ideological persuasiveness of the post-1945 consensus was evident in the growing influence within the two major parties of anti-consensual ideas: the neo-liberal New Right (Conservative) and the left-wing Alternative Economic Strategy (Labour) (see Chapter 5).

In both parties, the political centre was in retreat – in the Conservative Party because of the failure of Heathite Statism between 1972 and 1974; in the Labour Party because of dissatisfaction with Labour's record on welfare and the economy, and the rise of radical single-issue groups representing feminists, blacks, gays and CND. Governments had lost political authority because of their apparent incapacity to reverse national decline. In particular, they were increasingly perceived by the public as at the mercy of over-mighty interest groups and as unable to deal with Britain's long-term problems of low productivity, backward industry and strife-torn management-union relations. Wilson's attempt at trade union reform had been blocked by his own party (1969) while Heath's industrial relations legislation had collapsed in a wave of industrial militancy (1971–2). The breakdown of government union reforms and wage restraint policies in the decade before 1979

Table 2.2 Public expenditure as a proportion of GDP, 1955–76 (current prices)

	OECD average	United Kingdom
1955–7	28.5	32.5
1967–9	34.5	38.5
1974–6	41.4	44.5

Source: Pliatzky (1982, p. 166).

BOX 2.4
The ending of the consensus, 1979–97

The triumph of economic liberalism and mounting difficulties with Europe: the premierships of Margaret Thatcher and John Major.

Governments: Conservative 1979–97 (Thatcher, 1979–83; 1983–7; 1987–90; Major 1990–2; 1992–7).

Thatcher and Major years marked by pursuit of New Right policies.

In foreign affairs, Conservatives sought restoration of national prestige based on vigorous policy involving:

- Aggressive pursuit of British interests in EC;
- Revival of 'special relationship' with US;
- Robust anti-Soviet stance (in early 1980s);
- Emphasis on strong defence based on nuclear weapons;
- Willingness to use armed force in pursuit of national objectives (Falklands and Gulf War).

In domestic policy, Conservative Governments departed from consensus by:

- Economic policies giving priority to reduction of inflation over maintenance of high rate of employment;
- Tax cuts to encourage individual enterprise;
- Privatisation of public sector industries and services; legislative curbs on trade unions;
- Organisational reforms of welfare based on the introduction of 'quasi-markets';emphasis on 'selective' rather than 'universal' welfare and encouragement of private pensions, education and health;
- Constant search for reductions in public spending.

From the late 1980s,Conservative Governments experienced increasing difficulties with Europe,notably over the decision to join the ERM and Britain's ejection from it ('Black Wednesday', 16 September 1992), backbench rebelliousness over the ratification of the Treaty of Maastricht, 1993, and the implementation of a period of 'non-cooperation' with the EU(1995) following the EU ban on British beef after the outbreak of 'mad cow' disease.

broke through the Callaghan Government's 5 per cent pay norm in 1978–9, their actions seemed to symbolise the failure of consensus government.

The main objectives of Thatcherism between 1979 and 1990 were twofold: (1) to restore British prestige and assert British interests more vigorously abroad, and (2) to 'roll back the frontiers' of the state in economic and welfare (although not in law and order) policy. The full range of policies designed to implement the second of these goals was not present in its entirety in 1979 but emerged during the course of Thatcher's three administrations (privatisation, for example, mainly after 1983 and reform of the welfare state after 1987). Policies on the economy, industrial relations and welfare represented a deliberate reversal of the postwar consensus, a change of political tack aimed at turning the country round and halting decline. They were continued under John Major (1990–7), who retained low inflation as the central target of macroeconomic policy, implemented the more difficult privatisations and carried through the 'internal market' reforms in health and education. We now summarise these changes.

Foreign and defence policy

Arguably, the main elements of postwar foreign policy remained in place: what changed was that British interests (e.g. within the EEC) were asserted more aggressively, defence received greater emphasis and political rhetoric became more stridently nationalist. It is unlikely that any of Thatcher's immediate predecessors would have fought the Falklands War. No systematic revision of the Thatcher foreign policy ethos took place under Major,although in general his relations with the United States were less warm(especially after the advent of President Clinton) and more managerial than Thatcher's and he was less hostile to Germany and to the European Union (Wallace, 1994, pp.283–99; Peterson, 1997, p.40). However, the later years of his premiership were dogged by difficulties with Europe.

The European Community
In 1980 Britain's payments to the EEC exceeded its receipts by over £1 billion, and Thatcher, aiming at 'a broad balance' between contributions and

engendered a sense of ungovernability, chaos and mounting public frustration. When first the Ford workers, then the lorry drivers, then the public sector unions in a series of well-publicised strikes, receipts, fought a vigorous and largely successful campaign against the other eight countries to get 'our money' back (she eventually got about two-thirds of it). Later in the 1980s, having already signed the Single European Act (1986), she fiercely resisted 'Euro-federalism' (the idea of a United States of Europe) and significantly delayed Britain's entry into the European Exchange Rate Mechanism (ERM) until October 1990. Events proved that Britain had entered the ERM at too high an exchange rate but it was Major's Government that suffered the blow to its reputation when Britain was forced to leave it under two years later on 16 September 1992 ('Black Wednesday'). Major developed closer relationships with Germany's Chancellor Kohl which paved the way for his successful negotiation of concessions to the United Kingdom in the Treaty of Maastricht (1992–3), including British opt-outs on the Social Chapter and monetary union. However, in the later years of his term of office, Major's relations with the EU deteriorated. When, following the discovery of 'mad cow' disease in Britain, the EU declared a ban on exports of British beef, the Major Government riposted with a 'non-cooperation' policy, vetoing all proposed EU measures which required a unanimous vote (1995–6). Finally, Major's Government adopted a 'wait and see' policy on a single currency, maintaining it despite Eurosceptic dissent (Peterson, 1997, pp. 24–7).

The 'special relationship' with the United States

Margaret Thatcher's fierce anti-communism drew her into close support of US policy in the new Cold War of the early 1980s. In this revived 'special relationship' (seen as in decline from the late 1960s) she strongly backed the deployment of a new generation of American Cruise and Pershing missiles in Europe together with the 'dual track' NATO strategy of arms modernisation combined with negotiations for arms control. Thatcher's close personal relations (from 1981) with President Reagan cemented Britain's ties with the US and she repaid her debt for American intelligence and other support in the Falklands War by permitting the US to carry out retaliatory air strikes against Libya from its British bases (1986). In the mid-1980s, she used her ability to 'do business' with Soviet leader Gorbachev to flexibly broker détente between the US and the USSR, gaining her a (brief) high profile world role and a (more effective) resumption of the 'summitry' of earlier prime ministers.

Inheriting the Thatcher commitment of British troops to assist in a US-led United Nations operation to eject Iraq from Kuwait, Major's premiership began by underlining Britain's special role as the most dependable ally of the United States. After the successful conclusion of the Gulf War (1991), Major took the initiative in pressing for 'safe havens' for the Kurds, who were being savagely harassed by Saddam's defeated army. However, following the replacement of the Republican Bush by the Democrat Clinton as President, Britain's relationship with the US cooled. Already committed to military intervention in support of humanitarian aid in Bosnia, the Major Government resisted US pressure for a policy of 'lift and strike', i.e. lift the arms embargo on Bosnian Muslims and strike Bosnian Serbs with air power. Ultimately a NATO bombing campaign forced the Bosnian Serbs to negotiate a peace treaty under United States auspices (the Dayton Peace Accord (1995)), with Britain and other European powers playing no part.

Defence

Thatcher gave an increased commitment to defence, involving increased expenditure (the defence budget was one-fifth higher in the later 1980s than a decade earlier) and the commissioning from the United States of a new generation of more powerful nuclear weapons (Trident). However, with the collapse of the Soviet Union and the end of the Cold War (1989), Conservative Governments faced the task of scaling down Britain's military establishment whilst still retaining sufficient forces to enable Britain to play a world role in a much more unstable global situation. By 1996, defence spending was set to reach 3 per cent of GDP, compared with 5 per cent of GDP at its peak in 1986 (Freedman, 1994, pp. 270, 272–3).

The Falklands War (1982)

When the Argentinian President General Galtieri invaded the Falkland Islands, the Thatcher Government despatched a Task Force which successfully recaptured the islands at a cost of 255 British dead and 777 wounded. In addition, six

British ships were sunk. A 'Fortress Falklands' policy was then put in place for the defence of the islands at a cost of £5 billion. The result of the war – brought on to a significant extent by the Government's own diplomatic failings – enabled the Prime Minister to claim: 'Great Britain is great again'.

Decolonisation

The Conservative Government negotiated the independence of Southern Rhodesia as Zimbabwe (1980) and a special status for Hong Kong from 1997 within the People's Republic of China, but resisted Commonwealth pressure for wide-ranging sanctions against South Africa (1985–6).

Economic policy

The Government rejected full employment as the primary objective of economic policy in favour of the control of inflation. This meant the abandonment of Keynesian demand management in favour of monetarism (the control of the money supply) as the main mechanism of macroeconomic policy. By the mid-1980s, however, strict monetarism had been abandoned and the main counter-inflationary financial disciplines became first a stable exchange rate and then in 1990 entry to the European Exchange Rate Mechanism (ERM). Britain's ejection from the ERM in 1992, a devaluation of sterling from DM 2.95 to DM 2.65, led to the establishment of a new monetary framework involving publicly stated inflation targets and monthly meetings between the Chancellor and the Governor of the Bank of England to discuss monetary policy, the minutes of which were published six weeks later. By 1997, a low inflation economy seemed to have been achieved, with the inflation rate averaging 2.8 per cent between 1993 and 1997, still slightly higher than that of the UK's main trading partners (Kelly, 1997, p. 284). However, over the 1979–96 period the annual rate of inflation averaged 6 per cent in Britain, considerably higher than in France, Germany, the United States and Japan (*The Economist*, Election Briefing, 1997).

Public expenditure

The Conservative Government believed that *public expenditure was 'at the heart of Britain's present difficulties'* and came to power with the aim of reducing public expenditure as a proportion of GDP, promising substantial cuts in all areas except the National Health Service (NHS), defence and law and order. The overall purpose was to reduce the claims of the public sector on savings and to cut taxes in order to promote an 'enterprise culture'. By 1997, public spending had fallen, but not dramatically (from 44 per cent of GDP in 1979 to 41 per cent in 1997) and income tax rates had been reduced (the higher rate from 83 per cent to 40 per cent, standard rate from 33 per cent to 24 per cent), but owing to increases in indirect taxes such as VAT the overall burden of taxation had increased .

Privatisation

The 1979 manifesto promised only modest denationalisation (of aerospace and shipbuilding) but *privatisation emerged during the early 1980s as a central plank of the Government's programme*. Between 1979 and 1997 it carried out a massive transfer of assets from the public to the private sector, thereby virtually extinguishing the 'mixed economy' as it had existed since 1951. The goals were increased efficiency – the New Right believing as an article of faith that private enterprise was more efficient than public enterprise; the removal of a major burden from the taxpayer; and, more broadly, the creation of a free enterprise in place of a 'socialist' society. By 1997, 21 per cent of the adult population owned shares, compared with 7 per cent in 1979, and as a result of a large-scale sale of council houses, home-ownership had risen from 52 per cent of households in 1979 to 67 per cent in 1997.

Industry and trade unions

The Thatcher Governments *abandoned the corporatist, tripartite approach to industrial and incomes policy*, replacing it with an arm's length attitude to the employers and trade unions. The Conservatives also *sharply reduced the powers of the unions* both by legislation – which among other things outlawed secondary picketing, abolished the closed shop and made pre-strike ballots compulsory – and by winning bruising battles against the steel unions (1982) and (especially) the miners' union (1984–5). The Major Government continued these policies, further weakening the unions by legislation (1993) and abolishing tripartite institutions such as the National Economic Development Council (1992) and the Wages Councils which had laid down minimum wages for low-paid workers (1993). The goal of these policies was to shift responsibility away from the state on to 'the market' and within industry to move the balance of power towards management. Together with high unemployment, the reduction in union power resulted in an improvement in Britain's strike record, although it should be remembered that strike activity declined in most other advanced industrial countries in this period. During the 1990s, the Major Governments constantly extolled the virtues of Britain's flexible labour market in comparison with the more regulated, protected European labour markets.

The Welfare State

Conservative Governments in the 1980s would have liked to cut back severely on state-provided welfare but public support for the NHS, the social security system and free state education forced upon them *a less directly anti-consensual* approach. Nonetheless, the Thatcherite decade was a decisive one for social policy. Although the Thatcher Administrations failed to reduce the share of GDP taken by welfare expenditure, they ended its century-long increase, and did so despite the need to spend substantially more on unemployment benefits. They had three main goals: (1) the containment of costs and the search for greater efficiency and value for money in welfare provision; (2) the targeting of benefits on the most needy; and (3) encouragement of an enhanced role for the private sector in housing, health care,education and pensions provision. Before the late 1980s, *housing* represented the purest application of New Right principles, with significant but not revolutionary changes involving large-scale sales of council houses to sitting tenants, reductions in public sector house-building, the scaling down of council rent subsidies and the encouragement of house purchase (with mortgage interest relief trebling down to 1987–8). But after 1988 funda-

mental changes in the health service, education, community care and housing were brought about by the introduction of 'quasi-markets' into these services. The Education Act (1988), Housing Act (1988) and National Health Service and Community Care Act (1990) constituted really important legislation which rivalled that of the years 1944–48 in significance and represented the biggest break with social policy tradition since 1945 Glennerster, Power and Travers, 1992, p. 389–90). The changes were predominantly organisational and managerial and sought greater cost-consciousness, efficiency and diversity in the delivery of services rather than any erosion of the principles of taxpayer-financing or of free services at the point of use. The overall impact of the welfare reforms was to strengthen the role of central government, weaken the roles of local authorities and public sector professionals, and increase social inequality. They were continued by John Major, who added the 'Citizen's Charter' (1991), which sought to improve public sector services by establishing performance targets for them.

After May 1997: the emergence of a new consensus?

With the Conservatives moving emphatically to the right and Labour veering equally sharply to the left, the social, economic, foreign and defence policies of the major parties diverged sharply between 1979 and 1987. However, in the decade after 1987, their policies converged again, mainly owing to the shifts in Labour's policies engineered by party leaders Neil Kinnock, John Smith and Tony Blair. By the General Election of May 1997, a new, right-of-centre post-Thatcherite consensus seemed to have emerged, in sharp contrast to the left-of-centre Keynesian–Beveridgean consensus of the postwar era. Its arrival appeared to be confirmed by the early measures of the new Labour Government under Tony Blair. In broad terms, the new consensus was neo-liberal rather than social democratic, free market rather than mixed economy, and based on a vision of the state as enabler and regulator rather than direct provider of services (Box 2.5).

The Blair Government's early measures suggested firm commitment to the new **neo-liberal, right-of-centre consensus**. Major steps included the handing of control over monetary policy to an independent Bank of England, the acceptance of the previous Conservative Government's spending limits for the first two years and a pledge of no income tax increases for five years. A 'welfare to work' scheme was introduced aimed at getting the socially dependent unemployed and single parents into jobs, and state funding of university tuition fees was abandoned. This was a pro-market, pro-business, anti-inflationary government

committed to sound public finances and determined to eradicate its former 'tax and spend' reputation.

However, some differences remained between the major parties, just as they had done during the period of postwar consensus. Although determined to offer no concessions on essentials to trade unions, New Labour quickly removed the ban on union membership at GCHQ, signed the EU social chapter and promised a minimum wage, legislation to ensure union recognition where a majority of the workforce voted for a union, and enhanced employee rights at work. Although committed to tight control of public spending, the Labour Chancellor found an extra £2.2 billion from the contingency reserves for education and health. He also abolished tax credits on dividends (which critics argued would hit pension schemes) and imposed a £5.2 billion windfall tax on the privatised utilities, interventionist measures which no Conservative Chancellor would have adopted. Similarly, in education, Labour's abandonment of the selective places scheme outraged Conservatives. Labour also moved swiftly to 'constructive engagement' with Europe and pledged an 'ethical' foreign policy, one of its first steps being to accept an international ban on the

---

The neo-liberal post-Thatcherite consensus: The late-1990s' consensus involved a more modest role for Britain as a medium-sized state within the European Union; tight control of public spending with search for more targeted and more efficient, better value for money welfare services through quasi-markets and other means; and a free market economy with the role of the state limited to the supply side of the economy and priority given to low inflation.

BOX 2.5
The emergence of a new consensus: after 1997

Middle-ranking European state and free market economy

Governments: New Labour, 1997–

The new consensus was based on the acceptance by New Labour of the main social and economic changes of the Conservatives between 1979 and 1997.

External relations: Britain as middle-ranking, post-imperial European state but with nuclear weapons and still possessing cultural, diplomatic and military resources enabling it to play significant world role.

Relations with European Union of increasing significance: some change of style here between Major and Blair (who favours a more positive role for Britain) and differences on single currency between Labour and Hague, as Conservatives moved right after the election.

Good personal relationship between Blair and US President Clinton: close cooperation on Iraq crisis, 1998.

Post-Cold War search for defence cuts as part of peace dividend

Domestic policy: Labour's 1997 manifesto and first months in power showed clear commitment to 1979–97 'settlement':

- Priority to maintaining low inflation economy with emphasis on supply-side improvements in education and training;
- Low tax regime with tight control of public spending:
- Non-interventionist industrial policy, with no restoration of union power and privileges;
- Acceptance of free market economy produced by Conservative privatisations but with tighter regulation of privatised utilities;
- Support for 'quasi-market' reforms in education, health and housing;

Continuation of search for more efficient, more accountable public services.

import, export, transfer and manufacture of land mines. With Labour proposing to enter the European single currency soon after the next election and the Conservatives ruling out entry for at least ten years, there were also significant differences on the euro. Finally, New Labour's full programme of constitutional reform was far from welcome to the Conservatives.

Summary

- A political consensus on foreign, social and economic policy emerged between 1940 and 1955. Its main ingredients were: a major world role for Britain, a universalist welfare state and a mixed economy. But some inter-party differences remained, with Labour, for example, more public sector-orientated and the Conservatives more sympathetic to the private sector.
- Between 1955 and 1979, the consensus continued, despite the emergence of both external and domestic pressures. The main external pressures were the need for a radical reorientation towards Europe caused by rapid decolonisation, the erosion of the Commonwealth as a political and economic bloc and the success of the European Economic Community. The main internal pressures were the problems caused by slow economic growth, mounting inflation, industrial militancy and the rising taxation required to pay for ever-higher levels of public expenditure. These difficulties intensified during the 1970s and the Labour Government of 1974–9 began to move away from consensus policies on the economy.
- After 1979, the Conservative Governments of Margaret Thatcher and John Major, guided by New Right ideology, broke with the postwar consensus on social and economic policy. In foreign affairs, these years were marked by the aggressive pursuit of British interests in the European Union (within which Britain became, however, increasingly integrated) and a willingness to use armed force in pursuit of the national interest both with the assistance of the United States (the Falklands) or in support of the United States (the Gulf War). In domestic policy, the Conservatives departed from the consensus by prioritising the reduction of inflation over the maintenance of full employment and by 'rolling back the frontiers of the state' by, for example, privatising public sector industries and services, abandoning corporatist economic management, cutting direct taxes and implementing strict control of public expenditure. The search for greater efficiency, better value for money and higher standards lay behind reforms of the welfare state.
- Labour's move to the right in the late 1980s and 1990s underpinned the apparent emergence of a new consensus after 1997. Although sharply opposed to the Conservatives on its plans for constitutional reform, New Labour's 1997 general election manifesto and its behaviour in government after May 1997 showed that it had adopted most of the Thatcherite social and economic agenda while also seeking to combine this with the public demand for a more compassionate society.

Questions

1. Discuss the contention that the postwar consensus was a 'myth'.
2. How far did the Conservative Governments after 1979 break with the postwar consensus ?
3. How far in your view is it realistic to speak of the emergence of a new post-Thatcherite consensus in the late 1990s?

Assignment

Britain's post-1945 role in the world: delusions of grandeur versus genuine major player

Some historians and political commentators believe that *delusions of grandeur* stemming from Britain's possession of a great empire inhibited its adjustment to the postwar world, in particular persuading politicians of both major parties mistakenly to seek an independent and leading world role for Britain. This pursuit had the following adverse consequences for the country:

- *Excessive commitments*: Maintaining a large colonial empire and global system of military bases *plus* a welfare state *plus* a large house-building programme *plus* the development of nuclear weapons *plus* large conventional military forces, placed an excessive strain on the country's economy. Granted the strength of the political commitment to and the ethical desirability of better welfare and housing, it was the consistently high defence spending, compared with that of other comparable states, that proved such a mistake.

- *Missed opportunities*. (1) Failure to join the European Economic Community until 1973 rather than in 1957 meant that EEC institutional and arrangements were already shaped to suit Britain's partners rather than Britain itself, and (2) Britain missed the economic stimulus of participating directly in Europe during the most rapid phase of postwar economic growth. Instead of helping to build a new Europe, British politicians and officials were largely preoccupied with colonial crises and global defence whilst British industry, enjoying imperial preferences in 'soft' colonial markets, had no incentive to modernise. This 'lost generation' of industrial modernisation served Britain ill when its industry faced stronger European competitors in the 1970s.
- *A failure of political and cultural leadership*: Britain's political and cultural elites were well aware of the need to scale down its commitments to that of a medium-sized power after 1945, but instead political rhetoric ('world role', 'global leadership', 'making Britain great again') hampered rather than encouraged a more realistic understanding in the electorate whilst cultural elites (filmmakers, tabloid editors) fed nostalgic national myths (war films) and propagated suspicion of and hostility towards foreignors.
- *Liberal militarism*: Possession of a disproportionately large military establishment and defence industry (1) diverted economic resources from civilian to military purposes: in particular, Britain concentrated its research and development in the 1950s and 1960s on aircraft, military electronics and nuclear power whereas Britain's main competitors in Europe and Japan concentrated their innovative efforts on products such as vehicles, machinery and chemicals which provided the main impetus behind postwar economic growth; (2) led to Britain making disproportionately large commitments to international ventures: e.g. it provided the second largest contingents both in the Gulf War and Bosnia in the 1990s; (3) has made Britain excessively dependent on arms sales to developing countries (Britain controls one-fifth of the global market in arms sales and ranks second to the US as an arms exporter) and has led to scandals in the 1990s e.g. the Pergau Dam affair.

Opponents of this view argue as follows:

- *British exceptionalism*: It simply is not feasible to compare Britain with other medium-sized European countries especially in the decades immediately after the Second World War because its history (massive empire and wartime victory) and geography placed it in a comparatively much more influential position. The *political* importance of the imperial legacy (the global scope of British policy) is backed up by its *social* significance in people's lives (in December 1974, Prime Minister Harold Wilson pointed out that he had 43 relatives in Australia, over four times as many as he had in Britain; many British people have such links) and by its *cultural* impact (e.g. the English language is spoken by one-fifth of the world's population and the BBC has a large world audience)
- *Benign influence*: Britain's postwar commitments to, for example, a leading role in NATO, a large military establishment and the development of nuclear weapons have served Britain and the world well, enabling the country to play a significant role in the maintenance of world peace since 1945, in triggering the collapse of Soviet Communism and in resolving regional conflicts. 'No European power since the war has exerted more diplomatic influence more successfully' (A. Sked, the *Guardian,* 29 March, 1997).
- *The importance of historical context:* (1) A global power vacuum existed immediately after the war when it was far from clear whether the United States would be willing to undertake major international responsibilities and a new Cold War loomed: in the circumstances Britain was thrust into playing a major world role. (2) Once the

United States had assumed leadership of the West, British premiers were under frequent pressure to assist the US in the containment of world communism in Africa and Asia, in return receiving US assistance with nuclear weapons and support for sterling. (3) It is possible that, even though normally responsive to strong leadership, public opinion would not have supported an application for membership of the European Economic Community in the mid-1950s.

- *Britain's achievements*: Far from living in the past Britain adapted well to the postwar world and has much in which to take pride. (1) It had a comparatively smooth and relatively peaceful decolonisation from an empire population of 760 million (1945) to 168,000 (1997). Moreover, decolonisation left favourable legacies such as, first, the Commonwealth and, second, the fact that nearly a quarter of the world's democracies originated in the British Empire. In view of Britain's historical involvement in South Africa, Nelson Mandela in 1993 asked Britain to help his fellow citizens in rediscovering the practice of democracy. (2) It has the fifth largest economy in the world, with massive £1.7 trillion global investments and a very large proportion of American and Japanese investment in the European Union, together with world class institutions such as the National Health Service, the armed forces and an effective and uncorrupt civil service.

Questions

(i) Which of these two cases do you find most convincing, and why?

(ii) How well do you think these theses fit into a left and right wing perspective? Give reasons.

(iii) Assuming that you find neither case as pre-sented above completely convincing, state which individual components of each case you find persuasive, and why.

(iv) Does either case ignore any important factor (e.g. race relations)?

(v) Present a reasoned argument explaining the mistakes and successes in Britain's adjustment to the postwar world.

Further reading

On the postwar consensus, there is Kavanagh, D. and Morris, P. *Consensus Politics from Attlee to Thatcher*, 2nd edn. (Oxford: Blackwell) whilst Coxall, B and Robins, L. (1998) *British Politics since the War* (London: Macmillan) contains a chapter on the postwar consensus as well as chapters on postwar politics and social, economic and foreign policy. A critical view of the consensus thesis is offered by Pimlott, B. (1988) 'The Myth of Consensus', reprinted in *Frustrate Their Knavish Tricks* (London: Harper Collins, 1994). On the emergence of a post-Thatcherite consensus, see Dunleavy, P., Gamble, A., Holliday, I. and Peele, G. (1997) *Development in British Politics 5* (London: Macmillan), especially the Introduction and the chapters on 'Britain, Europe and the World', 'Economic Policy' and 'Social Policy'. Information on both the Thatcher and Major Governments is provided by Smith, M.J. and Ludlam, S. (eds) (1996) *Contemporary British Conservatism* (London: Macmillan) and Crewe, I. (1996) '1979–1996', in Seldon, A. (ed.), *How Tory Governments Fall* (London: Harper Collins).

Morgan, K. (1990) *The People's Peace: British History 1945–1989* (Oxford: Oxford University Press) provides a valuable account of the postwar period as in briefer compass does Dorey, P. (1995) *British Politics since 1945* (Oxford: Blackwell).

The social and economic context

The links between politics and society and politics and the economy are both close. Political issues such as the optimum organisation of the health service, how to tackle racial discrimination and how to encourage more women to enter politics are themselves thrown up by developments in society. Political scientists study voting behaviour in terms of the links between class and party, and institutions such as parties, Parliament, the civil service and the Cabinet are analysed in relationship to the social background of their members. Since 1945, when government assumed new responsibilities for management of the economy and even more since the 1960s when arresting British economic decline became a central concern of Cabinets, the disciplines of politics and economics have seemed ever more closely intertwined. Today's politics to a considerable extent is economic politics, with a high proportion of each day's news being economic news, concerned with inflation and unemployment rates, the trade figures, balance of payments, and so on.

This chapter examines the social and economic background to British politics. It focuses first on divisions in British society in terms of class, gender, race, nation and region; and second, on recent trends in the British economy.

Population

In terms of population, the United Kingdom (UK) is one of the larger states in the European Union (EU), smaller than the unified Germany but similar to France and Italy. In world terms, Britain ranks about seventeenth. UK population growth has slowed dramatically in the twentieth century in common with other industrialised nations, increasing from 41.46 million in 1901 to 49.2 million in 1945 and to 58.6 million in 1995.

Compared with slowing growth in the economically advanced countries, however, world population is growing at an ever faster rate. For example, in the 1920s it was 2 billion; 1960, 3 billion; 1974, 4 billion; 1996, 5.8 billion; and it is projected to reach 8.3 billion in 2010. The UK is one of the most densely populated nations in Europe , its population density of 242 people per square kilometre being well above the European Union average of about 153 people per square kilometre. Within the United Kingdom since the war there has been a redistribution of the population from Scotland and the North of England to the English South-East, East Anglia, the East Midlands and the South-West. Some international comparisons are given in Table 3.1.

Table 3.1 Population: some international comparisons, 1971 and 1996

	Population (millions)	
	1971	1996
United Kingdom	55.9	58.4
European Union	322.4	372.4
China	787.2	1,234.3
USA	207.0	265.8

Source: Extracted from *Social Trends* (1992 and 1997).

Social class in Britain

Class remains of great importance as the major source of social stratification in Britain. It is of central significance when considering individual life-chances, work experiences, political behaviour and popular perceptions of social division.

But there is no agreed method of allocating people into distinct classes. For example, Karl Marx (1818–83) stressed the schism between capital and labour, owners and workers, propertied and propertyless, as the fundamental class division. Max Weber, the German sociologist (1864–1920), variously emphasised the importance of status distinctions based on social recognition, differential life-chances grounded on different 'market' situations, and authority relations at work as determinants of social position. Both thinkers have latter-day followers who have developed more complex schema of stratification based respectively on relationships to the means of production and on status and 'life-chances'.

Some contemporary social commentators continue to use the 'language of class' first developed in the nineteenth century, referring to the upper, middle and working classes and to internal subdivisions (e.g. upper and lower) within the latter two categories. This classification has the merit of being easily comprehensible since it is the one people employ in everyday life. For example, respondents to social surveys normally have little difficulty in assigning themselves to a specific segment of a social class. But critics of this categorisation say that it lacks precision because it is not immediately apparent where particular occupational groups should be located.

Government, market researchers and sociologists agree in defining class in relation to work and in producing classificatory schemes based on *occupation*.

Social class: a group of people sharing a similar social position. Non-Marxists distinguish between classes on the basis of inequalities of income, status and occupation: e.g. middle class and working class, white collar and blue collar, manual and non-manual workers. Marxists see class divisions as the result of unequal economic power stemming from ownership/lack of ownership of the means of production.

The Registrar-General's five category classification is often seen as definitive. It forms the basis for social analysis of the ten-yearly census and is used in government publications. In 1997, however, a more elaborate eight-tier classification scheme was proposed by the Economic and Social Research Council (ESRC), which would extend the present scheme by including those on state benefits (the *Guardian*, 15 December , 1997). It is under consideration by the government. Market researchers divide people into six socioeconomic categories, but usually in practice reduce these to four: AB, C1, C2 and DE. This method of classification is employed in opinion polls.

Another influential system of social classification has been proposed by the social scientist John Goldthorpe and this is the one adopted by the political scientists Anthony Heath, Roger Jowell and John Curtice in their studies of voting behaviour (Table 3.2). This scheme distinguishes occupational classes by their economic interests rather than by their prestige and standing in the community (Registrar-General) or by their standard of living and lifestyle (market research). All of these classifications avoid the terms 'upper class' and 'middle class' and only one employs the term 'working class'. Unlike traditional descriptions of social class, categorisation by occupation avoids built-in value judgements. It is more specific and apparently more objective.

But, as reflections of social reality, occupational classifications face problems too. For example, only one of the listed schemes finds a place for the unemployed and other state dependents (although the ESRC scheme would do, if adopted) and none includes the wives of salaried or manual workers, or great landowners like the Duke of Devonshire. Clearly, despite possessing the advantage of a more 'neutral' language, occupational class cannot be equated with social class.

We conclude that both the traditional classification and the one based on occupations have value and that for political scientists their usefulness will depend to a large extent on the purpose for which they are required. Thus it may be feasible in discussions of voting behaviour to employ basically occupational categories (AB, C1, C2, DE) but it makes less sense to rely solely on these categories when analysing the social background of the Cabinet or

Table 3.2 Occupational class in Britain

Registrar-General	Market research	Oxford Mobility Study (John Goldthorpe)	Economic and Social Research Council proposal (1997)
I Professional	A Professional / senior managerial	I Higher professional (higher professionals and administrators; managers in large industrial establishments; large proprietors)	1. Professional/Employers, administrators and managers in large organisations (over 25 staff)
II Intermediate	B Middle managers / executives	II Lower professional (lower professionals and administrators; higher-grade technicians; managers in small industrial establishment; supervisors of non-manual workers)	2. Associate professionals (i.e. nurses, legal executives)/ Employers, administrators and managers in small organisations (under 25)/ Supervisors
III Skilled (subdivided into non-manual and manual	C1 Junior managers / non-manual	III Routine non-manual (clerical; sales; secretarial; services)	3. Intermediate administrative, clerical, sales and service occupations (i.e. secretaries, sales representatives, computer operators)
IV Partly-skilled manual	C2 Skilled manual	IV Petty bourgeoisie (farmers; small proprietors; self-employed)	4. Self-employed non-professionals (i.e. driving instructors, builders, carpenters)
V Unskilled manual	D Semi-skilled / unskilled manual	V Foremen and technicians (lower-grade technicians; supervisors of manual workers)	5. Skilled manual (plumbers, telephone fitters, craft and allied workers)
		VI Skilled manual	6. Semi-skilled and unskilled manual (lorry drivers, assembly-line workers, traffic wardens, routine manufacturing and service occupations)
		VII Semi skilled and unskilled manual; agricultural workers	7. All types of labourers, waiters, waitresses and cleaners and other elementary manufacturing and service occupations
			8. Long-term unemployed, or sick, on state benefits

Sources: Office of Population and Censuses; opinion poll surveys; Marshall, Swift and Roberts (1997); Economic and Social Research Council (1997).

the reasons for the decline of the pre-Blair Labour Party. The traditional classification, based on a division of British society into a small upper class, a middle class and a working class, with important sub-divisions within the two last-named classes, is of continued relevance.

The use of this classification is quite compatible with a recognition that the boundaries between classes are fluid and shifting and that this may lead on occasion to problems of definition. For example, in the 1960s it was often wondered whether the skilled worker as a result of greater affluence had become essentially middle class in lifestyle and attitude – the 'embourgeoisement' thesis. In the 1980s, new divisions were identified in both the middle and the working classes based on sectoral and other cleavages. For example, a contrast was drawn between a traditional and a 'new' working class, i.e between a trade unionist, public sector worker living in a council house in the North and a non-unionist, private sector worker buying his house on a mortgage in the South-East.

With the increase in unemployment and part-time (and temporary) working, other internal divisions within the classes have become important too – between the employed and the unemployed and between those in full-time and those in part-time work. But these complicate rather than erode the class structure. Factors of birth, education, social expectation, and professional training or trade skill which form the bases of class identity continue to operate whether a person has part-time or temporary work or is unemployed.

Social change since the war

The main change in the structure of British society since the war has been the growth of the middle class and the shrinkage of the working class. This has led to a considerable shift in the size and balance of classes. Broadly speaking, in 1951 the middle class constituted about one-third, the working class approximately two-thirds, of the working population. By the 1990s, the situation had been transformed, with the middle class having become a majority of the occupied population. Underlying this change has been the sharp increase in non-manual employment and a contraction of manual occupations (Table 3.3).

Table 3.3 Social class in Britain, 1964 and 1992 (percentages)

	1964	1992
Higher salariat	7.0	11.6
Lower salariat	12.3	16.3
Routine non-manual	16.5	24.2
Petty bourgeoisie	6.6	7.1
Foremen and technicians	7.6	4.8
Skilled manual	17.8	10.9
Unskilled manual	32.4	25.1

Source: Heath, cited in Adonis and Pollard (1997).

Some commentators – impressed by the growth of the professional, managerial, administrative and clerical strata – have suggested that Britain has become a 'middle class' society and is even in sight of becoming a 'classless' society. It is certainly the case that white-collar now outnumber blue-collar jobs and that, with the spread of affluence, standards of living and lifestyles formerly associated with the middle class are now enjoyed by the majority.

However, there are several arguments which tell against the thesis that Britain has become a 'middle class' or 'classless' society. First, all recent research points to the continuing sense of class identity in both the middle class and the working class;people not only perceive themselves as belonging to a particular class but also as occupying a certain position within it. Second, very large inequalities in wealth, income, housing, education and health – themselves related to class – remain, and may even have increased in recent years. Some writers, for example, have contrasted the rise of a new 'super rich' 'upper class' of top earners in business, the City and the private sector professions, on the one hand, with the emergence of a lower class or 'underclass' of the unemployed, the homeless, the poorly housed,and the ill-educated, on the other. Even if increasing general prosperity, improvements in diet and dress and the spread of consumerism have reduced the visible differences between classes, major class differences persist.

Table 3.4 The labour force, by gender, 1971–96

	1971 (millions)	% total	1981 (millions)	% total	1991 (millions)	% total	1996 (millions)	% total
Men	15.6	62	15.7	60	16.0	57	15.6	56
Women	9.4	38	10.6	40	12.1	43	12.3	44

Source: Extracted from *Social Trends* (1997) p. 74.

Gender

Social divisions based on **gender**, race, nation and region have increased in significance in recent decades. In the case of women, the reasons for this are, first, their growing prominence in the labour force and, second, the social and political impact of feminism since the later 1960s. (See further, Chapter 5.) In the immediate postwar period – before these developments took place – the role of women rarely achieved separate treatment in books like this, but was most often dealt with – if at all – under a theme such as 'the family'.

Women's participation in the workforce began to increase significantly after 1951 and accelerated after 1971. In 1951 men made up over two-thirds of the workforce and still constituted over three-fifths of it in 1971. By 1996, the situation was very different, with women making up well over two-fifths of the labour force (Table 3.4). A range of demographic, economic, social and cultural factors underlie women's increasing participation in waged work. These include comparatively low birth rates in the 1970s, the need of households for a second wage-earner in order to maintain living standards, improvements in women's health and educational qualifications, and changing attitudes to the employment of women by managements.

The rise in part-time working is closely connected with women's increasing participation in the labour force. In 1996 nearly a quarter of all jobs were part-time, and over four-fifths of part-time workers were women.

Women's activity in the labour workforce differs from men's in several ways. First, because of their role in raising young children, women spend a lower proportion – about two-thirds – of their potential working lives in the labour market. Second, the majority of employed women – two-thirds in 1996 – are in non-manual occupations, whereas under half of employed men are. Over a quarter of women workers are employed in clerical and secretarial occupations (compared with one-twelfth of male workers) and women also outnumber men in the health and social work sector (by four to one) and in education (by two to one) (Table 3.5). Third, as mentioned already, women are far more likely than men to work part-time: in spring 1996, 45 per cent of female employees but only 8 per cent of male employees worked part-time. Fourth, women's pay

Gender: Gender refers to the social and cultural allocation of different roles to men and women. Feminists stress gendered differences as being social constructs based on traditional social stereotypes and therefore as changeable compared with sexual, i.e. biological differences between men and women which cannot be altered.

Table 3.5 Employees, by gender and occupation, 1996 (percentages)

	Males	Females
Professional	12	10
Managers and administrators	19	10
Associate professional and technical	8	10
Clerical and secretarial	8	26
Personal and protective services	8	16
Sales	6	12
Craft and related	17	3
Plant and machine operatives	15	4
Other occupations	8	9

Source: *Social Trends* (1997) p.76.

Table 3.6 Weekly earnings, by gender, April 1995

	Average weekly earnings (all industries) (£)
Men	374.6
Women	269.6
Non-manual men	443.3
Non-manual women	288.1
Manual men	291.3
Manual women	188.1

Source: Extracted from *Key Data* (Office for National Statistics, 1996) p. 52.

lags significantly behind men's (Table 3.6). In April 1995, the average weekly wages of full-time women workers were only 72 per cent of the average weekly earnings of full-time male workers. Gender segregation in the labour market, with women relegated to badly paid, low-status jobs, is an important factor underlying this differential. However, this situation may be expected to change considerably in coming decades as a result of women's educational progress and of employer initiatives aimed at making better use of women's abilities (see further, Chapter 28).

Race

A further source of social division and inequality in Britain is **race**. In 1996, the ethnic minority population of Great Britain numbered 3.3 million, which represents just under 6 per cent of the total population. The ethnic minority population is made up as follows: Indian, about 27 per cent; Pakistani and Bangladeshi, 23 per cent; Afro-Caribbean and other

Race: a common form of social differentiation between groups based on superficial characteristics such as skin colour supposedly distinguishing people on biological grounds. In the absence of a fixed, objective category of race, the concept of ethnicity, defined as a shared cultural and historical identity, is often preferred to the term 'race' in this context.

groups, 26 per cent; and people of Arab, Chinese, mixed and other origins, 24 per cent.

This important change in the British population was brought about largely by immigration from the former colonial Caribbean and the South Asian subcontinent in the post-1945 period. Earlier labour migrations into Britain in the twentieth century – by the Irish and by the Jews and other displaced European nationals in the 1930s and 1940s – resulted in primarily *cultural* differences between the immigrants and the native population. The postwar immigration from the New Commonwealth and Pakistan, however, introduced ethnic differences of race as well as culture to the country for the first time, thereby challenging the traditional meanings attached to 'Britishness'.

Coloured immigration is not unique to Britain but common throughout the industrialised West. The large proportion of immigrant families who took up permanent residence, however, distinguished Britain from many other migrant labour-importing countries in Western Europe in the postwar era (Miles, 1982, in McDowell et al. (eds) 1989, pp. 93–110). Just under half of the ethnic minority population were born in Britain. The consequence of New Commonwealth immigration has been to make Britain into a multiracial, multicultural society.

The presence of a sizeable ethnic minority population, especially in the inner cities, has intensified social tensions in Britain, with racial discrimination, widespread although often hard to prove, overlapping and compounding inequalities based on class and gender. Opportunities for Britain's ethnic communities with regard to jobs, education and living their lives without victimisation are still much worse than for whites (*The Economist*, 8 February 1997). The ethnic minorities have presented British governments with the formidable challenge of achieving a racially non-discriminatory society (see further, Chapters 5 and 27 on the impact of race on British politics).

Nation and Region

Another source of differentiation within the UK is between the constituent **nations**. Quite simply, in population and wealth, England is hugely predominant. The Union is an asymmetrical one, with 83 per cent of the UK population living in England. In terms of population, England outnumbers Scotland by a ratio of over 9 to 1, Wales by over 17 to 1 and Northern Ireland by 30 to 1 (Table 3.7). This degree of domination was not always the case: in 1801, when the United Kingdom was formed, England contained 53 per cent of the UK population, Ireland, 33 per cent. Mass Irish emigration in the nineteenth century and the secession of Southern Ireland in 1922 produced the present imbalance. There is an equally marked economic disparity, with GDP per head and employment levels higher in England than in the other constituent countries of the UK (Table 3.8).

Cultural differences persist between the nations of the UK. These go beyond superficial differences, such as accent, to include patterns of religious observance, the speaking of Gaelic languages, educational systems and the mass media. Thus in England a majority identify with the Church of England, in Scotland with the Church of Scotland (Presbyterian), in Wales, where the Church of England was disestablished in 1920, with one of the Nonconformist sects, and in Northern Ireland with either the Protestant Episcopalian or Presbyterian Church. Only in Northern Ireland, where there is a sizeable minority of Roman Catholics, do religious divisions possess political salience.

Linguistic differences have also greatly diminished

from the early nineteenth century when about nine-tenths of Welsh people, half of the Irish and just under one-quarter of Scots spoke a variety of Gaelic as their first or only language. Today only a small minority (19 per cent in 1991) speak Welsh and a very much smaller proportion of Scots (under 2 per cent) speak Gaelic. Welsh schools were fully integrated with the English system after 1944, but education in Scotland and Northern Ireland is run on different lines, and in Northern Ireland is subject to strong sectarian influences. Finally newspapers produced in Northern Ireland and Scotland have large readerships in those countries (Birch, 1979, pp. 37–8).

During the 1980s a growing economic division between the relatively prosperous South and less well-off North attracted considerable attention. Included for the purposes of this analysis in 'the North' were the regions of Yorkshire and Humberside, the North-West, the North of England, Wales, Scotland and Northern Ireland; included in 'the South' were the South-East, East Anglia, the South-West, and the East and West Midlands. It was frequently observed that on a number of criteria, including income per head and unemployment rate, the gap between the North and the South increased during the 1980s (Table 3.8). During the early 1980s recession, many northern-based traditional industries disappeared whilst, especially in the late 1980s, the expansion of the business, financial and retailing sectors in the south increased employment opportunities. There are also striking regional disparities in health. The Black Report (1982) observed that 'death rates were highest in Scotland, followed by the north and north west regions of England, and were lowest in the south

---

> **Nation**: a group possessing a common language, history, customs, traditions, usually a territory and often, although not invariably, a state.

Table 3.7 The nations of the United Kingdom, 1995

	Population (millions)	% increase since 1961	% UK total	Population density (per square kilometre)
England	48.9	12.0	83.0	375
Wales	2.9	11.0	5.0	140
Scotland	5.1	−1.0	8.8	67
Northern Ireland	1.6	15.0	2.8	122
United Kingdom	58.6	11.0	100.0	242

Source: Extracted from *Social Trends* (1997) p. 28; *Britain: An Official Handbook* (HMSO, 1997) p. 31.

Table 3.8 Regional incomes and unemployment, United Kingdom, 1971–95

	Incomes (GDP per head) (percentages of UK figure)				Unemployment (%)				
	1971	1981	1991	1994	1979	1986	1990	1993	1995
North	87	94	89	89	6.5	14.7	10.4	11.3	10.8
Yorks and Humberside	93	92	92	89	4.1	12.4	7.7	10.0	8.7
North West	96	95	90	90	5.0	14.0	8.0	11.1	9.1
West Midlands	103	91	93	93	4.0	12.6	6.8	11.8	9.0
East Midlands	97	97	98	96	3.3	10.2	6.6	9.1	7.5
East Anglia	95	97	101	102	3.1	8.6	4.8	8.4	7.1
South West	95	93	95	96	4.0	8.9	5.0	9.2	7.8
South East	112	117	117	117	2.6	8.5	5.2	10.4	8.6
England	102	102	102	102	4.0	10.6	6.4	10.3	8.6
Wales	87	84	85	84	5.3	14.3	8.0	9.6	8.8
Scotland	94	97	97	100	5.7	13.9	9.3	10.2	8.3
Northern Ireland	78	79	82	82	7.9	15.8	11.6	12.5	11.0
United Kingdom	100	100	100	100	4.0	11.2	6.8	10.3	8.6

Source: Extracted from *Social Trends* (1997) p. 105; *Key Data* (Office for National Statistics (1996) p. 16.

east of England and East Anglia, confirming the long established North–South gradient' (Townsend, Davidson and Whitehead, 1990, p. 352).

The North–South divide in health, wealth and employment is a significant one, but should not be exaggerated. The gap in economic welfare – although not in health – is to some extent offset by a standard of living index, which evaluates regional living standards in terms of the relationship between average incomes and the cost of living, including house prices. On such a 'quality of life' calculation, the North of England region came top, with Yorkshire and Humberside second, whereas Greater London was at the bottom, with the South-East next to bottom (Reward Group Regional Cost of Living Report, 1988). Moreover, the early-1990s' recession hit the South-East far harder than the rest of the UK,with job losses in the year to June 1991 far higher than in the North, Yorkshire and Humberside, Wales, Scotland and Northern Ireland. Even in 1995, with economic recovery well under way, unemployment rates in the South-East were little different from elsewhere in the UK, and at 11.5 per cent in Greater London, they were considerably higher.

The changing British economy

Major developments in recent decades have been:

- A continuing decline in manufacturing industry and growth in the services sector;
- A large-scale shift of ownership from the public to the private sector and a significant increase in inward and outward investment;
- The discovery and development of offshore oil and gas resources;
- Important labour market changes, including declining employment in manufacturing and a rise in self-employment and part-time working;
- Changing long-term patterns of trade and changes in the 1980s in Britain's trade accounts and balance of payments;
- An economic performance which since 1945 has combined growing prosperity for the whole community with national economic decline.

The decline of manufacturing and the growth of services

The major trends in the British economy since the war have been a further decline in the already (by European standards) small agricultural sector, a reduction in the industrial sector and a sizeable expansion of the services sector (retailing, banking, tourism, public services). Thus agriculture generated 6 per cent of **Gross Domestic Product (GDP)** in 1951 but only 2 per cent in 1995; manufacturing contributed 36 per cent of national income at its peak in 1951, but had declined to just under 27 per cent in 1980 and just under 22 per cent in 1995 ; and services constituted 51 per cent of GDP in 1951 but had risen to 55.3 per cent in 1980 and further to 71 per cent in 1995. Table 3.8 shows GDP by sector between 1969 and 1995.

Economists and politicians disagree about the significance of the process of 'de-industrialisation' – another term for the decline of manufacturing industry – as it affects Britain. On the one hand, the overall trend is common to most advanced economies. On the other hand, the decline in British manufacturing has been sharper than elsewhere, with the result that by 1995 Britain had a smaller industrial base and a larger services sector than other advanced industrial nations. One opinion of this trend is that it need not be taken too seriously since improvements in the service sector can offset losses in employment and foreign earnings in manufacturing industry. Another view is that the decline of manufacturing matters a lot because services cannot be expanded at a sufficient rate to compensate for the decline in the capacity of manufacturing to earn foreign currency for Britain through exports.

The privatisation of nationalised industries

During the 1980s the British economy became more capitalist, with a massive transfer of assets taking place from the public to the private sector. Between 1979 and 1997, the Conservative Government privatised all the major industries nationalised by the Labour Government of 1945 to 1951, including gas, electricity, water, steel, coal, rail and the national airways. By 1996, the proceeds of these and other privatisations had raised £65 billion for the government.

As a result of privatisation, the proportion of GDP accounted for by the nationalised industries declined from 9 per cent to 3.5 per cent (1979–89) and the number of their employees dropped from 1.8 million to 700,000 over the same period. Individual share-ownership jumped from 3 million (about 7 per cent of the adult population) in 1979 to 10 million (22 per cent) in 1997. However, most shareholders in privatised companies owned shares in no more than two firms and over half owned shares in one company only. Moreover, as a proportion of total shareholding, individual share-ownership continued to decline, with the value of individual shares as a proportion of the value of all shares falling from 54 per cent in 1963 to 20 per cent in 1995 (see further, Chapter 17).

The 1980s were also marked by large-scale inward and outward investment. In 1982, foreign enterprises were already responsible for almost 15 per cent of total employment in Britain and just under 20 per cent of UK industrial output. However, as a consequence of a rise in inward investment from the late 1980s, overseas firms provided 18 per cent of all manufacturing jobs by 1996 and 24 per cent of net manufacturing output. Such inward investment,

Table 3.9 GDP, percentage by sector, 1969–95

	1969	1980	1985	1990	1995
Agriculture	3.1	2.1	1.9	1.5	2.0
Energy	4.9	9.7	10.6	5.1	5.0
Construction	7.0	6.1	5.8	7.6	5.3
Manufacturing	34.1	26.8	23.9	22.4	21.8
Private services	38.5	39.0	42.1	47.4	48.6
Public services	12.4	16.3	15.7	16.0	18.6

Note: Items in 1995 column total over 100 per cent (deduction for financial services in National Accounts omitted)

Source: UK National Accounts (1991 and 1996 editions).

Gross Domestic Product (GDP): A concept developed by economists to measure the size of a country's economy by aggregating the total value of transactions in goods and services over a fixed term(normally one year).The concept enables the measurement of year-on-year change and therefore of a national economy's growth.

especially by Japan, was a major factor in transforming Britain's motor and electronics industries. By the mid-1990s, 40 per cent of Japanese and US investment in the European Union went to the UK. At the same time, British overseas investment also leaped to exceptional levels in the late 1980s.In 1994,the bulk of it was in the EU (35 per cent) and United States (32 per cent).

The discovery and exploitation of North Sea oil

North Sea oil made a huge impact on the British economy in the 1980s. Before the mid-1970s, Britain was almost entirely dependent for its oil supplies upon imports. As a consequence, like most other advanced industrial countries, it was extremely vulnerable to sudden upward movements in the price of oil, as happened in 1973–4 when the Organisation of Petroleum Exporting Countries (OPEC) suddenly quadrupled its oil prices, immediately plunging Britain along with the rest of the industrialised world into recession. The first significant discovery of offshore oil was made in 1969 and the first oil came ashore from the North Sea in 1975. Within five years Britain became a major exporter of oil, with large current account surpluses. A trade deficit in oil of nearly £4 billion in 1976 became a relatively small surplus of £273 million in 1980, a massive one of £5.3 billion in 1984 and a more modest £1 billion surplus in 1995.

Oil production peaked in the mid-1980s – when Britain became the world's sixth largest producer – but declined steadily thereafter. However, Britain was still a net oil exporter in 1995 and the world's ninth largest producer .In1990, the UK was also the world's seventh largest producer of natural gas, with production mainly centred on fields in the North Sea. Oil and gas accounted for 2.1 per cent of GDP in 1995. In net terms, Britain is self-sufficient in energy and expects to remain so into the twenty-first century.

North Sea oil and gas had a considerable impact on government revenues in the 1980s. Over the whole decade they brought £65 billion into the Exchequer and helped keep government income buoyant in a period which saw a large increase in spending on unemployment benefits.

However, with falling production and a sharp decline in oil prices after 1986, government North Sea revenues dropped to £2.8 billion in 1990–1, compared with over £12 billion in 1984–5. North Sea oil also made a significant contribution to GDP and the balance of payments. In the mid-1980s, offshore oil production amounted to over 5 per cent of UK GDP, and after Britain in 1983 went into deficit on its trade balance in manufactures for the first time, the trade surplus in oil helped for a few years to compensate for this shortfall.

Changes in the labour market

The main recent trends in the workforce have been increased employment in services and declining employment in manufacturing, and a rise in self-employment and part-time working. The trend out of manufacturing into services is a long-term one. Between 1955 and 1996 employment in services rose from 36 per cent to almost 76 per cent whilst manufacturing employment declined from 43 per cent of all employment to just over 18 per cent. Services now account for three-quarters of all jobs, manufacturing for just under one-fifth. Underpinning the shift from manufacturing to services are changing patterns of consumption as a consequence of greater prosperity and the impact of new – especially computer-based – technology. Table 3.10 shows patterns of employment in the 1990s.

Both self-employment and part-time working rose during the 1980s. In part as a result of government

Table 3.10 Patterns of employment, by sector, 1991–6

	1991 (millions)	%	1996 (millions)	%
Service industries	16.2	72.8	16.8	75.9
Manufacturing industries	4.3	19.4	4.0	18.2
Mining, energy and water supply	0.4	1.7	0.2	0.9
Other industries	1.4	6.1	1.1	5.0

Source: Office for National Statistics in *Britain 1997: An Official Handbook* (HMSO, 1997) p. 187.

policy, the number of self-employed people increased by 75 per cent between 1979 and 1990, when there were 3.6 million self-employed, but this number fell to 3.3 million in spring 1996. Part-time work also increased – but more gradually – to 5.3 million in spring 1996, when over one-fifth of all jobs were part-time.

Trade and the balance of payments

Overseas trade is of vital importance to the British economy, exports of goods and services accounting for 28 per cent of GDP (1995). Britain is currently the fifth largest trading nation in the world and, as a member of the EU, part of a trading bloc which accounts for 40 per cent of world exports. From the late nineteenth century down to the 1960s, British trade with the rest of the world conformed to a particular pattern. Britain imported a large proportion of its food and raw materials and paid for these imports by exports of manufactured goods ('visibles') and services ('invisibles' – banking, insurance and the like). Over the last thirty years, however, this pattern has changed significantly. Imports of food and raw materials have declined – from 60 per cent of the total value of imports in 1956–63 to 13 per cent in 1995. Over the same period the value of manufactured (and semi-manufactured) goods as a proportion of the total value of UK imports increased from 28 per cent to 82 per cent. The long-term position with regard to exports has changed little, with manufactures constituting over four-fifths of the total value of exports in 1955 and in 1995.

The disappearance in 1983 of Britain's trade surplus in manufactures and the continuing trade deficit in manufactures from that year have been the subject of much comment. The reason for this occurrence was that despite strong growth in British manufacturing exports, imports of manufactures grew even faster. Import penetration (i.e. imported manufactures as a proportion of all manufactures sold in the UK) rose dramatically during the 1980s from 25 per cent (1980) to 37 per cent (1990).

The geographical distribution of Britain's trade has also changed considerably in recent decades. For example, exports to North America held steady at about one-sixth until the late 1980s and then fell to just over one eighth in 1995; while exports to former sterling-area countries (mainly Empire and Commonwealth) fell from about two-fifths to one-twentieth; and exports to Western Europe rose from about one-third to over three-fifths (62 per cent in 1995).

By the mid-1990s Western Europe – especially the EU – had replaced the Commonwealth as the major focus of British trade, supplying nearly two-thirds of UK imports. In 1995, EU countries provided seven of the UK's top ten export markets and six of the ten main exporters to Britain. For most of the 1980s the US was Britain's largest single market but it was overtaken in this respect in 1990 by Germany, which now accounts for about one-seventh of Britain's total trade. During the 1980s Britain's trade gap (excess of imports over exports) with the European Community grew steadily to a deficit of £9.8 billion in 1990.

Another significant trend has been a decline in Britain's trade with non-oil developing countries (since 1970) and with oil-exporting countries (since the early 1980s). Britain trades mainly with other developed countries, which supplied 83 per cent of Britain's imports and provided the destinations for 80 per cent of Britain's exports in 1995.

International comparisons

The British economic record since 1945 exhibits something of a paradox. On the one hand, the economy grew faster over the period 1948–73 than during any previous period of similar length in British history – at an annual average rate of 2.8 per cent. This compares with an annual average growth rate of 2 per cent between 1874 and 1914, and with just over 2 per cent between 1923 and 1937 (Cairncross, 1981, p. 376). The growth rate slowed to 1.4 per cent per annum between 1973 and 1979 but then increased slightly to an annual average of 1.9 per cent between 1979 and 1996 (*The Times*, 27 January, 1997). Over the period 1951 to 1995, Britain's GDP grew at an average rate of 2.4 per cent per annum (*Social Trends*, 1997, p. 104). Overall, income per head in the UK rose by about two and a half times between 1948 and 1996.

However, although the British economy grew at a historically rapid rate for much of the postwar period, it was outstripped by most other advanced industrial countries (Table 3.11). Britain's relative

Table 3.11 Rates of growth of the UK economy and some international comparisons, 1950–5 to 1974–95

	1950–5	1955–60	1960–73	1974–95
UK	2.9	2.5	3.2	1.8
USA	4.2	2.4	4.3	2.5
Germany[1]	9.1	6.4	4.4	2.6
France	4.4	4.8	5.4	2.2
Italy	6.3	5.4	5.3	2.4
Japan	7.1[2]	9.0	9.4	3.2

[1] West Germany to 1990.
[2] 1952–5.

Sources: Cairncross (1981) for 1950–60; OECD

economic decline – which many historians date back to the late nineteenth century – therefore continued. This is the postwar paradox for Britain: faster growth (for much of the period) and greatly increased per capita wealth has been combined with continuing relative economic decline.

Another index of Britain's decline has been its falling share of world trade, which declined from a 10.7 per cent of total world exports (by value) in 1950 to 6.7 per cent in 1970 and 5.3 per cent in 1989. With the exception of the USA, other major advanced nations have either held their own or increased their share.

Measuring the wealth of nations is of course a complex matter. In terms of income per head, Britain ranked third in 1950 but fell to thirteenth in 1979 (compared to the 24 other OECD countries), seventeenth in 1995 and nineteenth in 1996 (Figure 3.1 contains three non-OECD countries – Kuwait, Hong-Kong and Singapore). However, the decline since 1979 may be not so steep as Figure 3.1 suggests since the OECD's method of calculating Britain`s GDP per head changed in 1995 and, if the new method is used to re-calculate pre-1995 data, Britain already had slipped to seventeenth position in 1975 (*The Economist,* 26 April, 1997). According to this analysis, the rate of Britain's economic decline probably slowed down in the 1980s and 1990s, when the country lost ground mainly to some Far Eastern 'tiger economies' and oil-rich Kuwait. Some evaluations are based on more than narrowly

economic criteria. According to a United Nations report (1991), Britain ranked 11th out of 160 countries on a human development index which combines expectation of life, levels of education and basic purchasing power.

The main political consequence of Britain's comparative economic decline has been that from the early 1960s improving the country's economic performance has been a major issue between the parties and a leading goal of governments. Britain's lack of international competitiveness has stemmed in the long term from comparatively low productivity. However, partly as a result of the influx of foreign investment, British manufacturing productivity improved in the 1980s, and between 1979 and 1995 the gap between British manufacturing productivity

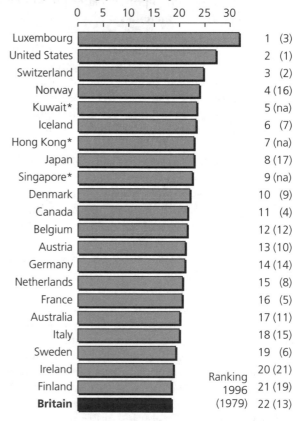

**GDP per person, 1996, $000
(OECD purchasing-power parity)**

*1995 World Bank data; not an OECD member

Source: *The Economist,* 26 April 1997.

Figure 3.1 GDP per head, 1996

and that of the USA, Japan, France and Germany narrowed considerably. However, Britain's investment record remains poor compared with other advanced industrial nations. Possible reasons include the facts that Britain has suffered from higher rates of inflation between 1979 and 1996 than its major competitors and also from much more severe recessions in the early 1980s and early 1990s. This meant that Britain's economy grew less smoothly than all of the group of seven largest industrial economies except for Canada, making it a less attractive centre for investment (*The Economist*, Election Briefing, 1997, p. 8). However, by 1997, according to the World Economic Forum, the UK had become the strongest performing country in the EU for the past year: in a ranking of 53 nations for economic competitiveness, the UK stood at seventh, compared with fifteenth in 1995 (the *Guardian*, 21 May 1997). But many commentators in the late 1990s still considered Britain needed to improve its levels of investment, its infrastructure and the education and skills of its labour force.

Summary

- Class remains of considerable importance in British society but disagreements over its definition continue. In addition to traditional methods of social classification, occupational schemes are useful,as devised for instance by the Registrar-General, market research (opinion polls) and leading sociologists.
- The main structural change in British society since 1945 has been the expansion of the middle class and the contraction of the working class as a result of the growth in professional and white collar and the decrease in manual occupations. Social mobility has occurred largely through this process rather than through the operation of greater equality of opportunity.
- Although visible differences between classes have decreased, largely owing to the spread of a consumer society, significant class differences remain, owing to the increase in income inequality since the late 1970s and to the persisting inequalities in access to health care, housing and education.
- In the period since 1960, social divisions based on gender, race and nation have become increasingly

significant,as a consequence both of continuing inequalities in these spheres and of intensifying ideological concentration on such divisions.
- Important structural changes have occurred in Britain's economy, involving the continuing decline of manufacturing industry, large-scale transfers of ownership from the public to the private sector (after 1979) and a redirection of UK trade away from the Commonwealth and former empire towards Western Europe, especially the European Union.
- Increasing prosperity helped to soften – and to some extent masked – the fact of continuing economic decline. Household incomes rose partly because of the occurrence of historically rapid rates of economic growth over much of the postwar period and partly because of the growing number of two-income households owing to the increase in married women workers.
- The rate of Britain's comparative decline appeared to slow down during the 1980s and although, in common with most other advanced western nations, losing ground to South-East Asian countries in the 1980s and 1990s, Britain had one of the strongest economies in Europe by 1997.

Questions

1. Gender inequalities are of growing significance in British society.' Explain and discuss.
2. Why is the state of the economy so important in politics?

Assignment

Social class in Britain
- *Infant mortality rates*: Deaths within one year of birth in 1994 averaged 4.5 per thousand live births for professional and managerial groups and 6.4 and 6.8 respectively for babies born to semi-skilled and unskilled manual workers (*Social Trends* 1997, p.122).
- *Housing tenure*: 87 per cent of professionals and 88 per cent of employers and managers but only 55 per cent of semi-skilled manuals and 43 per cent of unskilled manuals were owner-occupiers in 1995–6 (*Social Trends 1997*, p. 199).

- *Education*: Private schools cater for 7 per cent of school children but for approximately two-thirds of the children of professional and managerial groups. Their 'A' level performance is one-quarter superior to that of their state school counterparts and in 1996 178 of the top 200 schools in 'A' level performance were private schools. They provide half of all entrants to Oxford and Cambridge universities.
- *Income and wealth*: The gap between the best and worst-off groups in society widened in the 1980s. Thus (1) between 1980 and 1990, incomes of the top 10 per cent in the income scale grew by 47 per cent whilst those of the bottom 10 per cent increased by 6 per cent. (2) Professional incomes rose more rapidly than manual incomes after 1979: e.g. medical practitioners earned four and a half times as much as cleaners in April 1996 compared with three and a quarter times as much in April 1981; more generally, average earnings for non-manual occupations grew faster than for manual groups in this period and in 1996 stood at £390 per week compared with £272 per week (*Social Trends*, 1997, pp. 92–3). (3) Wealth is more unevenly distributed than income and its distribution has changed little in recent decades: in 1993, the wealthiest 10 per cent owned 48 per cent of marketable wealth compared with 50 per cent in 1976 and the wealthiest 25 per cent owned 72 per cent of marketable wealth compared with 71 per cent in 1976 (*Social Trends*, 1997, p. 102)

Questions

(i)   Comment on the statement that Britain has become or is becoming 'a classless society'.
(ii) In the immediate postwar period politicians of all parties sought to reduce social privilege and inequality. (a) Do you agree that this was a legitimate political objective? Explain your reasons. (b) What means were used to do so? (c) Why has the reduction of social inequality become a less important aim for all parties since the late 1970s?

Further reading

Halsey, A.H. (ed.) (1988) *Trends in British Society Since 1900*, 2nd. edn. (London: Macmillan) contains valuable information on a wide range of postwar social developments to the late 1980s. Adonis, A. and Pollard, S. (1997) *A Class Act: The Myth of Britain's Classless Society* (London: Hamish Hamilton) argues incisively that class divisions remain a reality in contemporary Britain and is particularly good on the last two decades. Rose, R. (1982) *Understanding the United Kingdom: The Territorial Dimension in Government* (London: Longman) explains the importance of national divisions in the UK; and Smith, D. (1994) *North and South: Britain's Economic, Social and Political Divide*, 2nd edn (Harmondsworth: Penguin) examines regional divisions.

On the economy, see Cairncross, A. (1992) *The British Economy since 1945* (Oxford: Blackwell) and on Britain's economic decline, Crafts, N. (1997) *Britain's Relative Economic Decline* (London: Social Market Foundation). Johnson, P. (1994) *Twentieth Century Britain* (London: Longman) contains useful essays on women, race relations and the economy since 1945. However, studies of society and the economy date rapidly and therefore these works should be supplemented by a reading of daily broadsheet newspapers and weeklies such as *The Economist* and by consultation of statistical publications such as *Social Trends* (HMSO) and the *Annual Abstract of Statistics*.

Power in Britain

In this chapter, we focus upon ideological approaches to understanding the political system, beginning with the relations between politics and society. We examine the social background of the people who make and influence the major political decisions and then proceed to an analysis of the main *interpretations* of the distribution of power – the theories of *the ruling class, power élite* and *competing élites*.

British social and political élites

Élites are the very small minority of people who play the key role in making decisions in their respective sectors and, if they are politicians, for society as a whole. The main point of studying them is to assess to what extent entrance to positions of power and social esteem is influenced by structural inequalities such as those deriving from class, gender or race. How far, for example, do power-holders in the various sectors reflect a broad cross-section of society? How far is society in practice as well as in theory a meritocracy?

A subsidiary but important question is the degree to which élite positions are changing. Are they, for example, becoming – however gradually – open to all comers? This needs to be asked not only in relation to their accessibility to the working class but also to women and ethnic groups. The essential

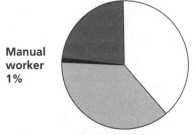

LABOUR

Miscellaneous 33%
(including miscellaneous white collar 17%, politician/political organiser 10% and publisher/journalist 7%)

Manual worker 13%

Business 9%
(including company directors and company executives 4%)

Professional 45%
(including teachers 27% and lawyers 7%)

CONSERVATIVE

Miscellaneous 23%
(including miscellaneous white collar 1.2%, politician/political organiser 9% and publisher/journalist 8%)

Manual worker 1%

Business 39%
(including company directors and company executives 32%)

Professional 37%
(including teachers 18% and lawyers 5%)

Source: Data from D. Butler and D. Kavanagh, *The British General Election of 1997 (1997)* p. 205.

Figure 4.1 The social background of MPs in the two major parties after the General Election of 1997

context to remember when considering the following analysis is the approximate percentage of the population which is privately educated (7 per cent), university-educated (7.1 per cent) and belongs to the A/B upper-middle and middle-class occupational grouping (19 per cent).

The most striking point to notice about Figure 4.1 is the contemporary predominance of professional and business groups in Parliament as a whole. These two groups alone have accounted for over three-fifths of the 'political class' since the war. Moreover, middle-class domination of the House of Commons is even more pronounced when it is borne in mind that professional groups such as political organisers, political researchers and journalists form a significant proportion of the 'miscellaneous white-collar' category. Today (1998) over four-fifths of MPs have professional, executive or managerial backgrounds.

A second important observation is the rise in the proportion of university-educated MPs between the interwar period – when half of Conservative MPs and under one-fifth of Labour MPs were university educated – and the postwar period, when the proportion of university-educated MPs in both parties has increased, most sharply in Labour (Figure 4.2).

That said, the two main parties present sharp contrasts. Labour is now largely and the Conservative Party almost totally middle class in composition, but each party is made up of a different sector of the middle class. Thus, the public sector middle class is dominant in the Labour Party, and the private sector middle class predominates in the Conservative Party. Over three-fifths of Tories were educated at public schools; the vast majority of Labour MPs attended state schools. Whereas graduates now form a majority in both parties, over 60 per cent of Conservative graduates went to Oxbridge; over 70 per cent of Labour graduates received their higher education at universities other than Oxbridge. Over a third of Conservative MPs but only 9 per cent Labour MPs have business backgrounds. Labour's working-class component has declined steadily since the war: well over one-third in 1951 (37 per cent), it fell to 28 per cent in October 1974 and had shrunk to a very small proportion in 1997 when, however, it was still significantly larger than the infinitesimal working-class element in the

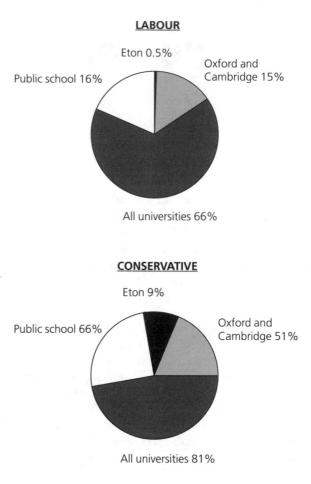

Source: Data from D. Butler and D. Kavanagh, *The British General Election of 1997* (1997) p. 203.

Figure 4.2 The educational background of MPs in the two major parties after the General Election of 1997

Conservatives. Whereas Conservative professionals are drawn mainly from the private sector and traditional professions (lawyers form 18 per cent of the party), Labour professionals generally have public sector occupations, with teachers and lecturers predominant (26 per cent of the Parliamentary Labour Party (PLP)).

Certain important trends are discernible over the century. The Conservatives have become less privileged in their recruitment, with the aristocratic and upper middle class drift away from the party being reflected in the decline in the public school element, especially in Old Etonians. During the same period, the Labour Party has moved sharply away from its working-class origins towards becoming a predominantly white-collar, university-educated, middle-class party. But this apparent convergence of the parties should not be pressed too far. The public–private sector division is an important one and is reflected in career patterns and lifestyles as well as in educational backgrounds. Thus, privately-educated themselves, Conservative MPs send their own children to public schools; state-educated for the most part, Labour MPs rarely do so. Accustomed to high earnings from business or the higher professions, Conservative MPs frequently supplement their parliamentary salaries with private incomes or consultancies: they do not expect to live on their remuneration as MPs. Labour MPs, by contrast, largely hailing from the less-well-paid public sector professions, exhibit less lavish lifestyles.

The social composition of the Cabinet reveals a tendency towards the growing embourgeoisement of party leaderships as well as a continuing contrast between the two party élites. Thus, since the early part of the century, Conservative Cabinets have become more middle class and *less aristocratic,* Labour Cabinets, more middle class and *less working class.*

But there are still sharp contrasts. Whereas the public school/Oxbridge element has increased in both Conservative and Labour Cabinets in the postwar period and also constitutes a higher proportion of them than it does of the respective parliamentary parties, it is much more pronounced in Conservative Cabinets. Thus, Tory Cabinets in the post-1945 era have been overwhelmingly composed of people of middle-class *origins,* but Labour Cabinets have been fairly evenly divided between ministers with working-class and those with middle-class backgrounds.

A comparison between the 1997 Blair Cabinet and the outgoing 1997 Major Cabinet reveals the main differences between the top echelons of the two parties (Table 4.1). Both élites were university-educated (over 95 per cent), but whereas approximately three-quarters of Major's Cabinet was educated at public school and Oxbridge, only two-fifths of the Labour Cabinet attended fee-paying schools and the great majority (86 per cent) went to universities other than Oxbridge.

Whilst some overlap existed in the occupational background of the two Cabinets, there were also sharp contrasts. Thus, over one-quarter of the Conservative Cabinet and just under one-third of the Labour Cabinet were lawyers. But whereas over half of the Conservative Cabinet was drawn from business and finance, the largest element in the Labour Cabinet (almost one-third) came from the world of teaching. Whereas the Conservative

Table 4.1 Educational and occupational backgrounds of the Conservative and Labour Cabinets, 1997

	Conservative Cabinet		Labour Cabinet	
	No.	Percentage	No.	Percentage
Education				
All fee paying schools	17	74	9	41
Eton	4	17	0	0
State school	6	26	13	59
Oxbridge	18	78	3	14
All universities	22	96	22	100
Occupations				
Business	12	52	0	0
Professions	10	43	21	91
Private sector occupations	6	23	14	64

Cabinet was predominantly private sector orientated, the Labour Cabinet is heavily biased towards the public sector. Whilst the Conservative élite was a blend of business and the professions, the Labour élite is wholly professional. It thus has negligible experience of finance, commerce and industry and is connected to the private sector only by the sizeable legal element in its composition. Correspondingly, with just two former university lecturers, a schools inspector and a psychiatric social worker, the Conservative élite had extremely limited experience of the public sector. There is a striking regional difference, with about three-quarters of the Blair Cabinet hailing from Wales, Scotland and the North of England, whereas the Major Cabinet was overwhelmingly from southern England.

The political élite – predominantly white, male and middle class – is therefore only a feeble reflection of society as a whole. However, there was a substantial increase in the proportion of women in the House of Commons elected in 1997 although not of the ethnic minorities. The Commons now contains 119 (18.05 per cent) women MPs, 9 MPs (1.4 per cent) from the ethnic minorities (who compose under 6 per cent of the population) and, in the three main parties, just under 9 per cent with a 'manual worker' background (manual jobs still constituted just under half (48 per cent) of all employment at the 1991 census).

Britain compares rather more favourably with the EU in terms of women's membership of the political élite after the 1997 general election (Table 4.2) and, despite the declining numbers of working-class MPs, still relatively well with regard to manual worker representation in the House of Commons (Adonis, 1993, pp. 51–2).

Other élites

We now turn to the educational background of other élites. Tables 4.3 and 4.4 show the proportion of a range of élites receiving private education between the late 1930s and the 1980s together with the percentage of the administrative élite which was recruited from Oxbridge over a slightly longer period. Table 4.3 shows that the *higher administrative grade* of the civil service has drawn decreasing proportions of its entrants from people educated at fee-paying schools as the century has progressed. The proportion of higher-grade entrants from Oxbridge has also declined, but again not uniformly: overall decline is compatible with a significant increase in the recruitment of the Oxbridge-educated to this grade in the 1980s (Table 4.4).

The civil service is more open than all other élites except the Air Force and the Navy. Table 4.3 reveals that the top posts in *the diplomatic service, the judiciary* and *the army* remain dominated by people educated in the private sector, and in the Army this predominance actually increased in the half-century down to the 1980s. This privileged background remained prevalent in the higher judiciary and the army in the mid-1990s: in 1997, thirty-three out of thirty-nine of the most senior judges and seven out of the nine foremost generals were privately educated. In contrast, by the early 1980s, both the Air Force and the civil service at the highest levels drew upon state-educated people to a significant extent and, in the Air Force, the majority of top officers were non-public school. This trend continued into the 1990s, by which time the recruitment of women and members of the ethnic minorities into top Whitehall posts had become an important issue. In 1995, half of the eighteen Permanent Secretaries in the civil service were educated at

Table 4.2 Women in political élites			
	UK (%)	EU average (%)	EU highest (%)
Women in parliament (lower and upper chambers)	12.5	13.2	33.0
In lower house	18.05	12.0	33.0
In upper house	7.0	9.4	28.0
In national governments	22.7	11.1	24.0

Note: UK figures for 1997: the House of Commons and Cabinet, 1997 general election; House of Lords, 22 May 1997. EU statistics, 1993.

private schools but two-thirds of them at Oxbridge (Adonis and Pollard, 1997, pp. 47, 59); and in 1995 Oxbridge accounted for 39 per cent of successful applicants for the 134 jobs in the Fast Stream Scheme for the administrative élite. In 1996, a mere 9 per cent of the top 577 posts at the three most senior grades of the civil service were held by women and just over 7 per cent of high court judges were women. In 1997, the ethnic minorities (6 per cent of the population) were scarcely represented in these professions, non-whites making up 1.2 per cent of QCs, 1 per cent of circuit judges, 2.3 per cent of solicitors, 1 per cent of army officers and 2.9 per cent of Metropolitan Police officers (Adonis and Pollard, 1997, pp. 249–50).

In considering the *business élite*, it is useful to distinguish between a financial élite and an industrial/commercial élite. The *financial élite* consists of the directors of the Bank of England together with the chairmen of the major clearing banks and leading merchant banks and the chairmen of the 12 largest insurance companies. The *industrial/commercial élite* may be defined narrowly as the chairmen or chief executives of the leading industrial and retailing enterprises and more broadly to include the directors as well as the chairmen/chief executives.

Studies of the financial élite suggest its social exclusivity. It is overwhelmingly privately and Oxbridge educated, with a particularly high proportion having been to Eton and other top public schools. Thus, in 1983, according to Moran, 81 per cent of the financial élite had been educated at fee-paying schools (32 per cent at Eton) and 68 per cent had gone to Oxbridge (Moran, 1989, p. 169).

An important reason for the closed nature of the financial élite is the rules of property inheritance which enable the transmission of wealth from one generation to the next, thereby protecting and preserving the positions of the top families.

Studies of the industrial/commercial élite reveal a similar educationally privileged background for the *chairmen of large companies* down to the 1970s although a rather less socially exclusive education for the directors of large industrial firms (Stanworth and Giddens, 1974).

However, there are signs that the domination of boardrooms by those educated at public school may be diminishing. An article in the *Financial Times* found that whereas nearly three-fifths (58 per cent)

Table 4.3 Percentage of selected administrative élites educated at fee paying schools, 1939–83

	1939	1950	1960	1970	1983
Ambassadors	73.5	72.6	82.6	82.5	76.3
High Court Judges	80.0	84.9	82.5	80.2	79.0
Major General and above	63.6	71.3	83.2	86.1	78.9
RAF Vice-Marshals and above	66.7	59.1	58.4	62.5	41.1
Civil Servants, Under-Secretary and above	84.5	58.7	65.0	61.7	58.8

Sources: Columns 1–4 calculated from D. Boyd, *Elites and their Education* (1973) pp. 93–5; column 5 from *Whitaker's Almanack* and *Who's Who*. Cited in Moran (1989) p. 166.

Table 4.4 Higher education of 'open competition' entrants to the administrative trainee grade of the home civil service (percentage), 1921–32 to 1985

	1921–32	1933–9	1949–50	1961–5	1971–5	1981	1982–3	1985
Oxbridge-educated	84	89	74	80	50	56	66	64

Sources: Data from Moran (1989) p. 163; Drewry and Butcher (1991) p. 71.

of the chairmen of the top 50 companies had been educated at leading public schools in 1979, by 1989 under one-quarter (24 per cent) had received such an education, and 70 per cent had attended either grammar schools (40 per cent) or other state schools (30 per cent). The writer also revealed that, compared with the situation a decade earlier, fewer top chairmen in 1989 had Oxbridge degrees (32 per cent), and a smaller proportion were non-graduate (only 28 per cent) (*Financial Times*, 3 November 1990).

This brief survey has shown varying degrees of exclusivity in the social background of British élites. Put another way, it may be said that élite recruitment in the various sectors of politics and society reflects differentially the principle of meritocracy. At one end of the privilege/meritocracy scale are groups such as the core financial élite – upper middle class in composition and educated at top public schools and Oxbridge. Close to this élite in terms of privileged social backgrounds are leading diplomats, judges and generals, and, only a short distance away again, top industrialists and the Conservative Party, both of which groups have become more meritocratic in recent years. The Conservatives' concessions to the principle of merit notably include their declining recruitment from public schools – especially top public schools such as Eton – and their election of leaders of working and lower-middle-class origins (the last three being the children respectively of a carpenter, a grocer and a circus artiste). Some way away from them are élite groups such as the Labour Party (mixed working/lower middle class, largely university-educated), and the upper ranks of the Royal Air Force (RAF) and home civil service (lower middle class, mainly state-educated and, in the case of the civil service, graduate).

The British social and political élite: recent trends

Two recent trends in the formation of the British social and political élite, both entrenching structured inequalities and making them more pronounced, require attention. First, a relatively long-term trend, beginning in the 1960s but intensifying in the 1980s, is the 'public school revolution'. Under political threat in the immediate postwar years, and

seemingly in decline, private sector establishments responded by adapting their curriculum (notably by devoting more attention to science) and by targeting their teaching more single-mindedly on examination (especially A-level) success. As a consequence, they became even more attractive to social élites, especially business élites, and their intake expanded from 5 to 7 per cent of the school population between the early 1960s and the late 1980s, despite the fact that their fees generally outpaced inflation (Sanderson, 1994, p. 386). Their proportion of Oxbridge places increased too. In 1969, 38 per cent but in 1995 about 50 per cent of places at Oxford University went to the privately educated (Adonis and Pollard, 1997, p. 56).

Second, the character of the British élite has been transformed owing to two major developments. First, it has become increasingly a graduate élite. Whereas formerly much of the social élite including the army officer class, the chartered professions and the world of finance did not require degrees, by the 1990s they did so. Britain's expanding professional class numbered 1.6 million in 1995–6, twice its size in 1955, and almost all its most recent entrants were graduates. Second, as a consequence of the huge surge in top private sector earnings in the 1980s and 1990s, the gap between top private and public sector professionals and managers became a chasm, and a new élite emerged – a 'super-class' of under 10,000 based on the private sector. It comprised leading individuals in the largest City law, accountancy, banking and investment finance groupings together with foremost barristers and company executives in industry. By the mid-1990s, earnings of this group had become several times as great as the earnings of the public sector élite (judges, officers in the armed forces, GPs, local government chiefs, university professors, headmasters of large secondary schools, even dentists). However, potential conflict between the public and private sector élites has been mitigated first by the switch of top university graduates from public to private sector careers and second by the overlap between public and private sector careers in the senior judiciary, hospital consultants, and increasingly the media, the military and the civil service, which has enabled professionals in these spheres to gain lucrative private sector employment for all or some of their careers.

Adonis and Pollard make two main points about

the implications of these developments for politics. First, most of the economic weight of this London-based élite is exerted 'at the very heart of the nation's culture and politics, ensuring it strong political clout' even though few of its members engage directly in politics. 'The City, the West End and Westminster are the boundaries of opinion-forming Britain'. Second, the political élite reflects changes in the broader social élite in two main ways: (1) the political élite itself has become increasingly composed of graduate professionals, a steadily rising proportion of whom are career politicians; (2) the public–private sector division in the social élite is echoed in the composition of the parties, with a pre-dominantly private sector Conservative party facing a primarily public sector Labour party (Adonis and Pollard, 1997, pp. 67–130). In the late 1990s, this division could be the basis of increasing pressure on the Labour leadership to redress the private–public sector imbalance in favour of pay-capped public sector professionals and workers at the lower but not the élite level.

Despite becoming less exclusive and more merito-cratic since the war, the British social and political élite remains fairly cohesive, united by its generally privileged public school, Oxbridge background and a self-confident belief that it has earned its privileges. Vestiges of a more traditional Establishment remain in the old public sector and especially aristocratic élite. Certainly compared with the United States, access to power in Britain remains limited rather than widely diffused, closed rather than open. The career of John Major, achieving power from outside the charmed circle of wealth, privilege and higher education, was the exception that proves this rule.

BOX 4.1
Elites in Britain: a summary

'Perhaps the most remarkable long-term feature of the social structure of élites in Britain is the limited scale of change in patterns of recruitment, and the slow pace at which that change has been accomplished. Change there has nevertheless been, the end result of which is a percep-tible widening in the social origins of many, though not all, élite groups.'

(Moran, 1989, p. 181)

Ruling class, power élite or competing élites?

There are three distinct approaches to the empiri-cally observable fact that the highest positions in British society and politics are in general recruited from a small and unrepresentative section of the population. These take the form of three models – the **ruling class** theory (Marxist), the 'power élite' theory (élitist) and the 'pluralist' theory (liberal). We consider and criticise each one in turn.

The 'ruling class' theory (Marxist)

In Marxist theory, there are two views of the rela-tionship between the state and particular classes. The first, associated with the early Marx (1848), is *instrumental* and *economically determinist*. On this view, the state is merely an instrument of the eco-nomically dominant class, the bourgeoisie, the owners of productive wealth. It is determinist because it views political power as flowing inevitably from economic domination, the state being seen as part of a mere 'superstructure' determined by the nature of the economic base. On this conception, the power of the ruling class rests on the control and ownership of capital. Divisions of interest may from time to time appear between sections of this ruling class – between finance capital (the City) and man-ufacturing industry, for example. Ultimately, however, the common interest of such groups in the continued existence and strength of capitalism takes precedence over apparently divergent interests.

This ruling class encompasses not only those most obviously involved in the ownership of wealth in all its forms (fixed and liquid assets, land, property and shares) but also those élites (Conservative politicians, judges, ambassadors, military chiefs) which possess a common privileged upper-class origin, education and life-style. Leading civil servants, too, belong to the upper class since they are 'filtered by a long pro-motion process' to ensure their identification with the interests of capital (Coates, 1984, p. 236).

Ruling class: the idea that there is a single cohesive ruling class whose power lies in its control and owner-ship of capital. In this theory, political power is closely allied to and, in its original Marxist formulation, deter-mined by the possession of economic power.

The fact that the ruling class is not particularly visible to people as they go about their everyday lives (it does not pose for a group photograph which then appears in television and the newspapers) does not mean, say Marxists, that it does not exist. On the traditional Marxist view, since the state is always and invariably under the domination of a capitalist ruling class, the apparatus of democracy – the holding of periodic elections, party competition for power, the political influence of pressure groups – makes no difference to the realities of power. It is a mere facade for the class rule of the big owners of property and capital. According to the early Marx (1848), 'the executive is but a committee for managing the common affairs of the whole bourgeoisie'. For Lenin, the state was 'an instrument for the oppression of the exploited class'.

To *classical Marxists* the British system of government is more appropriately entitled 'capitalist democracy' than 'liberal democracy', with the stress, moreover, on the word 'capitalist' rather than 'democracy'. This is because, in their view, economics takes precedence over politics. For them, the central fact bearing upon the working of the political system derives directly from the nature of the economic system. This is the inequality of wealth and income which flows from the workings of capitalism, a system whose essence is the accumulation of capital in the hands of the few. Such concentrations of wealth, in fact, place massive power in the hands of big financiers, financial institutions, industrial companies and the multinational corporations. Thus, constitutional and political rights and freedoms guaranteed to all by the liberal pluralist system are not really 'rights' and 'freedoms' at all, so long as glaring inequalities exist and the life-chances of the many are so overshadowed by the privileges of the few. Devolution, the strengthening of Parliament in relation to the government of the day and a Bill of Rights cannot affect the substance of social power and inequality. They cannot give the unemployed jobs, or the low-paid higher incomes, or prune the power of the financial and business élites.

To Marxists, elections are simply a ritual which confer neither real power nor even ultimate control on voters, merely the illusion of influence. Capitalist democracy contains 'a permanent and fundamental contradiction . . . between the promise of popular power, enshrined in popular suffrage, and the curbing or denial of that promise in practice' (Miliband, 1984, p. 1). Capitalism as an economic system requires the containment of 'pressure from below', and whilst the Conservatives might be expected to endorse such a goal enthusiastically, the Labour Party in practice has fallen in behind it also. It is formally committed to internal party democracy but in fact its parliamentary leadership has waged relentless war against the left-wing activists in the constituency parties and systematically ignored Conference decisions which it found distasteful. In reality, the word 'labourism' is a more accurate description of its practice than 'socialism'. In power, Labour has done nothing to weaken, let alone to destroy, capitalism; it exists merely to win concessions for the working class, concessions which, by making for a more contented labour force, strengthen rather than undermine the system. The formal rule by a particular party, then, is simply that – a formality which serves to conceal the fact that the ruling class is always in power. The same analysis is extended to the world of pressure groups. However diverse the character and activities of the groups appear to be, the diversity is only apparent. What seems to be the ebb and flow of influence between government and groups is just shadow-boxing. Behind governments of all complexions stands capitalism, national and international. Ultimately, whatever guise they may assume (the big banks, the finance houses, the insurance companies, the multinationals), capitalists always ensure that the major decisions promote the interests of capital. Rather than being responsive to public opinion, as democratic theory would have it, governments are agents of the economically dominant class.

Marxists perceive the state as inherently biased in favour of the middle class and against the working class. In its most unequivocal expression, this view holds that the state through its agents – judges, policemen and soldiers – is simply an instrument for ruling-class suppression of the working class. The liberal or pluralist claim that the law-enforcement agencies are neutral between classes cannot be true; the law exists to protect property – hence, by definition, its agents are biased towards the possessing classes and against those with little or no property. 'Equality before the law' and the 'legal rights of the citizen' are mere phrases with scant reference to reality for the majority of the population.

The second view of the relationship between state power and social class, the neo-Marxist (or modern Marxist) view, proposes 'the relative autonomy of the state'. It derives from the view of the later Marx (1852, 1871) that the capitalist class did not always dominate the state. At any given moment in history indeed the state might appear as the agency of another social group although it seems to have been Marx's view that in the longer term the state always does serve capitalist interests (Marsh and Stoker, 1995, pp. 248–87; Birch, 1993, pp. 186–95). It needs to be stressed that even though this later view moves away from the rigid economic determinism to be found in the Communist Manifesto, it still regards the distribution of economic power in society as 'ultimately decisive' in politics.

There are three main approaches under the heading of the relative autonomy of the state, the common thread being that rather than exercising power directly the capitalist class functions at one remove from the state. The first view is based on the concept of cultural hegemony developed by the Italian Socialist Antonio Gramsci in the 1930s; it maintains that class domination is a consequence of the manufacture of the consent of subordinate classes through ideological, cultural and political means as well as of coercion. Thus, by means of a continual indoctrination process taking place through education, the media, political institutions and the courts of law, the capitalist class gains the consent of non-bourgeois classes to its own rule and to the capitalist system. Some modern Marxists use this concept to account for the moderate reformist character of socialist parties in capitalist systems, arguing that the ideological acceptance of capitalist values in society at large sets limits to their goals and capacity to transform the system. A second modern Marxist approach focuses on government politicians as state managers whose primary goal is to further their self-interest rather than the interests of capital. Their self-interest lies in winning elections. However, since winning elections depends on economic success, governments must pursue policies which are in the interests of capitalists. Therefore, they are not in any real sense autonomous but severely constrained by their need to preside over a healthy capitalist economy to ensure their own political survival. Third, in the 'strategic relational' approach, the state at any given point in time simply

reflects the balance of social forces which include both the relationship between classes and between classes and non-class forces such as gender and ethnic divisions (Taylor, 1995, p. 261).

Common to both classical and modern Marxism is the emphasis on the way in which structures – usually but not invariably based on class – determine or strongly influence political outcomes. The structured inequalities based on class, gender or skin colour, rather than the institutions of democracy, provide the essential context in which the struggle for power takes place.

Power élite theories

Power élite theorists also challenge democracy, believing that whatever the ostensible distribution of power, all regimes are characterised by the rule of the few over the many. Power élite theorists rejected both the Marxist theory that political power is determined by the economic class structure and the pluralist idea of the diffusion of power. Power élite theory was developed in the early twentieth century by the Italian sociologists Vilfredo Pareto and Gaetano Mosca, and the German sociologist Robert Michels.

Pareto (1848–1923) identified an élite simply in terms of those exhibiting most skill in any area of activity. In politics, the most skilful politicians were the rulers, their political abilities being demonstrated in their superior deployment of cunning and force. Far from being exercised in terms of a certain economically determined pattern, as in the Marxist view, power is exercised by a continual succession (or *circulation*) of élites, with different groups exercising political authority in turn.

Mosca (1857–1941) considered that élite rule is inevitable, first because it is easier to achieve cohesion among the few than among the many, and second because the attributes necessary to rule are

---

Power élite: the idea that, whatever its formal distribution, power inevitably passes into the hands of the few. Élite domination may occur for social, organisational or psychological reasons: i.e. only a minority possesses the political resources, administrative and scientific expertise or qualities of cunning and ruthlessness required to gain and maintain power.

always unevenly distributed. Each ruling group possessed a 'political formula', or ideology, to legitimate its rule, such formulae including parliamentary sovereignty in Britain and the will of the people in the United States. One reason for the downfall of a political élite was a decline in popular belief in its political formula, e.g. the divine right of kings (cited Birch, 1993, pp. 173–4).

For Michels (1876–1936), whose main focus of study was political parties, the key reason for the inevitable emergence of a political élite was organisation. 'Who says organisation, says oligarchy', he asserted. Thus, in the modern age, parties need to be professionally organised and their leaders need to be accorded freedom of manoeuvre. Both needs spelt the death-knell for democracy. The requirements in modern mass parties of organisation and leadership led Michels to believe in the operation of an 'iron law of oligarchy'. The likelihood of any democratic control was further inhibited by the 'incompetence' of the apathetic rank-and-file.

Finally, the American sociologist C. Wright Mills (1916–1962) wrote *The Power Elite* (1956) in this tradition. It argued that power in the United States was distributed over three levels. At the top, an oligarchy of big business, the political executive and military chiefs held the reins of power; the 'middle level' was taken up with bargaining between interest groups and state and congressional politicians; at the lowest level were the politically fragmented masses. According to Mills, pluralist analysis focused only on the intermediate level of the power structure, totally ignoring the upper echelon where the real power lay.

The common thread then of élite theory is that power is inevitably exercised by a small ruling group which substitutes its own views and interests for those of the rest of society and, moreover, is effectively unaccountable because of its capacity to use force, intimidation, manipulation or indoctrination to sustain its power. Élitists believe élite rule is inevitable for a variety of reasons including the limitation of ruling abilities to a few; the administrative and leadership needs of large organisations; and the apathy and lack of capacity of the rank-and-file masses. Élite theorists rejected the Marxist idea that the political power is determined by the economic class structure and that the ruling class is simply a product of dominant economic forces. Rather, in their view, power can derive from a number of sources including education and political skill as well as wealth. But in élite theory as in ruling class theory, political democracy is impossible.

During the 1950s, a British version of power élite theory drew attention to the existence in Britain of an **Establishment**, a cohesive political class which pursues its own self-serving ends irrespective of the results of elections. This power élite or Establishment is held together less by shared economic interest (although its members do tend to possess similar socio-economic backgrounds) than by a common culture which separates it sharply from the rest of society. Sheltering behind the traditional rituals, norms of 'moderation' and strong adherence to confidentiality of British political culture, the Establishment governs Britain no matter which party is nominally in power. A permanent and pervasive psychological attitude characterises the 'Establishment'. New people – aspiring working-class and lower-middle-class politicians, for example – may enter it but never in sufficient numbers to change or dilute its enduring power and always at the price of the abandonment of radical principles. This is the way in which, historically, radicals and socialists who would challenge social inequality have been contained, tamed and ultimately absorbed. In the final analysis, this shared attitude comes down to a determination to remain in political control, come what may.

Pluralist theories

Pluralists disagree with both ruling class and élitist theories. According to pluralist theory, what matters about the distribution of power in society is not that it is uneven – since unevenness characterises all societies and is probably inevitable – but three other vital features:

(1) *Composition*: Whilst élites undoubtedly exist, they are to varying degrees open and relatively accessible to able people from below, rather than sealed into closed hierarchies. Pluralists do not deny that certain élite groups in Britain – the Conservative

> **The Establishment**: the notion that whatever the changes in government an unaccountable social élite largely drawn from the public schools is always in power is a British variant of power élite theory.

Party, the judiciary, the diplomatic service and the financial community in particular – are difficult to enter for those not born into the wealthy upper-middle (some would simply say 'upper') class. They argue, however, that élites vary greatly in composition. To set against those parts of society still dominated by upper-class individuals, there are other sectors in which people with working- and lower middle-class backgrounds can reach the top on merit. These include the Labour Party, the home civil service, local government, the police, the Royal Air Force and the trade union movement. Nor is it the case that the Conservative Party, judiciary, diplomatic service and the world of finance are exclusively upper-class preserves at the highest level. Change – however slow it may seem to reformers – has taken place in these sectors, as witness the fact, for example, that the last three leaders of the Conservative Party have come from modest social origins.

(2) *Competition*: Pluralists start from the proposition that 'The complexity of the modern liberal state means that no single group, class or organisation can dominate society' (Smith, 1995, p.209). Rather, pluralists argue, a number of élites compete for influence. Competition between a series of power blocs representing diverse interests rather than the rule of a single monolithic Establishment or ruling class is 'the name of the game'. Resources which can be deployed to influence decisions (money, numbers, organisational skills) are in practice widely dispersed. Thus, élite groups representing sectoral and occupational interests influence policy-making selectively within their specialised fields of concern (industrial, financial, military, academic). Moreover, since disagreements appear from time to time within élites, rank-and-file participation is possible as appeals for members' views have to be made. This type of wider appeal beyond the boundaries of the élite itself occurs quite frequently within political parties and trade unions. In parties, it tends to happen in the wake of electoral defeat, as in 1997 when William Hague replaced John Major as Conservative leader and immediately

---

Pluralism: the belief that power is widely and fairly evenly distributed rather than concentrated in the hands of a ruling class or power élite. This theory has increasingly acquired an élitist tinge (see below).

---

sought to democratise the party. Both the two major parties and trade unions – the first by reforming themselves, the second by legislation – have become more democratic since the 1960s.

(3) *Political power*: Pluralists argue that although many élites can be influential from time to time, the political élite, consisting largely of members of the Cabinet and top civil servants, is supreme. In their model, the power structure is rather like a range of mountain peaks among which one – the political – is discernibly higher than all the rest. Unlike the other two theories, which tend to locate power with hidden, behind-the-scenes manipulators, for pluralism, real power lies where it ostensibly lies or is supposed to lie – with the political élite. The political élite predominates over the leading business, financial, labour and other groups by virtue of the special authority afforded it by the democratic system of government. Moreover – and this point is fundamental in pluralist analysis – the governing élite acts within the powerful constraints of regular elections and, between elections, of the countervailing influence of public opinion. Small minorities make decisions in most areas but channels to the public are at least partially open. Included in public opinion in addition to the media and regular opinion polls are political institutions such as the civil service and the House of Lords and pressure groups such as the Confederation of British Industry (CBI), the Trades Union Congress (TUC) and the City. Far from considering democratic political machinery a mere facade, pluralists take it seriously. They maintain that although far from perfect it does ensure enough popular control, choice and participation to be regarded as a working or viable system. Whilst it is the case that in some important parts of the system, participation is low – only about 5 per cent of the electorate are members of political parties and an even smaller proportion are party activists – on the other hand, participation is high elsewhere in the system, and increasing. Minor parties now provide a wider base for political participation than was the case in the 1960s, and there has been a huge upsurge in pressure group activity, with participation in the environmental and women's movements becoming a major social phenomenon. In the view of pluralists, the present liberal democratic system has demonstrated a proven capacity to adapt over time in response to changing social needs and demands.

Criticisms of 'ruling class', 'power élite' and pluralist theories

Criticisms of Marxist theory

How far is it possible to agree with classical Marxism that in modern democracies all decisions are under the control of and in the interests of a capitalist ruling class? It can certainly be agreed that in Britain, for example, state élites are disproportionately drawn from the ranks of the propertied and privileged and that this creates a bias in favour of the maintenance of the capitalist system. But pluralists would also argue that all citizens benefit from the capitalist system, not just the ruling class, and hence they would not accept that the ruling class rules only in its own interests.

Second, granted that Marx wrote in a pre-democratic age, how do contemporary Marxists deal with the fact that modern democratic governments enact large-scale welfare programmes which are burdens on industry or intervene in industry on behalf of the environment? In other words, how can decisions which on the surface are against the interests of the capitalist class be explained? The Marxist response is that such policies serve to legitimise the capitalist system in the eyes of the poorest class in society and therefore are in the long-term interests of capitalism. Thus, a Marxist survey of the postwar period accepts that the political system is sufficiently open for lower-class people both to gain certain élite positions and as a class to negotiate benefits from it in the form of the welfare state. On the other hand, its author sees these gains as in effect illusory since they merely serve to stabilise the system and to consolidate the power of the capitalist class. The Conservative working-class vote is explained in terms of the penetration of working-class consciousness by a whole set of official orthodoxies reflecting 'the interests and preoccupations of the ruling strata' (Coates, 1984, pp. 114, 233, 151–2).

To liberal pluralists, this explanation itself seems élitist, as too dismissive of the working class, whose actual thoughts and wishes are not seen as in any sense their own but rather as a simple reflection of the ruling-class ideology. Their stated thoughts and actions, on this account, are not freely conceived but simply represent 'false consciousness' created by the ruling class. Liberal pluralists perceive the ruling-class model as too determinist, with each class simply 'programmed' to carry out its predestined role. and as too prone simply to *assume* the ideological cohesion and socio-economic uniformity of the capitalist class. Even modern Marxism, according to one interpretation,' remains involved in an unresolved struggle with economism', the notion that the economic structure structure of society determines the political (Marsh, 1995, p. 284).

Criticisms of élite theory

Inevitability?

Critics of élite theory also focus on the failure of élitists to substantiate their theory of the inevitability of élite rule in democratic societies with empirical evidence. A.H. Birch, an important critic of élitism, has suggested that in order to establish their theory, élitists would have to show one or other of the following propositions is true:

- Access to political office is strictly limited to members of a relatively small and cohesive group whose members share interests or values that have policy implications and that these interests and value are not shared by the majority of the people.
- Office-holders are rarely responsive to the views and interests of the public, habitually substitute their own views and interests for those of the people and avoid public accountability either because the machinery of accountability is inadequate or because they force compliance by coercion, threats or indoctrination.
- Office-holders may not necessarily look after their own interests but still regularly take decisions on behalf of a small class or group with a non-political power-base and interests different from those of the majority, e.g. the capitalist class in capitalist societies.

Birch concludes that none of the classical élitists produced sufficient evidence to support their claim of the inevitability of élite rule. Thus, Pareto failed to prove that governors always rule with their own ends in view, although that was the thrust of his argument. Mosca showed that past societies had often been ruled by self-serving élites but did not show, or even claim, that this must always be the case, especially in a democracy. Michels failed to demonstrate either that party leaderships are invariably aloof from and unaccountable to their members or that, if some parties did have such leaderships, this would necessarily make the political system as a whole undemocratic. Michels's so-called 'iron law of oligarchy' in political parties would require substantial empirical evidence to validate it, although his suggestion that electoral competition may lead parties to moderate their policies is an interesting one. Similarly, a modern élitist such as C. Wright Mills also failed to substantiate his thesis that a power élite in the USA took decisions which failed to reflect public interests and preferences. The secret military decisions he cited in evidence, including Roosevelt's decision to enter the Second World War, would all have have been supported by American public opinion (Birch, 1993, pp. 172–87).

It can be admitted that there is a tendency in all organisations for power to slide towards a few people – those with more than average commitment, capacity, experience and energy – and for such élites to escape control by the membership. However, in practice in democracies, leaderships of organisations like political parties and trade unions normally have to be rather more responsive to the wishes of their memberships than élite theory suggests. In democracies, moreover, membership of social organisations is voluntary, and members accordingly expect to be consulted, at least on major decisions and over the medium and long term. Élite theorists paid too little attention to the dynamics of the leader–follower relationship and to the context, in democratic systems, of that relationship.

Assumptions

The assumptions of élite theorists are also relevant. Their starting-point was pessimism about the possibility of democracy. They specifically wrote to refute what they saw as the false Utopianism of the democratic ideal of mass participation in decision-making. Beginning by simply assuming that people were selfish, ignorant and apolitical, they also posed a question – 'Who really rules?' – that invited an answer in terms of an undemocratic élite. It was scarcely surprising that they ended both by finding

an élite and by relegating the majority of people to political powerlessness as its dupes. They considered neither the possibility that people would grow in political understanding as society developed nor the possibility that it might make sense for ordinary members of organisations to delegate responsibility for decisions to a few, so long as *ultimate* control remained with the membership. At best, their case remains unproven (perhaps even impossible to establish). At worst, it consists of a sweeping generalisation which requires continual testing by reference to *specific* decisions and often disintegrates when faced by such a test.

Empirically, then, there seem to be better grounds for accepting the pluralist model – that different élites compete for influence with an overarching political élite; that élites are to some extent and differentially responsive to memberships; and, above all, that elections matter as a mechanism by which real power may change hands peaceably.

Criticisms of pluralist theory

However, the pluralist model can itself be criticised on the following grounds.

Elitism

With its focus on élite competition rather than any wider distribution of power, pluralism is itself élitist. Hence, the **élite pluralist or neo-pluralist model** might be considered a more appropriate term for it than simply 'pluralist'. Proponents of the other theories might well argue that pluralism – with its emphasis on detailed decision-making – fails 'to see the wood for the trees'. It exaggerates both rather minor disagreements between élites and relatively small changes in their composition. It ignores the extent to which all the élites share a common interest: the perpetuation of people like themselves in power (power élite theory) or of the

---

Élitist pluralism or neo-pluralism: this theory accepts that élite groups have privileged access to power but maintains that different groups dominate in different political sectors, that competition between élites helps keep government accountable and that a democratically elected élite – the government – predominates.

capitalist system (ruling-class theory). Evidence from Britain in the 1980s and early 1990s – e.g. *The Economist* survey (below, pp. 66–67) or the large-scale increase in social inequality or the huge pay rises taken by directors of the largest firms – can be read as pointing to the continued existence, social irresponsibility and political unaccountability of a power élite or ruling class.

Ideology

Underlying the debate about the distribution of power in society are *ideological* disagreements about ultimate values which arguably lie behind *all three* theories. Thus, with reference to ideology and values, proponents of the power élite were conservative 'mass society' theorists who regarded the majority as incompetent and apathetic 'masses'. They sought to refute the Marxist idea that the ruling class is doomed to be overthrown and replaced by a classless society by showing the inevitability of rule by a political élite in all societies at all times. In turn, the notion of the 'ruling class' represented an ideological response to what was perceived as classical liberalism's neglect of the vital role of economic power in society. Finally, pluralism as a form of political analysis developed out of a liberal perception and endorsement of the cultural and economic complexity of modern societies which make it both inevitable and desirable that power is dispersed among a multiplicity of interests and élites. Thus, pluralism, just like the other theories, had ideological roots.

BOX 4.2

Two dimensions of power for pluralists: making decisions and preventing decisions being made

The US political scientists Bachrach and Baratz have argued that 'Of course power is exercised when A participates in the making of decisions that affect B. But power is also exercised when A devotes his energies to creating or reinforcing social and political values and institutional practices that limit the scope of the political process to public consideration of only those issues which are comparatively innocuous to A.'

(cited Birch, 1993, p. 143)

Methodology

With regard to *methodology*, the question with which one begins an inquiry into the source of power in society plays a key role in shaping one's conclusion. Thus, to ask people the question 'Who rules?' invites an answer in terms of a power élite or ruling class. Similarly, to ask the question 'Who made that decision?' or 'Which people and/or groups influenced a particular decision?' invites a pluralist answer in terms of competing groups and interests, and even of the dispersion of power beyond an élite. Thus, the pluralist argument that power is dispersed rather than concentrated derives from their starting question. Moreover, pluralists have also to consider a second dimension of power defined by the US political scientists Bachrach and Baratz (1962) as 'non-decision-making'. This is the process by which issues, especially minority issues, are kept off the political agenda by, for example, the strength of consensual opinion against change or of an influential lobby (see Box 4.2 and Chapter 22).

The convergence of 'ruling class', 'power élite' and pluralist theories

In recent decades, Marxist, élitist and pluralist analyses have to a certain extent converged; and the direction of the convergence is towards an élitist position (Marsh, 1995, pp. 270–1). Economic determinism plays a much smaller role in Marxist theory, the concept of corporate power a greater role in pluralist theory. Always élitist, contemporary Marxists have moved away from seeing power in the state simply as a reflection of economic structure towards a perception of the state as a relatively autonomous arena in which gender, race and national as well as class struggles are played out. To modern Marxists, social and economic structures place severe constraints on political outcomes but do not determine them. Meanwhile, modern pluralists have had to acknowledge that power in society is concentrated rather than diffused and that certain groups such as business occupy a privileged position. Pluralism is brought about by competition between rival élites who may be situated within the government, e.g. different departments of state, or may be major producer groups linked to government through sponsoring departments (see Chapter 10). Finally, modern élitists have focused on élite domination both in the state itself and within the most powerful economic interests, the key feature of both state and private sector institutions being that they are hierarchically structured. In *competitive or democratic élitism,* élite rule and democratic institutions are combined with rival élites competing for the popular vote: this still ranks as élitist theory because élites always rule. In *neo-corporatism,* an influential contemporary theory with strong links to élitism, political power is exercised through a tripartite structure involving government and the peak organisations of capital and labour. A common feature of both contemporary Marxism and élitism is the way in which they regard political conflicts in contemporary western democracies as occurring in a context characterised by *structured inequalities* whilst pluralism has moved a significant distance towards accepting the privileged position of business in industrial democracies and the need to take structural constraints on decision-makers more seriously. However, convergence between the three approaches should not be overstressed. Élitist pluralists, for example, still focus centrally on the interplay between group pressures and elected governments that are accountable to public opinion.

Summary

- British élites are generally drawn from privileged social backgrounds although some élites do contain significant minorities of working class and lower-middle class people.
- Business and the professions predominate in the political élite – at parliamentary and Cabinet levels – and all but a small minority of the Conservative leadership stratum have been educated privately rather than in the state system.
- Whilst most British élites have become more open during the twentieth century, change has been only gradual, and in some traditional élites remarkably small.
- There are three major models of the distribution of power in Britain and other western democracies: Marxist, élitist and pluralist. Marxism devel-

oped as a criticism of liberal democracy, élitism as a criticism of socialism and democracy.

- Marxists argue that the distribution of economic power in society determines or in recent versions at least strongly influences politics, with power in the hands of an economic élite, the owners of capital, who form a ruling class.
- Élitists argue that rule by an élite is inevitable because the resources required for the successful exercise of political power are always unevenly distributed. In élite theory, the resources necessary for political rule are psychological, ideological and organisational as much as or more than economic, and these are possessed by an élite whose political expertise contrasts with the lack of organisation and apathy of the masses.
- Pluralists argue that modern societies are very diverse with a large number of groups competing to influence political decisions. Pluralism and democracy are compatible because governments offer many points of access to group influence and are ultimately accountable to electorates.
- In recent decades, there has been a certain amount of convergence between the three theories. Thus, whilst continuing to emphasise structural inequalities, neo-Marxists have abandoned the idea that the distribution of power within the state simply reflects the class structure and have recognised the significance of other groups based on gender and race. Twentieth-century élitists have focused on the way in which power in the state and other organisations is invariably hierarchically structured, on competition between rival élites for power in democracies and on the domination of political processes by corporate élites representing capital and labour. Finally, élite pluralists or neo-pluralists have come to accept that access to decision-makers is unequal and that certain groups such as business have privileged access to political power.

Questions

1. Compare and contrast the social and educational backgrounds of the Labour and Conservative parties in parliament (see Figures 4.1 and 4.2).
2. How far in your view would it make a real difference to British politics if women, ethnic minorities, and the poor were represented in par-

liament in proportion to their numbers in society?

3. Do you think that in modern western societies an élite based on class or its monopoly of political resources inevitably rules or that democratic arrangements and group competition guarantee the public responsiveness and accountability of governments?

Assignment

There are two views about the contemporary relevance of the British variant of power élite theory – the idea of a socially and culturally cohesive Establishment. These are summarised below. Which do you consider to be the most apt description of the relationship between politics and society in Britain? Support your arguments with evidence.

To some commentators, the idea of a British Establishment has declined in plausibility since it was first asserted in the 1950s. The Establishment, they argue, has been eroded by major social and political changes. Britain, as a consequence, is a less closed and more open, more meritocratic and less exclusive society, than at any time in its history.

- *Greater openness and less secrecy*: British government became more open and less secretive. By the 1980s, the public were far more aware of what went on in the inner counsels of the Cabinet and in the 'Whitehall village' than was the case a generation previously. This had happened as a result of such events as the publication of politicians' diaries and memoirs (Crossman, Castle), 'leaks' by civil servants (Tisdall, Ponting), revelations of goings-on inside secret institutions such as MI5 (Peter Wright), the decreasing anonymity of bureaucrats, and the light shed on the workings of government by the select committees.
- *Greater democracy*: Certain important sectors of British society became more democratic. In political parties, members played an increasingly important part in the election of leaders and the selection of party candidates; in trade unions, balloting on the choice of leaders and on strike decisions became the norm. Television contributed both to greater openness and greater democracy by providing continual public demonstrations that, far from being cohesive and united, the so-called Establishment spoke with many, often sharply divergent, voices.

- *Less deference*: Britain became a less deferential society. The willing submission to a social and political élite – and to authority figures generally – by the larger part of society virtually disappeared in the 1970s. A new populism emerged, most marked perhaps in the systematic revelations of the private lives of the 'great and the good' by the tabloid press. This profound cultural change, it has been argued, dealt a severe blow to Britain's formerly secure Establishment (Beer, 1982, esp. chs. 4 and 5).
- *The sudden weakening of the monarchy*: From being the most widely respected institution in British society, the Royal Family lost credit dramatically in the early 1990s. This was the consequence in part of the collapse of the royal marriages, in part of the critical intrusiveness of the 'tabloid' press and in part also of the failure of the monarchy to participate in voluntary reforms, especially with regard to such matters as the payment of tax (by the Queen) and royal claims on the civil list. Since the monarchy is centrally embedded in the traditional core of the Establishment – the Church of England, the Lords, the landowners, the top military men, the horse-racing world, the very wealthy – this crumbling of the mystique of the Royal Family seems likely to further undermine the Establishment as a whole (see Peele, 1993, pp. 38–9). It could be argued that events surrounding the death of Diana Princess of Wales weakened the monarchy even further at the end of a summer which saw public support for the monarchy dipping below 50 per cent for the first time.

However, other commentators, whilst accepting that postwar social change has made society more meritocratic and professionalised, argue that such change has been very gradual, that some change has reinforced rather than undermined class divisions, and that, although somewhat less exclusive than formerly, Britain's governing class or establishment remains powerfully entrenched.

- *The persistence of a social, cultural and political élite*: A survey of individuals in top jobs in 1992 by *The Economist* provided ammunition for those who argued that the Establishment had survived postwar social changes. The journal's survey compared the social backgrounds of a cross-section of top people (drawn from politics, business, the City, the learned professions and the arts) with those of their counterparts in 1972. It found that 66 per cent had attended public school (cf. 67 per cent, in 1972), 54 per cent were Oxbridge-educated (cf. 52 per cent, in 1972) and that only 4 per cent (cf. 2 per cent in 1972) were women. There were fewer Etonians in top posts (8 per cent, cf. 14 per cent in 1972) and fewer in such jobs who had not received higher education (11 per cent, cf. 22 per cent). In general, however, very little had changed. The old establishment had not given way to meritocrats. The 'social revolution' had 'not even started' (*The Economist*, 19 December 1992).

- *The enduring strength of Britain's* ancien régime: Critics also argue that, far from weakening, the core of the Establishment – the monarchy, the hereditary aristocracy in the House of Lords, and the public schools – remains strongly entrenched, and in the case of both the House of Lords and private education, has been revitalised over recent decades. As *The Economist* wrote in 1992: 'Feudal stratification lives on. The class of the past remains stronger in Britain than in most other countries, thanks to the monarchy, to the endurance of the landed gentry and to the private school system which perpetuates upper class apartheid.' Both monarchy and aristocracy are buttressed by huge wealth, large political influence, and popular obsession. Even removed, as in Labour's plans, from the House of Lords, the titles, houses and wealth of the hereditary peerage are safe: an attack on them, like abolition of the monarchy is inconceivable for any British government. As Adonis and Pollard point out, it is 'a laughable proposition' to suppose that the monarchy could be removed as easily as 'splitting the Department of the Environment'. It and its supportive hereditary aristocracy remain a powerful, closed caste seemingly immune to political erosion (*The Economist*, 5 September 1992; Adonis and Pollard, 1997, pp. 131–51).

Further reading

For up-to-date analyses of the social élite, see A. Adonis and Pollard, S. (1997) *A Class Act: The Myth of Britain's Classless Society* (London: Hamilton), and on the parliamentary élite, Norris, P. and Lovenduski, J. (1995) *Political Recruitment: Gender, Race and Class in the British Parliament* (Cambridge: Cambridge University Press) and Butler, D. and Kavanagh, D. (1998) *The British General Election of 1977* (London: Macmillan).

Still useful on the more recent history of British élites are Baker, D., Gamble, A. and Ludlam, S. (1992) 'More "Classless" and Less "Thatcherite"? Conservative Ministers and New Conservative MPs after the 1992 Election', *Parliamentary Affairs*, October; Burch, M. and Moran, M. (1985) 'The Changing British Political Elite, 1945–1983', *Parliamentary Affairs*, 38, winter; Coates, D. (1984) *The Context of British Politics* (London: Hutchinson); Coxall, B. (1992) 'The Social Context of British Politics: Class, Gender and Race in the Two Major Parties, 1970–1990' in B. Jones and L. Robins (eds) *Two Decades in British Politics* (Manchester: Manchester University Press); and Moran, M. (1989) *Politics and Society in Britain*, 2nd. edn (London: Macmillan).

Milibrand, R. (1984) *Capitalist Democracy in Britain* (Oxford: Oxford University Press) is a classic statement of Marxist Ruling Class theory, whilst Marsh, D. and Stoker, G. (1995) *Theories and Methods in Political Science* (London: Macmillan) provides excellent but advanced overviews of Marxist, Elitist and Pluralist theories. Birch, A. H. (1993) *The Concepts and Theories of Modern Democracy* (London: Routledge) is a thoughtful, very accessible consideration of these theories and is particularly useful in relating them to democracy.

Ideology and politics

We noticed in Chapter 1 that politics not only involves conflict over the distribution of scarce resources but also public competition between differing beliefs. These beliefs, when expressed as or forming part of systems of ideas, are called **ideologies.** Political change in recent decades has often been inspired by ideology – witness for example, the impact of feminism and the New Right – or by the displacement of the older ideologies of communism, socialism and conservatism in favour of a new politics of identity based on nationality, ethnicity, religion or gender. This chapter aims to look more closely at ideology. After offering a brief definition of the concept, it focuses on the leading ideologies of the contemporary world and the form they take in the British context.

The meaning and political significance of ideology

The term 'ideology' has often been used – and is still sometimes employed – in a pejorative sense. For example, Marx saw 'ideological' ideas as presenting false pictures of society compared with his own 'scientific' approach, whilst liberals have often used 'ideology' in a hostile sense to denote totalitarian systems of thought such as Soviet Communism pre-

1989. In everyday parlance in Britain, the term 'ideology' is often equated with rigid adherence to dogma in defiance of the facts, as for instance in attacks upon Thatcherism by the political centre or upon the 'loony left' by the tabloid press. These usages all deploy 'ideology' in a negative way, as offering (respectively) a fallacious, an intolerantly absolutist or an excessively dogmatic set of beliefs about society. Contemporary political scientists, however, prefer a *neutral* definition of the term which can include all systems and closely related sets of ideas. In this non-pejorative, comprehensive usage, an ideology is *any connected set* of beliefs. On this definition, conservatism, liberalism, socialism, fascism, nationalism and feminism are all ideologies. What general characteristics do they have in common? What are the defining features of ideology?

Political ideologies are *action-orientated*. They shape political behaviour in particular directions, e.g. to bring about national independence or resurgence (nationalism) or sexual equality (feminism). In serving as guides to political action, ideologies provide pictures of contemporary society which show how it has come to be as it is, what it ought to be like (and what it ought not to be like) and how it can achieve desirable changes and avoid undesirable ones. In other words, ideologies normally contain three elements: *description and interpretation* of the past and present; *prescription of an ideal* to be attained in the future; and *recommendation of strategies and policies* on how to achieve their goals.

Ideology is any system of interrelated ideas offering a comprehensive world-view and able to mobilise large numbers of people for or against political change.

Ideologies appeal to people as members of particular social groups – governing, business, ethnic, national, religious – as classes and as sexes. They aim to extend such groupings (which includes adding to them sympathisers who are not actually 'members') and to build up their morale. Typically, they combine conceptions of human nature; views on the process of history, including the roles of key social groupings such as class, race, gender and nation; and theories of the state.

An ideology may be distinguished from an academic discipline, a political idea and a party policy. In comparison with academic subjects such as history, philosophy or physics, which aim at *understanding*, the intention of ideology is to *persuade*. Unlike a political idea or ideas, an ideology provides a more or less systematic interrelated *set of ideas* or even *system of thought*. Finally, although an ideology may draw upon history and sociology and although it may influence policy, it generally operates at a more abstract level. Ideologies characteristically offer wide-ranging conceptions of human nature, society and the state.

Although its name may be the same, the form taken by an ideology varies from country to country. For example, socialism in Britain in its mainstream sense has meant social democracy. By contrast, in the pre-1989 USSR, it denoted Marxism-Leninism, social democracy having been extinguished by the Bolshevik Revolution of 1917.

Ideologies also change their function over time, the same ideology appearing as revolutionary in one age but as conservative in succeeding eras. Thus, liberalism was a revolutionary ideology in the late eighteenth century when pitted against the European *ancien régime,* but by the mid nineteenth century it had become the dominant ideology and was itself under attack from the new revolutionary ideology of socialism.

Sometimes, apparent lulls in ideological thought have been hailed as heralding the 'end of ideology', as for example when the US sociologist Daniel Bell (1960) argued this thesis about the consensual 1950s, or the US political commentator Francis Fukuyama (1992) maintained that the collapse of Soviet Communism had resulted in the final triumph of western liberal democracy thereby bringing about 'the end of history'. In fact, both writers focused on the weakening of one set of ideo-logical polarities but failed to observe the persistence, even resurgence, of others. Both theses therefore were premature, to say the least.

Liberalism

Liberalism has a strong claim to be regarded as the dominant ideology of modern times. Liberal capitalism and liberal democracy are the prevalent economic and political systems in the industrially advanced West and, in the wake of the collapse of communism, free market economies and pluralist political systems have been seen as emergent in Eastern Europe and the former USSR. Key liberal ideas such as freedom of conscience, freedom of expression, freedom of contract and the right to own property have entered the political culture in Western democracies and enjoy a 'taken for granted' status.

Liberalism is a complex ideology which has undergone considerable changes since the seventeenth century, but certain concepts remain fundamental to it.

Individualism

Whereas pre-modern societies took the community as the starting-point of their social analysis and modern ideologies take classes, nations, races or sexes as their starting-points, liberalism focuses on the individual, perceiving society primarily as a collection of separate individuals. Thus, in contrast to feudal society which saw people as possessed of social duties and obligations and defined them in terms of their social roles, as, for example, peasants, priests or lords, liberalism focused on the integrity of the individual personality – its distinctive needs, interests, rights, capacities, dignity and potential.

Liberalism: Liberals believe that the progress of societies depends on the talents and initiative of individuals and on the rigour with which inherited traditions and established authorities are examined and criticised. They consider that the quality of a society is reflected in the extent to which it accords individuals freedom to make their own choices, protects their rights and is open-minded and tolerant.

Because possessed of unique personalities, individuals, for the liberal, are not only worthy of respect in their own right, they are – or should be – autonomous, or self-directing; hence the evil of all social practices which destroy or threaten the intrinsic moral worth and autonomy of each individual, such as slavery, torture, violence, arranged marriages, and manipulation of other persons.

Rationalism

In forming their purposes, pursuing their interests, conducting their relationships and deciding by what principles to live their lives, individuals make use of their reason. They can calculate, adapt means to ends, deploy logic, analyse and compare – in short, they possess rationality. In addition to enabling individuals to live their private lives according to clear principles, this reasoning capacity can be directed at the analysis of social arrangements based on prejudice, custom or tradition. Liberals perceive individuals both as pursuing their own self-interest and as the best judges of their own interests.

Freedom

For many, freedom is the central liberal concept. In the liberal tradition, it has appeared in two guises: *negative freedom* and *positive freedom*. Because individuals are the best judges of their interests, it follows that they should be free to pursue them uncoerced by external pressures. Negative freedom is thus the absence of constraints upon individual activity in all spheres. It gives rise to the demand for specific 'freedoms' – of conscience, of worship, of association, of speech, of meeting, of trade, of contract, from arbitrary arrest, and so on. This aspect of liberalism is concerned with controlling the power of governments: it is a doctrine of constitutional limitations and safeguards. In the late nineteenth century another doctrine of freedom emphasising individual development or self-realisation emerged: positive freedom. By then, the practice of economic liberalism had led to considerable social deprivation, inequality and poverty: clearly, unregulated capitalism benefited the few, but not the many, who led stunted lives. In these circumstances, the 'New Liberalism' advocated a more 'interventionist' state in order to create the conditions for individual self-fulfilment – or positive liberty – by providing a decent education and some security against the contingencies of life, such as unemployment, ill-health and old age.

Box 5.1 explains how specific political doctrines flow from the central liberal ideological concepts of individualism, rationality and freedom.

Liberalism in Britain since 1945

With the Liberal Party remaining politically weak in this period, despite a revival in its electoral fortunes from the 1960s, the influence of liberal ideology has been necessarily through other parties. Thus, postwar British political history can plausibly be portrayed as playing out a conflict between two strands of liberalism – state interventionist New Liberalism and free market Neo-Liberalism, with the former in the ascendancy down to the 1970s and the latter predominant since then. The influence of liberalism, therefore, has been seminal and liberalism has a strong claim to be perceived as the dominant ideology of the postwar age. It has played a key role in each of the following phases:

(1) *Anti-totalitarianism*: In the period of the Cold War post-1945, liberalism became the doctrine of the West, advocating the values of social and political pluralism and diversity against the fascist and communist regimes which subordinated the individual to the state. These regimes were depicted as totalitarian – that is, as attempting the forced rebuilding of the whole of society in the light of an abstract goal – and were contrasted with the free societies of Western Europe and the United States with their variety of institutions and groups independent of the state.

(2) *Social democracy*: Liberal thinkers W. H. Beveridge (1879–1963) and J. M. Keynes (1883–1946) (who were also Liberals with a capital 'L') played a key role in the shaping of the postwar welfare state and managed economy that formed the basis of a two-party consensus which endured to the 1970s. Both were in the New Liberal tradition, believing in state intervention to offset the imperfections of free market capitalism by promoting welfare and employment, but they both favoured private ownership and were against nationalisation.

(3) *Social reforms of the 1960s and 1970s*: Traditional liberal ideas stressing the freedom of the

individual lay behind the so-called 'permissive society' reforms carried out during Labour rule in the 1960s, most notably the reform of the laws on divorce, abortion and homosexuality, the abolition of capital punishment and the relaxation of censorship in the arts. The equal pay for women and anti-racial discrimination legislation implemented by Labour in the 1970s were also rooted in liberal ideas.

(4) *Neo-liberalism*: New Right advocacy of free markets and opposition to government social and economic intervention, which formed the ideological core of Thatcherism, were indebted to an older strand of liberalism and lay behind the descriptions of Mrs Thatcher as a nineteenth-century liberal. The major postwar exponent of market liberalism, economic liberalism or neo-liberalism has been Friedrich von Hayek (1899–1992).

(5) *Constitutional reform*: Electoral reform, House of Lords reform and devolution have long been liberal causes, and when New Labour identified itself with these and other constitutional reforms, including freedom of information and a Bill of Rights, its programme recalled that of the 1906–14 Liberal Government, which also espoused constitutional reform.

The Liberal Party since 1945 has been in the New Liberal tradition of welfare capitalism and individual rights. The contemporary Liberal Democrats are a reforming party of the centre. They are

- for the market economy but balanced by strong government support for better education, the welfare state and protection of the environment;
- pro-European;
- internationalist (for reforming and strengthening the United Nations and increasing Britain's overseas aid);
- for greater toleration and rights for sexual minorities (legal equality for lesbians and gays);
- for constitutional reform, including proportional representation, devolution and a Bill of Rights to strengthen individual liberties.

Conservatism

There were conservatives before the late eighteenth century but modern **conservatism** began in the 1790s as a reaction against the French Revolution.

It originated in opposition to political radicalism – that is, to a particular set of doctrines about human nature, society and political change. These were, respectively: the inherent goodness and rationality of humanity; the idea of society as a mere collection of isolated individuals; and the feasibility and desirability of root-and-branch change, accomplished if necessary by revolution. Modern conservatism continued in the nineteenth century in opposition to political and economic liberalism, and in the twentieth century has seen its main enemy as statist and totalitarian socialism.

Nineteenth-century conservatives opposed political liberalism – the idea that the only legitimate form of government is self-government – because they believed that democracy would destroy the internal checks and balances of the traditional 'mixed constitution' (monarch, Lords and Commons) and that it would lead to the plunder of the rich by the poor majority. By the late nineteenth century, however, conservatives had accepted democratic government not only as inevitable but also as reconcilable with a privileged class, the constitution and the empire. Nineteenth-century conservatives opposed economic liberalism (the doctrine of *laissez-faire*) because they considered that an unrestricted market economy led to excessive and unnecessary suffering, especially of groups like women and children who could not defend themselves. In doing so, they drew upon a tradition of *paternalism,* which embodied the concern of the propertied for those worse off than themselves.

The 1920s and 1930s brought a major reorientation of conservatism – in domestic politics, to face the assertion of class interest by organised labour together with the socialist threat to use the state as an instrument of social levelling, and, internationally, to counter the menace of left totalitarianism following the Bolshevik Revolution. It became clear then that modern conservatism contained two strands – a libertarian, individualist and free market

> **Conservatism**: Conservatives emphasise the value of leadership by an experienced élite, regard property ownership as essential in order to give people independence of government as well as personal satisfaction and consider the defence of the nation the first task of statesmanship.

BOX 5.1
The ideology of liberalism

- **Government by consent**: Because human beings are autonomous creatures, no one can have authority over them except by their explicit consent: hence democracy is the only legitimate form of government.

- **Limited government**: A central concern is 'the taming of Leviathan' – i.e. guaranteeing the liberty of individuals against their rulers: hence constitutional concepts and mechanisms aimed at constraining government, such as the rule of law, the separation of powers, bicameralism, the legalisation of political opposition, Bills of Rights, and the Ombudsman and, in the twentieth century, an emphasis on pluralism – the legitimacy of a variety of competing groups in society and their role as a constraint on governmental power.

- **Freedom under the law**: The classic goal is a government of laws, not men. This is impossible since judges will always be necessary to interpret the law, but the phrase catches liberalism's fear of the individual becoming subject to the arbitrary power of another, and its consequent desire to establish a set of objective external limits over everyone – the law. Where the law, conceived in these impersonal terms as a body of rules applicable to everyone, is sovereign, no one need fear the power of another. As John Locke (1632–1704), one of the founders of liberalism, wrote: 'where there is no law, there is no freedom. For liberty is to be free of restraint and violence by others, which cannot be where there is no law.'

- **Rights**: Simply by virtue of their humanity, individuals possess rights, which it is the task of government to protect, sometimes by lengthy Bills of Rights as in the United States. In the eighteenth and nineteenth centuries, these rights were civil, legal, economic, political and religious; in the twentieth century, social rights – to health, education and a decent standard of living – have been added. Some commentators have seen these as socialist rather than liberal but others maintain that the welfare capitalism of New Liberals such as L. T. Hobhouse (1864–1929), J. M. Keynes and W. H. Beveridge remains within the liberal tradition.

- **Equality of opportunity**: Liberals are meritocrats, not egalitarians, advocating equality of opportunity, not absolute equality or equality of outcome. They favour a society in which what counts is individual ability, not inherited wealth or social position, and historically have fought against social privilege to secure 'a level playing field'.

- **Equality before the law**: As well as equality of opportunity, social justice requires legal equality, with no discrimination on the grounds of race, colour, creed, gender, or religion.

- **Toleration**: The goal is a plural society in which all individuals and groups have a right to express their views which, in practice, means toleration of the expression of views with which one may not agree. Anti-censorship of opinion, except for the views of those who would destroy the freedom of others: outraged by the *fatwa* (death sentence) declared by the Ayatollah Khomeini against Salman Rushdie, author of the *Satanic Verses*.

- **Devolution**: In the nineteenth century, support for movements for national independence abroad and Home Rule within the British Isles; in the twentieth century, for devolution of power within Britain both on the grounds of fairness to the smaller British nations and of more effective government.

- **Internationalism**: As a matter of fact the nation-state is being superseded and as a matter of principle ought to be superseded by supra-national and international organisations. Early support for Britain to join the European Economic Community (EEC, now EU) and consistent support for supra-national organisations such as the United Nations. Idealistic vision of an international community in which national identities are transcended rests upon a typical liberal perception of the individual, shorn of subordinate loyalties, as 'a citizen of the world'.

---

tradition, and a collectivist, paternalist and state interventionist one (Greenleaf, 1983).

The first strand, muted in the nineteenth century because of the need to oppose economic liberalism, goes back to Edmund Burke (1727–97), the founder of modern conservatism. Burke saw the free market as sacrosanct and any intervention in it by government as likely to undermine wealth-creation and harm the poor. After the First World War, as institutional liberalism (in the form of the Liberal Party) collapsed, conservatism drew upon the libertarian side of its inheritance, emphasising capitalist values and individual liberty against socialism in all its varieties.

After 1945, its paternalist, 'one nation' tradition, deriving from Disraeli, enabled conservatism to adapt to the interventionist welfare state and managed economy. This collectivist, interventionist vein became the dominant strand in the Conservative Party for the next thirty years. However, Enoch Powell kept alive the free market tradition of thought within conservatism until this was vigorously reasserted by Margaret Thatcher in the 1970s.

To sum up: Conservatism over two centuries has changed in various ways – most notably in the character of the élite it has defended (from territorial–aristocratic to business–professional–managerial) and in the nature of the state it has been required to endorse (from non-democratic to democratic). On the role of government, it contains two strands – libertarian and collectivist – one of which at any given time has been dominant. However, as an ideology, certain themes have been and remain of significance to conservatism:

- *Human nature*: Generally pessimistic: human beings seen as morally imperfect and as intellectually fallible, the practical implication of human frailties being a strong state to enforce order.
- *Society*: Seen in hierarchical terms as a command structure held together by people exercising their allotted duties as parents, teachers, employers,etc. Emphasis in social thought on inequality and variety and the 'naturalness' of certain groups, e.g. family, nation. Traditional conservatives see society as organic, i.e. as growing like a plant rather than being built like a machine.
- *Economy*: Capitalism endorsed as optimum economic system, both because of its capacity to generate wealth for societies and individuals and because of its close connection with political freedom.
- *Change*: Generally pro-gradual against radical change, but some exceptions; anti-revolutionary.
- *Nation*: Intensely patriotic and nationalistic, regarding the nation as the primary historical and political unit, the product of shared customs, traditions and values. The preservation of its integrity against internal and external threats is the first task of political leadership.
- *Property*: Unqualified regard for property as giving people independence, security, satisfaction and a means of expressing their personalities; consequent desire to extend property ownership. Unworried by social inequality because it is seen as result of differences in energy and ability. Private property seen as the main bulwark of political freedom and its security as in everyone's interest.
- *Leadership and authority*: Authority seen as social necessity at all levels – in the family, at work, in the nation – and as always flowing from the top, never emanating from the people. National leadership should be by an élite of the capable and experienced, formerly found largely in the aristocracy, now in the middle class.
- *Public order*: Strong emphasis on need to respect rule of law and on powerful law-enforcing agencies in order to preserve public order.
- *The Constitution*: Reverence for British Constitution as product of gradually evolving historical process which has proved its value over time. Traditionally believe in authoritative but limited government, restrained by rule of law, institutional checks, conventions, and tacit understandings.

The New Right

The 'New Right' is the term used to describe the combination of neo-liberal economic ideas with certain more traditional conservative themes which surfaced in Britain in the 1970s and became dominant under the Thatcher and Major Governments between 1979 and 1997. The major ingredients in what came to be termed Thatcherism were support for a free market economy and a nationalist desire to protect British sovereignty against European integration. Economic neo-liberals are anti-statist, regarding free markets as the best mechanism for the allocation of resources to their most profitable use. They believe that rather than practising large-scale intervention in the economy, governments should limit themselves to ensuring 'sound money' (i.e. controlling inflation), security of property and the enforceability of contracts. In practice, 'rolling back the frontiers of the state' under Margaret Thatcher's and John Major's Governments meant cutting direct taxes, seeking to reduce public expenditure, privatising publicly owned assets, ending 'corporatist' relationships with producer groups, and curbing the powers of the trade unions.

The New Right are anti-statist in social policy too: they see welfarism as undermining individual initiative and leading ultimately to a 'dependency' culture. The emphasis of their social policy is therefore on building up a country of more self-reliant individuals whose first question is not to ask what the state can do for them but what they can do for themselves. Some New Right Conservatives also reacted in matters of personal morality against the liberal 'permissiveness' of the 1960s, especially with regard to abortion, homosexuality and pornography. Major's ill-fated 'back to basics' campaign was an attempt to return to traditional family values.

Finally, a leading strand of Thatcherite Conservatism was support for a 'strong state' with regard to internal order, external defence and the protection of national interests. For example, Thatcherism in Britain involved strengthening the police, administering a tougher penal policy, and investing more heavily in defence. Abroad, Thatcherism began by backing US anti-Communism and ended by resisting what was perceived as the rush towards a federal Europe in the name of British sovereignty.

Academic debate has raged about whether Thatcher was truly a conservative. For some critics, her neo-liberal economics, radical rather than gradualist approach to change, rejection of moderation in favour of 'conviction' politics, dismissal of even the concept of 'society', and contempt for constitutional checks and balances (as in her assault upon local government, civil service neutrality and other traditional institutions) place her outside the conservative tradition. However, as already seen, modern conservatism contains both libertarian and collectivist strands of thought and it can therefore be plausibly argued that Thatcher's vigorous assertion of the merits of the free market economy, belief in private property and a powerful state (national defence and policing), and aggressive nationalism place her squarely in the tradition of libertarian conservatism. Box 5.2 compares the one-nation (paternalist) and Thatcherite New Right (libertarian) traditions in contemporary Conservatism.

BOX 5.2

Two strands in contemporary Conservatism

	One-nation (Paternalist)	New Right (Libertarian)
State	Interventionist	Limited
Economy	Mixed	Free market
Welfare	Universal right	Safety net
Civil society	Pluralistic	Individualistic
Change	Gradual	Rapid
Trade unions	Legitimate / Constructive	Undemocratic / Destructive
Morality	Liberal	Conservative
Nation State	European integration / pooling of sovereignty	Assert independence / retain sovereignty

Source: Adapted from Ludlam and Smith (1996) p.12.

The repositioning of Conservatism under William Hague

William Hague lost no time in seeking to adapt Conservative ideology in the wake of heavy electoral defeat and in the face of a Blair Government which it condemned for social and political authoritarianism. Early indications were that the new Conservatism possessed four major strands:

- *Neo-liberal economics*: the search for 'smaller government', involving lower taxes, lower public spending and reduced responsibilities for the state, would continue
- *Social libertarianism*: Hague proclaimed an 'open Conservatism' at ease with racial diversity and tolerant of a range of private sexual behaviour, whilst Michael Portillo took the role of defender of single-parent families and unmarried couples. Hague believed in a Conservatism that had 'compassion as its core', and Portillo suggested that 'concern for others and magnanimity are important qualities of Conservatism'.
- *Nationalist resistance to European integration*: the Conservatives under Hague ruled out British

membership of a single currency for ten years. Hague considered that 'there is a limit to European integration and . . . we are near that limit now'.

- *Constitutional conservatism*: the Conservatives opposed the radical reforms proposed by Labour.

Neo-liberalism on the economy reaffirmed Thatcherism, nationalist resistance to further European integration adopted a major element in Conservatism under Thatcher and Major and hardened it into the party's position, whilst conservativism on the constitution restated the traditional Conservative attitude. But commentators found the change in the party's social stance harder to interpret. To some, fastening on the rhetoric of 'caring' and 'compassion', it represented a return to 'one-nation Conservatism'. To others, it seemed less like a restatement of paternalist responsibility for those less fortunate and more a kind of right-wing liberal individualism expressing a belief in unfettered choice in personal lifestyle. This is probably closer to the truth: having for decades condemned the so-called 'permissive' social reforms of the 1960s, the Conservatives are searching for a more 'inclusive' liberal credo on a range of minorities including single parents, unmarried couples, homosexuals and the ethnic community.

Socialism

Like the other major ideologies, **socialism** emerged *in opposition* to a particular type of society and its ideological justification: nineteenth-century capitalism and *laissez-faire* liberalism. Like the other ideologies too, socialism has changed greatly through time, adapting to altered circumstances and different areas of the world.

> **Socialism**: Traditionally, there have been two major variants of socialism. Fundamentalist socialism has focused on the abolition of markets (capitalism) in favour of common ownership, whilst social democratic or reformist socialism has aimed to moderate the working of the market through state intervention. In recent decades, socialists have moved towards liberal ideas emphasising market socialism, democracy, citizenship, community and stakeholding.

Socialism as a world force

In the nineteenth century, Marx's socialism had many rivals, including the cooperative model proposed by the British mill-owner Robert Owen and the various strains of continental anarchism. But as a systematic theory of the new class society generated by industrial capitalism, Marx's socialism had no equal. The heart of his analysis is the notion of capitalism as exploitative of the working class. For Marx, capitalism as a system of production structured into society a fundamental and irreconcilable conflict of interest between the bourgeoisie – the owners of capital – and the property-less workers.

Because it was *systemic* – i.e. built into the system – this division of interest could lead only to class conflict: it could not be resolved by any change of heart by the capitalist, or trade union action to gain workers their fair rewards, or government intervention to palliate or remove the resultant social injustice and inequality. Eventually, as increasing competition between capitalists increased the misery of the workforce, the system would be overthrown by a workers' uprising. Proletarian revolution would end class rule and destroy the oppressive bourgeois state; after an interlude of worker dictatorship during which the last vestiges of bourgeois rule would be rooted out, a communist society characterised by democracy and social equality would follow.

By the early 1900s a fierce controversy had broken out among European socialists over whether Marx's aims would inevitably have to be accomplished by violent revolution or whether, in circumstances of rising working-class living standards, a revolutionary transformation could be attained by peaceful parliamentary methods. In 1917 occurred a major watershed in the history of socialism. The triumph of the Bolshevik Party during the Russian Revolution led to the division of socialism into two major strands, democratic socialism (Western) and communism (Eastern). With the victory of an anti-liberal, revolutionary party, the USSR became a one-party state with Marxism-Leninism as its official ideology.

World socialism thenceforth had a national base from which after 1945 it established itself in Eastern Europe and achieved considerable influence in the Third World. The success of the Chinese

Communists under Mao after 1949 provided not only a further variant of socialist ideology but also another – and for the Soviets, a rival – source of communist support in the underdeveloped countries. The revival of Marxist theory which gathered strength from the 1960s in the West looked for inspiration to the libertarian writings of the early Marx, to the Italian socialist of the 1920s, Antonio Gramsci, and to the exiled Bolshevik leader, Leon Trotsky, whose reputation survived the moral discredit into which Soviet communism fell under Stalin.

In the late 1980s, communism in the Soviet Union and Eastern Europe suddenly collapsed. The catalyst for the disintegration was the policy of political and economic liberalisation promoted by Mikhail Gorbachev, the General Secretary, after 1985. Within a tumultuous few years, communist governments in Eastern Europe and the USSR were swept away and replaced by multi-party political systems and embryonic free market economies. The Soviet Union itself fell apart and was succeeded by a looser confederation, the Commonwealth of Independent States (CIS). Confined to China, Cuba, North Korea and a few other countries mainly in the Far East, communism had been much diminished as a world force.

Socialism in Britain, 1900 to the 1980s

The central tenet of mainstream British socialism has been the idea of winning control of the state by democratic methods in order to eradicate poverty and create a more equal society. British socialism has been gradualist, parliamentary and reformist rather than revolutionary, and statist rather than decentralist. Its major vehicle has been the Labour Party. The three major influences upon Labour Party socialism were: the ethical socialism of the Independent Labour Party (ILP) (1893), which preached a new morality based on altruism and cooperation; the collectivism of the Fabian Society (1884), which equated socialism with state intervention; and the trade unions, which provided a 'labourist' ethos, tying the party to the pursuit of working-class interests.

Labour socialism shared with new liberalism a willingness to use the state to modify the operation of the market in favour of the poorer sections of society and has drawn upon it (Beveridge and Keynes). But it went beyond new liberalism in its preparedness to eliminate market forces altogether by nationalisation. Formed in 1900 by the trade unions and middle-class socialists (the ILP, Fabians and the Marxist Social Democratic Federation, which soon left), in 1918 the party adopted a socialist constitution which included a commitment to the public ownership of the means of production, distribution and exchange (clause 4).

The new party combined a moral critique of capitalism with labourism and statism. However, in the interwar period, imbued with a utopian vision of the ultimate disappearance of capitalism at some point in the future, Labour totally lacked policies to reform capitalism in the present, and, in office (1924 and 1929–31), could resort only to conventional panaceas. In the 1930s it gradually moved towards a reformist strategy which combined the public corporation form of nationalisation, improvements in social welfare and neo-Keynesian ideas on economic recovery.

There has always been tension within the Labour Party between its left and right wings. In the 1950s, with the party in opposition, having implemented its welfarist and nationalisation programme between 1945 and 1951, left–right conflict broke out again. The revisionists on the party right argued that the socialist goal of equality could be achieved by means other than public ownership, notably through a blend of economic growth to ensure full employment and growing prosperity, progressive taxation to enhance equality and fairness, and comprehensive welfare provision to eradicate poverty; hence, clause 4 should be abandoned. Fundamentalists countered by arguing that despite the social progress made by the Attlee Governments, Britain remained a predominantly capitalist society, and in order to complete its transformation into a socialist one, public ownership retained a key role. The revisionists failed in their attempt (1960) to remove clause 4 from the party constitution but Labour Governments in the 1960s and 1970s pursued revisionist policies based on high public spending, prices and incomes policies to counter inflation, industrial interventionism, the introduction of comprehensive schools and improvements in the rights of workers. The dominant Labour ideology between 1945 and the late 1970s may thus be described as *Keynesian social democracy – the desire to humanise capitalism by state intervention* (Heywood, 1997, p. 56).

During the 1970s, fuelled by disappointment with Labour's performance in government, the left emerged as a much more formidable force within the party. Fed from a variety of sources, including a resurgent Marxism, ethical socialism, neo-syndicalism, militant trade unionism, the new feminism, black activism, and a reborn peace movement, the left produced a wide range of reform proposals, which were later embodied in the 1983 manifesto. The high point of left-wing influence in the postwar period, it promised unilateralism, withdrawal from the EC, exchange controls, selective import controls, a new partnership with the unions, economic planning, industrial democracy and renationalisation of public assets privatised by the Conservatives (Shaw, 1996, p. 166). Labour's lurch to the left provoked a party split which saw the formation of the Social Democratic Party (SDP) (1981) but also triggered a long fightback by the party right.

The main strands in traditional socialism and social democracy were:

- *Human nature*: Human nature is inherently and potentially good but in capitalist economics human relationships are distorted and human goodness thwarted by an economic system which is geared to produce profits for the few rather than to satisfy the basic needs of the many. Capitalism makes people greedy, selfish and competitive rather than generous, altruistic and cooperative. It divides rather than unites people and dehumanises them by treating them as mere 'units' of production or 'consumers' rather than as individual human beings.
- *Society*: Individuals should be considered in the context of their social relationships. Language, knowledge, technology and capital are social products and human behaviour is fundamentally conditioned by the social environment.
- *Community*: People's sense of identity is defined by membership of groups and communities: this sense of belonging is of the highest value to their lives, and the communities they have built by their collective effort and sacrifices should be defended and not undermined.
- *Social class*: Social class is the most important source of social division and social inequality.

- *Equality*: The central socialist value. Socialists advocate the creation of a more equal society in which class differences in wealth, income, education, health and power are sharply reduced. Only greater equality, they believe, can produce genuine freedom for everyone.
- *Fraternity*: Another important socialist value. Socialists aspire to a society in which differentials of reward are justified in terms of social function, and differentials are allocated by a collective decision about the relative social worth of each job. They think such a society is likely to be a fraternal one, characterised by cooperativeness not individualism.
- *Social change*: Socialists call for a fundamental transformation of society whether by reform or revolution. A large-scale redistribution of income, wealth and power is required, but socialists have disagreed over how far this can be achieved by progressive taxation and welfare measures and whether public ownership is also required.
- *Representation*: Socialists see representation primarily in class terms, with power as a delegation from below and the function of the 'Labour' or 'Socialist' party as being to serve the interests of the working class. Politics has tended to be seen in collectivist terms as a matter of class loyalty or 'solidarity'. In practice, in Britain, Labour has always appealed to significant sections of the middle class, whilst over one-third of the working class has voted for non-socialist parties.
- *The state*: Although tainted by class interest, the state can be captured by democratic means and used as an instrument to improve the lives of the majority.

New Labour

Under the leadership of Neil Kinnock, John Smith and Tony Blair after 1983, Labour tacitly acknowledged that Thatcherism had transformed the political agenda and moved away from its traditional ideologies, both socialist and social democrat. Other contributory factors in its ideological shift were the collapse of Soviet Communism after 1989 and the growing impact of the global economy. The collapse of Socialism throughout the former Soviet empire was a major psychological defeat: it confirmed the supremacy of capitalism, free markets and liberal economics and discredited socialist state planning. At the same time it became widely accepted first that global economic forces had severely restricted the freedom of action of the traditional nation-state and, second, that global markets would quickly punish any government which deviated from economic liberalism by using tax and welfare systems for egalitarian redistribution. By the mid-1990s the party had repositioned itself ideologically in the political centre as 'New Labour'. The major symbol of this change was the substitution of the old clause IV public ownership commitment in the party constitution by a new clause 4 committing the party to work for 'a community in which power, wealth and opportunity are in the hands of the many not the few'. The New Labour ideology represents a blend of neo-liberal Thatcherite economics, a more traditional communitarian emphasis and a return to New Liberal-style interest in constitutional reform. The following are the key elements in New Labour ideology.

(1) *The 'competition state'*: New Labour abandoned its former support for publicly-run enterprise in favour of a firm commitment to the role of the market economy in wealth creation and distribution. It believes the central role of the state is to facilitate UK economic competitiveness by encouraging education, reskilling and flexible labour markets. A key New Labour goal is radical welfare reform aimed at ending welfare dependency and encouraging self-reliance and the work habit for which the main means suggested so far are welfare to work for single parents and the young unemployed and stakeholder pensions.

(2) *The idea of community*: Communitarianism represents one of New Labour's attempts (the other is stakeholding) to restate the relationship between the individual and society in an ideological and social situation in which older value systems seemed irrelevant: for example, the New Right's exclusive focus on individuals as consumers and Mrs Thatcher's assertion that 'there is no such thing as society' (laissez faire Conservatism) at one extreme, and Old Labour's focus on class solidarity, collectivism and statism at the other extreme. The social context is widespread concern about social atomisation and fragmentation. Hence, particularly in the realm of crime, education and the treatment of the young, New Labour stressed the ideas of social inter-

dependence, mutual obligation and social responsibility: individuals need strong communities to develop their talents to the full but communities can be strong only if they contain socially-responsible individuals.

(3) *The stakeholder society*: The basic concept of a 'stakeholder society' is that autonomous individuals possess rights, assets and opportunities but in return need to fulfil certain responsibilities and obligations and that governments need to develop policies on welfare, work and education to promote 'inclusion' and combat 'exclusion' (Gamble, 1997, p. 376). According to Tony Blair (1996), 'a stakeholder economy' is an economy in which 'opportunity is available to all, advancement is through merit and from which no group or class is set apart or excluded'; an 'underclass' is 'a moral and economic evil'. One application of the idea in business is that a company is more than a commodity to be bought and traded or make a profit (or loss): it is a partnership which should look after its employees (through good pay, perks and shares in the company), customers and suppliers as well as its shareholders.

(4) *Constitutional radicalism:* Whereas Old Labour had been constitutionally conservative, New Labour is constitutionally radical. The context for its new focus on constitutional reform (devolution, a bill of rights, electoral and parliamentary reform, freedom of information) was the centralisation of power under the Conservatives and a consequent desire to empower individuals against the state. These reform commitments represented a recognition on the left of the central value of according rights to individuals not just in the market-place as consumers (an idea New Labour adopted from the New Right) but also in the political sphere as *citizens*.

Feminism

Modern **feminism** has gone through two phases. The main objective of 'first wave' feminism was the

---

Feminism: Feminists argue that women's disadvantaged position compared with men does not derive primarily from biological difference but from deeply rooted social forces and that it is therefore an issue which can and should be challenged politically.

BOX 5.3
Old Labour and New Labour

	Old Labour	New Labour
State	Interventionist	Supply-side economics
Economy	Mixed	Free market
Economic priority	Low unemployment	Low inflation
Welfare	Universal right	Reduce welfare dependency
Social goal	Egalitarian	Equality of opportunity
Class	Pro-working class	Classless
Morality	Collectivist	Individualist
Trade unions	Public good	No return to pre-1979 privileges
Constitution	Keep status quo	Radical reform
Europe	Right was pro-Europe; left, anti-Europe in 1970s	Pro-Europe/pool sovereignty
Nation-state	Socialism in one country	Global economy

Source: Adapted from Smith and Ludlam (1996) p.12.

attainment of political and legal equality for women. This movement developed during the nineteenth century, drawing inspiration from such texts as Mary Wollstonecraft's *Vindication of the Rights of Woman* (1792) and John Stuart Mill's *The Subjection of Women* (1869). Wollstonecraft argued that women should possess the same civil rights as men on the basis of their fundamental equality as human beings, whilst Mill put the case for the legal equality of women and for women's right to vote on the same terms as men. This individualist or liberal variant of feminism was the dominant strand down to the late 1960s, when it included among its achievements the right to vote for women (1918/28 in the UK), the liberalisation of the laws on divorce and abortion (1967–9), equal-pay legislation, the right to education and the right to pursue a career on the same

terms as men. However, at that time, liberal feminism came under vociferous attack from 'second wave' feminists who argued that it had failed to address the root causes of women's exploitation and oppression.

Although 'second wave' feminism did continue to express the liberal demand for equal career opportunities for women, its main thrust was provided by socialist and radical feminists who felt that women's liberation required more far-reaching social change than civil equality. A resurgent socialist feminism focused on the continuing exploitation of women in the family and in the labour market: at home, women provided unwaged labour in the form of housework and childcare; at work, they are still to be found disproportionately in the lowest-paid, most insecure jobs.

For socialist feminists, women's inequality derives from capitalist property relations. Friedrich Engels stated the argument in his *The Origins of the Family, Private Property and the State* (1884): in history, as societies based on private property displaced communist societies in which property and social position could be inherited through the female line, women were relegated to subordinate positions in the patriarchal family. The transition from communism to capitalism thereby brought about what Engels called 'the world historical defeat of the female sex'. For traditional Marxist feminists, since the primary oppression is by class, women's liberation can come about only through the overthrow of capitalism, and the consequent liquidation of the bourgeois family.

A modern Socialist feminist, Juliet Mitchell, in *Women's Estate* (1971) – although writing in the Marxist tradition – gave sexual oppression as much emphasis as class exploitation. She analysed the role of women in terms of the part they played in four 'key structures': production (as members of the workforce), and, within the family, reproduction, sex and the socialisation of children. Women's liberation required the transformation of all four structures and should include the diversification of the family into a variety of differing forms, but not its abolition.

The most original and powerful element in the women's liberation movement, however, has been radical feminism. For *radical feminists* such as Eve Figes, Kate Millett, Germaine Greer and Shulamith

Firestone, the reason why women are exploited and oppressed is, quite simply, men. They see patriarchy – literally, the rule of the fathers – as the socially dominant concept, and patriarchal attitudes as culturally all-pervasive. For them, gender – not class, race or nation – is the most important social cleavage, but rather than being a 'natural' division, based on immutable biological differences between men and women, they regard it as a politically created and therefore removable one.

But gender differences – meaning superior male and subordinate female roles – are the consequence of a lengthy and deep-rooted process of social conditioning and as such cannot be eliminated either by liberal reformism or the socialist abolition of capitalism. Unless attacked directly, patriarchal attitudes can and would survive such changes; this is because so much of women's oppression takes place in the private sphere – in the family and in personal and sexual relationships. Hence radical feminists have sought to break down the traditional division in political thought between the public and private realms, arguing that 'the personal is the political'. For them, the two spheres cannot be separated since women are at the receiving end of male-dominated power relationships throughout all areas of life.

Feminism has offered a fundamental challenge to all other political ideologies. It characterises them as 'malestream' philosophies, arguing that they are based on the experiences, interests and perceptions of only half of the human race. In the 1990s, despite continuing disagreements among feminists about the way forward and feminism's only partial success to date, there could be no disputing the large-scale change in public consciousness achieved by second wave feminism. By the 1990s too, the radical feminist perception that the struggle against inequality should take place at all levels – in the private sphere as well as the public – had been widely accepted by feminists.

Fascism

Fascism is an extreme right-wing ideology which rose to prominence in inter-war Europe, declined with the defeat and death in war of Hitler and Mussolini, and has resurfaced in recent decades. Basically a doctrine of ultra-nationalism, fascism is a twentieth-century phenomenon (although with roots in the nineteenth century) whose precise form has varied according to different national histories and cultures. Fascism is commonly seen as a violent reaction against political principles and doctrines deriving from the European Enlightenment, such as rationalism, individualism, liberalism, parliamentary democracy and communism, all of which it rejects in the name of the cult of leadership, military-style authoritarianism and extreme nationalism and racism. It has tended to emerge in countries which are suffering from severe social dislocation owing to some combination of defeat in war, rapid industrialisation, the collapse of authoritarian leadership, frustrated nationalist ambitions, intense economic problems and the need to absorb large numbers of foreigners (Box 5.4).

Fascism in Britain

A version of fascism appeared in Britain in the 1930s associated with Oswald Mosley and the *British Union of Fascists* (BUF). Mosley's book *The Greater Britain* (1932) put forward a plan for British economic regeneration – 'Britain First' – which combined the idea of the corporate state with protectionism to guarantee industry a secure home market.

Mosley was thoroughly fascist in his attacks first on the politicians and parties of the parliamentary system (the 'Old Gang') for failing to measure up to the contemporary 'crisis', and second on the communists, seen as the major enemies of the state. Antisemitism is not a theme of the book but there is little doubt that Mosley was prepared to inveigh against the Jews opportunistically in his speeches or that his supporters in the BUF were virulently anti-semitic. Mosley himself stressed the significance of the Second World War in bringing British fascism to a halt, but the reality is that it never got going, held back by the strong support for the parliamentary system, by the respect for constitutionalism and

> **Fascism**: The fundamental goal of fascism is the creation of an organically united nation from which divisive individuals, classes and races have been eliminated and whose unified will is embodied in a forceful, charismatic leader.

moderation in the political culture, by the resilience of the class system, and most important of all perhaps, by the modesty of the economic problem, grave as it was, compared with the situation in Germany after 1918, and by the fact that Britain did not experience defeat in war.

In 1967 another racialist party of the extreme right emerged: the *National Front* (NF). Its central ideological idea was a redefinition of the 'real' or 'authentic' British community in terms of colour, with whites conceived as true Britons, and blacks denied this identity and blamed for social problems with regard to jobs, services and housing in the tradition of fascist 'scapegoating'. The party stood for the repatriation of New Commonwealth immigrants, and its leader for most of the 1970s, John Tyndall, advocated resistance to racial integration and the maintenance of racial separateness on apartheid lines.

The *British National Party* (1983), currently the leading party on the extreme right, emerged after the NF faded in the late 1970s and enjoyed a shortlived success in 1992 winning a local council seat (subsequently lost) in the Isle of Dogs (see Chapter 7). Throughout Europe, neo-fascists emerged in Germany in the wake of reunification, in France where Le Pen's *Front National* was similar to the BNP as a racist anti-immigrant party, and most virulently in the 'ethnic cleansing' practised in the former Yugoslavia.

Nationalism

The core of **nationalism** as an ideology is reducible to four propositions (Box 5.5). As is immediately apparent, the central concept of nationalist ideology is the idea of the 'nation'. Its basic political doctrine flows from this idea: that each nation should possess its own state. It has proved to be a doctrine of striking potency in the modern world.

For the emergence of nationalism as an ideology, the era of the French Revolution (*c.* 1789–1815) was decisive. During these years, three ideas fused to create the modern doctrine:

- The concept of the state as a particular form of territorially based civil association;
- The idea of the sovereignty of the people, popular government or democracy;
- The definition of a 'people' or 'nation' in terms of its culture, including, especially, its language.

The Revolution brought about a combination of the

Nationalism: The core doctrines of nationalism are that the nation defined by culture should either form a state or possess considerable autonomy within a state; and that the nation-state should protect its sovereignty against pressure from global forces and supra-national organisations.

BOX 5.4
Fascism: the main features

- **The 'new man'**: Fascists stress the malleability of human nature and seek to reshape it in a new mould. Fascist 'new man' is a Superman able to transcend materialist drives in pursuit of an ideal and subordinate selfish motives in the service of the Leader.
- **Ultra-nationalism and racialism**: Fascism exalts the consciousness of belonging to the nation, thriving on the contrast between its present state – perceived as corrupted by communists, traitors and Jews (or blacks) – and the true or authentic nation of its imagining, rid of these alien elements.
- **The leadership principle**: A charismatic leader is accorded absolute, dictatorial power as the embodiment of the will of the nation.
- **Dynamism and violence**: Fascism appeals overtly to bru-

tality and violence and glorifies physical force and strength. Fascist 'new man' is a dynamic individual constantly prepared to test his beliefs in action against the national enemies.
- **Irrationalism**: Fascism appeals to the irrational side of human nature – to instinct and to ties of blood and race.
- **Anti-liberal and anti-communist**: Fascism is contemptuous both of liberal parliamentary regimes – because they are based on majority rule and pluralism rather than élitism and the leadership principle – and of communist states – because they exalt class interests and class conflict above national unity.
- **Statism**: The fascist goal is to create a totally unified 'organic' community to which the individual owes complete unquestioning obedience.

first two of these ideas by extending the basis of a previously monarchical state to include the whole people; and the German writer J. G. Herder (1744–1803) suggested that the distinguishing mark of a 'people' or 'nation' was its possession of a unique culture – a distinctive blend of habits, customs, manners, literature, art, religion and notably language, which had grown up over the centuries.

The concept of the 'nation' is – in Benedict Anderson's phrase – an 'imagined community'. It is *imagined* because it is quite impossible for members of even the smallest nation to know any but a tiny proportion of their fellow nationals, yet each feels a sense of kinship with the rest – 'in the minds of each lives the image of their communion'. It is imagined as a *community* because, despite the social inequalities that may exist, the nation is always conceived as 'a deep, horizontal comradeship' – a sense of fraternity which ultimately makes it possible for people to sacrifice their lives for it (Anderson, 1985, pp. 15–16).

Superficially, the idea of nationalism is similar to an older concept like *patriotism*, but is distinguishable from it by its sharply political frame of reference. Whereas nationalism is a political doctrine which holds that all nations should govern themselves, patriotism is a sentiment, a feeling of love for one's country. As Orwell wrote, patriotism means 'devotion to a particular place, a particular way of life'. It may be a precondition of nationalism, but not the thing itself. Nor is nationalism to be identified with *national self-consciousness,* an awareness of separate identity by a nation, which predates it by hundreds of years – although nationalism may develop and use such a feeling.

Nationalism as a specific political doctrine almost invariably asserts the claims of a particular nationality against an external force, an alien, an outsider. In so doing, it normally relies on – and stimulates – the discovery, revival, systematisation and propagandist expounding of historic national cultures. This process then often culminates in the demand for political recognition of the national community by independence (separation), federalism or devolution.

A valuable typology of the main forms taken by nationalism in the modern world has been suggested by A.D. Smith (1979).

BOX 5.5
Nationalism: core ideas

- The world is naturally divided into nations.
- Each nation has its own unique character resulting from its history and culture.
- Each nation should be independent or possess a large degree of autonomy; only in running its own affairs can it achieve self-realisation.
- The primary allegiance of the individual is to the nation or, if it exists, to the nation-state.

- *Liberation struggles against empires*: These aim at independence and the creation of a new state – e.g. Latin America against Spain and Portugal in the nineteenth century, Afro-Asian countries against the European empires post-1945, Eastern European nations against the Soviet empire in the 1980s.
- *State 'renewal'*: The regeneration of an old-established state by an appeal to national pride, often associating this with a quest for economic revitalisation – e.g. de Gaulle in France in the 1950s and 1960s, Thatcher in Britain after 1979.
- *Nation-building in post-colonial societies*: The mobilisation of support for the new 'nation' (e.g. Kenya, Nigeria, Zimbabwe) is aimed at weakening tribalism and, often in combination with socialist principles and methods, achieving modernisation.
- *Ethnic separatism in old multinational states*: Separatist movements base themselves on traditional national identities and demand independence from or greater autonomy within the multinational state – e.g. the Bretons, Basques, Welsh and Scots.

Nationalities and nationalism within the United Kingdom

The circumstances of the formation of the British state – by means of the gradual absorption of Wales (1536), Scotland (1707) and Ireland (1801) into the core English state – profoundly shaped the character of the various nationalisms which emerged within it. Of particular significance were the facts that the UK was created by the assertion of English domination (against which peripheral nationalisms would later define themselves) and that the British Empire which emerged in the eighteenth and nineteenth centuries was for a lengthy period a unifying force within the new state (although not in Ireland). Other unifying factors were: the use of the English language; a party system found everywhere but in Northern Ireland; the Protestant religion; a shared experience of the economic benefits of industrialisation; the modern media and mass entertainments; and, above all, the British Crown and Parliament. These forces are still at work but the upsurge of support for Scottish and Welsh nationalism in the 1970s and the resurgence of Irish republicanism in Northern Ireland brought British nationalisms into unprecedented prominence.

English nationalism

The dominant strand in English nationalism is traditionalism. The slow, gradual and above all successful nature of English imperial expansion; the absence from English history since the seventeenth century of major popular uprisings, and since the eleventh century of invasion, despite the frequent threats of it; and the massive wealth generated by early industrialisation: all these factors contributed to the conservative, traditional character of English nationalism. It is insular – witness the arm's length attitude to 'Europe' – and non-popular, which is not to be confused with 'unpopular', but simply means that English nationalism lacks any symbolic association of the common people with the nation such as exists in the French celebration of the Fall of the Bastille (14 July) or the American celebration of Independence Day (4 July). What it celebrates are institutions and constitutional achievements (parliament, monarchy, common law) predominantly associated with élites, together with moments of national deliverance from invasion – the defeat of the Spanish Armada, of Napoleon, and of Hitler. The English national myth is – not unusually – 'freedom' ('Britons never, never, never shall be slaves').

Since the 1960s, English nationalism has been characterised by a traditionalist defence of the Union against peripheral nationalisms and of parliamentary sovereignty against the European Community; a call for economic modernisation and regeneration; and an assertion of the ethnic and cultural homogeneity of 'the English'.

Welsh nationalism

Welsh nationalism is at root cultural, a response to the threat to Welsh civilisation posed by industrialisation, centralisation and 'anglicisation'. Plaid Cymru, the 'Party of Wales' (1925), adopted the promotion of the Welsh language as its primary goal and favoured self-government (but not independence) as a means of enhancing the status of the language. The party founded by J. Saunders Lewis (1893 1985) was socially conservative; anti-materialist; and imbued with a romantic idealisation of the mediaeval European Order which permitted diverse local cultures to flourish. In the 1960s, the party moved to the left and adopted bilingualism as its ultimate goal.

Welsh nationalism has been profoundly shaped by the Welsh historical experience – by the fact that the national sense of identity never found political expression in a state; by the overwhelming predominance of religious Nonconformity; and by the survival of the language (one-tenth were Welsh speakers in 1991).

Scottish nationalism

In contrast to Welsh nationalism, Scottish nationalism is predominantly economic. Scottish nationalists blame neglect by remote Westminster governments for Scottish economic difficulties and argue that Scottish interests would be better served by the dissolution of the Act of Union (1707) with England and the establishment of an independent Scotland. Whereas the appeal of Plaid Cymru is limited by its divisive emphasis on the language issue, the SNP has invoked the traditional pride of the entire nation in its distinctive identity. Unlike Wales, Scotland was once a state and, after 1707, retained its own systems of law, education and local government and its own established (Presbyterian) Church. Nationalism in Scotland, therefore, has a strong foundation to build upon and has been a threat to the Union since the 1970s when it was further encouraged by the discovery of offshore oil. An important goal of Welsh and Scottish nationalists was achieved with the establishment of Welsh and Scottish parliaments in 1997 (see further, Chapters 7 and 18; also Coxall and Robins, 1998, Chapter 4).

Summary

- Ideologies are belief-systems which function as guides to action. Targeted at people as members of particular groups, they are of immense importance in shaping political behaviour and producing political change. They normally describe society from a particular perspective in the past and present, prescribe specific goals to be attained in the future and offer strategic advice on how to reach this destination. Although retaining identifiable features, ideologies themselves alter through time, assuming revolutionary form in one epoch, a conservative guise in the next, being dominant in one century, displaced and under attack in the following one. They also contain within themselves different traditions and emphases.

- The key concept of *liberalism* is individual freedom. Its thrust is individualist – towards the demarcation and protection of a sphere of activity in society against the claims of the state in which individuals may enjoy their rights and express their interests. Freedom of conscience, freedom of expression and freedom of association are key liberal freedoms. The expanded state recommended by New Liberalism is carefully defined in terms of the minimum functions compatible with a decent life for all. In the postwar period, New Liberalism, neo-liberalism and liberal constitutionalism have been influential, although through other parties, not the Liberal party.

- *Conservatism* has traditionally combined pessimism about human nature, a preference for gradual change, support for leadership by an experienced, able élite, assertive nationalism, and a strong commitment to the preservation of order. Two leading strands of modern British Conservatism are paternalism and libertarianism, the former predominant down to the 1970s as One Nation Conservatism and the latter dominant since then as Thatcherite economic liberalism. To Thatcherism's neo-liberalism, nationalism and constitutional conservatism, William Hague has added toleration for minority groups hitherto not well-regarded by traditional Conservatives.

- *Socialism*, like liberalism, is optimistic about human nature. It has traditionally held that societies which are based on a more equal distribution of wealth, income and power and on cooperation will be more humane, civilised and productive than societies founded on hierarchy, inequality and competition. Its major strands have been eastern communism based on Marxism and western democratic socialism based on Keynesian economic management and state welfare. Since the 1980s, under pressure from the success of neo-liberalism, the collapse of Soviet communism and globalisation, it has struck out in new directions. New Labour ideology combines economic liberalism with constitutional radicalism and a communitarian emphasis on social interdependence and individual social responsibility.

- For contemporary *feminists*, the inequality of women is socially rather than biologically created and hence it can and should be eliminated by ideological and political campaigning. Of the three main variants of feminism – liberal, socialist and radical, it is the latter, with its emphasis on removing male domination in both the private and the public spheres, which has become predominant among feminists in recent years.

- *Fascism* is an ideology of the extreme right: it is racist, élitist, authoritarian, and fiercely hostile both to liberalism and socialism. Its major expressions were in pre-war Hitlerian Germany and Mussolini's Italy. In postwar Europe, it has taken the form of anti-immigrant racism in Germany, France and Britain.

- The core doctrine of *nationalism* is that nations defined in cultural–linguistic terms should form states or possess considerable autonomy within multinational states. Contemporary nationalism takes four main forms: colonial liberation, state renewal and regeneration, nation-building in post-independence regimes, and ethnic separatism.

Questions

1. What do you understand by the concept of ideology? Explain its political significance.
2. Consider the ideological reasons for the formation of New Labour.
3. Discuss the influence of liberal ideas on both major parties since 1945.

Assignments

Assignment (1)

By drawing upon the analysis in the text and Box 5.2, explain the main differences between One Nation and neo-liberal Conservatism.

Assignment (2)
Ideological tensions within New Labour

Disagreement within the Labour Party on the ideological principles which should inform New Labour policy emerged soon after the 1997 General Election. The following summary of some leading themes is drawn largely from articles by Roy Hattersley and Gordon Brown, which appeared in *The Guardian* (see especially July 26, September 2 1997). Hattersley stated that he had become a 'reluctant dissenter' from the New Labour leadership and accused Tony Blair of looking for 'an alternative to socialism'. He made the following main points:

- The fundamental socialist principle is egalitarianism and New Labour has abandoned it by ruling out redistribution from rich to poor through progressive taxation because it argues global markets will not allow it. In fact, it is inequality which is the enemy of national prosperity.
- The tax system was used to redistribute income from poor to rich under Thatcher. This process could easily be put into reverse; British top tax (40 per cent) rates are below those of Germany, France and Italy (51–54 per cent).
- The poverty of single parents (and others) will not be ended by 'welfare to work' only by the increase of benefits; all four postwar Labour governments made the relief of poverty their top priority despite the adverse economic circumstances they inherited in contrast to New Labour which inherited a strong economy but left benefit rates unchanged (apart from abolishing the single parent supplement).
- The idea of 'flexible labour markets' is 'another denial of basic democratic socialist belief' which is that where the rights of the strong (employers) clash with those of the weak (workers) in the labour market place, democratic socialists should intervene on behalf of the weak.

In reply, Gordon Brown argued:

- Egalitarianism as equality of outcome is neither 'desirable not feasible': 'predetermined results applied, as they would have to be, by a central authority and decided irrespective of work, effort or contribution to the community, is not a socialist dream but other people's nightmare of socialism'. It denies rather than liberates humanity and aims to make people something they are not rather than helping them make the best of what they can be.
- Rather than equality of outcome, those on the left should stress equality of opportunity: based on the principle of the equal worth of every human being, it requires practical measures to be taken to ensure everyone achieves his or her potential.
- Roy Hattersley's solution to the problem of poverty – raising benefits by a few pounds – would only 'compensate people for their poverty, without tackling the causes', the main one being the lack of the opportunity of reasonably-paid work. People want the chance for real work, not welfare: hence New Labour's 'welfare to work' programme and minimum wage plans.
- Equality of opportunity should not be based as in the past on a single chance to get on the educational ladder at 11+ or 18+ but rather should be 'recurrent, life-long and comprehensive': government should 'relentlessly' pursue employment, educational, economic, cultural and political opportunities for all through improving employment prospects, modernising the tax and benefit system, increasing the staying-on rates at schools and colleges and enabling workers to gain more skills through a University of Industry.

Questions
(i)   Would it be fair to argue that Roy Hattersley's arguments restate democratic socialism('revisionist' Old Labour) whereas Gordon Brown's are more a modernisation of liberalism than any variant of socialism?

(ii) Why has New Labour ruled out alleviating poverty by increasing benefits? Is support for the 'welfare to work' programme compatible with arguing for increasing taxation to raise

benefits, as Roy Hattersley subsequently maintained?

(iii) Could New Labour's concept of the state more
aptly be termed an 'enabling state' rather than
a 'welfare state'?

(iv) Are the grounds for policy change within parties
ever 'purely ideological'? If not, what other
grounds might there be?

Further reading

The following books all continue valuable discus-
sions of all the major political ideologies as well as
useful considerations of the concept of ideology:
Eatwell, R. and Wright, A. (eds) (1993)
Contemporary Political Ideologies (London: Pinter);
Eccleshall, R., Geoghegan, V., Jay, R. and Wilford,
R. (1984) *Political Ideologies* (London: Hutchinson);
Heywood, A. (1998) *Political Ideologies: An
Introduction*, 2nd edn. (London: Macmillan); and
Leach, R. (1998) *British Political Ideologies* (London:
Macmillan).

On the New Right, see Gamble, A. (1994) *The
Free Economy and the Strong State: The Politics of
Thatcherism*, 2nd edn (London: Macmillan) and
Ludlam, S. and Smith, M.J. (eds) (1996)
Contemporary British Conservatism (London:
Macmillan); and on New Labour, Miliband, D.
(ed.) (1994) *Reinventing the Left* (Cambridge:
Polity). Stimulating, up-to-date analyses are
Marquand, D. and Seldon, A. (eds) (1996) *The Ideas
that Shaped Post-War Britain* (London: Fontana);
Garnett, M. (1996) *Principles and Policies in
Contemporary Britain* (London: Longman); and
Barker, R. (1997) *Political Ideas in Modern Britain*,
2nd edn. (London: Routledge).

PART 2

POLITICAL PARTICIPATION AND COMMUNICATION

Political participation

In Part I we considered the historical, sociological, economic and ideological context of British politics. In Part II, we examine the theme of **political participation** and communication:successive chapters consider parties, elections, voting behaviour, pressure groups and the mass media. This chapter begins our examination of political behaviour with a look at two key themes: political participation and political culture. We ask: what are the main forms of political participation, what proportion of the population may be considered active in politics and who are the active participants? We then turn to the beliefs and attitudes shaping political behaviour. We ask: what is political culture and, more specifically, what are the main characteristics of the British political culture and how have these changed?

Political participation

The most basic form of participation in a democracy is voting in elections. Voting in British general elections averaged 76.5 per cent between 1950 and 1997, but turnout has declined since the 1950s when it averaged over 80 per cent. In 1992, turnout

was 77.7 and in 1997, 71.5 (1990s average, 74.6). Voting turnout is lower at all other types of election, including referendums, and is especially low in Euro elections and local elections (see Table 6.1). A rather higher level of political commitment than voting is registered by joining a political party or a cause group. Membership of political parties stood at 2.3 million in 1992, approximately 7 per cent of the electorate, but was probably lower by 1997 because Conservative membership had almost certainly declined more than Labour membership had increased over the previous five years. The combined membership of the two major parties was about 700,000 in 1997 (Labour 400,000; Conservative 300,000). Membership of pressure groups numbers many millions and far exceeds membership of parties(see chapter 10).

Figure 6.1 divides the population into three main types of participant: a small number of *activists;* the majority – *just voters* – whose participation in politics is limited to voting in elections; and the *almost inactive,* who scarcely participate at all. It is based on the British Political Participation Survey (BPPS) (Parry et al., (1992)), which further subdivided political activists into five groups. These

---

Political participation: citizen involvement in politics through e.g. voting, group and party activity aimed at influencing government.

Table 6.1 Levels of political participation in Britain, 1950–1990s (percent)

General elections, 1950–97 (average)	76.5
European elections, 1970–94 (average)	34.7
Scottish devolution referendum, 1979	62.9
Scottish devolution referendum, 1997	60.1
Welsh devolution referendum, 1979	58.3
Welsh devolution referendum, 1997	50.6
Local government elections (average 1980–7)	42.0

were: *contacting activists* (7.7 per cent), who were politically involved through contacting officials and politicians by for example, phoning or writing a letter; *collective activists* (8.7 per cent), who participated as members of pressure groups; *direct activists* (3.1 per cent), who were protesters characterised mainly by the frequency of their direct action; and *party campaigners* (2.2 per cent), who were principally engaged in fund-raising, canvassing and clerical work and attending rallies. Only a tiny minority, the *complete activists* (1.5 per cent), were involved in a wide variety of political activities, encompassing voting, party campaigning, group activity, contacting and numerous kinds of protest. On this basis, it was estimated that real activists (the last-mentioned category) number about 625,000 in an adult population of about 41.6 million (Parry and Moyser, 1990, p. 150). However, political activity over such a wide field may be regarded as too 'heroic' a requirement for the active citizen. Perhaps it would be more reasonable to consider involvement on a fairly regular basis in any of the activities beyond voting and petition signing as an indicator of a politically active individual. On this less stringent criterion, a significant minority of Britons (between one-fifth and one-quarter) may be regarded as active citizens. Even so, the political participation of the vast majority is either minimal (voting in elections) or virtually non-existent.

Who participates?

Political activists are far from a microcosm of the nation, being found disproportionately among the well-educated middle class and those with stronger than average political opinions. The BPPS found that the salariat, those in professional or managerial occupations, were more likely than other social groups to be active politically. The reason for this is that the salariat possesses greater political resources in terms of wealth and education. Thus, graduates were among the top 12 per cent on the overall participation scale whereas those without formal qualifications had on average performed little in the way of political activity beyond voting and petitioning. Participation thus seemed to increase with education. A *BSA* (*British Social Attitudes*) investigation found that graduates were more likely to have contacted an MP, signed a petition and gone on a demonstration than those with intermediate qualifications, and the last-named group were more likely to have engaged in these three activities than those with no qualifications (Parry and Moyser, 1990, p. 155; Jowell et al., 1987, p. 65). Education builds self-confidence, increases political knowledge and provides literary skills, all of which are necessary for significant political participation. The BPPS also found that gender differences in political participation, once significant, have largely disappeared. Women are as well represented as men among the politically active, although not at élite level (Parry and Moyser, 1993, p. 21). In Norris's words, the traditional view that women participate in politics less than men 'is no longer valid today as women and men are remarkably similar in their mass behaviour and attitudes across all modes of participation' (Norris, 1991, p. 74).

Second, higher than average political participation is related to political values. Those holding strong or extreme political views tend to participate well above average, with overall participation highest on the extreme left. By contrast, the moderate centre tends to under-participate. In this sphere, political values associated with the 'new' or 'post-materialist' politics of environmentalism, peace and feminism are also linked to higher than average participation. But whereas holders of strong/extreme views on the traditional left–right spectrum are very active in all fields of political activity, strong adherents of the 'new' politics express their ideological commitments through collective and direct action far more than through more conventional forms of participation

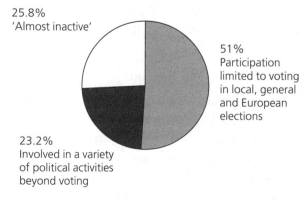

25.8%
'Almost inactive'

51%
Participation limited to voting in local, general and European elections

23.2%
Involved in a variety of political activities beyond voting

Source: Adapted from Parry and Moyser (1900) p. 150.

Figure 6.1 Types of political participation in Britain

(Parry et al., 1992, p. 216). Much of the new concern for the environment is expressed at the local level by people who have been described as 'sporadic interventionists' – individuals protesting about a threat to their own backyards who withdraw from the public arena once their purpose has been achieved. To the extent that 'green', internationalist, lifestyles and feminist issues continue to rise in political significance, it may be expected that political activism too will increase.

Public opinion and participation

The ideal for radical democrats such as John Stuart Mill is the active citizen, the person who is not only politically well informed but who also plays a vigorous part in the affairs of the community. To what extent, however, do people today themselves wish for a greater political role? How widespread are participatory values?

The BPPS tested the desire for more participation by asking respondents whether they thought (1) that ordinary citizens should have more say in the decisions made by government or whether those decisions were best left to elected representatives such as MPs or local councillors; (2) whether the public should be given more access to government documents even if it made the government's job more difficult; and (3) whether workers and employees should have more say in how the places where they work are run. These questions probed public opinion not only on political participation but also upon more open government, which may be seen as a prerequisite of a more participatory society, and on workplace democracy.

Only in the sphere of work did an overwhelming majority (four-fifths) express a wish for greater participation. This seems to be an issue which has steadily gained in public favour since the 1970s. According to the British Election Studies, the proportion of respondents agreeing that 'workers should be given more say in running the places where they work' rose from 56 per cent in 1974 to 80 per cent in 1986. (Jowell et al., 1987, p. 58). With regard to political participation, however, the majority – although a small one – favoured leaving decision-making to elected representatives. On the other hand, there was a majority (nearly three-fifths, 58.3 per cent) in support of more open government.

These findings suggest a widespread desire for greater involvement and autonomy at work combined with rather less widespread but still majority support for reforms that would bring about a more politically informed society. A sizeable minority (47.6 per cent) would like to play a greater role in government decision-making at local and/or national level.

To what extent do those who believe strongly in a more participatory society act on their principles by themselves participating politically more than the average? It has already been noticed that people who are strongly committed to a particular ideology tend to participate above the norm. The BPPS also found that a firm belief in the value of participation provided an impetus to greater activism, although a 'relatively modest' one. However, this generalisation requires careful analysis. A belief in greater participation did not increase participation in such matters as voting, contacting and party campaigning. Only with regard to collective action and, especially, direct action was there a strong link between holding participatory beliefs and greater political activism. Committed participationists were involved in direct action (e.g. strikes, demonstrations, road blocks) to a degree second only to the far left and higher than the most fervent supporters of feminism, environmentalism and the peace movement (Parry et al., 1992, pp. 218, 221–3).

Political competence and participation

Traditionally, citizen efficacy or competence – the belief by individuals that they are able to influence government decisions – has been seen as a vital element in an effective democratic society. How able to wield political influence do British citizens feel today, by what means would they seek to do so and how many of them have actually tried to act on their beliefs?

There are several measures of citizen competence or, put another way, individual political efficacy. The main ones are: people's perceptions of the efficacy of their votes in general, local and other elections; their perceptions of their ability acting both as individuals and in groups to influence Members of Parliament (MPs); and their notions of their capacity through individual and collective action to change an unjust law. The British Political

Participation Study found that about three-quarters of the sample believed that their individual votes could make a difference in elections. However, only about one-third believed that people like themselves *as individuals* could have any influence over MPs. But when asked what influence over MPs they might possess when acting *in a group,* people gave more optimistic responses, approximately two-thirds considering that in those circumstances they would be able to exercise some influence. This study concluded that 'feelings of political efficacy are fairly widely held in the population at large' (Parry et al., 1992, p. 174).

As already noticed, actual involvement in politics beyond voting is confined to a small minority – under one-quarter – of the adult population. However, judging from responses to the question about what respondents *would* do if they considered it necessary, *potential for action* is higher than actual involvement. Both the BPPS and the *BSA* surveys showed that an even larger proportion of people than actually participate feel confident in their ability to influence the political process if necessary

and also believe that effective mechanisms exist for them to do so. (Jowell et al., 1987, p. 56; Parry et al., 1992, p. 423). All this suggests that despite the political passivity of the majority, participation potential and a sense of political efficacy are relatively widespread.

Research published in the mid-1990s indicated that participation potential or propensity to protest against an unjust law may actually be increasing. Table 6.2 gives the answers over a period of time to a *British Social Attitudes* survey on actions respondents would take to an unjust law. The conclusion of the survey's authors was that over the eleven years between 1983 and 1994 there had been a 'fairly general' increase in the public's propensity to protest. On average, a larger proportion of the population at the later date would take some action against an unjust law; a larger proportion would undertake more actions than before; and a larger proportion would engage in unconventional political action, such as going on a protest march or a demonstration (Curtice and Jowell, 1995, pp. 154–5).

Table 6.2 Trends in potential political action, 1983–94

	1983	1984	1986	1989	1991	1994
% saying they would:						
Sign a petition	55	58	65	71	78	68
Contact their MP	46	56	52	55	49	58
Contact radio, TV or a newspaper	14	18	15	14	14	22
Go on a protest or demonstration	8	9	11	14	14	17
Speak to an influential person	10	15	15	15	17	17
Contact a government department	7	9	12	12	11	14
Form a group of like-minded people	6	8	8	10	7	10
Raise the issue in an organisation they already belong to	9	8	10	11	9	7
None of these	13	8	10	8	6	7
% saying they would undertake:						
Three or more actions	14	20	25	30	29	33
One or two actions	72	71	65	61	64	58
No action	12	8	10	8	6	7

Source: Curtice and Jowell (1995) p. 154.

Political culture

A **political culture** is the pattern of understandings, feelings and attitudes which dispose people towards behaving in a particular way politically. It is the collective expression of the political outlooks and values of the individuals who make up society. All societies possess a political culture.

In the immediate post-1945 period, it was customary to describe British political culture in terms of three main characteristics: homogeneity; consensus; and deference. These concepts may be summarised as follows:

- *Homogeneity*: the view that shared political values and a sense of community over and above cultural, national and political differences are prevalent in Britain. These facilitated political cooperation and fostered a widespread feeling of common purpose.
- *Consensus*: a reference to the way in which political divisions are held in check by common adherence to certain procedures for settling differences, to 'the rules of the democratic game', i.e. peaceful parliamentary methods and also by the pragmatism and feeling for compromise in moderate British political attitudes with their distaste for ideological extremes.
- *Deference*: this term in its most common meaning denotes the willing submission of the majority to a political élite often seen as 'born to rule'. Such an attitude is underpinned by a broader popular acceptance of social inequality and hierarchy.

Social, cultural and political change since the 1970s have led many to doubt the continuing validity of this theory of British political culture in the 1990s and also raised questions about its validity for any period other than the 1950s.

The '*homogeneity*' thesis underestimated the impact of differences of national culture upon the United Kingdom. Historically, diversity and plurality rather than homogeneity have been the rule.

Political Culture: the opinions, attitudes and beliefs which shape political behaviour. A country's political culture consists of the whole citizenry's collective attitudes to the political system and their role in it.

Since the 1960s, the effects of New Commonwealth immigration, the rise of Scottish and Welsh nationalism, and the recurrence of the Irish question have combined to undermine social homogeneity and fragment political values within the UK.

The *consensus* theory ignored the role played by military force and economic power in the making of the UK. In other words, it gave too little consideration to the historical dimension – and to the extent to which conflicts were settled by force rather than consensus. Procedural consensus remains important although since the 1970s it has been challenged 'on the streets' by groups using direct action such as striking miners, city rioters – in Toxteth, Brixton, Handsworth and North Tyneside – and poll tax protesters, and by groups using extreme violence such as the IRA (Irish Republican Army).

Traditionally, *deferential* attitudes depended upon the social isolation of the political élite supported by a powerful norm of secrecy. Increasingly, in recent decades, these attitudes have been eroded by the emergence of a populist culture characterised and shaped by media disrespect for authority figures. Pragmatic evaluations of governments' competence together with calculations of self-interest have displaced deference to a political élite as the main influence on voting behaviour (Kavanagh, 1971 and 1980; Moran, 1989). Respect for traditional élite institutions such as the monarchy has declined.

National identity and symbols of nationhood

The political culture of the United Kingdom is no longer – if it ever was – 'homogeneous', but rather multinational. Large numbers of people in the UK see themselves as primarily English, Welsh, Scottish, Northern Irish or Irish (Tables 6.3 and 6.4). But these national identities are not exclusive and for the great majority of inhabitants of the UK they coexist with a fundamental sense of 'Britishness'. Britons possess a dual loyalty – to a particular segment of the UK and to Britain as a whole. Over two-thirds of the English, over half of the Welsh and over one-third of Scots see themselves as equally or more British than English, Welsh or Scottish.

Each of the mainland UK nations has a different sense of 'Britishness'. The English identify more

Table 6.3 National identity in mainland Britain

(X = Scottish/Welsh/English)

	Scotland (%)	Wales (%)	England (%)
Thinks of self as:			
X, not British	37	28	16
More X than British	27	20	12
Equally X and British	25	30	43
More British than X	4	7	10
British, not X	6	14	15
None of these	2	1	3

Source: ICM/Rowntree Reform Trust (1992).

nature of the United Kingdom and its political consequences, see Chapters 5, 7 and 18.)

In various ways, then, the concept of 'Britishness' has become more problematic since 1945, more obviously a political and legal concept, less of a cultural one. In 1945, it has been argued, the term 'British' would have been coupled more easily with 'empire' than any specific national entity; now, having lost an empire, Britain has 'not yet found a nation' (Dowds and Young, 1996, p. 153). As the confused and divided loyalties of the inhabitants of the British Isles reveal, 'Britain' is far from being a "nation-state".

Today, 'Britishness' is threatened from below by peripheral nationalisms, but also from above by the development of the European Union. Large numbers of Britons continue to resist the EU as a source of loyalty. A *BSA* survey in 1995 showed that a 2:1 majority favoured protection of Britain's independence from the European Union over fuller integration with it (Table 6.5). A Gallup poll of 15,000 Europeans (1991) found that of the ten countries surveyed Britain was the most fearful of losing national identity and sacrificing national economic interests. As many as 68 per cent of Britons expressed their willingness 'to fight for their country', compared with the European average of 45 per cent, whilst 51.6 per cent of Britons were very proud of their nationality against a European average of just over 36 per cent. But the EU is more popular with the 18–24 age group than the rest of society so a sense of 'European-ness' is likely to

closely with 'Britishness' than the other two nations; traditionally, they have tended to equate, and even now often confuse, 'English' and 'British'. However, many Scots and Welsh have become cooler towards the 'British' identity in recent decades. Over two-thirds of Scots and nearly half of the Welsh now give priority to being Scottish or Welsh rather than British. The disappearance of the British Empire, a unifying force which bound the nations of the UK in a common enterprise, provided the psychological space for the growth of nationalism in the countries on the periphery of the UK. This movement has been strongest in Scotland where a substantial minority would like to shed the British connection altogether.

In Northern Ireland, the situation is different again. A larger proportion than on the mainland define themselves as 'British', although using the term in its legal and political rather than its cultural meaning; on the other hand, a sizeable minority think of themselves as 'Irish', thereby identifying themselves with a nation outside the United Kingdom, the Republic of Ireland. Religious differences underlie the divisions in the political culture (Table 6.4).

The strong correlation between religious affiliation and cultural/political identity in Northern Ireland is evident from Table 6.4. Two-thirds of Protestants think of themselves as British whilst three-fifths of Catholics consider themselves to be Irish. (For further discussion of the multinational

Table 6.4 Religious affiliation and cultural identity in Northern Ireland

	Total (%)	Protestant (%)	Roman Catholic (%)
Thinks of self as:			
British	44	66	10
Irish	25	4	60
Northern Irish	20	16	25
Sometimes British/ sometimes Irish	3	3	4

Source: Jowell *et al.* (eds) (1990) p. 198.

Table 6.5 Britain's relationship with the European Union, 1994 and 1995

	1994 (%)	1995 (%)
Britain's relationship with the European Union		
. . . should be closer	37	29
. . . should be less close	23	26
. . . is about right	34	39
Don't know	7	6
Britain should do all it can to . . .		
. . . unite fully with the European Union	40	32
. . . protect its independence from the European Union	53	60
Don't know	7	8
Britain's long-term policy should be to . . .		
. . . leave the European Union	11	14
. . . stay in the European Union and try to reduce European Union powers	25	23
. . . leave things as they are	20	20
. . . stay in the European Union and try to increase European Union powers	28	28
. . . work for the formation of a single European Government	8	8
Don't know	7	6

Source: Dowds and Young (1996) p. 150.

increase. In another very important sense, however, 'Britishness' has been an integrative force since the 1950s – in providing a focus for the allegiance of New Commonwealth immigrants and their descendants, who have become 'Black Britons' rather than 'Black English', 'Black Scots' or 'Black Welsh'.

The British monarchy

The UK has many national and ethnic subcultures but a sense of unity does exist. The major symbols of this national cohesion are the Union Jack – the United Kingdom flag – and the monarchy. Whereas the main focus of people's attachment in a republic such as the United States is the President, who combines the ceremonial role of head of state with that of effective head of government, in Britain it is the monarch, now almost reduced to a purely ceremonial function, who symbolises the nation. However, in early 1997, following much bad publicity surrounding royal finances and royal marriages, a Market and Opinion Research Institute (MORI) poll indicated that public support for the monarchy had declined with over one-third of respondents (35 per cent) agreeing with the statement that 'Britain no longer needs a monarchy' (the *Guardian*, 6 January 1997). An International Communication and Marketing (ICM) poll taken after the death of Diana Princess of Wales showed a strong public desire for reform: a mere 12 per cent wanted the monarchy to continue in its present form whilst 74 per cent expressed a wish for it to continue but be modernised (*The Observer*, 14 September 1997). By late 1997, the monarchy seemed to have made a limited comeback in the aftermath of the Princess's death, the proportion telling an ICM poll that Britain would be better off without a monarchy having fallen to 24 per cent (the *Guardian*, 12 November 1997).

Support for the political system

The British political culture is profoundly un-revolutionary and revolution is literally inconceivable to most of the population. In 1984, a mere 7 per cent said that they thought it likely that the Government would be overthrown in the next decade (Jowell and Airey, 1984, p. 31). It has been aptly stated that the British remain 'improbable revolutionaries' (Jowell and Topf, 1988). Support for the democratic system remains widespread. However, the proportion of the population believing that the British system of government works well has declined sharply from just under one-half in 1973 to just over one-fifth in 1995. Three-quarters of those surveyed in the mid-1990s thought the system needed to be improved compared with under one-half who did so in 1973 (Table 6.6). In 1995, against a background of public concern over political sleaze, a MORI poll for the Joseph Rowntree Reform Trust found that four

Table 6.6 Support for the British system of government, 1973–95

	1973 (%)	1991 (%)	1995 (%)	Change 1973–95 (%)
The British system of government				
Works extremely well and could not be improved	5	4	3	−2
Could be improved in small ways but mainly works well	43	29	19	−24
Could be improved quite a lot	35	40	41	+6
Needs a great deal of improvement	14	23	35	+21
Don't know	3	5	3	
Works well	48	33	22	−26
Could be improved	49	63	76	+27
Majority for works well	−1	−30	−54	

Sources: Report of the Royal Commission on the Constitution, 1973; Rowntree/MORI *State of the Nation* survey, 1991 and 1995. Cited Dunleavy and Weir (1995) p. 67.

fifths of respondents supported a written constitution, a Bill of Rights and a Freedom of Information Act (see further chapter 12). In the opinion of Patrick Dunleavy and Stuart Weir, the public reaction to sleaze issues reflects 'a groundswell of discontent amongst British citizens about the constitutionally ungrounded character of the UK's political system in general – the extent to which it is based on unspoken understandings, conventional limits, the self-restraint of political élites, and a 'muddling through' revisionism as a way of coping with emerging problems' (Dunleavy and Weir, 1995, p. 65).

Support for government

A widespread feeling that the political *system* could be improved is accompanied by fairly widespread public cynicism about governments and politicians.

Less than a quarter (22 per cent) of respondents to a *British Social Attitudes (BSA)* survey in 1996 trusted governments to put the needs of the nation above their own party 'just about always' or 'most of the time', compared with three-quarters who thought they would do so 'only some of the time' or 'almost never' (Curtice and Jowell, 1997, p.91). These responses revealed a sharp decline in trust in government over the previous two decades (Table 6.7). Large majorities of respondents to BSA surveys

agreed with the propositions that 'Generally speaking . . . MPs lose touch with people pretty quickly' (72 per cent) and that 'parties are only interested in people's votes, not in their opinions' (72 per cent) (Curtice and Jowell, 1995, p. 166). Whilst extremely cynical, disaffected attitudes are confined to a tiny minority (Parry et al., 1992, pp. 180–1), a degree of political cynicism is widespread.

In fact, however, political cynicism in British political culture is nothing new and has been found by virtually all political investigators going back to the 1940s. It was present but unstressed in the Civic Culture study in the 1950s, and it was also evident in a 1944 study which revealed that only 36 per cent of those questioned trusted politicians to do what was best for the country whereas 35 per cent saw them as out for themselves and 22 per cent as out for their party (Almond and Verba, 1965; Topf, 1989; Kavanagh, 1980). What seemed to be new in the mid-1990s was the *degree* of political cynicism being expressed by the public.

Comparative studies within and outside the UK shed further light on this aspect of the British political culture. Unsurprisingly, perhaps, trust in government is lower in Northern Ireland than in the UK as a whole: only just over one-fifth (21 per cent) of respondents to a survey of opinion in the Province, compared with a quarter in Great Britain, trusted government to place the needs of the nation

Table 6.7 Trust in government in Britain, 1974–96

	1974 (%)	1986 (%)	1991 (%)	1994 (%)	1996 (%)
Governments put needs of nation above interests of party					
. . . just about always/most of the time	39	38	33	24	22
. . . only some of the time/almost never	57	57	63	73	75

Sources: Political Action Study, 1974; *British Social Attitudes*, 1986–96. Cited Curtice and Jowell (1997) p. 91.

above party interests 'just about always' or 'most of the time' (Curtice and Jowell, 1995, p. 166). But a study comparing Britain with other advanced industrial democracies found Britain occupying a slightly below median position with regard to trust in government and politicians: less trusting and more cynical than West Germany, Austria and Switzerland but more trusting and less cynical than the USA and Italy (Parry et al., 1992, p. 181).

Support for political institutions

Public opinion surveys also showed declining confidence in Britain's political institutions in the 1990s. Public confidence in parliament and the legal system declined most steeply between 1983 and 1993 whilst trust in the civil service and police also fell by significant amounts; only the armed services retained a high degree of public confidence (Table 6.8). This

growing disillusion with central government and its institutions occurred across the political divide, with political trust declining to a similar extent among Conservative, Labour and Liberal Democrat identifiers (Curtice and Jowell, 1995, p. 149).

Thus, in Britain, trust in political authority – government and political institutions – is generally qualified and has declined over recent decades. The 'uncompromisingly irreverent and critical streak' which two late 1980s researchers found in British attitudes to their system of government appears to have become more pronounced (Jowell and Topf, 1988, p. 120). However, the greater scepticism about the political system and the decreased confidence in politicians and political institutions of the 1990s were combined with a keener public interest in constitutional reform (Curtice and Jowell, 1995, p.167; Curtice and Jowell, 1997, p. 100).

A changing political culture?

Has the often-remarked increasing resort to violence in British society in the 1980s and early 1990s with regard to rising levels of recorded crime, IRA terrorism and urban rioting at Brixton, Toxteth, Handsworth and elsewhere spilled over into the political culture? At least since the eighteenth century, Britain has been widely regarded as possessing a 'moderate' political culture, in which the norms of parliamentary government, an unwritten constitution based on tacit understandings, and the rule of law have enjoyed wide public endorsement. Even under the severe social strains and ideological pressures of the 1930s, there was no descent by more than a tiny minority into illegal or violent forms of protest. How far has this relatively mild political culture survived the impact of rapid and far-reaching postwar social change?

Table 6.8 Public confidence in institutions of government, 1983 and 1993

	Percentage having 'a great deal' or 'quite a lot' of confidence in institutions	
	1983	1993
Parliament	54	30
Civil Service	46	36
Legal system	58	36
The Police	83	70
Armed forces	88	84

Source: Extracted from Gallup poll, *Daily Telegraph*, 22 February 1993.

Table 6.9 Trends in attitudes towards the law, 1983–96 (percentages)

	1983	1984	1986	1989	1991	1994	1996
People should obey the law without exception	53	57	55	50	52	41	41
On exceptional occasions people should follow their consciences even if it means breaking the law	46	42	43	48	47	56	55

Source: Curtice and Jowell (1997) p. 95.

As already noticed, public dissatisfaction with British political institutions and its unwritten constitution increased in the 1980s and 1990s. Other signs of change in the political culture also became apparent in the mid-1990s. First, asked whether people should obey the law without exception or whether there are exceptional occasions in which people should follow their consciences even it it means breaking the law, a larger proportion than formerly opted for conscience over law (Table 6.9). Second, a dual trend occurred in public attitudes to different forms of protest. Support for *conventional* kinds of protest activity such as organising protest meetings, marches and demonstrations declined whilst support for *unconventional* forms of protest such as organising nationwide strikes and occupying government offices increased (Table 6.10). There remains widespread public support for orderly, peaceful methods of political protest and absolutely negligible positive support for protest activities involving violence against persons and property. But

willingness to engage in more threatening forms of direct action such as strikes, refusals to pay rent and taxes and blocking roads appears to have increased. Civil disobedience strategies have been most evident in animal rights, anti-poll tax and anti-roads and other environmental protests in the 1990s.

Thus, the conclusion reached by the British Political Participation Survey (BPPS) – that the only form of protest to have increased down to the mid-1980s was the signing of petitions (Parry et al., 1992 p. 420) – certainly requires modification in the 1990s in the light of the widespread discontent and protest generated against the poll tax (1989 to 1992), new roads (from 1991) and exports of live animals. The Anti-Poll Tax Movement employed a wide range of methods of protest, including lobbying of MPs and councillors, petitions and demonstrations; on occasion, it was involved in violent disturbances such as the riot in March 1990 at Trafalgar Square which ended with over 140 being injured. More significant still, its massive campaign

Table 6.10 Opinions on the legitimacy of types of public protest, 1985–96

	1985	1986	1990	1994	1996
Percentage saying that the following should definitely be allowed:					
Organising public meetings to protest against the government	59	55	62	48	54
Publishing pamphlets to protest against the government	55	43	53	41	
Organising protest marches and demonstrations	36	30	39	30	31
Percentage saying that the following should definitely not be allowed:					
Seriously damaging government buildings	91	91	91	83	83
Occupying a government office and stopping work for several days	61	61	58	50	47
Organising a nationwide strike of all workers against the government	52	54	43	39	35

Sources: Curtice and Jowell (1995) p. 157; Curtice and Jowell (1997) p. 94.

of non-payment 'tapped into' a long tradition of civil disobedience in Britain. In the first six months of 1992 alone, nearly 4 million people were summonsed for failing to pay the tax. This popular non-cooperation – fuelled by an admittedly rare combination of moral outrage and material self-interest – forced the Government to back down and withdraw the tax (Barr, 1992). Anti-roads protest was coordinated from 1991 by Alarm UK, an umbrella organisation for 250 groups. Peaceful direct action against a large number of road schemes, including extensions to the M3, M11 and A30, involved 'eco-warriors' in a large variety of obstructive activities on new road sites, including occupation of houses and tree-houses, barricading themselves in tunnels, chaining themselves to concrete lock-ins and occupying offices of construction companies. Protests against the export of live animals in 1995, involving demonstrations and obstruction, succeeded in reducing the number of ferry companies and ports handling the trade, but protesters were far from satisfied with the new EU rules on the live transport of animals agreed in July 1995. In February 1998, the Countryside Alliance mobilised over 250,000 in London on a protest march which, whilst mainly against a ban on foxhunting, also expressed concern against other threats to the rural way of life.

Political socialisation

The process by which people come to understand and mentally absorb the culture of their society is referred to as socialisation, and the process by which they acquire knowledge of their political culture is known as **political socialisation**. The notion of political socialisation holds that people's political knowledge, values, attitudes and beliefs are *learned* in a process which begins in childhood and continues throughout their adult lives. Although political socialisation is best seen as continuous, certain phases seem to be particularly important. Because of the malleability of the young and their greater

---

Political socialisation: The process by which political beliefs and attitudes are learned or acquired by experience and are transmitted from one generation to the next.

---

exposure and susceptibility to influences, it is generally held that the pre-adult years are of critical significance to political socialisation, even though political orientations learned when young may be modified or changed as a result of later experiences and pressures.

The sources which influence the political learning of an individual are called *the agencies of political socialisation*. These agencies supply a range of political information, values and attitudes which individuals may absorb both consciously and subconsciously. The most influential agencies are the family, education, peer groups and the media. Inevitably, they reflect a changing political context. The manner in which these agencies combine and in which one of them becomes the major influence, varies, of course, for each individual. Often, because of the depth and intensity of the emotional relationships it involves, the family is the predominating influence. It passes on an ethnic, religious and class identity, which normally is associated with a particular set of political orientations, and it powerfully shapes a child's attitude to authority, to gender roles, and to values (individualistic/cooperative, authoritarian/democratic, tough-minded/tender-minded) which have clear implications for political behaviour. But no influence, however powerful, is totally determinative of political outlooks. Even in the case of the family, people may rebel as teenagers or gradually grow away from its values as adults. Often the political 'messages' emitted by the various agencies of political socialisation overlap and mutually reinforce each other. They may be all the more influential as a result. But sometimes – from books, films or television, from friends or at work – an individual receives and has to accommodate a 'message' which conflicts with the overall view of the world derived from the other agencies. If it cannot be reconciled with the existing cultural perspective, it may bring about change in it.

The main agencies of political socialisation are themselves continually evolving. The considerable increase in recent decades of divorce and birth outside marriage may be weakening the family, thereby undermining its effectiveness as a mechanism for transmitting the political culture. In recent decades, also, the proportion of the population with qualifications at all levels has risen steadily and in the longer term an educated population may be expected to be a more participatory one. However, the young are more likely to participate in unconventional ways (protest politics) than conventional ones (voting in general elections). Significant mobilisers of youth in the 1990s have been the animal rights and environmental movements together with the civil rights issues involved in the Criminal Justice and Public Order Act (1994) (Evans, 1997, pp. 112–13).

Changes in the media may also be expected to have had an impact on the political socialisation process. The period since the 1970s has been characterised by the growing predominance of television as the major source of public information about politics, and by an increasing pro-Conservative bias in the press, which may, however, have been halted at the 1997 General Election (see Chapter 11).

Finally, an important theory of social change is the *generation theory:* the idea that the political outlook of each generation is powerfully shaped by the dominant ideas and institutions of the age into which it is born. Table 6.11 illustrates the changes – and the continuities – in the political contexts of people growing up over the last four decades. In seeking to understand political attitudes and behaviour, it makes sense to consider the often sharply contrasting experiences of political 'generations', and whether these are moulded respectively by the

---

Table 6.11 Political 'generations' and the political culture, 1960s–1990s

Political generation	Political context
1960s	Consensus over interventionist role of the state.
	Two party domination and prevalence of traditional left–right issues.
	'Permissive society' reforms: liberalisation of laws on abortion, divorce, homosexuality and capital punishment.
	Abroad: Cold War, USA in Vietnam.
1970s	Erosion of consensus.
	Two-party politics but rapid growth of third parties – Nationalists, Liberals.
	Emergence of new issues: Europe, feminism, environmentalism, peace, nationalism.
	Union militancy leading to 'ungovernability' debate.
	Northern Ireland issue again: IRA terrorism.
	Abroad: Cold War, USA pulls out of Vietnam
1980s	Thatcherite conviction politics; rejection of consensus.
	Sharply polarised politics as major parties move left and right; formation of Liberal–Social Democratic Alliance and strong electoral performance by centre.
	Continuing IRA terrorism. Falklands War.
	Abroad: intensification of nuclear rivalry between two major powers followed by disintegration of USSR, break-up of its East European empire and end of Cold War.
1990s	Conservative political domination undermined by economic failure (Britain's ejection from ERM, 1992) and 'sleaze' issue culminating in victory for New Labour in 1997 general election.
	New consensus based on Thatcherite economics and 'stakeholder' social values.
	Emergence of 'lifestyle' politics and growing prominence of environmental issues.
	Abroad: only one major power remaining (USA); Gulf War (1991) and disintegration of former Yugoslavia after Civil War.

carnage of the First World War, the 1930s Depression, the post-1945 welfare state, the 'permissive society' of the 1960s, the Thatcherite era of free markets and the 'enterprise culture', and the 'lifestyle' politics of the 1990s.

Anthony Heath and Alison Park tested this theory with reference to the 'Thatcher generation' of the 1980s, comparing it with three previous generations socialised in the 1920s/1930s, the 1940s/1950s and the 1960s/1970s respectively. They found that, whilst there was no evidence that Thatcherite values had had a formative effect on the 1980s generation, there were real differences between the generations in attitudes towards traditional British institutions and Britain's place in the world. Thus, the generation socialised in the 1980s was *less likely* to identify with the Conservatives than any previous generation and there was little evidence to support the notion that it was more materialistic in its economic attitudes than its predecessors. However, the authors did find a generation effect with regard to the monarchy and Europe. Support for the monarchy fell through each successive generation reaching its lowest support with the youngest age-group whilst the generations growing up in the 1960s and 1980s were more likely than those growing up before or just after the second world war to favour a closer relationship with Europe. Other political differences, in their view, were more likely to reflect *life cycle* than generational differences. Thus, they attribute the greater apathy about traditional politics characterising those growing up in the 1980s compared with earlier generations not to 'a fundamental generation gap' but rather to the stage in the life-cycle of this group. In other words, 'political interest increases with age', and is likely to do so for the 1980s generation too (Heath and Park, 1997, pp. 4, 6, 7, 9, 16, 18).

Heath and Park concluded that their study substantiated other findings that the Thatcherite crusade for a fundamental change in values had failed. For example, despite the Thatcherite attack on statism, support for state welfare provision remained undiminished among the general public and among the young in the late 1980s and the 1990s. Opinion polls showed consistent public support for socialised values over more individualistic ones: in a MORI poll in March 1989, respondents by a massive five to one ratio endorsed a society in which 'caring for others' was more highly rewarded than 'the creation of wealth' (cited Crewe, 1996, p. 406).

Summary

- Political participation in Britain takes place mainly in elections. Around three-quarters of the electorate normally vote in general elections but turnout is much lower in local elections, Euro elections and referendums. Apart from voting and petitioning, politics is very much a minority activity involving less than a quarter of the adult population. A far smaller proportion – 1.5 per cent – are 'complete activists', engaged in a wide range of political activities.

- Political activists are far from a microcosm of the nation, being found disproportionately among the educated middle class and those with extreme political opinions, especially on the left. New movements such as feminism, environmentalism and animal rights triggered increased political participation in the 1980s and 1990s.

- Citizen political competence or efficacy is the belief by individuals that they can exercise political influence should they wish to do so. It is of central importance in a democratic society. Traditionally, political efficacy has been widespread in Britain and, moreover, research evidence on the period between 1983 and 1994 suggested that it was increasing, with more people than formerly prepared to take action against an unjust law and to become involved in unconventional political action.

- Political culture consists of the pattern of feelings, attitudes and understandings that dispose people to behave in particular ways politically; it embodies people's collective perceptions of the political system and their place in it. Key attitudes are those relating to the political unit, the nation, the regime, the government, parties, politicians and public officials, political efficacy and political participation.

- British political culture has traditionally been described in terms of its homogeneity, consensus and deference but by the 1990s these terms had come to seem less appropriate. The rise of peripheral nationalisms and growth of ethnic cultures had undermined cultural homogeneity, the resort to political violence (the IRA) and the increase in unconventional forms of protest had eroded procedural consensus; and declining public trust in British institutions had revealed the spread of more egalitarian and less deferential attitudes.

- In the UK more people think of themselves as primarily English, Scots, Welsh or 'Irish' than as British, although many, especially in England, combine a sense of loyalty to their particular nation with a sense of Britishness. The British in general do not feel 'European' and resistance to full political and cultural involvement in Europe remained strong in the 1990s. The monarchy is an important source of cohesion within the political unit, but support for it declined in the 1990s, when public debate intensified on the need for an 'imperial monarchy' to reform itself in order to survive.

- There is strong support for the liberal democratic regime within a moderate political culture profoundly addicted to parliamentary methods. However, public confidence that major British political institutions were working well declined in the 1990s and public cynicism about politicians increased. This declining public trust when combined with growing public support for institutional and constitutional reform could be interpreted as revealing the underlying strength of British political culture.

- In the 1990s, growing numbers of people used civil disobedience strategies in protests over the poll tax, animal rights and new road-building projects, and public tolerance of unconventional methods of protest increased. But public support for protests involving violence against persons or the destruction of property remained negligible.

- The process by which people learn the norms of their political culture is known as political socialisation, the main agencies of which are the family, education, peer groups and the media. These agencies themselves are subject to continual change and are responsive to developments in the political context itself.

Questions

1. To what extent has public confidence in British political institutions declined in the 1980s and 1990s? Account for any changes you find.

2. Define political culture and discuss its significance for political behaviour. Use the information provided in this chapter, especially Tables 6.6–6.10, to discuss British political culture and changes in it in recent decades.

3. Examine your own political attitudes to the political unit, nation, regime, government, party allegiance, public officials and participation, and attempt an analysis of the main influences on their formation.

Assignment

Consider the main features of the British political culture as traditionally described (p. 93). Then examine how far the traditional theory has been undermined by these developments, and answer the questions which follow.

Homogeneity
Less homogeneity now because of:

- growth of nationalism leading to devolution (1997) in Scotland and Wales and IRA success in placing constitutional future of Northern Ireland on political agenda;
- rise of multicultural society in Britain as a consequence of postwar immigration from Commonwealth; establishment of Muslim parliament (1992) and issue of state provision of Muslim schools;
- increase in social inequality in 1980s, with widening income and wealth gap between most well-off and least well-off sections of society and growth of social alienation amongst those excluded from benefits of affluent, consumer society such as the unemployed, the homeless, inner-city dwellers, the badly educated and poorly housed;
- diminished power of the old symbols of national unity such as the Crown, the flag and parliament, in part for the above reasons.

Consensus
Less consensus now because of:

- failure to replace conception of Britain as a great

imperial power with an alternative vision of the country's role in the world: question of British membership of European Community/Union is an issue which produces divisions both within and between parties;

- emergence of more pluralistic politics as a result of the erosion of the dominant two-party politics of the 1950s and its partial displacement by new multi-party system and massive upsurge of participation through pressure groups; development of a 'new politics' based on post-materialist 'life-style' issues, involving for example the environment and feminism. This development has implications for both the content and structure of politics as 'postmaterialists are not satisfied with a loaf of bread; they also insist that it should be wholemeal and additive-free!" and "Post-materialists are also more attracted to organisations giving real opportunities for individual participation' (Hague, Harrop and Breslin, 1992, p. 141);

- increasing public scepticism about politicians and rising concern about the working of political institutions coupled with growing demand for constitutional reform. Greater practice of and more public tolerance for unconventional methods of participation and protest.

Deference
Less deference now because of:

- post-1960s growth of more tolerant and less repressive public attitudes on a wide range of social issues, including divorce, abortion, sexual relationships and censorship in the arts;
- greater equality for women based on better access to education and opportunities for paid employment;
- displacement of conventional morality based on duty and automatic respect for authority by romantic individualistic values calling for personal fulfilment;
- impact of tabloid press which since 1970s has propagated populist anti-élitist and, in certain sections, anti-monarchist values: see, for example, *The Sun* which on 29 July 1993 asked 'Will the

country be any worse off without MPs? No, of course not . . . .'

Questions
(i) Which do you see as the most important factors in the undermining of the picture of Britain as a homogeneous, consensual and deferential society, and why?
(ii) How much homogeneity and deference remain in Britain today? Give examples.
(iii) What do you understand by the distinction between procedural consensus and substantive consensus? How far do you think a procedural consensus based on respect for parliamentary norms and the unwritten British Constitution still exists? Give your reasons.

Further reading

On political participation, the major work is Parry, G., Moyser, G. and Day, N. (1992) *Political Participation and Democracy in Britain* (Cambridge: Cambridge University Press). Its main findings are summarised in Parry, G., Moyser G. and Day, N. (1992) 'Political Participation and Democracy in Britain', *Politics Review*, 3:2, November. For a useful discussion of changes in the 1990s, see Evans, M. (1997) 'Political Participation', in Dunleavy, P. et al. (eds), *Developments in British Politics 5* (London: Macmillan).

On political culture, the classic work is Almond, G. and Verba, S. (1965) *The Civic Culture* (Boston and Toronto: Little, Brown) on which Kavanagh, D. (1980) 'Political Culture in Great Britain: The Decline of the Civic Culture', in G. Almond and S. Verba, *The Civic Culture Revisited* (Boston: Little Brown), provides an incisive critique. Further critical overviews of Almond and Verba's thesis are provided by Topf, R. (1989) 'Political Change and Political Culture in Britain, 1959–87', in J. R.Gibbins (ed.), *Contemporary Political Culture* (London: Sage) and Eatwell, R. (1997) 'Britain' in R. Eatwell (ed.) *European Political Cultures* (London: Routledge).

The *British Social Attitudes* surveys, produced annually since 1983, provide essential analyses of changes in British political culture: see, in particular, Curtice, J. and Jowell, R., 'The Sceptical

Electorate', in R. Jowell, J. Curtice, A. Park, L. Brook and D. Ahrendt (eds), *British Social Attitudes: The 12th Report* (Aldershot: Dartmouth). The Joseph Rowntree Trust's *State of the Nation* surveys in 1991 and 1995 also furnish useful evidence to changing public attitudes to the political system and institutions: see for an analysis of the 1995 survey on the impact of political sleaze, Dunleavy, P. and Weir, S. (1995) 'Media, Opinion and the Constitution', in F. F. Ridley and A. Doig (1995) (eds) *Sleaze: Politicians, Private Interests and Public Reaction* (Oxford: Oxford University Press). For information on political protest, see Jenkins, J. and Klandermans, B. (eds) (1995) *The Politics of Social Protest* (London: University College London Press). On the question of national identity, there are Crick, B. (ed.) (1991) *National Identities* (Oxford: Blackwell) and Dowds, L. and Young, K. (1997) 'National Identity', in *British Social Attitudes: the 13th Report* (Aldershot: Dartmouth).

Political parties

Parties are encountered at several points in this book. In Chapter 1 we saw that democratic government was basically party government; Chapter 12 notes that, although unknown to the British Constitution, voluntary organisations such as parties are in fact essential to its working; Chapter 14 examines the role of party in government and Chapter 16 explains the functions and organisation of the parties in parliament with special reference to their tasks in opposition. The next two chapters – 8 and 9 – will consider voting behaviour and the role of parties in the electoral system. This chapter focuses on the **parties** themselves, explaining both the overall working of the British party system and the internal organisation, financing and membership of the parties together with recent trends in their popular support. We begin, however, by briefly summarising the major functions of party, which are to provide government and opposition; to serve as agencies of representation; and, alongside other means such as pressure groups, to enable popular participation in politics to take place.

> **Political parties** are broad-based coalitions of opinions and interests with permanent organisations which aim to win power alone or in coalition through elections.

The functions of party in Britain

Government and Opposition

Parties form governments – not all parties have an equal chance of forming a government, but government is always by *some* party. Parties recruit the politicians by their selection of party candidates, develop the programmes expressed in manifestos on which government policy is (largely) based and run the major offices of state.

Opposition, as we have seen, is also by party. The party with the second highest number of seats forms both the official Opposition and the alternative government. All the non-governing parties in parliament are collectively said to be in opposition.

Representation

Parties are the single most important agency of political **representation**. They organise a mass electorate by enabling it to make meaningful choices. Parties in the UK enable voters to elect governments by grouping parliamentary candidates together in a coherent way (i.e. under a limited range of 'labels') so that votes in one constituency can be related to votes in another: voters, in other words, vote for a party first and foremost, and for a particular candidate only to an extremely small extent. The elector has probably never heard of most if not all of the candidates on the ballot paper, but he or she *has* heard of the Conservative and Labour parties, the Liberal Democrats, and the various nationalist

> **Representation**: acting on behalf of a group of people. In democratic societies a representative acts on behalf of the voters.

parties. In voting, electors are (largely) expressing an opinion on which party would form the most effective government and which party leader would make the most capable Prime Minister. Parties are important instruments of communication between governments and governed. Parties shape the ideas of groups and individuals to their purposes and bring them into the public arena and into government. Conversely, through their conferences, their canvassing of voters at election time and in the meetings of MPs with party 'activists' and with constituents, parties take the concerns of government to their supporters and the electorate at large.

Participation

Parties are also important agencies of political participation. Participation can range from the fairly minimal – voting in elections – to the maximal – joining a party and working for it by canvassing, attending meetings and conferences and even – for a few – representing it in parliament and government. Parties enable individuals to assert their distinctive political identities; to register a commitment to what can be an important cause in their lives; ultimately, at the deepest level, to express a preference for one kind of society rather than another. Parties can represent classes, ethnic groups, regions, economic interests and ideologies. Parties offer the opportunity to participate in politics from the

---

BOX 7.1
Party functions in a democratic society

- **Government and Opposition**: parties provide coherent government and disciplined opposition
- **Political recruitment**: parties recruit and train politicians
- **Political representation**: parties are the main vehicle of popular representation in assemblies
- **Political communication**: parties provide upward and downward links between governments and governed
- **Interest aggregation**: parties select and shape group proposals and present them to electorates
- **Political participation**: parties are a leading mechanism enabling people to participate in politics
- **Political choice**: parties are the main method by which voters choose between policies and goals at elections

---

highest level to the most moderate and are the sole agencies of comprehensive choice at elections.

The party system in the UK

Is UK politics best described as a two-party system, a dominant party system, a two-and-a-half party system, a three-party system, or a multi-party system? Answers to this question depend to a considerable extent on the criteria, perspective and time period adopted.

A two-party system?

Britain has been traditionally regarded as a two-party system. The academic orthodoxy has held that Britain has a system in which two major parties – each of them willing to govern alone – have regularly competed for all seats in the country and alternated in power with working majorities. The period between 1945 and 1979 – when the political pendulum did swing at fairly regular intervals between Labour and the Conservatives – seems to confirm this notion (Table 7.1). However, even though occupying government after six general elections in this period, Labour was elected only twice with working majorities (defined as an overall advantage of 20 or more seats). Moreover, if we consider the period between 1979 and 1997 – and before 1945 – the situation is even less clear-cut. Labour lost four consecutive general elections after 1979 and by 1997 had been out of office for eighteen years; between the wars, it held power for only the briefest periods (1924 and 1929–31), and did not begin to contest over 80 per cent of constituencies until 1924 or all constituencies until 1945.

Finally, sometimes neither major party has achieved an overall majority and the minority party taking office has become dependent for its continuation in power upon the support of a third party. Periods of minority government (each time involving Labour) occurred in 1924, 1929–31, 1974 (February–October) and again in 1977. In 1977, Labour lost its overall majority and, in order to prevent continual defeats in the House of Commons, made a pact with the Liberal Party. This arrangement fell short of being a formal coalition as

Table 7.1 The major parties: parliamentary majorities, 1945–97

Election	Party returned to office	Size of overall majority
1945	Labour	146
1950	Labour	5
1951	Conservative	17
1955	Conservative	58
1959	Conservative	100
1964	Labour	4
1966	Labour	96
1970	Conservative	30
1974 (Feb)	Labour	–33
1974 (Oct)	Labour	3
1979	Conservative	43
1983	Conservative	144
1987	Conservative	101
1992	Conservative	21
1997	Labour	179

A dominant party system?

Some commentators consider that the most appropriate term to describe the British polity is 'dominant party system'. Between 1918 and 1997, the Conservatives were in government for fifty-eight years – 73 per cent of the time – ruling either alone or as the dominant partner in national coalitions and enjoying several lengthy uninterrupted spells in power – 1931–45; 1951–64; and 1979–97, this latter spell in office being the longest period of unbroken rule by a single party since 1832 (Table 7.2). Put in these terms, the dominant party thesis appears persuasive. But critics argue that Conservative dominance in government was the consequence of specific factors, namely a divided opposition and the employment of a majoritarian electoral system which routinely translates a minority of votes into a majority of seats. Only twice since 1918 – in 1931 and 1935 – have the Conservatives gained over 50 per cent of the vote and in their four election victories after 1979 they failed to achieve over 44 per cent total share. Moreover, the lowest percentage by which the Conservative share of the vote was exceeded by the combined share of the main national opposition parties (Labour/Liberal/Alliance/Liberal Democrat) between 1974 and 1992 was 6.8 per cent in 1979; in other years the difference in percentage share of the vote between the Conservatives and the combined share of its two major rivals was: 18.5 per cent (1974 Feb.), 21.7 per cent (1974 Oct.), 10.6 per cent (1983), 11.1 per cent (1987) and 10.3 per cent (1992). In 1992, nearly 58 per cent of voters cast their votes for parties other than the Conservatives and in 1997 69.3 per cent of voters did so. Is Labour a new hegemonic party then? It is impossible to say at present, but in 1997, despite the

the Liberals did not enter the Government. But it constitutes another exception to a purported 'normal' situation in which one or other major party rules alone without the tolerance or assistance of a third party. In short, if Britain has a two-way party system, it is not a particularly well-balanced one: often, the electoral pendulum has failed to swing sufficiently either to give the main opposition power at all or to provide it with a working majority. In 1997, the pendulum swung violently to give New Labour a massive majority which many analysts see as proof even against defeat in 2002.

Table 7.2 One-party dominance, 1979–92

	1979	1983	1987	1992
Conservative MPs elected	339	397	376	336
Labour MPs elected	269	209	229	271
Conservative majority over Labour	70	188	147	65
Conservative percentage share of the UK vote	43.9	42.4	42.3	41.9
Labour percentage share of the UK vote	36.9	27.6	30.8	34.4
Conservative percentage majority over Labour	7	14.8	11.5	7.5

Table 7.3 The major parties: seats, votes and share of the total vote, 1945–97

General election	Seats		Votes in millions		Percentage share of total vote	
	Lab.	Con.	Lab.	Con.	Lab.	Con.
1945	393	213	11.9	9.9	47.8	39.8
1950	315	298	13.2	12.5	46.1	43.5
1951	295	321	13.9	13.7	48.8	48.0
1955	277	344	12.4	13.2	46.4	49.7
1959	258	365	12.2	13.7	43.8	49.4
1964	317	304	12.2	12.0	44.1	43.4
1966	363	253	13.0	11.4	47.9	41.9
1970	287	330	12.1	13.1	43.0	46.4
1974 (Feb.)	301	297	11.6	11.8	37.1	37.9
1974 (Oct.)	319	277	11.4	10.4	39.2	35.8
1979	268	339	11.5	13.6	36.9	43.9
1983	209	397	8.4	13.0	27.6	42.4
1987	229	375	10.0	13.7	30.8	42.3
1992	271	336	11.5	14.1	34.4	41.9
1997	419	165	13.5	9.6	43.2	30.7

huge margin of its victory in terms of seats, it achieved only 43.2 per cent of vote, broadly comparable to the Conservative share between 1979 and 1992. In terms of electoral votes, Britain is far from possessing a 'dominant party' system.

A two-and-a-half or three-party system?

The case for saying that Britain has a two-and-a-half or three-party system rests on the proposition that the Liberal Democrats (pre-1989 Liberals) are

BOX 7.2
Party systems

The relationship between parties has a significant effect on the way a political system works. The pattern of relationships between parties is called the party system. Several types of party system have been identified.

One party: a single party possesses a monopoly of power through political or constitutional proscription of other parties, e.g. Communist parties in China and former Soviet Union

Dominant party: several parties compete for power and gain representation in the legislature but one party dominates government, ruling alone or in coalition e.g. Japan; Italy, 1945–93

Two party: there may be several parties but two parties alternate in power; often found in 'first past the post' electoral systems, e.g. Britain, Canada, New Zealand and the United States

Multi-party: more than two parties compete for power but the larger parties normally fail to achieve power alone, thus necessitating coalition government often formed of a major party with one of the smaller parties, e.g. Germany, Belgium, the Netherlands.

virtually or in reality a major party. The main arguments for this proposition are that since the general election of February 1974, either alone or together with the Social Democrats as 'the Alliance', the party has contested all or nearly all constituencies nation-wide and regularly polled very highly, 4.3 million in 1979 being its lowest in this period and 7.8 million (with the SDP) in 1983 its highest vote. Its 46 seats for 16.8 per cent of the total vote constituted its lowest under-representation since 1970 (Dunleavy and Margetts, 1997, p. 735). The party is very strong at the political grass-roots, as indicated by its successes in by-elections and local elections, and is the main opposition party to the Conservatives in 145 constituencies. However, despite a willingness to serve in government, the Liberals have not held power alone as a party since 1915. In parliamentary terms, they are a minor party, victims of the remorseless 'squeeze' exercised by the British 'first past the post' electoral system on third parties. However, the possibility that a third party might gain rough parity in seats as well as votes with the two other parties remains, and was almost certainly increased by the refusal of many millions to vote Conservative in 1997. This happened during the first half of the century as Labour rose to the position of alternative governing party while the Liberal party declined. For a time during this process – in the early 1920s – the Liberals were 'neck and neck' with Labour, gaining seats (159 in 1923, for example) roughly commensurate with their total vote, and people spoke and wrote of the 'naturalness' of the three-party system.

A multi-party system?

Like the argument that Britain has a two-and-a-half or three-party system, the case that it possesses a multi-party system focuses on *electoral choice*. Thus, at the constituency level, the system is to a considerable extent regionalised, with differing patterns of parties confronting electors in each geographical area of the UK. Indeed, the Ulster parties, the Scottish National Party (SNP) and the Welsh Nationalists (Plaid Cymru) exist only in their particular regions. Alongside the other UK parties, the Nationalists increase the range of electoral choice in Scotland and Wales. In Northern Ireland, where down to 1992

the mainland parties had no presence, the regional (Ulster) parties constitute almost the entire choice. But although a vote for the nationalist parties or for other small parties like the Green Party, expresses a political preference, it does not help to choose a government since none of these puts forward enough candidates to have any chance of gaining a UK majority. Nor would contesting more constituencies necessarily bring any electoral rewards: for example, the SNP would be unlikely to pick up many votes in South East England.

The answer to the question with which we began this section may be expressed as follows. Britain is still best described as a two-party system (Table 7.3). But two qualifications need to be borne in mind. First, and most important, is the 1979 to 1997 period of one-party domination which led to the suggestion that the system consists of 'a natural party of government and a natural party of opposition' (Crewe, 1992, p. 254). After Labour's sweeping victory in the 1997 general election, this argument is less heard today but is still relevant with respect to Conservative dominance since 1945 (in power for 35 out of the 52 years to 1997), since 1918 or since 1884. Second, at the constituency level, voters are offered a range of electoral choice extending well beyond the two main parties to encompass, particularly, one minor party of importance throughout the mainland and nationalist parties of purely regional significance.

The two major trends since 1970 have been a decline in support for the two major parties and an increase in the followings of the minor parties. In 1951, at the 'peak' of two-party electoral dominance, the Conservative and Labour parties together received 96.8 per cent of the total vote and minor parties a negligible 3.2 per cent. By 1997, the combined vote of the two major parties had dropped to 73.9 per cent of the total vote and that of the minor parties had risen dramatically to 23.7 per cent (Tables 7.3 and 7.4). Between 1951 and 1997, therefore, the two major parties had lost the support of over one-fifth of voters. The main landmark in the break-up of major party domination was the general election of February 1974 when the mainland minor parties almost doubled their parliamentary representation and more than doubled their share of the vote (Table 7.4).

BOX 7.3
The 1997 General Election manifestos on the main issues

	Economy	Industry	Employment and training
Labour	Maintain *public spending plans* of present govt. for first two years. Inflation target of $2^1/_2$%, or less. Reform Bank of England to ensure monetary policy is free of short term manipulation. No increase in top tax rates throughout next parliament. Reduce starting rate of income tax to 10p in £ as long-term aim. Cut VAT on fuel to 5%: no extension of VAT to food, books, children's clothes, newspapers or public transport fares. New individual savings account. Review of corporate and capital gains taxes to promote long-term investment. Early budget to get young and long-term unemployed back to work.	Retain 1980s changes in industrial relations and enterprise. Promotes competition in utilities and tough regulation wherever competition is not an effective discipline. Give Post Office (and similar public sector organisations) greater commercial freedom. Introduce tough competition law. Promote flexible labour markets but plus e.g. national minimum wage and increased infrastructure investment. Help small business by e.g. statutory interest on late debt payments. Encourage employee share ownership. Regional Employment Agencies to coordinate regional development.	'Welfare to work' programme for $1/_4$ million under 25s: four options – private sector job; non profit voluntary sector job; full-time study on approved course; job with environmental task force. Full or part-time education for all over 16s. Any over 18 year-old in work to have right to study on an approved course at college. Attack on long-term joblessness by encouraging employers to take on over two-year unemployed with £75 a week tax rebate paid for by windfall levy. Help lone parents back to work (once youngest is in second term) with package of job search, training and after-school care.
Conservative	Maintain tight control of public spending: goal of reducing it to under 40% of National Income by 2002 and virtually eliminating public borrowing by 2000AD. Inflation target $2^1/_2$%, or less. Goal of 20p basic rate income tax. Tax reform to help families looking after dependent children or relatives. Overall aim to double living standards between 1995 and 2020.	More curbs on trade unions: remove the legal immunity from strikes in essential services, which have disproportionate or excessive effect. Privatisation of Parcelforce, London Underground and Air Traffic Control; consider options to introduce private capital and management skills into Post Office. New Competition Bill to protect companies against price fixing, and other restrictive practices by larger competitors. Help small businesses by cutting corporation tax and reforming business rates. Reduce capital gains and inheritance tax.	Schemes already in place to provide targeted help and training, including remedial education in literacy and numeracy. New incentives being developed, alongside Family Credit, to help people move off benefit and into work. Jobseekers' Allowance ensures no one can refuse reasonable work and remain on benefit. Will focus on long-term unemployed: Project Work currently helping over two-year unemployed. Will use Millenium Lottery Fund to transform computer facilities and information links in schools, libraries, museums and voluntary organisations. 'IT for All' programme with industry.

Welfare

Education: no. 1 priority: increase proportion of National Income on education; 'setting' in comprehensives; no closure of good schools; scrap Assisted Places Scheme and use money to cut class sizes to 30 for all 5–7 year olds; scrap nursery vouchers and use money to guarantee nursery places for all 4 year olds; literacy summer schools; educational establishments wired up free to information super highway; new university of Industry.
Health: continue access to NHS based on need alone; end internal market; end waiting for cancer surgery; new Patients' Charter to concentrate on success and quality of treatment; new public health drive;end tobacco advertising; new independent Food Standards Agency. New forms of public/private partnership to raise funds for NHS in place of failed Private Finance Initiative.
Social Security: partnership of public and private pension provision; retain state pension and increase in line with prices; stakeholder pensions for those who cannot afford good value second pensions; help poorest pensioners; strengthen occupational pensions and retain SERPS; prevent pension mis-selling; fair system of long-term care for elderly; retain universal child benefit and raise in line with prices. Support for pro-family rights such as maximum 48-hour working week, annual holiday and limited unpaid parental leave.
Housing: Encourage more flexible mortgages; action on gazumping; reinvest capital receipts from council house sales in building new houses and rehabilitating old ones; new 'common-hold' tenure for flat-owners. New duty on LAs to protect the homeless through no fault of their own and in priority need.

Education: national targets for schools and action on underperforming schools; all schools to be allowed to select some of their pupils; help schools become grammar schools in all major towns; expand Assisted Places Scheme; help one in five schools become specialist schools by 2001; extend self-governance to all LEA schools
Health: Year by year real terms increase in NHS resources; large expansion of trained doctors and nurses; encourage spread of GP fundholding; enable GPs to provide wider range of patient services; full range of services to cater for mentally ill; promote Private Finance Initiative to unleash funds for NHS. Improve food safety by appointing Chief Food Safety Advisor and Food Safety Council.
Social Security: Basic Pensions Plus scheme to build up private pensions for all; all young people currently entering workforce to enter personal pension fund paid for by rebate on National Insurance Contributions; at retirement get 'significantly' higher pension than currently get from state but guaranteed pension at least equal to present state pension. Phase in policy over next 40 years; will eventually produce massive public expenditure savings. Facilitate small employer pension plans for employees; also 'portable pensions'. Respite Care Programme to enable breaks for carers. Make it easier for old to afford cost of care without giving up life savings. Raise standards in social services by new regulatory framework. Protect value of Family Credit and Child Credit. Bring lone-parent benefits into line with two-parent benefits.
Housing: 'Commonhold' ownership for flat buyers. Force public landlords to sell properties available for occupation but empty without good reason. Clean up housing estates by raising £25 billion new investment by encouraging over half of remaining public sector tenants to transfer homes to new landlords.

Europe

Against European federal state
Priorities for EU
– enlargement
– constitutional reform including PR in Euro elections
– reform of Common Agricultural Policy; 'thorough overhaul' of Common Fisheries Policy
– more competitive markets
Sign Social Chapter
Single currency: Britain should not join in first wave.
Referendum as approval condition for joining
Retain national veto over matters of national interest but consider extending Qualified Majority Voting in limited areas.

Against European federal state
Priorities for EU
– enlargement
– constitutional reform including reform of Court of Justice and stronger role for national parliaments
– completion of single market
– reform of Common Agricultural Policy
– incorporation of principle of subsidiarity into Treaty
Maintain opt-out on Social Chapter and insist on exemption from Working Time Directive
Single Currency: keep options open; no joining without referendum
Retain national veto and oppose extension of Qualified Majority Voting.

Contd ⟩⟩⟩

BOX 7.3 *(continued)*
The 1997 General Election manifestos on the main issues

	Economy	Industry	Employment and training
Liberal Democrat	Keep to 'golden rule' of public finance: total borrowing not to exceed total investment over the economic cycle. Turn Bank of England into UK Reserve Bank free from political interference. Increase basic rate of income tax by 1p to 24p to help finance investment in education. Take nearly 2m. people out of tax by raising tax thresholds. New top tax rate of 50p on incomes of over £100,000 a year. Half of all tax payers to be better off or no worse off by these proposals. Extend benefits of TESSAs and PEPs to wide range of savers.	Reform privatised utilities: combine existing regulations into single office of utility regulation responsible to a cabinet minister. Strengthen competition law e.g. by tightening rules on monopolies and creating single powerful body to promote competition. Strengthen consumer and investor protection. Encourage flexible labour market but protect low-paid with regional variable minimum rate. Support small and medium businesses by e.g. right to interest on late debt payments. Abolish Uniform Business Rate in long term. Major measures against environmental pollution.	Enable long-term unemployed to turn their unemployment benefits into 'working benefits' paid to an employer to recruit and train them. Create hundreds of thousands of new jobs with plans to boost infrastructure investment, promote small businesses and encourage energy conservation. Lower taxes will increase incentives to work. Extra £2 billion a year investment in education and training. New Low Income Benefit to replace Income Support and Family Credit to increase incentives to return to work. Help parents return to work. Extend tax relief on workplace nurseries to other forms of day nursery care.

Choice at elections

In the heyday of political consensus thirty years ago, it was often said that parties at elections merely offered electors the choice between Tweedledum and Tweedledee. This view faded during the Thatcher years when both major parties veered sharply away from the centre, the Conservatives to the right and Labour to the left. Adversarial politics characterised the 1980s. In the 1983 general election, for example, the parties put forward sharply contrasting policies on all the main areas of public concern: the economy, defence, the EEC and the welfare state. However, in order to compete electorally, Labour moved rightwards into the political centre in the late 1980s and 1990s, and party policies converged again. Richard Rose's theory of the *moving consensus*, which suggests that the initiatives of the party in government are gradually accepted by the other major party, helps explain this phenomenon. In a mainly two-party system, the pressure of electoral competition forces parties to the centre and usually brings defeat to parties which become more extreme. Box 7.3, comparing the manifestos of the nationwide parties on the main issues in 1997, reveals the extent to which party convergence had narrowed choice for the voter. Both main parties were Thatcherite on the economy and promised referendums on the single currency (although there were also differences). However, party competition extends far beyond the manifestoes. In 1997, people voted on the political record of the Conservatives'

Welfare

Education: Additional £2 billion a year on education; in first year, double spending on books and equipment to offset recent cuts. Extra £500 million over 5 years to tackle backlog of repairs and maintenance of buildings. Phase out Assisted Places Scheme and use money for LA-Independent Schools partnerships. Reduce primary class sizes to 30 or less in 5 years. Scrap nursery voucher scheme. General Teaching Council to improve teaching standards. Special literacy programme. Improve skills and qualifications of adults.

Health: invest at least an extra £540 million a year in NHS; £2 million a year to provide large number of extra doctors and nurses; cut hospital waiting lists to 6 months maximum over 3 years; end two-tier system in NHS; restore free eye and dental checks; freeze prescription charges; 6 month halt on ward and bed closures. New National Inspectorate for Health and Social Care and new Food Commission independent of MAFF. support for pro-family rights, such as maximum 48-hour working week, annual holiday and limited unpaid parental leave.

Social security: guarantee all an acceptable standard of living in retirement. Retain basic state pension indexed to prices plus additional top-up pension for pensioners with incomes below Income Support level. Phase out expensive, unfair contributory system and base right to state pensions and give people more control over their pensions. Replace SERPS with scheme under which all workers have personal or occupational pension. Protect pension rights by "portable pensions' New carers' benefit to replace Independent Living Allowance to meet more of the financial cost of caring. Extend Carer's Benefit to those over retirement age, as circumstances allow. Increase access to respite care. Codes of practice for residential and care homes. Raise threshold at which older people contribute to their long-term care. New Charter of Rights for Disabled; new Partial Capacity Benefit for working disabled, more support for disabled who cannot find work. New code of practice to improve disabled access to buildings and transport. New statutory right to parental leave. Maternity Benefit to be developed into new flexible parental benefit to be shared between partners.

Housing: new Mortgage Benefit for first-time buyers. Encourage partnerships between public and private sectors and housing associations to build more homes to rent and buy. Allow LAs to raise finance for new homes directly on market; and begin phased release of council house sales receipts to build new homes. More power and responsibility to councils to remove homeless from streets by 2000.

Europe

Priorities for EU – constitutional reform with larger roles for House of Commons, EU Parliament; PR in 1999 Euroelections – reform of Common Agricultural Policy; scrapping of Common Fisheries Policy

Sign Social Chapter

Single Currency: Britain should join but approval in referendum a condition

Retain national veto over constitutional and budgetary matters but extend Qualified Majority Voting

---

over eighteen years of government and the credibility of Labour as a potential government. Voters' *perceptions* of the major parties were far apart on the key issues, their leaderships and the extent to which they were united. Table 7.5 shows public opinion on some leading issues in the 1997 general election. On the key issue of the economy, Labour matched the Conservatives, even had a small lead, compared with 1992 when it lagged by 20 points. On income tax, an even greater shift had occurred, with a 22-point Conservative lead in 1992 being transformed into an 8-point lead for Labour. This change reflected not only voter unhappiness with the Conservative tax record over the previous five years but also the work Labour had done to reassure the electorate on an issue which had inflicted severe damage on its

prospects in 1992. Traditionally a strong issue for Labour, education provided a 22-point lead for the party in 1997, whilst a new issue, sleaze, was also good for Labour and damaging for the Conservatives. Voters' preference for Blair over Major as Prime Minister (Table 14.2) provided Labour with a 'Blair premium' which helped it to nullify the way in which the 'feelgood' factor might have assisted the Conservatives once the economic recovery got under way after 1994 (Kellner, 1997, p. 628). Finally, as Table 7.6 reveals, New Labour's adoption of a 'one nation' stance and its strong internal discipline gave it a considerable advantage over the Conservatives, who were widely perceived as serving only the better-off sections of society and as disunited, notably on Europe.

Both party policies and public perceptions of parties, of course, are shaped by a broad complex of factors, including ideology, ethos, institutional interests, party groups, organisation and personalities.

Table 7.4 The minor parties: seats, votes and share of total vote, 1945–97

General election	Seats	Votes in millions	Percentage share of total vote
1945	34	3.1	11.8
1950	12	3.0	10.4
1951	9	0.9	5.8
1955	9	1.0	3.9
1959	7	1.7	6.8
1964	9	3.4	12.5
1966	14	2.7	9.7
1970	13	3.0	10.7
1974 (Feb.)			
GB	25	7.1	22.7
NI	12	0.7	2.3
1974 (Oct.)			
GB	27	6.5	22.6
NI	12	0.7	2.4
1979			
GB	15	5.2	16.9
NI	12	0.6	2.2
1983			
GB	27	8.4	27.5
NI	17	0.7	2.5
1987			
GB	28	8.0	24.8
NI	17	0.7	2.5
1992			
GB	27	6.8	20.1
NI	17	0.7	2.2
1997			
GB	56	6.0	19.3
NI	18	0.8	2.5

Note: Before 1974 Ulster Unionists were affiliated to the Conservative Party but they broke this link in that year. From 1974, their results (together with those of smaller Ulster groupings) appear separately from the other British minor parties.

We now examine more closely the character of the parties which make up the British party system.

The Labour Party

The Labour Party originated in a decision of representatives of socialist societies and trade unions in 1900 to press for independent working-class representation in Parliament. A Labour Representation Committee with five representatives from the socialist societies and seven from the trade unions was established to guide this enterprise and gained its first major success in 1906, when 29 Labour MPs were elected. After the large-scale franchise extensions of 1918 and 1928, Labour gained ground steadily, displacing the Liberals in the 1920s as the second largest party and forming minority governments in 1924 and 1929–31. Labour did not achieve an absolute majority over the other parties until 1945, however, and although alternating in power with the Conservatives down to 1979 by ruling for seventeen out of the thirty-four years, the party gained a working majority only once more (1966) in this entire period (Table 7.1). Nonetheless, from the vantage-point of the 1980s and early 1990s, the pre-1979 era came to seem like the 'good times' for Labour. Four successive election defeats between 1979 and 1992 underlined the need for radical changes in ideology, policy and organisation if the party were ever again to exercise power. These changes were achieved at first gradually, then more rapidly, under the leadership of Neil Kinnock

BOX 7.4
Party structure

The nature of parties differs considerably, ranging from extremely centralised disciplined machines mobilised by an ideology, such as the Communist Party in the former Soviet Union, to highly decentralised, weakly disciplined coalitions with minimal ideology held together largely by the need to contest presidential elections, such as the Republicans and Democrats in the USA. Britain's parties are more centralised and disciplined than US parties; they have a permanent existence between elections and play a larger role both in the recruitment of politicians and in providing coherent programmatic government and disciplined political opposition.

Table 7.5 Party ratings on the main issues in the 1997 General Election (percentages)

(Responses are to the question: 'Which party do you trust to take the right decision about . . . ?')

	Conservative		Labour	
	1997	Change since 1992	1997	Change since 1992
The economy	42	−11	44	+11
Income tax	36	−19	44	+13
Schools/education	26	−14	48	+9
Dealing with sleaze	23	n/a	49	n/a

Source: BBC/NOP exit poll, abstracted from Kellner (1997b) p. 621.

(1983–92), John Smith(1992–94) and Tony Blair (1994–).

Neil Kinnock began the process, purging the extreme left, dropping unilateralism and withdrawal from the European Community, and accepting much Thatcherite change as permanent, especially privatisation, council house sales and the curbing of trade union powers. He also launched reform of the party organisation with a series of measures which helped to reassert the power of the leader against traditional power bases such as the unions, the National Executive Committee (NEC) and party conference. Thus, Kinnock set up a Shadow Communications Agency to develop campaign strategy and used the campaign management team and the campaign strategy committee which were responsible to him to bypass the NEC. He gained agreement to the reduction of the trade union vote at conference from 90 per cent to 70 per cent and took powers to intervene in the selection of by-election candidates (Kavanagh, 1997, p.534). Yet Labour achieved little more than 34 per cent of the vote in 1992, once again failing to gain as much as half the vote of the working class – its 'natural' constituency. The party had travelled a considerable distance towards electability since 1983, but not far enough. Kinnock, whose popularity as leader consistently lagged behind that of John Major, resigned.

Although moving less swiftly, the modernising strategy continued under the new party leader, the 'consolidationist' John Smith. His main achievement was to persuade Conference to introduce one member, one vote (OMOV) in the selection of parliamentary candidates and in elections to the constituency section of the NEC. He gave the party three years to rethink its entire policy and established a Commission on Social Justice to examine reform of the tax and benefit systems. Following the report of the party's internal working group on electoral reform (the Plant Committee), which recommended in favour of the supplementary vote, he proposed a referendum on the issue and this was party policy in 1997. By the time Tony Blair became leader following John Smith's sudden death, Labour had a 20 per cent lead in the polls and a growing reputation as a reformed party. But it was under Blair's leadership that the main transformation of the party

Table 7.6 Party images in the 1997 General Election (percentages)

(Responses are to the questions: 'Regardless of how you voted today, do you think the Conservative Party/Labour Party is good for one class or all classes?' and 'Regardless of how you voted today, do you think the Conservative Party/Labour Party is united or divided?')

	Conservative	Labour
Good for one class	68	31
Good for all classes	32	69
United	16	66
Divided	84	34

Source: BBC/NOP exit poll, abstracted from Kellner (1997b) p. 627.

into New Labour (a term Neil Kinnock would not use) took place.

For Blair and his close ally Gordon Brown, much still needed to be done before Labour could face a general election with confidence. These tasks included: reassurance of the public that Labour was no longer a tax-and-spend party; elimination of the party image as a socialist party in hock to the unions; removal of its automatic association with declining social groups such as the working class and the unions and association of the party with the aspirations of the middle and upper working classes throughout the country but especially in London and the South-East; further organisational reform aimed at increasing the power of the leadership; and a determined effort to gain the support – or at least subdue the active hostility – of the tabloid press. By

the 1997 general election, building rapidly on the achievements of their predecessors, Blair and Brown had reinvented the party, transforming it from a federal and delegated democracy to a strongly led mass membership party based on the use of plebiscites of the membership to approve leadership initiatives.

Key features of New Labour are:

- *increased power of leadership*: Blair in particular has concentrated power in the leadership by being prepared to bypass NEC and Conference and appeal directly to membership to back clause 4 change (1995) and draft manifesto (1996), to bypass the Parliamentary Party (PLP) in directly appointing Chief Whip (Donald Dewar) and to give strong leads on policy and strategy

Figure 7.1 Tony Blair, modernising Labour leader and Prime Minister from 1997

- *reduced role for NEC*: turned into 'partner' of a Labour Government, forced to work with it, rather than alternative party voice (January 1997); also, balance of power on NEC shifted away from trade unions towards ordinary members
- *reduced trade union influence* at all levels of the party including conference, selection of parliamentary candidates and funding
- *ideological change*: abandonment of the clause 4 public ownership (socialist) clause in the party constitution in favour of a vaguer statement of 'aims and values'
- *policy change*: removal of tax-and-spend image by pre-election adoption of Conservative public spending plans and existing tax rates for two years of new parliament;endorsement of free markets and equal opportunity replaced former emphasis on redistribution and public ownership
- *strenuous fund-raising from individuals and companies*: £15 million raised from private business between June 1996 and March 1997; trade union contribution to party funds declined from 75 per cent to 50 per cent of the total between 1986 and 1996
- *mass membership party:* membership rose by 140,000 between 1994 (280,000) and 1997 (420,000); computerised membership list used for direct mailing and fundraising
- *support of tabloid press*: serious cultivation of formerly hostile tabloid press such as *The Sun* and *Daily Mail* included Blair's meeting with News International (Murdoch) executives in Australia; rewarded with support of *The Sun* and *News of the World* in 1997 election
- *campaigning party*: New Labour studied and sought to draw lessons from methods employed by Clinton's Democrats in the US and Keating's Labour in Australia; ran election campaign from media centre at Millbank Tower, which had a 'war room' containing the key campaign personnel, a 'rebuttal unit' to respond immediately to opponents' attacks and a key seats task force; tight control of shadow ministers who were kept 'on message' by chief Blair aide Peter Mandelson as chair of the General Election Planning Group
- *increasing role of women*: 38 women candidates had already been selected from women-only shortlists before a legal decision forced Labour to abandon its women-only shortlists in January 1996; Labour's policy of 'positive discrimination' and sympathetic attitude towards women candidates was rewarded with the election of 102 women MPs in May 1997. As well as forming 24 per cent of the parliamentary party, women form 48 per cent of Labour's National Executive Committee and from 1993 Labour set goals of half of Constituency Labour Party (CLP) officers and from 1995 half of representatives on the National Policy Forum being women.

The Labour leader

Traditionally, Labour's egalitarian ethos and federalistic constitution – which gave a dominant role to the trade unions – made leadership of the party a more complex task than that of the Conservative Party. The leader has had to balance the claims of parliamentarians, trade unionists and constituency activists and since the 1970s has also had to cope with the clamorous demands of women's groups and black activists. Moreover, each element within the party contains its own divisions between left and right with shades of opinion within each subdivision, which have to be taken into account. In conducting this balancing act and defusing actual and potential conflicts, Labour leaders have normally commanded certain resources: personal prestige, the authority inherent in the position, the power to appoint the Cabinet (in government) and allocate shadow cabinet portfolios and form shadow teams in opposition, and ex-officio membership of the NEC; above all, perhaps, the leader could exploit the desire of the party for office, which has often provided a motive for compromise. However, a series of strong leaders culminating in Tony Blair have used the party's desperation for office ruthlessly to tilt the balance of power in the party away from the traditional and formal power-bases – the unions, the National Executive Committee and Annual Conference – towards the leadership itself. Beginning in the mid-1980s, they have rooted out extremist groups such as Militant, got rid of the party's socialist commitment, driven party policy hard towards the centre, and by radical organisational reforms created a more compliant party. They have imposed firm discipline from the centre upon all sections of the party. New disciplinary rules adopted in late 1996 permit the withdrawal of the whip from any Labour MP for voting against the leadership or bringing the party into disrepute. The months following the 1997 general election saw the suspension of two Labour MPs accused respectively of bribery and running a smear campaign, the suspension of four Labour MEPs for flouting the new code gagging them from publicly criticising government policies, and the suspension of local councillors in Doncaster and Glasgow for misconduct. In addition, Scottish Labour MP Tam Dalyell and Welsh Labour MP Llew Smith faced uncertain futures as a result of their sustained opposition to the Government's devolution plans. To the party leadership, stern action against dissent within the party was necessary because indiscipline had destroyed both the last Labour Government and the previous Conservative Administration. But critics, not only from the party left, believed that a totally compliant party would be incapable of emitting warning signals should things go wrong, and that that situation could be as dangerous to the government as excessive dissent.

Party divisions and groups

With the new 1997 parliament in its infancy and with the Blair Government enjoying a massive majority, it was difficult to predict precisely what the internal battle lines would be or how vigorous existing or any newly-formed groups would be. It was reasonable to suppose however that individuals and groups would take sides on five issues: (1) the relationship between the leader and the party; (2) the relationship between the party and civil society, including other parties like the Liberal Democrats; (3) the party's traditional core principles, in particular how far the party should move away from equality and redistribution; (4) Europe, especially the single currency; and (5) the actions and policies of the Blair Government. Early indications were that, whilst new Labour MPs saw themselves as slightly more right-wing than Old Labour, and were slightly more right-wing on privatisation, taxation, and inflation, they were slightly more in favour of Britain's membership of the EU and more egalitarian on gender equality. In general, the differences in attitude between old and new Labour MPs were modest. As the party had moved centre-left, this tide

'had swept most Labour politicians in the same direction' (Norris, 1997, pp.529–30). No doubt, in a largely Blairite party with many new MPs grateful to the modernisers for their seats, divisions would take a little time to emerge. The Tribune Group, for example, had not reconstituted itself by the summer recess 1997 (Butler and Kavanagh, 1997, p. 207).

But some Old Labour and left-wing dissenting voices had already been heard by late 1997. A former Old Labour right-winger, Roy Hattersley, who generally supported the modernising project, defended the principles of egalitarianism, redistribution and higher state spending in the relief of poverty against Government ministers. From the left, Tony Benn criticised the Government's close relationships with the Liberal Democrats whilst Ken Livingstone attacked the introduction of tuition fees at universities and the raising of interest rates. He also called for the reform of corporate taxation to favour long-term investment and for reductions in excessive defence spending. Livingstone's defeat of a chief Blair aide, the Minister without Portfolio, Peter Mandelson, for a place in the constituency section of the NEC in September 1997 was widely seen as a blow on behalf of Old Labour against New Labour and a warning to the modernising leadership. The first serious parliamentary revolt against the Labour Government came in December 1997 when 61 Labour backbenchers abstained or voted against the cuts in single-parent benefits.

Both Benn and Livingstone are members of the far-left *Campaign Group,* which numbers about 30 MPs, and has strenuously, albeit ineffectively, opposed the rightward drift of the party, including the organisational changes which have concentrated power in the leadership and reduced the role of the unions. A more mainstream-left group is *New Left in New Labour,* an informal grouping of supporters of Robin Cook and John Prescott which from the mid-1990s met fortnightly in the House of Commons. It also argued for the retention of greater union influence in key party institutions against the sweeping proposals of the leadership in the document *Party into Power.* A traditional group which remains active in the party is the *Fabian Society* (1884), one of Labour's founding groups, which has a local as well as parliamentary membership and whose main function is to float ideas through the publication of pamphlets and through providing a forum for discussion. A Fabian pamphlet in summer 1997 called for the ending of trade union affiliation fees from which the party derives large financial support. It was a leading advocate of modernisation, including abolishing the trade union block vote and replacing clause 4 with a new clause simply stating the party's aims and objects as a social democratic party. Finally, the *Tribune Group* is a former leading 'soft left' faction which takes its name from the weekly newspaper, *Tribune,* which it still publishes and which dates back to 1937. Its editor Mark Seddon has expressed concern that New Labour's developing relations with the Liberal Democrats would alienate trade unions and democratic socialists and that traditional concerns for redistribution of wealth, fairness and the relief of poverty were disappearing from the party.

The two most influential 'think-tanks' on New Labour are the *Institute for Public Policy Research* (1988) and *Demos* (1993). The IPPR is a left-of-centre unit, whose initial goal was to challenge Thatcherite free market ideas. It was subsequently influential on Labour's Commission on Social Justice, for which it served as the secretariat. Demos was launched by Martin Jacques, the former editor of *Marxism Today;* its director Geoff Mulgan has links with New Labour and is credited with importing the idea of communitarianism into Britain.

Organisation

In *formal* terms, by its original constitution (1918) the distribution of power within the Labour Party reflected its origins in a mass movement, with the party outside Westminster accorded a significant role in key party institutions such as conference and the National Executive Committee (NEC). However, the most radical reform ever of party structure was carried out by the 1997 party conference based on the modernising document *Party into Power* (Figure 7.2). Whilst Conference remained officially 'the supreme policy-making body', the key institutions in reality are now the new Joint Policy Committee (JPC), chaired by the Prime Minister and composed of equal numbers from an expanded NEC and Government. The JPC directs an expanded National Policy Forum which consists of representatives from all sections of the party and reviews all party policy on a two-year rolling pro-

gramme. Conference retains final say on what is and what is not adopted as party policy but loses its former powers to initiate debate over a wide range of policy. The New Labour leadership hopes the new system will avoid the divisions between government and party which proved so damaging to the previous Labour Government. Supporters of the change argue that the new system will produce more effective policy-making because it gives the leader and ministers such a prominent role and is also democratic because it gives all sections of the party a continuous say in policy making. But critics argue that the changes are simply aimed at transferring powers from Conference and the NEC to the party leadership. Overall, they maintain that the changes are intended to stifle debate. In early 1998, the leadership responded to criticisms of over-centralisation by announcing its intention to broaden grass-roots par-

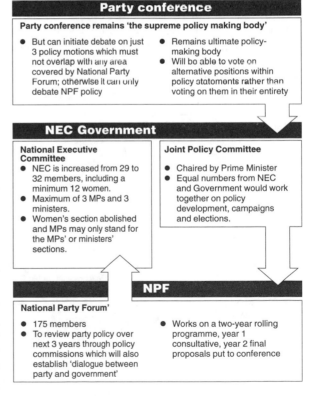

Chain of command

Party conference

Party conference remains 'the supreme policy making body'

- But can initiate debate on just 3 policy motions which must not overlap with any area covered by National Party Forum; otherwise it can only debate NPF policy

- Remains ultimate policy-making body
- Will be able to vote on alternative positions within policy statements rather than voting on them in their entirety

NEC Government

National Executive Committee
- NEC is increased from 29 to 32 members, including a minimum 12 women.
- Maximum of 3 MPs and 3 ministers.
- Women's section abolished and MPs may only stand for the MPs' or ministers' sections.

Joint Policy Committee
- Chaired by Prime Minister
- Equal numbers from NEC and Government would work together on policy development, campaigns and elections.

NPF

National Party Forum'
- 175 members
- To review party policy over next 3 years through policy commissions which will also establish 'dialogue between party and government'

- Works on a two-year rolling programme, year 1 consultative, year 2 final proposals put to conference

Source: The Guardian, 30 September 1997.

Figure 7.2 Labour Party structure after the 1997 reforms

ticipation by establishing 45 policy forums at which ordinary party members would be invited to express their views on all aspects of policy.

The election of the Labour leader

Labour's leader is elected by an *electoral college*, a system which dates from 1981. For twelve years the system of weighting allocated a greater role to the trade unions (40 per cent) than to the PLP (30 per cent), and the Constituency Labour Parties (CLPs) (30 per cent) but from 1993 the share of the trade unions was reduced and that of the other two components slightly raised so that unions, PLP and CLPs now each possess a one-third share. Voting is open, not secret, and since 1988 MEPs have been able to vote in the parliamentary section. In order to stand for the leadership in Labour's electoral college, candidates need the support of 12.5 per cent of PLP but a challenge to an incumbent since 1988 has required 20 per cent support. Only political levy-paying Labour supporters may vote in the trade union section. MPs, MEPs and ordinary members vote by postal ballot; trade unions are not required to use postal ballots but may do so if they wish. Voting is by one member one vote (OMOV) in each section and a preferential voting system is employed (AV) with party members voting 1 for first choice, 2 for second choice and 3 for third choice. Candidates are allocated their proportional share of the vote in each section and these shares are then added together to provide a winner. If an overall majority is not achieved by one candidate on the first count, the third-placed candidate is eliminated and the second choices of voters who had put that candidate first are redistributed among the other two candidates to produce a winner. This system was last used in 1994, when after the sudden death of John Smith, Tony Blair defeated John Prescott and Margaret Beckett for the leadership (Table 7.7).

Annual Conference

According to the Constitution of 1918, Conference is the ruling body of the party but, although this formally remains the position, its *de facto* role was much reduced by the changes introduced in 1997 (see above). It still decides the policies which compose the party programme but its role both in initiating debate and deciding final policy has been severely scaled down. In practice, the influence of Conference on Labour policy in government was normally considerably less than its formal powers

---

Table 7.7 Labour leadership elections, 1983–94

	PLP section (30%) (%)	Constituency section (30%) (%)	Trade union section (40%) (%)	Total (%)
1983				
Neil Kinnock	14.8	27.5	29.0	71.3
Roy Hattersley	7.8	0.6	10.9	19.3
Eric Heffer	4.3	2.0	0.1	6.3
Peter Shore	3.1	0.0	0.1	3.1
1988				
Neil Kinnock	24.8	24.3	39.7	88.6
Tony Benn	5.2	5.9	0.3	11.4
1992				
John Smith	23.2	29.3	38.5	91.0
Bryan Gould	6.8	0.7	1.5	9.0
1994				
Tony Blair	60.5	58.2	52.3	57
John Prescott	19.6	24.4	28.4	24.1
Margaret Beckett	19.9	17.4	19.3	18.9

might lead one to believe. Policies agreed at Conference were regularly ignored or toned down by the parliamentary leaders when drawing up the manifesto or, even if they did appear in the manifesto, jettisoned by a Labour Government. Traditionally, the alliance between the PLP leaders and the union 'bosses' ran the party and gave it stability. The period between 1968 and 1979, when the unions resisted the party leadership over industrial relations reform and incomes policy, was a relatively unusual break with this pattern. However, although not the ultimate arbiter of party policy, Conference was the major forum of grass-roots opinion, shaping and constraining the initiatives of the leadership, and it is this potential power which the leadership hopes and critics fear has been lost by the 1997 changes.

Despite recent changes, the trade unions remain influential if much less dominant at Conference. They now cast 50 per cent of the Conference vote (reduced from 90 per cent by a rule change beginning in 1991) and, in 1993, accepted a further reform of the block vote system. From 1994, the votes of affiliated unions were no longer cast as a block but divided up among the members of union delegations. CLPs cast the remaining 50 per cent of Conference votes. From 1997, the union influence on the composition of the NEC (32) was also reduced: previously, in addition to electing twelve members to its trade union section, they had – through their domination of Conference – a major role in the election of five women's representatives and the party treasurer, who are elected by the conference as a whole. But the unions now simply elect 12 members of the 32-strong NEC. In addition, in 1997 the role of the CLPs was also reduced: formerly, they were able to vote directly for MPs in the constituency section but now MPs may no longer stand in this section, and the CLPs' direct influence over the parliamentary party through this route has been lost. Rather, the leader and the PLP now have greater direct influence on the NEC through their ability to choose three ministers and three MPs respectively. The leader and deputy-leader are ex-officio members and the party secretary is also secretary of the NEC.

Previously, according to the constitution, any proposal receiving a two-thirds majority at conference went into the party programme. Of course, the programme was not the manifesto, which was the joint responsibility of NEC and Cabinet or, when in opposition, of the NEC and Parliamentary Committee of the PLP. In practice, whether in government or opposition, the leader always played a decisive role in drawing up the manifesto and because of this was often subject to charges of betrayal from left-wing trade unionists and party activists at conference. However, in 1996, having gained NEC approval for the draft manifesto, Tony Blair took the unprecedented step of putting the manifesto to a vote of party members after the 1996 conference, despite protests that this devalued the role of Conference. Blair wanted to bind the members to the manifesto in a way that would enable him to refute any subsequent allegations of betrayal.

Constituency Labour parties (CLPs)

Selection of parliamentary candidates

Selection of Labour parliamentary candidates is done by the constituency parties (CLPs). CLPs consist of delegates from a wide variety of labour organisations and societies and are run by General Management Committees (GMCs). Selection of parliamentary candidates cannot begin without permission from the NEC which automatically forwards its Approved List of candidates (the former A, B, C and W Lists covering trade-union-sponsored and CLP, affiliated society and Women's Section recommended candidates respectively) to the constituency party concerned. Nominations are made and usually include many names not on the Approved List. Next, CLP General Committees shortlist candidates. Shortlists must include: the sitting Labour MP (if the constituency has one); any candidate receiving 25 per cent of the nominations or any candidate with 50 per cent of the nominations from affiliated organisations; at least four candidates where no Labour MP is in contention; and at least one woman. If the sitting MP is nominated by two-thirds of nominating bodies, he or she is automatically reselected; and if he or she has at least one nomination the CLP may vote for automatic reselection anyway. Since 1993, the final selection of Labour parliamentary candidates has been in a full meeting of the CLP by one member one vote (OMOV). Entitled to vote are full members of twelve months' standing together with members of affiliated trade unions who agree to pay an additional levy of £3 on top of the political levy (the Levy Plus scheme). Voting is by the alternative vote. Successful candidates must then seek endorsement by the NEC.

CLPs have been subject to considerable NEC intervention in their selection processes in recent years. The main example of this centralisation was the imposition of all-women shortlists in half of 'winnable' seats between 1993 and 1996. But there have been many instances of tough action by the NEC where it has found local party choices or processes unacceptable: for example, Denis McShane was imposed on the local party in Rotherham (1994), Phil Woolas on the new Oldham and Saddleworth CLP (1995) and, most controversially, the candidature of Liz Davies, the choice of the Leeds NE CLP, was overruled (1995) on the grounds of her political 'disloyalty'. The NEC has also suspended CLPs it suspects of dubious practices, as for example when four Birmingham CLPs were suspended pending investigation of allegations of mass recruitment of Asian members, and there were other race-tinged selection disputes involving NEC intervention in Bradford West, Bethnal Green and Bow and Glasgow Govan. The NEC also imposed its will on the selection process at Exeter and Swindon North as well as ensuring the shortlisting of the Conservative defector, Alan Howarth, at Newport East. Labour's Consolidated Rule Book (1995) gives the NEC the power 'to take whatever action is necessary' to ensure a suitable candidate is selected in by-elections,a power that began in 1989.

The trade unions sponsored 53 per cent of Labour MPs in the 1992–7 parliament, but trade union sponsorship of Labour MPs was discontinued in 1995 and this move further undermined local CLP independence as well as trade union influence. Direct union sponsorship was replaced by 'Constituency plan agreements' between trade unions and selected CLPs by which, in return for paying money into a central pool to support the activities of constituency parties, unions received representation on the CLP general committees. One hundred such agreements had been made by summer 1997, largely with CLPs in key marginals, with the aim of building up Labour strength in such vital areas. Twenty-six 'Labour and Cooperative'

MPs were elected in May 1997 but, as with the trade unions, Cooperative Party sponsorship has ceased and it is now a 'sister' party rather than a sponsoring organisation (Butler and Kavanagh, 1997, p. 206).

Party central headquarters

The leading official of the Party (General Secretary), a moderniser with a trade union background, Tom Sawyer, works from Walworth Road, the Labour Party headquarters. Following the 1992 general election, sweeping changes shifted major responsibility for policy-making away from the NEC and the Walworth Road professionals to front-bench spokesmen, the leader's office, and a new joint policy commission agreed at the 1992 Conference. From 1995, key staff moved to the party's new campaign and media centre at Millbank Tower, marginalising Walworth Road. The Millbank Tower operation was directed by the Shadow Minister for Election Planning, Peter Mandelson, who was directly responsible to Tony Blair. A key position is that of National Agent but the party normally has fewer agents than the Conservatives and had 60 in 1997 compared with 287. However, in 1997 this disadvantage was more than offset by a larger campaigning membership and by effective 'spin-doctoring' from Millbank Tower i.e. persuading the media to carry a favourable interpretation of the party 'message'.

Finance and membership

During most of the period since 1945, the trade unions contributed over three-quarters of both Labour's central income and its General Election funds but this source of the party's income declined sharply after 1986 to half of party funds in 1996. Income from rising membership (420,000 in 1997), from the Thousand Club which raised money through dinners for wealthy members and from the vigorously sought donations from leading businessmen offset the smaller union contribution. A more buoyant income enabled the party to spend over £13 million from central party funds in the year before the 1997 general election.

The Conservative Party

The Conservative Party is the most successful modern party. Since the Third Reform Act (1884), it has dominated its rivals, being in power, either singly, in coalition or in some looser form of alliance, for just over two-thirds of the time. On the face of it, this fact requires some explanation. How has a party drawn predominantly from the upper and upper middle classes and whose political reason for existence is the defence of property and the Constitution consistently gained the support of one-third of the working class? The answer lies in a combination of its own merits, political circumstances and the misfortunes of its rivals.

Conservative strengths

- *Cohesiveness*: The party puts a high premium on party loyalty and overall has been less subject to damaging faction fights than its rivals, or to splits, although it did split over the Corn Laws in 1846 and over Tariff Reform in the first quarter of the twentieth century, and some commentators have suggested it may split over Europe in the next decade.
- *Adaptability*: Traditionally, Conservatives have valued pragmatism, a non-doctrinaire approach to politics combined with an ability to adapt to changing circumstances, and this quality served the party well in helping it adjust to the post-1945 transition to a 'managed economy' and 'Welfare State', the loss of empire and British entry into Europe.
- *Ethos*: The party's ethos blends nationalism ('Putting Britain first'), individualism ('making the best of your talents and circumstances') and the claim to good government (the country's 'natural' and most competent rulers) and consistently translates these elements into policies which sound like common sense in a political culture in which symbols and values of nation, individual striving and leadership retain a firm hold.
- *Leadership*: Conservatives have continually produced leaders able to dominate their political generations, in part by coining, or latching on to, phrases expressive of the popular mood – for example, Macmillan ('You've never had it so good') in an age of dawning affluence (the 1950s); and Mrs Thatcher ('Roll back the Frontiers of the State') at a time of growing public anxiety about high levels of government spending and taxation (the 1970s and 1980s).

Favouring political circumstances

Also, the party has benefited from political circumstances which favoured its appeal to nationalism. These have occurred quite frequently and include threats to the integrity of the British state from within (Home Rule in the late nineteenth and early twentieth centuries) or from outside (the Kaiser's Germany in 1914–18, Hitler's Germany, 1939–45) or to its economy (the World Economic Depression of the 1930s).

Rivals' misfortunes

The Conservatives have derived indirect assistance from the misfortunes of their main rivals and from a divided opposition. Both in the 1920s and 1930s and again between the 1970s and the early 1990s the Conservatives profited from the drawn-out struggle between Labour and the Liberals to be the major force on the political left whilst in the 1980s they gained from the turmoil in the Labour Party which produced the secession of the SDP.

However, this combination of favourable factors ceased to operate after 1992 for a number of reasons and Conservative fortunes collapsed into the kind of severe decline which has afflicted the party periodically throughout its history. The reverse the Conservatives suffered in the 1997 general election necessitated radical reform of all sections of the party. In considering party organisation, this section examines the background to the 1997 electoral disaster and the programme of far-reaching reform immediately launched by the new leader, William Hague.

> **Party faction**: a group within a group often within a political party. Factions are normally fairly enduring and possess a degree of organisation; they are formed to press for a particular policy or ideology to persist or prevail. Broader strands of opinion – normally without formal organisation – are termed tendencies.

BOX 7.5
Conservative Party: the main internal groups

	Progressive	Neo-Liberal	Nationalist
Groups	One Nation group	Selsdon Group	Monday Club
	Tory Reform Group	No Turning Back group	Salisbury Group
	Macleod Group	Conservative Way Forward	Fresh Start group
	Conservative Group for Europe	Conservative 2000 Foundation	Freedom Association
	Positive European Group	Bruges Group	Tory Action
	Action Centre for Europe	Conservatives Against Federal	European Foundation
	Conservative Mainstream	Europe (CAFE)	
	The Lollards	Bow Group	
	Charter Movement	92 Group	
	Social Market Foundation	Institute for Economic Affairs	
		Adam Smith Institute	
		Centre for Policy Studies	
		Social Affairs Unit	
		European Research Group	
Causes	Moderate social reform; British membership of European Union; European integration; Christian Democracy	Free market economics; privatisation, deregulation and popular capitalism; Euroscepticism; defence of British sovereignty in Europe	Anti-immigration; Anti-European integration; Pro-integrity of UK; Free market economics; Sceptical about international institutions
Leading figures	Kenneth Clarke	John Redwood	
	Michael Heseltine	Peter Lilley	Teddy Taylor
	Edward Heath	Norman Lamont	Nicholas Budgen
	Ian Gilmour	Margaret Thatcher	Michael Spicer
		William Hague	Roger Scruton

Sources: Adapted from McKee (1996) p. 32.

The Conservative Party to date (1997) has consisted of three main elements – the parliamentary party; the National Union together with the Constituency Associations (the members, the 'party in the country'); and Central Office (the professional side, the party bureaucracy). Of these, the parliamentary party is pre-eminent with the other two parts of the party having come into existence historically as its 'servants'. Traditionally seen, pre-Thatcher, as a party of 'tendencies' rather than factions, the Conservatives became increasingly ideological under Thatcher and during the 1990s this factional struggle between the right and left in parliament intensified. There were two main trends. First, one of the main issues dividing the party in the late 1980s and early 1990s – preservation or movement away from the neo-liberal Thatcherite

social and economic legacy – ended effectively in victory for the neo-liberal right. The main reason for this was that the Major Government pursued fundamentally Thatcherite neo-liberal policies, carrying out the more difficult privatisations and continuing the marketisation of the public sector. However, faction-fighting intensified over the other main source of internal division, with pro-Europeans supporting Britain's growing integration within the EC and Euro-sceptics bitterly opposed to it. Euroscepticism drew upon both the economic libertarian and the nationalist strands within Conservatism. The factional groupings which provided focal points for the the ideological struggle within the party are detailed in Box 7.5. Some are fundamentally research groups; some promote a particular strand of thought; some are formally independent 'think-tanks' sympathetic to the party; some – but not many – are exclusively parliamentary; some have lengthy existences; some are more recent formations. From time to time, older groups are re-launched e.g. the One Nation group in 1992. There is considerable overlapping of memberships.

Conservative organisation

The Conservative Party is an autocracy tempered by consent. Thus, authority is concentrated in the leader who appoints the Party Chairman, the party's Shadow Cabinet when it is in opposition, and, after consultation only with the close colleagues, decides party policy. Between 1965 and 1997, the leader was elected by a relatively restricted constituency: Conservative MPs. However, a change in the method of electing the leader seemed likely to form one of the many organisational changes launched after the 1997 general election defeat, and hence the system described in Box 7.6 may not last much longer. Firm leadership is expected by the party and this involves establishing definite priorities of policy and strategy and communicating them clearly downwards through the party organisation. Leaders need to deliver political success. Electoral defeat or even the threat of it places the position of the leader in immediate jeopardy. Defeat in October 1974 – his third in four elections – led to the swift deposition of Edward Heath. In 1990, in unprecedented fashion, the party ousted its leader, Margaret Thatcher, when Prime Minister; even though Mrs Thatcher had won three consecutive general elections, this was insufficient to offset her unwillingness to reverse the policies, especially on the poll tax and the economy, which had brought about the Government's unpopularity and the threat of defeat in the next General Election. Defeat in the 1997 general election was followed by the immediate resignation of John Major.

A third ballot has been necessary only once in the six contests held under the system which began in 1965 – in the fiercely contested 1997 election to decide John Major's successor. In 1965, when Edward Heath gained an overall majority but only a 5.7 per cent lead over his nearest rival, his opponents withdrew and no new candidates were forthcoming. In 1975, Mrs Thatcher – who, on the first ballot, lacked both an overall majority and a sufficient lead

---

BOX 7.6
How the Conservative Party elected its leader, 1965–98

Unless the Party leadership was already vacant, an election could be launched by 10 per cent of Conservative MPs who notified the Chairman of the 1922 Committee that they considered a contest is desirable. If there was a vacancy, a contestant required the backing of only two MPs. The notification had to be made within three months of the opening of a new parliament or fourteen days of the start of a new session. Names of the 10 per cent of MPs backing a challenger were kept secret. Before the first ballot, constituency associations informed MPs of their views and the opinions of Conservative peers were also canvassed by the Conservative leader and Chief Whip in the Lords.

First ballot	Winner needed an overall majority of those eligible to vote (i.e. all Conservative MPs) plus a 15 per cent lead over nearest rival. If not achieved by any candidate, contest went to a second ballot.
Second ballot	New candidates could now stand. Original candidates could continue or withdraw. Winner needed overall majority; if not achieved, candidates were allowed 24 hours to withdraw, and if a third ballot was required only the top two candidates went forward.
Third ballot	In the event of a tie, a fourth ballot was held unless candidates could 'resolve the matter between themselves'.

The winner (after whichever ballot) was confirmed at a party meeting attended by MPs, MEPs, Peers, parliamentary candidates and members of the National Union executive.

---

over her nearest rival – decisively defeated her opponents in the second ballot. In 1989, she easily beat off the challenge from a 'stalking-horse' candidate, although a surprisingly large number of her parliamentary party (60) opposed her. Finally, in 1990, although Mrs. Thatcher obtained an overall majority on the first ballot, she was four votes short of gaining the required 15 per cent lead and, with her authority already damaged and her support reportedly ebbing, was persuaded to stand down by the Cabinet (whose members she consulted individually). In the second ballot, John Major lacked an overall majority but a third ballot was declared to be

BOX 7.7
Conservative leadership elections, 1965–97

1965	Sir Alec Douglas-Home resigned and the leadership became vacant			
	First ballot	Edward Heath	150	(49.3%)
		Reginald Maudling	133	(43.8%)
		Enoch Powell	15	(4.9%)
		Abstentions/spoiled papers	6	(2%)
1975	Heath's leadership was challenged			
	First ballot	Margaret Thatcher	130	(47.1%)
		Edward Heath	119	(43.6%)
		Hugh Fraser	16	(5.8%)
		Abstentions	11	(4%)
	Fraser withdrew; Whitelaw, Prior, Howe and Peyton came forward			
	Second ballot	Margaret Thatcher	146	(52.9%)
		William Whitelaw	76	(28.6%)
		Geoffrey Howe	19	(6.9%)
		James Prior	19	(6.9%)
		John Peyton	11	(4%)
		Abstentions/spoiled papers	2	(0.7%)
1989	Sir Anthony Meyer challenged for the leadership			
	First ballot	Margaret Thatcher	314	(84%)
		Sir Anthony Meyer	33	(8.8%)
		Spoilt ballots	24	(6%)
		Absent	3	(1%)
1990	Michael Heseltine challenged for the leadership			
	First ballot	Margaret Thatcher	204	(54.8%)
		Michael Heseltine	152	(40.9%)
		Spoilt ballots	16	(4.3%)
	Thatcher withdrew; Major and Hurd entered the contest			
	Second ballot	John Major	185	(49.7%)
		Michael Heseltine	131	(35.2%)
		Douglas Hurd	56	(15.1%)
1995	John Major resigned the leadership and was challenged by John Redwood			
	First ballot	John Major	218	(66.3%)
		John Redwood	89	(27.1%)
		Abstentions	8	(2.4%)
		Spoilt papers	12	(3.7%)
		Absent	2	(0.6%)
	Major re-elected.			
1997	John Major resigned and the leadership became vacant			
	First ballot	Kenneth Clarke	49	(29.9%)
		William Hague	41	(25%)
		John Redwood	27	(16.5%)
		Peter Lilley	24	(14.6%)
		Michael Howard	23	(14.0%)
	Howard and Lilley withdrew			
	Second ballot	Kenneth Clarke	64	(39.0%)
		William Hague	62	(37.8%)
		John Redwood	38	(23.2%)
	Redwood withdrew			
	Third ballot	William Hague	92	(56.1%)
		Kenneth Clarke	70	(42.7%)
		Abstentions	2	(1.2%)
	Hague had overall majority and became leader.			

unnecessary as his two rivals conceded defeat. In 1995, Major resigned the leadership, calling upon his critics to 'put up or shut up', and John Redwood resigned from the Cabinet to fight on a platform of outright opposition to the single currency and Major's opt-out strategy. Major won a first-round victory but Redwood's supporters claimed that, setting on one side the Major 'payroll' vote of members of the government, nearly half the parliamentary party had voted against Major (Ludlam and Smith, 1996, p. 120). In 1997, the leadership contest was fought out between the pro-European centre-left Kenneth Clarke, the centre-right William Hague and three right-wing Eurosceptics, John Redwood, Peter Lilley and Michael Howard. With the last-named three eliminated over the first two rounds, round three was contested between Clarke, who had overwhelming grass-roots support amongst the constituency chairmen, MEPs, peers and top-level party volunteer workers, and Hague, who, however, won by taking most of the votes of Redwood's supporters in round two. This occurred despite an unusual and surprising pact between the arch-European Clarke and the Eurosceptic Redwood after round two, made possible on the basis of an agreement to differ and the promise of a free vote on Europe (Box 7.7).

The National Union

The National Union of Conservative Associations (1867) is the second (voluntary) side of the Conservative Party's three main components, representing and supervising the party membership. The aims of the party leadership which established it were to create a nationwide Conservative organisation which would coordinate the work of existing Associations, encourage the formation of new ones and disseminate Conservative publicity to the new working-class electors.

Established in order to assist but definitely not to control the party leaders, in formal terms the National Union exercises a purely 'advisory' role (Maxwell-Fyfe Report, 1949). Its main task is to convene an annual conference, whose proceedings are often dismissed as bland, uncritical affairs where votes are rarely taken and which are carefully stage-managed to avoid any appearance of disunity. However, this negative view undoubtedly underes-

timates the role of the National Union and its annual conference as *a two-way channel of communication* between party members and the leadership. Although provision for intra-party democracy is conspicuously absent from its formal arrangements, the actual practice of the party is more complex. The influence of the 'feedback' from party members upon the leadership is hard to measure because conference is always more a matter of 'mood' than specific resolutions, but, historically, conference debates have played an important part in preparing the way in the 1880s and 1890s for the party's later adoption of protectionism, in bringing about the downfall of the Coalition Government (and of Austen Chamberlain) in 1922 and in the passing of the Trades Disputes Act in 1927.

The increase in the importance of Conference in the 1980s and 1990s, which was the result first of a populist then of a less decisive style of leadership, social levelling between the platform and the conference hall, and the decline of 'deference', may constitute a permanent trend. Recent research suggests that far from being a 'one-off' event, the annual conference is more appropriately depicted as the culmination of a series of less publicised area and sectional conferences at which senior party figures invite and receive frank and critical advice from representative 'experts' in, for example, regional Conservatism or trade unionism. According to this thesis, applause at annual conference, rather than registering unthinking loyalty, records grass-roots Conservatives' perceptions that ministers have listened to the advice offered at these earlier meetings; expressions of dissent occur when a minister has failed to make concessions on a matter of importance. Since 1983, the influence of this largely hidden 'system' of grass-roots representation may be discerned in government policies on trade union reform, married women's taxation, disability pensions and the revival of interest in rates reform (Kelly, 1989, 1992).

To summarise: Conservative Party conferences have more than one 'face'. They are certainly exercises in public relations but this is only one aspect. They are demonstrations of enthusiasm and solidarity with the leadership, inspirers of the party 'activists' and occasions for their letting off steam on such matters as law and order and immigration, but also vehicles for the expression of serious dissent (e.g. in 1997 over the parliamentary party whose squabbling was considered to have undermined the party's general election chances) and occasionally for policy influence.

Constituency Associations

The major roles of Conservative constituency associations are threefold: campaigning for the party in local and national elections; fund-raising; and the selection of parliamentary candidates.

Local Conservative Associations possess considerable freedom from outside interference in choosing a parliamentary candidate. Candidates must either be on the party's approved list of candidates or, if not, gain acceptance by the party's Standing Advisory Committee on candidates. A Vice-Chairman at Central Office is in charge of the 800-strong candidates' list. As soon as they are on the list, candidates can apply for advertised vacancies. Applications are considered by a sub-committee of the local Association's Executive Council: it draws up a shortlist of about 20 candidates, whom it interviews and reduces to a final short-list of about three, who then go before a final selection meeting of the full Executive Council. The Council then must recommend at least two candidates for final choice by a special general meeting of the Association. Local associations have largely resisted Central Office pressure to select more working-class and women candidates: in 1997 the Conservatives fielded only 66 women candidates (10 per cent of all their candidates), less than half the number nominated by Labour (155: 24 per cent) and the Liberal Democrats (139: 21 per cent).

Re-adoption struggles have been relatively rare. In 1997, however, three Conservative MPs were deselected – David Ashby (Leicestershire North West), after press exposure of his private life, Sir Nicholas Scott (Kensington and Chelsea), after a series of incidents involving drink, and Sir George Gardiner (Reigate), following his support for Redwood's challenge to the leader in 1995. Two others – Robert Banks (Harrogate) and Roy Thomason (Bromsgrove) – retired rather than face reselection ballots. But the greatest controversy occurred over the re-adoption of Neil Hamilton, who was strongly linked to the sleaze issue, as parliamentary candidate for Tatton. His candidature together with the withdrawal of the official Labour and Liberal Democrat candidates in favour of an anti-corruption Independent candidate, Martin Bell, the BBC war correspondent, helped ensure that the sleaze issue remained alive throughout the campaign. This episode underlined in the starkest manner the autonomy of local Conservative Associations in the selection of candidates. The party leadership was deeply embarrassed by Hamilton but, despite bringing pressure on him, could not force his withdrawal. Rather it was dependent on his doing 'the decent thing' and withdrawing as did Tim Smith, the MP for Beaconsfield, who had also taken money from the lobbyist Ian Greer in support of Mahammed Al Fayed's bid to control Harrods (Butler and Kavanagh, 1997, pp. 95–7, 199). Nominally, the power to disaffiliate an obstructive local Association was streamlined in 1993 when it passed from the large and rather unwieldy National Union Executive Committee to the smaller and potentially more effective General Purposes Committee. But no action was taken to disaffiliate the nine Conservative MPs who lost the Conservative whip in 1994–5, all of whom had the strong backing of their local Associations.

Central Office

Conservative Central Office (CCO), founded in 1870, is the party's third main component: it constitutes the professional element, the party bureaucracy, and is staffed by officials many of whom make their work a full-time career. Its Chairman (normally a leading politician) is appointed by and responsible to the party leader, a fact which has led to the description of Central Office as 'the personal machine of the Leader'. Its main tasks are money-raising, the organisation of election campaigns, assistance with the selection of candidates, research and political education and, in carrying out these functions, it must liaise both with the parliamentary party and with the party outside Westminster. A particularly vital role performed by CCO is the training, certification and promotion of agents. Agents are the key professionals in politics and another aspect in which the Conservatives enjoy an advantage over their rivals; they employed 287 full-time agents in the 1997 general election compared with Labour's 60 and the Liberal Democrats' 30. Normally employed by the constituency associations, agents play an important part in liaising between the party's central headquarters and its regional, area and local bodies; in fund raising; and in election campaigns, especially in marginal seats.

Central Office was substantially restructured after 1987 and now consists of three Departments (Communications, Campaigning and Research), and a Board of Finance, whose Heads are responsible to the Party Chairman. After the 1992 general election, there were further changes with the appointment of a Director General and Finance Director and a new Board of Management, containing senior figures from the parliamentary party, the National Union and Central Office. However, Central Office 'did not work well for much of the 1990s' (Peele, 1997, p.107). The main relationship is between Central Office top staff and those of the Prime Minister at No.10, but this has not always been smooth. There was tension between the Party Chairman, Chris Patten, and key staff at No.10 during the 1992 general election campaign whilst the usefulness of the next Chairman, Sir Norman Fowler (1992–4), as a link between Central Office and No.10 and as a public defender of the government's policies was reduced by his unwillingness to serve in the Cabinet. His successor, Jeremy Hanley (1994–5) also proved unsuccessful as a communicator and he was soon replaced by Brian Mawhinney, but problems of effective communication and publicity persisted. This was another section of the party which seemed ripe for reform after 1997. Central Office also faced severe criticisms during the 1990s from the *Charter Movement*, which was set up in 1981 by activists in Kent to campaign for greater democracy and accountability within the party. The Movement, through its journal *Charter News*, regards Central Office 'waste, carelessness and profligacy' as largely to blame for the party's huge deficit, considers large donations from foreign backers 'a degredation' and calls for an elected Chairman.

Party finances

The Conservative Party is the wealthiest party, its money being provided by business, the constituency membership and gifts from individuals. Its formidable capacity to raise funds enables the party to outspend its opponents by significant amounts at general elections. At the 1997 general election, for

example, the party spent more (£20 million) than Labour (£13 million) and the Liberal Democrats (£0.7 million) combined.

However, huge increases in expenditure during the 1980s and early 1990s led to an accumulated deficit reportedly in the region of £19 million in 1993. But Lord Harris of Peckham proved an effective fundraiser and by May 1997 the revenue deficit had been transformed into a surplus of £2 million(Butler and Kavanagh, 1997, p. 26).

Nonetheless, problems remain. In recent years, contributions from the constituencies and from companies have both declined and private donations increased as a proportion of central party income. Local contributions have suffered because of the decline in membership and gifts from industry have declined partly because of the recession, partly because of the attraction of New Labour. There is political controversy both over business contributions (Table 7.8) and over the scale, secrecy and source of individual donations (usually concealed in the 'unspecified' category). Labour argues that the Conservatives are over-dependent on business, the Conservatives say Labour is 'in hock' to the unions. Labour maintains that company contributions to the Conservatives are not published and companies are not legally required to seek shareholders' approval of such gifts (as trade unions, since 1984, have been legally required to ballot members before making political donations). The Conservatives reply that companies may seek shareholders' authority for political gifts if they wish. Labour admits this but ripostes that very few do so: only the National Freight Corporation – out of 38 large companies making gifts to the Conservatives – gave its shareholders a vote on its political donation in 1991, and the result was an 87 per cent majority against such gifts. In late 1997 the Committee on Standards in Public Life required the Conservatives to disclose amounts received over the previous five years but did not require the party to reveal the identity of the donors.

Finally, large individual donations especially from foreign sources aroused intense political controversy in the 1990s especially after the Nolan Report (1995), which made such donations suspect (see below for further discussion). The Labour Government plans to introduce legislation banning overseas political donations and may also cap

Table 7.8 Top business donations to the Conservative Party, 1995–6

	£
Hanson	100,000
P&O	100,000
Chubb	75,000
Racal	75,000
Vodafone	75,000
Pearson	75,000
Hambros	56,000
Caledonia Inv	55,000
Vickers	55,000
GRE	50,000
Sun Alliance	50,000
Scottish and Newcastle	50,000

election expenditure. A recommendation from the Committee on Standards in Public Life on party funding was expected in summer 1998.

A party in decline

There was evidence of severe decline in the Conservative Party during 1997, consisting of the following factors:

- *electoral collapse*: from 336 MPs (1992) to 165 MPs (1997).
- *lack of parliamentary discipline*: public squabbles between MPs discredited the party and helped to bring about defeat in 1997.
- *falling and ageing membership*: party membership declined from 1.5 million(1979) to 750,000 in 1987 to 300,000 in 1997; average age of members is 62, and 84 per cent are over 45. The Young Conservatives are near extinction with under 3,000 members.The lack of a central register of membership was exposed in July 1997 when Neil Hamilton admitted he was not even a member of the Conservative party.
- *too few campaigners*: 50,000 compared with Labour's 200,000 in the 1997 general election (P. Seyd, quoted in the *Guardian*, 8 October 1997).
- *too few councillors*: the party collapsed in local

elections, with its number of councillors falling from 12,100 in 1979 to 4,400 in 1997.
- *standards of conduct*: discredited 'cash for questions' MPs Graham Riddick and David Tredinnick and disgraced MPs Neil Hamilton, Tim Smith and Jonathan Aitken helped bring the party into disrepute.
- *method of leadership election*: seen by many as too élitist with widespread grass-roots discontent about lack of formal involvement in 1997.
- *declining constituency income*: as a proportion of party income, constituency income declined from 13.8 per cent of party income in 1988–9 to 5.7 per cent in 1994–5, whilst company and individual donations rose from 77.7 per cent to 83.2 per cent over the same period.

William Hague's proposals for party reform

Following his election as leader in June 1997, William Hague immediately set out to build a unified national party ending the divisions between the parliamentary party, central office and the National Union, which would be wound up. The main proposals, which largely appeared in *Blueprint for Change* published during the 1997 party conference, were:

- streamlined management at all levels of the party organisation with a single governing body ('the Board'), headed by the party chairman and including 12 other members, six of whom would be elected by the membership;
- a mass membership party with a central data base of all members: aim to double the membership in two years and become 'the most effective volunteer movement in Western Europe';
- a new democratic system for the election of the party leader in which MPs choose the candidates in a Westminster primary and then the leader is chosen by the party membership by a simple majority on a one member/one vote principle;
- constituency chairman to be elected by one member one vote;
- parliamentary candidates: constituency parties to retain the right to select candidates but in by-elections they will be given a list to choose from;
- women MPs: aim to get more women MPs: 25

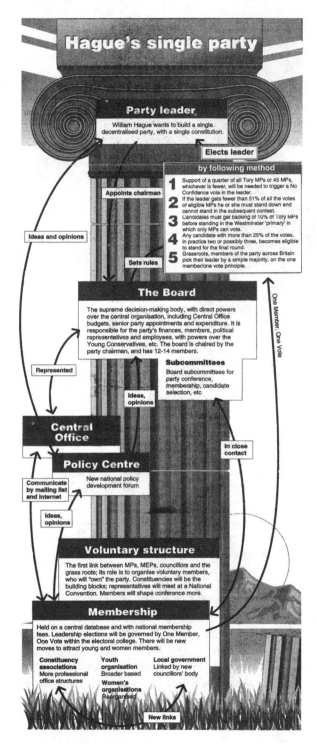

Hague's single party

Party leader

William Hague wants to build a single decentralised party, with a single constitution.

Elects leader

by following method

1 Support of a quarter of all Tory MPs or 45 MPs, whichever is fewer, will be needed to trigger a No Confidence vote in the leader.

2 If the leader gets fewer than 51% of all the votes of eligible MPs he or she must stand down and cannot stand in the subsequent contest.

3 Candidates must get backing of 10% of Tory MPs before standing in the Westminster 'primary' in which only MPs can vote.

4 Any candidate with more than 25% of the votes, in practice two or possibly three, becomes eligible to stand for the final round.

5 Grassroots, members of the party across Britain pick their leader by a simple majority, on the one member/one vote principle.

Appoints chairman

Ideas and opinions

Sets rules

One Member, One Vote

The Board

The supreme decision-making body, with direct powers over the central organisation, including Central Office budgets, senior party appointments and expenditure. It is responsible for the party's finances, members, political representatives and employees, with powers over the Young Conservatives, etc. The Board is chaired by the party chairman, and has 12-14 members.

Subcommittees

Board subcommittees for party conference, membership, candidate selection, etc

Represented

Ideas, opinions

Central Office

In close contact

Policy Centre

New national policy development forum

Communicate by mailing list and Internet

Ideas, opinions

Voluntary structure

The first link between MPs, MEPs, councillors and the grass roots; its role is to organise voluntary members, who will "own" the party. Constituencies will be the building blocks; representatives will meet at a National Convention. Members will shape conference more.

Membership

Held on a central database and with national membership fees. Leadership elections will be governed by One Member, One Vote within the electoral college. There will be new moves to attract young and women members.

Constituency associations
More professional office structures

Youth organisation
Broader based
Women's organisations
Reorganised

Local government
Linked by new councillors' body

New links

Source: The Guardian, 8 October 1997; 8 and 15 January 1998.

Figure 7.3 Conservative Party organisation: the 1997 proposals

per cent of candidates interviewed should be women out of a minimum of eight candidates interviewed;

- standards of conduct: new ethics and integrity committee to stiffen party discipline. The committee will include the chairmen of the national convention and the 1922 committee with an independent chairman and will be expected to take 'swift, effective and fair action' where the reputation of the party may be threatened. It will have the power to suspend or expel party members;
- more open party funding with names of major donors published and foreign gifts banned.

Under William Hague, the Thatcherite grip on the party tightened. In Hague's first shadow cabinet, neo-liberal Eurosceptic right-wingers got the key posts, with Peter Lilley as shadow chancellor, Michael Howard as shadow foreign secretary and John Redwood as shadow trade and industry secretary. Moderate Tory Reform Group Conservatives were relegated to minor shadow cabinet roles. Conservative divisions on Europe reopened in late autumn 1997. First, William Hague imposed a new harder line on the single currency on the shadow cabinet of 'not for the next ten years' in place of the earlier 'not for the forseeable future'. Then, following a statement by the Labour Chancellor that the Government backed the single currency in principle but Britain would not join in the first wave in 1999, a lower-ranking pro-European shadow minister, Ian Taylor, resigned, whilst from the Conservative backbenches Kenneth Clarke expressed the opinion that if the Labour Cabinet campaigned hard on a cross-party basis with the support of the CBI, the TUC and the City, it could win a referendum on the single currency.

The Liberal Democrats

The Liberal Democrats emerged in 1988, the product of a merger between the Liberal Party and its former partner in the Alliance, the Social Democratic Party (SDP). The merger imposed severe strains on both former parties: although 88 per cent of Liberals and 65 per cent of SDP members who voted supported it, nearly half of each party did not vote. Disgruntled minorities refused

Figure 7.4 The Liberal Democrat leader, Paddy Ashdown, with his colleagues at the first meeting of a joint Labour-Lib Dem cabinet committee in September 1997.

to accept the new party, Michael Meadowcroft leading a small group of 'old Liberals' and David Owen the 'continuing SDP'. However, neither grouping proved to be viable. The 'old Liberals' performed very badly in the 1992 general election, with only Meadowcroft of its 73 candidates saving his deposit, whilst the Owenite SDP decided to disband in 1990, Owen himself shortly afterwards announcing his retirement from politics and the two remaining SDP MPs being defeated in 1992.

Meanwhile, the new merged party, which began with 19 MPs (17 of them former Liberals) and a claimed 3,500 councillors and 100,000 members, moved quickly to appoint a new leader to replace the interim joint leadership of David Steel and Robert Maclennan. In a ballot of the whole membership in July 1988, Paddy Ashdown was elected leader, gaining 71.9 per cent of the vote to Alan Beith's 28.1 per cent. By November 1990, the Liberal Democrats had recovered from their inauspicious start: good local election results in May had been followed in November with a classic by-election victory at Eastbourne. Yet another phase was under way in the turbulent twentieth-century history of the Liberal Party which saw the party a major governing party until 1922, and subsequently relegated to the third-party status that has persisted down to the present day. The Liberals faced near-extinction in the immediate post-1945 period, but then revived in the

1960s and 1970s before forging an Alliance with the Social Democratic Party, formed in 1981 largely of former Labour right-wingers, in an attempt to 'break the mould' of two-party British politics by creating a viable third force in the political centre. The attempt was seen to have broken down in 1987 in large part because the working of the first past the post electoral system favoured the major parties with their regionally concentrated support and disadvantaged the Alliance whose vote was evenly spread (Table 7.9).

The Liberal Democrats are a non-socialist reforming party of the centre, enthusiastically European, environmentalist (they propose a pollution added tax), in favour of constitutional reform, and supportive both of a free enterprise culture and an increase in income tax to fund investment in education. Before 1992, they adopted a stance of 'equidistance' from the two major parties, criticising them as respectively in hock to the unions (Labour) and to business (the Conservatives) but after 1994 they abandoned this position and moved closer to the Blairite Labour Party, cooperating with New Labour particularly on constitutional reform. Traditionally strong in local politics and in by-elections, by May 1997 they controlled four times as many local councils as the Conservatives and had raised their parliamentary representation from 20 to 26 by by-election victories. Party membership remained firm

Table 7.9 The Liberal Party: votes, candidates, seats and share of vote, 1945–97

	Votes (m.)	Candidates	Seats	Share of the vote (%)
1945	2.25	306	12	9.0
1950	2.62	475	9	9.1
1951	0.74	109	6	2.6
1955	0.72	110	6	2.7
1959	1.64	216	6	5.9
1964	3.10	365	9	11.2
1966	2.33	311	12	8.5
1970	2.12	332	6	7.5
1974 (Feb)	6.06	517	14	19.3
1974 Oct)	5.35	619	13	18.3
1979	4.31	577	11	13.8
1983*	7.78	633	23	25.4
1987*	7.34	633	22	22.6
1992**	5.99	632	20	17.8
1997**	5.24	637	46	16.8

* The Liberal–Social Democrat Alliance
** The Liberal Democrats

at over 100,000. Their tactic of targeting winnable seats was rewarded in the 1997 general election when they won 46 seats – all of them in competition with the two major parties – although on a slightly lower proportion of the total vote than in 1992. By late 1997, the Labour Government had enacted devolution and incorporated the European Convention on Human Rights, two changes long sought by Liberals/Liberal Democrats; leading Liberal Democrats had been given places alongside Labour on a cabinet committee on constitutional reform; and Labour had promised proportional representation not only in elections for the new Scottish and Welsh Assemblies but also in the 1999 Euro-elections. However, there were already indications that the Labour Government might be moving away from the pre-election Labour–Lib Dem agreement that the Electoral Commission should look only at a proportional voting system as a substitute for the present first-past-the-post voting method and were

preparing to allow the Commission to consider the Alternative Vote (not a proportional system). There are two potential difficulties for Liberal Democrats. First, the party is vulnerable to a Conservative recovery. Second, whilst at the top leading Liberal Democrats are close to New Labour, at grass-roots level Liberal Democrat activists and councillors are more accustomed to seeing Labour as the political enemy. This may make the leadership-driven national accord with Labour hard to sustain within the party, especially if the Liberal Democrats fail to get proportional representation.

The Scottish and Welsh nationalist parties

Both nationalist parties want independence for their countries within the European Union and both took what they saw as the first step on this road when Scotland and Wales voted 'yes' to the Scottish Parliament and Welsh Assembly in September 1997. Although it had refused to participate in the Scottish Constitutional Convention, the *Scottish National Party* (SNP) campaigned for a 'double yes' vote (to tax powers as well as to an assembly) in the devolution referendum. After the successful devolution campaign, with a gradualist road to independence having replaced its former 'free by 1993' strategy, the party aimed to take a full part in the new Scottish Assembly. Although criticising the Welsh Assembly proposals as feeble, the Welsh nationalist party, *Plaid Cymru*, supported the successful campaign for Welsh devolution and then aimed to form the main opposition to Labour in the new Assembly.

To a certain extent, the two nationalist parties have experienced similar electoral fortunes since 1945 (Table 7.10). However, once the parties had achieved parliamentary representation in the 1970s, SNP support remained at a much higher level than that for Plaid Cymru, reflecting the greater potential of Scottish nationalism. Plaid Cymru's close links with the language issue effectively confines its appeal to the regions containing a high percentage of Welsh-language speakers in the North-West and West of the country. In 1997, it won at least one-third of the vote in all five seats where the majority speak Welsh but less than one-fifth of the vote everywhere else in Wales. It retained the four MPs it had

had since 1992. By contrast, the SNP could aim realistically at becoming the second party to Labour in Scotland, a position it achieved in 1997 when the Conservative Party vote collapsed and it lost all its MPs north of the border. In 1997, the SNP pulled ahead of the Conservatives in seats (6, compared with 0), total vote (over 600,000, compared with under 500,000) and share of the vote (22.1 per cent, compared with 17.5 per cent).

Other minor parties

Of the other minor parties in the 1997 general election, only the *Referendum Party* made a significant impact, although a lesser one than its founder the multi-millionaire Sir James Goldsmith hoped or its political opponents feared. The party put forward 547 candidates, spent £20 million and distributed several million free videos in an attempt to force a referendum on Britain's future in Europe. Overall, the party gained 810,000 votes – less than the one million vote target it set itself – and its candidates

achieved an average vote of 3.1 per cent, but despite early comments that it had helped to topple about 20 Conservative MPs, the net effect of its intervention and that of the *UK Independence Party* probably only cost the Conservatives three seats (Butler and Kavanagh, 1997, p.251). Arguably, however, the Referendum Party had helped to push Europe up the list of issues to third and helped to force almost one-third of Conservative MPs to defy the party leadership on the single currency in their campaign literature. Other minor parties, which included the *Natural Law* party (196 candidates), the *Liberal Party* (54), Arthur Scargill's *Socialist Labour Party* (64), the *Pro-Life Alliance* (53), the *British National Party* (57) and the *Green Party* (95), achieved the usual results of minor parties in the British electoral system, namely almost inevitable lost deposits and a minuscule fraction of the vote. Of these, the *Green Party* considered not standing any candidates in the 1997 election largely to conserve resources to fight the 1999 Euro elections where the party could expect to make a greater impact. Its most considerable success indeed had been in the 1989 European elec-

Table 7.10 The Scottish National Party and Plaid Cymru: candidates, seats and share of the vote, 1945–97

	SNP			Plaid Cymru		
	Candidates	Seats	Share of Scottish vote	Candidates	Seats	Share of Welsh vote
1945	8	0	1.2	7	0	1.2
1950	3	0	0.4	7	0	1.2
1951	2	0	0.3	4	0	0.7
1955	2	0	0.5	11	0	3.1
1959	5	0	0.8	20	0	5.2
1964	15	0	2.4	23	0	4.8
1966	23	0	5.0	20	0	4.3
1970	65	1	11.4	36	0	11.5
1974 (1)	70	7	21.9	36	2	10.7
1974 (2)	71	11	30.4	36	3	10.8
1979	71	2	17.3	36	2	8.1
1983	71	2	11.8	38	2	7.8
1987	71	3	14.0	38	3	7.3
1992	72	3	21.5	38	4	8.8
1997	72	6	22.1	40	4	9.9

tions when it gained 2.3 million votes and 15 per cent of the total vote. Since 1990, its membership had declined from 20,000 to about 5,000, and in addition to lack of resources, the party had suffered asset-stripping of its ideas and policies by the main parties and internal squabbling between pragmatists and fundamentalists. The extreme right-wing *British National Party* (BNP) sought to build on sporadic local successes by concentrating its candidates in the inner cities but achieved a mere 36,000 votes and a 0.1 per cent of the total vote. But it is on the streets rather than in elections that the BNP and its violent neo-Nazi splinter group, Combat 18, have made an impact. Recent events affecting these groupings have been in keeping with the turbulent history of racist politics. In 1995, the BNP's Bexley headquarters were closed down by the Government but not before its presence had provoked a sharp rise in racist attacks in south-east London whilst Combat 18 waged a campaign of assaults and arson against members of ethnic groups, the Anti-Nazi League and others it defined as its enemies throughout the country.

On the far left, electoral activity declined after 1987, with the 28 far-left candidates mustering under 6,500 votes in 1992. *The Communist Party of Great Britain* (1920) disappeared in 1991, when it changed its name to *Democratic Left*, whilst of Trotskyist groups which stood for elections, the *Workers' Revolutionary Party* (WRP) was weakened by splits in the 1980s leaving the *Socialist Workers' Party* (SWP) as the most influential far-left group, notably on the anti-poll-tax campaign. *Militant Labour* (1993) is a successor to Militant tendency, the far-left Trotskyist grouping, which infiltrated the Labour Party using entryist tactics after 1973, causing considerable disruption which culminated in large numbers of expulsions, the deselection of two Militant Labour MPs and and the purging of the Liverpool Labour Party. With the collapse of Communism in the USSR making such labels as 'Stalinism', 'Trotskyism' and 'Eurocommunism' virtually redundant, neither entryism nor independent party-building has brought the far left much reward in the 1990s.

Summary

- Political parties play a key role in democratic systems: they provide government and opposition, recruit and train politicians, form the leading agencies of political representation, serve as very important agencies of political participation, play a decisive role in political communication by linking rulers and ruled, aggregate different interests and offer electorates political choice.

- Both party systems and the structure of parties themselves differ considerably, affecting and being affected by the nature and working of the political systems in which they operate. Party systems include one-party, dominant-party, two-party and multi-party. Party structure varies from, at one extreme, the highly disciplined,extremely centralised party serving an all-embracing ideology found in Communist systems like the former Soviet Union, to the weakly disciplined,very decentralised groupings with minimal ideological baggage found in the USA, at the other.

- Britain still has a two-party system in the sense that only two parties stand a realistic chance of exercising government, alone or (possibly) in some form of agreement with a third party. The increasing success of minor parties since the 1970s, which intensified in 1997 when minor parties won 56 seats in Great Britain, still produces multi-partyism at constituency level but not a three-party system.

- With the run of Conservative victories – and Labour failures – having been ended by the sweeping Labour victory in the 1997 general election, less is now heard of the thesis that Britain has 'a natural party of government' and 'a natural party of opposition' operating in 'a dominant party system'. However, over the post-1945 period (and earlier) this thesis is still tenable, but may need re-thinking if the Blair Government wins a second term (or more).

- In terms of party structure, Britain's parties are more centralised, more disciplined and cohesive, more permanent (i.e. more than election fighting forces), more ideological and more programmatic than parties in the US.

- Although important differences of ideology, policy, ethos and organisation remain between the two major parties, a certain convergence occurred in the 1990s. The convergence occurred especially on ideology, policy and organisation and was influenced by 'outside' factors such as the growing importance of the global economy, increasing integration in Europe and, in party terms, the enhanced 'presidentialism' of British politics which spotlighted the roles of the party leaders. But other key reasons for the change were electoral.

- In order to compete electorally, Labour 're-invented' itself as New Labour, moving into the political centre ground and in particular appropriating much of Conservative neo-liberalism on the role of the state, public spending and economic policy. It jettisoned its old clause 4 (socialist commitment) and adopted a new structure which centralised power in the leadership, shifting it away from the NEC and Conference.

- After its severe reverse in the 1997 general election and the period of intense faction-fighting within the party which preceded it, the Conservative Party under a new leader sought the changes within the party which would make it electable again. In particular, it sought a more 'inclusive' stance on minority groups not previously acceptable to the party, stronger internal discipline especially among MPs, and party reforms which would make the party more democratic but also increase membership, provide central lists of members and give the central organisation more influence over candidate selection. These last-mentioned two reforms were required in order to avoid further embarrassments such as the Hamilton affair. Much would depend on the success of these reforms and also on the extent to which the party could avoid further factionalism on Europe.

- Each major party remains a broad coalition with groups representing different strands of opinion competing for influence. In the 1990s, Conservative differences over Europe intensified and became the main focus of struggle between (broadly) neo-liberals and one-nation Conservatives. In the quest for power, Labour modernisers had the support of a compliant party desperate for office, but in government, as it enacts a rather minimalist, neo-liberal manifesto, the New Labour Cabinet may have to face greater internal opposition from a still predominantly public sector, trade-union-orientated, pro-local government party, which still has much sympathy for Old Labour ideas and values and is by no means united on Europe.

- Multi-partyism at constituency level enhances electoral choice and increases pressure on the major parties. The Liberal Democrats won 46 seats in 1997 all in competition with the major parties. In Scotland and Wales, the nationalist parties made significant contributions to the extinction of Conservative representation in those countries. First steps towards the achievement of Liberal Democrat and nationalist objectives have already been taken. The Green Party has failed to relive its 1989 Euro-election success but it can claim some influence – within the broader environmental movement – in the qualified 'greening' of the major parties. The political and electoral challenge of both extreme left and extreme right has faded in the 1990s but sections within them both have had a presence at street level.

Questions

1. How far has the Labour Party changed its internal organisation since the 1980s, and why?
2. How important is the leader to the electoral success of the main parties?
3. Does the Conservative Party deserve its reputation as a more united party than Labour?

Assignment

Consider Box 7.3 (above) on party manifestos in 1997:

(i) Why are party manifestos important?
(ii) How much choice was offered to voters on Europe and the economy by the policy proposals of the three parties?
(iii) How much choice did the three parties offer on social, industrial and employment policy?
(iv) What are the reasons for the convergence or divergence you find in party policies in your answers to questions (ii). and (iii)?
(v) Why might a political party in government depart from its manifesto?

Further reading

On British political parties, Garner, R. and Kelly, R. (1993) *British Political Parties Today* (Manchester University Press), Fisher, J. (1996) *British Political Parties* (London: Harvester Wheatsheaf), Robins, L., Blackmore, H. and Pyper, R. (eds) (1994) *Britain's Changing Party System* (London: Leicester University Press); Peele, G., 'Political Parties', in Dunleavy, P., Gamble, A., Holliday, I. and Peele, G. (eds) (1997) *Developments in British Politics 5* (London: Macmillan) can be recommended.

For valuable surveys of recent developments in Britain's parties, see *Parliamentary Affairs*, vol. 50, no. 4, October 1997 (the whole edition is on the theme 'Britain Votes 1997') and Butler, D. and Kavanagh, D. (1997) *The British General Election of 1997* (London: Macmillan). The theme of political parties is a rapidly changing scene: try to keep up-to-date by consulting specialist journals such as *Talking Politics* and *Politics Review*, quality dailies, and weeklies such as *The Economist*.

Elections and electoral reform

Elections play an important and complex role in most political systems. Even undemocratic societies hold elections in order to legitimise the existing political order. In democratic societies elections help resolve political conflict in a non-violent way, for even the losers may accept that their defeat was fair. Because elections are held regularly there is always the chance that the losers will do better next time, especially if the winners do poorly in government. In this way, elections help hold government accountable to the people. Generally, elections offer people a choice in who is to represent them, which then gives the winning candidates a mandate to govern. But the way in which the people's votes are translated into winning seats – the electoral system – influences who will win and who will lose. This chapter examines electoral behaviour as well as electoral systems used in Britain. There is much debate in Britain about the need for electoral reform and the electorate may be given a choice, through a referendum, regarding which system should be used in future elections. This chapter also explores the referendum as an alternative means of expressing voters' opinions.

Electoral statistics

British elections have produced some results which,

at face value, appear perplexing. Some of these 'strange but true' electoral facts include the following:

- In the 1951 general election Labour won 49 per cent of all votes cast (the popular vote) yet lost to the Conservatives. In 1997 Labour won 44 per cent of the popular vote and beat the Conservatives with a massive majority of 179 seats.
- Labour went on to win a larger share of the popular vote in the 1955 and 1959 general elections than it did in 1997, but it also lost these elections to the Conservatives.
- In 1983 the Labour Party received 27.6 per cent of the popular vote and won 209 seats. The recently formed Liberal–SDP Alliance were close behind with 25.4 per cent of the popular vote, yet won only 23 seats. In terms of averages, Labour was rewarded with one MP for every 40,000 votes it won, whereas the Liberal–SDP Alliance gained an MP at the cost of 338,000 votes cast for it.
- In 1997 the Liberal Democrats' popular vote fell by over 700,000 from 1992, yet they won an additional 26 seats.
- In 1992 John Major's party won a record 14,091,891 votes which gave the Conservatives a 21-seat majority in the Commons. In 1997 Tony Blair won 13,516,632 votes which gave new Labour the largest post-war majority of 179 seats.

Of course all of these apparently contradictory 'facts' can be explained. The strength of third party intervention can vary from one election to another, making it either easier or harder for the 'favourite' party to win. In tightly fought contests a third party might encourage tactical voting which results in the defeat of the favourite party, or a fourth party might draw a small yet critical amount of support from the favourite party which again contributes to its defeat. The pattern of party support – the spread of votes – is also important in understanding election results. Whilst piling up votes in safe constituencies will increase a party's share of the **popular vote**, it may not win it any extra seats. On the other hand, if a party's support is spread too thinly across the constituencies it risks coming second everywhere and not winning any seats. The level of turnout can be an important factor, particularly in marginal seats. And in all cases, the fate of the parties depended in great part on the first-past-the-post electoral system. Had another system been in place, election results would have differed; the chances of one party dominating government for long periods might be reduced while the chances of parties having to form coalitions in order to govern might be increased. Some recent examples, from a variety of elections, will help unravel some of these complexities.

Turnout and outcomes

In terms of winning popular support and gaining seats, the 1997 general election was a disaster for the Conservatives; not since the 1830s had they been so unpopular, and not since the Liberal landslide in

1906 had they won so few seats. Yet few commentators interpret Labour's 1997 landslide in terms of popular enthusiasm for Tony Blair's modernised party. What factors might explain this and other recent results?

The first contrast, shown in Table 8.1, is in the drop in turnout between the 1992 and 1997 general elections. Labour gained around 2 million additional votes, but the Conservatives lost over 4.5 million votes. Some commentators argued that the 1997 general election could be explained in large part by the 2 million Conservatives who abstained, the 1.5 million former Conservatives who switched to Labour, and the million or so that switched to the Liberal Democrats or voted for the Referendum Party.

The problem with this simple explanation is that the pattern of turnout varies a great deal geographically – from a low of 52 per cent in Liverpool Riverside to a high of 82 per cent in Brecon and Radnor. Furthermore, as David Denver argued, the fall in turnout was smaller in Conservative-held seats (–6 per cent on average) than in those that were Labour-held (–8 per cent). Moreover, 'the decline was greatest in typically Labour-supporting areas . . . This is a sobering counter to the euphoria generated by Labour's landslide victory. The landslide was won on the lowest turnout since the war and it was lowest of all, and fell most sharply, in Labour areas' (Denver, 1997, p. 8).

Table 8.2 shows the results of election to the European Parliament which were based on a much lower level of turnout than general elections. Although extrapolating the results from one election

> **Popular vote**: is the percentage of Britain's voters which supports each party, regardless of constituency boundaries or seats.

Table 8.1 The 1992 and 1997 General Elections

	1992				1997		
	Votes (%)	Seats No.	Seats (%)		Votes (%)	Seats No.	Seats (%)
Conservative	43	336	53		31	165	26
Labour	35	271	43		44	419	65
Liberal Democrat	18	20	3		17	46	7
Others	4	7	1		4	11	2
Referendum Party					3	0	0
Turnout 78%				Turnout 72%			

Table 8.2 The 1989 and 1994 British elections to the European Parliament

	1989				1994		
	Votes (%)	Seats No.	Seats (%)		Votes (%)	Seats No.	Seats (%)
Conservative	35	32	41		27	18	21
Labour	40	45	58		45	62	74
Liberal Democrat	6	0	0		16	2	2
Greens	15	0	0		3	0	0
SNP/PC	4	1	1		4	2	2
Turnout 36%				Turnout 36%			

to predict another is sometimes inappropriate, the 1994 European Parliament election results contained a warning to Conservatives. Based on a low yet regionally variable turnout, one commentator calculated that 'if the same thing were to happen at the next general election, the Conservatives would be reduced to just 146 seats – their lowest this century – while the Liberals would win 39 seats and Labour 432' (the *Guardian*, 14 June 1994).

Turnout at local authority elections can vary considerably; in 1997 it was over 70 per cent because local elections were held alongside the general election, but normally turnout is closer to half this level. Nevertheless, local election results have been used by politicians to calculate how well their party would have done had it been a general election. Conservative Party Chairmen used the May local elections in 1983 and 1987 as an electoral test, and given the good results advised their leader to call a general election in the following month. Rather than count the number of council seats each party has won or lost, or the number of councils where overall control has been won or lost, party managers calculate an 'equivalent popular vote' in order to extrapolate from local to national levels.

Proportionality

First-past-the-post is said to exaggerate the lead of the winning party when translating votes into seats. Table 8.1 shows that the party which won both the 1992 and 1997 general elections received a greater share of seats than their share of votes. In its 1997 landslide, Labour won 128 seats more than proportional to its share of votes. The winning party in the 1989 and 1994 elections to the European Parliament, Labour on both occasions, also won a greater share of seats than its share of votes (see Table 8.2).

Some argue that first-past-the-post over-represents both the leading parties – Labour and Conservative – whilst under-representing the Liberal Democrats. Table 8.2 shows that in 1992 both Labour and Conservative were over-rewarded in terms of the number of seats they won. In 1997, however, the Conservatives received a smaller share of seats than their share of votes. A proportional share would have meant another 39 MPs on the Conservative backbenches. A similar situation for the Conservatives of being proportionally under-represented occurred in the 1994 European Parliament election (Table 8.2).

The Liberal Democrats were less penalised by first-past-the-post in 1997 than in 1992, but strict proportionality would have resulted in 112 MPs rather than 46. However, some commentators have pointed to the anomalous result for the Liberal Democrats in Scotland (see Table 8.3). The Conservatives did not win a single Scottish seat; Liberal Democrats won ten on a much smaller share of the vote. Again, the SNP's much larger share of the popular vote provided them with four fewer MPs than won by the Liberal Democrats.

In the past, psephologists calculated the impact of the electoral system in exaggerating the lead of the winning party in terms of the cube law: 'if votes are

Table 8.3 The 1997 General Election Scottish results

	Votes (%)	Seats No.
Conservative	17	0
Labour	46	56
Liberal Democrat	13	10
SNP	22	6
Others	2	0
Turnout 71%		

in the ratio a:b then the electoral system will convert this into the ratio a^3:b^3 in terms of seats' (Denver, 1997, p. 8). The cube law has, for over thirty years been of declining usefulness in calculating the lead of the winning party. However, in 1997 'the ratio of Labour to Conservative seats was 72:28 on the basis of a vote split of 59:41. This exaggeration of Labour's lead was almost as large as implied by the "cube rule"' (Denver, 1997, p. 4).

Tactical voting

The electorate appears to be using the electoral system in an increasingly sophisticated way in order to register its political preferences. By-elections, for example, have long seen safe seats for the party of government overturned by disgruntled voters wanting to 'send a message to Number Ten'. The impact of the Liberal–SDP Alliance in 1983 showed that the electorate was prepared to vote tactically in a general election. Labour's 'landslide' victory shown in Table 8.1 might be explained in large part by the ability of both Labour and the Liberal Democrats to have won seats outside their list of target marginals. There is evidence that this occurred because of **tactical voting** against the government on an unprecedented scale' in 1997 (Norris, 1997, p.521). Although it is difficult to measure the exact extent

Tactical voting: this involves voting for a second choice party in order to defeat the party which is most disliked.

of tactical voting, Pippa Norris found that the electorate behaved differently according to the type of local contest: 'in Conservative seats where Labour was in second place in 1992, Labour's share of the vote went up by 13 per cent on average, while the Liberal Democrat share declined by about three per cent. In sharp contrast, in marginal seats where the Liberal Democrats were in second place in 1992, the Liberal Democrat vote increased by about two to three per cent, while the Labour share rose by less than average' (Norris, ibid). She concluded that this was remarkable because the constituency boundary changes since 1992 meant that many voters must have been unsure which party stood the best chance against the Conservative candidate.

Using different methods of analysis, Ian McAllister found evidence of tactical voting in 324 English constituencies, over half of which were judged to be 'very safe' (see Table 8.4). His study of tactical voting in 1997 showed that Conservative seats with either Labour or Liberal Democrat in second place were mainly found in the South East, East Anglia and the South West, with few in the

Table 8.4 Tactical voting, England, 1997

	Actual minus predicted vote		
	Labour	Liberal Democrat	N
Con/Lab contest			
Very marginal	+6.7	−5.8	(27)
Fairly marginal	+7.7	−7.0	(29)
Semi marginal	+3.2	−4.7	(16)
Fairly safe	+6.8	−7.5	(24)
Very safe	+2.5	−6.3	(76)
Con/Lib Dem contest			
Very marginal	−18.6	+22.5	(5)
Fairly marginal	−18.0	+18.0	(8)
Semi marginal	−11.6	+14.3	(14)
Fairly safe	−7.2	+10.4	(23)
Very safe	−5.0	+2.1	(102)

Source: Based on McAllister (1997) p. 652.

North and, because of nationalist candidates, few in Scotland and Wales. His evidence (see Table 8.4) is of modest tactical voting where Labour challenges Conservative candidates, but by contrast 'high levels of tactical voting in the constituencies where a Liberal Democrat candidate was running second to a Conservative incumbent, and most particularly where the contest was marginal' (McAllister, 1997 p. 652). He concluded that tactical voting was a 'very significant factor' in the Liberal Democrats' success in winning 46 seats.

Electoral systems

Should so many of Britain's electorate have to resort to tactical voting in order to get the electoral system to produce a result which is acceptable? Is it preferable to have an electoral system which enables the electorate to vote 'strategically' by targeting their votes on their main choices rather than having to make complex 'tactical' voting decisions on the best way of defeating the party they dislike most?

There are a considerable number of **electoral systems**; some differ only in terms of detail, others differ in terms of fundamental characteristics. A main characteristic which distinguishes electoral systems is the electoral formula of how votes are translated into seats. Giovanni Sartori distinguishes between majoritarian and proportional systems; 'in majoritarian systems the voter's choice is funnelled and ultimately narrowed into one alternative; in proportional systems voters are not forced into concentrating their vote and their range of choice might be quite extensive' (Sartori, 1994, p. 3).

Majoritarian electoral systems

The 'majority' can be an absolute majority of 50 per cent (plus one vote) of all votes cast, or the 'majority' can be a simple plurality with the winner being the candidate with the highest vote. In a tightly contested election of three or more candidates, the winner will receive well under 50 per cent of votes cast. Sartori describes Britain's first-past-the-post as

> **Electoral system**: an electoral system is the means by which voters elect candidates to political office.

a 'one-shot plurality' system. To become truly majoritarian there would need to be a second ballot in all seats which were not won with 50 per cent of all votes or more. Only the two front-runners would appear in the second ballot, ensuring that the final winner would receive over half the votes cast. Majoritarian systems include:

- *First-past-the-post*, also known as 'simple majority' or 'single member simple plurality' (Farrell, 1997, p. 12). As well as Britain, it is used in the USA, Canada, India and, until recently, New Zealand. As David Farrell comments, three arguments are customarily made about the advantages of this 'winner takes all' system: (i) simplicity – the act of voting is simple, the system is straightforward and the results are easily understood (ii) stability – because the system exaggerates the lead of the winning party it does away with the need for parties to form coalitions in order to govern. In all post-war British general elections except those in 1964 and 1974, governments have been returned with workable, often large, parliamentary majorities. (iii) Constituency representation – each MP represents a constituency. This is in contrast with some proportional systems where there is no constituency link between voters and their elected representatives. The main losers under this system are parties whose support is spread evenly but too thinly across the country; they may lose few deposits but win few seats. The winners are parties which can pile up their votes in particular parts of the country and so gain seats.

- The *two-ballot* or *second ballot system* is primarily associated with France. Should a candidate win more than 50 per cent of votes cast there is no need for a second ballot. Where this is not the case a second ballot is held, generally a week later, from which the least popular candidates have been eliminated. In practice, depending upon how many candidates qualify (by meeting rules which can vary) for the second ballot, it is possible that the winner of the second ballot may still not achieve a true majority. Sartori argues that the interval between the two ballots is important because it allows voters to reconsider their voting intentions and 'reorient their choices on the basis of the returns of the first round' (Sartori, 1994, p.11).

- The *alternative vote* is described by Sartori as a 'preferential' voting system within single-member constituencies which requires every voter to number all candidates in order of preference: 'the candidates with fewest first preferences are eliminated and preferences are redistributed until an absolute majority winner emerges' (Sartori, 1994, p. 6). This system is associated with Australia. As Farrell states, at first glance the alternative vote system seems fairer than first-past-the-post: 'the candidate elected has more votes than all the other candidates combined . . . This system also allows the voters a greater say over who they want to represent them: if it is not to be their first choice, then they can choose a second' (Farrell, 1997, p. 49). Farrell, unlike Sartori, sees the absence of second ballot as an advantage since it denies parties the opportunity to manipulate the electorate.
- The *supplementary vote* was recommended by a Labour Party working party into electoral reform chaired by Lord Plant. An elaboration of the alternative vote, the voter would have just two preference votes. Where no candidate receives at least 50 per cent of the vote 'then all but the top two candidates are eliminated and the second' preferences are redistributed (Farrell, 1997, p. 56). The winning candidate will have a majority of votes cast.

Proportional electoral systems

Systems of **proportional representation** may be more or less proportional in nature, ranging from a perfect correspondence between votes cast and seats won to a much looser approximation between votes and seats. Some political scientists have argued that majoritarian systems tend to result in two-party systems as in the UK and USA, whereas proportional systems result in multi-party systems. So whilst proportional representation systems may be 'fairer', they may also result in greater governmental

---

Proportional representation: proportional representation systems produce a stronger arithmetic link between the way in which votes are cast and the candidates which get elected than do either majoritarian or first-past-the-post systems.

---

instability and the formation of coalition governments with policies based on compromise and negotiation which no electors voted for. PR systems include:

- *List systems* are party-based rather than candidate-based, and are used in most European countries. There is great variation within the list systems but the basic principle they all share is that 'each party draws up a list of candidates in each constituency. The size of the lists is based on the number of seats to be filled . . . The proportion of votes each party receives determines the number of seats it can fill' (Farrell, 1997, p. 60). Had a list system been used in the 1997 general election, rather than enjoying a landslide Labour would have been the largest party but still 89 seats short of a majority. Liberal Democrats, with over a hundred seats, would have been the obvious coalition partners. Lists may be open, with no rank ordering of candidates so that voters express their preferences. Or lists may be closed with the parties placing their senior candidates at the top of the list. In Israel, which treats the whole country as a single constituency, parties determine the rank ordering of candidates on the lists. Variations are based on establishing thresholds, calculating quotas and using unused votes to decide remaining seats. The d'Hondt system, used in Belgium, the Netherlands, Portugal and Spain, attempts to ensure 'that the average number of votes taken to elect any one candidate from a party is as nearly as possible equal to any other in that party. This is often called the "highest-average formula"' (Jones, 1994, p. 181). The Hagenbach-Bischoff system is a derivative of the d'Hondt using a different formula to calculate the quota, used in Greece. Finally, the Sainte-Lague system uses the highest average formula to translate votes into seats and is used, in modified form, in Sweden and Norway.
- The *single transferable vote system* (STV) is interesting in-so-far as some political scientists see it as a pure system of proportional representation whereas others argue that in practice constituencies are too small and STV does not work proportionally. STV is based on multi-member constituencies and electors rank candidates in order of preference. A quota is established as a thresh-

Table 8.5 Replaying the 1997 General Election

	First past-the-post	Pure proportionality (list)	Alternative vote	Single transferable vote	Additional member	Supplementary vote
Conservative	165	202	110	144	203	110
Labour	419	285	436	342	303	436
Liberal Democrats	46	110	84	131	115	84
SNP/Plaid Cymru	10	46	10	24	20	10
Others (including Northern Ireland)	19	18	19	18	18	19
Result	Labour majority 179	Labour 89 seats short	Labour majority 213	Labour majority 25	Labour 27 seats short	Labour majority 213

Source: Based on Kellner in *The Observer* (21 September 1997).

old for winning a seat; in a 5-member constituency, each party would need around 20 per cent of the vote to win a seat, 40 per cent to win two seats, and so on. The formula for calculating the quota varies; here the Droop formula is shown.

$$\left[\frac{\text{total number of votes}}{(\text{total number of seats} +1)} \right] +1$$

Votes that a candidate wins surplus to the quota are redistributed according to second, third and fourth preferences, etc. As the bottom candidates are successively eliminated, their preferences are also redistributed to remaining candidates. If STV is to be proportional, it requires more rather than fewer seats to be contested in large constituencies. STV is used in Ireland and for European Parliamentary and local elections in Northern Ireland. But, as Farrell recounts, STV as operated in Ireland includes an element of chance. Surplus votes happen to be the ones counted last before their preferences are redistributed. The preferences expressed in the winning pile of votes might be quite different. Some argue that STV is preferable to the list system since it retains constituency links with the electorate with electors voting for candidates rather than parties, whilst retaining proportionality.

The *additional member system* is a combination of two other systems in order to get the advantages of local constituency links together with greater proportionality. Each voter has two votes – one for a constituency MP and the other for a party list. The constituency MP would be voted in under the alternative vote or first-past-the-post system, with the other MPs getting elected from a regional or national list. The list seats are allocated so as to help compensate for the disproportionality of the constituency vote. One disadvantage of this system is the creation of two classes of MPs.

Electoral reform

The wisdom of electoral reform has been discussed since well into the last century, and in 1917 many believed that the campaign to introduce STV in some constituencies, AV in others, was as good as won. In the event Parliament rejected electoral reform, except for STV being used in a small number of (now abolished) university seats. For a variety of reasons public interest in electoral reform has intensified over recent decades. STV was introduced to some elections in Northern Ireland as a visibly 'fairer' system for representing the two traditions; the revival of the Liberals in the polls but not in the Commons portrayed the unfairness of first-past-the-post; feminists argued that proportional representation would result in women contesting more seats and with greater success; Britain's membership of the European Community/Union raised questions about reforming elections to the European Parliament; and finally electoral reform was seen as crucial for making elected local government more representative through breaking up one-party domination and attendant problems of poor quality candidates and unacceptable standards of government.

The new Labour Government's constitutionally radical programme included consideration of electoral reform for general elections, local government elections, elections to the European Parliament as well as changed systems for electing the devolved assemblies. In addition to all this, some reforms would be preceded by a referendum seeking approval, which itself represented a form of electoral reform.

A study by London and Essex academics, *Making Votes Count*, could result in some Liberal Democrats having second thoughts. Immediately after the general election 8,000 voters were asked to complete mock ballot papers from other electoral systems. The results are shown in Table 8.5 and suggest that under STV Liberal Democrats would draw close to challenging the Conservatives for the status of the 'official' opposition, although Labour would still have had a workable majority. Under the additional member system Liberal Democrats would have won less seats but so too would Labour, with the Liberal Democrats likely to enter government as coalition partners.

Referendums

In the past, Britain's politicians viewed **referendums** with much suspicion; Labour's postwar prime minister, Clement Attlee, described them as 'devices alien to our traditions'. Nevertheless, along with other EU members and the US, Britain is resorting to increasing use of the referendum. Referendums have been used on more than one occasion regard-

> A **referendum** allows voters to register their opinions on specific questions regarding policy issues.

ing the relationship of Northern Ireland, Scotland and Wales within the United Kingdom, with a nationwide referendum in 1975 on Britain's continued membership of the European Community. All political parties are pledged to holding a referendum prior to Britain joining EMU and adopting the single currency. Britain's referendums have focused on seeking legitimacy for constitutional change, but other countries have held referendums to resolve moral issues or miscellaneous debates such as whether smoking should be allowed in public places.

Referendums may differ in technical detail; a referendum may be a 'top down' consultation exercise by government simply to find out the electorate's opinion on an issue, or it may be a 'bottom up' exercise in which the decision made by voters is binding. Thresholds may be introduced, as in the first devolution referendums in 1979, when at least 40 per cent of the electorate (not just voters) had to vote 'yes' before the new assemblies would be set up. Sometimes the term 'plebiscite' is used to refer to a referendum, and in the United States, particularly California, 'initiatives' are held which are a form of referendum. Before an issue is put to the state's electorate, it must have already have the support of a required number of voters who will have signed the 'petition' (see Box 8.1).

Some support referendums as a means of achieving direct democracy; others feel that referendums have undesirable effects. It has been argued that a referendum polarises political opinion into two opposed camps rather than attempting to seek a compromise. Also the choice of voting 'yes' or 'no' may be too simple for the complex issue being decided. For example, those opposed to holding a referendum on Britain entering EMU argue that the decision may depend upon the rate at which sterling enters, or whether or not Britain is the only EU member not to join, and these conditions are not easily reduced to a 'yes/no' answer.

The difficulties in framing a satisfactory referendum question were illuminated in the run-up to the 1997 general election. The major parties were committed to holding a referendum prior to joining EMU but another party sponsored by the financier, the late Sir James Goldsmith, was committed to letting the people answer a wider question. The Referendum Party campaigned for a referendum to be held as 'who should run Britain – Westminster or

BOX 8.1
Direct democracy: a Californian contrast

The British electorate is voting in referendums with increasing frequency. However, British electors still lag far behind the voting habits of some Americans. For example, Californians voted on a number of Propositions in November 1994 – they defeated by more than 2-1 the tobacco industry's Proposition 188 which would have weakened anti-smoking legislation. Also rejected was Proposition 186 which would have created a Californian health care system based on Canada's. Proposition 184 was passed, which endorsed existing state law which mandates 25-year or longer prison sentences to anyone convicted of a third serious felony ('three strikes, you're out') thus making it harder for any future reformers to change this policy. But the most controversial Proposition since the Proposition 13 tax revolt of the late 1970s was Proposition 187. This was aimed at denying public schooling and other services funded by tax-payers to illegal immigrants and their children.

California, once governed by Mexico, has absorbed a large number of illegal immigrants during recent years. During California's boom years they were economically useful but politically 'invisible'. In hard times, however, they have been identified as an economic burden which is driving California towards bankruptcy. Proposition 187 was publicly supported by Gov. Wilson, and approved by a large 59–41 majority. Voters in more liberal Northern California rejected Proposition 187 but the conservative areas of Southern California, such as Orange and San Diego, passed it by an overwhelming margin. Exit poles show that whites supported it 3–2, blacks were split evenly, and Latinos rejected it 3–1. Just under half of Democrat and three-quarters of Republican voters supported Proposition 187.

BOX 8.2
The devolution referendums of 1997

	For (%)	Against (%)	Turnout (%)
The Scottish parliament	74.3	25.7	60.1
With taxation powers	63.5	36.5	
The Welsh assembly	50.3	49.7	50.1

Europe'. They were unsure whether he had the EU of today in mind, or some hypothetical superstate not yet planned. (Although the Referendum Party failed to win a seat, some political analysts argued that its small share of the Euro-sceptic vote resulted in the defeat of 17 Conservative MPs.)

Similar difficulties were encountered by Euro-sceptic Conservative MP, Bill Cash, when he attempted to steer a referendum bill through Parliament. His proposed wording was

- Do you want the United Kingdom to propose and insist on irreversible changes in the treaty on European Union, so that the United Kingdom retains its powers of government and is not part of a federal Europe nor part of a European Monetary Union, including a single currency?

Again, critics argued that this was not a neutral question so much as a politically biased statement. Also, its premises were false since Britain could not 'insist' on any changes to the Maastricht Treaty.

On occasions a referendum may not resolve an issue so much as show that an electorate is split down the middle. This happened in two referendums held in November 1995: a referendum in Ireland supported legalising divorce by only 9,124 votes, less than half of one per cent of those who voted; in Quebec a referendum on independence was lost by only 53,000 votes out of 4.5 million cast. Even worse in some ways was the devolution referendum held in Wales (see Box 8.2) where the largest group was the 'stay at homes'. The vote which cleared the way for Welsh devolution was made by only one in four of the electorate, hardly comprising a moral mandate for constitutional change.

Brussels?' Sir James encountered problems when he attempted to flesh out the precise wording for his proposed referendum. He proposed that two questions be included:

- Do you want the United Kingdom to be part of a Federal Europe?
or
- Do you want the United Kingdom to return to an association of sovereign states that are part of a common trading market?

Critics argued that Sir James's questions were flawed. What, they asked, did Sir James mean by 'Federal

Summary

- British citizens vote in elections at local, national and European levels. With some exceptions, these elections utilise the first-past-the-post system, which has come under increasing criticism during the 1980s and 1990s.
- First-past-the-post exaggerates the lead of the winning party and so has resulted in the over-representation of both the Labour and Conservative parties in Parliament.
- Alternative voting systems include both majoritarian and proportional systems.
- An increasing proportion of British voters are voting tactically or prepared to split-ticket vote when two elections are held on the same day.
- The new devolved assemblies will not be elected by first-past-the-post, and the prospects for electoral reform before the next general election and elections to the European Parliament seem favourable.
- The debate concerning which electoral system will replace first-past-the-post will consider alternatives which are either majoritarian or proportional in nature. Like other issues concerned with significant constitutional change, a referendum is likely to precede any electoral reform.

Questions

1. Discuss the case for and against electoral reform in Britain.
2. Refer to the information in Table 8.5 and describe how different electoral systems may have changed the outcome of the 1997 general election.
3. Some electoral systems are more democratic than others' . . . 'The choice is either good government and FPTP or unstable coalition government with PR' . . . 'The most important feature of any electoral system is that electors understand how it works.' Discuss the validity of these statements.

Assignments

Assignment (1)
The merits and disadvantages of initiatives and referendums

Many who exercise power are reluctant to opt for more direct democracy, and argue that whilst it may be appropriate for deciding local and state issues it has disadvantages in national politics.

Conservatives tend to fear its use on key questions of defence and foreign affairs; liberals worry about the repercussions for minority groups. Many members of both categories feel safer with traditional methods of representative democracy.

In favour of votes on a single issue, it may be said that;

- They give people a chance to take decisions which affect their lives, whereas in a general election they can only offer a general verdict.
- They stimulate interest and involvement in public policy.
- They may exert pressure on the legislature to act responsibly, and in the public interest.
- They may help counter the special interests to which legislators can be beholden.
- They help overcome the obstructionism of out-of-touch legislators and therefore make reform more likely.

Against such consultation, it may be said that;

- Proposals can be ill-thought-out, and badly drafted.
- Campaigns can be expensive and therefore to the advantage of well-funded groups; money is too dominant in the process, business interests have far more scope to influence the outcome.
- There are too many issues for voters to handle, and many of them are too complex for popular understanding. The rash of tax-limitation measures and similar ones which starve the schools and other essential public services (as in the US) are ones where the mass of people are too ill-informed and apathetic to make a wise decision. They elect representatives to decide. This

is what representative democracy is all about. If the voter dislikes the decisions made, he or she can turn against the controlling party in the next election.

- Initiatives and allied devices undermine political parties and therefore weaken the democratic process.
- They reflect an unwarranted mistrust of legislative bodies, and lessen their sense of responsibility for public policy.
- They encourage single-issue politics, rather than debate based on a conflict of broad principles.
- They can work to the disadvantage of minorities who can be persecuted by the majority – e.g., blacks and gays.

(*Source*: Watts, 1997, p.47)

Questions

(i)   Why might those who exercise power at national level oppose the use of referendums?

(ii) What is meant by the phrase 'traditional methods of representative democracy'?

(iii) Incorporate either the points made in favour or the points made against use of the referendum into a tabloid-style newspaper article of 300 words.

Assignment (2)
Four constituency results in the general election

1.   LIVERPOOL WALTON

P. Kilfoyle(LAB)	31,516
R. Roberts (LIB DEM)	4,478
M. Kotecha (CON)	2,551
C. Grundy (REF)	620
L. Mahmood (SOC)	447
H. Williams (LIB)	352
V. Mearn (PRO-LIFE)	246

LAB HOLD	Majority	27,038

Turnout 59.5%

2.   TEWKESBURY

L. Robertson (CON)	23,859
J. Sewell (LIB DEM)	14,625
K. Tustin (LAB)	13,665

CON HOLD	Majority	9,234

Turnout 76.5%

3.   CASTLE POINT

C. Butler (LAB)	20,605
R. Spink (CON)	19,489
D. Baker (LIB DEM)	4,477
H. Maulkin (REF)	2,700
L. Kendall (IND DEM)	1,301

LAB GAIN	Majority	1,116

Turnout 72.3%

4.   MORAY

M. Ewing (SNP)	16,529
A. Finlay (CON)	10,963
D. Storr (LIB DEM)	3,548
P Mieklejohn (REF)	840

SNP HOLD	Majority	5,566

Turnout 68.2%

Questions

(i)   Identify two 'single issue' parties. In which constituency might the vote won by a single issue party have cost the Conservative candidate his/her seat?

(ii) Consider the results for Liverpool Walton and Tewkesbury. Discuss possible reasons for the large difference in the levels of turnout. In what sense does the Labour MP have a stronger claim to represent Liverpool Walton than the Conservative MP to represent Tewkesbury? Discuss how electoral reform might change these situations.

(iii) Consider 'third party' intervention in the four results above. Why might SNP intervention in Moray have been more successful than Liberal Democrat intervention in all constituencies? Despite their postwar record of returning 46 MPs, to what extent did first-past-the-post discriminate against Liberal Democrats?

Further reading

Denver, D. (1997) 'The 1997 General Election Results', *Talking Politics*, 10:1, pp. 2–8. Includes analysis of the electoral system effect and the return of the 'cube' rule. Farrell, D. (1997) *Comparing Electoral Systems* (London: Macmillan) is a detailed examination of alternatives which also considers historical origins. Jones, A (1994) 'European Electoral Systems', *Talking Politics*, 6:3, pp. 181–3 is a comprehensive guide to the alternatives in current usage.

Sartori, G. (1994) *Comparative Constitutional Engineering* (London: Macmillan) is a controversial account of the workings of alternative electoral systems.

Voting behaviour

In the late 1960s a political scientist could observe with considerable justification that in Britain 'class is the basis of party politics; all else is embellishment and detail'. Thirty years later social class appears to explain much less about variations in political behaviour and today political scientists talk of 'class dealignment' as having taken place. But, as we shall see, there is much disagreement about the extent to which dealignment has occurred. Political scientists have developed various models to help explain the changes which have taken place in voting behaviour. Each model is useful in that it explains some aspect or other of voting, but none explains voting patterns entirely. How far do they help in analysing the general election of 1997? On the surface, Labour enjoyed a landslide victory of historic proportions but are there other explanations which put Tony Blair's success into perspective? Finally, this chapter examines the reliability of opinion poll data on which political scientists base much of their research.

The decline of the two-party system

The electorate is not an unchanging entity, nor is it stable. Some changes will occur because its composition is changing as young people attain voting age and become included, whilst others die. Other changes will occur because of movements in attitudes, values and behaviour from one election to the next.

Thus there may be long-term and short-term changes which help explain voting trends. Although it is a basic point, it has to be remembered that when comparing the electorate of the 1950s with that of the 1990s very different groups of voters are involved. Many voters in the 1950s would have remembered the Boer War as well as two World Wars; they might have experienced great economic hardship during the 1930s or been involved in the suffragette movement; they would certainly have witnessed the election of the Attlee government. None of these voters will have lived long enough to vote in the 1990s. In contrast, first-time young voters in 1997 will have no real memories of the last Labour government which left office in 1979. But these young voters may well be aware of short-term changes in the political agenda on which elections have been fought; they may have noticed, for example, that the defence issue seemed to play a smaller role in the 1997 campaign than it did in 1987. The impact of these processes on voting behaviour has contributed to the decline of two-party voting. This can be seen in three closely related developments which have occurred during the last forty years.

Firstly, there has been a more or less steady decline in the percentage of the total vote won in general elections by the Conservative and Labour parties.

For example, in 1951 nearly 97 per cent of voters supported either Labour or Conservative. After touching a low point of 72 per cent in 1983, the percentage rose to 78 per cent in 1992, and fell back to 74 per cent in 1997, all far below the 1951 level.

Secondly, one of the major causes for this decline has been the weakening of *party identification*. In other words, the links between voters and parties have grown weaker and weaker as fewer and fewer voters identified with particular political parties. As party loyalties have weakened so electoral *volatility* has increased. Because an increasing number of voters do not have such strong emotional ties to particular parties, they find it easier to switch their vote to another party or decide not to vote at all. In 1997 this was reflected in two particular behaviours:

- Table 9.1 shows that three out of ten Labour voters and four out of ten Conservative voters decided which party to support as late as during the election campaign. Two-thirds of Liberal Democrat support came from 'late deciders'. This compares with the elections of 1983 and 1987 when only one in five of all voters decided during the last two or three weeks of the campaigns. In 1992 the equivalent figure rose to one in four.
- Evidence since 1979 shows that an increasing number of voters are prepared to support different parties in local and general elections. In 1997 around half Britain's electors had the opportunity of voting in both elections on May 1st, and a Mori poll found that at least 10 per cent of Conservative and Labour general election supporters intended to vote Liberal Democrat in the local elections. 'Split ticket' voting accounted for the Liberal Democrat vote being 'seven per cent higher than

the party's general election vote, with the Conservatives down by four per cent and Labour by five' (Rallings and Thrasher, 1997, p.687).

Thirdly, there has been a decline in class-based voting during the post-war years. In the 1950s approximately two-thirds of the working class voted Labour, and four-fifths of the middle-class voted Conservative.

Since those early post-war years the links between class and party have weakened. Political scientists refer to this process as **dealignment**. What processes have been at work to cause the weakening of class and party links, voter and party links, resulting in greater volatility with a quarter of voters switching their support away from the two major parties? As might be expected of such a complex question, no single theory can explain adequately all the changes that have occurred in recent decades. Various explanations, however, can be grouped into two main types – those sharing the primacy approach and those sharing the recency approach.

The primacy approach: the social basis of voting behaviour

Much human behaviour reflects social divisions. For example, in terms of leisure and cultural behaviour patterns, almost all those attending a rave will be

> **Dealignment** occurs when voters from a particular social class background no longer support the party which traditionally claims to represent the interests of that social class.

Table 9.1 When the voting decision was made in 1997 (per cent)

Question: 'When did you make up your mind how you would vote today?'

	All	*Conservative*	*Labour*	*Lib Dem*
Before election was called	57	58	65	34
Since election was called	18	18	15	25
Within the last week	14	12	10	25
Today	11	11	9	16

Source: Kellner (1997b) p. 619.

young people: far more elderly than young will spend a night at bingo. Only the more affluent in society will be found picnicking at Glyndebourne. Many more men than women go fishing. Can voting behaviour be explained in this way by social divisions – such as age, gender, ethnicity, and class? How far are the very different experiences of individuals living in society reflected in their voting behaviour?

If the way in which individuals vote is an expression of their position in the social structure, then voting would tend to be stable. This is because an individual's sex, ethnicity, etc. is fixed. Of course an individual's voting habits might well change from time to time but such changes that occur do so within an overall pattern of stability. It might be argued, for example, that this stability in voting behaviour was shown in practice by the long period of Conservative government from 1979 to 1997 being achieved on around 42 per cent of the vote in four consecutive election victories.

In order to analyse the loyalties of voters, Richard Rose and Ian McAllister devised a theoretical framework for exploring how a lifetime of learning steadily shapes how an individual might vote (*The Loyalties of Voters*, 1990). A modified version of their framework is shown in Figure 9.1. The process begins with childhood political socialisation, since young children develop attitudes towards authority based on their own experience within the family. Some children will learn about authority in a strict authoritarian family where they are punished if they disobey the rules, whereas others will learn in a more open or democratic family where they may even be involved in making family decisions. Each individual's family is located in the class structure, and so provides a social class identity and value system. All the learning experiences shown in the framework may influence a particular voter, whilst another voter might only be influenced by one or two of the experiences. The framework does not attempt to analyse voting loyalty in terms of one explanation only, but is flexible enough for new findings to be 'hung' on the framework in order to build up a fuller understanding of voting behaviour. A well-known American book, *The American Voter* (1960), influenced political scientists into believing that long-term factors in an individual's life were the most important in influencing his or her vote. The authors, Angus Campbell, Philip E. Converse, Warren E. Miller and Donald E. Stokes, set out a framework similar in principle to Rose and McAllister's but referred to theirs as the 'funnel of causality'.

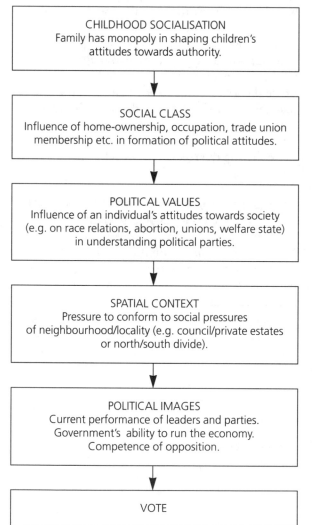

Source: Adapted from Rose and McAllister (1990).

Figure 9.1 A framework for analysis of voting behaviour

Social class and voting behaviour

Of all the social divisions – such as age, gender, ethnicity, and the urban–rural split – it is social class that has preoccupied political scientists. As Table 9.2 indicates, in the early post-war years there was a fairly positive relationship between social class membership and voting behaviour. Political scientists of the time were more interested in the 'class defectors' – the middle-class socialists and the working-class Tories – than they were in the majorities of voters who supported their 'natural' class party. Most research focused on the working-class Tories since this was the most extensive of the deviant behaviour. Did a third of the working class vote Tory because they were **deferential** and preferred being governed by their social superiors? Was society – in the form of the mass media and education – undermining working-class consciousness and thereby confusing a minority of working people as to which political party they ought to support? Had other social processes, such as slum clearance, the decline of occupational communities and the decline in workplace contacts brought about by increasing automation, resulted in weakening the ties for some between class and party? Or, finally, were some workers motivated more than others by affluence and voting Tory on pragmatic or instrumental grounds because they believed they would be better off in material terms under a Conservative government? These were the sort of questions that political scientists posed and set about answering.

During the 1960s and particularly during the 1970s the relationship between class and party weakened. This process of class *dealignment* was reflected in a reduction in Conservative support from the professional and managerial classes and a reduction in Labour support from the working classes. Table 9.3 indicates the voting behaviour of social classes in the 1997 general election.

It can be seen that new Labour's appeal to what journalist dubbed 'Middle Britain' was very successful. Labour increased its support across all social classes, increasing its core support in the working classes as well as among the professional and managerial AB voters and especially among the clerical C1 voters. Pippa Norris described new Labour as 'a catch-all' party with Tony Blair's Labour Party doing much better in constituencies with a high concen-

> **Deference** is an attitude of respect towards social superiors which is not extended to social equals.

Table 9.2 Class percentages voting Labour and Conservative, 1945–58

	AB	C1	C2	DE
Conservative	85	70	35	30
Labour	10	25	60	65

Source: Tapper and Bowles (1982) p. 175.

tration of professional and managerial workers than Neil Kinnock's Labour Party in 1992, and 'while seats with many skilled non-manuals (C1s) swung sharply towards Thatcher in 1979, these areas shifted most strongly towards Labour in the 1990s . . . Labour has triumphed by maintaining its traditional base and yet simultaneously widening its appeal to middle England' (Norris, 1997 p.523). It is possible to interpret Labour's gains in class support and Conservative losses in different ways:

- In terms of the Alford Index (measuring Labour's share of the vote among non-manual voters minus its share among manual workers), 1992 to 1997 saw a drop from 27 to 21 points (Norris, ibid. p. 524). This is the lowest score in any postwar election and represents a continuation in the trend of dealignment.

- It is possible to argue that the pattern of party support from the classes in 1997 has remained much the same, but what has differed is that Labour has gained additional support from every class. In other words, Conservatives still won more support from the professional and managerial classes than Labour and Labour won more working-class support than the Conservatives. The dealignment process has not been reversed in any degree, and remains much the same as in 1992.

- Finally, it can be argued that attempting to identify trends in class support are of limited use since it is not possible to compare like with like. Those who supported Blair's new Labour were voting for a party which was ideologically much closer to the Liberal Democrats or the defunct SDP than to the old 'socialist' Labour Party of the past. The image of new Labour, with its new non-ideological *Clause Four* and weaker links with the unions, is more important in explaining the

Table 9.3 Class voting in the 1997 General Election (per cent)

(change from 1992 shown in brackets)

	All voters	AB	C1	C2	DE
Conservative	31 (–12)	42 (–11)	26 (–22)	25 (–15)	21 (–8)
Labour	44 (+9)	31 (+9)	47 (+19)	54 (+15)	61 (+9)
Liberal Democrat	17 (–1)	21 (0)	19 (–1)	14 (–4)	13 (0)

Source: *The Sunday Times* 4 May 1997.

changes shown in Table 9.3 than any long-term social trend.

The analysis of electoral trends during the 1980s resulted in many political scientists believing that Labour was becoming a northern rather than national party, and in terminal decline. Much research effort was put into analysing Labour's shrinking core vote which, after affluent workers increasingly defected to Thatcherism, comprised, typically, that part of the

---

BOX 9.1
New Labour and Middle England

Middle England is primarily a political invention, an attempt to capture the concerns of those voters who deserted Labour for the Conservatives in the Thatcher era. It is about suburbia, middle-class aspirations, holding down taxation and public expenditure. But it also has a cultural meaning, as the *Daily Mail*, the foremost protagonist of Middle England, knows well.

Middle England is a metaphor for respectability, the nuclear family, heterosexuality, conservatism, whiteness, middle age and the status quo. It is a culture fearful of change and the unknown, which prefers the certainties of the past to the uncertainties of the future.

At the very moment when Britain is displaying an energy which is the envy of many in the western world, our political leaders have their gaze fixed elsewhere, on a culture which is dead from the neck upwards, which is incapable of radicalism and experimentation. In 1964, one at least had the sense that Labour, however vaguely, was on the side of the cultural radicals. In 1997 one cannot – to put it mildly – be sure. The besuited young men of New Labour, respectable to their fingertips (or so they would have us believe), display not a hint of radicalism in their politics, their culture – or their dress.

Source: Extract from Martin Jacques writing in *The Guardian*, 20.2.97

Scottish and northern working class which lived in council houses and had joined a trade union. However, after 1997 journalists speculated whether it was the Conservatives who were now in near-terminal decline, having won their lowest share of the vote since 1832 and the smallest number of MPs since 1906 (see Chapter 8). Labour won 1997 with almost double the largest swing any party had received in postwar general elections. And despite their slight drop in the popular vote, Liberal Democrats returned their biggest number of MPs since 1929. The questions about the future of Labour, crucial in the 1980s, seemed redundant after 1997.

Table 9.4 shows that Labour had strengthened or maintained its core supporters whilst the Conservatives had lost their once traditional core supporters. Labour won back 7 per cent of the trade union vote since 1992. This was particularly significant given the changing nature of trade unionism, with the decline of industrial trade unionism and the rise of white-collar trade unionism. Labour maintained its already high level of support among council tenants. In contrast the Conservatives lost the support of one in four home-owners and one in three mortgage-payers since 1992. Traditionally Conservatives have seen themselves as the 'party of home-ownership' but the hardship many people had experienced during the Major years as a result of high interest rates, negative equity and repossessions led to much support being switched to Labour.

Gender and voting

The pattern of gender and voting has changed considerably over recent years. Writing in 1967 it was possible to argue that 'there is overwhelming

Table 9.4 Social characteristics of voters in 1997 (per cent)

(change from 1992 shown in brackets)

	Trade unionists	Home-owners	Mortgage-payers	Council tenants
Conservative	16 (–9)	39 (–14)	29 (–16)	12 (–8)
Labour	59 (+7)	37 (+10)	46 (+15)	66 (+1)
Liberal Democrat	20 (+2)	17 (–2)	19 (–2)	16 (+4)

Source: Cowling (1997) p. 14 and Kellner (1997b) p. 617; Sunday Times, 4 May 1997.

evidence that women are more Conservatively inclined than men' (Pulzer, 1967, p. 107). There appeared to be sound reasons why this situation existed. Some argued that since women stayed at home more than men, it was natural that their attitudes should be shaped by the traditional values of the family. It was likely that women were more religious and more deferential than men. Also, not having a job meant that such women never experienced industrial conflict at the workplace and so did not value the role of trade unions. All these factors were believed to produce a political outlook amongst women that was more inclined towards supporting Conservatives.

From 1979 onwards the gender gap narrowed until it disappeared in 1987 (see Table 9.5). The great mystery is why it returned in such a marked way in 1992. For Labour campaigned hard in order to win female support, and many of the issues at the top of its political agenda were 'women's issues'. Part of the answer may lie in the different ways different age groups of women voted. In a survey conducted between 1986 and 1988 David Denver and Gordon Hands revealed that a gender gap existed amongst young people, but it represented a reversal of the traditional picture. Boys gave more support (50 per cent) to the Conservatives than girls (35 per cent). It appeared that young males were attracted by Margaret Thatcher's 'macho' image whereas young females were attracted more by Labour's 'caring' image on health and education (surprisingly, attitudes on 'women's issues', such as abortion and divorce, accounted for little difference). In 1997 the gender gap closed as in 1987, but with women showing a 10 per cent swing to Labour compared with 6 per cent for men.

Joni Lovenduski's analysis of the 1997 campaign drew a useful distinction between women's issues (which mainly affect women) and women's perspectives (which are women's views on all political issues). An example of the former is party policy on nursery-school provision; an example of the latter is policy towards the EU, where men focus on issues of sovereignty and the single currency whilst women are more concerned with social rights. Although women do not represent a solid voting bloc whose support is either to be won or lost, all the major parties made some attempt to develop policies for women but it was Labour which 'made a sustained effort to convince women voters' (Lovenduski, 1997, p. 715). But by other measures women played a low profile in the campaign: the presidential nature of the campaigning focused on men; the party manifestos did not feature women's issues to the same extent as such issues had featured in party debates during the years prior to 1997; and a study of TV coverage during a week of the campaign found that

Table 9.5 Sex and party choice in General Elections, 1987–97 (per cent)

		Conservative	Labour	Liberal Democrat
1987	Men	44	33	25
	Women	44	31	25
1992	Men	38	36	19
	Women	44	34	16
1997	Men	31	44	17
	Women	32	44	17

Source: The Guardian, 15 June 1987; Daily Telegraph, 14 April 1992; Sunday Times, 4 May 1997.

Source: *The Observer* 4.5.97

Figure 9.2 Hard stare from Michael Portillo as Labour MP Stephen Twigg acknowledges victory

Table 9.6 The 1997 General Election: party support, by age (percent)

Age	Conservative	Labour	Liberal Democrat
18–29	22	57	17
30–44	26	49	17
45–64	33	43	18
65+	44	34	16

Source: *Sunday Times*, 4 May 1997.

male politicians made 169 appearances compared with 8 for females. The result, however, was a triumph for women with a record 120 female MPs entering the Commons (see Chapter 28).

Age and voting

There has been a long recognised association between increasing age and Conservative support. Why should age be an influence on voting behaviour? It has been argued that for most people property and wealth increase as they grow older, and as their families grow up so aspects of the welfare state become less important to them, resulting in a more Conservative outlook. Others have suggested that age is an influence on voting in terms of 'political generations' passing through the electorate. Each generation forms its views and votes for the first time in a distinct political climate.

Table 9.6 confirms the generalisation with the 65-year-olds and over, being the only age group giving the Conservatives more support than Labour. Of all the age groups, the 65+ swung least from supporting Conservative candidates. This group also swung marginally away from voting Labour compared with 1992, the only age group to do so. Support for Labour was strongest from the youngest group in the electorate – first-time voters – which voted 18

per cent Conservative, 59 per cent Labour and 19 per cent Liberal Democrat (Cowling, 1997, p.14).

Compared with 1992, when voters under 44 voted Conservative and Labour in roughly equal proportions and voters aged 44 and over much preferred the Conservatives, Labour in 1997 enjoyed a much improved position. Peter Kellner speculated on the impact of this age-related pattern on future elections: 'Half of Labour's voters were under 45, whilst half were over 45; however only a third of Conservative voters were under 45, while fully two-thirds were over 45 . . . If past demographic trends continue . . . 1.1 million people who voted Conservative at this year's election are likely to die before the next general election, compared with 800,000 Labour voters . . . Labour will start with a 25% lead among the survivors from 1997 (Kellner, 1997b, p. 617).

Ethnicity and voting

In his book, *Immigration and 'Race' Politics in Post-War Britain* (1992), Zig Layton-Henry made the point that participation by the ethnic minorities in elections can be used as a measure of political integration and support for democratic politics. At the same time, discrimination against ethnic minorities could result in political responses such as apathy, alienation or even rebellion. Others examine the ethnic minority vote in terms of its potential impact on election results. One in twenty Britons comes from an ethnic minority but their votes are concentrated in a limited number of urban, mainly inner-city, constituencies. Some estimates suggest that in

Table 9.7 Asian and Black voting intentions, 1996–7 (percent)

	Asian	Black
Conservative	25	8
Labour	70	86
Liberal Democrat	4	4
Other/undecided/not voting	23	22

Source: Based on Saggar (1997) p. 699.

fear that the 'race card' might be played during the campaign in a desperate bid to exploit anti-immigrant attitudes in order to rebuild Conservative support. In the event such fears were ill-founded. Indeed, the Conservatives made great efforts to woo the Asian vote which included a high-profile tour of India by the party leader, John Major. Table 9.7 suggests that Conservative tactics may have resulted in some success. Conservatives had the support of a quarter of traditionally Labour-supporting Asians, compared with only 10 per cent support from black ethnic minorities.

as many as 49 seats the majority of the sitting MP was less than the local ethnic minority vote.

Tough Conservative legislation on asylum-seekers and immigration debated and passed prior to the 1997 general election led some commentators to

The geography of voting

At the micro-level of political geography, there is an influence on voting behaviour which political scien-

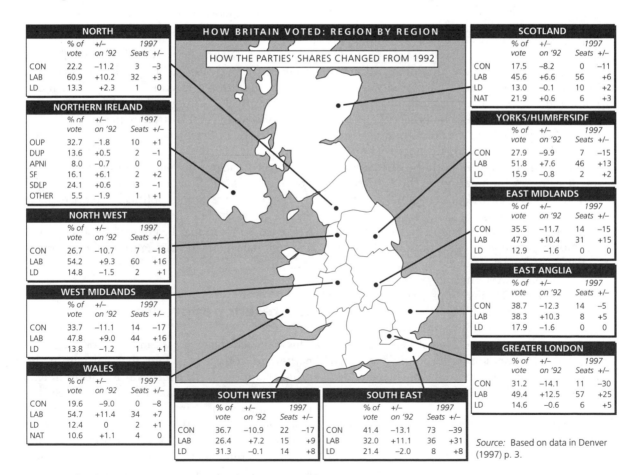

HOW BRITAIN VOTED: REGION BY REGION

HOW THE PARTIES' SHARES CHANGED FROM 1992

NORTH

	% of vote	+/– on '92	1997 Seats	+/–
CON	22.2	–11.2	3	–3
LAB	60.9	+10.2	32	+3
LD	13.3	+2.3	1	0

NORTHERN IRELAND

	% of vote	+/– on '92	1997 Seats	+/–
OUP	32.7	–1.8	10	+1
DUP	13.6	+0.5	2	–1
APNI	8.0	–0.7	0	0
SF	16.1	+6.1	2	+2
SDLP	24.1	+0.6	3	–1
OTHER	5.5	–1.9	1	+1

NORTH WEST

	% of vote	+/– on '92	1997 Seats	+/–
CON	26.7	–10.7	7	–18
LAB	54.2	+9.3	60	+16
LD	14.8	–1.5	2	+1

WEST MIDLANDS

	% of vote	+/– on '92	1997 Seats	+/–
CON	33.7	–11.1	14	–17
LAB	47.8	+9.0	44	+16
LD	13.8	–1.2	1	+1

WALES

	% of vote	+/– on '92	1997 Seats	+/–
CON	19.6	–9.0	0	–8
LAB	54.7	+11.4	34	+7
LD	12.4	0	2	+1
NAT	10.6	+1.1	4	0

SOUTH WEST

	% of vote	+/– on '92	1997 Seats	+/–
CON	36.7	–10.9	22	–17
LAB	26.4	+7.2	15	+9
LD	31.3	–0.1	14	+8

SOUTH EAST

	% of vote	+/– on '92	1997 Seats	+/–
CON	41.4	–13.1	73	–39
LAB	32.0	+11.1	36	+31
LD	21.4	–2.0	8	+8

SCOTLAND

	% of vote	+/– on '92	1997 Seats	+/–
CON	17.5	–8.2	0	–11
LAB	45.6	+6.6	56	+6
LD	13.0	–0.1	10	+2
NAT	21.9	+0.6	6	+3

YORKS/HUMBERSIDE

	% of vote	+/– on '92	1997 Seats	+/–
CON	27.9	–9.9	7	–15
LAB	51.8	+7.6	46	+13
LD	15.9	–0.8	2	+2

EAST MIDLANDS

	% of vote	+/– on '92	1997 Seats	+/–
CON	35.5	–11.7	14	–15
LAB	47.9	+10.4	31	+15
LD	12.9	–1.6	0	0

EAST ANGLIA

	% of vote	+/– on '92	1997 Seats	+/–
CON	38.7	–12.3	14	–5
LAB	38.3	+10.3	8	+5
LD	17.9	–1.6	0	0

GREATER LONDON

	% of vote	+/– on '92	1997 Seats	+/–
CON	31.2	–14.1	11	–30
LAB	49.4	+12.5	57	+25
LD	14.6	–0.6	6	+5

Source: Based on data in Denver (1997) p. 3.

Figure 9.3 How Britain voted in 1997: region by region

tists refer to as the 'neighbourhood effect'. This effect is far too detailed to appear on the map since it occurs within local communities. Essentially it is argued that the dominant characteristic of a community will influence all voters. Denver has stated that 'The more middle-class an area was, then the more Conservative were both middle-class and working-class voters; the more working-class an area the more strongly Labour were both groups of voters . . . Voters, then, tend to conform to the locally dominant political norm' (Denver, 1989, p. 39).

Regional voting emerged as an important factor which contributed to the Conservative defeat in 1997: it took only modest swings against the Conservatives to leave them without a seat in Scotland and Wales, the most important regional factor being 'the swing against them in large parts of the South of England and the Midlands, where they had found strong support during the Thatcher period' (McAllister, 1997 p.641).

Psephologists are interested in the level of support each party receives, since this may vary from one region to the next. They are also interested in the movement of votes between parties between one election and the next. They may calculate national or regional average swings in order to discover patterns of deviation from the norm. In reality there is not a uniform average swing to one party from the others, but much variety in both the direction and scope of swings. Commenting on the 1997 result, McAllister stressed the extent of regional variation:

'The Labour vote ranged from a high of 60.9% in the North of England – a substantial 16.5% higher than the Britain-wide figure – to a low of 26.4% in South West England . . . By contrast, the Conservatives vote varied from lows of 17.5% and 19.6% in Scotland and Wales, respectively . . . to a high of 41.4% in the South East . . . The regional variation in the Liberal Democrat vote was, with the exception of the South West where their support is concentrated, considerably less. (McAllister, 1997, p. 642)

General regional patterns revealed that the North–South divide remains a characteristic of Britain's electoral politics, although it has narrowed still further since 1992: 'The Conservatives were 29.4 per cent behind Labour in the North but 1.9%

Table 9.8 The North–South and urban–rural divides, 1992–7 (percent)

	Conservative 'lead' over Labour		
	North	Midlands	South
1992	−11.7	+7.4	+25.3
1997	−29.4	−13.5	+1.9
Change	−17.7	−20.9	−23.4
	Very urban	Mixed	Rural
1992	−4.9	+14.1	+24.6
1997	−27.3	−5.8	+5.1
Change	−22.4	−19.9	−19.5

Source: Based on Denver (1997) p.6. Note that where the Conservative lead is shown as positive it is a real lead. A negative lead for the Conservatives indicates that in reality Labour is leading.

ahead in the South, with the Midlands falling in between' (Denver, 1997, p. 6). Table 9.8 also reveals that the traditional electoral pattern, of Labour being relatively stronger in urban areas and Conservatives in rural areas, remained in 1997.

The causes of regional variation in voting are complex and related to the different socio-economic structures of the regions in terms of social class composition, levels of affluence, unemployment, social deprivation, etc. Some political scientists have argued that as the links between class and party have weakened, so voters may be influenced more by local and regional factors in shaping their political orientations.

The recency approach

This approach challenges the ideas behind the explanations of voting behaviour that fall within the primacy approach. In other words, the argument that long-term factors influence voting is largely dismissed, and much greater stress is put on the importance of recent events as explanations of voting behaviour. In terms of Figure 9.1 the recency approach would focus on perceptions of parties, leaders, issues, the campaign, and the government's ability to run the economy. These perceptions can,

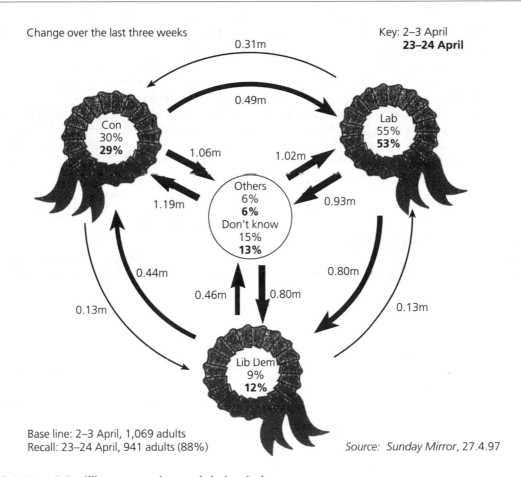

Change over the last three weeks

Key: 2–3 April
23–24 April

Con
30%
29%

Lab
55%
53%

Others
6%
6%
Don't know
15%
13%

Lib Dem
9%
12%

0.31m

0.49m

1.06m

1.02m

1.19m

0.93m

0.44m

0.80m

0.13m

0.46m

0.80m

0.13m

Base line: 2–3 April, 1,069 adults
Recall: 23–24 April, 941 adults (88%)

Source: Sunday Mirror, 27.4.97

Figure 9.4 How 8.5 million voters changed their minds

of course, change quite quickly. A new party leader, a fall in the interest rate or a period of poor industrial relations can result in large swings of support from one party to another. Unlike the primacy approach which embraces lifelong characteristics, such as gender, class and ethnicity, and so focuses on the relative stability of voting behaviour, the recency approach emphasises the volatility of voting behaviour which can result from relatively minor events which occur in politics.

The resounding electoral victory of new Labour, with its new constitution, new policies and new leader, swept to power on a 10 per cent national swing suggests that primacy explanations of voting behaviour is no longer particularly useful. However, it is counter-argued that Labour's victory was not the result of an electoral tidal wave of changed voting – only one in three of the electorate voted Labour – but the result of tactical voting and the electoral system

effect (see Chapter 8) which gave Labour a landslide in seats. The primacy approach continues to make the point that Conservative governments throughout the 1980s and 1992 were elected on a stable 42 per cent of the popular vote. Also, Labour's victory was not a sudden or unexpected event since opinion polls had been reflecting Labour's growing popularity during the five years prior to the general election.

These arguments are dismissed by political scientists who support the recency approach. The similar levels of support won by the Conservatives in 1979, 1983, 1987 and 1992 does not mean that it was the same people voting for them at each election. A great deal of 'churn' takes place which is not revealed in simple statistics. Figure 9.4 illustrates the degree of churn which occurred during a three-week period in the 1997 campaign when an estimated 8.5 million voters changed their minds about how they would vote. Yet during this three-week period the total level of support received by the major parties appeared fairly stable. A quarter of all voters made their final decision on which party to support in the final week of the campaign or on election day itself. In other words, unlike the primacy approach, the recency approach does not reveal an analysis of electoral stability. Rather the balance of support between the major parties is identified as being highly unstable, with support swinging from one party to another in response to economic events, personalities, political images, etc.

The image of the party leader

With the growth in the importance of television in political communication, and the emphasis on 'spin control' by the parties in order to project the most favourable image, are voters now influenced principally by their judgements on party leaders? Was there a 'Blair effect' in 1997 whereby a vote for Labour really meant a vote for Tony Blair as Prime Minister? In other words, was the 1997 general election in reality a presidential battle fought between Major, Blair and Ashdown?

Some political commentators do not believe that the image of the party leader is so crucial in influencing voters. Only if there is not much to choose between the parties in terms of policies will the qualities of their respective leaders become more important to voters. Also, they argue, the experience of past elections shows that unpopular leaders can win. For example, in 1970 Labour Prime Minister Harold Wilson with a 51 per cent approval rating was far more popular than Conservative leader Edward Heath with only 28 per cent approval. Yet Heath won the 1970 general election.

Pollsters found that in 1997 only 7 per cent of voters believed that the party leader was their main reason for voting as they did, the same percentage as in 1992 (Cowling, 1997, p. 14). The 'approval ratings' for the respective party leaders rose and fell during the weeks of the campaign. When asked mid-way during the campaign who would make best prime minister, 35 per cent answered Blair, 28 per cent Major and 22 per cent Ashdown (the *Guardian*, 16 April 1997). The final election day figures were, however, very close to party shares of the popular vote, with Blair thought best by 47 per cent, Major

by 33 per cent and Ashdown by 20 per cent (Kellner, 1997b, p. 626).

Peter Kellner also found that Conservatives were more loyal to Major (89 per cent) than Labour supporters to Blair (84 per cent). While only 5 per cent of Conservatives felt that Ashdown would make the best prime minister, 12 per cent of Labour supporters held this opinion. At the same time, 30 per cent Liberal Democrats thought that Blair would make the best premier.

Party images

The Conservatives in government had experienced a number of image problems ranging from sleaze, a leadership crisis, and party indiscipline, to incompetence on policies such as sterling and the ERM and BSE ('mad cow disease'). Conservative ex-Chancellor, Norman Lamont, struck a chord with many in his party when he accused the government of giving the impression of 'being in office but not in power'. A private party poll of 'natural Tory voters', leaked to the press in a memorandum written by the party's deputy chairman, John Maples, revealed that they perceived the government as 'ineffectual and unable to deliver its promises'. These general feelings of dissatisfaction with the Conservatives were reflected in a poll total of 67 per cent which agreed 'it's time for a change' (Kellner, 1997b p. 620).

The Maples memorandum concluded its grim news for the Conservative leadership with the warning that 'if Blair turns out to be as good as he looks, we have a problem'. Up to and during the election campaign, Conservative strategists were in two minds on how best to deal with the electoral threat posed by new Labour and Blair. A message based on 'New Labour, New Danger', featuring Labour politicians with superimposed demon eyes, conveyed that under the superficial PR gloss of Labour lurked a more sinister party. This propaganda was at odds, however, with Blair's new Labour accused of stealing traditional Conservative policies. Here Labour was not projected as a party of demons but as an inadequate imitation of the Conservatives.

Tony Blair continued and accelerated the modernisation of Labour begun by Neil Kinnock and John Smith. A new party constitution and acceptance of much of the market-based Thatcherite agenda resulted in the emergence of 'new' Labour. Labour had drawn ideas not just from the Conservatives, but from American Democrats where Clinton's political renewal had successfully won back the support of the 'Reagan Democrats', an approximate US equivalent of the 'Thatcherite C2s'.

Labour's campaign was boosted by the support of the biggest selling tabloids as well as by a massive telephone campaign. Here Labour party workers in safe Northern constituencies could canvass electors in marginal seats many hundreds of miles away. Labour's attempt to win the support of 'Middle Britain' with its new image appeared successful insofar as one poll found that 69 per cent felt Labour was 'good for all classes' whereas only 31 per cent felt that Conservatives were best (Kellner, 1997b, p. 627).

Can issue preferences explain voting behaviour?

New issues can arise on the political agenda which do not fit into the traditional class interests of the parties, and can therefore blur the lines linking party and voter. For example, advocates and opponents of nuclear power development cross party lines causing divisions amongst trade unionists in particular. The miners have an interest in actually closing existing nuclear power stations, whilst workers in the nuclear power industry support its expansion. The issue of Britain's role inside the European Union has caused deep divisions within and between the major parties as well as within public opinion at large. Moral issues, such as the abortion issue or health education, can become salient issues which have little relation to party positions and are better understood in terms of authoritarian or libertarian orientations.

With the weakening of class influences on voting and the emergence of new issues which did not fit traditional partisan splits, some political scientists argued that an increasing number of the electorate were voting on the basis of issue preferences. Mark Franklin found, for example, that the effect of voters deciding which party to vote for according to issue preferences more than doubled between 1964 and 1983 (Franklin, 1985). Some political scientists argued that Labour's electoral defeats between 1979 and 1992 were accounted for in part because its

policies were no longer popular, even with its long-standing supporters. For example, Ivor Crewe considered that trends in public opinion revealed a quite exceptional movement of opinion away from Labour's traditional positions amongst Labour supporters over the past twenty or thirty years. There has been a spectacular decline in support for the 'collectivist trinity' of public ownership, trade union power and social welfare.

A 'consumer model' of voting behaviour has been constructed by H. Himmelweit and colleagues which is derived from an issue-based theory of voting (Himmelweit et al., 1984). Voters 'shop around' to find the party with a programme of policies which offers the closest fit to their own policy preferences. Of course, voters may not have perfect information about various parties' policies, and even when they do have the relevant information, they may suspect that a party, if elected to office, would not implement its manifesto proposals. Although past studies showed that party support could be predicted with 80 per cent accuracy from consumer preferences, the 1987 general election raised some doubts about seeing voters as analogous to shoppers in the political market-place. As Ivor Crewe commented in the *Guardian*, 'Labour's poor performance remains a puzzle because its campaign did succeed in placing its favourable issues much further up the agenda than in 1983 . . . Had electors voted solely on the main issues Labour would have won' (the *Guardian*, 16 June 1987).

However, the 1992 general election once again raised the possibility that issue-voting was an important factor which explained aspects of voting behaviour such as party choice and volatility. Although Labour succeeded in pushing some of its campaign issues – such as health, pensions and transport – well up amongst those the electorate saw as important, the top issues were inflation and taxation which lay at the heart of the Conservative's 'double whammy' propaganda drive.

In the 1997 campaign, Labour neutralised any repeat of the Conservatives' 'double whammy' by stating that a future Labour government would accept Conservative spending limits and not raise income tax. Indeed, after their tax-raising government it was now the Conservatives who were vulnerable on the tax issue. According to Mori, the top six important issues in the minds of electors were

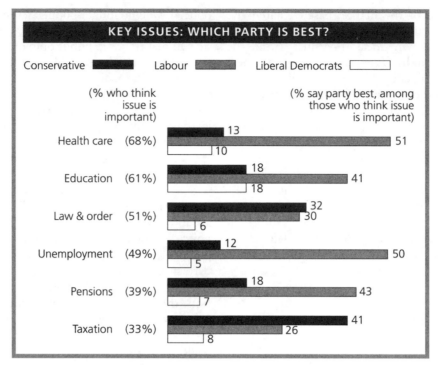

Source: MORI poll in The Times, 10.4.97

Figure 9.5 Top six key issues: which party is best?

health care (68 per cent), education (61 per cent), law and order (51 per cent), unemployment (49 per cent), pensions (39 per cent), and taxation (33 per cent). As Figure 9.5 indicates, on all but law and order where Conservatives enjoyed a small lead, and taxation, the sixth issue, Labour had substantial leads. Labour was successful in ensuring that its traditional issues were amongst the most important election issues, and had big leads on four of the six biggest issues. Unlike the situation Ivor Crewe described in 1983, had electors voted on the main issues in 1997 then this would help explain Labour's victory in the popular vote.

An econometric explanation of voting preference

Relatively minor events, such as a public sector strike or movements in inflation and interest rates, will have an undue influence on a volatile electorate. In the language of journalists, such events will cause the electorate to either 'feel good' or 'feel bad'. David Sanders analysed the relationship between public support for the government and changes in the key 'feel good' economic factors. He found that there was a time-lag of three to four months between voters experiencing improved economic conditions and a decision to change the party they were supporting. Using past patterns of the 'feel good' factor and government support as well as economic forecasts, Sanders predicted in August 1991 an outcome which was very close to the actual result in April 1992.

It can be argued that John Major lost the 1997 general election on 16 September 1992 when, after an international loss of confidence in sterling, Britain was forced to withdraw from the ERM. Public perceptions of the Conservatives' competence to manage the economy were dented and never recovered sufficiently to deliver a fifth consecutive election victory. Sanders's statistical analysis showed that after the ERM crisis 'the competence graph plunges downwards and continues to trend downwards thereafter' (Sanders, 1995, p. 161).

Withdrawal from the straitjacket of the ERM resulted in a sustained economic recovery. By January 1997 regular monthly falls in unemployment figures brought the total below 2 million, inflation was at 2.7 per cent, and interest rates had fallen to 6 per cent. Conventional political wisdom would have predicted that a grateful electorate, now 'feeling good', would have rewarded John Major's government with another term in office. However, this was not to be the case. As Gavin and Sanders explain, the government was forced to drop all the arguments in favour of Britain being in the ERM in order to get low inflation and economic growth since Britain was now enjoying these conditions outside the ERM. Indeed, it was the countries remaining in the ERM which were suffering from rising unemployment, public spending cuts and slow growth:

Indeed in the wake of Black Wednesday, the government was obliged to argue that economic growth could best be achieved by Britain's remaining outside the ERM. Such a policy U-turn, without a plausible story to justify it, engendered a loss of public confidence in the government's managerial capabilities. (Gavin and Sanders, 1997, p. 633)

Measuring public opinion

Many politicians believe that they can measure public opinion informally by reading newspapers, talking to party workers or listening to the views of their constituents. There are also more 'scientific' methods that are used by party managers who measure the response of the public to numerous aspects of their party's image. In terms of measuring the level of public support a party enjoys, local election (and local by-election) results can provide a guide. Opinion polls provide greater flexibility in measuring public attitudes since they can be conducted any time. Newspapers and TV sponsor pollsters such as Mori, Gallup, NOP, ICM and Harris to carry out research. Many published findings report on the general level of support for each of the main parties based on answers from a representative sample of around a thousand people. The sample, balanced in terms of social class, sex, age and region to represent the electorate as a whole, is asked which party it would vote for if there was an election.

In some countries, opinion polls have been banned in the last days of the election campaign on the grounds that they interfere with the way people vote. The effects of polls can vary according to particular circumstances, but a 'bandwagon effect' can result from more and more people supporting a party because they want to see its support increase still further. Or if one party has a large lead in the polls there can be a 'boomerang effect' on election day as overconfident voters stay at home because the polls have convinced them their party is going to win.

Predicting how the whole electorate will vote from the responses of a small sample of electors is bound to include a margin of error. This is usually estimated at 3 per cent plus or minus the published finding. Occasionally a 'rogue' poll may be published which is based on faulty fieldwork and it will be far out of line with the results from other polls. In any election the most accurate poll is likely to be an 'exit' poll on election day which asks voters which way they *actually* voted rather than which way they *intend* to vote.

During the 1992 general election campaign pollsters consistently predicted that the outcome would be a hung parliament, with most predicting that Labour would be the largest party. The fact that the Conservatives won with a respectable majority was the cause of considerable embarrassment for the polling organisations. Inquests into 'why did the pollsters get it wrong?' revealed a number of possible problems in both the fieldwork stage of collecting people's opinions and later in interpreting the results. An enquiry by the polling organisations into why they had failed to forecast a Conservative victory found:

- The sampling quotas did not match the composition of the electorate since they contained too few middle-class interviewees. Those organisations which used quotas, such as Mori and ICM, drew up more sophisticated quotas in order to better reflect the stratification of the electorate.
- Older Conservative supporters appeared more reluctant than their Labour counterparts to disclose their voting intentions face-to-face to an interviewer. ICM attempted to overcome this by experimenting with respondents completing a secret mock ballot form not seen by the inter-

Table 9.9 Opinion polls and 1997 General Election result (percent)

Pollster	Final opinion polls					Poll of polls	Exit polls		Final result
	Harris	NOP	ICM	Gallup	MORI		MORI	NOP	
Con	31	28	33	33	29	31	30	29	31
Lab	48	50	43	47	47	47	46	47	45
Lib Dem	15	14	18	14	19	15	18	18	17
Others	6	8	6	6	5	7	6	6	7
Av error	1.5	3.0	1.5	2.0	2.0	1.0	1.0	1.5	–

Source: New Statesman, May 1997.

viewer. Later ICM, along with Gallup, adopted random telephone polling. Respondents are more likely to be candid to an unseen interviewer than during a face-to-face interview.

- There was a late swing to the Conservatives in 1992 which most pollsters missed.

Pollsters also adjusted their findings in order to increase their accuracy. Respondents were asked to recall how they voted in the last general election, and the whole sample was adjusted to match the actual vote in 1992. Table 9.9 shows that pollsters have done much to repair the damage done to their reputation by their poor performance in 1992. It can be seen that there is still a tendency to overestimate the Labour vote and underestimate the Conservative vote, but that overall the margins of error are quite small.

Although the pollsters celebrated their improved performance in 1997, some critics pointed out that they still had problems with their methods. Using average errors during the campaign, one poll still overestimated Labour's lead by 9 per cent; 44 polls published during the campaign predicted that Labour would win by a bigger margin than it did; had the 1997 general election been a closer contest, the pollsters would have got it wrong again. Finally, because of increased variation in constituency swings and greater tactical voting, it was argued that pollsters must pay greater attention in converting the 'popular support' percentages into parliamentary seats.

Summary

- During the postwar years, there has been a declin-

ing attachment of voters to parties, and a subsequent increase in the volatility of voting behaviour. There has been a decline in the class basis of voting.

- Models of class and gender socialisation and issue-based consumerism add to our understanding of voting behaviour although each explanation has weaknesses which limit its explanatory power.
- Labour's landslide victory in 1997 was more in terms of seats won in Parliament than its share of the popular vote.
- Turnout was low and there were large regional variations in party support, with Conservatives winning no representation in Scotland and Wales.
- There was increased tactical voting, which helped the Liberal Democrats win twenty-eight extra seats on a smaller vote.
- Some political scientists felt that the seeds of the Conservative defeat were sown on Black Wednesday in 1992 when the government lost its reputation for competence in managing the economy.
- Pollsters did better in predicting the final outcome in 1997 than in 1992, although the tendency to overestimate Labour support and underestimate Conservative support was still evident.

Questions

1. Evaluate the usefulness of the primacy and recency approaches in explaining voting behaviour.
2. Describe and account for the changing relationship between class and voting.

3. During early postwar elections 'to know the swing in Cornwall was to know, within a percentage or two, the swing in Caithness' (I. Crewe). To what extent was this the case in 1997?

4. 'Having a successful economic policy guarantees the re-election of the government.' Discuss this assertion.

5. Comment on the performance of the opinion polls during the 1997 general election campaign.

Assignment

Assignment (1)
Myth of the missing voters

'They say: the Conservatives were trounced on election day chiefly because two million Tory supporters stayed at home. They say: the Referendum Party's 800,000 votes came almost entirely from the Tories and cost them a number of key marginals. They say: next time, all these voters will flock back to the Tories, so the task of regaining power is not nearly as great as it seems.

I say: rubbish. All elections are apt to produce myths; but the myth of the missing Tories has acquired a special potency during the past fortnight . . . as many as 3.1 million people who voted Tory in 1992 switched to a different party this time: 1.4 million to Labour, 1.2 million to the Lib Dems, 400,000 to the Referendum Party and 200,000 to nationalists and other minority parties. Against that, the Tories gained only 500,000 votes from other parties.

It is these figures that Tory strategists need to attend to as they seek to rebuild their party, not the reduced turnout. That is a red herring. Turnout fell in every kind of seat and among every kind of voter.

Did the Referendum Party's 800,000 votes come almost entirely from ex-Tories?

No. According to the NOP/BBC exit poll, 45 per cent of people who backed the Referendum Party this time recalled voting Tory in 1992; 18 per cent recalled voting Labour, 11 per cent were ex-Liberal Democrat, 4 per cent came from other parties, and 12 per cent from those who did not vote in 1992. This leaves 9 per cent who could not remember, or refused to say, how they voted in 1992.

These figures show that ex-Tories did provide the biggest single pool of Referendum Party voters; but about half came from elsewhere. Furthermore, it is wrong to assume that these ex-Tories would have voted Conservative had the Referendum Party not existed. There is no evidence that the Tory–Labour swing was any higher in seats with Referendum candidates than elsewhere.

Source: extracts from Peter Kellner's article in *The Observer*, 18 May 1997.

Questions

(i) Peter Kellner argues that 1997 has already produced two 'election myths.' Identify both of them.

(ii) Outline the reasons given why Conservative losses were not caused by support moving to the Referendum Party.

(iii) Why does the author advise Tory strategists not to concentrate overly on low turnout as the reason for their party's defeat?

(iv) What advice would you give the Conservative Party in order for it to regain lost ground in the next general election?

Assignment (2)

Advantage Labour

Gallup asked voters which party would handle each problem best. Figures below are proportions of voters replying Conservative in each case minus proportions replying Labour. Conservative leads are given in minus proportions replying Labour. Conservative leads are given in black on white. Labour leads in white on black. The right-hand column reports the change in Labour's favour.

	1992	1997	Change
Defence	35	12	+23
Relations with Europe	27	-3	+20
Strikes, industrial disputes	17	-4	+21
Law and order	16	-11	+27
Inflation and prices	14	2	+12
Taxation	10	-9	+19
Environment	5	-15	+20
Education, schools	-12	-26	+14
Pensions	-16	-26	+10
Unemployment	-22	-29	+7
National Health Service	-26	-40	+14
Unity of the United Kingdom	na	-2	
High standards in public life	na	-24	

Source: Daily Telegraph, 10 April 1997

Questions

(i)   On what issue did Labour make the biggest gain in public support since 1992?

(ii) Identify the issues in the 1997 campaign which voters believe would be dealt with best by a Conservative Government.

(iii) Some issues are more electorally important than others. Using your own knowledge, identify the most important four issues in the mind of the electorate.

(iv) Using the table as well as your own knowledge, assess the impact of issue-voting in the 1997 general election.

Further reading

Cowling, David (1997) 'A Landslide without Illusions' *New Statesman*, May special edition, pp. 12–14 is a stimulating journalistic account of the 1997 general election. Curtice, John (1997) 'Anatomy of a Non-Landslide', *Politics Review*, 7:1, Sept. pp. 2–8 is an academic account of Labour's victory. Denver, David (1994) *Elections and Voting Behaviour in Britain,* (Hemel Hempstead: Harvester Wheatsheaf) gives a comprehensive account of the theory of voting used to explain election outcomes, and Denver, David (1997) 'The 1997 General Election Results', *Talking Politics*, 10: 1 autumn, pp. 2–8 is an academic account which summarises the main lessons to be drawn from the 1997 general election.

CHAPTER **10** | # Pressure groups

Pressure groups are important institutions in modern democratic societies. They cover a broad spectrum, from the large business in high-level contacts at national government and European level to the smallest local group, and embrace an equally wide range of activities, from the secret, behind-the-scenes consultations of the sectional interest to the highly visible operations of the road protesters. More people belong to pressure groups than to political parties. Study of the groups and their influence is therefore vital to an understanding of how the political system works. Starting with a definition and some leading examples of pressure groups, this chapter analyses their role in the political system and considers key recent trends in their activities before moving to a consideration of their targets for influence and the factors on which that influence depends. There follows a discussion of the debate on 'pressure groups and democracy'. The chapter concludes with a consideration of pressure groups and New Labour.

What are pressure groups?

Pressure groups, like parties, are informal political institutions which seek to influence the making and implementation of public policy. However, pressure groups are unlike parties in (at least) three important

respects. First, they do not normally contest elections. Second, when they do stand for election, they do not do so with the aim of forming a government or part of a government (like the nation-wide parties) or even of changing the constitution (like the nationalist parties) but to make a political point, by indicating the level of public concern on an issue (e.g. the environment) or by drawing support away from the government on a key issue like Sir James Goldsmith's Referendum Party. Third, pressure groups typically have narrower concerns than parties. They generally contribute selectively to the political debate from a particular standpoint or in a specific field of concern; they do not adopt a comprehensive programme which seeks to cover the whole field of politics, as parties do.

Although not normally aiming to exercise power directly or adopting an all-embracing perspective, however, pressure groups do share some characteristics with parties. In particular, they are agencies of *representation* and *participation:* they are mechanisms for the expression of people's interests and opinions and for popular involvement in politics. Also, even though they are not elected to it, they often play an important role in *government,* wielding influence through hundreds of regulatory and supervisory bodies which depend on the groups' cooperation to function at all. Finally, pressure groups can sometimes overlap with parties in important ways: for example, by providing funds, sponsoring candidates and enjoying a large amount of constitutionally

> **Pressure group**: any organisation which – normally working through lobbying rather than standing for office – seeks to influence public policy and decisions at local, national, European or international levels usually within a particular, quite limited sphere.

sanctioned influence in shaping their policies, as, for example, the trade unions do in the Labour Party.

Types of pressure group

Two main approaches to characterising pressure groups have been developed: the first describes groups in terms of *what they represent,* the second in terms of *their strategies and relations with government.*

The first approach distinguishes two main types of pressure group: (1) sectional (or interest) groups; and (2) cause (or promotional) groups.

Sectional groups arise out of the performance of an economic function: they exist to further the interests of people as engaged in certain professions, trades and occupations – as, for example, teachers, shopkeepers, miners and company directors. Examples of sectional groups are the Confederation of British Industry, the Trades Union Congress, the British Medical Association, the Law Society and the National Union of Teachers.

Cause groups in contrast come into existence to promote some belief, attitude or principle. They are also referred to as attitude, ideological or preference groups. Examples are Greenpeace, the Child Poverty Action Group, Amnesty International, Shelter and Charter 88.

There are two main differences between the two types of group. First, whereas membership of a sectional group is limited to those with a shared background, membership of a cause group is open to all those sharing the same values. Second, whereas the purpose of the sectional group is to protect the interests of its own members, the aim of the cause group is generally to advance the public welfare as perceived by its members.

Although largely valid, the distinction between sectional and cause groups is not an absolute one. First, sectional groups may pursue causes: the British Medical Association, for example, as well as acting as a sectional professional interest on behalf of the terms and conditions of service of doctors also campaigns on more general health issues such as drinking, smoking and the safety of boxing. Second,

whilst in terms of their overall goals and motives many groups are clearly cause groups, such groups also often have material interests to defend. A charity such as Oxfam, for example, owns property, employs professional staff with careers to advance, and, although as a charity precluded from engaging in overt political activity, needs to ensure that changes in the tax law do not impede its fund-raising activities. Finally, some groups are difficult to classify as either sectional or cause: protest groups, for instance, often have some features of each, local Nimby (Not in my Backyard) groups being both altruistic and protective of an interest.

Despite these complications, the straightforward classification of groups into sectional and cause remains important, valuable and widely used. However, increasingly employed instead or in addition to this typology are the categories **insider** and **outsider**, which Wyn Grant has developed (Grant, 1995, p. 15).

One important virtue of this typology is that it sets groups firmly within *a relationship with government.* It refers both to the *strategy* pursued by a group- whether or not it seeks acceptance by government- and to the *status* achieved or not achieved as a result of its efforts. This classification cuts across the sectional/cause distinction. Whilst it is probable that most insiders are sectional groups, it is also the case that not all sectional groups will be insiders. Also, cause groups can gain insider status, e.g. MENCAP and the Howard League for Penal Reform. The line between 'insider' and 'outsider' status is not an unchanging one and in practice is often crossed. This is first because classic insider groups such as the British Medical Association do not hesitate to campaign publicly when occasion demands – that is, they adopt a combination of insider and outsider tactics. Second, groups move into and out of insider status: Grant cites the National Federation of Retirement Pensions Associations as a group which has lost insider status.

Finally, the distinction needs to be made between *primary groups* whose only reason for existence is

---

Sectional groups are based on the performance of an economic function whereas **cause groups** are based on a shared attitude or values.

Insider groups are consulted on a regular basis by government whilst **outsider groups** either do not want to become closely involved with government or are unable to gain government recognition.

political lobbying and *secondary groups* which are not primarily political. Examples of primary groups include professional lobbying companies, national cause groups such as Charter 88, specific issue groups such as Doctors for Tobacco Law(against TV advertising), one-off national campaigns such as the Campaign to save Radio 4 Longwave, and local amenity and 'nimby' groups. Secondary groups include the churches, the universities, trade unions, the motoring organisations and charities. Their main purposes are respectively religious, educational, economic, motoring and charitable but they all from time to time make political repesentations on behalf of their members.

Pressure politics

The term 'pressure' can describe a type of activity as well as a kind of organisation. All institutions whatever their purpose are subject to attempts at influencing their activities by individuals and groups. Pressure groups themselves are not immune: an example is the division of opinion within the National Trust on the attempt by radicals to get the institution to ban stag-hunting on Trust land. All this activity may be termed 'pressure politics', even if these groups within an organisation are impermanent, fluctuating in membership and relatively transient. This chapter focuses on the pressure exercised by pressure groups as organisations but it is worth remembering that the goals and policies they pursue are normally the consequence of pressure politics within the groups themselves.

Pressure groups and the political system

This section deals first with the analytical models which help us understand the role of pressure groups in politics (Box 10.1) and second, with the ideological perceptions which have helped to shape that role (Box 10.2). The broad distinction to be made here is that Box 10.1 examines *analytical* theories of pressure groups, i.e. those which set out to describe and explain their activities, whilst Box 10.2 considers *normative* theories of pressure groups, i.e. those which seek to recommend a particular set of political relationships. It is worth noting that quite often

theories can be used in both senses – analytical and normative, to refer both to what is and what ought to be. For example, pluralism both describes and prescribes pressure group behaviour, being a leading analysis of the actual role of groups in the political system and also a term of approval employed by liberals for the system described in the analysis. Similarly, corporatism can be used both to describe the system of group–government relationships prevalent in the 1960s and 1970s and to refer to the approving attitude to such relationships ('prescriptive corporatism') taken by both Labour and Conservative Governments at that time (see further, Grant, 1995, pp. 27–8).

History and recent trends

Before 1939, although a large number of well-organised *sectional* groups already existed, it was relatively uncommon for groups to develop close relations with government. However, the wartime needs of the state, especially for higher production in industry and agriculture and for an emergency hospital service, made it dependent on group cooperation and close government–group relations developed in a number of fields (Smith, 1995, pp. 31–3). The post-1945 period saw a continuation and expansion of such relationships as well as a considerable growth in the activities of pressure groups. There have been three main phases: (1) 1945–1960s; (2) 1960s–1970s; (3) 1980s–1990s.

1945–1960s

The close wartime relationship between government and pressure groups continued and developed in the postwar period. It became recognised practice for governments to consult groups before making decisions affecting their interests and a widely accepted norm that they *should* do so. The consolidation and extension of this relationship occurred because the new responsibilities assumed by government – particularly with regard to management of the economy and the welfare state – created a situation of mutual dependence between government and groups. Governments sought the advice and cooperation of interested groups in order to be able to carry out their policies effectively and with the minimum of

BOX 10.1

Pressure groups and the political system: the main models

Model	Features	Comments
Pluralism	• Decision-making in modern democracies is a process of continuous interaction between a wide range of groups and governing institutions at all levels • Groups have unequal resources but no group becomes completely dominant. This is because: (1) groups counter-balance each other e.g. the CBI is offset by the TUC, pro-abortion groups by anti-abortion groups; (2) no group attempts influence in more than a limited area; hence its influence will be counterbalanced by that of another group elsewhere; (3) membership of groups overlaps e.g. workers and consumers so that it is in no group's interest to become completely dominant; (4) even if an interest is not organised a 'potential' for organisation makes government wary of threatening it.	• Main approach to study of pressure groups and still more comprehensive than rivals • Criticised for overestimating both the ease with which groups can be formed and the accessibility of the political system to groups • Criticism that it underestimates the power of capital has led to formulation of theory of neo-pluralism recognising superior resources of business • Large-scale expansion of cause groups since 1960s supports pluralist theory.
Corporatism	• System of consultation (also, especially in its British form, called tripartism or neo-corporatism) between government and major sectional groups over economic policy • The process arose out of the need of governments which required the cooperation of the main representative groups of business (the Confederation of British Industry) and the unions (Trades Union Congress) for the successful implementation of counter-inflationary prices and incomes policies. In return for consultation, the CBI and TUC were required to ensure the compliance of their members to agreed policies.	• Limited as a general theory because applies only to producer groups and to fairly short phase of history ended by Conservatives in 1979 • Post-Thatcher Governments unlikely to return to neo-corporatist relations with CBI and TUC.
Policy Networks	• Developed in the late 1970s by the political scientists J. J. Richardson and G. Jordan out of the pluralist notion of distinct issue areas • Policy-making in modern government is compartmentalised in a series of separate areas based on government departments, each of which has a distinct pattern of relationships between civil servants and groups. • The concept of policy networks is a generic term denoting a continuum of relationships from *policy communities* to *issue networks* • Policy communities involve close, stable relationships between government officials and a relatively small number of groups, with participants usually sharing the same ideology • Issue networks at the opposite end of the continuum are characterised by a larger number of groups, relatively open access to groups, less close, more discontinuous group – official relationships, and greater conflict over policy and values.	• Widely accepted as accurate picture of decision-making in government departments in Britain • Fits in well with insider/outsider group concept developed by Grant • Criticised as rather static model, more useful for describing existing networks than for explaining how they emerge or change.

conflict whilst groups needed to lobby government to ensure that their members' interests were taken into account when decisions affecting them were made. Accordingly, pressure groups – especially *sectional* groups – became better organised and acquired larger memberships. Particularly strong relationships developed between government and pressure groups in agriculture, health and industrial relations. Functional representation (the representation of sectional interests) developed alongside the more traditional system of parliamentary representation in the postwar era not solely because it suited the mutual interests of governments and producer groups but also because it fitted in with the ethos of the two major parties. Both Labour and the Conservatives had collectivist rather than individualist theories of representation: both saw it as legitimate for important social and economic interests such as business and the trade unions to seek influence not only within the parties themselves but also directly at the level of government.

1960s and 1970s

This phase brought two main changes: the development of the relationship between government and the main economic groups into a neo-corporatist one; and a considerable expansion of the numbers and memberships of cause groups.

(i) *Neo-corporatism*. A very close relationships between government and the leading producer groups developed, with the latter involved in both the formulation and the implementation of policy. Neo-corporatism was largely a product of the need of government to increase economic growth and maintain price stability against a background of comparative economic decline, rising inflation and increasing trade union militancy. Key areas of 'tripartite' government–CBI–TUC consultation were economic growth and prices and incomes policies. Having helped to make 'deals' with government on such matters as prices and incomes policy, the representative business and trade union organisations were required to 'sell' these deals to their members,

---

Neo-corporatism: a weak variant of corporatism which appeared in Britain in the 1960s and 1970s. It denotes the practice of close consultation between government, business and trade unions over economic policy and in particular the making of bargains, e.g. over prices and incomes restraint, which the producer groups were required to keep by ensuring the compliance of their members (also referred to as tripartism).

---

i.e. ensure their compliance. The major indications of the neo-corporatist relations prevalent between 1961 and 1979 were:

- The establishment of key institutions of tripartite economic cooperation such as the National Economic Development Council (NEDC) and the more shortlived National Incomes Commission (NIC). The NEDC provided a forum for government to discuss economic problems and possible solutions with the CBI and TUC.
- The frequent appearance of the main producer groups at 'No.10' in top-level consultations aimed at, e.g., averting or ending strikes.
- Government arrangements with business or the unions which went beyond prior consultation on policy, such as the 1976 Budget which made income tax cuts dependent on the success of pay talks with the TUC on Stage 2 of the government's wage restraint policy.

Although neo-corporatism had the effect of politicising industrial relations and economic policymaking, its overall impact was limited first by the fact that the Treasury remained in control of economic policy and second by the fact that the main producer groups, especially the unions, had relatively weak central bodies (the CBI and TUC) which found it difficult and sometimes impossible to enforce national agreements on their members.

(ii) *The expansion of cause groups*. In this period, joining a cause group or enlisting in a new social movement became for many people a more effective way of achieving a desired political end than joining a political party. As membership of the two major political parties declined, membership of pressure groups (and of the smaller parties) increased. People were attracted to a wide range of causes and movements:feminism, anti-nuclear protest, the relief of poverty and deprivation, environmentalism, and international aid and rights. Much of this upsurge of activity took place at local level. Some groups such as tenants' associations, neighbourhood councils and 'nimbies' ('not in my backyard' protesters) have a naturally local context. But, in addition, many new social movements such as the Campaign for Nuclear Disarmament, environmentalism and women's liberation have a participant ethos and decentralised structure which encourages local membership.

BOX 10.2

Pressure groups and the political system: the main ideological approaches

Model	Features	Comments
Liberal	• Pressure groups essential to democracy because embody fundamental principle of freedom of association • Pressure groups contribute to civil society by providing additional methods of participation and representation (to political parties); vital intermediary institutions and agencies which help protect the individual against an over-mighty state; and the means by which the intensity of public feeling on issues can be expressed. • Improve government by increasing information at its disposal and bringing new issues on to the political agenda. • Sympathetic to groups advocating individual and minority rights, constitutional reform, internationalism and environmentalism.	• The normative side of pluralism: i.e. where pluralism *analyses society* in terms of the division of power amongst competing groups, liberals endorse this situation • Most influential ideology on role of groups in a democratic society • Has penetrated all except radical socialist (Marxist) ideologies.
Democratic Socialist	• Accepts liberal view of groups as playing valuable role in democratic society • Democratic socialist Labour governments helped develop corporatism in 1960s and 1970s engaging in regular tripartite consultations with business and unions; a key point was 'social contract' with unions (1974) by which Labour agreed to maintain living standards in return for wage restraint by the unions • Special sympathy for trade unions whose rights democratic socialists seek to defend and enhance; also pro-welfare, individual rights and environmental lobbies.	• Dominant view on the left between 1940s and 1970s • As ideology of government relations with major sectional interests ('prescriptive corporatism') undermined by post-1979 triumph of the New Right • Liberal attitudes to groups and union sympathies continue to influence New Labour despite official arm's length stance towards big sectional interests.
One nation Conservative	• Represents further development post 1945 of traditional Conservative view of society as composed of legitimate interests – landowners, farmers, business, tradesmen, shopkeepers – which merit consultation and conciliation by government: 'the greatest number and variety of legitimate interests are all welcome and all have an assured place' (Sir David Eccles, 1948) • Postwar One Nation Conservative governments (like Labour) pursued policies of close consultation of interests and then, in the belief an even closer partnership with major groups was necessary	• Dominant view on the right down to late 1970s when displaced by New Right • Like democratic socialist Labour accepted primary need for government to consolidate major interests but cf Labour, pro-business rather than pro-union.

Contd ⇒

Why did cause groups and social movements increase so dramatically during this period? Explanations refer to aspects of social change post-1945 and include:

• the spread of affluence and education: in contemporary society in which the majority are both economically more secure and better educated than before, post-material values such as the quality of life are able to displace the materialist concerns with economic improvement which had hitherto dominated politics; new social movements recruit from those influenced by post-materialist values

• the growth of the information society: contemporary society has become an 'information' society, with new technologies of storing and diffusing information serving as the pace-setters of social change. Such a society not only provides independent data-bases of global information

BOX 10.2 *(continued)*

Model	Features	Comments
	for economic growth, 'prescriptive corporatism' in 1960s and 1970s • Also see voluntary groups as valuable because provide outlets for altruism and improve social cohesion by giving individual sense of belonging and encouraging community spirit • Sympathetic to business, especially small business, landowners, farmers, shopkeepers.	
New Right	• Hostile attitude to groups, especially major producer groups, as 'strangling serpents' throttling the life out of democratic politics and the national economy • Opposed to corporatist government deals with sectional interests as undemocratic because such deals bypass and thereby undermine parliament and continual bargaining with interests erodes the authority of government • Also opposed to corporatism on economic grounds because excessive power of sectional interests has inflationary consequences and puts brake on social and economic progress by creating mass of vested interests (e.g. public sector unions and professions) in favour of bloated, interventionist state and against social and economic reform.	• Underpinned new anti-corporatist Conservative government (1979–97) which kept business and unions at arm's length and destroyed union privileges. • Not hostile to all pressure groups and some increased their influence e.g. New Right 'think tanks', right wing Institute of Directors, commercial lobbyists.
Radical socialist	• Distrusts pressure groups as ineffective because unable to alter the grossly unequal distribution of wealth and power in capitalist society: i.e. groups only influential *at the margins*, leaving intact central capitalist structure of class power, private property and social inequality • Pro-labour groups such as trade unions have had negligible effect in challenging capitalism or even in providing effective counterbalance to business • Concession to working class in postwar welfare state stabilised capitalism without empowering working class	• Democratic socialist critics say capitalist economics have produced real gains for workers in past through activities of trade unions • Radical socialist (Marxist) influential as analysis in pointing to preeminent position of business in western societies

upon which groups may draw but also creates new centres of power such as the mass media which provide direct access to public opinion for pressure groups

• the welfare state: the post-1945 welfare state set standards of comprehensive social progress involving the banishment of poverty and optimum provision in health, education and housing for all citizens: its failure always to meet these targets and its lack of inclusiveness lay behind the emergence of new groups representing the children of poor families, the mentally and physically handicapped, the homeless and the old from the mid-1960s

• the multi-cultural society: as society has acquired a greater ethnic mix, a large number of new groups have emerged from within the ethnic minorities such as the many, often locally based, Muslim groups and the British Sikh Federation; in addition, libertarian groups have been involved in countering racial discrimination and groups like the anti-Nazi League have been formed to fight racism

- the decline of class: with the shrinkage of the traditional working class and the general weakening of social class in structuring political attitudes and loyalties, people have become more open to other influences such as gender, race, intellectual conviction, personal tastes and moral viewpoints as guides to political action
- the emergence of individualist and libertarian philosophies: the radical student protest movement of the late 1960s began a new 'life-style' politics based on personal freedom and self-fulfilment; as well as fuelling some of the new social movements – women's liberation and environmentalism, for example – it also legitimated the participatory, anti-hierarchical, decentralised and localised character of such groupings
- the nuclear threat: the development of weapons of mass destruction on a hitherto unparalleled scale, such as the H-Bomb in the context of the Cold War between the superpowers, lay behind the large membership achieved in the late 1950s and again in the early 1980s by the Campaign for Nuclear Disarmament

1979–97: the Conservative Governments

Changes affecting pressure groups in this phase derived to a considerable extent from the impact of Thatcherism but there were also other changes.

The impact of Thatcherism

Thatcherite Conservatism was hostile to pressure groups, with Ministers in this period referring to them variously as 'strangling serpents' (Douglas Hurd), and as being as essential to democracy as the 'sewage system' in any big city (Michael Portillo). Accordingly, important changes were bought about in government–pressure group relations by the Thatcher Governments, changes which broadly continued under the premiership of John Major (see Box 10.2).

(i) *The ending of neo-corporatism*. Perceiving neo-corporatism as a major cause of Britain's economic decline, the Conservative Government abruptly broke with this system after 1979. First, it ended the system of 'tripartite' consultation in economic policy-making by moving to an arm's-length relationship with business and trade unions and by downgrading and then abolishing (1992) the National Economic Development Council. Second, it severely curtailed trade union powers by legislation (Acts of 1980, 1982, 1984, 1988, 1990, 1992, 1993) and by engaging in major industrial confrontations and winning them, e.g. the 1984–5 Miners' Strike. Third, it pursued economic policies which gave higher priority to curbing inflation than to conquering unemployment, thereby allowing unemployment to increase rapidly.

(ii) *The challenge to certain intermediate institutions, professional bodies and welfare cause groups*. The Conservative Governments saw institutions such as local government, the universities and the BBC and more broadly the welfare state as in need of radical reform and were not prepared to allow representatives of the affected organisations and causes to deflect their aims. Accordingly, local government associations, professional groups such as doctors and teachers, and the cause groups involved in the poverty lobby lost influence in this period.

(iii) *The growth in influence of ideological sympathisers*. The Conservatives were not hostile to *all* pressure groups and some groups increased their influence in the 1980s. These included, first, groups which supported New Right aims such as the Institute of Directors, financial institutions in the City and right-wing think-tanks, and second, groups which could assist in the implementation of Conservative policies such as independent schools, private health providers and housing associations. (Table 10.1).

Although important changes occurred, it should not be assumed that relations between the executive and pressure groups broke down during these years. Even where relations with Ministers broke down, groups often retained contact with civil servants. There was much continuity – as well as significant discontinuities – between the Thatcher Government and its predecessors in terms of government-group relations. As one researcher has pointed out: 'in a large proportion of cases the relations between groups and the executive neither improved nor deteriorated' (Baggott, 1995, p. 123).

Table 10.1 Organisations and groups gaining and losing influence, 1979–97	
Gaining influence	*Losing influence*
Right-wing 'think-tanks' such as the Centre for Policy Studies, the Adam Smith Institute and the Institute of Economic Affairs	The Trades Union Congress
Institute of Directors	National Union of Mineworkers
Merchant bankers	Trade unions
Insurance companies	British Medical Association
Association of British Chambers of Commerce	National Union of Teachers, and other teacher unions
Large retailers	The Law Society
Oil companies	British Broadcasting Corporation
Advertising agencies	The Poverty lobby, e.g. Low Pay Unit, Child Poverty Action Group, Shelter
Estate agents	Local government associations
Brewery companies	
Groups representing the police	
National Viewers' and Listeners' Association	
Conservative Family Campaign	

Other changes

Other changes included a continuing rise in the political profile of cause groups and the growing importance of parliament, public campaigns and Europe as foci of pressure group effort.

(i) *The continuing rise of cause groups.* For the reasons listed above (pp. 172–4) and for other reasons, cause and single-issue pressure groups continued to be politically prominent. In the 1990s, Greenpeace's campaign against the deep sea dumping of the North Sea oil-rig, Brent Spar, a vigorous campaign by animal rights groups against the live export of veal calves, a succession of anti-roads protests over, for example, the M3 extension through Twyford Down and the Newbury by-pass, and the Snowdrop petitioners' campaign for the abolition of handguns in private homes after the Dunblane massacre, hit the headlines. Many of these campaigns – e.g. veal calves and anti-roads protests – brought together temporary coalitions of animal rights and environmental pressure groups and local action groups, including many of the concerned middle classes. New factors prompting pressure group activity included legislation: the Anti-Poll Tax Federation campaigned against the poll tax whilst the Criminal Justice and Public Order Act (1994),

which introduced new public order offences aimed to curb hunt saboteurs, New Age travellers, mass rave parties and anti-road protesters, was resisted by civil rights, environmental and other affected groups in a campaign organised by the Freedom Network.

(ii) *Changes in the direction of pressure group activity.* With the activities of professional lobbyists intensifying, Parliament became a more important target for pressure groups whilst publicity campaigns relying upon skilful use of the media became more prominent. As Britain became further integrated into the European Union as a result of the Single European Act (1986) and the Treaty of Maastricht (1993), pressure groups increasingly targeted European institutions such as the Brussels Commission and the European Parliament.

Pressure group targets

At which points in the political system do pressure groups seek to exert influence? British pressure groups have five main target areas: the 'core executive' – government ministers (including the Prime Minister) and civil servants (Whitehall); Parliament (both Houses); public opinion (mainly through the media); local institutions, including local government; and the European Union. As already noticed (p. 168 above), the terms 'insider' and 'outsider' usefully refer both to the *status* of groups – insiders acceptable to government, outsiders not so – and to *strategy* – whether a group seeks acceptance at core executive level or, through necessity or choice, remains an outsider. Research suggests that many groups – sectional and cause – pursue multiple strategies, seeking to exercise influence – as resources permit – at a variety of points in the system. Thus, Baggott's study of a cross-section of pressure groups at national level (both sectional and cause) found that whilst insider groups had more frequent contacts with the political system at all points than outsider groups, a relatively large number of outsider groups were *in quite frequent contact with the executive to junior civil servant level* (Table 10.2). This finding fits in well with Grant's further sub-division of insider and outsider groups in which only two of the six sub-categories – insider 'prisoner' groups and 'ideological' outsiders – never cross the insider/outsider boundary line (Box 10.3). In fact, this line is often crossed – first because, as already mentioned, groups adopt more than one strategy; second, because insider status can be lost as well as gained.

Pressure groups and government

The concentration of power in the executive makes government the main target for pressure groups in Britain. A well-established system of formal and informal contacts links insider groups with government. Increasingly, formal contacts have become institutionalised through pressure group membership of a wide variety of government-established committees; through the circulation of government consultative documents;and through widespread consultation with groups over the contents of delegated legislation (statutory instruments).

- government committees with pressure group representation include executive bodies able to make regulations and dispense money (358 with over 4,000 appointees in 1995); advisory committees (829 with over 10,000 appointees in 1995);tribunals(over 2,000 in 1994); Committees of Inquiry (over 2,000 since 1900); and Royal Commissions (35 between 1944 and 1995);
- pre-legislative consultative documents (286 per year between 1991–3) and Green Papers (31 per year between 1991 and 1993) are circulated to pressure groups inviting comment within a specified time – normally about two months;

Table 10.2 Pressure groups and the political system

| | % of groups in contact | | | |
| | Weekly | | Monthly | |
	Outsider	Insider	Outsider	Insider
Prime minister	–	2	10	14
Cabinet ministers	5	12	37	45
Junior ministers	10	14	38	67
Senior civil servants	12	25	45	49
Junior civil servants	12	55	62	76
House of Commons	20	39	51	72
House of Lords	8	23	36	63
Political parties	13	27	34	51
Media	74	86	84	94

Source: Baggott (1992) p. 20.

BOX 10.3
Insider and outsider groups

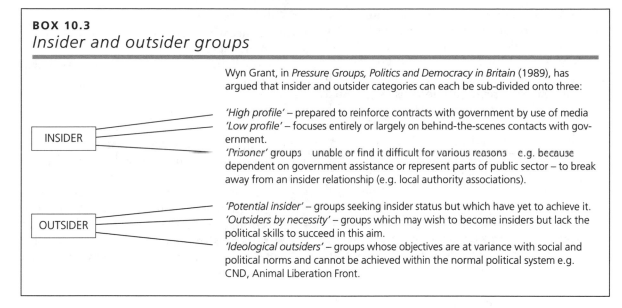

Wyn Grant, in *Pressure Groups, Politics and Democracy in Britain* (1989), has argued that insider and outsider categories can each be sub-divided onto three:

'High profile' – prepared to reinforce contracts with government by use of media
'Low profile' – focuses entirely or largely on behind-the-scenes contacts with government.
'Prisoner' groups – unable or find it difficult for various reasons – e.g. because dependent on government assistance or represent parts of public sector – to break away from an insider relationship (e.g. local authority associations).

'Potential insider' – groups seeking insider status but which have yet to achieve it.
'Outsiders by necessity' – groups which may wish to become insiders but lack the political skills to succeed in this aim.
'Ideological outsiders' – groups whose objectives are at variance with social and political norms and cannot be achieved within the normal political system e.g. CND, Animal Liberation Front.

- most of the annual 2,500 Statutory Instruments are laid before parliament only after extensive consultation with affected interests.

Even though formal consultation between government and groups is very extensive, the great majority of contacts are informal and typically occur at quite a low level (assistant secretary and principal) of the civil service (see Table 10.2). Indeed, much business is done informally by telephone and face-to-face discussions between civil servants and representatives of the groups.

Two major features of insider groups' relationship of regular consultation and negotiation with government departments invite comment. First, the acceptability of a group to government – its recognition as an insider – depends upon its *credibility*. This rests upon such factors as

- *A group's representativeness* – its genuine capacity to speak for a large number of people in its section of society
- *The reasonableness of its demands and their compatibility with the aims of government* – realism, responsibility and negotiability are the watchwords
- *The reliability and quality of its advice* – past 'track' record and the extent of government need can both be important
- *Its ability to 'talk the same language' as government*

– i.e. its familiarity with government procedures
- *Economic leverage and veto power* – diminished for some groups in the 1980s, e.g. TUC, but still can be a factor, e.g. the boycott of Standard Assessment Tests by the teachers' unions in 1993.

Conversely, characteristics which make for a group's *unacceptability* to government (thereby ensuring that it remains an outsider) include:

- *Incompatibility* – possessing aims incompatible with those of government, e.g. the Marxist-inspired Radical Alternatives to Prison (RAP), which calls for the abolition of prison;and
- *Contentiousness* – the likelihood that a group will be opposed by other groups, e.g.the Abortion Law Reform Association (ALRA) by the Society for the Protection of the Unborn Child (SPUCC).

Second, there is the extent to which pressure groups in their linkages with government departments form *policy networks*, a concept which expresses a variety of relationships on a continuum between *policy communities and issue networks* (see above, p. 170). In a *policy community*, relationships between a group or groups and a government department are close, relatively exclusive, consensual and cooperative. The best example of a policy community in the postwar period is agriculture, where a close and generally harmonious relationship existed between the two main parties involved, the Ministry of Agriculture, Food and Fisheries (MAFF) and the National Farmers' Union (NFU). Health and transport are two further examples in which policy is made in semi-autonomous, segmented communities between departments and groups with privileged access. In policy communities, Ministers, permanent officials and groups share an interest in increasing the resources devoted to a given policy area and departments often identify closely with group viewpoints. The Department of Transport, for example, has often been cited as being both pro-road and pro-lorry, the former Department of Energy tended to side with energy-producers against energy users whilst MAFF invariably supported the interests of producers of food against its consumers. *Issue networks* are less stable than policy communities and contain a larger number of participants – often several ministries as well as numerous pressure groups-, who often find it difficult to agree on policy. The numerous Departments – Treasury, Home Office, Employment, Education, Social Security – and pressure groups involved in inner-city policy in the 1980s provide an example of an issue network (Smith, 1995, p. 28).

In return for regular consultation by government, for being taken into the confidence of officials and allowed to state their case and conceivably gain concessions, groups are expected to conform to certain patterns of behaviour. They are expected at all times to be discreet about discussions in Whitehall and to refrain, even where they feel aggrieved, from 'going public' and, especially,from criticising ministers. They may also be expected to sell the policy to their members. Occasionally, this cosy, symbiotic relationship will break down and a group will attack its governmental 'patron': this happened in 1992 when the Engineering Employers' Federation publicly called for 'a more effective and committed champion' than Michael Heseltine at the Department of Trade and Industry

The benefits to government of this system of group representation include:

- up-to-date, often technical and highly specialised advice

- 'market' information in the various sectors
- compliance with their policies by the main interests in each specific field
- assistance in the administration of projects (where required)

In return, groups get

- a hearing for their case (at the least)
- the chance to influence policy (including legislation) and decisions in their formative, early stages
- the possibility of gaining an executive role alongside government in the implementation of policy
- funds from government: studies have shown that government is an important source of funds for large numbers of groups in the environmental and poverty lobbies.

Pressure groups and parliament

Survey evidence suggests the increased importance of parliament as a target for pressure group lobbying in recent years. In the Study of Parliament Group Survey, 75 per cent of groups claimed to be in regular or frequent contact with MPs and 59 per cent of groups claimed regular or frequent dealings with peers (Rush, 1990, p. 14). Factors facilitating the growing use of parliament by groups included: the discernible increase in backbench independence; the establishment of the new select committees after 1979 which provided another channel of potential influence; the growth of specialist political influence; the increased number of political consultancy firms;the distancing of government from pressure groups by Conservative Governments after 1979; and the large majorities enjoyed by Conservative Governments in the 1980s which directed attention to Conservative backbenchers and the House of Lords as the main obstacles to legislation. However, groups remain realistic in their perceptions of where power lies in the political system, ranking parliament below government departments/civil servants, ministers and the media as influences upon public policy (Table 10.3)

Nonetheless, because parliament is perceived as a policy-influencer, no pressure group can ignore it. Indeed, an important conclusion of the Study

Table 10.3 Groups' ranking of influences on public policy

Civil servants/government departments	1
Ministers	2
The media	3
Parliament	4
Particular sections of public opinion	5
Public opinion generally	6
Other pressure groups	7
Political parties generally	8
One political party in particular	9

Source: Rush (1990) p. 272.

of Parliament Group survey is that, 'contrary to what might be expected', more of the attention received by Parliament 'comes from insider than outsider, and more from sectional than promotional groups' (Rush, 1990, p. 277; see also Table 10.2).

Groups seek contact with parliament for three main purposes:

- To amend legislation – or change policy – in often slight but, for the affected interest or cause, significant ways;
- To sponsor legislation;
- To influence the climate of public opinion by gaining additional publicity and support for an issue first raised or raised concurrently outside Parliament.

Characteristic activities of groups concerned about legislation include – circularising MPs, wining and dining them to encourage sympathy for the group's viewpoint, requesting an MP to arrange a meeting with the minister responsible for a bill, asking an MP to speak in a second reading debate, and asking an MP to propose an amendment during the committee or report stages of a bill. In the Lords, too, peers regularly put down questions, speak in debates and table legislative amendments on behalf of groups. By prompting MPs or peers to act along such lines, groups can hope to persuade ministers to adopt a favourable amendment, back down on a

controversial detail, clarify an ambiguous point, or give an assurance on the interpretation of a particular clause.

The time allocated to private members' legislation (although small – under 5 per cent) gives groups an opportunity to promote change rather than simply react to it. In the 1960s, sympathetic MPs sponsored much social legislation, liberalising the law on divorce, abortion, homosexuality, theatre censorship and capital punishment. Between 1979 and 1986, pressure groups promoted 25 bills – just under a quarter (23 per cent) of private members' bills introduced in this period (Rush, 1990, pp. 202–3). One such item of backbench legislation was the House Buyers Bill (1983–4): promoted by the Consumers' Association and sponsored by the Labour MP, Austin Mitchell, it aimed to remove the solicitors' monopoly over conveyancing, and eventually became government policy. In order to succeed on free votes, groups have to build cross-bench support and often fail to do so, e.g. the defeat of the private members' bills seeking to outlaw fox-hunting (1992 and 1998) and reduce the age of consent for homosexuals to 16 (1994; a compromise lowering it to 18 succeeded). In 1998, the Labour backbencher Mike Foster's anti-foxhunting bill was 'talked out' by Conservative MPs who as part of their time-wasting tactics debated the definition of a dog, with one insisting that if the bill went through, 'dogs' would be banned from hunting but not bitches. Private Members' bills also sometimes encounter opposition from the government, which effectively blocked the Civil Rights (Disabled Persons) Bill in 1994.

Finally, groups can use parliament in a broader way – often in combination with other strategies – to publicise their cause and shape public policy in their interest over a longer time-span. Such mechanisms include working through party committees, all-party committees and select committees, prompting parliamentary questions and gaining the maximum number of signatures to an Early Day Motion. For example, the Wing Airport Resistance Association (formed to resist an inland site for London's third airport in 1970) used parliamentary contacts skilfully – first, through the good offices of sympathetic local MPs to set up an all-party committee of backbenchers and then to launch an Early Day Motion with an eventual 219 signatures. In

1988, organised interests provided secretarial assistance for 25 of the 103 all-party subject – e.g. the RSPCA services the Animal Welfare Parliamentary Group.

The various ways in which outside interests can be financially linked with MPs are explored in Chapter 16. It is sufficient merely to underline here the growth of professional lobbying companies in the 1980s. By 1990, such political consultancy firms had an estimated annual turnover of over £10 million. A lobbying firm allegedly secured the blocking of a private member's bill banning tobacco advertising in 1994. However, following the Nolan Report (1995), MPs were banned from holding consultancies with lobbying companies and, in addition, the new 'paid advocacy' rule prevents them from helping fee-paying interests by tabling questions, presenting bills, speaking in debates, moving motions or changing reports of Select Committees (see further, Chapter 16).

The benefits derived by groups from their contacts with parliament range over a spectrum from the very considerable to the quite modest to the minimal and negligible. At the former end are the occasional sponsorship of private members' bills together with such events as the successful campaign waged against the Shops Bill (1986) by the shopworkers' union, the churches and various voluntary organisations and by the large brewers against the DTI plan which would have forced owners of more than 2,000 public houses to sell their 'surplus' outlets. In the middle of the range are the amendments to legislation which groups quite frequently obtain, such as the amendment achieved by gay pressure groups to the Criminal Justice and Public Order Bill (1994) which reduced the age of consent for homosexuals from 21 to 18. Many groups, however, derive much less from their lobbying activities. When questioned by the Study of Parliament Group, just under 39 per cent of groups saw themselves as 'not very successful' at influencing legislation, and just under 6 per cent as 'unsuccessful'. In contrast, over 55 per cent claimed to be 'very' successful (7.2 per cent) or 'quite' successful (48.3 per cent). In return, the input by groups to the legislative process gives MPs a 'critical capacity' they would otherwise lack and, in addition, it increases the legitimacy of measures by securing wider consent to them than would otherwise be achieved (Norton, 1990b, pp. 193, 196–7).

Beyond Whitehall and Westminster

Because power in Britain is concentrated at the centre, most pressure group activity is directed at government and parliament. Nonetheless, a good deal of group activity takes place outside Westminster and Whitehall, with pressure groups running public campaigns and seeking influence in political parties, through the courts and at local level.

Public campaigns

Many groups seek to increase public awareness of their causes by running national campaigns. These include *long-term educational campaigns* designed to produce significant shifts in public opinion, such as the Campaign for Lead Free Air (CLEAR), and *short-term 'fire-brigade' campaigns* warning about and seeking to avert a specific threat, such as the NUM campaign against pit closures in 1992. Whilst public campaigning remains the leading strategy of outsider groups, insiders – and sectional groups – increasingly employ public campaigns in combination with parliamentary and Whitehall strategies. Gaining media attention – for example, through a well-researched press release, letters to the quality newspapers or sometimes a carefully-staged 'event' – is central to the success of a public campaigning strategy. Groups can also seek to raise public awareness of an issue by various forms of protest and direct action. These include legal and non-violent methods such as marches and demonstrations – e.g. the massive London demonstration organised by the Countryside Alliance against the anti-foxhunting bill and other perceived threats to rural life in 1998; the anti-racism demonstrations organised by the Anti-Nazi League; and consumer boycotts, such as that organised against South African goods by the anti-apartheid campaign. But they also include the illegal but non-violent non-payment tactics used by the Anti-Poll Tax Federation, the sit-ins employed by the anti-roads protesters and the disruptive methods deployed by hunt saboteurs and anti-whalers, as well as the violent and illegal methods employed by, for example, some animal rights groups, such as the Animal Liberation Front, which break into laboratories, release animals and destroy equipment.

Political parties

Groups may also attempt to bring pressure on the political parties. They may do this in a number of ways. The most obvious way is to make donations to political parties, as do both the trade unions (to Labour) and business (to the Conservatives) (see further, Chapter 16). In the 1990s, trade union contributions to the Labour Party declined (from three-quarters to half its total funds, 1986–96) whilst business contributions have grown. At the same time, business contributions to the Conservatives declined sharply in the 1990s. Another method is to sponsor candidates as the trade unions did before 1995 in the Labour Party. Some cause groups – e.g. the anti-hunting and anti-abortion lobbies – try to influence parties' choice of parliamentary candidates. Others again attempt to persuade parties to place detailed commitments in their manifestos. In return for influence, such groups campaign for the party supporting their cause. Sometimes group and party membership overlaps, and this may help the groups achieve a favourable reception from parties. For example, most of the 418 Labour MPs elected in 1997 belong to trade unions (Butler and Kavanagh, 1997, p. 206). In addition, the Labour Party also contains many members of campaigning organisations such as CND, Greenpeace and Friends of the Earth, and of local community action, tenants' and women's groups (Seyd and Whiteley, 1992, pp. 91–2). In late 1997 New Labour's simultaneous receptiveness to certain cause group demands combined with its desire to attract business funds produced embarrassment for the party over its exemption of Formula One from its proposed tobacco advertising ban.

The courts

On occasion, pressure groups may turn to the courts. This happens relatively rarely, but bringing test cases provided the poverty lobby with an opportunity 'to politicize an issue and to exert pressure for changes in the law' (Whiteley and Winyard, 1987, p. 108); a legal challenge by Greenpeace (together with Lancashire County Council) in 1994 to the opening and commissioning of the Thorp nuclear processing plant by British Nuclear Fuels failed, but gained valuable publicity for the issue as well as something of a moral victory since Greenpeace were not required to pay the BNF's costs; and the Council

for the Protection of Rural England played a major part in thwarting the government's intention to transfer pollution control to the private sector by pointing out that the move was illegal in European law (Garner, 1996, p. 164).

Local groups

A wide variety of groups are active at local level, including economic (trade unions and chambers of commerce), community (tenants' associations, ethnic groupings), cause groups and social movements (Friends of the Earth, anti-hunting, women's groups)) and the voluntary sector (Rural Community Councils, Age Concern, the churches, MIND). Many seek insider status at local level, the pattern of their representation in local government reflecting the political complexion of councils: thus, farming and landowning interests are well established in Conservative rural areas, local business interests and amenity and middle class residents' groups predominate in suburban Conservative councils whilst trade unions, community and ethnic minority representatives are influential in leftwing Labour urban authorities, and so on (Stoker, 1991, pp. 133–4). Local areas are also the scene of well-publicised campaigns by Nimby (Not in my backyard) groups against such matters as unwanted schemes (e.g. the Channel Tunnel rail link, new roads, the construction of greenfield superstores, the dumping of toxic waste) and by local residents against the closure of schools, hospitals and playing fields.

Pressure groups and Europe

The growing integration of Britain in the European Union has brought a considerable increase in lobbying at European level by British pressure groups. According to one estimate, the number of pressure group employees in Brussels doubled from 5,000 to 10,000 between the late 1980s and 1994 (Grant, 1995, p. 98). The Single European Act (1986) and the Treaty of Maastricht (1993) gave considerable encouragement to this trend by increasing the number of policy areas in which decisions are made at European level, by extending the use of qualified majority voting and by giving additional legislative powers to the European parliament (see Chapter 12). Business and farming interests, trade

BOX 10.4

Comparative pressure groups: the UK, USA, France and the European Union

The character and behaviour of pressure groups are shaped by the national context, in particular the nature of the political system and the political culture.

(1) The political system

(a) *Unitary/Federal*

In unitary systems of government such as the UK, pressure groups aim primarily at central institutions; in a federal system like the United States, groups target both federal *and* regional governments at state and local levels. In the confederal European Union, groups also divide their attention between two main foci – the European Commission and national governments (in order to exert influence on the Council of Ministers).

(b) *Executive-dominated systems/balanced constitutions, based on the separation of powers*

In executive-dominated systems such as the UK, pressure groups aim mainly at the Executive (Ministers and Whitehall); in systems with a relatively even balance between Executive and Legislature such as the US, organised groups focus on both the Presidency and Congress.

(c) *Codified/uncodified constitutions*

In Britain's uncodified constitution, groups have relatively rare recourse to the courts but in the US and the European Union, which have codified constitutions, groups often invoke legal means of redress. In the United States, groups turn to the judicial system to bring test cases, challenge the regulatory agencies and compel implementation of congressional legislation whilst in Europe, women's and environmental groups have used the European Court of Justice to force national governments to carry out European legislation on equality between male and female workers and standards of drinking water.

(2) Political culture

(a) *cf. UK and USA*

US society is more individualistic, less collectivist and more decentralised than British society. It contains a greater diversity of ethnic groups and religious faiths but its class system is much less pronounced. When combined with constitutional support for the right of citizens to assemble and petition and to practise their religion, these social and cultural differences have produced a pressure group system which is more competitive, diverse and fragmented than the British system. In the United States, pressure groups are more favoured than political parties for representing interests and beliefs and achieving political goals whereas the reverse is the case in the UK. Non-economic groups such as those representing women, social causes, environmental concerns, the Christian Right and specific foreign policy interests have been particularly prominent in recent decades.

An interesting case-study is the relative strength of the gun lobbies. Despite possessing a murder rate many times higher than that of the UK and a public opinion in favour of firmer gun control, US governments have been unable to strengthen gun laws significantly and guns remain more available to the average American than to citizens in other countries. Stronger gun control is hard to achieve in the USA in large part because of the effective lobbying of the National Rifle Association backed by forces shaped by the frontier mentality and by the constitutional enshrinement of 'the right of the people to keep and bear arms'. Contrast the speed with which anti-gun ownership forces in Britain, building on outraged public opinion after the Dunblane shootings, overwhelmed the gun lobby in 1996 (see Assignment).

(b) *cf. US/UK/France*

The greater numbers, competitiveness and fragmentation of US pressure groups can be contrasted with pressure group behaviour in more statist countries such as the UK and France. Both have strong executive traditions, with governments in both countries capable of exercising a shaping influence on organised interests – for example, by forcing groups into merger and developing patron–client relationships with them. Furthermore, governments in both countries attempted to change the balance of power between organised interests in the 1980s, a move which was more successful in Britain than in France partly because of the differing strengths of the traditions of popular protest in the two countries. Thus, whilst a tide of legislative and economic change undermined the strength of British labour in the 1980s and 1990s, French labour, whilst also weakened by privatisation and falling union membership, could draw upon a revolutionary tradition and proved capable of more resistance – as indicated by the successful strike of private sector road hauliers in 1996. The ability to bring thousands of protesters on to the streets gives formidable political leverage to many French groups. More broadly, the French pressure group system stands mid-way between the UK and US systems, more centralised than the US but also providing a larger number of accessible power centres than the UK.

Finally, EU membership is producing a similarity between pressure group behaviour in Britain and France which is likely to increase in the future. Organised groups in these and other EU countries already devote considerable resources to building alliances with national officials to fight their cases in Brussels and to building European-wide federations of interests to maximise their lobbying power at the Brussels Commission. With large EU resources devoted to regional development, government–pressure group relations are developing at three levels: regions; nation-states; and Brussels bureaucracy. The term 'competitive federalism' has been coined to describe this trend.

unions, professional associations such as the BMA and the Law Society, and environmental groups all lobby at European Union level. Groups may lobby directly – many have offices in Brussels, with business groups predominating, by employing consultancy firms and through Europe-wide groups such as UNICE (Union of Industrial and Employers' Confederations of Europe), ETUC (European Trade Union Confederation), COPA (Committee of Professional Agricultural Organisations), BEUC (European Bureau of Consumers' Associations) and EEB (European Environmental Bureau).

Pressure groups target European institutions in this order: the European Commission, the Council of Ministers, the European Parliament, and the European Court of Justice. Since groups cannot exert direct pressure on the Council of Ministers but must rely on their own government to protect their interests, they frequently combine lobbying their own ministers with a 'Brussels strategy'. This tendency was reinforced after 1993 by a reduction of the influence of national governments following the extension of qualified majority voting (QMV), which made it even more imperative for groups to develop contacts with the Commission. Although far less significant than the Commission as a focus of lobbying activity, the European Parliament 's increased legislative powers following the SEA and Maastricht enhanced its attractiveness to pressure groups, especially to those representing consumer, environmental and animal welfare interests. The European Court of Justice has been used by groups both to force the UK government to implement EU legislation, e.g. over the quality of drinking water, and to challenge domestic measures, e.g. pit closures by the miners' union (1992) and the proposed legal aid regulations by the Law Society (1993) (see further, Box 10.4).

Pressure group influence

Figure 10.1 sums up in diagrammatic form the stages at which groups may seek to influence policy and legislation. Summarised schematically, these are:

- *Agenda-setting*: getting an item on to the policy agenda

- *Policy-formation*: helping to shape policy/legislation at the consultation and (for Acts of Parliament) drafting stages
- *Passage through Parliament (Commons and Lords) including Statutory Instruments*
- *Implementation*: groups help identify flaws in the policy/legislation and suggest remedies.

Whether and how far pressure groups succeed in influencing political decision-making depends upon several factors including their resources, strategies and social and economic leverage.

Resources

Resources include finances, organisation, staffing, membership, expertise and leadership. It is generally believed that sectional groups possess an advantage over cause groups in terms of resources, and this is both normally the case and affords such groups a considerable bargaining advantage. Business groups such as the motor industry, weapons manufacturers, and the tobacco and brewing industries have far greater resources than consumers and pensioners, for example. However, well-resourced campaigns by major sectional groups have sometimes failed – e.g. the very expensive anti-nationalisation campaigns run by business between 1945 and 1979 and also the campaign against pit closures by the mineworkers' union in 1984–5, which was undermined by poor leadership and inadequate strategy. By contrast, groups representing single parents, the disabled, the unemployed and the elderly deployed much more modest resources between 1965 and 1985 but made important gains through 'painstaking and persistent lobbying' (Whiteley and Winyard, 1987, p. 138). Again, some environmental groups are now as well-resourced as the larger sectional groups: for example, Greenpeace spent £350,000 on TV equipment for its Brent Spar campaign, running a 24-hour news operation, equipped with its own film crews, editing suites and satellite technology (the *Guardian*, 28 August 1995). However, lack of resources undoubtedly handicapped the anti-nuclear lobby in its protest against the Conservatives' extensive nuclear energy programme, which had the backing of the major forces in the energy industry, including the Central Electricity Generating Board, the Atomic Energy Authority, large national firms such as the

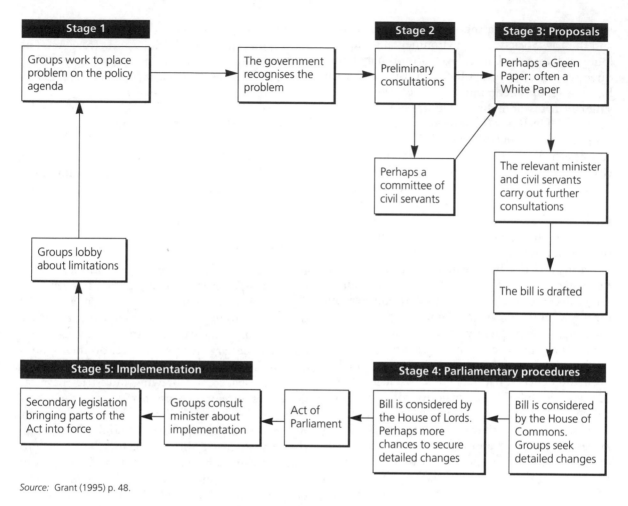

Source: Grant (1995) p. 48.

Figure 10.1 Pressure group influence: the main stages

General Electric Company (GEC) and big multinationals like Westinghouse and Rio Tinto Zinc.

Resources – whether slender or considerable – need to be expertly deployed if a group is to achieve its aims. The quality of the information it provides to government guarantees Amnesty International 'insider' status. Environmental groups such as Friends of the Earth have focused increasingly on providing reliable information to policy-makers but may suffer loss of credibility if their test figures turn out to be mistaken and their solutions contested, as happened to Greenpeace in the wake of its successful campaign to avert the deep-sea dumping of the redundant Brent Spar oil rig. Parliamentary know-how is essential if groups are to influence legislation at the standing committee stage, but much of the briefing material they provide for MPs is over-long, too generalised and too late to be effective. Consumer groups, local government associations and certain trade unions possess such expertise but City institutions demonstrated ignorance of such procedure over the Financial Services Bill (1986) (Norton, 1990, pp. 194–6). Its knowledge of parliamentary procedure enabled the pro-abortion lobby first to liberalise the abortion law and then to resist the campaign by anti-abortion groups to amend it between 1967 and 1975. Pro-abortionists attribute the failure of the pro-life lobby to reduce the abortion limit to the counter-productive tactics adopted by the Society for the Protection of the Unborn Child (SPUC), which sent a plastic foetus to every MP.

With regard to pressure group membership, size, density, solidarity, and quality have to be considered. Sometimes, as in the case of demonstrations, absolute numbers can be important, to show that a group is as well-supported as its proponents – or as poorly supported as its opponents – respectively claim. For example, the potential influence of the Countryside March (1 March 1998) was strengthened by its being able to claim a turnout of over 280,000. Just as often, it is important to a group to show that it represents a high proportion of potential members. Thus, trade associations are strengthened by being able to claim – as they often can – that they represent over 90 per cent of an industry, whereas the authority of the CBI is undermined by its inability to speak for a wide range of diverse interests, and trade unionism is weakened by the fact that only a third of workers are members of trade unions. The solidarity of its membership can reinforce a group's case, especially if it can be demonstrated by ballot or opinion poll. Failure by the NUM to hold a strike ballot in 1984 enabled the government to speculate about divisions within the union. Similarly cause groups such as the anti-hunting and disablement lobbies have suffered from internal rivalries and differences over tactics. Finally, quality of membership matters, with cause groups often offsetting the handicap of small size by the dedication, enthusiasm and knowledge of their memberships.

Strategy

Adoption of an appropriate strategy can be a vital ingredient in group success. The way in which a group allocates its efforts between government departments, parliament and public campaigns depends upon the nature of the group, its cause and the congruence (or lack of congruence) of its goals with public opinion. The degree of choice is often more limited than this suggests: thus, trade associations generally have little option but to adopt an 'insider' strategy, whereas 'ideological' groups like CND or oppositional movements like the Anti-Poll Tax Federation are forced by necessity into 'outsider' strategies. Within the field of law reform, a respectable group such as the Howard League for Penal Reform, which directs its efforts for liberal reforms within an acceptance of the legitimacy of the criminal law, has achieved 'insider' status with the Home Office to which the left-inspired Radical Alternatives to Prison (RAP) and Preservation of the Rights of Prisoners (PROP) can never aspire. Some sectional groups pursue 'insider' and 'outsider' strategies simultaneously: for example, the TUC continued its institutionalised relationship with Whitehall while running effective national campaigns, involving parliamentary, legal and mass action, against industrial relations legislation in the late 1960s and early 1970s. Congruence with public opinion also affects a group's choice of strategy: workers enjoying widespread public sympathy such as firemen and nurses were able to run public campaigns over pay in the 1980s but other industrial groups and the TUC had to take into account the likelihood of lukewarm, indifferent or even hostile public reactions when considering public campaigns.

Sanctions

A group's capacity to employ sanctions in pursuit of its goals depends upon its general importance in the national economy and, more specifically, its capacity to disrupt government plans by resistance and/or non-compliance. With regard to economic leverage and veto power, sectional groups are generally considered more powerful than promotional groups because they possess stronger weapons. Whilst largely true, this needs to be treated with caution. Generally, the more powerful a group and the more essential its policy-compliance is to government, the less overt its threat of sanctions need be: the City, for instance, with its ability to talk down the pound, often gains decisions in its favour without any overt lobbying at all. However, the power of sectional interests can fluctuate, in large part because of shifts in government needs and changing political circumstances, as shown by the declining influence of farming, manufacturing and professional groups in the 1980s. At the same time, campaigns of non-compliance, delay and disruption can be formidable weapons in the hands of promotional groups, as demonstrated by the anti-poll-tax non-payment campaign, the physical obstruction of anti-roads protesters and the spoiling tactics of hunt saboteurs.

Pressure groups and democracy

There is a serious debate about whether pressure groups (PGs) enhance or distort democracy. The main arguments on each side are summarised in Box 10.5.

New Labour and pressure groups

What changes are discernible in government–pressure group relationships under New Labour?

New Labour and the trade unions

New Labour relationships with the unions promised to be less close than under previous Labour Administrations but also closer than those of the previous Conservative Governments. Part of the modernising project of the party leadership was to weaken Labour's union links by reducing union influence at all levels of the party (Chapter 7). Also, before the 1997 general election, Blair made clear that if Labour were elected there would be no return to the neo-corporatist style of government–union relations of the 1970s and that there would be no

---

BOX 10.5
Pressure groups and democracy: for and against

For

- **Participation and political access** PGs increase participation and access to political system, thereby enhancing the quality of democracy. They complement and supplement electoral democracy in two main ways: first, by providing an important mechanism by which citizens can influence government *between elections*; and second, by enabling the *intensity* of feeling on issues to be considered, opinions to be weighed as well as counted.
- **Improvement of government** Consultation with affected groups is the rational way to make decisions in a free society. It makes government more efficient by enhancing the quality of the decision-making process: the information and advice provided by groups helps to improve the quality of government policy and legislation.
- **Pluralism** PGs are a product of freedom of association, which is a fundamental principle of liberal democracy: its obverse is autocratic or tyrannical suppression of interests. Freely operating pressure groups are essential to the effective functioning of liberal democracy in three main ways: (1) they serve as vital intermediary institutions between government and society; (2) they assist in the dispersal of political power; and (3) they provide important counterweights to undue concentration of power.
- **Social progress** PGs enable new concerns and issues to reach the political agenda, thereby facilitating social progress and preventing social stagnation: e.g. the women's and environmentalist movements.
- **Social cohesion** PGs increase social cohesion and political stability by providing a 'safety-valve' outlet for individual and collective grievances and demands.
- **Opposition** PGs assist surveillance of government by exposing information it would rather keep secret, thereby reinforcing and complementing work of opposition through political parties. PGs thereby improve the accountability of decision-makers to electorates.

Against

- **Sectionalism and selfishness** PGs improve participation, but *unequally*, benefiting the well-organised but disadvantaging the weakly-organised. In this sense, they work against – not in favour of – the public interest.
- **Anti-parliamentary democracy** Groups and government form policy networks and policy communities, engaging in secret behind-the-scenes consultation: the resulting covert 'deals' detract both from open government and the authority of elected legislators in parliament. Also, many groups are not themselves democratic organisations as they offer their members little opportunity for effective participation.
- **Elitism** Group system only *apparently* functions on a 'level playing field'; in practice, it reinforces the existing class and power structure – 'in the pluralist heaven the heavenly choir sings with a strong upper class accent' (Schnattsneider, 1960, cited Grant, 1995, p. 33).
- **Pluralistic stagnation** Group opposition can slow down or block desirable changes, thereby contributing to social immobilism.
- **Social disharmony and dislocation** Inegalitarian operation of groups increases social discontent and political instability by intensifying sense of social frustration and injustice felt by disadvantaged and excluded sections of the population
- **Failure of opposition** True in theory but only to a limited extent in practice: in Britain's secretive political system, groups and parties combined are unable to mount effective opposition to government policies because they generally lack adequate information.

repeal of Conservative trade union legislation. On the other hand, New Labour made manifesto promises attractive to the unions including a statutory minimum wage, the signing of the European Social Chapter and the promise of union recognition where the majority of the workforce vote for a union to represent them. Moreover, despite the reduction of their role, the unions' influence within the party remained considerable and they contributed £11 million to the party's election campaign. By early 1998, the Labour Government had pleased the unions by signing the Social Chapter, removing the ban on unions at GCHQ, and setting up a Low Pay Commission to examine the minimum wage. But talks between the CBI and TUC had failed to reach agreement on union recognition, an issue vital to the unions' hopes of increasing their membership and influence.

New Labour and business

New Labour made a determined pre-election effort to reassure business and where possible to gain its active support with promises of a low-tax, low-inflation regime committed to maintaining Conservative public spending levels for two years. It promised flexible labour markets and help for small businesses. It sought and reputedly received large financial support from business, together with the political backing of some chairmen of leading companies and substantial support in a poll of businessmen. After the election, Labour's pro-business sympathies were further demonstrated by its appointment of leading businessmen Geoffrey Robinson, formerly head of Jaguar cars, and Sir David Simon, the former chairman of BP, to leading posts in the government. Its decision to join the European single currency found favour with the CBI which also expressed concern about the Conservatives' move to hardline opposition to it.

Cause groups

The advent of the New Labour Government shifted the balance of advantage among causes and interests as indicated by the fierce conflicts generated over its manifesto promises of a ban on tobacco advertising, greater freedom for people to explore the countryside and a free vote on a ban on foxhunting. First,

Labour's exemption of Formula One motor racing from its tobacco advertising ban in November 1997 led to a public furore after it simultaneously leaked out that the party had received a pre-election gift of £1 million from the Formula One chief, Bernie Ecclestone. Ecclestone had had talks with Blair a few weeks before the decision was announced. Formula One argued that tobacco sponsorship was vital to the sport and proceeding with the ban would lead to the loss to Britain of 50,000 full time jobs and £900,000 a year in exports as well as the possible removal of Formula One to Asia. Against this, the anti-smoking lobby, which included ASH (Action on Smoking and Health), the BMA and several charities, countered that the association of tobacco advertising with motor racing glamorised smoking and helped make it attractive to young people. The key political issues involved the suspicion of party favours on policy in return for funding, and the power of powerful commercial interests to sway government decisions by behind-the-scenes lobbying. Labour was particularly vulnerable to such allegations in view of its pre-election attacks on Conservative sleaze and its criticisms of Conservative Governments for failing to cut teenage smoking by banning tobacco advertising and receipt of large contributions to party funds from the tobacco industry. In retreating from the ban, Labour argued that it had not been the victim of insider lobbying but rather had been won over by the strength of the argument that the global nature of the sport made a ban counter-productive. The upshot of the affair was that, on the advice of the chairman of the Committee on Standards and Privileges, the party returned the money to Bernie Ecclestone. The EU directive's ban on sports advertising exempted Formula One from the ban until 2006.

Second, rural interests joined in a massive Countryside March through London organised by the Countryside Alliance early in spring 1998. The major focus of rural alarm was the backbench anti-foxhunting bill which had received a large majority at its second reading and which, if it were to gain the backing of the government, had a strong chance of success. The aim of the demonstration was to pressurise the government not to make parliamentary time for the bill and, in addition, to express a variety of other discontents including the impact of the BSE

BOX 10.6
The 'cash for access' affair

The so-called 'cash for access affair' embarrassed the Labour Government in July 1998. An undercover *Observer* investigation alleged that key Labour advisers when the party was in opposition were now working for lobbying companies and had passed confidential government information to large corporations. Lobbyists told *Observer* reporters posing as representatives of US energy companies that those buying their services could receive advance word of the contents of speeches by the Chancellor, help in securing a place on government task forces formulating policy, pre-publication sight of reports of parliamentary select committees, lunch at No. 10, meetings with ministers and special advisers, and help with winning approval for takeover bids. Derek Draper, a director of lobbying company GPC Market Access and former adviser to Peter Mandelson, then Minister without Portfolio, claimed that he had passed on important financial information to a US investment bank. He also claimed that he was close to the '17 people who count' in the Blair Government. Also implicated was Roger Liddle, a senior member of the PM's Policy Unit, who allegedly said to the reporters posing as businessmen: 'Tell me who you want to meet and Derek [Draper] and I will make the call for you'. Liddle was co-founder of a lobbying company that had merged with GPC but had no financial interest in the company at the time of the revelations.

The Prime Minister responded by denying the allegations but also stated that the rules on ministerial contacts with lobbyists were being tightened. Draft guidance to Permanent Secretaries from the Cabinet Secretary proposed that civil servants and special advisers should refuse lobbyists' invitations to social functions and that civil servants should never offer inside information to a lobbyist and in addition should log all contacts with lobbyists. Meanwhile the Opposition leader William Hague condemned Labour's 'culture of croneyism' and Draper resigned from GPC Market Access. Although by no means a scandal of the 'cash for questions' kind, the 'cash for access' affair had nonetheless embarrassed the government by revealing a covert network of influence linking former Labour policy advisers-turned-lobbyists to current policy advisers, civil servants and some key ministers, with lobbyists using their insider contacts to sell privileged access to government to corporations and other clients. The episode led to a renewal of calls for a statutory code of practice governing lobbying companies and for a three-year interval between party advisers leaving their posts and taking up jobs with lobbying companies.

Source: The Observer, 5 and 12 July, 1998; *Guardian* 9 July 1998; *Daily Telegraph*, 9 July 1998.

crisis on the beef industry, the Government's recent ban on sales of beef-on-the-bone, cheap meat imports, the threat of legislation on the right to roam, possible further restrictions on shooting, the likelihood of more housing on rural land, and the steady erosion of rural schools, hospitals, public transport and village shops. The Countryside Alliance argued that what was at stake was the right of a minority to pursue its way of life without infringement by the majority and that a ban on fox-hunting would destroy large numbers of jobs in an already imperilled countryside. Critics claimed that the march was essentially a pro-hunting lobby, that public and parliamentary opinion favoured a ban, and that the majority of those marching were Conservative voters who would not have marched against a Conservative Government even though most of the matters complained of (apart from the possible hunting ban) had taken place over several decades under Conservative Governments. The Labour Government, however, responded with concessions, which included more financial help for beef farmers, raising the proportion of new houses to be built on urban sites and softening its position on the right to roam by allowing landowners two years to reach voluntary agreements giving more access to the open countryside. The anti-hunting bill was talked out but the government in its defence claimed that this was a private member's bill which it had made no pledges to support.

Summary

- Pressure groups play a key role in contemporary democratic society especially in the making but also in the implementation of policy.
- The two major types of pressure group are sectional groups which seek to further the interests of people as engaged in particular occupations and cause groups which are formed to promote some attitude, belief or principle.
- The main developments in the post-1945 period have been (1) the institutionalisation of consultation between sectional groups and government, an arrangement seen as advantageous by both sides; (2) a rapid upsurge since the 1960s of cause group activity – often linked to the growth of new social movements; and (3) the systematic dismantling by government of corporatist-style con-

sultation with the 'peak' producer groups together with a significant reorientation of group lobbying efforts towards the European Union in the 1980s and 1990s.

- The distinction between 'insider' groups, which are regarded as legitimate by government and consulted on a regular basis, and 'outsider' groups, which are unable or unwilling to gain such recognition, is a useful one.
- Specific liberal, democratic socialist, one-nation conservative, new right conservative and radical socialist ideological approaches to pressure groups can be identified and all except the marxist have influenced the relationship between government and groups in the postwar era.
- Concepts such as pluralism, corporatism and policy networks provide valuable tools with which to analyse the role of groups in society and government.
- A group's decisions about strategies and methods of influence are dependent on the nature and aims of the group and its perceptions of the location of power in the political system.
- The major channels of influence for groups are the executive (ministers and civil servants), parliament, public opinion, and the European Union but groups may also target the political parties, the courts and local institutions, including local government.
- The debate continues about how far and in what ways pressure groups improve or detract from democracy.

Questions

1. Which groups gained – and which groups lost – influence after 1979 and for what reasons?
2. Evaluate the role of pressure groups under New Labour.
3. Account for the growth of cause groups in recent decades.
4. Examine the arguments for and against pressure groups in a democratic society.

Assignment

The Snowdrop Campaign

The murder of 16 schoolchildren and their teacher at a school in Dunblane, Scotland on 13 March 1996 led to one of the most successful pressure group campaigns in recent times. Within a few days of the Dunblane massacre a group of bereaved parents began a campaign for a complete ban on handguns. Their campaign faced considerable opposition from the powerful handgun lobby which was adept at parliamentary lobbying and had valuable allies in 25 pro-shooting Conservative MPs. Almost immediately the Conservative-dominated Home Affairs Select Committee issued a report rejecting the case for a complete ban on handguns. The government appointed a senior Scottish judge, Lord Cullen, to report on Dunblane and make recommendations. Over the next seven months, the pro- and anti-gun lobbies fought to win over Cabinet, parliament and public opinion to their respective cases.

The gun lobby consisted of prominent groups such as the Shooters' Rights Association, the British Shooting Sports Council, the British Field Sports Society, the National Rifle Association and the National Pistol Association; it represented the interests of 2,118 approved gun clubs and a £60 million per annum gun trade, with 2,470 gun dealers and 10,000 employees. The gun lobby employed professional lobbyists. It argued that the situation called for careful gun licensing rather than a ban and pointed out the danger of hasty legislation driven by emotion.

The anti-gun lobby included the Snowdrop campaigners, who presented a petition containing 750,000 signatures to the Prime Minister in July 1996; the Gun Control Network; the Police Federation; and the Association of Chief Police Officers (ACPO). All these groups advocated a complete handgun ban except ACPO, which supported a ban on all pistols over .22 calibre. The anti-gun lobby did not employ professional lobbyists. It argued that Britain could no longer rely on stringent licensing control to keep guns out of the hands of mentally unstable people such as Thomas Hamilton, the Dunblane murderer, and that, with 200,000 licensed handguns, pistol shooting as one of the fastest-growing pastimes, and an average 54 homicides per year (1989–93) resulting from shooting incidents, Britain was degenerating into a violent gun culture.

The Cullen Report on 16 October called for a range of measures designed to improve public security but stopped short of advocating a ban on any kind of handgun. However, the report had been overtaken by events,and the following day the government announced a ban on all handguns of over .22 calibre, a step which would involve the surrender of 160,000 legally-held guns. Snowdrop immediately announced that it would continue to campaign for a total ban. A total ban was supported by Labour, the Scottish Nationalists and the Liberal Democrats. Key factors in the Government's decision were:

- the persistence of the Snowdrop Campaign and its possession of an articulate spokesperson in Ann Pearston. Her moving speech at the Labour Conference prompted the Labour leader Tony Blair to declare himself in favour of a total handgun ban
- media support for the campaign bolstered by interviews with the bereaved Dunblane parents
- the uncompromising attitude of the gun lobby, which was unwilling to find out if any restrictions less drastic than a total ban could be made to work
- Cabinet politics: Michael Forsyth, the Scottish Secretary, was the MP for the constituency of Stirling, which included Dunblane, and his majority in 1992 was a mere 703 (his notional majority in the new constituency was only 236). From the outset, Forsyth favoured a strong measure and the Cabinet committee chaired by John Major which discussed the matter was aware that anything less would make his political situation very difficult; therefore, the government was prepared to move further than its previous position of a ban on keeping handguns at home.

Questions

(i) Evaluate the arguments of the pro- and anti-handgun lobbies.

(ii) Is this a case of a majority imposing its views on a minority? If so, how far is it right that the majority should destroy what is for most of its practitioners a peaceful pastime?

(iii) 'An affecting picture has been painted of a distressed but determined group of parents in Dunblane banding together to force a timorous government to take firm action against guns. It was not quite like that. What the Government did was dictated by party politics' (Alan Watkins, *The Times*, 26 October 1996). Discuss this view of the main reason for the government action over handguns? What in your view was the main factor in its decision?

Further reading

Good recent texts on pressure groups in Britain are those by Baggott, R. (1995) *Pressure Groups Today* (Manchester: Manchester University Press) and W. Grant (1995, 2nd edn) *Pressure Groups, Politics and Democracy in Britain* (Hemel Hempstead: Prentice-Hall/Harvester Wheatsheaf). A. J. Jordan and J. J. Richardson (1987) *Government and Pressure Groups in Britain* (Oxford; Clarendon) and D. March and R. Rhodes (1992) *Policy Networks and British Government* (Oxford: Oxford University Press) are classic expositions of the policy networks approach and M.J. Smith (1995) *Pressure Politics* (Manchester: Baseline Books) a more recent one. S. Mazey and J. Richardson (eds) (1993) *Lobbying in the European Community* (Oxford: Oxford University Press) provides valuable insights into the developing world of Euro-lobbying, whilst J. J. Richardson (ed.) (1993) *Pressure Groups* (Oxford: Oxford University Press) affords a useful comparative perspective.

The mass media

The communication of political information is an important process in the political system, and the **mass media** play a central role in this activity. Some political scientists believe that the mass media in Britain help democracy work through allowing a wide variety of views to be expressed. Others believe that the media are anti-democratic because of their power to manipulate the way people think about politics at home and abroad. The media, in other words, are politically biased.

Other critics have accused the mass media of trivialising politics. Because different television channels and newspapers find that they are competing for a limited number of viewers and readers, there is the tendency to make the news more attractive by treating it as entertainment rather than as a serious business.

The chapter concludes by considering the impact of election television and newspaper reporting.

The mass media and society

Only a small proportion of Britain's population is actively engaged in politics and therefore learns about political affairs from first-hand experience. What the majority 'know' about politics is made up principally from what they learn from the mass media. In other words, for those individuals who do not participate directly in politics the mass media define their 'real world' of politics. Peter Golding has argued that 'The media are central in the provision of ideas and images which people use to interpret and understand a great deal of their everyday experience' (Golding, 1974, p. 178). This, of course, gives the mass media enormous power since they can either set people's minds against the political system or help to generate popular support for it.

Events following the death of the Princess of Wales in August 1997 will be analysed by media sociologists and social psychologists in terms of understanding the role of the mass media in society. Very crudely, the public seemed to divide into those who reacted to news of her death with sadness (reflected in the relatively low-key tribute paid by William Hague) and those who were engulfed by genuine grief (reflected in Tony Blair's emotional tribute). In many ways Diana's death was a phenomenon like no other, exciting mass emotion, with people setting up local 'shrines' of flowers to her memory up and down the country. Amongst the questions that academics will raise are: how far did the mass media direct and orchestrate the public's response; how far was highly emotional saturation coverage by the media simply a reflection of the public's feelings; and to what extent and by which means did the mass media create a cultural icon out of Diana's image?

> The **mass media** provide the ideas and images which help most people to understand the world they live in and their place in that world.

Some went so far as arguing that the nature of British society changed during summer 1997, a new Britain emerging after Diana's death which was less formal, less deferential and more expressive. Can such arguments be substantiated and, if so, how far did the media contribute towards the 'reinvention' of Britain? (see Box 11.1).

The 'media as part of democracy' viewpoint

There are two basic viewpoints concerning the relationship between the mass media and society. First, there is the view that the media are part of democracy since they are themselves a 'free' institution. The media assist the working of a democratic system through facilitating free speech and unrestricted public debate. In Britain, there is no state control of either the press or broadcasting, although the latter is regulated so that it always serves the interests of the community as a whole. This results in a great variety of political opinions being given an airing, and many of them are hostile to the government of the day.

Broadcasting is bound by law to be 'impartial'. For example the Independent Broadcasting Authority is legally required to ensure that all news is presented with due accuracy and impartiality and that 'due impartiality is preserved on the part of persons providing the programmes as respects matters of political or industrial controversy or relating to current public policy'. During times of national emergency the government may extend greater control over broadcasting as part of its strategy for coping. John Whale has pointed out that the laws relating to both the BBC and ITA make it clear that ministers could instruct them to broadcast or withhold whatever government wanted. He added 'That particular cannon has seldom been fired. It is not much use to party politicians: it was meant to guard the interests of the state (especially in wartime), not of any one political party' (Whale, 1977, p. 12). Direct intervention in broadcasting by the government is rare but we shall see that governments can be extremely sensitive about what is broadcast.

The government has no substantial role in the newspaper business. There is no censorship apart from D (Defence) Notices. Thus, unlike broadcast-ing, there is no obligation for newspapers to be politically impartial. The press provide what can be seen as a 'market place for ideas' in which a wide spectrum of political opinion is made available to the public. As might be expected, some newspapers will be bought more than others, with the popular papers providing the public with what they want to read. These papers will thrive, whilst unpopular and unread papers will struggle and eventually cease being published. The fact that the majority of British newspapers generally supported the Conservative Party does not undermine this democratic view of the press; indeed, it provides crucial evidence that Britain does have a politically representative press.

John Whale argued that 'the media do more towards corroborating opinion than creating it', and with reference to newspapers, he used the *Morning Star* (a communist paper originally published as the *Daily Worker*) with its low circulation as an example: 'if any substantial number of people seriously wanted the structure of society rebuilt from the bottom, the *Morning Star* would sell more copies than it does' (ibid., p. 85). The same argument can be applied to a long list of pro-Labour newspapers: the *Daily Herald, Reynolds News* (which became the *Sunday Citizen*), and *News on Sunday* – all of which closed because they did not sell enough copies. Even the tabloid *Star* dropped its support for Labour in order to improve its circulation. The marketplace had consistently supported only one pro-Labour paper, the *Daily Mirror,* and the non-aligned *Guardian* and *Independent*. In other words, the British press is predominantly conservative in tone because its readers are.

The bias in the press towards parties which support the status quo of a free enterprise system is inevitable since the newspaper industry is under private control and is part of the free enterprise system. In the past the interests of free enterprise were pursued most strongly by the Conservative Party, and for this reason it followed that the press was predominantly Conservative in its sympathies. In 1997, however, newspapers which had traditionally supported the Conservatives either reduced their enthusiasm for recommending that their readers vote Tory or switched to recommending Labour. Some commentators argued that the political sympathies of newspapers had changed less than

BOX 11.1
The masses, the media and the monarchy

The week following the death of the Princess of Wales was remarkable in terms of interaction between the tabloids, a large section of the public, senior officials at Buckingham Palace and the Queen. Through the tabloids, the public 'demanded' that the Queen dumped protocol and expressed the sadness which many felt. The palace concluded that it had badly misjudged the mood of the nation as represented in the headlines below and unprecedented Royal U-turns were made.

The Queen complied and a week of silence ended

The Queen returned to London, and the flag flew

The Queen complied

The palace complied

appeared on the surface since 'new' Labour was in fact a conservative, free-market supporting party. Having said this, the press plays an important 'watchdog' role for democracy, and has not shied away from criticising the Conservative Party or Conservative governments in the past nor Labour today.

The media's 'watchdog' role can, as might be expected, be the source of tension between journalists and the government. This is because government in Britain has grown accustomed to operating in a climate of greater secrecy than some other Western governments, notably the US administration. As a consequence there can be much greater political embarrassment when investigative journalism unearths information which might threaten the government's standing. Governments in the past have frequently tried to suppress such information. For example, Labour and Conservative governments alike have been very sensitive about documentary television programmes which probe beyond the 'bombs and bullets' level of news reporting on Northern Ireland. The biggest uproar came in response to Thames Television's 'Death on the Rock'. This programme explored the circumstances surrounding the killing of three IRA (Irish

Republican Army) terrorists in Gibraltar by the SAS (Special Air Service). On the one hand, the then Prime Minister, Margaret Thatcher, had suffered the assassination of her close colleague, Airey Neave MP, by an IRA bomb and she could not understand why journalists did not battle against the IRA as she did. She felt that the media provided terrorists with the 'oxygen of publicity' and attempted to counteract this by imposing a ban on broadcast interviews with individuals connected with terrorist groups. Roger Bolton, Series Director for 'Death on the Rock', defined the media's watchdog role:

> We, on the other hand, did not see ourselves as agents of the State. Our job was to ask what, why and how, to give the public in a democracy the information to which it is entitled. Put another way our job was not to further government policy but to report the facts, to get the truth. (Bolton, 1990, p. 4 1)

John Major's Conservative government was embarrassed by a series of media disclosures regarding sleaze; most publicity was devoted to the *Guardian*'s accusations that ex-minister Neil Hamilton had received 'cash for questions' from

Harrods' owner Mahamed Al Fayed. Tony Blair's government was embarrassed by press scrutiny of 'influence for cash' suspicions when, after making an exception of Formula One motor racing from a ban on the tobacco sponsorship of sport, it was revealed that Formula One boss, Bernie Ecclestone, made a million pound pre-election donation to Labour.

Newspapers, particularly the tabloids, confronted the government in 1992 over new legislation which also threatened the public's 'right to know'. But in this case, the 'right to know' concerned details of people's private lives rather than details of directly political issues which the government would prefer kept confidential. This conflict was important, however, because it concerned both the power and the freedom of tabloid editors who felt that the government, which owed them a favour for their loyal support during the election campaign, should now not be threatening them with restrictive laws. The Secretary of State for National Heritage, David Mellor, would be responsible for the new privacy legislation, and he had already warned the tabloids that they had broken too many promises about self-regulation and were now 'drinking in the Last Chance Saloon'. Mellor had projected a strong family image during the election campaign, and it was a great embarrassment to him when the *People* alleged that he was having an affair with an actress. In 1997, following the death of the Princess of Wales, attention focused on the press imposing restrictions on the activities of the paparazzi.

Finally, the mass media play an important role in the democratic process by helping to set the political agenda. The agenda-setting function – defined as the correspondence between 'the order of importance in the media given to issues and the order of significance attached to the same issues by the public and politicians' (McQuail, 1987, p. 275) – is complex. Sometimes the agenda set in the media is for the media and far removed from the concerns of the electorate, other times not. Along with politicians, the public, parties and other organisations, the media play a crucial role in structuring and widening political debate in Britain so that issues such as the environment, industrial relations or the 'poll tax' receive attention until the problems are addressed by the government. See Chapter 22 for a discussion of the new morality agenda which emerged during the years running up to the 1997 general election, much to the disadvantage of the Conservative government.

Through these functions the media, it can be argued, enhance and strengthen the quality of democracy in Britain. Despite concern expressed by politicians from the left and right that there is political bias in television, TV and radio maintain a careful balance between the parties. The BBC defines this balance in practice as coverage which should reflect the support obtained by the parties in the preceding election. It is true that newspapers are partisan, mostly supporting the Conservatives in the past, but even then this has not prevented the election of Labour governments.

The 'media as a tool of the ruling class' viewpoint

An alternative view of the mass media in relation to society sees *the media playing a much more creative role in shaping people's ideas, attitudes, beliefs and actions.* In other words, the mass media do not simply reflect public opinion so much as help to mould it in the first place.

The mass media structure the complexities of the social world and make it understandable to readers, viewers and listeners. For example, journalists invariably use a consensus view of society as a framework which is imposed on their reporting in order to explain or make sense out of events. In doing this, the media tend to give authority to certain institutions – such as Parliament – whilst making those who advocate non-parliamentary or direct political action appear as extremists or irresponsible fanatics. Journalists frequently consult or interview 'experts' for their opinions on issues; and these experts are invariably powerful people in society and naturally support the system which gives them power. Although experts may be seen to disagree with each other on specific issues, they are unlikely ever to challenge the consensus view of society in a fundamental way.

The mass media in Britain, even television and radio, cannot be neutral or impartial. This is because the media are a product of Britain's culture, a culture which is biased like any other culture, with assumptions and prejudices of its own. The imposition of this cultural framework is seen in what is referred to as the 'social manufacture' or 'social production' of the news. News does not 'just happen', rather 'it is made'. News programmes and newspapers have a number of predefined categories to be filled by 'the news' – e.g. sport, human interest, politics, economics, and so on. Visually interesting material is more likely to become 'news' than are abstract developments. The selection process of what will become news is known as 'agenda setting'.

Agenda-setting is important politically because of the consequences of an issue being placed on the agenda. If industrial strikes are put on the agenda rather than industrial accidents, it will lead to demands for tighter trade union legislation rather than stricter factory regulations. News about 'social security scroungers' or 'New Age' travellers will stir up different feelings about society than news about 'tax evaders'. Sometimes there is an over-reaction to what is seen as a threat to society and this is referred to as a 'moral panic'. During the 1970s there was a feeling that mugging was a new, violent and increasingly common street crime. The reaction was out of all proportion to the threat, which was not new, but nevertheless demands for more policing and tougher penalties were fed into the political system.

The leading stories in national newspapers influence the choice of issues covered by television and radio later in the day. In other words, the agenda set by television, which people see as being 'objective', takes its lead from stories in the national press. Invariably, since they come from a generally pro-Conservative press, there is a marked tendency for these stories to be anti-Labour and anti-union. At the same time, newspapers followed by television will be relatively uncritical of the Conservative Party or a Conservative government. For example, the media in general failed to question the logic of Thatcherite monetarism in the early 1980s, accepted the 1981–2 recession as inevitable, repeated the government's mid-1980s view of Britain being an 'economic miracle' and failed to scrutinise policies which resulted by the early 1990s in the longest and deepest recession since the war.

The media values of professional journalists together with the traditionally pro-Conservative bias found most explicitly in the press mean that the mass media fail to reflect the values found in society at large. In particular, working-class views do not find expression in the media. From time to time, Labour and the unions have considered launching their own papers in order to remedy this situation. But there are problems in publishing 'working-class' papers, already experienced by the defunct *Daily Herald, Daily Sketch* and *Sunday Graphic:* 'They all had a predominantly working-class readership and, in terms of marketing, relatively "small" circulations. They thus fell between two stools: they had neither the quantity nor the social "quality" of readership needed to attract sufficient advertising for them to survive' (Curran and Seaton, 1990, p. 97). In its analysis of media values, the Glasgow Group found an underlying ideology within the media which attacked working-class institutions. In particular, the researchers' study of industrial relations reporting of strikes on television was 'clearly skewed against the interests of the working class and organised labour' and 'in favour of the managers of industry' (Glasgow Media Group, 1980, p. 400).

Newspapers and much of television and radio are commercial enterprises concerned with making a profit for their shareholders. Put simply, they form part of the capitalist system and this shapes the values which they promote. Indeed, the mass media are very big business. Six leading newspaper publishers – Reed International, News International, Beaverbrook, Associated Newspapers, Thomson, and S. Pearson and Son – account for some 80 per cent of all daily, Sunday and local newspaper sales. Most of these concerns are conglomerates which have financial interests in other sectors of the communication industry. For example, S. Pearson and Son publish *The Financial Times* but also have interests in Longman, Ladybird Books and Penguin Books. Some concerns, such as Thomson, have considerable interests in independent television and commercial radio. Other conglomerates have an even wider base in industry and commerce (see Box 11.2). This pattern of ownership can represent a threat to democracy:

First, concentration limits the range and diversity of views and opinions which are able to find public expression. More significantly, it is those views and opinions representing the least powerful social groups which are systematically excluded by the process of concentration . . . Second, concentration of control over the media into the hands of large conglomerates emphasises production for maximum profit at the necessary expense of other

BOX 11.2
Ownership and control of the media

In countries like Germany and the United States, newspapers are regionally rather than nationally based. Although Britain has local and regional newspapers, it also has a large national newspaper market. This is reflected in the fact that of the 11 biggest circulation newspapers in Europe, 9 are British. Although there is a downward trend, about two-thirds of all British adults regularly read a daily national paper.

There has been a general trend in Britain of there being fewer and fewer national newspapers. Although new newspapers are launched from time to time, the number of daily papers has declined from 21 in 1900 to 11 today. The number of regional and local papers has also declined; in 1900 London had 9 daily evening papers whereas today it has only one. By contrast the United States, with roughly four times the population of Britain, has only one national paper and around 11,000 regional and local papers of which 400 are in the Los Angeles area alone.

Similarly television and radio are highly centralised in Britain. Although there are regional programmes and local radio, most viewers and listeners tune in to national stations such as BBC and ITV. Again, in contrast, the United States has roughly 9,000 radio stations and 1,000 TV stations. What has concerned many political scientists is the concentrated pattern of ownership in Britain's newspapers – five big companies sell well over 80 per cent of all daily national newspapers. They are concerned that this places much power in relatively few hands. The same five big companies have also increased their ownership of local and regional newspapers. Furthermore, these companies own other media such as television and film companies, books, magazines, etc. An example is Rupert Murdoch's News Corporation with financial interests around the world. His British company, News International, publishes *The Times, The Sunday Times, The Times* supplements, the *Sun, News of the World*, as well as books, magazines and journals published by Collins, Fontana and Granada Books. His company has interests in cable TV, satellite TV and LWT, with film interests in Metromedia and Twentieth Century Fox. Finally, News International has interests in the Reuters news agency, property, oil, gas and transport. Political scientists are concerned that the growth of large companies such as this has resulted in 'too much power in too few hands' which puts democracy at risk. As we have already seen, a small number of media conglomerates, such as News International, control the newspapers which are read by a very large proportion of the electorate. Also, as we have seen, newspapers not controlled by any of the media conglomerates, such as the *Independent*, can be put at risk through an aggressive price war.

social goals that should be a vital aspect of communication media. Third, such concentration is undemocratic in two senses. It removes the media from public surveillance and accountability, that is, it renders them externally undemocratic. (Murdoch and Golding, 1977, pp. 105–6)

John Whale was considerably less worried about the effects of ownership on communication. For, at the time he was writing, the 'press baron' who owned papers and who personally dictated editorial policy had disappeared. There were no proprietors like Lord Beaverbrook or Lord Northcliffe, who used to instruct their editors what to put in the *Daily Express* and *Daily Mail* respectively. Contents and policy were determined by professional staff journalists who decided what items to cover, and what items to comment about. However, events were to overtake this argument with the emergence of a new generation of press barons such as Rupert Murdoch and the late Robert Maxwell. There was concern that not only were these new proprietors so powerful that they could intervene in the same ways as the old press barons but also that they did not usually have to intervene since editorial staff anticipated and wrote what they knew would find the approval of their respective proprietors. In addition John Whale saw the pattern of ownership as something which was inevitable in the modern communications newspapers.

However, issues of ownership and control have made a dramatic impact upon the press. The case of the *Sun* shows how a newspaper can be redirected away from the political views of its established readership. Rupert Murdoch purchased the broadsheet *Sun*, which developed from the pro-Labour *Daily Herald*. Murdoch had a reputation for moving his newspapers to the right, and in 1974 this was to happen to the *Sun* 'in opposition to the opinion of its readers', the majority of whom supported Labour (Curran and Seaton, 1990 p. 81). Thus in a little over a decade, Labour had lost the support of a mass circulation daily paper and the Conservatives gained yet another supporter in Fleet Street which a further decade later was to be the most ardent champion of Thatcherism. The values of groups such as the ethnic minorities, unions, feminists and others beyond the Conservative domain are marginalised by the media and remain unrepresented. Even the major opposition party, Labour, was generally portrayed as a dangerous and unpatriotic enemy within. Only when 'new' Labour endorsed the Thatcherite agenda and accepted free-market economics, did the *Sun* change sides.

There is no comparison between the sycophantic British press at national and local level and the US press which scrutinises Republican and Democrat administrations with equal rigour on behalf of American citizens. In this sense, therefore, the British media fails miserably in performing its 'watchdog' role. Indeed, the 'lobby system' is an expression of the cosy relationship between the media and the government, with the former depending on the latter for the supply of 'news' items. This dependency relationship between journalists and politicians is in sharp contrast to the American tradition of investigative journalism.

Television politics

Most people rely on television as their main source of information. As long ago as 1962 a BBC survey showed that 58 per cent of the sample learned the news primarily from TV whereas only 33 per cent learned it mainly from newspapers. Another study ten years later revealed that 85 per cent named television as their main source of information. There is a tendency for people to believe what they 'see' on TV but to be sceptical about what they read in the press. Nearly 70 per cent think that television is the 'most trustworthy' news source whilst only 6 per cent are prepared to rank newspapers so highly.

Since television is perceived by so many as providing a source of objective political information, it is not surprising that there are tensions between politicians and personnel in the media. Examples have been provided above of specific programmes in which the government of the day did not feel it was being treated fairly. Politicians have also complained about the aggressive questioning they receive on Radio Four's *Today* programme.

It is not only specific programmes which have interested politicians but the general 'tone' of a network which has, from time to time, been examined by a 'bias monitoring unit'. Some commentators felt that during the period when the last Conservative government was deciding the future of the BBC – whether its Royal Charter should be renewed or whether it should be privatised – broadcasters were so anxious not to upset the government that their reporting of government policies was noticeably uncritical. In a rather similar way it has been argued that the independent television companies are 'controlled' by the periodic franchise renewal process (see Box 11.3).

Government ministers sometimes come to see policy failure in terms of poor presentation in the media. In other words, rather than recognising that the policies in question are ill-thought-out, inappropriate or not working, it is argued that for some reason 'the message is not getting across'. This logic places the blame with the media for communicating poorly rather than with ministers for governing poorly. In order to receive favourable treatment, politicians and their parties will attempt to manipulate the media in a number of ways. Firstly, accusing television journalists of being biased may produce positive results:

A party can try to bias television in its favour by alleging that the broadcasters are biased against them. If that produces any response at all it may encourage the broadcasters to alter the balance in its favour. Even if the *broadcasters do nothing it may* encourage the *viewers* to regard television as biased against the party and to make allowances for that when they watch. The political effectiveness of the press is much reduced because its readers often see it as 'the Tory press' and adjust their reactions to press stories accordingly. If they can be persuaded that television is not impartial but is dominated by trendy lefties, then the credibility of television reporting will go down and the credibility of press reporting will increase – to the advantage of the Conservatives. (Miller et al., 1990, p. 72)

Secondly, parties will attempt to manipulate the media, particularly television, by what is known as 'spin control'. This involves dealing with events, particularly potentially damaging ones, in order to get

> **BOX 11.3**
> ## How independent is Independent Television?
>
> The former head of London Weekend Television, Greg Dyke, argued that independent television was no more 'independent' than the BBC. In just the same way as the BBC depended on government to get its Charter renewed, so ITV depended on the government to get its franchise renewed. Because both BBC and ITV depended on the government for their survival, they had to be careful and not upset government. This resulted in a 'culture of dependency' which weakened television's 'watchdog' role by eroding the freedom of journalists to effectively question government. In the 1980s, the threats to broadcasters' freedoms came from a general Thatcherite attack on the 'liberal establishment'. Greg Dyke commented that 'as one ardent Thatcherite described it, they needed to get rid of liberal broadcasters in the same way as Henry VIII dissolved the monasteries'. In the 1990s the threats to the political independence of television
>
> are caused by the growth of a dependency culture, in which broadcasters are increasingly dependent on the
>
> actions of government in some cases for their very existence and, in the commercial sector, for their financial success. This is not healthy for broadcasting . . . For a range of reasons – a combination I suspect of the inadequacies of the Broadcasting Act, the business ambitions of some of the ITV companies, and the changing face of competition – the larger ITV companies now always want something more out of government. This is a potential threat to a politically free broadcasting system and potentially gives enormous power to the government of the day.
>
> To illustrate some of the points he was making in his lecture, Greg Dyke mentioned that ITV could not even change the timing of its *News at Ten* programme because of pressure from the then prime minister, John Major, not to alter the scheduling of their nightly news programme.

them interpreted in a favourable way by journalists. The Conservative government put a positive spin on the conclusions of the Scott Report into the sale of British arms to Iraq. On the surface Scott found ministers not guilty of misconduct and this was the conclusion which the government chose to emphasise in Parliament and in the media: 'Scott accepts there was no deliberate misleading of Parliament . . . the government welcomes the clearing of its good name.' Sir Richard Scott made it known that he was annoyed by the spin that government ministers put on his report by selectively quoting him as well as quoting him out of context in order to give the wrong impression of what he found. For it was in the detail of his report that there was much criticism of government conduct.

Labour came to power with a reputation for skilful spin control but in office found that news management could 'spin out of control'. On the issue of Britain's membership of the European single currency, the Chancellor was known to be more enthusiastic over early entry than the Prime Minister. Press stories talked about splits between them. In order to give the impression of unity, the Chancellor, Gordon Brown, gave an interview to *The Times* in which he expressed greater caution. His press secretary, Charlie Whelan, was reported to have put a populist spin on this for the tabloids

along the lines of 'Brown saves sterling'. This gave the impression that the Chancellor was swinging from one extreme position on the euro to another, which resulted in much uncertainty, as a result of unsuccessful spin.

The 'tabloidisation' of the mass media

It has been argued that Western culture is in a crisis; some have identified a process in the mass media which involves reducing the intellectual demands made on viewers, listeners or readers. Americans call it 'dumbing down'. It is argued that film-makers, TV producers, and newspaper editors reduce standards in order to increase their share of the market.

Some political commentators are convinced that the dumbing-down process has affected the quality broadsheet newspapers as well as the tabloids. They argue that 20 or 30 years ago, quality broadsheets like *The Times*, *Guardian* and *Telegraph* made much greater demands on readers by assuming a higher level of knowledge and greater concentration in reading their contents. (In the 1930s *The Times* occasionally printed news stories in ancient Greek, knowing that most of its readers would be able to read them.) It is argued that in the last ten years or so, quality broadsheet newspapers have become more like the tabloids.

Anthony Sampson has argued that 'the frontier between the qualities and popular papers has virtually disappeared'. He noted that the amount of foreign news, parliamentary reporting and serious investigative reporting has declined. The quality broadsheets now include stories about celebrities – 'Gazza', the Spice Girls, Paula Yates, Liam Gallaher, etc. – in a way that they used not to do. When film star Hugh Grant became involved with a Los Angeles woman, the four quality broadsheets devoted an amazing total of 1,752 column inches to report the incident.

It is argued that today's quality press are trivialising the news, which deadens intellect and harms critical thought, which is not good for democracy. An example of this is found in the way serious newspapers devoted much space to covering Tony Blair's changed hairstyle, including computer graphics of his appearance at various stages of baldness. Is this just 'a bit of fun' or does it trivialise politics and put serious political debate at risk?

At the same time, it is also argued that the tabloid papers have become more tabloid. For example, during the 1960s the middle-market papers – the *Daily Mail* and the *Daily Express* – had as much written text on their front pages as today's broadsheets. The reporting was serious; the *Daily Mirror* devoted considerable space to foreign affairs, once giving 15 pages to cover the political crisis in Cambodia. Finally, it is noted that even regional and local newspapers are going tabloid, mixing gossip with news coverage.

Tabloid television

It is argued that serious television programmes are also influenced by tabloid values. This is because news programmes have become seen as 'entertainment' rather than 'education'. As a result, programmes focus on 'human interest' stories at the expense of more complex or abstract news items. Many political commentators were surprised when the tabloid papers' obsession with the Princess of Wales appeared to be shared by the BBC's flagship documentary programme, *Panorama*, which devoted a programme-long interview to exploring her problems and ambitions.

Why are media values now tabloid values?

- Circulation battles: quality broadsheets are locked into a bitter struggle to win readers. There are fears that because of a declining market, one of the quality newspapers will disappear in the near future. Hence they are all attempting to maximise their sales, which means moving 'down market'. Similar arguments might be applied to television.
- Newspapers are trying to get younger readers. Therefore papers now use snappier headlines and shorter sentences to report 'soundbite' politics. Others argue that such techniques are an insult to the young because editors are treating them as if they really are dumb.
- The influence of Rupert Murdoch's style on journalism on the mass media. An example may be useful to covey the new media culture associated with Murdoch; when Elvis Presley died in 1977, *The Times* was owned by Lord Thomson. No *Times* reporter was sent to Memphis to cover the funeral, since it was decided that it was not an appropriate story for a serious newspaper. Murdoch bought *The Times* in 1981, and two journalists were sent to Jamaica to cover the death of Bob Marley. *The Times* then introduced its own style of bingo game, again unthinkable when under its previous owner.
- The influence of greater competition in the electronic media from satellite and cable television. Their impact has resulted in pressures to lower standards.

Newspaper readership

The rack of papers seen outside any newsagents symbolises the British class system. The quality press is read overwhelmingly by the higher socio-economic groups whilst the mass-circulation *Sun*, *Mirror* and *Star* have predominantly working-class readers. Between the 'haughties' and the 'naughties' are the *Mail* and *Express* which, reflecting their lower-middle-class pitch, are read across the social spectrum (see Table 11.1).

Table 11.1 Reading of national newspapers; by social class

Great Britain

| | \multicolumn{4}{c}{Percentage reading each paper} | Readership (millions) |
	AB	C1	C2	DE	
Daily newspapers					
The Sun	7	18	29	30	9.9
Daily Mirror	7	13	22	20	7.1
Daily Mail	14	13	8	6	4.5
Daily Express	9	10	8	5	3.5
The Daily Telegraph	6	6	2	1	2.6
Daily Star	1	4	7	7	2.2
Today	3	4	5	3	1.8
The Guardian	8	3	1	1	1.3
The Times	8	3	1	1	1.3
The Independent	6	3	1	1	1.1
Financial Times	5	2	–	–	7.4
Sunday newspapers					
News of the World	11	23	36	36	12.4
Sunday Mirror	9	16	24	21	8.1
The Mail on Sunday	18	17	11	6	5.9
The People	6	12	16	15	5.6
Sunday Express	13	13	9	5	4.6
The Sunday Times	21	8	3	2	3.7
Sunday Telegraph	11	4	2	1	1.9
The Observer	9	4	2	1	1.6
Independent on Sunday	7	3	1	1	1.2
Sunday Sport	1	2	3	3	9.0

Source: Social Trends 25, 1995, (HMSO).

Treatment of the news varies enormously between papers. The quality papers contain much more of what might be described as 'hard news' in addition to comment and editorial. The mass circulation papers more closely resemble adult comics and are designed for 'looking at' rather than 'reading', containing 'soft news' features which have interest but not immediate newsworthiness. Much space is taken up with photographs and large-print headlines. Where the quality press focuses on international events and city news, the mass circulation papers rarely fail to devote considerable space to 'scandal' of one sort or another.

Only 21 per cent of the adult male population reads a quality broadsheet newspaper, and only 12 per cent of adult females do so. Anxiety has been expressed about the declining quality of the tabloid press. Frequently the tabloids pander to basic prejudices – the 'Gotcha!' headline which reported the sinking of the *Belgrano* during the Falklands War and, the 'Up Yours, Delors' headline on EC policy, are frequently mentioned examples likely to have kindled jingoistic feelings. Some argue that this situation is particularly significant in so far as most tabloid readers are working class. Put another way, rather than inform their readers about the facts of political life, the tabloids maintain their working-class readership in a state of relative political ignorance. The class with the greatest interest in political change is fed a biased, anti-left and trivialised account of politics in Britain and the wider world.

Not only has the tabloid press become more tabloid in nature over recent years, but the press has generally undergone political change: 'national newspapers became markedly more partisan from 1974 onwards. This was partly due in response to the growing polarization of British politics. But it also reflected the cumulative impact of a new generation of partisan, interventionist proprietors' (Curran and Seaton, 1990, p. 80). It was once assumed that such changes would have little impact upon the political behaviour of the electorate. But, as we shall see, this view has been challenged by the findings of recent research.

The political impact of the mass media

There is a view that the mass media can actually create news by 'setting up' newsworthy events that otherwise could not have taken place. Some think that the mere presence of TV cameras at a demonstration increases the risks that it will develop into a riot. If such a riot is shown on the TV news some people think that this creates 'copycat' riots in other areas. There is another view that the mass media may enhance or reduce the importance of events, but those events cannot be created by the media. For example, Colin Seymour-Ure argues that the media were influential in making Enoch Powell into a major political figure in 1968 'as the result of intense, sustained publicity for his views on immigration' (Seymour-Ure, 1974, p. 21). Yet 'that status depended also on the distinctive character of his views and the existence of a political crisis that gave them point' (ibid., p. 21). He continues by arguing that the political impact of any communication will be influenced by its timing, frequency and intensity.

Timing

One of the most interesting examples of political impact resulting from the timing of news took place during the General Election campaign of 1924 with the publication of the Zinoviev letter. The letter, commonly believed to be a fake, was marked 'Very Secret' and was sent from the Third Communist International in Moscow to the Central Committee of the British Communist Party. It urged the need to stir the British working class into revolutionary action and form them into a British Red Army. The letter was published in the Press on 25 October and dominated the campaign until polling day on 29 October. The *Daily Mail* gave the letter the most sensational treatment and amongst the remaining papers only the *Herald* declared it to be a forgery. Some argue that the 'Red Scare' resulting from the Zinoviev letter lost Labour the election. In other words, had the news of this letter which had been known for some considerable period been released at a different time, then Labour would have won the General Election.

Frequency

The constant repetition of messages over a period of time may make an impact on the political climate. Colin Seymour-Ure argues that the habit of the mass media in presenting a 'Westminster' view of British politics can mislead the public:

The construction regularly put upon the nature of British politics by the mass media stresses heavily the 'Westminster' as opposed to the 'Whitehall' elements. The power of Parliament, and the extent to which it figures in political processes at all, are arguably emphasised more than they should be if an accurate impression of events is to be given. If that is so, the frequency of media coverage has much to do with it. (Seymour-Ure, 1974, p. 36)

Intensity

When one story dominates all others, it is said to be communicated more intensely.

An unexpected or urgent event can be turned into a crisis by the intensity of media coverage, such as the untimely death of the Princess of Wales. The Falklands War of 1982 is another interesting example of a high-intensity media event. But because lives were at risk, there was a conflict of interests between the government and the mass media. The essence of successful warfare is secrecy whereas the essence of successful journalism is publicity and disclosure. Despite the intensity of communication, there was relatively little raw information to transmit. It seems likely, also, that the British government was bearing in mind that TV coverage of the war in Vietnam had undermined public support amongst Americans for the conflict to be pursued. Thus, whilst there was the technical capacity to send Falklands War pictures back to Britain from the South Atlantic, these facilities were denied to journalists. In the absence of 'live' coverage, news and current affairs programmes relied on military 'experts' to speculate on events with the aid of cartoons and models. The Gulf War, in which Saddam Hussein's Iraqi invasion of Kuwait was reversed by an alliance of American, British and Arab forces dominated the world's news media in January 1991. The intensity of reporting in Britain was reflected in a round-the-clock BBC radio channel being devoted to reporting the conflict.

Election television and press coverage

Despite the extraordinary outcome of the 1997 general election, coverage of events on television fell flat. Some commentators concluded that in 1997, 'British election television news was voluminous,

Table 11.2 National daily and Sunday press; circulation by partisanship at the time of the 1997 General Election

Paper	Preferred winner (1992 in brackets)	% readers intending to vote (actual result in brackets)			
		Con	Lab	L-D	Others
Daily papers					
Daily Mail	Conservative (same)	49	29	14	8
Daily Mirror	Labour (same)	14	72	11	3
Daily Star	Labour (implicitly Conservative)	17	66	12	5
Daily Telegraph	Conservative (same)	57	20	17	6
Express	Conservative (same)	49	29	16	6
Financial Times	Labour (not a Conservative majority)	48	29	19	4
Guardian	Labour (Lab; more Lib Dems)	8	67	22	3
Independent	Labour (uncommitted)	16	47	30	7
Sun	Labour (Conservative)	30	52	12	6
The Times	Eurosceptic (Conservative)	42	28	25	5

Total circulation (000)
  pro-Conservative: 4,504 (33%)
Total circulation pro-Labour: 8,533 (62%)
Total circulation: 13,757

Sunday papers					
Express on Sunday	Conservative (same)	53	27	14	6
Independent on Sunday	Labour (not a Conservative majority)	14	48	32	6
Mail on Sunday	Conservative (same)	49	28	15	8
News of the World	Labour (Conservative)	28	55	11	6
Observer	Labour (same)	11	63	22	4
People	Labour (same)	21	62	11	6
Sunday Mirror	Labour (same)	18	67	12	3
Sunday Telegraph	Conservative (same)	56	19	17	8
Sunday Times	Conservative (same)	43	30	21	6

Total circulation(000)
  pro-Conservative (%):   5,490 (37%)
Total circulation pro-Labour (%):   9,311 (63%)
Total circulation: 14,801

Source: Seymour-Ure (1997) pp. 590–1.

substantive, and more detailed than in many other countries. Nevertheless . . . the news was more negative in 1997 than in previous campaigns, and this process may turn voters off' (Semetko et al., 1997, p. 614). Politicians launched attacks on their opponents on a daily basis, faithfully reported by television journalists, and the 'balance requirement' of the Representation of the People Act 'despite all its good intentions, often resulted in regimented soundbites and negative conflict that may in fact have conspired against understanding' (ibid., p. 615).

Labour enjoyed its greatest level of endorsement by the daily and Sunday national press in the 1997 general election campaign (see Table 11.2):

- In 1945, when Labour's parliamentary landslide was won on 48 per cent of the popular vote, it was supported by daily national papers which had a combined 35 per cent of all newspaper circulation.
- In 1964, when Labour was returned to power on 44 per cent of the popular vote, it had the support of 3 national dailies which together had 42 per cent of all newspaper circulation.
- In 1983, Labour won only 28 per cent of the popular vote, and was supported only by the loyal *Daily Mirror*, which accounted for 22 per cent of newspaper circulation.
- In Labour's 1997 parliamentary landslide, achieved on 44 per cent of the popular vote, the party was supported by 6 dailies which represented 62 per cent of all newspaper circulation.

(*Source*: Seymour-Ure, 1997, p. 588)

Labour's leader, Tony Blair, had carefully established good relations with Rupert Murdoch's News Corporation and it was not a surprise when the *Sun* changed sides (Box 11.4). On reflection the *Sun* had been a Thatcherite rather than pro-Conservative paper and in changing its allegiance it was pro-Blair rather than pro-Labour (see Figure 11.1). Another press baron, Lord Rothermere, whose publishing empire included the *Daily Mail* and London's *Evening Standard*, announced his conversion to new Labour.

What factors encouraged six of Britain's ten daily papers and five of nine Sunday papers to endorse Labour? Apart from the Major government's inability to devise a policy on the EU which won the support of its backbenchers and the party's poor record on sleaze, two factors are critical:

- In July 1995 John Major resigned as party leader and put himself up to re-election in a 'back me or sack me' contest. The *Sun* declared that 'Major could not lead a cinema queue. He is damaged goods, a loser.' The *Daily Mail*'s front-page headlines said 'Time to ditch the Captain' above a cartoon of a ship 'Toryanic' sinking after striking

Figure 11.1 The *Sun* backs Blair

an iceberg in the shape of Tony Blair. Only the *Daily Express* backed John Major in his re-election bid. It would have been very difficult for these papers to reject John Major in 1995 yet give him enthusiastic endorsement in 1997. The *Sun*, especially, did not want to be on the losing side in the 1997 election for commercial reasons.

- Labour's long-held and substantial lead in the opinion polls was reflected in the readership of the Conservative press. By 1995, for example, the percentage of *Times* readers which supported the Conservatives had fallen to 37 per cent from 64 per cent in 1992; Conservative support fell from 72 per cent to 52 per cent amongst *Daily Telegraph* readers during the same period. With 45 per cent of *Times* readers and almost a third of *Telegraph* readers now supporting Labour, respective editors were put in a difficult position. They wanted to acknowledge the changing politics of their readers; whilst not wishing to make a *Sun*-like change of political loyalty, they toned down their Conservative support compared with earlier elections.

BOX 11.4
Looking back to 1992: did the Sun win it?

The influence of tabloid newspapers, the *Sun* in particular, on voting behaviour in the 1992 general election is still discussed by political scientists. The day following the election the *Sun* headline told readers 'It's the Sun Wot Won It' and some journalists agreed that the claim was largely justified. Poll data indicated that during the last week of the campaign the anti-Labour blitz in the Tory tabloids had produced swings to the Conservatives of 4 per cent amongst *Sun* readers, 3 per cent amongst *Daily Express* readers and 2 per cent amongst *Daily Mail* readers. Oddly enough, there had also been a 2.5 per cent swing to the Conservatives amongst readers of the pro-Labour *Mirror* although there had been no last-minute Conservative swing amongst readers of the relatively apolitical *Star*. Although the evidence is far from being conclusive, there is a case that the tabloids determined which candidate was to win, particularly in the South, on 'bonus' votes produced in the main by the *Sun* 'effect'.

A study published by the Institute of Public Policy Research written by Martin Linton, *Money and Votes*, measured the financial value of favourable press coverage for a party as if it had been paid for at commercial advertising rates. During the 1992 general election campaign the Conservatives had 40 pages of positive coverage in the *Sun*, 87 in the *Mail* and 94 in the *Daily Express*, while Labour received 60 pages in the *Daily Mirror*. The report calculated that if this positive publicity had been paid for at advertising rates, the Conservatives would have paid £1,342,000 to the *Sun*, £1,973,160 to the *Mail* and £2,233,900 to the *Express*, while the Labour Party would have paid £1,788,000 to the *Mirror*. The report also calculated the figures in a different way on the basis that advertising agencies believe that favourable coverage on the editorial page of a paper is worth three times as much as the equivalent advertising space on any other page. If this assumption is accepted, the Conservatives received free publicity worth £16 million and Labour £5 million in the 1992 campaign.

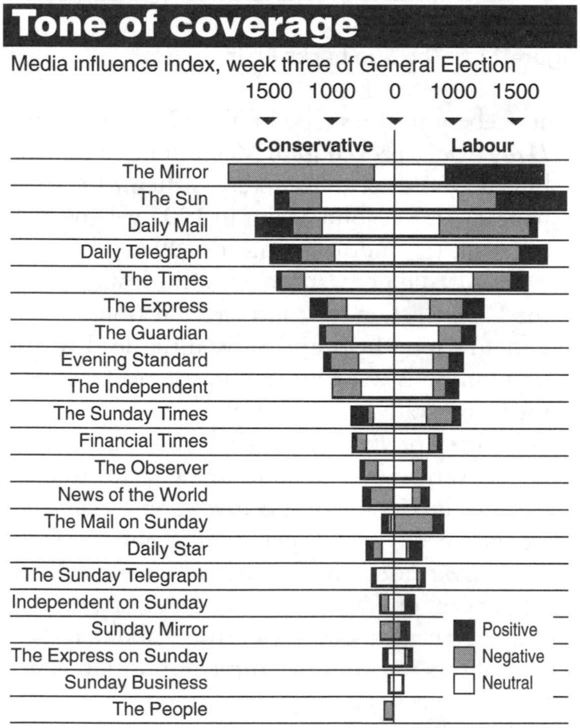

Tone of coverage
Media influence index, week three of General Election

Source: The Guardian, 17 April 1997.

Figure 11.2 The tone of press coverage of the 1997 General Election (week 3)

A team of media analysts working for CMS Precis studied national daily and Sunday papers and constructed a 'media influence index' based on a combination of factors such as circulation, the amount of space devoted to the 1997 election issues and the impact of photographs and headlines (see Figure 11.2). According to their findings, the most biased election coverage was in the traditionally Labour-loyal *Daily Mirror*, with no pro-Conservative stories and no anti-Labour stories. Their analysis clearly revealed the *Sun*'s conversion to Blair's new Labour, whilst the *Times* and the *Guardian* were amongst the most balanced and neutral in their reporting of the election.

Backbench exposure: parliament or the media?

Some politicians opposed TV cameras entering the Lords and then the Commons because they thought that televising proceedings would 'devalue' Parliament in the eyes of the electorate. Oddly enough TV has reduced the importance of Parliament in some ways, but not so much in the eyes of the public as in the actions of politicians. Close to Parliament are the TV and radio studios at 4 Millbank. Which venue, the Commons or Millbank, is the more important for a backbench MP who wants publicity for his or her views?

- Many MPs find that it is much easier to get a hearing at Millbank than it is in the Commons. This is particularly true for maverick backbenchers such as Ken Livingstone who frequently have a controversial view which they want to communicate to the public yet rarely have the opportunity of being called to speak in Commons debates.
- There are now many more opportunities for MPs to appear on TV and radio than existed in the past. The number of political programmes, such as those broadcast at lunchtime on Sunday, has increased during the last twenty years.
- MPs reach a wider audience more quickly by appearing on TV or radio than by speaking in a Commons debate. Many Ministers feel that a twelve-second 'soundbite' on Radio 4's *Today* programme or the TV news is more effective than a lengthy speech in Parliament.
- Newspapers now monitor TV and radio more closely than they follow proceedings in Parliament. In recent years there has been a sharp decline in the reporting of Parliamentary debates in the quality broadsheet newspapers (see assignment 1). A consequence of this is that the Press follows up TV and radio news items in the next day's papers. Hence MPs are more likely to push their concerns on to the political agenda through appearing in the TV and radio studios at Millbank than on the floor of the House of Commons.
- Finally, MPs gain greater recognition through appearing on TV and radio than through debating in the Commons. This may be because TV and radio stresses the 'entertainment' or 'soap opera' ingredients of politics – conflict between individuals, clashes of personality, and aspects of scandal – whereas the focus of Parliament is on the more routine legislative process. In short, politicians on TV and radio come across as colourful personalities who capture the attention of viewers and listeners, whereas in the Commons they are more 'grey' and much less attractive.

Summary

- The mass media are amongst the most powerful political institutions in society although it is difficult to be precise about the extent of their influence.
- Some academics see the mass media as free institutions which are part of democracy, whilst others see them as manipulators of public opinion in the interests of the ruling class.
- The general population seem to be sceptical about the political content in newspapers but to trust what they see on television. Despite this, recent research suggests that newspapers, particularly the tabloid press, have a greater influence on political behaviour than was previously believed to be the case.
- For the first time in its history Labour had the majority backing of the British press in the general election of 1997, including renewed support from the *Sun*.

Questions

1. To what extent if any did the media's 'watchdog' role contribute to the defeat of the Conservatives in 1997?
2. How far and in what ways can the media be used by politicians to project a favourable image?
3. Why did the majority of British newspapers support Labour in 1997 after supporting the Conservatives in previous general elections?
4. Conduct a 'content analysis' of a tabloid and a broadsheet newspaper, and calculate the percentage of each paper devoted to reporting politics. Devise your own categories (such as the economy, overseas news) and show your results as pie-charts or bar-graphs together with a brief commentary on your findings.
5. Consider whether 'balanced' political reporting on television undermines or strengthens the influence of a partisan tabloid press.
6. 'Televising the Commons has had no impact upon British politics.' Discuss.
7. 'The main impact of the media on politics has been to trivialise politics.' Discuss.

Assignments

Assignment (1) The decline in newspaper reporting of Parliament

A study conducted by Labour MP, Jack Straw, revealed a sharp decline in the reporting of Parliamentary debates in the quality broadsheet newspapers. He stated that 'Until the late 1980s, the broadsheet press devoted substantial space to the straightforward reporting of Parliament . . . In the past five years, systematic reporting of debate has all but been abandoned. Between 1933 and 1988, debates took between 400 and 800 lines each day in the *Times*, and between 300 and 700 lines in the *Guardian*. By 1992 coverage was fewer than 100 lines in both papers.' Although the *Times* and *Guardian* were singled out for special criticism, he also noted that the *Daily Telegraph* had halved its coverage; he thought Parliament was best reported in the *Independent*.

Jack Straw argued that the decline in reporting Parliament reduces the public's understanding of politics, because political argument is a vital ingredient in democracy. He went as far as saying that 'argument lies at the heart of the democratic system'. He pointed out how the speeches in the Maastricht debate had changed attitudes on Labour and Conservative backbenches. The more Maastricht was debated, the greater the opposition to economic and monetary union on both sides.

But is Jack Straw right to be so concerned about this development? Others have argued that his point about speeches being at the heart of democracy is a myth. Journalist Martin Kettle asked 'How many

Figure 11.3 The reporters' room in the House of Commons in the 1860s. It is argued that today parliament is served poorly by the press.

political speeches a year actually matter? I doubt the number exceeds two dozen, and most of them are made at party conferences . . . In Parliament, only the Budget speech, and the occasional set piece from the parliamentary party leaders retain any civic interest or importance.'

What factors have led to the recent decline in reporting Parliament in newspapers? There are probably two basic causes; firstly, the impact of televising the Commons despite the fact that only snippets of speeches are ever televised; secondly, MPs making greater use of press releases to publicise their arguments rather than relying on speeches made in the Commons (Figure 11.3).

Questions
(i) Identify the papers Jack Straw picked out for special criticism in their reporting of Parliament, and his reasons for so doing.
(ii) Which paper did Straw believe to be the best in reporting the business of Parliament?
(iii) Why did journalist Martin Kettle disagree with Jack Straw over the importance of reporting Parliament?
(iv) Apart from newspaper reporting, by what other means can be public learn which issues concern politicians? Are these alternative means satisfactory?

Assignment (2) Doctoring the news?
The use of the American term 'spin doctor' is relatively recent, but in reality spin doctors have operated in British politics for a long time. For example, Harold Wilson's spin doctors included Joe Haines and Marcia Williams. It is probably true to say that the growth in the mass media has increased the number of spin doctors.

What do spin doctors do? Basically, spin doctors are concerned with political news management. It is their job to get the best possible outcome for their party in any situation. A typical example of the spin doctor's craft was seen in how the Conservatives handled the May 1996 local election results. Central Office knew that the party was going to suffer badly

at the polls, and yet wanted to present the results in a positive way. Skilful news management lowered media (and therefore public) expectations which then enabled poor results to look like good ones. In other words, Conservative spin doctors stated that 800 losses would be a disastrous result for the party; in the event, Conservatives lost *only* 573 seats.

There has been much discontent inside Labour over the growing influence of spin doctors – particularly Peter Mandelson (nicknamed 'the prince of darkness') and Alistair Campbell. Typical is Brian Sedgemore, who argued that 'their job seems to be to distort; to give serious political issues a populist appeal and slant, in a way that is often simplistic – or even offensive – to those who have spent their lives trying to get difficult points across. The spin doctor is trying to convert everything into 25 second soundbites, for televisual consumption.'

Questions
(i) Identify three 'spin doctors'. To what extent, if any, do spin doctors assist public understanding of political issues? How far do you agree with Brian Sedgemore's criticism?
(ii) Discuss another example of political 'spin' being put on a negative event experienced by any of the parties.
(iii) Explain how political news is 'made'.

Further reading
Curran, J. and Seaton, J. (1990) *Power Without Responsibility: The Press and Broadcasting in Britain* (London: Routledge). An interesting discussion of the position of the contemporary media. Glasgow Media Group (1980) *More Bad News* (London: Routledge & Kegan Paul). A radical critique of Britain's mass media. Harrison, M. (1985) *TV News: Whose Bias?* (Hermitage, Policy Journals): a rejoinder to the conclusions of the Glasgow Media Group. Whale, J. (1977) *The Politics of the Media* (London: Fontana): an interesting discussion of the political context within which the media operates and yet influences.

PART 3

INSTITUTIONS AND THE POLITICAL PROCESS

The changing British Constitution

This chapter discusses the distribution of power and authority within Britain. We begin by examining constitutions in general, including the meaning of the term **constitution**, how a constitution may be distinguished from a 'political system', differing types of constitution, and the reasons why constitutional issues are inherently political. We then consider the major sources, leading principles, actual working of and recent developments in the British Constitution before looking at how it is perceived by the main political ideologies. Finally, we examine the constitutional reform movement which began in the late 1980s before concluding with a consideration of the prospects for constitutional reform under the Labour Government.

Constitution: a constitution allocates political authority within a state: it states where power is legally located and how it is to be made accountable to the ruled. It defines the composition and powers of the main offices and institutions of state and regulates their relations with each other and with the citizen.

What is a constitution?

Political science has sometimes neglected the study of constitutions. This is for two main reasons. First, formal constitutions are imperfect guides to political reality – to the *actual* as compared with the *supposed* distribution of power within a state. For example, many constitutions either omit or scarcely mention the roles in the political process of such important institutions as parties, pressure groups and civil services. In fact, the structure and number of parties are so influential upon the way political systems work that some leading political scientists see these factors as the major determinants of the whole nature of political regimes. Clearly, much important political behaviour occurs outside the formal legal framework. Second, formal constitutions have been frequently and easily flouted and overthrown. The constant demolition of allegedly binding constitutions since 1918 appears to mock the nineteenth-century belief in the capacity of written codes of rules to mould political actions. The tearing-up of written constitutions by dictators are merely dramatic examples of this process.

Yet, powerful though these considerations undoubtedly are, they represent arguments for not expecting too much from the study of formal constitutions rather than for abandoning the exercise altogether. Even though formal constitutions are *incomplete* as guides to political practice, this lack of comprehensiveness is not a sound reason to neglect their study altogether. For one thing, no document or limited set of documents could ever incorporate the whole of a country's political system in its vastly complex entirety. For another, constitutions' lack of correspondence with political realities can be – and has been – exaggerated. As S. E. Finer has commented, few formal constitutions bear 'no relationship whatsoever to what goes on' in a political system and in some countries – the USA, France and Germany, for example – 'the practice of politics does not widely diverge from the guidelines in the constitutional texts' (Finer, 1979, pp. 13–14, 16).

Formal constitutions, then, do matter for a number of reasons. They contain the most important – if not all – of the procedural rules of a political system. They serve as revelations – and reminders – of the political principles a particular people considers important, and wishes to live up to. Alongside moral codes and cultural norms, they provide a means of restraint on politicians and civil servants. And finally, they are the major way of giving legitimacy to a particular system of government, to a particular way of organising the distribution of power within a state.

Students of politics, then, need to distinguish between the formal and informal elements in a political system, between the 'public' constitution, normally contained in a specific document or a number of documents, and the 'private' constitution, the unspecified activities of individuals, groups, parties and other institutions. Both elements are necessary to a comprehensive description of the structure and operations of power and authority in a political community.

It is customary to classify constitutions according to whether they are **unitary** or **federal**, 'written' or 'unwritten', and 'flexible' or 'inflexible'.

Unitary and federal systems

Constitutions seek to create a viable order out of the diversity which confronts them – a diversity of

---

In a **unitary** state, supreme authority remains in the hands of a single source; devolved power is always subject to supervision by the sovereign body and can be revoked by it.

In a **federal** state, authority is constitutionally divided between several coordinate agencies. The central government may have the more important responsibilities but the provincial governments are all-powerful within their constitutionally allocated spheres of responsibility. Clashes between coordinate governments are resolved by means such as a court or similar institution.

---

classes, regions and ethnic groups. All these various subgroups demand from the framers of constitutions inclusion in the state in a manner which accords with their self-respect. The claims of ethnic and regional groupings are normally the hardest to accommodate constitutionally. Where the differing cultures and races in a state are not physically separate from the rest of the community – e.g. blacks in the United States, West Indians, Indians and Pakistanis in the United Kingdom – they may seek protection of their civil rights by special constitutional guarantees and legislation. Where ethnic, cultural and national groups are located in geographically distinct areas – e.g. the Bretons, Basques, Walloons, Welsh and Scots – a classic problem of state-making exists: that of providing a single government for several territorial regions each with its own culture.

The two major forms of political union are unitary and federal systems. Each recognises the territorial aspect of government – the need to provide for regional cultural diversity – in a different way. In the contemporary world, the United Kingdom, France and Japan are unitary states; the USA, Australia and Germany have federal constitutions.

Written and unwritten constitutions

All formal constitutions are selections of the most important legal and political rules and practices. Countries with 'written' constitutions encapsulate the main body of their constitutional law in a single document. Britain, which does not encapsulate its constitutional rules in a single, authoritative document, has on this conception an 'unwritten' constitution. However, in fact, much of the UK constitution is 'written' although it is not 'codified' in a single document. In popular, everyday parlance, the British Constitution will probably continue to be referred to as 'unwritten'. But a more precise form of classification would be to use terms such as 'codified' and 'uncodified' to distinguish between those countries which incorporate their major constitutional rules into a single document and those like Britain which, apart from a few Middle Eastern kingdoms, is the only country in the world which does not do so.

Flexible and inflexible constitutions

It is a major characteristic of 'written' or 'codified' constitutions that the constitutional law they embody has the status of a higher form of law. For example, Article VI, Clause 2 of the US Constitution states: 'This Constitution . . . shall be the supreme law of the land.' Whereas written constitutions are normally only alterable by special procedures, uncodified constitutions like Britain's can be amended by the same process as the ordinary law. In the matter of ease of amendment, therefore, codified constitutions are generally described as inflexible, uncodified constitutions as flexible.

What makes constitutions political?

Sometimes textbooks on this subject have given the impression that constitutions are somehow 'above politics'. But, in fact, this is not the case. Constitutions are both *about* politics and *in* politics. Constitutions are *about* politics because they provide the framework of rules which shape political behaviour – the main 'rules of the game'. No more than in football or cricket do you have to learn long lists of such rules in order to be able to play the political 'game'. But a grasp of their main features is essential for an understanding of the 'play'. Second, constitutions are *in* politics because as bodies of the most important rules in a country they are subject to pressure from the competing individuals, groups and classes whose activities they constrain. Constitutions at any given moment are always more or less advantageous to some and disadvantageous to others. For example, the single-member, simple majority electoral system benefits the major parties but operates against the Liberal Democrats. A constitution, therefore, is something which politicians and political activists are always seeking to change, radically modify, keep the same or, if they are revolutionaries, overthrow.

Because constitutions are inherently political, they have to be seen in a dynamic rather than a static way. The British Constitution, like other constitutions to a lesser extent, is a *historical* formation. Its provisions reflect a continually changing balance of power between classes, groups and interests. This balance and those constitutional provisions have been changed as a result of *political* action by 'new' groups using such means as demonstrating, lobbying and marching in order to bring about concessions from the established order. Thus the aristocratic 'balanced' constitution of the eighteenth century became the middle-class liberal constitution of the nineteenth century which in turn – as a consequence particularly of the franchise extensions of 1918 and 1928 – became the liberal democratic constitution of the twentieth century.

These changes have involved major shifts of power between the leading national institutions. By the mid-nineteenth century the monarchy and the House of Lords had been supplanted as dominative bodies by the House of Commons which – one hundred years later – had itself been in part displaced from the centre of the constitutional scene by a large bureaucracy and by a vast web of outside interests. Clearly rules which have changed so often and so dramatically over the past two centuries will change again, and change considerably.

One point is worth stressing about the *process* of constitutional change and about the *nature* of the constitutional 'settlement' which results from any period of intense constitutional activity. The process itself always consists of a kind of dialogue between (crudely) the forces of conservation and the forces of transformation, and the upshot – *the* constitution at any particular moment – represents in essentials a compromise between them. In that sense, the constitution represents the terms, the arrangements, on which a country can be ruled.

In this quite abstract but very important sense, constitution-making is about engineering consent to government. Thus, in Britain agitation by the middle and working classes and by women broke the constitutional settlements prevailing respectively in the early nineteenth, late nineteenth and early twentieth centuries. At each point in time, public consent to the constitution was no longer possible on the old terms; change was a condition of political stability. In essence, the nature of constitutions is to express the conditions under which people will consent to be governed.

The main sources of the British Constitution

It is clear from the discussion so far that Britain neither lacks a constitution – as sometimes used to be said – nor that its constitution is unwritten – as also used to be said. In fact, the British Constitution can best be described as partly written, but uncodified, i.e. not set down in a single document. It is not codified because, although often compelled to alter course, the country's political authorities have never in modern times faced the kind of crisis which forced them to think the constitution through to first principles, and to set these down. However, there is, of course, a British Constitution in the sense of a set of 'rules, customs and understandings empowering and limiting government'. It is a constitution which, as we have seen, 'was never invented or designed but just grew, so that political facts became constitutional rules' (Madgwick and Woodhouse, 1995, pp.11, 18). The major sources of the British Constitution are: legislation; common law; conventions; European Union law; the law and custom of Parliament; and works of authority. These are defined and described in more detail – with examples – in Box 12.1.

The main characteristics of the British Constitution

As well as being flexible and partly written but uncodified, the British Constitution is unitary rather than federal, based on the principle of parliamentary sovereignty, and generally considered to enshrine the rule of law.

A unitary constitution

The United Kingdom of Great Britain and Northern Ireland is a political union of several countries, each with a different constitutional status. Legally, it consists of the Kingdoms of England and Scotland, the Principality of Wales and two-thirds of the province of Ulster (Northern Ireland) which remained loyal to the British Crown in 1922 when the rest of Ireland split away to form what eventually became the Republic of Ireland (1949).

However, although the national sub-divisions of the British Isles lend themselves in theory to a federal constitution, the United Kingdom has become – and remains – a unitary state. The major reason for this is the strength of political will displayed by mediaeval and early modern English ruling groups in successively incorporating Wales (1536), Scotland (1707) and Ireland (1801) into a political union on terms dictated by its most powerful member.

The argument that the UK is not a true unitary state is unconvincing. This claim rests in particular upon Scotland's retention of its own legal system and upon the degree of devolution to Northern Ireland between 1921 and 1972 which allegedly made it more like a provincial unit in a federal system than a constitutionally subordinate part of a unitary state. However, the constitutionally subordinate status of Scotland and Wales was revealed over the issue of devolution in 1978 when, having legislated devolved powers upon Scottish and Welsh assemblies, the Westminster Parliament repealed them in the following year. In 1997, devolution to Scotland and Wales took place within the framework of the continuing **sovereignty** of the Westminster Parliament. The fundamentally subordinate position of Stormont, the Northern Ireland parliament, within the UK was shown in 1972 when the Westminster government revoked its powers and reasserted direct rule over the province from Westminster. The Westminster Parliament (in strict legal terms, the Crown-in-Parliament) remains the supreme constitutional authority in the United Kingdom.

Parliamentary sovereignty

In formal terms, parliamentary authority in the United Kingdom is unlimited: parliament can make or unmake law on any subject whatsoever; and it can do so retrospectively. The classic statement of its omnicompetence derives from William Blackstone, the eighteenth-century jurist, who declared that parliament 'can do everything that is not naturally impossible'. No person may question its legislative competence and the courts must give effect to its

> **Sovereignty**: within a state, it refers to the source of ultimate legal authority; when used of states in their external relations, it means a state's ability to function as an independent entity.

BOX 12.1
The British constitution: the major sources

Legislation: Easily the most significant source of British constitutional law. It consists both of Acts of Parliament and of subordinate legislation such as Orders in Council (made by the Queen in her Privy Council) and rules and regulations made by Ministers under statutory authority. Key constitutional matters regulated by legislation include:

- The composition of the electorate (Representation of the People Acts, 1832–1928);
- Relations between the Crown and Parliament (Bill of Rights, 1689); between the two Houses of Parliament (Parliament Acts, 1911 and 1949); between the component parts of the UK (Act of Union with Scotland, 1707); between the UK and the EEC (European Communities Act, 1972) and between the individual and the state (Habeas Corpus Act, 1679, and the Administration of Justice Act, 1960).

Common law: Common law means case law and custom, the law made by the decisions of courts or which has grown up as accepted practice over the years. Having declined over the centuries, it is now less important than legislation but remains significant in three main ways:

- The fundamental constitutional principle of parliamentary sovereignty derives from a small number of customary rules (now in part qualified by legislation).
- The remaining prerogative powers exercised by or in the name of the Crown derive from common law, e.g. the appointment of Ministers, the dissolution of Parliament, the power of pardon and the award of honours. By convention, these powers are now predominantly exercised on the advice of ministers.
- Decisions made by the courts under the principle of judicial review of administrative action.

Conventions: Conventions have been persuasively defined as 'certain rules of constitutional behaviour which are considered to be binding by and upon those who operate the Constitution, but which are not enforced by the law courts (although the courts may recognise their existence), nor by the presiding officers in the Houses of Parliament' (Marshall and Moodie, 1967, p. 26).

Conventions are a major means by which the constitution adapts to changing circumstances and are absolutely essential to its working. Many relate to the powers of the monarch, including those that the Queen must appoint as prime minister a person who has the confidence of the House of Commons (this will normally be the leader of the majority party), must assent to measures passed by both Houses of Parliament, and must exercise her powers on Ministerial advice. Other conventions regulate the relations between the executive and legislature (e.g. Ministerial

responsibility), and the operation of the two Houses of Parliament, the civil service and the judiciary.

Conventions are observed largely because of the political difficulties which would follow if they were not: for example, for the monarchy if it refused a request for a dissolution, for a prime minister if he or she came from the Lords. Conventions are vaguer than laws and sometimes – when challenged – are superseded by legislation: for example, in 1910, a convention that the upper House should defer to the lower House on matters of finance was threatened by the Lords' rejection of a budget, which led to this aspect of relations between the two Houses being settled by legislation (Parliament Act, 1911) Normally, a rule becomes a convention once it has been accepted and operated by governments of differing political persuasions.

European Union Law: From 1973, when Britain joined the European Economic Community, Community law (now Union law) and the judgements of the European Court of Justice have been a source of British constitutional law. Some EU rules – mainly regulations made by the Council of Ministers and the Commission – are 'directly applicable' in the UK: this means that they are applied by British courts without re-enactment as though they are Acts of Parliament. Membership of the EU has general constitutional implications with regard to the doctrine of parliamentary sovereignty (discussed in text). More specifically, the EU can levy certain customs duties directly in the United Kingdom (UK) and the UK may not restrict the employment or occupation of any EU national given leave to enter the country.

The law and custom of Parliament: The rules relating to the functions, procedure, privileges and immunities of each House of Parliament: sources of these are the resolutions of each House, conventions (e.g. the duty of impartiality required of the Speaker of the House of Commons) and other informal understandings (e.g. relating to the allocation of time to the Opposition), and to a lesser extent statute law and judicial interpretation.

Works of authority: Its partly written and uncodified character means that constitutional experts and works of authority such as Walter Bagehot, *The English Constitution* (1967), Edward Dicey, *The Law of the Constitution* (1885) and Sir Ivor Jennings, *The Law and the Constitution* (1933) have occasionally to be consulted for guidance on the British Constitution. Post-1945, constitutional authorities have been turned to on such matters as peerage law, aspects of the royal prerogative, the law of treason and constitutional conventions. On the law and custom of Parliament, Sir Thomas Erskine May's treatise on the *Law, Privileges, Proceedings and Usage of Parliament* is regarded as definitive.

legislation. **Parliamentary sovereignty** is the 'dominating characteristic' of the British Constitution (Bogdanor, 1988, p. 55).

However, it is necessary to consider how far the sovereignty of the UK Parliament has been impaired by membership of the European Union (EU). The European Communities Act (1972) gave the force of law in the United Kingdom to obligations arising under the EC treaties; it gave EC law general and binding authority within the United Kingdom; it provided that Community law should take precedence over all inconsistent UK law; and it precluded the UK Parliament from legislating on matters within EC competence where the Community had formulated rules to 'occupy the field'.

It might be argued on two grounds that parliamentary sovereignty is not impaired. First, membership of the EU has not broken the principle that Parliament cannot bind its future action. Thus, the European Communities Act was overturnable and indeed had the 1975 Referendum on continuing membership of the EC gone the other way, the United Kingdom would probably have withdrawn from the Community. Second, what happens should a member state refuse to pass amending legislation where its law is inconsistent with EU law? It seems clear that the European Court of Justice cannot hold national legislation void because it is inconsistent with European law. In fact, this is an 'extreme' case which normally would not arise because the amending legislation would be passed (de Smith and Brazier, 1990, p. 82).

Despite these qualifications, however, a reasonable summary of the present constitutional position would be that Britain's membership of the European Union has impaired the doctrine of parliamentary sovereignty which can only be restored to its pre-1973 state by Britain's withdrawal from the Union. Britain's legal subordination to Brussels was underlined by an important legal case in 1991, *R. v. Secretary of State for Transport ex parte Factortame Ltd no 2.* (The Factortame case). The European Court of Justice in effect quashed sections of a British Act of Parliament (the Merchant Shipping Act 1988) which provided that UK-registered boats must be 75 per cent British-owned and have 75 per cent of crew resident in the UK. The Act had been designed to prevent boats from Spain and other EC countries 'quota-hopping' by registering under the British flag and using the UK's EC fishing quotas. British legislation had been overturned before by the Court but no earlier case had provoked such an outcry. This was mainly because *Factortame* concerned a matter traditionally associated with national sovereignty – the registration of vessels (See further, Peele, 1993, pp. 25–6.) This position was further confirmed by a subsequent case (*R. v. Secretary of State for Employment, ex parte Equal Opportunities Commission,* (1994) 2 WLR 409), in which the House of Lords struck down aspects of the Employment Protection (Consolidation) Act 1978 as incompatible with EU law.

In effect, the UK Parliament has bound itself procedurally by the 1972 European Communities Act so that in areas of EU legislative competence, EU law is supreme and the British courts will give it precedence over national UK law where the two conflict. Thus, since 1973, Britain has possessed 'dual constitutional arrangements, as an independent state and as a member of the European Community (Union)'. Since then, it has had, and still has, 'a parallel constitution' (Madgwick and Woodhouse, 1995, p. 42).

The UK Parliament is subject to *political* constraints on what it can actually – as opposed to what it may legally – do. In addition to needing to take into account a wide variety of day-to-day pressures, the government is inhibited by obligations assumed under treaties, for example as a member of the North Atlantic Treaty Organisation (NATO), or even by the terms of foreign loans. In addition, although it may occasionally pass legislation which is genuinely unpopular, such as suspending capital punishment, the government must also govern in broad accordance with public opinion. This is largely what is meant by saying that whereas Parliament is the legal sovereign (or possesses constitutional supremacy), the electorate is the *political* sovereign. Governments must therefore pay some regard to pressure-group views and to the opinion polls. Trade union resistance wrecked the 1971

Parliamentary sovereignty: ultimate legitimate authority resides in parliament (the 'Queen-in-Parliament'), which is the supreme law-making body. Statute law overrides all other sources of law and the sovereignty of parliament is recognised by the courts.

Trade Union Act and widespread popular revolt destroyed the poll tax. The prohibition of alcoholic liquor would be as unpopular in Britain as it was for a brief spell in the USA, and no government has ever tried it.

The rule of law

The British Constitution is commonly said to be based on the principle of *the rule of law* but this principle has proved hard to define precisely. It broadly comprises the following meanings:

- The powers exercised by politicians and public servants must have a legitimate foundation, i.e. they must be exercised in accordance with authorised procedures.
- Redress – i.e. legal remedy for wrongs – is available to all citizens both against any other citizen, no matter how powerful, and against officers of the state.

The leading jurist A. V. Dicey (1835–1922) saw the rule of law as a fundamental characteristic of the British Constitution, viewing it as of equal importance to the doctrine of parliamentary sovereignty. Although in strict constitutional terms, the rule of law is subordinate to parliamentary sovereignty which could be used to remove the rights it entails, the rule of law remains of key significance. In particular, it underpins the very important constitutional principle of the partial *separation of powers,* whereby, although executive and legislative branches are 'fused', the judicial branch is largely independent and separate and can check the executive. Second, the rule of law enshrines principles such as natural justice, fairness and reasonableness which can be applied by the courts.

Certain twentieth-century developments have led to concern about the contemporary validity of the principle of the rule of law. Anxieties have been expressed in these areas:

- The wide range of discretionary powers assumed and exercised by public authorities;
- The powers and accountability of the police and security services;
- The ability of the state to guarantee equality of rights to blacks and other minority groups;

- The impartiality of the courts especially in trade union and race relations cases.

At the same time, from the 1970s the rule of law came under threat increasingly from terrorists and other groups prepared to resort to illegal methods to change the law. In response, the state was propelled into detention without trial and other abuses of legal procedure. Concern about the threat to individual liberties has led to calls for a Bill of Rights to protect basic freedoms such as freedom of expression, association and movement (see Chapter 20).

The general characteristics of the British Constitution as discussed so far are summarised in Box 12.2.

The working of the Constitution

Parliamentary government under a constitutional monarchy

This phrase is the most apt description of the British liberal democratic state. Its leading features are as follows. At least once every five years, everyone over 18 votes either for the party in government or one of the opposition parties in a general election, the main purpose of which is to elect a government. The party which gains the majority of seats in the House of Commons wins the election. By convention, the monarch then asks the leader of the majority party to form a government. If the leader lacks an overall majority, he or she may consult with other party leaders about the possibility of a coalition, but need not do so.

The victorious party leader normally becomes the prime minister and forms a Cabinet and then a government from party colleagues. Names are submitted to the monarch who, by convention, assents to the prime minister's choice. The Cabinet is the committee which governs the country. Its major tasks are to make decisions on policy and legislation and submit these decisions to Parliament for its assent. It also controls and coordinates the major Departments of State. The Cabinet is collectively responsible to the House of Commons for its decisions and, if defeated on a vote of confidence, must either request a dissolution of Parliament – i.e. call a general election – or resign. Although this did occur in March 1979, in normal circumstances it happens only rarely because party discipline ensures that the party in government, which normally commands a majority in the House of Commons, is secure against parliamentary defeat. All government Ministers are formally responsible to the monarch and, by convention, through the doctrine of ministerial responsibility, to Parliament.

The Cabinet is assisted in the policy-making process by the civil service and during this process there is consultation between government and outside interests (pressure groups). The House of Commons is the major legislative chamber but the House of Lords retains a significant largely amending role in the parliamentary process. Once it has been passed by both Houses of Parliament, a bill goes to the monarch for assent which, by convention, is never refused. The bill is now an Act of Parliament (statute), has binding authority (it cannot be challenged in the courts) and is enforced by the agencies of state.

So far we have been dealing with the major institutions of central decision-making – Cabinet Ministers, other Ministers, Civil Service, Parliament. This emphasis is a fair reflection of a highly centralised political system: Britain is a unitary state with the power of policy-making for the entire UK located in a Cabinet responsible to the Westminster Parliament. Parliamentary Sovereignty means that parliament can both give and remove powers from subordinate units of government. In recent years, it has undoubtedly removed more powers from than it has given to such institutions. Nevertheless, subordinate units of government operating at national, regional and local levels remain of constitutional significance.

Nationally, the main subordinate institutions are the few remaining nationalised industries and the non-departmental bodies known as 'quangos' (quasi-autonomous non-governmental organisations). Although the boards which run them are appointed by the appropriate Ministers, the *nationalised industries* are able to function in considerable independence from detailed day-to-day political control.

'*Quangos*' are public bodies established by government to advise on or administer matters of public concern which carry out their work at arm's length from government. Good examples are the New

---

> **BOX 12.2**
> ## *Main features of the British constitution*
>
> - Unitary
> - Flexible
> - Partly written but uncodified
> - Parliamentary sovereignty
> - Rule of law

Town Development Corporations, the UK Atomic Energy Authority, the British Broadcasting Corporation (BBC), the Arts Council of Great Britain and the Higher Education Funding Council. An important difference emerged during the 1990s between the Government's exclusive definition of a 'quango' as a 'non-departmental body' (NDPB) with a role in national government but operating at arm's length from it and the inclusive definition of the Democratic Audit as an 'extra-governmental organisation' (EGO). According to the government's definition, there were fewer quangos (NDPBs) in 1995 (1,227) than in 1979 (2,167). However, according to the Democratic Audit, which included NHS trusts, Training and Enterprise Councils, registered housing associations, grant maintained schools, and further and higher education corporations in its definition, there were 5,521 quangos (EGOs) in 1995 (Wilson, 1996, p. 27).

Regionally, the highest subordinate institutions are the government departments responsible for the administration of a wide range of functions in Northern Ireland, Scotland and Wales. In each country, the respective Department or Office is given the responsibility for such matters as health, housing, education and environmental services (although from 1998, devolved assemblies will be responsible for these functions in Scotland and Wales). At an intermediate level, non-elected quasi-governmental bodies administer certain services throughout England, Scotland and Wales. The best examples are the 14 regional health authorities (eight from 1994) created under the 1973 Health Service Reorganisation Act. In addition, government departments such as the Department of the Environment and the Department of Trade and Industry devolve authority to regional offices.

Finally, the only elected form of government below

BOX 12.3
Constitutionalism

Constitutionalism is linked in liberal theory with the desire to avoid concentrations of power, for which purpose the doctrine of the separation of powers was developed in the eighteenth century: the idea that the institutions that make, carry out and adjudicate the laws should be both separate and in the hands of different persons. The only way in which the British system embodies this theory is in the independence of the judiciary; executive and legislature overlap in that the government (executive) is elected through the House of Commons (lower house of legislature) not separately as in the USA, and Ministers are drawn from and remain within parliament. A related concept with the similar purpose of preventing the growth of absolute power is checks and balances, the idea of the division of authority between numerous governing institutions so that they provide curbs upon each other; such devices include judicial review and a bicameral legislature. Britain has judicial review in the sense of the capacity of the courts to review executive action for going beyond the powers but not in the stronger sense which exists in codified constitutions of the courts being able to strike down legislative and executive acts as unconstitutional. Britain has a bicameral legislature (two Houses of Parliament), but the second chamber is by far the inferior house and only a very weak check upon the Commons.

national level on the British mainland (but not in Northern Ireland) exists in local government. The powers of local authorities are strictly curtailed: they can exercise only those functions authorised by law; they have to operate within the framework set by national government; and a high proportion of their expenditure is provided by central government. During the 1980s the large-scale transformation of the responsibilities of local government by the Conservative Administrations did not require any special procedures. However, some argued that an important constitutional 'understanding', if not convention, had been breached: that fundamental changes in the balance of central–local power and in local democracy should not be made in haste but only after the considered reflection generated by a public inquiry.

This deliberately brief summary of the main features of the British system of parliamentary government is intended to provide a succinct framework for the fuller discussions in the rest of the book. It has brought out the close inter-dependence between institutions like Parliament, the monarchy and the electorate with a formal constitutional role and those informal institutions like parties, without which the formal constitution could not work, and pressure groups, without which no realistic description of the contemporary system would be possible.

The major liberal democratic concepts employed in describing the British Constitution are **constitutional government**; responsible government; parliamentary government; representative government; and party government. The cluster of ideas around the key concept of constitutional government are

examined below and in Box 12.3; Chapter 14 considers responsible government and Chapter 16 the other three concepts.

The changing Constitution

In the last two decades, constitutional change and pressures for further change have mounted steadily. From being considered a settled matter, the Constitution is now firmly on the political agenda.

Parliamentary sovereignty

Britain's membership of the European Community (1973) has had a fundamental impact on this central doctrine of the Constitution. Acceptance of the European Treaties means that 'it is part of the law of the land' that, in areas covered by European Union law, 'that law is superior to British law' (Mount,

Constitutional government: constitutional government is government according to recognised rules which provide limits on its power and means of redress for citizens.
Unconstitutional: behaviour which breaks or threatens to break the constitution, or part of it.
Anti-constitutional: the effort to undermine the whole constitution out of a disbelief in the desirability of any constitutional restraints or a wish to produce a superior one more representative of the will of the people.

1992, p. 221). Legal judgements in the 1990s such as *Factortame* made this clear, with the House of Lords acting in effect as a constitutional court and overturning British statutes which were incompatible with European Community law. Thus, in passing the European Communities Act (1973), parliament entrenched a superior source of authority, which will last so long as Britain's membership of the European Union lasts. Equally, national sovereignty is retained in the sense that, should public opinion wish it, the UK can withdraw (secede) from the Union (see further the discussion in Madgwick and Woodhouse, 1995, pp. 28–31; Mount, 1992, pp. 61–2, 218–25).

Centralisation of government

Relations between the Westminster government and the periphery

This question became an issue in the 1970s with the upsurge of nationalism in Wales and Scotland and the resumption of direct rule over Northern Ireland by the British Government in 1972. However, devolution proposals for Wales and Scotland were rejected in 1979 but accepted in referendums in 1997, and their effects, together with some devolution to the English regions, seemed likely partly to offset territorial centralisation. However, this particular solution to the problem of metropolitan concentration of power also unleashes a shoal of potential problems, including Scottish and Welsh over-representation at Westminster, the West Lothian question and relationships between the Scottish and Welsh assemblies and the UK government. Equally, devolution may well achieve its intended effect of invigorating the British nations and regions, so creating a more balanced political system (see further, Chapter 18).

Central–local relations

The existence of a vigorous local government as a counterweight to the power of the centre has no firm embodiment in the Constitution but was for a long time considered to be a pluralist check. Between 1979 and 1997, however, Conservative Governments by means of over fifty legislative enactments introduced sweeping changes in local government which weakened its constitutional status. The main changes included the abolition of the Greater London Council and the metropolitan counties and the transfer of responsibilities and functions of local government to non-elected institutions or commercial enterprises. Along with civil service reform, the reformation of local government was the second major Conservative reform of the period. It was informed less by constitutional theory than by a political desire to get local councils under firmer central control in the cause of lower spending and greater efficiency and by an ideological intention to roll back the frontiers of the local state in favour of a set of alternative institutions responsible to the citizen as consumer rather than as voter. Labour came to power in 1997 pledged to reinvigorate local government (see further, Chapter 19)

Intermediary institutions

Organisations as diverse as trade unions, the BBC, the universities and the nationalised industries were the subject of restrictive government intervention in the 1980s, having their influence pruned or, in the latter case, being largely eliminated. Some commentators believed that these developments cumulatively eroded political pluralism – the idea of the value of a range of vital intermediate institutions standing as buffers between the state and the citizen. At the same time, the growth of what was described as the 'quango state' exacerbated this situation by producing a new range of unaccountable executive bodies disbursing large amounts of public money and massively expanding the patronage in the hands of ministers. According to one academic commentator, 'this hastily erected apparatus of appointive government lacks the essential democratic underpinnings of scrutiny, openness and accountability' (Weir, 1995, p. 143; see further, Chapter 17).

Executive power

> **Executive**: the branch of the constitution charged with carrying out laws and policies.
> **Legislature**: the branch of the constitution responsible for making laws.
> **Judiciary**: the branch of the constitution responsible for adjudicating legal disputes and pronouncing on the meaning of the law.

There were two major sources of constitutional attention.

Relations between parliament and the executive

Despite certain changes aimed at increasing the capacity of Parliament to hold the **executive** to account, such as the establishment of Commons Select Committees, the concern persisted that Parliament remained an ineffective critic of and check upon government. The large-scale hiving-off of civil service functions to executive agencies throughout the 1980s and 1990s undermined the principle of ministerial responsibility, whilst the aftermath of the Scott Report on the arms to Iraq affair (1996) starkly revealed the impotence of the House of Commons in holding to account a government determined to brazen out serious criticisms by an independent outsider. The House of Lords at times showed surprising vigour, but its hereditary basis continued to be widely criticised as an anachronism in a democratic society (see further, Chapters 15 and 16).

The 'politicisation' of government

This phrase became increasingly used in the 1980s and 1990s to denote anxiety at what was felt to be improper use of governmental powers in the interests of party rather than nation. Fears expressed under this umbrella term include the alleged 'politicisation' of the higher ranks of the civil service, the use of patronage to 'pack' quangos with politically sympathetic people and the employment of the honours system and the award of peerages to reward MPs for political services and company chairmen for donations to party funds. The 'revolving door' syndrome whereby ministers moved out of government into 'plum' jobs in newly-privatised industries with which they had previously had dealings was a further example of lowered standards in public life. So, even more blatantly, was the apparent willingness of some MPs to ask parliamentary questions for 'cash' and more generally to augment their parliamentary salaries by paid services to lobbyists. These matters – appointments to quangos, ministerial moves into business jobs and MPs' outside interests – were all the subject of recommendations by the Nolan Committee (1995) before the 1997 general election (see further, Chapters 15 and 16).

Parliamentary government

On two occasions during the 1970s – in 1975 to vote on the renegotiated terms of British membership of the EC and in 1979 for the Scots and Welsh to vote on devolution legislation – British governments used referendums. Traditionally, referendums had been considered an alien constitutional mechanism quite out of keeping with a parliamentary system, an argument which was heard again in 1993 in opposition to calls for a referendum on the ratification of the Maastricht Treaty. However, in 1997 referendums were used on the Scottish and Welsh devolution proposals and further referendums were promised on new elected authorities for London and English regions, a change in voting system for parliamentary elections and the European single currency. Some would maintain still that referendums are unconstitutional because incompatible with parliamentary sovereignty and further that 'government by referendum' constitutes an abdication of governmental responsibility. Against this, however, it may be said that referendums do not invade parliamentary sovereignty because they do not determine the law, and further that they enhance legitimacy for a particularly important change, e.g. a fundamental constitutional change.

The electoral system

Electoral reform mattered to few outside the Liberal Party before the 1970s but Labour interest grew in the early 1990s as consecutive Conservative election victories threatened to condemn it to permanent opposition. From 1979, government was by a party which gained only just over two-fifths of the popular vote whilst the very sizeable proportion of the vote gained by smaller parties was not reflected in parliamentary seats. The British system has been described as 'one of the most disproportional electoral systems anywhere in the western world' and its operation in particular sections, e.g. South-East England outside London in 1992, when the Conservatives won 97 per cent of seats there on the basis of 55 per cent of votes, as 'just about as unrepresentative as it is possible for a voting system to become and still count as "democratic"' (Dunleavy, 1997, pp. 148–9). Labour entered office pledged to hold a referendum on electoral reform (see further, Chapter 8).

Civil liberties

Civil liberties as a political issue became increasingly prominent from the early 1970s as a consequence of a series of cases involving individual rights against the state. Controversy arose over such matters as the use of police powers, the banning of trade unions at the government communications headquarters (GCHQ), the prosecution of civil servants for 'leaking' information classified under the Official Secrets Acts, restrictions on freedom of movement during the Miners' Strike (1984–5) and government pressure on the broadcasting authorities (BBC and ITV) over programmes involving state security. Political pressures from the opposition parties for more open government and for a more secure system of rights mounted during the long period of Conservative hegemony. They were given additional impetus by examination of the workings of freedom of information measures in other democracies and by the 'growing authority' of the European Convention and the judgements of the European Court of Human Rights (Mount, 1992, pp. 230–1; see further, Chapters 20 and 21).

A 'hung' parliament

Most powers remaining within the royal prerogative are now governed by convention: for example, the monarch formally assents to legislation passed by both Houses of Parliament and accepts ministerial advice on the making of treaties and the declaring of war. However, some uncertainty remains in two areas in which no settled convention has emerged: the power to appoint a prime minister and to grant a dissolution of parliament. The first of these concerns appears as a subject of debate among constitutional commentators on the eve of general elections but tends to sink out of sight once a party has gained an electoral majority. In such circumstances, no problem exists because the Queen by convention simply invites the leader of the majority party to form a government. However, it is unclear what the monarch would do if a general election resulted in a 'hung parliament' in which no party had an overall majority. The three alternatives available to the Queen appear to be:

- To permit the leader of the previously largest party to continue;
- To invite the leader of the largest party to attempt to form a government (assuming, of course, this were not the existing governing party);
- To invite any individual from the House of Commons to try to constitute a government with a Commons majority.

Events in February 1974 may be taken as a precedent, when, after the Conservative Government failed to gain an overall majority at the general election, Edward Heath, the existing Prime Minister, remained in office for four days whilst he sought support from the Liberals to enable him to form a government. He failed, and Harold Wilson, the leader of the largest party, formed a minority Labour Government which he led as Prime Minister for eight months until seeking a dissolution in order to obtain an overall majority.

On the other hand, the Labour Party believes that the largest party in such a situation is entitled to form a minority government whilst the Liberal Democrats and the Nationalists consider that one or other of the major parties should try to form a Coalition Government.

Opinions also differ about how soon and in what circumstances the Queen would grant a dissolution. Would she invite more than one party leader to attempt to form a government or would she grant a dissolution to the first person to fail? Labour believes that a prime minister leading a minority government is automatically entitled to a dissolution, whilst the Liberal Democrats consider that the Queen might grant a dissolution only if she was convinced that another government could not be formed from the existing House of Commons.

Much depends upon the view her advisers take about the degree of independent authority remaining to the monarch. Some constitutional experts argue that very little remains of the royal prerogative; others maintain that in such circumstances sufficient residual power exists to justify the monarch playing a decisive role. A further consideration is the extent to which the monarch might be willing to be seen to be acting politically. One prominent view is that she would not wish her influence to be a crucial factor in resolving a crisis since this would impair her neutral stance 'above politics' and that consequently she would be likely to grant an immediate dissolution to whoever requested it in order that the electorate should decide.

Ideological perceptions of the British Constitution

The political parties have differing perceptions of the British Constitution, both of how it works and of how – if at all – it should be changed.

The Labour Party

The mainstream Labour tradition has traditionally endorsed the strong executive embodied in British constitutional arrangements, but for a different reason from the Conservatives. It perceived the Labour Party as a vehicle for the parliamentary representation of the working class and argued that, once having gained an electoral majority for its programme, the party has a mandate to enact it without check or hindrance. In addition to ideological reasons, as a major party, Labour possessed strong grounds of self-interest to support the constitutional status quo which guaranteed it and the Conservatives such great advantages. These advantages included an electoral system which both protected the two major parties from third-party competition and helped to hold them together; executive control of parliament which ensured the passage of party programmes; strong central control over subordinate levels of government; and virtual freedom from judicial interference (Dunleavy, 1997, p. 130).

However, during the 1990s, the mainstream Labour Party took up the cause of radical constitutional reform. The reasons for this dramatic shift were both ideological and pragmatic. Ideologically, after the ideological collapse of statist socialism in the 1980s, Labour, in common with many left wing parties, renewed its interest in a pro-democracy, civil rights agenda. A growing individualism replaced the traditional collectivism in Labour's constitutional thought, a concern to protect the rights of the individual against institutions of government at all levels. The main pragmatic reason for adopting constitutional reform was the declining legitimacy of the centralised Westminster state – at the periphery, where Scotland and Wales had not been ruled by a

government of their dominant political persuasion for nearly twenty years; for individual citizens, forced to seek justice in Strasbourg rather than at home; and at Westminster itself, where political sleaze had brought parliament and government into disrepute. On the grounds that a two-party agreement to constitutional reform would both enhance the chances of reform in the parliamentary division lobbies and give it a broader legitimacy with the electorate, Labour established a Joint Consultative Committee on Constitutional Reform with the Liberals. The Committee's Report (March 1997) formed the basis of both parties' 1997 manifesto proposals (Table 12.1)

The Conservative Party

Conservatives see authority as flowing from above: they emphasise strong government and accord popular participation a minimal role. So government, backed by a loyal party, governs; and the electorate, through Parliament, consents to this firm leadership. Conservatives regard loyalty to the party leader as a primary political virtue and party as a socially integrative force, enabling people of ability to bind the nation together by drawing support for their policies from all classes and groups. By tradition and instinct, Conservatives are committed to the preservation of the Union and, in office, reluctant to disturb the historical constitution, although, as already noted, they put into practice an anti-statist programme of reform concerned to diminish the scope of government activity between 1979 and 1997. However, although their programme did have an impact on the Constitution, they made no attempt to launch any discussion of this nor did they regard themselves as constitutional reformers. For most of the postwar period, their constitutional conservatism did not differentiate them too much from Labour but, with Labour adopting a programme of radical constitutional reform in the 1990s, the two major parties diverged sharply on constitutional issues (Table 12.1). The Conservatives' position in the 1997 general election blended support for small-scale evolutionary change with opposition to Labour's radical programme. Their 1997 manifesto maintained that Conservative Governments had taken 'significant steps' towards open, accountable government, had decentralised government, strengthened parliament and adopted measures which recognised national diversity within the Union.

Open, accountable government
- publishing previously secret information on the composition of Cabinet committees and the structure of the security and intelligence services;
- appointing the Nolan Committee and implementing its proposals;
- introducing a new civil service code and reforming the process for public appointments;
- introducing code on access to government information policed by the ombudsman.

Decentralisation of government
- transferring power to local organisations such as school governors and hospital trusts;
- introducing the Citizen's Charter;
- requiring local organisations to publish information on their performance.

Strengthening of parliament
- select committees;
- new procedures to scrutinise European legislation;
- reform of parliament's working day;
- reform of budget to include tax and spending;
- put before the Commons a clear new statement of the principles underlying ministerial accountability to parliament.

Reinforcing the position of Scotland, Wales and Northern Ireland in the Union
- new powers given to Scottish Grand Committee and Welsh Grand Committee enabling Scottish and Welsh MPs to call ministers to account and debate legislation affecting their countries;
- extension of basic powers of the Northern Ireland Grand Committee.

The Conservative 1997 General Election manifesto strongly opposed the other parties' proposals for radical constitutional reform which included a Bill of Rights, a new electoral system, devolution to Scotland, Wales and the English regions, and reform of the House of Lords. After the election, however, as Labour's constitutional reforms proceeded, the Conservatives were forced to adopt a more prag-

matic position on certain reforms – for example, to accept a Scottish Parliament as an accomplished fact by putting forward their own candidates for election to it and to refrain from defence of the hereditary peerage whilst attacking increased prime ministerial patronage over the House of Lords.

The Liberal Democrats

The Liberal Democrats have traditionally placed radical constitutional reform at the centre of their programme, seeing it as the major precondition of social and economic progress. Strong supporters of parliamentary government, they consider that the role of Parliament has been downgraded in the twentieth century by the growth of executive power, the main contributory factors being the emergence of programmatic parties each with a collectivist ethos together with a massive bureaucracy. In addition, they regard the electoral system as unfair because it produces minority governments and penalises the smaller parties.

Adherents of individual liberties and the rights of minorities, Liberal Democrats believe that political over-centralisation combined with the emergence of a multicultural society have eroded individual liberties and produced problems in the protection of national, regional and black minorities. In 1997, they advocated a far-reaching programme of constitutional reform including proportional representation, a Bill of Rights, the strengthening of Parliament, and large-scale devolution and decentralisation of power away from Westminster and Whitehall (see Table 12.1).

The movement for constitutional reform

Constitutional reform moved to the centre of the political stage in the late 1980s in a way not seen since before 1914. Compared with the earlier period of constitutional concern in the 1960s and 1970s, this new phase was about fundamentals, and produced radical proposals for reform. An important step was the formation of Charter 88 (Box 12.4), but although deriving mainly from individuals, groups and parties of the centre and left and from the nationalist parties, constitutional reform

Table 12.1 The parties and the constitution: the main manifesto proposals in 1997

LABOUR	CONSERVATIVE	LIBERAL DEMOCRAT
General approach	**General approach**	**General approach**
Measured, sensible reforms of 'centralised, inefficient and bureaucratic' system of government.	Gradual improvement not radical change.	Priority to restoring trust between people and government, renewing Britain's democracy and giving government back to the people.
Parliament	**Parliament**	**Parliament**
House of Commons	*House of Commons*	*House of Commons*
Modernise House of Commons. Special Commons Select Committee to review House of Commons procedures. Make PM's Questions more effective. Review ministerial accountability to remove recent abuses. Fully implement Nolan proposals obliging parties to declare all donations above a minimum figure. Ban foreign funding of parties. Ask Nolan to consider how party funding can be regulated and reformed.	Extend Queen's Speech to cover legislation not only for year ahead but for year after that. This will make more draft bills subject to public scrutiny before they reach the floor of the House of Commons.	Modernise House of Commons by reducing House to 200 MPs and introducing tougher rules for conduct, behaviour and outside sources of income . Fixed parliamentary term of four years. Improve drafting and consultation on legislation and strengthen MPs' ability to hold government to account. Reform party funding and limit national spending on campaigns. Each party will publish its accounts and list all large donors.
House of Lords	*House of Lords*	*House of Lords*
End right of hereditary peers to sit and vote in upper house as first stage in process of reform to make Lords more democratic and representative. Review system of appointment of life peers with overall aim of ensuring party appointees as life peers more accurately reflect votes cast at the previous general election. No one party should seek a House of Lords majority. Committee of both Houses to undertake wide-ranging review and produce proposals for reform.	Opposition proposals on the House of Lords represent 'fundamental changes which have not been thought through' and 'would be extremely damaging'.	Transform House of Lords into mainly elected second capable of representing UK nations and regions and of playing key role in scrutiny of EU legislation.
Devolution	**Devolution**	**Devolution**
Referendums on devolution not later than Autumn 1997, with simple majority of those voting sufficient to endorse Scottish and Welsh devolution. Proposals: Scottish parliament elected by additional member system with law-making powers and defined and limited powers to vary revenue. It will have power over the areas of responsibility currently exercised by the Scottish office. Welsh assembly also elected by AMS, with power	Against devolution to Scotland and Wales: would create strains that could pull the Union part, create a new power-hungry layer of government, risk conflict between assemblies and Westminster and raise questions about whether present Scottish and Welsh representation at Westminster	Introduce Home Rule for Scotland and Wales with a Scottish Parliament and Welsh Senedd elected by proportional representation and able to raise and reduce income tax. Scrap unnecessary quangos and hand functions to elected bodies. Remaining quangos to

Contd ⟶

Table 12.1 *(continued)*

LABOUR	CONSERVATIVE	LIBERAL DEMOCRAT
over existing Welsh Office functions, powers of secondary legislation and specific powers to reform and democratise the 'quango state'.	should be changed.	meet in public and list their members' interests.
Regional chambers to coordinate transport, planning, economic development, bids for European funding and land use planning.	Devolution not in the interests of Scotland, Wales or the Union as a whole.	More open and representative appointment process for quangos.
In time region by region referendums to decide on elected regional governments.	Against regional government which would be 'a dangerously centralising measure'. Instead,want to shift power to the local neighbourhood by e.g. giving more power to parish councils.	Elected regional assemblies in England where there is demonstrated public demand for them.
Referendum to confirm popular support for an elected government for London, followed by a new directly-elected mayor and strategic authority.		Strategic authority for London.
New duty on local councils to promote the economic, social and environmental of their areas.		Strengthen local government, with councils given wider scope for action.
Proportion of councillors elected annually to ensure greater accountability.		Will allow local authorities to raise more of their funds locally, give them greater discretion over spending, and permit them, within strict limits to raise funds for capital projects directly from the market.
Pilot schemes of elected mayors with executive powers in cities.		
Retain reserve powers to control excessive rate rises.		
Will require all councils to publish a local performance plan with targets for service improvement which they will be expected to achieve.		Long-term aims of replacing Council Tax with a Local Income Tax and replacing the Uniform Business Rate with a fairer system.
A Labour government will join with local government to mount a concerted attack on the multiple causes of social and economic decline – unemployment, bad housing, crime, poor health and a degraded environment.		

Electoral reform

Referendum on electoral reform:

early appointment of an independent commission to recommend a a proportional alternative to the first-past-the-post system

Electoral reform

Against changes in the voting system which would break the link between an MP and his constituents

A system of proportional representation (PR) would be likely to produce unstable, coalition governments unable to provide effective leadership, with crucial decisions being dependent on compromise deals hammered out behind closed doors.

'This is not the British way.'

Electoral reform

Introduce proportional representation for all elections.

Greater use of referendums for constitutional issues, e.g. changing the voting system or any further transfer of power to European institutions.

Referendums on local issues where there is public demand.

Contd ⟹

Table 12.1 *(continued)*

LABOUR	CONSERVATIVE	LIBERAL DEMOCRAT
Individual rights	**Individual rights**	**Individual rights**
Incorporation of the European Convention on Human Rights into British law to establish 'a floor, not a ceiling, for human rights'. End unjustifiable discrimination, e.g. by enacting comprehensive, enforceable civil rights for the disabled. Immigration: reform system to remove arbitrariness and unfairness of 'primary purpose rule' and streamline appeals system for those denied a visa. Swift and fair decisions on asylum seekers, control of unscrupulous and crackdown on fraudulent use birth certificates.	Against a Bill of Rights, which would risk transferring power away from parliament to the courts, thereby undermining the democratic supremacy of parliament. This may be necessary in other countries which depend upon more formalised written constitutions but 'we do not believe it appropriate for the UK'.	Incorporation of European Convention on Human Rights as 'first step' to Bill of Rights. Will establish Human Rights Commission to strengthen protection of individual rights. Will create a Ministry of Justice for protecting human rights, overseeing the administration of the legal system, the courts and legal aid.
Open government	**Open government**	**Open government**
Incorporate European Convention on Human Rights into British law to establish 'a floor, not a ceiling, for human rights'. Introduce Freedom of Information Act and an independent National Statistical Service. Reform civil justice system and Legal Aid.	Build on steps already taken to more open government by by legislating on commitments in 1993 White Paper to create a statutory right of access by citizens to personal records held about them by the government and other public authorities.	Introduce Freedom of Information Act establishing citizens' right to know.
Northern Ireland	**Northern Ireland**	**Northern Ireland**
Seek a new political settlement which can command the support of the Unionist and Nationalist traditions.	Aim is to end direct rule and restore local accountable democracy. To this end continue to pursue policy of dialogue and negotiation with and between the democratic Northern Ireland parties.	Set up a power-sharing Executive elected by PR. Build on Joint Declaration and Framework Document.

proposals also came from the political right, e.g. *The Economist* weekly newspaper, the Institute of Economic Affairs (IEA) and a former head of Margaret Thatcher's Political Unit, Ferdinand Mount. By 1991, when a Charter 88 convention met to consider how to fuse a consensus out of them, draft codified constitutions had been proposed by the Labour left-winger, Tony Benn, the left-of-centre Institute for Public Policy Research,

the Liberal Democrat, John MacDonald, and the Conservative-leaning think-tank, the Institute of Economic Affairs. In March 1997, the two centre-left parties, Labour and the Liberal Democrats produced an agreed raft of piecemeal proposals for constitutional reform (Box 12.5).

The reforming mood also gained some endorsement by public opinion. A 'State of the Nation' poll commissioned by the Joseph Rowntree Trust in

---

BOX 12.4
Charter 88

The time has come to demand political, civil and human rights in the United Kingdom. The first step is to establish them in constitutional form, so that they are no longer subject to the arbitrary dictat of Westminster and Whitehall.

We call, therefore, for a new constitutional settlement which would: Enshrine, by means of a Bill of Rights, such civil liberties as the right to peaceful assembly, to freedom of association, to freedom from discrimination, to freedom from detention without trial by jury, to privacy and to freedom of expression.

Subject executive powers and prerogatives, by whomsoever exercised, to the rule of law.

Establish freedom of information and open government.

Create a fair electoral system of proportional representation.

Reform the upper house to establish a democratic, non-hereditary second chamber.

Place the executive under the power of a democratically renewed parliament and all agencies of the state under the rule of law.

Ensure the independence of a reformed judiciary.

Provide legal remedies for all abuses of power by the state and the officials of central, regional and local government.

Guarantee an equitable distribution of power between local, regional and national government.

Draw up a written constitution, anchored in the idea of universal citizenship, that incorporates these reforms.

Our central concern is the law. No country can be considered free in which the government is above the law. No democracy can be considered safe whose freedoms are not encoded in a basic constitution.

We, the undersigned, have called this document Charter 88. First, to mark our rejection of the complacency with which the tercentenary of the Revolution of 1688 has been celebrated. Second, to reassert a tradition of demands for constitutional rights in Britain, which stretches from the barons who forced the Magna Carta on King John, to the working men who drew up the People's Charter in 1838, to the women at the beginning of this century who demanded universal suffrage. Third, to salute the courage of those in Eastern Europe who still fight for their fundamental freedoms.

1995 found that the proportion of people believing the system of government works well had dropped to a mere 22 per cent, whilst 81 per cent were in favour of a Freedom of Information Act, and 79 per cent wanted a Bill of Rights and a written constitution. There was strong support also for greater use of referendums, the enforcement of the MPs' code of conduct by the courts, civil or criminal, and the investigation of ministerial misconduct by people other than politicians. Although most people considered that MPs should be allowed to carry on their trade or profession, they also thought that MPs should not have a paid job or be paid to write articles or represent interest groups.

Although there is a significant overlap between the specific reforms they advocate, the most important difference between reformers is between those who advocate piecemeal reform and those who favour a written constitution. Even though the adoption by Labour of a constitutional reform programme in 1997, followed by its sweeping electoral victory,

gave a decisive advantage to piecemeal reform of the constitution, it is worth considering briefly the differences between piecemeal reform,

---

BOX 12.5
Constitutional reform: the Labour–Liberal Democrat proposals, 1997

- Select Committee on modernisation of House of Commons.
- Abolition of hereditary peers
- Scottish Parliament and Welsh assembly elected by proportional representation
- Referendums on creation of an elected London authority and elected regional governments in England
- Incorporation of European Convention of Human Rights into UK law .
- Electoral commission to produce alternative to present voting system.
- Freedom of Information Act.

however radical, and the enactment of a written constitution.

If enacted piecemeal, the reform proposals would make a very great difference to the working of the British Constitution but they would not transform it completely. Even if eroded by EC membership, parliamentary sovereignty would remain its cardinal principle. However, the proposal that constitutional reforms should be codified in a single document would make an enormous difference, if accomplished. Parliamentary sovereignty would no longer be the basic principle of the British Constitution: rather, the Constitution itself would be supreme.

Two further consequences are worthy of note. First, constitutional change itself would require a special procedure and would therefore be more difficult to achieve than under the present system. Second, judges – their authority institutionalised in a supreme or a high court – would play a decisive role in the interpretation of the Constitution. What then are the arguments for and against a codified constitution for Britain? Constitutional radicals argue that a codified constitution would:

- Replace the uncertainty of the existing Constitution with constitutional rules which have far greater clarity thereby (a) providing a fixed point of reference for constitutional debate; (b) encouraging a citizen rather than subject-based political culture in which people know and feel able to assert their rights; and (c) bringing the UK into line with other advanced democracies.
- Eliminate the doctrine of parliamentary sovereignty which, however liberating in the seventeenth century, has been the means not only of the development of an insufficiently accountable and over-powerful executive but also of difficulties in the acceptance of the binding force of supra-national treaties such as those with the EC.
- Provide secure legal limitations upon the powers of governments; greater protection for the rights of individuals and groups; and firm obstacles against further centralisation of power in Westminster. The constitution would form a kind of higher law only changeable by special procedures and therefore removed from easy modification by the government of the day.

Constitutional conservatives argue that a codified constitution is:

- Unnecessary because the present Constitution is still serving the country well, with both Parliament and pressure groups more capable than they were earlier in the century of checking government and individual rights as secure as in regimes which specify and entrench them.
- Undesirable because (a) the existing 'flexible' constitution is well able to respond to new demands. That new demands have so far not been accommodated reveals only that they are insufficiently urgent and deeply felt to gain constitutional recognition. Therefore, to replace a constitution which is simple to modify in accordance with popular wishes with one that is not is a retrograde step. (b) Written constitutions tend to place too much power in the hands of an unelected, unaccountable judiciary; and (c) piecemeal reform is preferable to sweeping change.
- Impractical because (a) there is no agreement even among its advocates over what it should contain; and (b) both major parties are opposed to the idea even though Labour now supports some constitutional reforms. In no readily foreseeable circumstances could a 'written constitution' be achievable.

Labour and the Constitution: a government of radical reform?

New Labour came to power with the most considerable programme of constitutional reform of any government since the war. By late 1997 much of it was under way, with affirmative referendums already held on Scottish and Welsh Assemblies, white papers published outlining the details of a Human Rights Act to incorporate the European Convention on Human Rights into British law and of a Freedom of Information Act, and an Electoral Commission established to produce an alternative to the first-past-the-post system by late 1998. Of these reforms, and intended reforms, the most problematic was the last-mentioned – electoral reform, mainly because Prime Minister and Cabinet seemed unlikely to favour a fully-fledged PR alternative to first-past-the-post to include in a referendum, but instead non-proportional changes such as the Supplementary Vote or the Alternative Vote. However, if the reforms well down the pipeline by this point were an earnest of Labour's intentions, then it seemed likely that elected authorities for London and (if publicly endorsed) the English regions together with parliamentary reform, including reform of the composition of the House of Lords, would follow during the course of the Labour Administration. At the same time, other reforms, already in train, such as those proposed by the Nolan Committee, could be expected to continue, in particular an investigation into the funding of political parties. How radical an impact on the Constitution are these reforms likely to have?

The strong likelihood is that their overall impact will be 'considerable' but not 'revolutionary'. This thesis can be argued for two main reasons. First, Labour's reform package agreed with the Liberal Democrats included two types of reforms: liberal constitutionalist and electoral reformist. Of these, it is the liberal constitutionalist reforms which are the most likely to be carried out, but the electoral reformist which, if fully implemented by the introduction of a genuine PR system, would have the greatest impact. It would do so because its probable effect would be to replace majority government by coalition government, which in turn would have radical consequences for the operation of the Westminster model, especially the role of parliament (Madgwick and Woodhouse, 1995, pp. 334–5). In other words, in contrast to the major thread of Labour's reforms which is to continue, through such measures as incorporation of the ECHR, to 'judicialise' the constitution, PR would be more likely to achieve a real shift of power from the executive to parliament. There are, however, conceivable circumstances in which reforms in the liberal constitutionalist vein would have a very great impact, too. This would be if devolution to Scotland and Wales led either to federalism or break-up of the Union, the last-mentioned outcome being certainly the aim of the SNP.

The second reason for expressing caution about the probable impact of the reforms is because Labour's constitutional programme, radical in British terms though it is, omits much which would have to change in order to encompass a constitutional transformation. Thus, there are no plans to adopt a codified constitution, in which regard British exceptionalism will continue and parliamentary sovereignty, qualified by the 'parallel constitution' provided by the European Union, will persist as the cardinal constitutional doctrine of the UK. Nor, seemingly, are there any plans for major reform of the monarchy, although, after the death of Diana, Princess of Wales, a discreet and gradual scaling down may be expected. Above all, in all likelihood, the 'strong executive' embodying the residual prerogative powers, large-scale prime ministerial patronage, including the honours system, and especially its total domination of parliament, will remain. So will, in most essentials, the unaccountable 'quango state'. On balance, therefore, the model of constitutional change will remain evolutionary, albeit an accelerated evolution. And the most important impact on the British Constitution will continue to be exerted by the pressure from an integrationist European Union.

Summary

- Constitutions deserve close attention even though they form imperfect guides to political reality and are often overthrown. They need to be complemented by the study of the actual working of key political institutions such as parties, pressure groups and civil services and their roles in the political process, and by the study of political cultures.

- Constitutions contain the most important procedural rules of a political system; form valuable guides to countries' political aspirations and, in varying degrees, to their political practices; help, alongside moral codes and cultural norms, to restrain politicians; and serve as sources of legitimacy for political systems.

- The main broad classification of constitutions is as unitary or federal; codified or uncodified (generally preferable terms to 'written' and 'unwritten'); and flexible and inflexible.

- The British Constitution may be categorised as unitary, partly written but uncodified, and flexible. Its main sources are: legislation, common law, conventions, European Union law, the law and customs of Parliament, and works of authority. It is based on the principle of parliamentary sovereignty although this is modified by membership of the EU, which since 1973, has provided Britain with a dual or 'parallel' constitution.

- The rule of law is also often said to be an underlying principle of the Constitution. It means, first, that the powers of the authorities must be conferred by law and exercised according to authorised procedures; and, second, that redress of wrongs is available to all citizens against other citizens and against officers of the state. But as a constitutional principle the rule of law is inferior to parliamentary sovereignty because parliamentary sovereignty could be used to undermine it.
- Parliamentary government under a constitutional monarch is the most appropriate description of the particular form taken by the British liberal democratic state. The main concepts required for its analysis include constitutional, parliamentary, representative, responsible and party government.
- Constitutions are part of rather than above politics and are constantly subject to political pressures for change. Each party approaches the constitution from a different ideological perspective of what it is and should be. Down to the late 1980s, the major parties broadly agreed, for different reasons, in supporting Britain's historical constitution. However, their views diverged from that moment, as Labour moved towards adopting a programme of reform in a liberal constitutionalist vein.
- Constitutional innovations and pressures for reform which emerged in the 1960s and 1970s intensified in the 1980s and early 1990s and included proposals for a 'written constitution'. However, with Labour and the Liberal Democrats adopting an agreed package of constitutional reforms before the 1997 general election, significant piecemeal reforms were soon being introduced by the new Labour Government. For at least two main reasons, these reforms, although important, were unlikely to transform the British Constitution.

Questions

1. What is a 'constitution'? How far are constitutions influenced by politics?
2. How democratic is the British Constitution?

3. List the main characteristics of the rule of law and discuss the extent to which the British Constitution is based on this principle. (It would be helpful to read Chapters 20 and 21 before attempting this question.)
4. Compare the constitutional proposals put forward by Labour, the Liberal Democrats and the Conservatives in their 1997 General Election manifestos (Table 12.1).

Assignments

Assignment (1)
Study the statement by Charter 88 (Box 12.4) and then discuss how far you agree with it and for what reasons.

Assignment (2) The British Constitution: for and against
It has been suggested that the British Constitution somewhat resembles a camel – a horse designed by a committee – although without 'the camel's fitness for purpose and its visual appeal'. According to Peter Madgwick and Diana Woodhouse, its defects are obvious and include:

- lack of certainty and precision about what it includes – hence constant doubt about what is constitutional and what is not constitutional;
- the lack of a higher authority (such as a supreme court) and hence doubt about the enforceability of constitutional rules;
- the inadequacy of institutional provision for the limitation and accountability of power;
- inadequate procedures for amendment, lack of procedure for formal amendment and the absence of barriers to informal amendment by practice;
- the lack of a basis for and encouragement of constitutional awareness and understanding in the political culture.

But the British Constitution does have two substantial virtues:

- The principle and political fact of parliamentary sovereignty means that power resides in the

House of Commons and, because the House has to be re-elected periodically, it rests ultimately with the people. Hence, even though the government can increase its own power, in the end popular vote is able to reduce it.

● Although it has many faults, the historical British Constitution does not induce the fondness for going to law and the domination by lawyers that normally results from a codified constitution.

Source: Adapted from Madgwick and Woodhouse (1995), pp. 12–13.

Questions

(i) Can you add any defects or advantages to those listed above for the British Constitution?

(ii) What do you consider to be the most important defect, and the greatest advantage, of Britain's constitution?

(iii) Where, in your view, does the balance of advantage lie between the British Constitution and codified constitutions?

(iv) Should Britain have a codified constitution?

Further reading

The most accessible, up-to-date account of the British Constitution is Madgwick, P. and Woodhouse, D. (1995) *The Law and Politics of the Constitution of the United Kingdom* (London: Harvester Wheatsheaf). It can be supplemented by the authoritative de Smith, S. and Brazier, R. (1994) *Constitutional and Administrative Law*, 7th edn (Harmondsworth: Penguin). A useful overview of contemporary developments is Dunleavy, P. (1997) 'The Constitution', in P. Dunleavy et al., *Developments in British Politics 5* (London: Macmillan) whilst Mount, F. (1992 *The British Constitution Now* (London: Heinemann) and Hennessy, P. (1995) *The Hidden Wiring Unearthing the British Constitution* (London: Gollancz) both provide stimulating, if hardly introductory, analyses.

On the comparative aspect: Finer, S. E., Bogdanor, V. and Rudden, B. (1995) *Comparing Constitutions* (Oxford: Clarendon); on the European context specifically, Hesse, J. J. and Johnson, N. (eds) (1995) *Constitutional Policy and Change in Europe* (Oxford: Oxford University Press); and on the EU impact on UK government and politics, Kingdom, J. (1995) 'The European Context', in M. Mullard (ed) *Policy Making in Britain* (London: Routledge) can be recommended.

On constitutional reform see: Barnett, A., Ellis, C. and Hirst, P. (eds) (1993) *Debating the Constitution* (Oxford: Polity Press); Brazier, R. (1991) *Constitutional Reform* (Oxford: Clarendon); Norton, P. (1994) 'The Constitution in Question', *Politics Review*, 3:4, April; Ridley, F. F. (1988) 'There Is No British Constitution: A Dangerous Case of the Emperor's Clothes', *Parliamentary Affairs*, 41:3 July; Ridley, F. F. (1991) 'Using Power to Keep Power: The Need for Constitutional Checks', *Parliamentary Affairs*, 44:4, October; and Wright, A. (1993) *Citizens and Subjects* (London: Routledge).

Britain and the European Union

The creation of a single market within the European Union (EU), together with other goals including the creation of a single currency, has caused serious divisions within British opinion. What is it about the way in which the EU operates which frequently results in Britain being the most reluctant member? In which directions might the EU develop in order to solve both the old pressures which have been present since its formation and the new challenges it now faces? Will it be possible for Britain to remain 'at the heart of Europe', even with Labour in office?

From European Community to European Union

In the ruins of post-war Europe the French Foreign Minister, Robert Schuman, devised a plan to unite the coal and steel industries of France and Germany in the cause of peace. The Treaty of Paris, signed by six countries but not by Britain, set up the European Coal and Steel Community from which the European Community was to develop (see Coxall and Robins, 1998, ch. 5). The economies of the six prospered during the 1950s and 1960s, but harder times lay ahead.

The national economies of the European Community's member states were hard hit by recession during the 1970s and 1980s, and some resorted to protectionist measures in order to promote recovery. The protection of national markets was, of course, a barrier to European economic integration. By 1985 the Commission, chaired by Jacques Delors, decided it was timely to relaunch the original ideal of a truly common market. The Single European Act of 1986 amended the founding treaties by extending the principle of majority voting, strengthening the power of the European Parliament in the legislative process, but most importantly by creating 'an area without frontiers in which the free movement of goods, persons, services and capital is ensured' as from 31 December 1992. The Single European Act also included a general commitment to improve cooperation over matters of economic and monetary policy. A report written by Paolo Cecchini predicted that the effects of creating a single market would help solve the problems being experienced by national economies by raising output, creating more jobs, reducing prices and increasing European competitiveness abroad.

The Single European Act represented a huge stride forward in the cause of **Europeanism**. As before, major reforms towards economic integration took the Community closer to the threshold of political unity. For a single European market would never be totally achieved without a single European currency, and a single currency would mean that much freedom in economic policy-making would be lost by the governments of the member states. It was argued that this sacrifice of sovereignty by the twelve

> **Europeanism** is an attitude which puts the interests of developing the European Union before developing other links, such as Atlanticist preferences which put greater value on developing links with the United States.

national governments would be replaced by increasing federal decision-making powers inside Community institutions.

The Delors Plan for economic and monetary union (EMU) was presented to the Council by Ministers in 1989, and was based on a three-stage progression. Stage One included the establishment of the single European market by the end of 1992, with closer coordination of different countries' economic and monetary policies. This was to be achieved by all member states joining the Exchange Rate Mechanism (ERM) of the European Monetary System (EMS). The effect of the ERM was that each country's currency became fixed more tightly to the values of other currencies in the EC. Implementing the EMS also involved making greater use of the European Currency Unit (ECU) which is best thought of as a theoretical unit of currency the value of which is calculated from the values of members' currencies in agreed proportions.

Stage Two of the Delors Plan will involve setting up a new European central bank to coordinate the monetary policies of individual member states. This would mean that a number of important functions performed by national central banks, such as the Bank of England, would from this stage onwards be performed by a European central bank. This development would also have implications for taxation policy and the setting of interest rates, which would also move towards being decided at the European rather than member state level. Stage Three will be a crucial one in the history of the EU for the exchange rates of member countries will be firmly locked together with a view to their being replaced by a single European currency, the euro.

A number of 'convergence criteria' were devised to draw the economies of EU members closer together (based on interest rates, growth, inflation rates, the budget deficit and national debt) so that countries that complied could participate in the single currency on January 1st 1999. However, in order to meet the convergence criteria some European governments undertook programmes of economic austerity which pushed EU unemployment to over 18 million, and reduced welfare benefits which pushed another 50 million into poverty. As Larry Elliott commented, such hardship inflicted on ordinary people was 'typical of the arrogant way in which Europe's political class has ploughed on with

monetary union, despite a mountain of evidence that it is bureaucratic and riddled with flaws.' (*Guardian*, 16 June 1997). Popular resentment led to calls for the EU to develop as a 'people's Europe' rather than the Europe of a technocratic elite.

The ERM came under great stress, with Britain withdrawing in September 1992 (see page 441). Nevertheless the drive towards economic and monetary union continued within the EU. By 1998 all EU members except Greece were on course to meet the convergence criteria. Britain, under John Major, had negotiated an opt-out from EMU and, despite hints to the contrary, would not join within the life of Blair's first Labour government. It was argued that Britain's economy was out of step with continental economies, making participation difficult but, in any case, it seemed wise to delay and ensure that the single currency was successful before Britain joined.

A group of over 300 economists, who were not opposed to a single currency in principle, argued that the plans to introduce the euro were deeply flawed (see Box 13.1). Critics saw EMU as a triumph of politics over economics. It was argued that the convergence criteria should be more realistic, more rigorously applied, and should include consideration of unemployment totals. Also the economies of Europe, Britain apart, were in rather weak shape leading to fears that the euro would quickly become a 'soft' currency. As such the euro would inevitably become the target of international speculation and would require high interest rates to defend it, bringing dangers of lower growth, higher taxation and still higher unemployment. Outright opponents of monetary union argued that the EU was not suited to having a single currency; it was not an 'optimal currency area' since member countries had such differently structured economies.

Supporters of EMU argued that in the long term a single currency will increase prosperity and bring more jobs to Europe. Also it would make a reality of the EU, which would truly become the world's largest trading area, replacing currency fluctuation and devaluations with stability. Also the establishment of a European Central Bank to set interest rates, taking away from governments the political temptation of stop–go economics, would help deliver low inflation. Finally, a single currency would make it easier for companies to trade in the EU since

BOX 13.1
A euro for the people

European Union heads of government were presented at the Amsterdam summit with a letter from 331 economists across Europe demanding radical changes to the plans for monetary union. This is an edited version of their letter:

'Europe is contending with high unemployment, poverty, social marginalisation and ecological deterioration. The current design of Europe's economy does not provide adequate prospects of reining in these problems.

Your economic advisers have told you that EMU, as laid out in the Maastricht Treaty and further regulated in the Dublin Stability Pact, will bring Europe more jobs and prosperity. We, economists in the EU's member states, are afraid

that the opposite is true. This project for economic and monetary integration not only falls short from a social, ecological, and democratic perspective, but also from an economic one. This is a missed opportunity.

A single European currency could be very advantageous and help to find the way to full employment with good quality jobs and social security. But this EMU is not a starting point for a modern European welfare state; instead it institutionalises the dismantling of the public sector and reduces the manoeuvring room for active social and fiscal policy.'

Source: *The Guardian*, (13 June 1997).

---

there would be no 'transactional costs' involved in buying and selling currencies.

During the 1980s the Labour Opposition became increasingly committed to the European cause. To a large extent this was because the only hope of defeating the Thatcher government's policies on issues such as trade union rights or welfare rights was in the context of European Community laws. Margaret Thatcher did not disagree with Labour on this, for in her eyes the EC seemed to be developing into a semi-socialist, highly bureaucratic, federal Euro-state which increasingly threatened to curtail her government's freedom of action. The Social Charter – or 'Socialist Charter' as Thatcher insisted on calling it – together with proposals to harmonise social policies, were both interventionist and egalitarian in purpose and clearly at odds with the free-market philosophy of Thatcherism. The EMS was also opposed by Thatcher, who preferred exchange rates to move freely. Her personal economic adviser, Sir Alan Walters, described the EMS as a 'half-baked' idea, and Thatcher agreed with him, arguing that the pound sterling was 'the most powerful expression of sovereignty you can have'. Thatcher's hostility to Britain's closer involvement with the EC, particularly Britain's full membership of the EMS in 1990, led to the resignation of her Chancellor, and later her Deputy Prime Minister, which then contributed to her own downfall.

At the outset, John Major's government was more positive generally towards the EC although there were aspects of federalism and centralisation in the proposed development of the Community which

were opposed. When he was Chancellor of the Exchequer, John Major challenged Delors' concept of Europe having a *single* currency with an alternative of Europe having a *common* currency. Major's rival plan centred around what was known as the 'hard ECU' which would be legal tender in each country alongside national currencies. As Prime Minister, Major 'opted out' of specific aspects the Maastricht deal (see later) which reassured the Euro-sceptics in the Bruges Group. In the Treaty on European Union, all references to 'federalism' were removed; Britain alone won the right to opt out of joining a single currency if the other EU members decided to go ahead as planned in 1999; and the Social Chapter, which was akin to the Social Charter, was dropped from the Maastricht Treaty. In debating the European Communities (Amendment) Bill which ratified the Maastricht Treaty, Major stressed his victory in getting the principle of 'subsidiarity' enshrined in the Treaty: by which is meant that 'the Community only tackles tasks which it is able to deal with more effectively than the Member States acting alone' (Commission of the European Communities, 1991, p. 32).

Parliamentary arithmetic resulted in John Major's government becoming vulnerable to pressure from various party cliques. With a slim parliamentary majority of 21 after the 1992 general election, John Major was in a weak position and came to lack authority within his own party. Twenty-two Conservative MPs voted against the second reading of the Maastricht Bill, forty-one voted against the third reading, with five abstaining. Eventually Major was forced to resort to a motion of confidence in his government in order to get legislation through parliament.

John Major's efforts to discipline his party generally failed; eight hard-line Euro-sceptic Conservative backbenchers had the whip withdrawn but 'free from the constraints of party discipline, the 'Sceptic Eight' were now able to wage guerrilla warfare on Major's government, helping to defeat its VAT increase on fuel in December 1994 and impeding it on the EU fishing rules vote of January 1995' (Kelly, 1995 p. 15). His efforts to forge compromises on European policy also failed; for concessions to Euro-sceptics led to further demands whilst raising the anxiety of a minority of Conservatives who supported Maastricht. Events were to go from bad to worse as a result of the EU ban on British beef exports resulting from the BSE crisis, with John Major forced into taking the desperate measure of blocking EU business for two months. John Major entered office with the ambition of 'Britain being at the heart of Europe' but left with Britain on the margins of Europe, with the Conservative party split from top to bottom on European policy. The party's new leader, William Hague, has indicated that whilst many Conservative policies may be reviewed during the years of opposition, the party's European policy will remain cast in the Euro-sceptic mould. Only the Liberal Democrats are committed to the development of a federal EU. Whilst being less hostile than the Conservatives, Labour has reservations on harmonising a number of policies. Labour is committed to signing the Social Chapter, and not opposed in principle to EMU participation which will be judged pragmatically and tested in a referendum. Basically, however, Labour prefers the 'Nato' European process of enlargement based on intergovernmentalism rather than the EU process of federal deepening, with some members involved in different areas and at different stages than others. Labour has retained traditional Conservative demands to retain control of UK borders, no integration of Nato into European structures, changes demanded on fishing policy and recognition of the need for flexible labour markets.

BOX 13.2
The six professions of an EU official

President Delors said that a Commission official has six professions:

- to innovate, as the needs of the Community change;

- to be a law-maker, preparing the legal texts needed for Community decisions;

- to manage the growing number of Community policies;

- to control respect for Community decisions at all levels;

- to negotiate constantly with all the different actors in the Community process;

- to be a diplomat in order to be successful in the five other professions.

The institutions of the European Union

The European Commission

The image of the Commission with the general public is that of the 'Brussels bureaucrats'. Indeed, the Commission is the biggest of the European Union's institutions and employs around 16,000 people. But considering the scope of the Commission's role in the Union, this is a relatively small number of employees. At the apex of the Commission are 20 Commissioners, with larger EU countries appointing two Commissioners and small members one. They are appointed to serve for a four-year term of office, which is renewable. Commissioners generally come from the ranks of senior politicians, but as members of the Commission they are guardians of the EU treaties rather than representatives of their own country's national interest. Individual Commissioners are in charge of specific policy areas, and they meet once a week in a forum known as the College of Commissioners.

At the head of the Commission is its President, a post which is currently filled by Jacques Santer. The President's duties include coordinating the work of the Commission, but the position also provides an opportunity to inject political direction into the way the Community develops.

Whilst his predecessor, Jacques Delors, was a controversial President who predicted that within years the Commission would be responsible for 80 per cent of all members' social and economic legislation, Santer has been less ambitious. He has been concerned that the Commission does less than under Delors, but does it better. In 1996 this resulted in the Commission making only 12 new legislative proposals. Critics argue that the Commission has lost its way within the EU's structure; it has too many commissioners, of variable quality, from different administrative cultures to work effectively. In terms of power, some feel that the Commission has lost much policy initiative to the Inter-governmental Conferences (IGC) attended by heads of state every six months.

The Commission is often described as being the 'civil service of the European Union'. There is some truth in this, although at the higher levels it has wider responsibilities than many national civil services, but at lower levels it delivers far fewer services. Rather like national civil services, the work of the Commission is divided up into a number of 'ministries' called Directorates General. Most of the work of the Commission is completed by 23 Directorates General – the biggest of which has responsibility for agriculture, but others cover areas such as transport, environment, fisheries, energy, regional policies – as well as by some specialised agencies such as a statistical office, translation service, and Office for Official Publications (which supplied some of the illustrations in this chapter). As might be expected, the work of the Commission is serviced by a complex committee structure, which no doubt contributes to its bureaucratic image. Each Commissioner is assisted by a small *cabinet* or team of officials, usually civil servants seconded to work in Brussels. There is also a large and complex web of committees set up to provide advice, consultation and expert opinion as a form of input into the EU's legislative process.

What, then, is the nature of the Commission's contribution to the running of the Union? Firstly, the Commission acts as the Union's watchdog by ensuring that EU Treaties are respected by all the member states. The Commission can, if necessary, refer cases where states contravene Union law to the Court of Justice. There have been newspaper reports in recent years that 'Britain will be taken to court by the Commission' over failing to implement Union law on the purity of drinking water and the safety of coastal bathing water. Rather than flagrantly breaking these laws, Britain, like other countries in a similar position, will play for time and act very slowly in conforming to EU standards since British Ministers know that it will be many years before either the Commission or the Court of Justice will act and bring matters to a head. The Commission does, however, have much sharper claws when it comes to regulating competition policy since it can fine individuals or firms which break EU rules. In 1986 a number of large European companies, including ICI (Imperial Chemical Industries) and Shell, were fined for fixing the market so that consumers were paying too much for one of their products.

Secondly, the Commission initiates EU policy. It does this principally by formulating proposals which

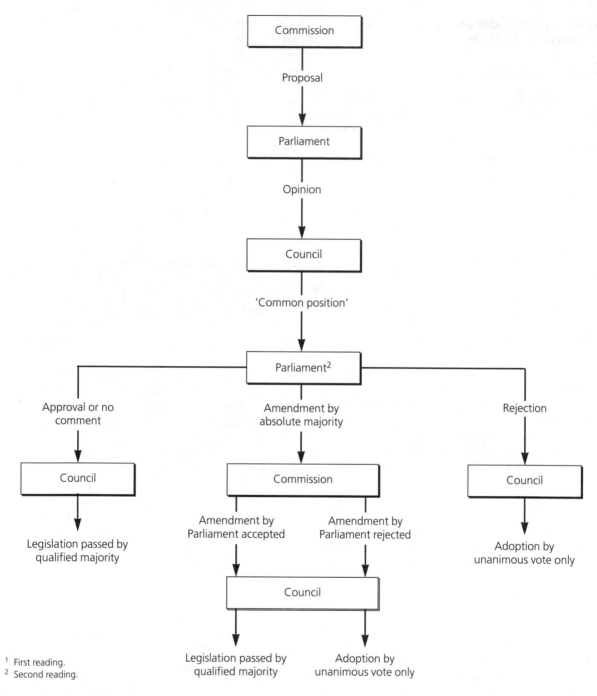

¹ First reading.
² Second reading.

Source: Borchhardt (1990) p. 32.

Figure 13.1 Decision-making in the European Union

are put to the Council of Ministers. As Nugent has commented,

> What this means, in practice, is that the Council's legislative capacity is heavily dependent on the willingness and ability of the Commission to put proposals before it. The Council cannot initiate and draft legislation itself. Furthermore, if the Council wishes to amend a Commission proposal, Article 149 of the EEC Treaty states that it can only do so either with the Commission's agreement or by acting unanimously if the Commission disagrees. If either of these two routes are open, the Council must accept the Commission's proposal as it stands, reject it, or refer it back to the Commission for reconsideration and resubmission at a later date. (Nugent, 1991, p. 73)

Thirdly, the Commission has a broad executive role in terms of supervising and implementing EU policies. It is called upon to make rules for situations where no rules yet exist. Fourthly, the Commission has the task of managing the Community's budget. Finally, the Commission negotiates with other international organisations, such as the UN and GATT, and with other countries, such as with developing countries through the Lomé Agreement.

The Commission is responsible for relatively little public administration, since as long as the domestic law of member states is parallel with European law that will be performed by the twelve public sectors of members. However, there is more politics involved in the work of the Commission than implied by the treaties. Much of its work in preparing, liaising and consulting requires the Commission to be aware of what is possible in political terms. Added to this is the increasing cultural diversity of EU members, which necessarily means that values or practices which are traditional and accepted by one member are unacceptable to others. The Commission has to be constantly mindful of this and conduct its business in a diplomatically sensitive manner. Developing the EU, through harmonisation, involves the Commission creating a general consensus in those areas where there is scope for the Union to move forward whilst at the same time tolerating diversity in other areas where

---

BOX 13.3
Legal instruments of the European Union

(Article 189 of the EEC Treaty)

The Council and the Commission issue regulations, directives and decisions, make recommendations and deliver opinions.

Regulations are directly applicable in every Member State. They are comparable to national laws.

Directives are addressed to Member States. They are binding as to the result to be achieved but leave the choice of form and methods for incorporating them into national legislation to the national authorities.

Decisions are binding on those to whom they are addressed (e.g. a government or a company).

Recommendations and opinions are not binding.

Source: Commission of the European Communities (1991).

---

nationalistic attitudes and values are deeply ingrained.

The Council of the European Union

If the work of the Commission reflects the federal process of the EU, then the Council of the European Union, more commonly known as the Council of Ministers, reflects the intergovernmental process. For in the Council of Ministers national governments are able to exert greatest influence and thereby protect their respective national interests. Because national sovereignty is a sensitive matter and because the Council of Ministers is a crucial decision-making body within the EU, the voting method by which the Council of Ministers reaches its decisions has sometimes been a contested issue. The Council can make decisions by (1) **unanimity**, particularly appropriate when a new policy is being considered, (2) a **qualified majority**, where an already established policy is being modified – Britain, along with Germany, France and Italy, has 10 'weighted' votes out of a total of 76; and the minimum requirement for a qualified majority is 54 votes which must be cast by at least 8 members – and (3) a **simple**

majority, which is usually used only where procedural issues are being decided upon.

The Luxembourg Compromise, which focused on agriculture but extended to wider issues, enshrined the principle that any member had the right to exercise a veto on Council decisions if it affected a vital national interest. This seemed to be challenged in 1982 when the Council of Ministers used a majority vote to force through farm price increases despite Britain's protests. Britain argued that its national interests were being damaged by the Common Agricultural Policy, but other members argued that this was not the case and Britain was simply holding up agricultural policy as a means of exerting influence to get its way on other issues. The Single European Act envisaged that the Commission should make an increasing number of decisions through majority voting.

The central function of the Council of Ministers is to decide European Union law on the basis of proposals it receives from the Commission. It is important to note that although the Council converts proposals into legislation, normally it does not have the constitutional right to initiate those proposals. In reality, however, the Council can guide and influence the shape of the proposals made to it by the Commission despite not having the right to draft those proposals itself. The work of the Council is divided up into 23 policy areas – such as agriculture, transport or foreign affairs – with the appropriate Ministers attending meetings depending upon the nature of the business in hand. As might be imagined, the meetings of the Council of Agricultural Ministers have included some of the most acrimonious sessions.

The business of the Council of Ministers is organised in large part by its President, a position which rotates between member states on a six-monthly basis. It is an influential role in terms of shaping the agenda of the Council, conducting negotiations with the Commission and Parliament, and thereby steering the direction and deciding the speed at which the Union develops. Much of the Council's business is conducted in secrecy.

Each member country has a permanent delegation of diplomats to assist in the work of the Council. These delegations meet together as the 'Committee of Permanent Representatives' (referred to by the French abbreviation of COREPER). These diplomats are relatively permanent and they tend to know each other well on a personal basis. Much of the work of COREPER involves completing tasks unfinished by the Council and preparing the political and technical ground for future Council meetings. It has been estimated that around 90 per cent of the Council's work is completed in advance by COREPER.

The European Parliament

The European Parliament has 626 directly elected MEPs of which 87 are elected to represent British constituencies (Figure 13.2). In the 1994 elections, British turnout was 36.4 per cent; and when compared with other national electorates Britain was firmly at the bottom of the turnout league table. In some ways the apathy of British voters towards the elections to the European Parliament was a healthy reaction since it is not really a Parliament which produces a government or has a pro-active legislative role. It is as if the British electorate realised that whether it returned Labour or Conservative MEPs made no impact on the European order. At the same time it is the case that since MEPs have been directly elected rather than appointed, they have behaved in a more assertive manner yet found that they can still be overruled or ignored whenever it suits the convenience of the Union's executive. Why is this?

There is no doubt that the European Parliament has more influence within European structures than used to be the case. It has more influence over the budget, along with the Council of Ministers, and these 'co-decision' powers have enhanced its ability to amend or reject draft laws. Having said this, the European Parliament does not exert democratic control over either the Commission or the Council of Ministers. The so-called 'democratic deficit' remains a characteristic of EU politics. Basically, it remains a democratically elected bogus institution with its MEPs (Members of the European Parliament) walking, as one journalist put it, the cor-

---

Unanimity involves obtaining the support of all countries; a **qualified majority** involves obtaining the support of more than half of all votes to a predetermined level; a **simple majority** is a half of all votes plus at least one extra vote.

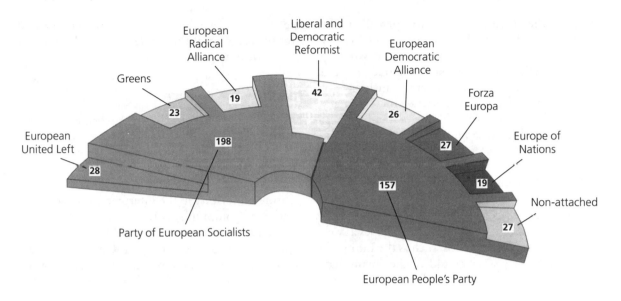

Figure 13.2 The European Parliament

ridors of weakness. Basically, then, the European Parliament (EP) plays a consultative role in the legislative process. Such influence as it has is won not only through formal channels but also informally in behind-the-scene negotiations.

It is very difficult to estimate the precise effect of EP deliberations on the final form of legislative acts. One reason for this is that a great deal of EP persuading and lobbying is impossible to monitor because it is carried out via informal contacts with the Commission and Council representatives. Another reason is that the Commission and the Council often go halfway in agreeing to the sense of EP amendments, but object to the way in which they are phrased or to specific parts of them. In general, however, it is clear that the Commission is more sympathetic than is the Council: so, whereas the Commission, on average, accepts between about 65–80 per cent of EP amendments at the first or the single reading stage, with much of the remaining 20–30 per cent being rejected for technical rather than political reasons, the Council's acceptance rate is considerably lower, especially where there is only a single reading. Sometimes less than 20 per cent of EP amendments appear in the final legislative text (Nugent, 1991, p. 133).

The exceptional circumstances in which the MEPs wield power concern the EU budget and dismissal of the Commission. The European Parliament can play a creative role in the budget process as well as having the power to reject draft budgets, a power that has been used on a number of occasions. However, when the Parliament does confront the Council of Ministers over budget proposals, MEPs find that they are more restricted by Treaty obligations than are the Council of Ministers. Also the European Parliament has the power, which it has not yet used, to dismiss the Commission. The European Parliament has no formal powers over the Council of Ministers, whose members see themselves as generally responsible to their national governments. Even the access of MEPs to the Council can prove difficult, depending on the membership of the Council at any particular time.

The European Parliament offers opinions on legislative proposals put before it, with MEPs doing much of their work in one of the 18 standing committees or one of the *ad hoc* committees. Their deliberations result in having some influence on European Union affairs, but the absence of democratic accountability inside the EU – the 'democratic deficit' – is a source of embarrassment to the EU. The powers of the European Parliament have been increased marginally from time to time. For example, the Maastricht Treaty provided the European Parliament with greater powers of scrutiny as well as a new 'negative assent' procedure whereby certain legislation can be blocked should it be found unacceptable. It seems likely that the influence of the European Parliament will increase incrementally in this manner, unless the EU moves in a federalist direction, in which case reforms giving an increase in real power can be anticipated, (Figure 13.1).

Party organisation within the European Parliament

Party organisation is complex in so far as parties or political groups come in all ideological shapes as well as different sizes. Some groups, such as the European right, are relatively small and ideologically unified. Others, such as the socialists, are large and contain a number of distinct ideological factions. Labour MEPs have joined the largest group, the socialists, which has members from every member country. Labour's recently found enthusiasm for the EU can be explained in part by the changing balance of power within the European Parliament. In the past the centre-right held sway, but over a period of years influence slipped to the left, putting the socialist group, including Labour, into the ascendancy.

The Economic and Social Committee

This advisory body was established within the EU to ensure the representation of important sectional interests and the general public. The Economic and Social Committee (ESC) has 189 members, of which the UK supplies 24. Around half the members are drawn from industry, commerce or other business organisations. Trade unions are represented also along with other interests such as the professions, local authorities and consumer groups. Trade unionists have long complained that they are outnumbered on the ESC by employers of one sort or another.

The ESC has been described as the 'other Parliament' of the Union, but this comparison flatters the significance of the ESC in European affairs. For if the European Parliament is weak, then the ESC is occasionally heard but rarely listened to. It is consulted, but often at such an advanced stage in the decision-making process that it is too late to amend or modify. It is possible, however, that the

role of the ESC will become a little more influential after the creation of the single market, should that lead, in turn, to greater union in general.

The Court of Justice

Thirteen judges, assisted by six Advocates-General, provide the judicial authority of the Union and ensure that European law is uniformly enacted. The Court of Justice's task is to

> ensure uniformity in the interpretation and application of Community law, to review the legality of acts adopted by the Council and the Commission, and to rule on questions of Community law referred to it by national courts. Any Member State may, if it considers that another Member State has failed to comply with an obligation under the Treaties, bring the matter before the Court, as may the Commission. The Court of Justice also rules on complaints by natural and legal persons who wish to challenge decisions affecting them taken by the Community. (*The European Community 1992 and Beyond,* 1991, p. 25)

The Court of Justice has dealt with cases which cover a wide range of areas, such as social welfare and agriculture, but the main thrust of its activities is concerned with business law. As the EU developed, so the workload of the Court has increased in both the number and complexity of the cases brought before it.

Where the domestic law of a member state clashes with EU law, the latter takes precedence over the former. The primacy of EU law was once challenged by the Italian constitutional court which argued that since the Treaty of Rome had been ratified by an ordinary law, any later laws which conflicted with the Rome Treaty would take precedence. European judges disagreed and argued the formal case which exists today, namely, 'By creating a Community of unlimited duration . . . the Members States have limited their sovereign rights, albeit within limited fields, and have thus created a body of laws which binds both their nationals and themselves' (OPEC, 1986, p. 37).

Britain and the European process

The terms in which the EU has been discussed in domestic politics have differed very widely. On the one hand, there has been a debate concerning the future of European Union which has involved aspirations about whether or not the EC and later EU should develop into a federal superstate. On the other hand, there have been arguments over the 'nuts and bolts' of the Common Agricultural Policy (CAP) and the EU budget. With what seemed equal degrees of commitment concerning the EU, politicians may have been discussing either the destiny of our continent or the price of sugarbeet.

This puzzling situation can be explained in part because (1) from the outset agriculture was one of the 'foundations of the Community' and has accounted for the largest proportion of EU legislation and spending (65.3 per cent of the EC's total budget in 1990 falling to 49.3 per cent in 1993) and (2) agriculture is not just 'domestic policy' but is caught up in world politics in terms of GATT world trade regulations and Third World development. The American agricultural lobby, in particular, has argued that the protectionist CAP blocks US imports into the EU whilst at the same time European surpluses are dumped at artificially cheap prices on world markets, again making it difficult for American farmers to compete.

Before Britain joined the EC it had a 'cheap food' policy, in sharp contrast to the CAP which is based on artificially high food prices to encourage production. Whereas Britain's system of agricultural support generally provided a balance in the demand and supply of food, the CAP results in a surplus of food production which has to be either destroyed, stored or sold off cheaply to consumers outside the EU. Not surprisingly, the CAP was popular with Britain's farmers but had many enemies on the political left and right. Labour politicians pointed out that because of the effects of the CAP, British families were paying by 1992 an extra £17 a week for food through higher prices and extra tax. Conservatives, with their preference for free markets and low public spending detested the highly interventionist and wasteful CAP.

There were also divisions on the CAP within Whitehall. The Ministry of Agriculture, reflecting farmers' interests rather more than consumers', generally supported the CAP; the Treasury, concerned at the CAP's rapidly increasing costs, were anxious that it should be reformed. This split was reflected within the Council of Ministers, with Finance Ministers generally sharing the Treasury's view on the need for reform, whilst Agriculture Ministers, having greater responsibility in the making of agricultural policy, were much more inclined to leave the CAP intact. However, by the mid-1980s the cost of the CAP was rising rapidly, with Britain paying into the EC far more than it got out. Attitudes hardened inside the Ministry of Agriculture with the Minister telling the Conservative Conference that 'The CAP has grown obese and needs slimming ... we cannot go on producing more and more food which we cannot either eat or sell.'

At the same time public attitudes towards the farming community were changing. In the past the public held farmers in high regard and appeared willing to subsidise the family farm. Pressure groups have helped to inform the public that most farming is now done by large mechanised undertakings controlled by 'farm managers' rather than 'yeoman farmers'. The intensive methods used in both the stock and arable sectors have increased efficiency but at a cost to the environment. Greater reliance on agrochemicals has resulted in the pollution of waterways as well as increased levels of mineral residues in meat, cereals and other products, with public confidence in farming shattered by the BSE crisis. Given these changes, it is not surprising that public sympathy for the farming community has weakened together with support for high levels of subsidy.

The Commission and Council of Ministers agreed that the CAP was in fact a bankrupt policy and that its reform was essential. The agriculture Commissioner, Ray McSharry, led the negotiations which resulted in the reform of the CAP in 1992. The reform involved a new mix of subsidies together with reduced farm incomes. Much more land was to be taken out of agricultural production, with the subsidies being switched from agricultural output to farm incomes. Quotas for dairy farmers were to be cut still further, with a 29 per cent reduction in the prices paid for cereals. Thus the new method for subsidising agriculture no longer encouraged farmers to produce ever larger surpluses of meat, cereals, milk, etc.

A Federal Structure?

A Confederal Structure?

A Twin-Track Structure?

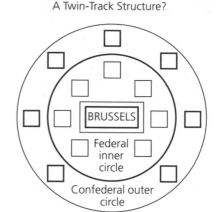

Weak national governments

Strong national governments

Euro-sceptics fear the gradual loss of national sovereignty if the EU develops into a 'United States of Europe'. If the UK had signed the Treaty of Maastricht like the other 11 members, it would have led to one market, single currency, and common defence and foreign policies. But their critics point to the principle of 'subsidiarity' which, like devolution, means that decisions are made at levels as close to the people as appropriate. Sceptics reply that employment law is best made at Westminster, so why did federalists want it included in the Social Chapter?

Rather than 'supra-nationalism' or 'federalism', Eurosceptics prefer 'intergovernmental' policy making and decision-taking. This could take place in a confederal structure, with a relatively weak centre and national governments which are strong and play the dominant roles. Some EU enthusiasts feel that the Union institutions would stagnate, or even disintegrate, if future developments were to follow this pattern. They argue that the chance of making the EU a world power would then be lost.

As prime minister John Major stated that he wanted Britain at the heart of the EU. His critics argued that his opting out of the single currency and Social Chapter would have sidelined the UK. Whilst others move towards a federal future, Britain and some other, mostly poorer countries, will be left in the slow lane. Others argue that this is unthinkable, since Britain could not afford to stay in the slow lane. The Blair Government has signed the Social Chapter and supports joining the single currency in principle, although not in the first wave for pragmatic reasons.

Figure 13.3 Which future for the European Union?

The CAP was the most federalist, most integrated, and most completely community-wide of all EC policies. It was also the most absurd. This was a great political convenience for Mrs Thatcher during the 1980s: 'The right and Mrs Thatcher used the issue of agricultural policy as a means of attacking the EC and its profligacy' (Martin J. Smith, 1992, p 141.) Thatcher's hostility was also directed towards the EC in general, not just the CAP in particular, which she saw as a socialist bureaucracy wanting to reintroduce to Britain many features of economic intervention, trade union privileges and socialist principles which her governments had banished.

The CAP has also been a long established grievance in Labour party politics. Labour wants further CAP finance reforms which will redirect EU budget from agriculture to industry and training.

The Maastricht summit

The summit meeting held in Maastricht in 1991 was proclaimed by some commentators as being the latter-day equivalent of the Congress of Vienna (1815) or Yalta (1945) in terms of its influence over the shaping of Europe. The Danish referendum, which subsequently rejected the Maastricht Treaty, dented this sort of media-hype and proved useful in providing time for governments to have further thoughts about European development whilst reminding themselves of the political dangers which existed when the integration process became detached from the democratic process.

The Maastricht summit was held when important developments were taking place both inside and outside the EU. Within the EU there had been efforts, pursued by Jacques Delors, to *deepen* the institutions of the EU. This involved the EU developing along federal lines, with a single European market being followed by a single European currency, leading eventually to common economic, social, foreign and defence policies. The deepening process had accelerated since the creation of the single market, with economic and monetary union seeming feasible by the end of the century.

Outside the EU were two sets of potential members, the admission of which would *widen* the Community. Firstly, the members of EFTA (Switzerland, Austria, Norway, Sweden, Finland, Iceland and Liechtenstein) had made an agreement with the EU to form the world's largest trade zone, the European Economic Area (EEA). The EEA will be made up of 380 million people from 19 countries and account for 40 per cent of the world's trade. The democratic revolution in Eastern Europe has also produced a dozen or so candidates for EU membership, with East Germany having already entered through German unification and with Poland and Hungary expecting to follow by the end of the decade.

The crucial question regarding the EU's future is whether the widening process and the deepening process are politically compatible. In other words, can both these processes work within the Union or only one of them? Some argue that some institutional reforms inside the EU will facilitate both processes. The original EC, it is argued, was designed for six members and could not operate with around thirty members. A new streamlined supra-national executive body, balanced by a more powerful European Parliament, would be needed to integrate the economies and policies of an expanded Union. Others argue that any significant widening of the EU automatically means that it will become a looser, less federal and more intergovernmental type of organisation. This is primarily because new member states, particularly those from Eastern Europe, could not share a single currency with the more powerful economies to the West for the foreseeable future. And a single currency, it is argued, is

---

BOX 13.4
British attitudes towards the European Union

	EURO-ENTHUSIASTIC	EURO-SCEPTIC
Federalism	Supports development of a European super-state with common European policies, even on foreign affairs and defence. Supports creation of European armed forces, possibly outside Nato. Supports extended Qualified Majority Voting.	Opposed to federalism. Preference for international co-operation between members rather than supra-national decision-making. National government seen as main location of power. Supports national veto on policies opposed to the national interest. Opposed to QMV.
Democracy	Supports European Parliament playing a more prominent role with powers which equal or exceed those of national governments. In short term, the elected Parliament should have greater power in setting the EU budget.	Content with the European Parliament having limited powers. Euro-sceptics prefer the Parliament to remain as a consultative body rather than evolve into a genuine parliament.
Enlargement	Supports new nations joining the EU but not at the expense of slowing down federal developments.	Supports enlargement in the belief that this will act as a brake on federal developments. Some believe that eventually the EU will become too big and will collapse in disarray. New members are welcomed as seeds of EU's destruction.
Single currency	Supports full economic and monetary union in order to make a reality of the single market and to facilitate common policies.	Supports the single market in order to increase competition, but opposes the single currency since it involves a major loss of parliamentary sovereignty.

a minimum prerequisite for federal deepening (Figure 13.3).

The first important decision of Blair's Labour government was negotiation of the Treaty of Amsterdam, which extended EU jurisdiction over aspects of immigration and border policy, human rights and employment policy as well as reducing the 'Luxembourg Compromise' national veto (see p. 240) and extending some powers of the European Parliament. In many ways this Treaty represented EU members doing 'routine' business, and the biggest decision facing Labour was the one which crippled the previous Conservative government: should Britain replace sterling with the euro and, if so, when? And would such a move result in the decline of the British nation state and a more federal Europe? (see Box 13.1, Box 13.4).

Summary

- Martin Westlake has commented on how the original structure of the first European experiment in 1951, the European Coal and Steel Community, still influences the configuration of the EU nearly 50 years later: 'a High Authority (later to become the Commission); a parliamentary assembly (later to become the European Parliament); a Special Council of Ministers (later to become the Council); and the Court of Justice' (Westlake, 1997, p. 148).
- Britain's relations with the original body, the ECSC, as well as its successors have played an increasingly important role in party politics. Both before and after Britain joined the European Community in 1973 there were deep splits of opinion within and between the parties. In the past Labour was the party most deeply divided over the European issue, but since Margaret Thatcher's leadership the Conservatives have become increasingly split over the direction in which the EU was developing. John Major was unable to build policy compromises on the EU which united Conservative factions.
- Party divisions on Europe in new Labour are less deep, but they are still present. The Labour government is committed to constitutionally radical reform in its project to construct 'new Britain'; how far will this radicalism be channelled in a European direction to build a 'People's Europe'

which is more popular and in touch with its citizens than the current EU?

Questions

1. To what extent has Britain been a 'bad European' inside the EU?
2. 'The EU is no more than an undemocratic and highly interventionist bureaucracy.' How valid is this criticism? What sort of reforms might improve the reputation of the Union?
3. Why has the EU issue divided opinion within and between Britain's main political parties?

Assignment

The 'United States of Europe' and the United States of America

How similar is the EU's political system to that of the United States? Read the following arguments before answering the questions.

Argument One: The two systems are surprisingly similar

- Both systems are democracies and have fixed-term elections. Although the European Parliament is not yet as influential as Congress, it does represent various regional interests spread across a continent and successive reforms are increasing its power within the European decision-making system.
- The EU and USA each have a political culture which contains common values as well as diversity. The USA is multi-ethnic, with an increasing number of its citizens being non-English speakers. Political parties are relatively weak organisations in both the EU and the USA; just as members of the Party of European Socialists hold very different views, so too do Democrats (and Republicans) depending upon their regional loyalties. Both systems endure relatively low turnouts in important elections; 56.8 per cent turned out in the 1994 European elections and 49.0 per cent in the 1996 US presidential elections. Pressure group representation plays a large role in both systems; the lobby in Brussels is as influential as that in Washington.

- Both systems recognise the Rule of Law and protect their citizens with a Bill of Rights. The European Court of Justice judges on compliance with treaties, directives and regulations in ways very similar to the Supreme Court. The American Bill of Rights is enshrined in the Constitution, whereas European rights are contained in the Social Chapter as well as by arrangements outside the EU. Although not part of the EU's formal structure, all citizens are protected by the European Court of Human Rights.
- Although the formal power structures of the EU and USA differ, they share similar characteristics in the way they operate. Too often the executive branch can become remote from the needs of citizens; both systems are complex and sometimes inaccessible; and legislative logjams are common to both, with consequent inability at times in both Washington and Brussels to make policy.
- Both the EU and USA have multi-layers of government. Whether or not both systems are strictly federal or not is irrelevant. What is important is that both European and American citizens can express their views through the ballot box at the local level, at national/state level, and at supranational federal level.

Argument Two: The two systems are very different
- The USA is a democracy in ways in which the EU is not. Direct elections to Congress represent the opportunity to vote for powerful decision-makers whereas direct elections to the European Parliament are for choosing relatively powerless non-decision-makers. Americans can vote, through an electoral college, for the executive in ways not available to Europeans in the EU. An unpopular president may be removed in ways in which an unpopular Commission and its President cannot.
- The USA has one dominant political culture which enables all citizens to engage in meaningful political debate. Citizens articulate their views through political parties which are substantial political organisations when compared with the 'political groupings' inside the European Parliament. For example European citizens cannot identify with the Party of European Socialists, for whom they

may never vote since its members may contest elections under different party labels, in ways which Americans can identify with either the Republicans or Democrats.
- Government in the USA is based on a separation of powers; the executive branch (the presidency); the legislative branch (Congress); and the judicial branch (the Supreme Court and court system). This facilitates a system of checks and balances so that no one branch of government can dominate the others. The structure of EU government is opaque, with much depending on relations between member states at any particular time and their negotiations for occupants of key positions. Power is diffused within and between the different institutions in a changing and unpredictable way.
- The USA has a federal system of government with national and state sharing responsibilities as well as having distinct responsibilities. The EU is not federal, neither is subsidiarity a concept which means much the same as federalism.
- The differences between the USA, a country, and the EU, a diplomatic invention, are at their starkest when considering the role of the President. The US President is 'commander in chief' of American armed forces. Neither the President of the Commission nor any other EU official has such powers, since there are no 'European' armed forces to command. In reality, through Nato, the US President dominates many European military decisions. The EU will always remain far behind the US in terms of governmental development, since there is no compelling 'supranational interest' guiding the EU in so far as there is a 'national interest' which guides the USA. The EU remains prisoner of 15 separate national interests, which will act as a constant brake on democratic developments and further federalism.

Questions
(i) Examine argument one and two. Identify the weakest and strongest points made, giving reasons for your choice.
(ii) To what extent, if any, does the EU and USA share a similar political culture?

(iii) After completing some library research, compare and contrast 'federalism' in the USA and EU.

(iv) To what extent would the adoption of the euro throughout the EU inevitably produce a more politically united organisation?

Further reading

Jones, B. and Robins, L. (eds) (1992) *Two Decades in British Politics* (Manchester University Press) explores Mrs Thatcher's vision of inter-governmental Europeanism. Nugent, N. (1994) *The Govern-* *ment and Politics of the European Community,* 3rd edn (Basingstoke: Macmillan) is a comprehensive examination of European institutions with a fair degree of technical detail. Pilkington, C. (1995) *Britain in the European Union Today* (Manchester: MUP) gives a cogent account of the major institutions and how they work. Watts, D. (1996) *Introducing the European Union* (Sheffield Hallam University, PAVIC Publications) is an illustrated, easily accessible account of the EU.

Website
Europa homepage (links to EU institutions and policy websites):

http://europa.eu.int/index–en.htm

Prime Minister and Cabinet

In this chapter and in Chapters 15 and 21 we consider the institutions which make up what has been aptly termed **the core executive**. This complex of offices and institutions at the pinnacle of the central decision-making process goes beyond the prime minister and Cabinet to include both their support institutions (the Prime Minister's Office and the Cabinet Office) and, in addition, the Departments themselves, headed by Ministers assisted by a small number of senior civil servants. Our focus in this chapter is on the Prime Minister and Cabinet system. We describe its principal features, consider the controversy over prime ministerial or Cabinet government before concluding with an examination of its strengths and weaknesses, and of proposals for reform.

The prime minister

The modern office of prime minister (PM) embodies a formidable concentration of power. In summary, the prime minister is responsible for

> **Core executive**: The term 'core executive' refers to the key institutions at the centre of government. It covers major institutions such as the Prime Minister, Cabinet and its committees, the Prime Minister's Office and the Cabinet Office, coordinating departments such as the Treasury, the government law officers and the security and intelligence services.

forming a government; for directing and coordinating its work; and for general supervision of the civil service. The prime minister takes particular interest in – and exercises strong influence over – decisions on the economy (as first lord of the Treasury) and on defence and foreign affairs; the prime minister also has special responsibilities in the sphere of national security. The prime minister decides upon the date for a general election (normally after consultation with senior colleagues) and, subject to the formality of royal assent, dissolves Parliament. Finally, the prime minister is the national leader, as evidenced by his or her role in representing the country at international conferences and meetings, signing treaties and playing host to leaders of other states.

The role of the prime minister

Patronage

The most important element of prime ministerial patronage is the power to select the one hundred or so politicians – drawn mainly from the House of Commons but also from the House of Lords – who at any given moment form the government. The prime minister appoints not just the Cabinet of normally 20–22 members but also ministers of state, under-secretaries of state, whips and law officers such as the attorney-general and solicitor-general.

Three points are worthy of note here. First, there is the sheer extent of the patronage. Between one-third and one-quarter (depending on the number of seats won) of the victorious party at a general election can realistically expect office. By no means all politicians seek office but a large number, probably the majority, do. The fact that so many share this goal is a formidable source of control for the prime minister. Second, this particular responsibility is not a once-for-all affair but a continuing one, with ministerial changes – by forced or deliberate reshuffle – occurring quite frequently. For example, under half of John Major's first Cabinet of November 1990 remained in his final Cabinet at the 1997 General Election and only one of the remaining ten Ministers – Lord Mackay – was in the same post. The frequency of government changes keeps this aspect of prime ministerial power firmly in the forefront of public attention. Third, despite the constraints on the prime minister's power of appointment (see below, pp. 267–9), it is a real power. Swift promotion – such as John Major's rapid advance to Foreign Secretary and then Chancellor of the Exchequer by Margaret Thatcher – is in the PM's hands, as is equally rapid demotion. By the end of 1981, only two and a half years after taking office, Margaret Thatcher had moved five 'wets' (i.e. one-nation Conservatives) out of the Cabinet whilst John Major sacked his Chancellor, Norman Lamont, a mere two and a half years after first appointing him to the post in November 1990.

The prime minister also plays a key role in the selection of individuals to fill a wide variety of other leading posts in national life. This influence extends over the creation of peers as well as over the appointment of top civil servants at the permanent secretary and deputy secretary levels, the heads of the security services and the chairmen of royal commissions. In addition, the prime minister has ultimate responsibility for recommendations of baronetcies, knighthoods, CBEs (Commander of the British Empire), MBEs (Member of the Order of the British Empire) and the like in the various New Year, Queen's Birthday and special honours lists.

Direction and organisation of the government

The prime minister is responsible for directing and organising the work of the government at the highest level (Figures 14.1 and 14.2). The PM must steer the government: colleagues expect such leadership and governments tend to drift without it. This involves setting broad policy objectives (within the framework of party ideology and the party manifesto) and devising short-term and long-term strategies for attaining these goals. The leadership, of course, is always in a collective context: the PM is not a single executive like the US President. Within that framework, there are clearly differences in style.

Margaret Thatcher is well known for having led from the front. Harold Wilson, on the other hand, although a good short-term tactician, was generally more concerned to conjure consensus from his colleagues than to lead them in a particular direction (Madgwick, 1991, pp. 140–1). Unless he or she specifically exempts them, the PM expects ministerial colleagues to support government policy according to the convention of collective responsibility.

The steering role means that the prime minister with his or her top adviser must decide upon the allocation of work between the Cabinet, its committees, ministerial groups, and bilateral meetings and consultations. Structuring the framework of decision-making involves the PM in drawing up the Cabinet agenda, and in deciding the composition, terms of reference and chairmanship of Cabinet committees. The special status of the prime minister is also evident in his or her special responsibility for and strong personal involvement in certain key policy areas. Thus, the PM plays a decisive role in the determination of economic policy in consultation with the chancellor of the exchequer and the treasury and of important foreign policy and defence matters in concert with the foreign secretary and defence secretary respectively. The prime minister alone is ultimately responsible for matters of national security which never go before Cabinet.

Finally, issues may arise over the whole field of governmental concern in which the prime minister either has to get involved or chooses to take a particular interest. Thus, prime ministers in the 1960s and 1970s were unavoidably involved in industrial, trade union and pay policies; they have consistently taken leading roles in the development of initiatives in Northern Ireland; and, more recently, John Major had to take a close interest in the abolition of the 'poll tax'. They may choose to become involved in any area which attracts their interest, although they risk upsetting the departmental minister concerned: thus, James Callaghan intervened in the fields of education, hospitals, personal tax reform, nuclear policy and aircraft purchasing policy, whilst Margaret Thatcher on her own initiative cancelled a research programme on the transmission of Aids, pushed for more British history in the National Curriculum, insisted on the introduction of market principles into the NHS (National Health Service), and put her weight behind a national identity card scheme to curb football hooliganism (Donoughue, 1987, pp. 5–6; Young, 1990, pp. 548–9).

As well as playing a key part in deciding the nature, timing and ordering of issues reaching the Cabinet agenda, the prime minister chairs Cabinet meetings. Prime ministerial 'styles' of chairmanship have included the clipped and businesslike (Attlee), the dominant but discursive (Churchill), the relaxed yet efficient (Macmillan), the non-directive consensual (Wilson), the aloof (Heath), the managerial (Callaghan), the directive non-consensual (Thatcher) and the collegial (John Major) (James, 1992, pp. 128–9). Whatever their particular style, the chairmanship gives prime ministers the capacity to shape the direction and result of policy discussions, for example by making their views known before and during the meeting, by their handling of Cabinet (who is called to speak and in what order) and by their summing up of 'the sense of the meeting' at the end. In the process, they may deploy various manipulative 'arts' of chairmanship including delay, obfuscation of the issue, verbosity, deliberate ambiguity, adjournment (followed by 'arm-twisting'), briskness (sometimes Cabinets have complained of being 'bounced' into decisions), sheer persistence, and authoritativeness. For all these wiles, they may not always succeed and examples abound of premiers failing to get their way (see below, pp. 267–9). Votes are almost never taken in Cabinet: they encourage division, dilute collective responsibility, and are vulnerable to 'leaks' and misleading reports in the media. But it is the task of the prime minister to summarise the decisions reached, taking into account the weight of opinion for or against a course of action as well as the numerical balance of opinion, and sometimes concluding against what appears to be the majority view. After the meeting, Cabinet conclusions are recorded by the Cabinet secretary in consultation with the prime minister.

The prime minister also makes decisions about the *structure* of the government, involving in particular the allocation of duties between the departments of state. The fluctuations in the number of departments – 30 in 1951, 21 in 1983, 19 in 1993 – and the changes in their functions are evidence of considerable prime ministerial activity in this sphere. The recent history of the departments concerned with trade, industry and power provides a good example. Edward Heath brought the Board of Trade and the Ministries of Technology and Power together in 1970 to form a new 'super-ministry', the Department of Trade and Industry (DTI), only to hive off Power to form the Department of Energy after the oil crisis in 1973. On gaining office in 1974, Harold Wilson broke up the DTI into separate Departments of Trade and Industry again and, in addition, created a new Ministry of Prices and Consumer Affairs. Margaret Thatcher, after 1979, merged Trade and Industry again, gave Prices and Consumer Affairs back to Trade, and kept Energy separate. John Major after his 1992 election victory abolished Energy, handing over its functions to Trade and Industry, and also created a new National Heritage department. Tony Blair as premier created a new super-ministry of Transport, Environment and the Regions and a new Department of International Development.

Finally in this regard, the prime minister has overall responsibility for the work of the civil service (the Cabinet Secretary is head of the civil service). This power has three main aspects – appointments, organisation, and practices. Developments since 1979 have seen a significant strengthening of the prime minister's position in relation to Whitehall. On top appointments, prime ministers are frequently willing simply to endorse the recommendations of the Senior Appointments Selection Committee although on occasion have been more closely involved. But on organisation and tasks, the Thatcher–Major era saw large-scale change launched and carried through, with a series of reforms initiated and supervised by advisers and personnel at the centre of government. Thus, the massive reorganisation of the civil service involved by the Next Steps programme was proposed by Mrs Thatcher's Efficiency Unit, a group within the Prime Minister's Office, whilst under John Major the package of reforms involving the Citizens' Charters and the market testing or contracting out of some civil service functions to the private sector were carried out by a unit within the Cabinet Office (Burch, 1995a, p. 131).

The power of dissolution

The prime minister has the exclusive right to recommend to the monarch the timing of the dissolution of Parliament within a five-year period. Whilst not an important power in relation to Cabinet and

Figure 14.1 The Labour Cabinet, May 1997

the prime minister's own party, the ability to call for a dissolution undoubtedly strengthens a prime minister's hand against the opposition parties. However, it is a weapon that may backfire since misjudgements like those of Edward Heath in calling a general election in February 1974 and of James Callaghan in failing to call one in autumn 1978 can contribute to a party's electoral defeat and, in doing so, lose many MPs their seats. Normally, the PM consults with senior ministers, including the chief whip, before making a decision about an election date and then informing Cabinet of the final choice.

National leadership

The prime minister occupies a special role in the life of the country which quite distinguishes the

occupant of the office from other Cabinet members – as national leader. This is always the case but becomes especially apparent at times of national crisis such as war – for example, Churchill's role in 1940–5, Thatcher's in the Falklands War (1982) and Major's during the Gulf War (1991). But the public spotlight focuses upon the PM at other times, too – during general elections, at times of political difficulty (e.g. during the row over tobacco sponsorship in November 1997) and when key decisions affecting the nation's future are being made (e.g. during EU inter-governmental negotiations). Prime ministers must please more than their close associates and their parties if they are to succeed. Ultimately they are judged by their success in providing effective national leadership by opponents and neutrals as well as friends. Failure in key areas of policy destroyed the premierships of Heath, Callaghan and Thatcher and severely weakened Wilson.

The prime minister's relations with party, Parliament and the media are often closely linked to the authority with which prime ministers are able to carry out their executive and national leadership roles. It is as the leader of the party which has gained a parliamentary majority in a general election that a prime minister gains office in the first place; it is as a consequence of the regular support of that party in Parliament that the prime minister can expect to govern and in particular to translate the party programme into legislation. Relationships with the party, therefore, are of the greatest significance and these are two-way. The prime minister seeks to maximise control of the party while the party strives for influence over the prime minister. The long-running battle between Major and the Conservative Euro-dissidents first over the ratification of the Maastricht Treaty and then over the European single currency, with the PM constantly appealing for party unity and the rebels demanding concessions, well illustrates this point.

Faced by recalcitrant backbenchers, the PM can appeal to personal ambition (the power of patronage is a potent weapon) and party loyalty (a general desire to do nothing to assist the 'other side'). In general, prime ministers are strongest in their relations with their parties in the months following victory in a general election or leadership election. Such 'honeymoon' periods may be very brief indeed, as John Major's experience in 1992 showed. In April, the fact that he enjoyed much greater popularity than Neil Kinnock made an important contribution to the Conservatives' election victory, but by early November he had become the most unpopular prime minister since records began.

PMs are at their weakest when government policies seem not to be working and provoke popular hostility and opposition. It was Thatcher's mounting unpopularity as a result of high interest rates, a stagnant economy and the 'poll tax', that led the party to revolt against her in November 1990.

The prime minister's performance in Parliament is always the subject of close scrutiny. Every Wednesday for half an hour the premier appears in the House of Commons to answer 'Prime Minister's Questions'. 'Question Time' is by far the most common prime ministerial activity in Parliament.

Prime ministers can expect to answer about 1,000 questions per session, a large proportion of them on economic and foreign affairs. Many of the questions appear as supplementaries which are more difficult to prepare for. Question Time is a testing ordeal, therefore, at which much is at stake, including personal reputation, command of party, and the authority of the government. Between 1974 and 1979 Labour premiers Harold Wilson and James Callaghan faced 400 Question Times whilst Margaret Thatcher answered 7,500 oral questions in her eleven years as PM (Madgwick, 1991, p. 174).

Whilst Parliament is sitting, premiers may expect to be constantly preoccupied with it in other ways, too. Their concerns include the progress of government legislation, set-piece speeches in full-dress parliamentary debates and, more generally, the state of party morale. 'Parliamentary business' is always an item on Cabinet agenda. A recent study has suggested that, whereas before 1940 prime ministers were often 'multi-faceted parliamentary performers who would, for example, both make a speech in a debate and then intervene subsequently', in the period after 1940 they have tended to attend the Commons 'only for a set and specific purpose, especially the effectively mandatory Prime Minister's question time' (Dunleavy, Jones and O'Leary (1990); see Box 14.1).

Contemporary prime ministers need to pay particular attention to the way they and their governments are presented in the media. They inevitably spend much of their lives in public – being interviewed on television, briefing lobby correspondents, making speeches at this or that public function, responding impromptu in the street or airport lounge or on the doorstep to queries about the latest crisis, scandal or leak. If they succeed in presenting a decisive image, they will be given credit for their handling – or, more pejoratively, for their 'manipulation' – of the media; if they are tripped up, or fluff their lines, or in any way give a less than positive impression, not only their own reputation but also that of the government will suffer. In other words, self-presentation through newspapers, radio and television has become another vital prime ministerial concern. Tony Blair was rarely out of the headlines during 1997.

Prime ministers need also to be concerned about their personal standing in the opinion polls. The

---

BOX 14.1
Prime ministers and parliament, 1945–94

Recent research has shown that:

- **Answering questions** at Question Time is far more common than any other kind of prime ministerial parliamentary activity; from the early 1960s there was considerable continuity in the extent to which prime ministers answered parliamentary questions until a slight fall under Thatcher in the 1980s and a further fall under Major.
- **Statements** to the House by prime ministers become more frequent in the post-1940 period but fell dramatically under Thatcher – 'a sporadic performer by postwar standards', and rose only slightly from that much lower base under Major.
- **Speeches** have become much rarer, with postwar PMs on average making speeches about half as often as PMs before 1940; however, prime ministerial speeches fell sharply under Thatcher from the postwar plateau and

although recovering under Major to not far below the postwar pre-Thatcher level, 'unusual wartime or crisis performances' may account for nearly half of that increase.
- **Interventions** in debates – in a spontaneous, unscripted way – was the second most common type of parliamentary activity by PMs down to the mid-1970s but this activity declined under Callaghan, fell even further under Thatcher and Major, and may be said to have 'completely withered and died'.
- Taking all these kinds of parliamentary activity together (namely, answering questions, statements, speeches and interventions), there has been a clear long-term decline in prime ministerial accountability to Parliament.

Sources: Dunleavy, Jones and O'Leary (1990); Dunleavy and Jones (1993); Burnham and Jones, with Elgie (1995).

---

polling organisations – Mori, Gallup, Marplan and the like – repeatedly sound public opinion on such matters as the moral qualities (toughness, integrity, truthfulness and compassion), leadership style (dictatorial/consensual) and policy achievements of the prime minister. They compare the premier's political standing with that of his or her main rivals (Table 14.1) and then often compare these ratings with

party support. These relative positions – prime ministers compared with other leaders; party leaders compared with their parties – fluctuate continually during the lifetime of a Parliament.

We are now in a position to summarise the role of the prime minister in the British political system (Box 14.2). It is worth noting that the main reason that the prime minister is more powerful in the British system of government than the US president is in the US system is because of the political consequences of a 'fused' executive–legislature (Britain) compared with a constitutionally separate executive and legislature (USA). Thus, a British prime minister normally has control of the legislature whereas an American president faces a constitutionally independent Congress in which, moreover, the president's party may not be in a majority.

Table 14.1 The political popularity of the party leaders in 1997

(1) 1997 General Election

Who would make the best prime minister, Mr Blair, Mr Major or Mr Ashdown?

Blair	36.7%
Major	26.6%
Ashdown	14.0%

(2) Summer 1997

Who would make the best prime minister, Mr Blair, Mr Major or Mr Ashdown?

	July	August
Blair	60.7%	58.7%
Major	10.5%	11.4%
Ashdown	14.9%	15.0%

Source: Gallup, *Daily Telegraph*, 12 September 1997

The Prime Minister's Office

The **prime minister** has a personal staff of around 100 people, about one-third of whom are senior officials and advisers. The Prime Minister's Office includes the following: the Private Office; the Press

---

The prime minister: a head of government whose power derives from leadership of the largest party in the legislature.

BOX 14.2
The role of the prime minister

- **Elected by the people**: authority of PM derives from being leader of the party which gains a parliamentary majority in a general election. Leader of party with overall majority gains constitutional status of the monarch's first minister.
- **Appoints government**: (and many more people to positions of national eminence): PM hires, reshuffles and dismisses ministers; decides order of rank – 'pecking order' – of Cabinet, signified by seating arrangements in Cabinet room.
- **Steers government**: PM directs and coordinates government policy and strategy; provides motive force of Cabinet system, exerting significant influence over Cabinet agenda, meetings and conclusions, and also determining pattern of decision-making at top (i.e. specific use of Cabinet committees, *ad hoc* ministerial groups, bilateral meetings). PM has special interest in economic, defence and foreign policy and may intervene in particular Departments. PM has special responsibilities in the field of national security.

- **Organises government**: this may involve abolition of old and creation of new Departments of State. As head of civil service, PM oversees appointments, organisation and practices.
- **Requests dissolution of Parliament from the monarch,** normally after consultation with senior ministers. This is an important power, enabling PM (within certain time limits) to call a general election at a moment of maximum advantage to his or her party.
- **Controls House of Commons** through leadership of majority party combined with (in most circumstances) its disciplined voting behaviour.
- **Gives leadership to the nation**: this is most obvious during national crises (e.g. wars) and key international negotiations (e.g. EU treaty-making and budget discussions) but in fact is continuous, as shown by the PM's constant activity in hosting receptions of foreign leaders and in making official visits abroad. PM has continuous high political profile because of frequent appearances on TV and radio and in press.

Office; the Political Office; the Policy Unit; and Special Advisers. Often from within the PM's Office, a number of close confidants and friends, a so-called 'Kitchen Cabinet', will emerge. (Figure 14.2). As two academic analysts have commented: 'The extension of the Prime Ministership from a post for an individual to a specialised micro-department of state is a significant constitutional development' (Madgwick and Woodhouse, 1995, p. 129).

The Private Office

The task of the Private Office is to support the PM in any way required. This involves it in ensuring that the PM's relationships as head of government with Whitehall, Parliament and public function as smoothly and efficiently as possible. The Private Office acts as a 'gate-keeper' for all incoming communications to the PM, forwarding them with appropriate comments; shadows the PM in his or her dealings with the outside world, including ministers; and, finally, provides any other support services needed, including advice, information, and the drafting of letters and speeches. The Private Office is headed by the prime minister's principal

private secretary and has five other private secretaries – all senior civil servants on secondment from their departments – backed up by a number of secretaries, executive officers and duty clerks. Of the private secretaries, four each cover a particular area of prime ministerial business – overseas, economic, parliamentary and home affairs – whilst a fifth keeps the prime minister's diary (Burch, 1995b, p. 31).

The Press Office

As already seen, media management is now considered an essential task of government and the role of the Press Office (the first press officer was appointed in 1931) is to handle the prime minister's relations with the media and the flow of government information. It holds briefing sessions with lobby correspondents 'off the record' on a daily basis and plans the PM's media appearances. Because of the central role of the press officer in presenting government policy to the media, recent holders of the job have been close confidants of the prime minister. Tony Blair's chief press officer Alistair Campbell became renowned for his efforts to run a tightly controlled presentation of government policies.

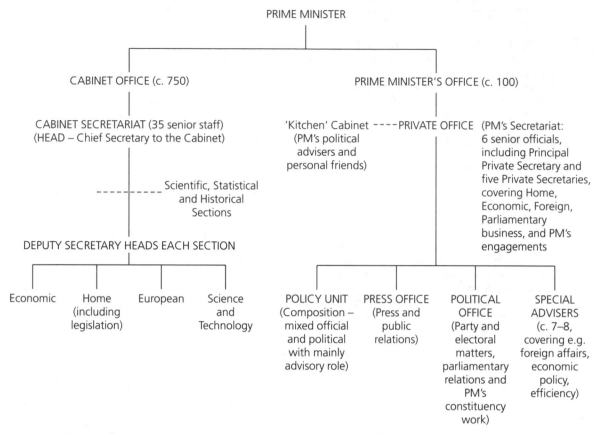

Figure 14.2 The executive centre of British government

The Political Office

The task of the Political Office, which is staffed not by civil servants but by temporary outsiders, is to deal with all matters concerning the prime minister as a party politician. It keeps in constant contact with party headquarters, with constituency parties – including the PM's own constituency – and generally with party developments at Westminster and in the country.

The Policy Unit

The Policy Unit, which was founded in 1974, provides policy and analysis and advice for the prime minister. Under the Conservative governments, it had eight or nine staff but was expanded by Tony Blair. Its main purposes are:

- commenting critically upon Departmental proposals;
- bringing forward new ideas and identifying new areas requiring attention;
- following up policy proposals.

In order to be effective the Unit needs and generally gets privileged access to Departmental officials and to ministers, including the right to attend top-level Cabinet and official committees. Its members are mostly politically partisan outsiders, usually recruited from business and academic life, but also include some career civil servants. The Policy Unit has been an undoubted success in providing prime ministers with an alternative source of policy advice to that emanating from the Departments on all areas except foreign policy. Its head under Labour is Rachel Lomax, a former high-flying civil servant who left to become Chief of Staff at the World Bank before her appointment by Tony Blair.

Special advisers

Modern prime ministers also appoint specialist advisers. John Major appointed special advisers on foreign affairs and efficiency and competition. Among those appointed by Margaret Thatcher were Sir Anthony Parsons, a former diplomat, to advise on foreign policy, and Sir Alan Walters, to advise on economic affairs. The continuing influence of Walters with the prime minister in the late 1980s created difficulties in the relationship between No. 10 and the Chancellor of the Exchequer, Nigel Lawson, ultimately leading to Lawson's resignation in October 1989. At the heart of the differences between the two men was the desirability of joining the ERM, which Lawson favoured and Walters opposed. Lawson's resignation letter stated:

> The successful conduct of economic policy is possible only if there is, and is seen to be, full agreement between the Prime Minister and the Chancellor of the Exchequer. Recent events have confirmed that this essential requirement cannot be met so long as Sir Alan Walters remains your personal economic adviser.

The recent events referred to included the publication of an article by Walters in which he described the European Monetary system as half-baked. Thatcher's response to a query about Walter's position by the Leader of the Opposition earlier in the week of the resignation had drawn attention to the constitutional position: 'Advisers advise, ministers decide.' Whilst true, this was also evasive about the particular significance of the role of *this* adviser. Lawson's relationship with Thatcher had been deteriorating for 18 months when he resigned and would probably have ended in resignation at some later point anyway. But there is little doubt either that Walters' advice had not only strengthened Thatcher's resistance to her Chancellor, thereby widening the division between them, but also contributed signally to her habit of covertly distancing herself from the policy of her own government. In this particular case, she had gone along with British membership of the EMS but, by failing to repudiate

Walters' attacks on it, encouraged the view among Conservative anti-Europeans and the public at large that she really opposed it. This tactic led first to policy confusion and then to political disaster, with Walters vacating his part-time £31,000-a-year job immediately after Lawson's resignation.

The 'Kitchen Cabinet'

Finally, most prime ministers have had a 'kitchen Cabinet' of close confidants, a circle of 'friends' to whom they can look for personal support. Margaret Thatcher's most trusted aides came from the PM's Office, in fact, and included Charles Powell, a foreign affairs adviser in her Private Office, Bernard Ingham, her Chief Press Secretary, and – over a much shorter period of time – her Parliamentary Private Secretary, Ian Gow. For close support, John Major looked mainly to people within the Prime Minister's Office: to Stephen Wall (Powell's successor in 1991) and Alex Allan, his principal private secretary from 1993, both in his Private Office, to Judith Chaplin and Jonathan Hill in the Political Office as well as to Norman Fowler, Party Chairman, 1992–4, a friend from Major's early years in government (Seldon, 1994, p. 160). Tony Blair's close circle of trusted advisers included Peter Mandelson, the Minister without Portfolio, Derry Irvine, the Lord Chancellor and Alastair Campbell, his Press Secretary.

The Cabinet

The Cabinet is the country's top executive committee. It usually consists of between 20 and 22 members. In May 1997 the Labour Cabinet contained 23 members (Table 14.2). Status within the Cabinet is not equal and most Cabinets divide into a small circle of ministers who may expect to be frequently consulted by the prime minister and an outer circle who count for less. John Major, for example, paid particular attention to the views of his most senior ministers, Douglas Hurd, Kenneth Clarke, Michael Heseltine, Michael Howard and Lord Wakeham (Seldon, 1994, p. 164). The 'plum' jobs are the chancellorship of the Exchequer and the foreign and home secretaryships, which a victorious party's leading few politicians may expect to occupy.

Table 14.2 The Labour Cabinet in July 1998

Prime Minister	Tony Blair
Deputy Prime Minister and Environment, Transport and the Regions Secretary	John Prescott
Chancellor of the Exchequer	Gordon Brown
Foreign Secretary	Robin Cook
Home Secretary	Jack Straw
Lord Chancellor	Lord Irvine
President of the Council and Leader of the House of Commons	Margaret Beckett
Minister for the Cabinet Office and Chancellor of the Duchy of Lancaster	Jack Cunningham
Education and Employment	David Blunkett
Health	Frank Dobson
Social Security	Alistair Darling
Scotland	Donald Dewar
Defence	George Robertson
Northern Ireland	Marjorie Mowlam
Agriculture, Fisheries and Food	Nick Brown
Wales	Ron Davies
National Heritage	Chris Smith
International Development	Claire Short
Chief Whip	Ann Taylor
Trade and Industry	Peter Mandelson
Leader of the Lords and Minister for Women	Baroness Jay
Chief Secretary to the Treasury	Stephen Byers

Non members of the Cabinet but attend Cabinet meetings: Minister for Transport – Dr John Reid and Government chief whip, House of Lords – Lord Carter.

meetings became more numerous throughout the century down to the 1960s but declined thereafter, slowly at first but then dramatically under Thatcher to a much lower level which was continued by Major (Table 14.3).

Cabinet business

Very few decisions in the modern Cabinet system are actually *made* by Cabinet although virtually all the major policy issues come before it in some form. Its agenda over a period of time consists predominantly of three kinds of matter: *routine items* such as forthcoming parliamentary business, reports on foreign affairs and major economic decisions, e.g. the budget, interest rate changes; from the 1980s regular slots have been found for EU matters and home affairs; *disagreements referred upwards for Cabinet arbitration,* e.g. from Cabinet committees or from a departmental minister in dispute; and *important contemporary concerns* – a broad range, including national crises such as a war, issues of major controversy such as a large-scale strike and matters of considerable political sensitivity, such as pit closures in 1992. Not only does the Cabinet itself not make many of the major policy decisions, it does not itself *initiate* policy either. In the 1990s, under John

Table 14.3 Frequency of Cabinet meetings, 1914–90

Period/prime minister	Meetings: total per year/ average number per week
Pre 1914	40 per year: under one per week
1918–1939	60 per year: just over one per week
1946–54	90 per year: two per week
Harold Wilson (1964–70, 74–6)	59 per year: just over one per week 472 meetings in approx. 8 years
Margaret Thatcher (1979–90)	35 per year: under one per week 394 meetings in over 11 years
John Major (1990–7)	30–40 per year: under one per week

Sources: Data from Hennessy (1986) p. 100; Madgwick (1991) p. 53.

On occasion, and notably in times of war, a small inner Cabinet has been formed, as in the Falklands War, for example. Thus, although the decision to commit the Task Force in 1981 was taken by full Cabinet, Margaret Thatcher formed a small War Cabinet of five to run the war on a day-to-day basis.

The full Cabinet meets once a week when parliament is sitting – under Major, on Thursday mornings for between an hour and an hour and a half. In times of crisis, it tends to meet more frequently and on other days of the week. Cabinet

Major, more extensive use was made of political Cabinets, where the Cabinet secretariat withdraws and the party chairman joins the meeting (Seldon, 1994, p. 165). Box 14.3 summarises the role of the modern Cabinet.

Cabinet committees

Because of the sheer volume and complexity of modern governmental business, the bulk of decisions within the Cabinet system are taken by *Cabinet committees* (either ministerial standing committees or ministerial *ad hoc* committees). Cabinet committees either take decisions themselves or prepare matters for higher-level decision, possibly at Cabinet. Official committees (of civil servants) shadow ministerial committees and prepare papers for their consideration (Burch and Holliday, 1996, p. 44). Cabinet committee decisions have the status of Cabinet decisions and only when they are unable to reach agreement is a matter referred to full Cabinet. The committee chairman must agree any request to take a dispute to full Cabinet, but in general such appeals are strongly discouraged. Treasury ministers however, in 1975, gained the right of automatic appeal to Cabinet if defeated on public spending in committee (James, 1992, p. 69).

The establishment, composition, terms of reference and chairmanship of Cabinet committees are the responsibility of the prime minister. Before 1992, their structure was supposedly a secret, although they did gradually come to light from the 1970s as a result of ministerial memoirs and partial statements by the prime minister. After the 1992 general election, however, John Major decided to make public the entire system of Cabinet standing committees and the subjects they deal with. Table 14.4 shows the ministerial standing committees established by Tony Blair .

In addition to the Cabinet standing committees, there are also a number of *ad hoc* committees set up by the prime minister to deal with particular issues as they arise. Table 14.5 gives some examples of *ad hoc* committees in the 1980s. Standing committees are normally classified under a set of code letters (e.g. DOP for 'Defence and Overseas Policy), *ad hoc* committees under the term 'GEN' for 'General' or 'MISC' for 'Miscellaneous', followed by a number. By the end of her second term, Mrs Thatcher had set

> **BOX 14.3**
> ## *The role of the Cabinet*
>
> **Formal approval**: Formal approval of decisions taken elsewhere.
>
> **Final court of appeal**: Final court of appeal for disagreements referred from below.
>
> **Crisis management**: Management of crises and issues of major political controversy.
>
> **Brake**: Blocking, slowing down, amending and qualifying policies and legislation.
>
> **Debating forum**: Sounding board for general debate by leading ministers.
>
> **Legitimiser**: Conferment of authority upon government decisions.
>
> **Symbol of collective executive**: Ultimate symbol of collective rather than single executive in Britain.

up about 200 *ad hoc* committees but John Major established far fewer – only 34 by July 1995, after over four years in office. For obvious reasons, ad hoc committees usually have a short life: in April 1995, out of over 20 appointed, only three ministerial *ad hoc* committees were still in being – those dealing with sanctions against Yugoslavia (GEN 27), competitiveness (GEN 29) and card technology (GEN 34) – and these too had disappeared by July 1995 (Burch and Holliday, 1996, pp. 43–4).

The prime minister and senior members of the Cabinet chair the most important Cabinet committees. Table 14.4, for example, shows the PM and Deputy Prime Minister each presiding over four standing committees and the Chancellor of the Exchequer, Lord Chancellor and Lord President of the Council responsible for a further five between them. Key standing committees are Defence and Overseas Policy (DOP), Home and Social Affairs (HS), Economic Affairs (EA), Public Expenditure (PX) and Legislation (LEG). The role of the Public Expenditure committee, which developed out of an *ad hoc* committee (the so-called 'Star Chamber'), is to arbitrate between the claims of spending departments and the Treasury's demand for economy.

Cabinet committees have become central to

Table 14.4 Ministerial standing committees of the Cabinet in June 1997

Chair	Committees: policy area (and designation), number of members
Prime Minister	Defence and Overseas Policy (DOP), 6 Constitutional Reform Policy (CRP), 13 Intelligence Services (IS), 6 Northern Ireland (IN), 6
Deputy Prime Minister and Secretary of State for the Environment, Transport and Regions	Home and Social Affairs (HS), 20 Environment (ENV), 18 Local Government (GL), 19 Sub-committee on London (GL(L), 12
Chancellor of the Exchequer	Economic Affairs (EA), 17 Public Expenditure (PX), 9 Sub-committee on Welfare to Work (EA(WW)), 13
Lord Chancellor	Queen's speeches and Future Legislation (QFL), 11 Devolution to Scotland and Wales and the English Regions (DSWR), 19 Sub-committee on Incorporation of the European Convention on Human rights (CRP(EC)), 17
President of the Council and Leader of the House	Legislation (LEG), 14 Sub-committee on Drug Misuse (HS(D)), 12 Sub-committee on Health Strategy (HS(H)), 15
Other Ministers (chair indicated)	Sub-committee on European Issues ((E) DOP), chair: Secretary of State for Foreign and Commonweath affairs, 19 Sub-committee on Women's Issues (HS (W)), chair: Secretary of State for Social Security, 14

Source: Cabinet Office (June 1997).

decision-making in the postwar period, even though in recent years their number and frequency of meeting have fallen. Thus, Mrs Thatcher reduced the number of committees, establishing a mere 30–35 standing committees and 120 *ad hoc* committees in six and a half years between 1979 and 1987. She also reduced the frequency of Cabinet committee meetings with the result that by 1990 the average annual frequency of meeting was only just over half that registered in the late 1970s. This trend continued under Major, who however tended to use ministerial standing committees more, and ministerial *ad hoc* committees less, than his predecessor. These figures may be compared with the 148 standing and 313 *ad hoc* committees established by Attlee in six and a quarter years between 1945 and 1951, and the 137 standing committees and 109 *ad hoc* committees set up by Churchill in three and a

half years between 1951 and 1954. The consequence of the fall in the number of committees and in the frequency of their meetings has been 'a more regularised and streamlined Cabinet committee system' (Burch and Holliday, 1996, p. 45).

The Cabinet Office

The Cabinet Office is another institution at the heart of the core executive which has developed in response to the large growth in the volume of government business. Dating from 1916, its most important component so far as central government is concerned is the *Cabinet Secretariat*, a group of about 28 senior civil servants on secondment from other Departments working under the direction of the Cabinet secretary. The Cabinet Secretariat is organised in five secretariats, each corresponding to

Table 14.5 Some key *ad hoc* Cabinet committees in the 1980s

Committee	Functions
MISC 62 ('Star Chamber')	Adjudication of public expenditure disputes between 'spending' departments and the Treasury and enforcement of spending cuts.
MISC 7	Replacement of the Polaris force with Trident.
MISC 57	Contingency planning for a miners' strike.
MISC 95	Abolition of the GLC and the metropolitan counties.
MISC 101	Day-to-day planning of the 1984–5 miners' strike.
MISC 107	Youth training.
MISC 111	Future of the Welfare State.
MISC 122	Handling of the teachers' dispute 1985–6.

a main area of Cabinet (Cabinet Committee) business, namely economic policy; home and social affairs (including legislation); overseas and defence affairs; European, and, operating rather differently from the other secretariats, joint intelligence. Its main tasks are threefold:

- to service Cabinet and its committees, preparing agendas, briefing Chairmen, taking minutes, circulating conclusions and chairing official committees which 'shadow' Cabinet committees;
- to coordinate and plan Cabinet business: there are weekly meetings to plan Cabinet and Cabinet committee business over the next 2–4 weeks with a periodic 'forward look' to 3–6 months ahead for future business and where it should be handled;
- to supervise the implementation of decisions emanating from the Cabinet system.

From 1992, the Cabinet Secretariat has also included the Office of Public Service which is headed by a Cabinet Minister answering to the Deputy Prime Minister and the Prime Minister. It is responsible for civil service management, raising the standard of public services, senior public appointments and promotion of greater openness in government.

Collective responsibility

Like the office of prime minister, the Cabinet lacks formal constitutional existence. Both institutions are creations of convention. The document *A Code of*

Conduct and Guidance on Procedure for Ministers ((1997), previously *Questions of Procedure for Ministers* – which is the first Cabinet paper a new minister is handed – has been described as the nearest thing to a written constitution for Cabinet government in Britain (Box 14.4). This document was also published in May 1992 along with the details about Cabinet ministerial committees; prior to that, knowledge of it had been available only through leaked editions. An important concern of *A Code of Conduct and Guidance on Procedure for Ministers* is the collective responsibility of ministers. It states: 'Decisions reached by the cabinet or ministerial committees are binding on all members of the government', that is, not just on members of the Cabinet. The doctrine of **collective responsibility,** which holds that all ministers accept responsibility collectively for decisions made in Cabinet and its committees, is the main convention influencing the operation of the Cabinet. The practical implications of the doctrine are as follows:

- *Cabinet solidarity.* Ministers may disagree until a decision is made, but are expected then to support it publicly or, at least, not express their lack of support for it. If they feel they must dissent publicly, they are expected to resign; if they fail to

> **Collective responsibility**: the convention of Cabinet Government that requires all ministers to support publicly decisions of cabinet and its committees or resign.

BOX 14.4

Cabinet practice: A Code of Conduct and Guidance on Procedure for Ministers

This paper lays down guidelines to ministers and civil servants in the operation of Cabinet government. It requires ministers

- To uphold the practice of collective responsibility;
- To account to and be held to account by Parliament for the policies, decisions and actions of their Departments and Next Steps Agencies;
- To give accurate and truthful information to Parliament, correcting any inadvertent error at the earliest possible opportunity; ministers who knowingly mislead Parliament are expected to offer their resignations to the Prime Minister;
- To be as open as possible with Parliament and the public, refusing to provide information only when disclosure would not be in the public interest;
- To require civil servants who give evidence before Parliamentary Committees on their behalf or under their direction to provide accurate, truthful and full information in accordance with the duties set out in the Civil Service Code;
- To scrupulously avoid any actual or apparent conflicts of interest between the public duties entailed by their ministerial position and their private financial interests; they should not accept any gift or hospitality which might or might reasonably appear to compromise their judgement or place them under an improper obligation;
- Not to disclose either the internal process through which a decision has been made or the level of committee by which it was taken;
- To maintain complete secrecy about opinions expressed in Cabinet and ministerial committees and, subject to the guidelines set out in Code of Practice on Access to Government Information (January 1997), to protect the privacy of Cabinet business and the security of government documents; if Privy Councillors, to give precedence to meetings with the Queen over all other matters;

- To make important announcements in the first instance in Parliament and to channel all announcements through the Downing Street Press Office;
- To pay particular attention in making appointments to securing on merit proper representation of women and members of ethnic minorities on public bodies;
- Not to use resources for party political purposes; to uphold the political impartiality of the Civil Service and not ask civil servants to act in any way which would conflict with the Civil Service Code;
- If in receipt of gifts over £140 from a foreign government to hand them over to their department (gifts under £140 may be retained so long as reported to the permanent secretary).

The document also informs ministers about Cabinet procedure:

- That minutes of Cabinet and Cabinet committees are restricted to summaries and that the Cabinet Office is instructed to avoid as far as practicable recording the opinions expressed by individual ministers;
- That Ministerial Committees (standing and *ad hoc*) may take important decisions which never reach the Cabinet but which the Government as a whole must accept responsibility for;
- That only Treasury ministers have an automatic right of appeal to full Cabinet from lower committees over spending decisions with which they disagree;
- That a minister wishing to raise a matter in Cabinet or in Cabinet committee must give the Cabinet Secretary at least seven days notice of it.

Source: Cabinet Office (July 1997)

---

resign, it falls to the prime minister to require them to do so. The underlying purpose of this is to create and maintain the authority of the government which public squabbling between ministers could be expected to damage.

- *Cabinet secrecy.* A precondition of Cabinet solidarity is that Cabinet discussion is secret. Ministers need to feel free to speak their minds secure in the knowledge that their views will not be divulged to the media. Ministers who are known to disagree with a policy may be expected

to have little commitment to it: well-publicised disagreements, therefore, have potentially damaging consequences for public confidence in government.

- *Cabinet resignation if defeated on a Commons vote of confidence.* The convention requires that the Cabinet – and therefore the entire government – should resign if defeated on a vote of confidence in the House of Commons. This aspect of the convention still operates unambiguously: when the Labour government elected in October 1974 was defeated on a vote of confidence on 28 March 1979, the Prime Minister James Callaghan immediately requested a dissolution. However, it rarely happens because the circumstances of a government lacking an overall majority are so infrequent.

The doctrine of collective responsibility is clearly of value to the prime minister in the control of Cabinet colleagues. On the other hand, it does lay reciprocal obligations on the PM, first, not to leak decisions and, second, to run the government in a collegial way, making sure that ministers have reasonable opportunities to discuss issues. This latter point has implications not only for the conduct of Cabinet itself but also for the composition of Cabinet committees which – if they are to take authoritative decisions in the name of the Cabinet – must be representative of the Cabinet as a whole (James, 1992, p. 9).

In recent times, the convention of collective responsibility has been repeatedly broken in several ways. These are:

* *Suspension by the PM*: Labour Prime Minister Harold Wilson in 1975 suspended the convention on the issue of Britain's continued membership of the European Community rather than risk public squabbling between members of the government and resignations by ministerial opponents of the Community. James Callaghan also did so in 1977 on the question of the most suitable electoral system for the European Parliament.
* *Leaks and memoirs*: unattributable leaks of confidential information by ministers, including the prime minister, and the publication of diaries by former Cabinet ministers such as Richard Crossman, Barbara Castle and Tony Benn which reveal details of Cabinet discussions.
* *Non-resignation despite serious disagreement with Cabinet policy over major issues*: In theory, dissent on an important aspect of government policy should be a resigning matter but there are fewer resignations than serious divisions within the Cabinet. Thus, James Callaghan campaigned openly against trade union reform in 1969 and Sir Geoffrey Howe openly argued in favour of joining the ERM after his demotion from the

Foreign Office in summer 1989 but whilst still a member of a Cabinet which officially did not support joining it. In late 1974 Tony Benn announced his opposition to EC membership in open defiance of a Cabinet agreement to observe collective responsibility until the process of renegotiation of entry terms had been completed. (Callaghan, 1987, p. 318).

Nonetheless, the habitual practice of Cabinet government is still best described in terms of 'the unanimity rule and the confidentiality rule' (Marshall, 1984, p. 55), respectively solidarity and secrecy. Between 1964 and 1990, 21 ministers left governments on the grounds of collective responsibility, including six (one dismissed, five resigned) from governments led by Thatcher (Pyper, 1991, pp. 243–4). Table 14.6 shows collective responsibility resignations between 1985 and 1990.

Thatcher's high-handedness as PM and failure to run the Cabinet in a collegial way culminated in the resignations of three Cabinet 'heavy weights', Michael Heseltine, Nigel Lawson and Sir Geoffrey Howe, in her last four years of office.

Heseltine resigned in 1986, maintaining that 'the basis of trust' necessary in the relationship between the Prime Minister and Defence Secretary had broken down. Thatcher had summoned two *ad hoc* ministerial meetings followed by a meeting of the Cabinet's Economic Affairs (EA) Committee in order to resolve the widely publicised dispute about the best solution for the problems of an ailing helicopter company, Westland. Later Heseltine claimed that his case for a 'European' – against the case for an American – solution had not been given a fair hearing within the Cabinet system, alleging in particular (a) that a further meeting of the Economic Affairs Committee promised at the 9 December meeting for 13 December 1985 had not been held (the PM denied that such a meeting was ever fixed), and (b) that his request to discuss Westland at a Cabinet meeting on 12 December was refused by the PM and that his protest about this was not recorded in the Cabinet minutes as he asked and nor was it recorded after he had complained to the Cabinet Secretary about the matter. He then felt justified in arguing his case about Westland helicopters publicly – in breach of Cabinet confidentiality – and when, after

Table 14.6 Resignations on grounds of collective responsibility, 1985–90

	Position	Reason for resignation
Ian Gow	Minister of State, Treasury, November 1985	Opposed to Anglo-Irish Agreement
Michael Heseltine	Secretary of State for Defence, January 1986	Opposed to PM's management of Westland Affair
Nigel Lawson	Chancellor of the Exchequer, October 1989	Opposed to PM's conduct of economic policy and to role of special adviser Sir Alan Walters
Nicholas Ridley	Secretary of State, Trade and Industry, July 1990	Resigned after pressure from PM following controversy over his comments on Germany
Sir Geoffrey Howe	Lord President of the Council Leader of the House of Commons ('Deputy Prime Minister') , November 1990	Opposed to PM's conduct of policy on Europe

a further controversy involving the leaking of a vital letter by the DTI (see Chapter 15), the PM sought to restrain him by the requirement that all future statements on Westland would have to be cleared with the Cabinet Office, he resigned (9 January 1986).

Like Heseltine, *Nigel Lawson* in resigning (see above, p. 257) argued that there had been a breakdown in the constitutional principle of collective Cabinet government. Shortly after resigning he stated in the House of Commons: 'For our system of Cabinet government to work effectively, the prime minister of the day must appoint ministers that he or she trusts and then leave them to carry out the policy. When differences of view emerge, as they are bound to do from time to time, they should be resolved privately and, wherever appropriate, collectively.' The political reality, however, was that in this case there was no agreed policy (on whether to join the ERM), and the PM – probably fearing that her own preference for remaining outside the ERM was the minority view – was unwilling to put the matter to the test of collegial discussion.

Sir Geoffrey Howe's resignation one year later (1 November 1990) occurred after Britain had joined the ERM but also immediately in the wake of vigorous prime ministerial attacks on European federal ideals and monetary integration. Sir Geoffrey avowed his belief that Cabinet government was 'all about trying to persuade one another from within'. He resigned because he believed that the PM's

negative attitudes on Europe prevented him from any longer being able to resolve the conflict between his loyalty to the PM and his loyalty to what he perceived as the true interests of the nation from within the government.

It has been argued that two of these resignations (Heseltine and Howe) were not straightforward examples of collective responsibility resignations, since in Heseltine's case, personal ambition, and in both cases, clashes of personality with the Prime Minister, were also involved as well as policy disagreements. Furthermore, both resignations were linked to a power struggle in the Conservative Party concerning the replacement of Margaret Thatcher as party leader (Dorey, 1994/5, pp. 105–6). These ministers, it is contended, simply used the doctrine of collective responsibility to legitimise and give credence to their actions. Whether the argument in these particular cases is accepted or not, it is hard to disagree that the doctrine of collective responsibility has been weakened in recent times. Further examples occurred in the 1990s of ministers – e.g. Michael Portillo – being prepared to make speeches or write articles revealing their disagreements with aspects of government policy without resigning or being required to resign (Dorey, ibid, p. 106). One problem for ministers is certainly the extent to which as individuals they have played little part in making the decisions to which they are required to assent: the reduction of time spent in Cabinet and the rising incidence of discretionary powers given to ministers and the prime minister when negotiating in the European Union place clear limits on collective decision-making (James, 1995, p. 83).

Cabinet minutes

Cabinet minutes – which are the responsibility of the Cabinet Secretariat – aim not to record every shift and turn of Cabinet debate but simply to reflect, in the words of a former Cabinet Secretary, Sir John Hunt, 'as much agreement as is there'. Controversy has occurred over the extent of prime ministerial involvement in the process, with certain members of Labour Cabinets suggesting that this could be considerable (Castle, 1980, p. 252; Crossman, 1979, p. 702). But the then Prime Minister, Harold Wilson, denied it, maintaining at the time (1970) that only 'very, very occasionally' was he consulted about the minutes before issue. He later stated that 'the writing of the conclusions is the unique responsibility of the Secretary of the

Cabinet . . . The conclusions are circulated very promptly after Cabinet, and up to that that time no minister, certainly not the Prime Minister, sees them, asks to see them or conditions them in any way' (cited in King, 1985, p. 40). This later statement is widely accepted now as a correct account of routine procedure.

A recent detailed account of practice in the 1980s states:

On most items before Cabinet, the Cabinet Secretary and at least one member . . . of the secretariat most directly responsible . . . would record a full record of the discussion in their notebooks. From their notes, the officials would compile a draft minute to send to Armstrong's office later on the day of the meeting . . . Armstrong then collated and edited the drafts sent in by the secretariats, and produced a final copy of the Cabinet's minutes . . . *His final record was never cleared with the PM or with the individual ministers concerned,*

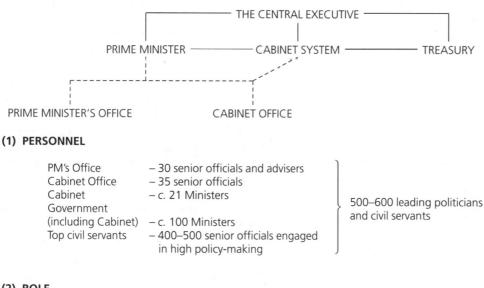

(1) PERSONNEL

PM's Office	– 30 senior officials and advisers	
Cabinet Office	– 35 senior officials	
Cabinet	– c. 21 Ministers	500–600 leading politicians and civil servants
Government (including Cabinet)	– c. 100 Ministers	
Top civil servants	– 400–500 senior officials engaged in high policy-making	

(2) ROLE

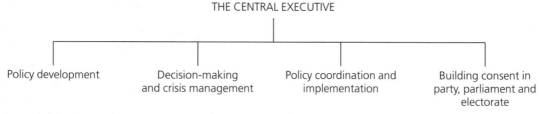

Figure 14.3 The central executive: personnel and role

contrary to the views of some (Seldon, 1990, our italics).

Figure 14.3 provides a summary overview of the personnel and role of the main institutions in the central executive territory.

Prime ministerial or Cabinet government?

Some commentators have argued that the British system of government has evolved towards **prime ministerial government** (Crossman, 1964; Benn, 1980) or even 'presidential' government (Foley, 1993) in the postwar period. Margaret Thatcher's premiership, which stretched the power of the office to the limit, has been seen as validating this thesis. Briefly, these writers argue that a considerable concentration of power in the premiership has occurred, resulting in 'a system of personal rule in the very heart of our parliamentary democracy' (Benn, 1980). The prime minister's powers of appointment and dismissal of ministers, control over government business, special responsibilities in the spheres of strategic economic matters, defence, foreign policy and security, command over government information and publicity, and constitutional capacity to request a dissolution of parliament are considered to have elevated the premiership at the expense of the Cabinet. By making decisions through informal ministerial groups and bilateral meetings with a minister and officials, the prime minister can bypass – and downgrade – Cabinet. The prime minister has a direct relationship with all ministers and expects to

---

Prime Ministerial Government: the argument that the Prime Minister dominates governmental decision-making, using the powers of the office to decide policy in any area with whomsoever s/he chooses, to decide key issues and to set the ideological framework for ministerial policies.

Cabinet Government: a system of government by a collective executive, the Cabinet, whose members share in the making of decisions and are equally accountable for them.

---

be informed about all new policy initiatives, which makes it possible to kill off those he or she dislikes. Whereas if he or she wishes, a prime minister can intervene selectively over the entire field of policy-making, the cabinet can deal only with the material which is put before it. Very recent trends have reinforced prime ministerial dominance. These include:

- Fewer and shorter meetings of Cabinet and fewer Cabinet papers. In the period since 1974, 'formal Cabinet has been progressively used less and less' (Burch and Holliday, 1996, p. 45). As a consequence Cabinet's role has been diminished to the extent that ' no one informed about British politics believes that a great deal of business can be transacted at weekly meetings of 23 ministers lasting for around an hour and a half' (Dunleavy, 1995, p. 298).

- The expansion and increased status of the Prime Minister's Office since the 1970s, especially the formation of the Prime Minister's Policy Unit, has increased the prime minister's capacity ' to oversee government strategy, to monitor departmental work and to initiate policy from the centre'. Contemporary prime ministers are better informed about what is happening across the whole range of government and there is an increased tendency for business to flow to the Prime Minister's Office and for ministers to consult No.10 before launching policy initiatives (Burch and Holliday, 1996, p. 45).

- The impact of British membership of the EU on top decision-making has strengthened the prime minister's hand and weakened Cabinet. As the leading British negotiator in EU treaty-making the PM has to be given considerable latitude to make deals in Britain's interests and, when other ministers are involved in European policy-making, to assent to any changes in negotiating positions This point extends beyond Europe to the general enhancement of the PM's position by the impact of international summit meetings, e.g. Group of Seven (G7) meetings (James, 1995, p.75; Lee, 1995, pp. 214–5).

- The prime minister's position at the centre of the Cabinet committee system enhances his or her power. After identifying eight main policy networks in the British Cabinet system (such as domestic policy, overseas policy and European

Union policy), Burch and Holliday found the prime minister to be 'a core member of seven networks' and also that the prime minister's power potential 'has been increased in in all networks of which he or she is core' (Burch and Holliday, 1996, pp. 105–6). Dunleavy's study of positional influence in Cabinet committees under Major concluded that the Prime Minister is in 'a powerful coalitional position', that is in a strong position to build blocs of influence involving top ministers such as the Chancellor or foreign secretary plus non-departmental ministers (Dunleavy, 1995, pp. 318–19).

- More intense media focus on the prime minister has increased the need for the prime minister constantly to demonstrate leadership, control of party, a political vision, and personal charisma. Premiers' ability to do all these things is vital to the success of their parties (and to their own continuance in office); hence, their emphasis on presentation of their policies and relationships with the media, and the key role in their premierships of the Downing Street press officers and their ability to put a favourable 'spin' or gloss on events (Burch and Holliday, 1996, pp. 100–2; Seymour-Ure, 1995, p. 197).

However, despite the comprehensive assertion of the powers of the PM's office by Margaret Thatcher, it remains inappropriate to describe the British system as 'prime ministerial government'. In practice, prime ministerial power can vary considerably according to the disposition of the individual prime minister to exploit the capacities of the office and political circumstances such as size of parliamentary majority and simply how 'events' fall out. Figure 14.4 sets out the range of styles of prime minister–Cabinet relationship in the postwar period. It shows that neither the pure model of prime ministerial power nor of collective **Cabinet government** has been achieved, but rather, in each premiership, something in between, with biases towards the one or the other (Burch and Holliday, 1996, p. 146; Figure 14.4). Its creators, Martin Burch and Ian Holliday, consider prime ministerial styles only to John Major, but already by early 1998, after less than a year in power, Tony Blair appears to fit into the diagram next to Thatcher as an active, singular style of Prime Minister (Box 14.5).

Constitutional, political, administrative and personal constraints prevent the prime minister from achieving the degree of predominance suggested by the prime ministerial government thesis.

Constitutional constraints

Britain's top decision-making body remains a collective not a single executive and the prime minister's role therefore is to provide leadership within a Cabinet context in which collective responsibility remains the rule. In the final analysis, the 'mortal wound' to Margaret Thatcher was struck by the Cabinet, which 'rejected her' (Jones, 1995, p. 87).

Political constraints

Appointment and dismissals: Constitutionally the PM has a free hand in the making of government appointments but *politically* selection is constrained by the pool of talent within a particular party, by party standing and by the need to please sections of the party (left and right, 'wets' and 'dries', Euro-enthusiasts and Euro-sceptics). This means in practice that Cabinets contain individuals whom the PM would rather be without and also that many Cabinets contain one or two politicians of the highest calibre and with a following in the party who may be rivals for the party leadership: 'these are people whom the Prime Minister needs as much, or maybe more sometimes, than they need the Prime Minister' (Roy Jenkins, cit. James, 1992, p. 133). Political considerations also constrain the PM's power of dismissal and demotion: Macmillan in dismissing seven Cabinet ministers and nine ministers outside the Cabinet in July 1962 (the so-called 'Night of the Long Knives') damaged his own standing as the brutality of the sackings caused resentment in the party and gave the appearance of panic to the country. Thatcher's big Cabinet reshuffle of July 1989 which included the demotion of the reluctant Sir Geoffrey Howe from the post of Foreign Secretary also had very damaging consequences (Young, 1990, pp. 555–7).

Policy: Party also serves as a constraint in matters of policy. A good illustration of this is policy towards Europe which has caused a series of PMs from Macmillan to Major often acute problems of party management. Wilson suspended collective responsibility and held a referendum to avoid splitting Labour and Major resigned the party leadership in 1995 in an attempt to put to rest incessant Cabinet and party dissension over Europe. Moreover, the PM heads an executive whose collective task is to implement the party manifesto, in which inevitably individual ministers play key roles.

Tenure: Ultimately the party may remove a sitting PM, but this is a rare event, having been the fate of just four of the seventeen PMs in the twentieth century: in addition to Thatcher (1990), Asquith (1916), Lloyd George (1922) and Chamberlain (1940) resigned after losing the support of senior colleagues and a sizeable section of the majority parliamentary party. The very unusual combination of circumstances which led to the downfall of Thatcher included the availability of a strong prime ministerial candidate outside the Cabinet (Heseltine), the recent resignations of two Cabinet 'heavyweights' (Lawson and Howe), with Howe giving a particularly wounding resignation speech, a by-election disaster at a normally safe Conservative seat (Eastbourne), adverse economic indicators, public anger at the 'poll tax' for which Thatcher was generally blamed, and the considerable unpopularity of the Prime Minister and the party she led in the polls.

Administrative constraints

The Cabinet: The major institutional constraint upon a PM is the Cabinet: however great their powers of manipulation, PMs have often suffered defeats in Cabinet, e.g. Wilson on trade union reform (1969), Callaghan on his wish to declare a state of emergency during the 'Winter of Discontent' (1979) and Margaret Thatcher on a number of issues including public expenditure cuts, radical anti-union and privatisation measures (early 1980s), a Northern Ireland assembly, and the sale of Ford Motors to Austin Motors (1986); major settlements such as those relating to Rhodesia/Zimbabwe (1981) and Hong Kong (1984) and the decision to enter the ERM (1990) were pushed through against her resistance. On crucial issues, PMs are careful to bind the whole Cabinet to a decision: on the sending of the Task Force to the Falklands, Thatcher asked every member of the Cabinet individually to indicate a view. John Major, especially in his first two

years before acquiring a personal mandate in 1992, was careful to take decisions collectively in order to bind his colleagues to the final outcome.

Government Departments and the civil service: The PM can also be restrained in a number of ways by the Departments and the civil service. Government Departments are 'the key policy-making institutions in British politics' and the PM/'Core executive' 'does not play a decisive role in all, or even in most of, the stages of the policy process' (Smith, Marsh and Richards, 1995, p. 38). Characteristically, in relation to the Departments, the prime minister is in ' the position of a bargainer rather than of a leader enjoying a significant power of command' (Burch, 1995a, p. 136). Thus, policy tends to arrive at the PM at such a late stage that effective challenge becomes difficult. Thus, the prime minister may be able to squash ministerial policy initiatives but would find it hard to impose a policy on a minister. As Harold Wilson said, 'I'm tired of asking for this or that suggestion to be followed up only to have Michael (Stewart's) or Jim's (Callaghan) officials report back three weeks later that nothing could be done' (cited James, 1992, p. 220). With expertise, knowledge of the facts and policy networks concentrated in the Departments, any policy that is 'to last the course' must come from a departmental minister (James, 1995, p. 76).

Personal constraints

Finally, there are *personal limits* upon the power of the prime minister – the limits of any single individual's ability, energy, resources and time, together with the (very considerable) extent to which decisions are shaped by circumstances beyond any individual's ability to control. A survey of the prime minister's 'diary' during the 1970s has shown how stretched a single individual is to fulfil such a punishing schedule of consultations, meetings, appointments, conferences, receptions, and visits: according to this estimate – assuming a 13-hour day, a five-day Whitehall week and a Cabinet year of 44 weeks – only about one day per week is available to the PM for 'the Cabinet role', rising to over one and a half days when time spent with civil servants is taken into account; the rest of the time is spent on party matters, Parliament, and hosting and visiting (Donoughue, 1988). Moreover, the PM's special

BOX 14.5
Tony Blair's style of premiership

- **Intentions**: Some pre-election rhetoric suggested Blair intended to run a 'presidentialist' government lacking in collegiality. One of his advisers suggested there would be greater prime ministerial drive: 'You may see a change from a feudal system of barons to a more Napoleonic system.' The phrase 'the Blair Presidency' is often used by his inner circle in private.

- **Practice**: 'The system is driven more from No. 10 under Blair even than under her (Mrs Thatcher) at her height' (Hennessy, 1998, p. 16). There are several signs of greater control from the centre: (a) Changes in the Prime Minister's Office and the Cabinet Office enable the PM to exercise more control throughout Whitehall and to take 'strategic direction of his government': e.g. a closer relationship between the No.10 Policy Unit and the Cabinet Office; the appointment of over 50 task forces, advisory groups and reviews by August 1997, with all the major review teams including a representative from No. 10; and the new Social Exclusion Unit, located in the Cabinet Office, reporting directly to the PM. (b) There has been a further reduction in the role of Cabinet (although still too early for more than very provisional judgement): Blair Cabinets have been short (rarely lasting more than an hour), very informal ('call me Tony'), and have broken with custom by having no formal agenda. (c) There is an enhanced role for 'spin doctors'. Three measures ensure tight central control of government policy and its presentation: (i) daily meetings on policy presentation under Blair of a team of top advisers including Peter Mandelson, the Minister without Portfolio, Alastair Campbell, the PM's Press Secretary, and Jonathan Powell, the PM's chief of staff; (ii) new emphasis in *A Code of Conduct and Guidance on Procedure for Ministers* on ministers' need to agree all major interviews and media appearances with the No. 10 Press Office before any commitments are entered into whilst the policy content of all major speeches, press releases and new policy initiatives also need to be cleared with the No. 10 Press Office in good time (paragraph 88); (iii) new machinery to centralise government information service with political advisers increasingly supplanting career civil servants within departments and working to the No. 10 Press Office under Campbell.

- **Qualifications of 'presidentialism'**: (a) As in previous governments, the political influence of Cabinet 'heavyweights' sets limits to the power of the PM, notably the Chancellor of the Exchequer, Gordon Brown, the deputy Prime Minister, John Prescott, and the Foreign Secretary, Robin Cook. These, with Blair, form the Labour Government's 'Big Four': only these four knew about the decision to move control of interest rates to the Bank of England, which was announced before Cabinet had met once. The 'Big Four' meet once a week without civil servants present. Again as in previous administrations, the relationship between the occupants of No. 10 and No. 11 Downing Street, between Blair and Brown, is particularly important for the fortunes of the government. (b) The importance of Cabinet is likely to increase with time, once manifesto promises have been delivered and disagreements among senior ministers need resolution.

Sources: Hennessy (1998); The *Guardian*, 3 June 1997.

---

concerns (foreign affairs, the economy and security) are particularly vulnerable to setbacks which rebound swiftly on the popularity and even credibility of the premier: thus, security services disasters undermined Macmillan, pay policy problems leading to industrial conflict helped to destroy Callaghan, whilst difficulties over Europe ultimately eroded the authority of Thatcher and Major. Indeed, it was not only problems with Europe over such matters as 'mad cow disease' but also an almost continuous series of public relations failures over political 'sleaze' which undermined Major.

To summarise: the British prime minister has very considerable powers – and these were stretched to the limit by a dynamic PM such as Thatcher and are being stretched by Blair also. But the constraints upon the premier make 'prime ministerial government' an inappropriate description. Is 'Cabinet government' a more apt one? Our earlier discussion suggested that the Cabinet itself neither originates policy nor takes more than a small proportion of major decisions. Most policy decisions in British government are taken by the Departments. However, the Cabinet retains what may be described as 'a residual and irreducible' authority; it has not sunk into merely 'dignified' status (Madgwick, 1991, p. 259). It remains strong enough to help depose a dominant PM and also to provide a collective shield to protect both a prime minister and his or her leading ministers when they get into political difficulties. The British system of decision-making at the top has grown more complex, diffuse, and extensive but it is still a collective executive in which the prime minister provides leadership within a Cabinet system. However, political commentators have drawn attention to two main weaknesses at the

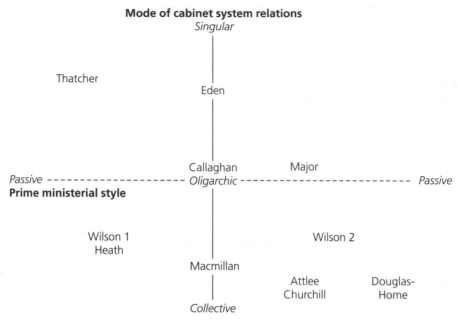

Source: Burch and Holliday, 1996, p.146.

Figure 14.4 Styles of Prime Minister–Cabinet relations, 1945–95

centre of British government. First, despite the undoubted strengthening of the central executive machine over the last twenty years (mainly through the development of the Prime Minister's Office and the Cabinet Office), a single executive capable of providing policy leadership and coherence has not emerged (Burch, 1995b, p. 33). There is 'a hole in the centre of government' (Bogdanor, the *Guardian*, 4 June 1997). Second, policy remains largely the preserve of the Departments, thereby – in default of a corrective mechanism – undermining *collective* decision-making and accountability.

Proposals for reform

Ministers in Cabinet rarely look at the totality of their responsibilities, at the balance of policy, at the progress of government towards its objectives as a whole ... The form and structure of a modern Cabinet and the diet it consumes almost oblige it to function like a group of individuals, and not as a unity (Sir Douglas Wass, 1983).

One of the most frequent criticisms of the operation of modern Cabinet government is the weakness of

coordination and strategic direction at the top. Recent examples of confusion and lack of direction include the unresolved tension between PM and Chancellor of the Exchequer over European policy in the late 1980s, the failure of government to reconcile its free market ideology with the pursuit of 'green' objectives in the same period, and the two-month gap which appeared in government economic policy when Britain was forced out of the ERM in mid-September 1992. Many reform proposals therefore have focused on strengthening the capacity of prime minister and/or Cabinet to provide improved policy-making coordination and better long-term strategic direction. Reformers argue that there is a crying need to overcome the 'short-termism' seemingly endemic in postwar British government, which has had especially damaging consequences in the fields of foreign and economic policy.

Reforms aimed at strengthening the administrative capacity and competence of Cabinet include: reviving the Central Policy Review Staff, the 'think tank' created by Edward Heath but abolished by Margaret Thatcher; augmenting the Cabinet Office by adding analysis and strategy units; holding special strategy and monitoring sessions of Cabinet; and increasing the number of political advisers for

Table 14.7 Proposals for reform: Prime Minister and Cabinet

Reform proposal	Aims	Comments
• Revive Central Policy Review Staff (CPRS)		Founded by Edward Heath (1971); abolished (1983) by Thatcher.
• Strengthen Cabinet Office by adding analysis and strategy units		Had some success.
• Ministerial 'Cabinets'	To improve coordination and long-term strategic direction at the top of central government by increasing the time and resources available to Cabinet Ministers to consider general policy	To brief ministers for Cabinet on general policy.
• Create small inner Cabinet to coordinate and steer government business		
• Cabinet Review Committees		To relate policy areas to overall Government strategy.
• Reduce Ministerial workloads and increase length of time spent in posts		
• Prime Minister's Department	To increase the capacity of the PM to provide well-informed leadership of the Cabinet system.	Proposed by Lord Hunt (1984). Critics say might strengthen PM *against* Cabinet.
• Strengthen Prime Minister's Office		
• Fixed-term Parliament/PM to take dissolution request to full Cabinet	To curtail the PM's dissolution power.	
• Curb PM's patronage by party elections to Cabinet and making most public appointments subject to parliamentary confirmation	To reduce PM's patronage powers and make PM more accountable to party and government.	PM would retain power to allocate Ministerial portfolios.
• More open government including Freedom of Information Act	Increase governmental accountability and improve quality of policies by requiring leading politicians to argue their cases publicly.	Small start made by Major and significant step taken by Blair Government with passing of Freedom of Information Act in conflict with long tradition of secrecy in British government

Ministers. A further possibility, in view of the reductions in the size of Departments following the removal of a large part of the Civil Service into executive agencies, might be amalgamation of some of the smaller ministries in order to create a small inner Cabinet charged with the overall coordination and steering of government business (Burch, 1995b, p. 39).

With the appointment of 53 political advisers (compared with 38 under the Conservatives), Tony Blair's early steps were to improve ministers' capacity to contribute to the general strategy of the government by improving the advice available to them in their departments. The role of the political advisers is to assist ministers carry out their part of the manifesto and to enable them to contribute more knowledgeably to issues outside their departmental remits.

A second reforming approach seeks to strengthen the central institutions, especially the Prime Minister's Office and the Cabinet Office. With the largest increase in the number of political advisers appointed by Tony Blair going into No. 10 Downing Street, it seems likely that the Labour Prime Minister was further bolstering recent trends to augment the capacity of the centre.

A third line of criticism developed by the left focuses less on improving the administrative capacity of government than in increasing its accountability and curbing its power. It maintains that too much power has become concentrated in the prime minister, who has developed into an 'elected monarch'. Reforms proposed by this school of thought focus on limiting the premier's political and other patronage, circumscribing his/her power to recommend a dissolution and making the premiership more accountable to Parliament.

Finally, many critics argue that government would be both stronger – in the sense of better able to deliver its objectives – and more publicly accountable if it were less secretive and more open. Noting the start made by the Major Government in this direction in May 1992, they argue that this process needs to be taken much further, and welcome the Labour Government's plans for a Freedom of Information Act.

Summary

- The modern premiership is a powerful office, its formidable array of powers and responsibilities making the prime minister very much more than 'first among equals' in relation to the rest of the Cabinet. Nonetheless, Britain does not have 'prime ministerial government'; rather, it has a Cabinet system of government driven and organised by the prime minister.
- The Cabinet itself, although neither initiating policy nor making more than a small number of important decisions, retains a vital core of authority. Although not always observed, the principle of collective responsibility – Cabinet solidarity and confidentiality – still applies. The vast majority of government decisions continue to be made in the departments.
- *A Code of Conduct and Guidance on Procedure for Ministers* is the key constitutional document on prime minister and Cabinet. Previously entitled *Questions of Procedure for Ministers,* it was made public officially for the first time in 1992 by John Major. It prescribes rules on matters such as the nature of Cabinet and Cabinet committee business, collective responsibility (the requirements of solidarity and confidentiality) and the central responsibility of the prime minister for the overall organisation of the executive.
- In the twentieth century, and especially after 1945, with the growth in the scope of complexity of government, the Prime Minister's Office, the Cabinet Secretariat (Cabinet Office) and an extensive Cabinet committee system have developed to enable the core executive to deal with its vastly increased volume of business.
- The main trends in the core executive level since the 1970s have been a reduction in the number of Cabinet meetings, a streamlining of the Cabinet committee system and an enlargement – and consequent increased capacity – of both the Prime Minister's Office and the Cabinet Office. The formation of the Prime Minister's Policy Unit and the Office of Public Service are important developments.
- Despite the trends to centralisation in the core executive, political analysts still consider that there is 'a hole in the centre 'of the British Cabinet system. The prime minister lacks sufficient administrative resources, especially with regard to policy and long-term strategy, to steer the government effectively, whilst Cabinet ministers are well-equipped for their departmental tasks but inadequate for their collective, Cabinet role.
- Proposals for reform focus on strengthening strategic direction and policy coordination within the Cabinet system and making British government more open and more accountable. The Labour Government took early steps to increase the number of political advisers both of the prime minister and of members of the Cabinet and to continue the work begun by Major of opening up government by passing a Freedom of Information Act.

Questions

1. How appropriate is it to describe the modern

British prime minister as 'an elective dictator'?

2. How far do you agree with the proposition that the Cabinet has been reduced to a merely 'dignified' institution in British government?

3. Evaluate the resignations of Michael Heseltine, Nigel Lawson and Sir Geoffrey Howe. How far were these collective responsibility resignations and how far were other factors at stake?

Assignment

Prime minister and Cabinet
Re-read the discussion of prime ministerial or Cabinet government (above, pp. 266–70).

Questions

(i) What are the main factors which have increased the power of the prime minister in recent decades?

(ii) What are the major constraints upon the prime minister's power?

(iii) How far does the PM's power vary according to such factors as size of parliamentary majority, phase of the electoral cycle and political strength and ambition of leading colleagues? Give some examples.

(iv) How far does the term 'Cabinet government' remain an appropriate description of the British system?

Further reading

On the prime minister, there are Shell, D. and Hodder-Williams, R. (eds) (1995) *Churchill to Major: The British Prime Ministership since 1945*

(London: Hurst and Company); Jones, G. W. (1990) 'Mrs Thatcher and the Power of the Prime Minister', *Contemporary Record*, 3:4; King, Anthony (1985) *The British Prime Minister* (London: Macmillan); and Kavanagh, D. (1991) 'Prime Ministerial Power Revisited', *Social Studies Review*, 6:4, March.

On the Cabinet, Burch, M. and Holliday, I. (1996) *The British Cabinet System* (London: Harvester Wheatsheaf) is an authoritative study. Valuable discussions are provided by Madgwick, Peter (1991) *British Government: The Central Executive Territory* (London: Philip Allan), and James, Simon (1992) *British Cabinet Government* (London: Routledge) whilst there is much valuable historical information in Hennessy, Peter (1987) *Cabinet* (Oxford: Blackwell).

Finally, useful analyses of prime minister–Cabinet relationships are contained in Rhodes, R.A.W. and Dunleavy, P. (eds) (1995) *Prime Minister, Cabinet and Core Executive* (London: Macmillan); Seldon, A. (1994) 'Policy Making and Cabinet', in D. Kavanagh and A. Seldon (eds), *The Major Effect* (London: Macmillan); Hood, C. and James, O. (1997) 'The Central Executive', in Dunleavy et al. (eds), *Developments in British Politics 5* (London: Macmillan) and Burch, M. (1995) 'Prime Minister and Cabinet: An Executive in Transition?', in R. Pyper and L. Robins (eds), *Governing the UK in the 1990s* (London: Macmillan).

Websites:
10 Downing Street:
http;//www.number-10.gov.uk/

Cabinet Office:
http://www.open.gov.uk/co/cohome.htm

Ministers, departments and the civil service

This chapter continues our examination of the 'core executive' by considering the major Departments of State. We begin by characterising them in terms of structure, size and recruitment. We then turn to the two leading themes of this chapter – first, to a consideration of the roles of ministers and civil servants, with special emphasis upon the nature of the relationship between them; and second, to an analysis of the convention of ministerial responsibility, which in traditional accounts is held to describe the accountability of ministerial heads of Departments to Parliament. We examine the precise meanings that are attached to this convention today. Our dual focus, therefore, is upon how decisions are made throughout the bulk of British government and how those decisions are made constitutionally accountable. We examine the implications of mid-1990s Reports (Nolan and Scott) for civil service and ministerial relations, conduct and accountability. Finally, we explore the radical changes in the **civil service** introduced by the Conservatives between 1979 and 1997 in the course of the chapter which concludes with a consideration of the impact of these and other developments on the cardinal principles of permanence, neutrality and anonymity characterising the traditional civil service.

The main departments of state

In forming an administration, as already noted (Chapter 14, above), a prime minister makes over 100 appointments. In addition to government whips, these include ministers who head Departments – most of whom are of Cabinet rank, non-Departmental ministers such as the lord president of the council and the chancellor of the Duchy of Lancaster, and a large number of junior ministers, i.e. ministers of state and parliamentary under-secretaries of state. As well as a Departmental head (secretary of state), each ministry frequently contains at least one minister of state and two or more parliamentary under-secretaries of state: these junior ministerial appointments are the route by which aspiring politicians gain experience of government and often but not invariably lead in time to promotion to full ministerial rank. The Department of Education and Employments – a large department – has a Cabinet minister at its head assisted by three ministers of state and three parliamentary under-secretaries of state. By contrast, a very small ministry like the Welsh Office has one Cabinet minister and two parliamentary under secretaries of state. Junior ministers (ministers of state and parliamentary under-secretaries) normally assume responsibility for

> **Civil Service:** the state bureaucracy, the civil public administration of the state. A civil servant is a Crown servant working in a civil capacity who is not a political or judicial office-holder or a member of the Royal Household.

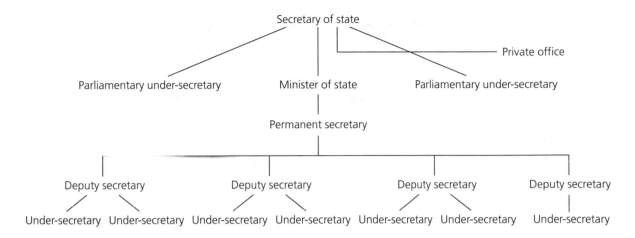

Figure 15.1 Structure of a typical department of state

specific tasks: in the Department of Education and Employment, for example, they cover employment and disability rights, further and higher education, school standards, life-long learning and welfare to work.

Ministers are the political and constitutional heads of Departments. Departments, however, are largely composed of permanent officials. Below the ministerial 'team' there is a body of civil servants headed by the permanent secretary, the most senior official in the departmental hierarchy. In addition to acting as the minister's top policy adviser, the permanent secretary is in charge of the daily work of the Department, is responsible for its staffing and organisation, and is also its accounting officer. Below the permanent secretary, in order of rank, are the deputy secretaries, under-secretaries and three other grades down to principal. Broadly speaking, each Department is normally divided up, first into several areas of policy, with each the responsibility of a deputy secretary, and then into a number of functional units (or branches), each with an under-secretary in charge. Figure 15.1 brings together the points made so far about departmental structure in diagrammatic form.

There are nineteen major Whitehall departments, including the three legal ones. Table 15.1 sets out their main responsibilities together with the size of their staff (1996) and projected budgets for 1997–8. For top politicians, the most coveted Departments are the three mentioned first – the Treasury, the Foreign Office and the Home Office. However, in terms of size these are surpassed by the big spending departments such as Defence, Education and Employment and Social Security. Table 15.1 brings out the disparities not only in size but also in budgets between these Departmental giants and Departmental 'minnows' such as the Northern Ireland Office.

The Tomlin Commission (1931) suggested a definition of 'civil servant' which has become widely used: civil servants are 'Servants of the Crown, other than holders of political or judicial offices, who are employed in a civil capacity and whose remuneration is paid wholly and directly out of moneys voted by Parliament'. This definition covered 494,300 individuals on 1 April 1996 who collectively constituted about 10 per cent of all public sector employees and about 2 per cent of the working population. Their numbers had declined from 735,000 in 1979 as a result of a deliberate policy designed to prune the bureaucracy carried out by Conservative governments between 1979 and 1997.

Within the civil service as a whole it is useful to distinguish between the non-industrial and the industrial civil servants – i.e. those employed in factories and workshops. As a proportion of the whole, industrial civil servants – who numbered a mere 36,000 in 1996 – have declined from 53 per cent in 1939 to just over 7 per cent in 1996; correspondingly, non-industrial civil servants now constitute over 92 per cent of the total service. Of the non-industrial civil servants, one-fifth (21 per cent) work in London; just under one-seventh (15 per cent)

Table 15.1 The main government departments: responsibilities, size, budgets, 1996

Department (headed by)	Responsibilities	Size (number of personnel)	Budget (£bn) November 1996 plans for 1997–8
The Treasury (Chancellor of the Exchequer)	Economic policy	958	1.1
Foreign and Commonwealth Office (Foreign Secretary)	Foreign policy	5,015	1.1
Home Office (Home Secretary)	Administration of justice, police, prisons, immigration, public safety, public morals	11,938	6.8
Trade and Industry (President of the Board of Trade)	Trade policy, industrial policy technology and civil research and development, monopolies	9,234	3.1
Health (Secretary of State)	National Health Service	4,795	34.9
Environment (Secretary of State)	Housing, local government and inner cities, environment and countryside	4,678	39.0
Defence (Secretary of State)	Defence policy, armed services	109,858	21.1
Agriculture (Secretary of State)	Agriculture, fisheries and food	9,995	3.6
Education and Employment (Secretary of State)	Employment policy; industrial relations, job training; primary, secondary, further and higher education, science policy	40,327	14.0
Social Security (Secretary of State)	Social security benefits of all kinds.	91,516	79.7
Transport (Secretary of State)	Transport policy	11,071	5.2
Scottish Office (Secretary of State)	Social and economic policies	5,054	14.3
Welsh Office (Secretary of State)	Wide range of policies and services	2,139	6.9
Northern Ireland Office (Secretary of State)	Economic and social policies, law and order, security policy, constitutional developments relating to Northern Ireland.	215	8.2
National Heritage (Secretary of State)	Arts, media, heritage, sport	1,003	0.7
Lord Chancellor's Department	Administration of the law and the courts	11,227	3.56
Law Officer's Department (Attorney-General)	Enforcement of criminal law; advice to government on legal matters; represents Crown in major court cases	26	–
Lord Advocate's Department	Has same functions in Scotland as Law Officer's Department in England	20	–

Sources: Treasury figures, *Civil Service Statistics* (1996) pp. 21–3.

Figure 15.2 Whitehall

work in the rest of the South East whilst the remaining two-thirds work in the provinces.

It is also important to notice that most executive functions of the civil service are now carried out by executive agencies which have been established under the Next Steps programme (1988) to improve management in government and the delivery of services. In total, nearly 71 per cent of the civil service was working in Next Steps agencies or on Next Steps lines by 1 April 1996. Each agency is headed by a Chief Executive who generally reports to a Minister. The Minister sets the Chief Executive output, financial and quality of service targets for each year.

This chapter is primarily concerned with a tiny fraction of the non-industrial civil service – the top policy-making grades who mostly work in London and who since April 1996 have been banded together as the Senior Civil Service (SCS). There were just under 4,000 (3,900) in the SCS in 1996. As well as what were formerly the first five grades, the SCS also includes senior diplomatic personnel

and a number of other staff at a similar level. It constitutes a mere 0.8 per cent of the entire non-industrial civil service (494,300) (Figure 15.3). Members of this group form the administrative élite who, in cooperation with their ministerial superiors, 'run the country'.

Recruitment to the ranks of the leading administrators is mainly at graduate level by a qualifying literacy and numeracy test followed by an extremely rigorous series of written appreciations, drafting tests and simulated committee work over two days at the Civil Service Selection Board (CSSB). Successful candidates at this stage then go before a Final Selection Board (FSB). The Fulton Report (1968) called for changes in civil service recruitment, promotion and training, recommending preference to be given to graduates with more relevant degrees, a considerable expansion of late entry in order to enable people from many walks of life to bring in their experience, and the widening of the social and educational base from which top civil servants were recruited. The idea of demanding 'relevance' was rejected but, although expansion of late entry had disappointing results, from the mid-1980s there was a significant programme of two-way temporary secondments between Whitehall and industry, commerce and other institutions (Hennessy, 1990, pp. 523–4). By 1996, there had been a dramatic increase in recruitment from the private sector, with a quarter of the 63 posts advertised in the senior civil service going to private sector applicants.

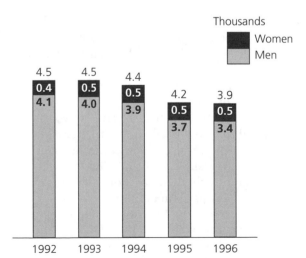

Figure 15.3 The senior civil service, 1992–96

Secondments outside Whitehall had also increased, with 1,500 civil servants on medium to long-term attachments in 1996. The Blair government established a new group headed by the Cabinet Secretary and the President of the CBI to oversee the development of shorter, more flexible secondments from the civil service into industry, especially of junior level civil servants from outside London (*Daily Telegraph,* 25 September 1997). Broadening the base of recruitment away from Oxbridge-educated arts graduates has occurred very gradually, although canvassing for recruits at 'redbrick' universities intensified in 1991. In 1993, 59 per cent of fast-stream entrants were Oxbridge compared with 85 per cent in the early 1960s, and Oxbridge accounted for a mere 39 per cent of the successful fast-stream applicants in 1996, a considerable but probably untypical fall (the *Guardian,* 13 June 1996).

The British civil service – three major features

British constitutional theory makes a clear distinction between the *political* role of ministers and the *administrative* role of civil servants. Ministers are in charge of Departments and responsible to Parliament for running them, whilst civil servants advise ministers on policy and implement government decisions. Three major features of civil servants are linked to this distinction:

- *Permanence*: Unlike the position in the United States, where large numbers of administrative posts change hands when the political complexion of the government changes, in Britain civil servants are career officials prepared to serve governments of any party.
- *Political neutrality*: British civil servants are required to be politically impartial, not allowing their own political opinions to influence their actions and loyally carrying out decisions whether they agree with them or not; they must not engage in any partisan political activity.
- *Anonymity*: It is the function of ministers to be politically answerable for their Departments to Parliament and public, whereas it is the role of civil servants to offer confidential advice in secret. If civil servants became public figures, this might

compromise their neutrality since they would become associated in the public mind with a particular policy; it also might undermine the frankness of the advice offered to ministers.

These general points are valuable as guidelines but also need to be handled with care. For example, civil servants, although not allowed to play a formal (party) political role, are much more involved in the political process than the description of their work in terms of 'administration' suggests. They are obviously heavily involved in the politics of bargaining for influence *within* Departments, *between* Departments, *with* outside interests and *in their relations with* ministers. They are centrally concerned with policy advice to ministers. This inherently political (and problematic) aspect of the role of civil servants will become amply evident in the discussion of decision making within Departments in the next section. Moreover, in the postwar period, and with increasing rapidity in the 1980s and 1990s, traditional features of the civil service have been to a significant degree eroded, especially its neutrality and anonymity, and this is examined in the final section.

Decision-making within departments

The vast majority of governmental decisions nowadays are made in Departments. As already noted in Chapter 14, the proportion of Departmental decisions which are either sufficiently important or controversial to be taken to Cabinet has become very small indeed. An examination of decision-making in Departments, therefore, takes us to the centre of contemporary British government. Not only do Departments take the bulk of decisions – from the relatively minor to the undeniably major – it is no accident that they do so. For whenever new responsibilities are created by legislation, Parliament confers them squarely upon Departments. New powers developed by statute are given to ministers, not to the Cabinet or the prime minister. The political and administrative importance of Departments stems directly from their legal-constitutional preeminence.

How decisions are taken within Departments is consequently of vital significance in British govern-

BOX 15.1
Models of minister–civil servant relations

- The traditional public administration or liberal-democratic.
- The new public administration or liberal-bureaucratic.
- The 'Whitehall village'.
- The power bloc.
- The bureaucratic over-supply or New Right.

ment. To what extent are ministers the real decision-makers or, to put the question in another way, how far does the real power lie with civil servants? There are five models of the minister–civil servant relationship (Box 15.1).

The *traditional public administration* model expresses the perception of minister–civil servant relations which is embedded in formal constitutional theory. It is the orthodox account according to which ministers take policy decisions and defend them publicly, whilst civil servants brief ministers, processing information so that their political superiors can choose between options in an informed way and then unquestioningly implementing ministerial decisions. In this view, ministers always have the final say whilst civil servants are neutral advisers who are permanently 'on tap but never on top'.

This model assumes a clear dividing-line between political decision-making, which is what ministers do, and administration, which is the job of civil servants in tendering advice and carrying out decisions. This is not only the traditional textbook view but also predominates within the civil service itself and among ministers. It is the model reaffirmed by the Cabinet Secretary, Sir Robert Armstrong in his *Note of Guidance on the Duties and Responsibilities of Civil Servants in Relation to Ministers* (1985) in the wake of the Ponting case (see below, p. 418). The Armstrong Memorandum asserted that the civil service has '*no constitutional personality or responsibility separate from the duly elected government of the day*' and stressed that the duty of the civil servant was first and foremost to the ministerial head of Department. A new version of the memorandum issued after the Westland affair in 1987 also stated the traditional view that ministers are responsible to Parliament for the conduct of their Depart-

ments whilst civil servants are answerable to ministers.

Many observers believe that the traditional model simply describes the norm to which participants in government aspire but ignores the political realities of a situation in which the 'Departmental view' often prevails. The *liberal-bureaucratic model* best expresses the fact of civil service power in a context in which lip-service is still paid to the textbook theory of ministerial–civil servant relations. This approach does not exclude the possibility that a minister can dominate a Department. But it does suggest that a variety of factors often tilt the balance of power in a Department away from the minister and towards the permanent officials. And it portrays the ministerial–civil servant relationship in adversarial terms as a constant power struggle in which civil servants often obstruct and sabotage ministerial policy instructions (Theakston, 1995a, p. 47).

The *'Whitehall Village' model* draws attention to aspects of the minister–civil servant relationship largely ignored by the other models. It posits that the relationship is much more complex than can be expressed by a theory suggesting simple domination by either elected politician or official. In practice, in the enclosed world of Whitehall, relationships between ministers and mandarins are cooperative as well as conflictual and in addition operate *across* Departments as well as within them. The central focus of this model is on the way in which civil servants sharing a common language and culture 'prepare the ground' for ministerial decisions through their own networks of informal contacts and official committees. This theory was first developed by two American academics, Hugh Heclo and Aaron Wildavsky in their book, *The Private Government of Public Money* (1974). Applied by them to public expenditure decision-making, the relevance of the model to virtually all areas of Whitehall was soon realised.

According to the *power-bloc model*, the civil service functions as an Establishment veto group. On this view, the civil service comprises an administrative cadre whose conservative bias reflects the interests of the privileged sections of society from which it is largely recruited. It deploys its administrative expertise and exploits its permanency of tenure to thwart radical policy moves by socialist governments. Important advocates of this far-left view of the civil service are Ralph Miliband in *The State in Capitalist Society* (1973), Brian Sedgemore in *The Secret Constitution* (1980) and Tony Benn (1982). This view is an extreme version of the liberal-bureaucratic model.

The *bureaucratic over-supply model* came to the fore in the 1970s and is mainly but not exclusively linked with the New Right critique of civil service expansionism in previous decades. The views of this school of thought do not bear directly on the minister–civil servant relationship but focus rather on the disastrous *consequences* of a situation in which a self-interested civil service holds the upper hand. The result of its single-minded pursuit of its own interests with regard to pay, pensions, conditions of service and its own size and status was a bloated, inefficient and wasteful bureaucracy. This analysis was also linked to the right-wing view in the 1970s and 1980s that the civil service was wedded to the social democratic consensus and believed in interventionist government and big public spending. This analysis produced its own programme: both the bureaucracy and 'big government', according to the Thatcherite right, needed 'cutting down to size'.

The resurgence of the traditional model

In 1979 the liberal-bureaucratic, power-bloc and bureaucratic over-supply theories held the field, the traditional liberal-democratic model of the civil service was in eclipse. By the late 1990s, as a result of the changes in Whitehall produced by the Conservative governments between 1979 and 1997, this situation had been largely reversed: little was heard of the far left critique, and the reassertion of political control over the civil service by Conservative governments inspired by New Right Theory had brought about a resurgence of the traditional, liberal-democratic theory. Indeed some commentators went further, arguing that its traditional detachment and impartiality had been eroded and that the civil service had been politicised. This section briefly traces the history of these evolving interpretations.

By the late 1970s, in large part in order to explain Labour's failures in office, theories stressing the obstructiveness and the potential for obstruction of the British bureaucracy had become commonplace.

The liberal-bureaucratic model, and its more extreme variant the power-bloc theory, were often invoked in academic discussion. The main factors tilting the balance away from ministers towards civil servants were considered to be as follows:

- *Numbers*: Ministers are heavily outnumbered in their contacts with leading mandarins: there are roughly six leading civil servants to every minister.
- *Permanence*: Civil servants are permanent and, moreover, often spend their entire careers in the same Department; by contrast, ministers are 'birds of passage' who change jobs frequently. The average tenure of ministerial office since 1945 is just over two years: there were twelve Trade and Industry Secretaries between 1979 and 1997. It takes ministers a lengthy period to master the business of their Departments (according to Crossman about 18 months) and during this time they are largely dependent on briefing by their officials.
- *Expertise*: Few ministers, on taking office, have specialised knowledge of their Departments, a situation which increases civil service influence. Some ministers have 'shadowed' their Departments in Opposition, but this became of even less significance during the Conservative hegemony: Kenneth Clarke held no less than five Cabinet posts between 1987 and 1997, being successively Chancellor of the Duchy of Lancaster, Health Secretary, Education Secretary, Home Secretary and Chancellor of the Exchequer.
- *Coordinating role*: Both formally through official committees and through informal contacts with their opposite numbers in other Departments, top civil servants prepare and to a varying extent predetermine the work of ministers. As Crossman wrote in his *Diaries,* 'very often the whole job is pre-cooked in the official committees to a point from which it is difficult to reach any other conclusion than that already determined by officials in advance' (p. 92). Civil servants can also use their contacts with other officials to delay and obstruct ministerial wishes if that is what they decide to do: they can do so by contacting colleagues in other Departments (say B, C and D) to brief ministers in those Departments to resist policies emanating from their own minister (Department A) in Cabinet and elsewhere.

- *Control of information*: Top civil servants control the *content* of the information going before ministers, the *way* in which it is presented and its *timing*, all of which gives them a formidable capacity to shape decisions. Thus officials decide what ministers learn and also what they do not learn, can manipulate the presentation of policy options in order to suggest one policy rather than another, and can 'bounce' ministers into a particular decision by submitting papers at the last minute. They can also influence public opinion by the secret briefing of known opponents of their minister's policy or by 'leaking' to the media.

- *Implementation*: Civil servants can employ a variety of tactics to thwart implementation of policy including delay, finding practical difficulties and even 'losing things'.

- *Ministerial workload*: Another factor weighting the scales of influence towards civil servants is ministers' massive workloads. Ministers face multiple demands upon their time – from Cabinet, Parliament, constituency, media and increasingly from the EU in addition to their Departments; on average, they spend about two-thirds of their working week on other than departmental matters.

- *Weak preparation for office*: Ministers rarely come to office with clearly defined policies, priorities or objectives. Moreover, they invariably confront unexpected situations during their terms of office which further increases their dependence upon officials: these include policies which become more significant than originally envisaged (e.g. privatisation), pressure group-promoted initiatives (e.g. anti-smoking and lead-free petrol legislation) and the emergence of new problems (e.g. AIDS, child abuse and cable and satellite television) (James, 1992, p. 39).

- *Lack of alternative policy advice*: The practice of importing special political advisers into Departments to provide an alternative source of policy advice for ministers and to strengthen their hand against permanent officials effectively began in the mid-1960s; Labour brought in 38 such advisers between 1974 and 1979, the Conservatives had 42 special advisers in 1993 and Labour immediately moved 58 special advisers into place in 1997, 37 of them into the Departments. It has been suggested that political advisers 'have added an extra dimension to the support that officials provide ministers, keeping in touch with the party and generating alternative ideas on policy within a framework of political values shared with the minister' (Theakston, 1995b, p. 15).

An extreme variant of the liberal bureaucratic theory, the *power-bloc model* became popular on the far left in the 1970s and was heard on occasion on the political right in the early 1980s. But it has virtually disappeared since then. It remains broadly true that the higher civil service is largely recruited from socially privileged groups. But it clearly does not follow (1) that it will refuse to carry out the radical policies of left and right governments; (2) that it invariably curbs the reformist impulses of radical politicians; or (3) that it constitutes a monolithic bloc in terms of views and perceptions.

With regard to (1): arguably, the two most radical governments since 1945 have been the Labour Administrations of 1945–51 and the Conservative Administrations of 1979–97, yet the civil service can scarcely be said to have blocked either the Keynesian, welfare and nationalisation policies of the one or the monetarist, anti-welfare and privatisation policies of the other. (2) Tony Benn as Secretary of State for Industry in the Labour Government of February 1974 is often cited as an example of a radical minister whose schemes for sweeping nationalisation of shipbuilding, aircraft and pharmaceuticals and for planning agreements with industry were thwarted largely by civil service resistance. In fact, however, it is much more likely that Benn failed (he was eventually transferred to Energy in June 1975) because of the opposition he encountered from the prime minister and other Labour ministers, i.e. from his own colleagues in government. Finally, if argument (3) were the case, the sharp inter-Departmental struggles which are a frequent occurrence in Whitehall could hardly be expected to take place. In the words of a recent study, 'Whitehall is a seething mass of discrete departmental interests', in which Departments – each with its own distinctive 'view' and 'ethos' – continually bargain and compete with each other for, amongst other things, larger shares of public expenditure and a place in the parliamentary legislative timetable (Drewry and Butcher, 1991, pp. 84–5).

Thus, the lines of conflict are not usually between ministers and civil servants within a department but between departments, with each department's ministers and civil servants combining to advance and defend departmental interests against ministers and officials in other departments combining to do the same.

The *liberal-bureaucratic theory* retains some validity as an approach to the relationship between ministers and civil servants. It remains relevant in situations in which weak ministers are 'captured' by their officials and also to describe occasions when the scales of departmental power tilt towards the officials. The value of the model consists in bringing out that minister–civil service relations are a matter of balance rather than automatically accepted authority (as the traditional theory holds) and also in pointing out the factors which *may* operate in various combinations to give the advantage to the bureaucrat. In the apt conclusion of one study: 'The exact balance between ministerial and civil service power will very much depend on what is being decided, the political circumstances surrounding it, and the relative abilities of civil servants and Ministers' (Kellner and Crowther-Hunt, 1980, p. 234).

However, the reassertion of political control over the civil service by the Thatcher governments in the 1980s meant that the theory was applicable in far fewer instances by the early 1990s. The combined effect of the Thatcherite assault on the size and privileges of the civil service, of intervention in its workings on a broad scale by a strong-willed Prime Minister and of the pervasive influence of the radical New Right ideology (see below) was the re-establishment of the traditional public administration model. In the words of Hugo Young: 'The constitutional textbooks are truer now than they have been for some time' (cited Theakston, 1991–2, p. 94).

The resurgence of the traditional public administration model does not mean, of course, that policy-making is totally the preserve of ministers whilst civil servants are limited to a purely administrative role. During the Scott Inquiry, ministers (including two prime ministers) admitted that they could not possibly see every paper passing through their offices and hence had to rely on officials to filter the paperwork (Madgwick and Woodhouse, 1995, p. 147). In fact, ministers actually see only a tiny fraction (under 1 per cent, according to one estimate) of their Departments' work. Thus, their influence is primarily in terms of making the very small number of top departmental decisions together with 'setting the climate' of policy-making so that officials can predict their intentions and make policy accordingly.

The *Whitehall village model* usefully draws attention to the inner life of the political administrative community at the centre of British government. Its emphases – on cooperation between ministers and mandarins within Departments and on the role of inter-departmental collaboration between civil servants in the preparation of decisions – capture much of the reality of top-level policy-making. There is a sense in which a single 'government community' exists characterised by agreement on the rules of the game and the desirability of excluding outsiders. But this model has been justly criticised as inherently too limited in focus to capture that reality in its entirety. For example, in focusing on life in the Whitehall village, it largely ignores that 'community's' external relationships, both in terms of policy inputs from pressure groups, ideological 'think-tanks', party manifestos and so on, and in terms of the way in which ministers' need to defend policies before Parliament and public actually helps to shape the policies themselves (Pliatzky, 1982, pp. 35, 37; Theakston, 1995a, p. 52). The shaping effect of party and ideological influences on ministerial–civil servants relations may be gauged from the fact that no department concerned with domestic policy had a 'departmental view' at odds with Thatcherism by the early 1990s (G.K. Wilson, 1991, cited Theakston, 1995a, p. 19).

Finally, the *bureaucratic over-supply model* was the inspiration for a sustained, successful attack on the power, prestige and privileges of the civil service by Conservative Governments after 1979. It provided the political and ideological thrust for the Conservative reforms of the civil service in the 1980s and 1990s. Margaret Thatcher came to power in 1979 convinced that the civil service was too big, too expensive, too negative and too consensual. She believed it had become an overblown bureaucracy, wasteful and inefficient, more adapted to finding problems in new initiatives that to solving them, and compromised by the failures of postwar British governments. The reform process she launched in the 1980s – which continues today – aimed at curtailing the privileges, increasing the efficiency and transforming the culture of the civil service. Although this bureaucratic expansionism model was politically influential, few academics now consider it of value in explaining the behaviour of civil servants. The motivation of officials cannot be reduced to departmental empire-building and the key Whitehall departments have always been – and remain – small departments such as the Treasury.

The Conservative reforms: a revolution in government

The Conservative reforms between 1979 and 1997 constitute the most radical change in the civil service since the Northcote–Trevelyan reforms of 1854. Reforms proceeded piecemeal in line with the manifesto commitment to reduce 'waste, bureaucracy and over-government' but gathered speed after 1988.

Size

The Conservatives achieved a very large reduction in civil service numbers (735,000 to 494,300) between April 1979 and April 1996, a drop of over 32 per cent. The lower manpower targets were attained by a combination of natural wastage, early retirement, the non-filling of vacant posts, the transfer of civil service functions to appointed public sector boards, and privatisation. Much larger cuts were achieved in the industrial civil service, which fell by 132,000 from 168,000 to 36,000 (80 per cent) in this period, than in the non-industrial civil service, where numbers dropped by 110,000 from 568,000 to 458,000 (19 per cent).

Curtailment of privileges

The Thatcher government 'de-privileged' the civil service by setting aside the settlement of pay based on the system of 'fair comparison' and then offering relatively low increases related to 'market forces' and introducing performance-related pay; holding out successfully against the 21-week strike by civil service unions in support of their pay claim (1981); banning trade union membership at the Government Communications Headquarters

(GCHQ), which had been shut down for a short period in 1981 as a result of the strike action; and abolishing the Civil Service Department (1981), which Thatcher regarded as too much the champion of the civil service and as insufficiently supportive of the government's efforts to defeat the civil service strike. Its responsibility for civil service pay, conditions of service and manpower was transferred to the Treasury, and the Cabinet Secretary became the official head of the Civil Service.

Improving efficiency

In a series of managerial reforms, the Rayner Scrutinies (1979) were followed by the Financial Management Initiative (1982), the 'Next Steps' programme (1988), and market testing, privatisation and the Citizens' Charters in the 1990s.

The Rayner Scrutinies

The quest for greater efficiency and the elimination of 'waste' in government began in 1979 with the establishment in the Cabinet Office of a small Efficiency Unit headed by Sir Derek (later Lord) Rayner, who was then the joint Managing Director of Marks and Spencer. Rayner initiated a series of Scrutinies of Departments with the aim of reducing costs and streamlining procedure. The Scrutinies led to huge savings, amounting to £1.5 billion by 1993. Raynor also launched an attack on unnecessary paperwork which led to the scrapping of 27,000 forms and the redesigning of 41,000 more.

The Financial Management Initiative (FMI)

Begun in 1982, the FMI sought to improve financial management in all Departments by laying down three principles. Managers at all levels were to have: (1) a clear view of their objectives and the means to assess and, wherever possible, measure outputs of performance in relation to those objectives; (2) well-defined responsibility for making the best use of their resources, including a critical scrutiny of output and value for money; and (3) the information (particularly about costs), the training and the access to expert advice that they need to exercise their responsibilities effectively.

A variety of management information systems designed to enable ministers to discover 'who does what, why and at what cost?' in their Departments developed under the Rayner and FMI approaches, e.g. MINIS (Management Information System for Ministers) at the Department of Environment (DOE) and Activity and Resource Management (ARM) at the Department of Trade and Industry (DTI). MINIS-style systems soon spread throughout Whitehall. The overall aim was to transform civil service culture along business lines, to enhance the role of civil servants as managers of people and resources and to downgrade their role as policy advisers. The reforms reflected the Thatcherite ethos that the task of the civil service was to manage resources with maximum effectiveness in pursuit of policy goals set by ministers.

The 'Next Steps' programme (1988)

This programme originated in a certain disappointment at the slow progress of the FMI and other 'managerial' reforms, as a result of which the Efficiency Unit – now headed by Sir Robin Ibbs, a former Imperial Chemical Industries (ICI) executive – produced a report focusing on the obstacles to further improvement in civil service management. Entitled 'Improving Management in Government: The Next Steps', it argued that there had been insufficient focus on the delivery of services, even though the vast majority of civil servants (95 per cent) were in service delivery or executive rather than policy advice roles. Believing that the civil service was too large and diverse to be run as a single entity, the report advocated its division into (1) a small 'core' engaged in supporting ministers with policy advice within the traditional Departments; and (2) a wide range of executive agencies responsible for the delivery of services, each headed by a chief executive. Departments would set the policy and budgetary objectives and monitor the work of the agencies, but within that framework, agencies would have considerable managerial independence, with chief executives controlling the recruitment, grading, organisation and pay of their staffs. Another advantage claimed for the move was the reduction in ministerial overload.

By April 1996, huge progress had been made on the Next Steps programme: altogether, with 102 agencies already established in the Home Civil Service, nearly 71 per cent of the civil service (350,000) was working in Next Steps Agencies or along Next Steps lines and there were plans to add a further 6 per cent to this number. Some Next Steps Agencies – such as the massive Benefits Agency (71,000) – considerably reduce the size of their 'parent' Departments (the Department of Social Security (DSS)). Most of them, however, are small or medium-sized: for example, the Vehicle Inspectorate (1,471), the Royal Mint (997), the Public Record Office (455) and the Teachers' Pensions Agency (370).

Market-testing (1991)

During the 1980s, compulsory competitive tendering (CCT) had been introduced in local government and the NHS. Following a white paper *Competing for Quality* (1991), CCT or market-resting was extended to the civil service. The first part of a rolling programme of market testing (November 1992) put out nearly £1.5 billion of civil service work to competitive tender, requiring over 44,000 civil servants to compete with outsiders for their jobs. By January 1995, when ministers were claiming that market testing had brought savings of £400 million a year over the previous two years, over £1 billion of work had been transferred to the private sector. Half of the work had been put out to the private sector without any competing in-house bid but in-house teams had won 73 per cent of the contracts they were allowed to tender for. A further £1.1 billion worth of work was to be tendered and competed for over the following year (Theakston, 1995b, pp. 150–1). Privatisation of some agencies had been envisaged by the Ibbs Report from the outset. Part of the 'prior options' tests applied within departments included the contracting out or privatisation of a part of their activities. Thus, the initial presumption that most civil service activities would remain within the public sector seems to have been reversed from autumn 1992, although only eight small central government organisations were transferred to the private sector between 1992 and 1995.

The Citizen's Charter (1991)

The Citizen's Charter was the 'big idea' of John Major and essentially consisted of a campaign to raise standards in the public services. It applied to public services generally and included, for example, health and education as well as services delivered by the civil service. Each service was required to publish performance targets and results against set targets and there would be well-publicised and readily available complaints and redress procedures. The aim was to improve standards of service without injecting extra resources. By 1995, nine Agencies had published individual charters specifying standards that customers and clients were entitled to expect e.g. the Jobseekers' Charter published by the Employment Service Agency.

Overall Impact of the civil service reforms

Supporters of the 'new public management' reforms argue that the reforms have improved delivery of service, increased cost-effectiveness and produced significant savings so far (1998) and will continue to deliver improvements in the future. The Driver and Vehicle Licensing Agency – an agency since 1990 – may be cited as an example: it sets itself clear targets, e.g. to reduce average waiting time for a driving test from 8–9 weeks (1991) to 6 weeks and to issue 90 per cent of driving licenses within 13 days (1992) instead of 16 days (1991); has shown considerable enthusiasm for marketing, e.g. customised number-plates; and cut costs by putting provision of security and cleaning services out to private tender. However, *critics* point to the potential dangers of the programme, especially to the erosion of civil service morale by constant changes involving a deterioration in pay and conditions of service and to the further weakening in ministerial accountability resulting from the division between the policy core and executive agencies (see below, pp. 293, 294–5).

The Nolan and Scott Reports

The Nolan Report (1995)

The Nolan Committee on Standards in Public Life was set up in October 1994 by Prime Minister John Major in response to widespread public concern about declining ethical standards among politicians and other public figures. Nolan's terms of reference were to examine current concerns about standards of conduct in public office-holders and to make recommendations as to any changes required to ensure the highest standards of propriety in public life. His brief covered parliament (see Chapter 16); ministerial appointments to quangos (see Chapter 17); and central government. Nolan responded (Report,

1995) by laying down the 'seven principles of public life' (Box15.2). His recommendations with regard to central government are summariseable under three main headings.

Standards of conduct of officeholders

- The ethical principles contained in *Questions of Procedure for Ministers* should be drawn together into a separate section of *QPM* or a separate document.
- It should spell out clearly that Ministers of the Crown are expected to behave according to the highest standards of constitutional and personal conduct.
- Specific prescriptions included: ministers must ensure that no conflict arises between their public duties and their private interests; they must not mislead parliament; and they must keep their party and ministerial roles separate, and not ask civil servants to carry out party political duties or to act in any way that would conflict with the civil service code.
- It would be for individual ministers to judge how best to act in order to uphold the highest standards and for the prime minister to determine whether or not they had done so in any particular circumstance.

A Civil Service Code

Nolan recommended a tough Civil Service Code, of which the main features would be:

- to facilitate 'whistleblowing' by enabling civil servants to make known examples of 'wrongdoing and maladministration' even if not personally involved in it and to require them to ensure 'the proper, effective and efficient use of public money' even if that expenditure is not within their direct control;
- to appoint a senior official outside the line management to investigate civil service concerns and complaints; and
- to ensure that all complaints upheld by the Civil Service Commissioners are reported to Parliament.

Transition of ministers to outside appointments

- cabinet ministers automatically to wait a

BOX 15.2

The Nolan Report, 1995: the seven principles of public life

- **Selflessness.** Holders of public office should take decisions solely in the public interest. They should not do so in order to gain financial or other material benefits for themselves, their family or their friends.
- **Integrity.** Holders of public office should not place themselves under under any financial or other obligation to outside individuals or organisations that might influence them in the performance of their official duties.
- **Objectivity.** In carrying out public business, including making public appointments, awarding contracts, or recommending individuals for rewards and benefits, holders of public office should make choices on merit.
- **Accountability.** Holders of public office are accountable for their decisions and actions to the public and must

submit themselves to whatever scrutiny is appropriate to their office.
- **Openness.** Holders of public office should be as open as possible about all the decisions and actions that they take. They should give reasons for their decisions and restrict information only when the wider public interest clearly demands.
- **Honesty.** Holders of public office have a duty to declare any private interests relating to their public duties and to take steps to resolve any conflicts arising in a way that protects the public interest.
- **Leadership.** Holders of public office should promote and support these principles by leadership and example.

---

minimum of three months before taking up a private sector job in areas in which they have a direct ministerial interest and a maximum two years if a longer waiting period is recommended; and

- the rules applicable to civil service business appointments should also apply to ministers.

In its white paper *The Government's Response to the First Report from the Committee on Standards in Public Life* (1995), the Conservative Government largely accepted Nolan's recommendations with regard to the executive. First, a Civil Service Code was already in the offing (see below) but Nolan prompted the government to strengthen procedure on issues of conscience and political neutrality. On the former, civil servants were enjoined to report illegal or criminal behaviour to the appropriate authorities and to report other breaches of the Code or instructions raising fundamental issues of conscience according to departmental procedures. On the latter, a new section of the Code laid a duty on ministers 'not to act for party political purposes, to uphold the political impartiality of the Civil Service, and not to ask civil servants to act in any other way which would conflict with the Civil Service Code'. Second, the government conceded that ministers would be covered by similar requirements as top civil servants when moving to private sector posts. Finally, and more controversially, whilst not accepting Nolan's suggestion of a separate ethical code, the

government reworded paragraph 27 of *Questions of Procedure for Ministers* (re-named *Conduct and Procedure for Ministers*) to read 'Ministers must not *knowingly* mislead Parliament *and the public and should correct any inadvertent errors at the earliest possible opportunity.* They must be as open as possible with Parliament and the public, *withholding information only when disclosure would not be in the public interest'* (italics where the white paper redrafted Nolan). Critics jibbed in particular at the use of the vague phrase 'public interest', which clearly gave rise to the possibility of a broad definition in its own favour by government (Hennessy, 1995, pp. 195–6).

The Code of Conduct for Civil Servants (1995)

Revelations during the Ponting, Westland and arms to Iraq affairs on civil service ethics and standards of behaviour, the managerial reforms and allegations about the politicisation of the service during the long period of Conservative rule led to demands for a new code of conduct for civil servants. In 1994, the Civil Service First Division Association (FDA) published a draft code of ethics whilst the Treasury and Civil Service Committee also called for a statutory code of ethics. Against the background of the transfer of three-quarters of the civil service into agencies, devolution and delegation of authority, the breakup of centralised pay bargaining and the further erosion of a unitary civil service by the injection of commercial values, market-testing, contracting out and privatisation, the Committee saw the traditional values as a unifying force (*The Independent*, 25 November 1994). The First Report of the Nolan Committee on Standards in Public Life (1995) recommended an even tougher Code (see above). The new Code (January 1995), which was outlined in the white paper *The Civil Service: Taking Forward Continuity and Change* (1995), stated that officials should act with 'integrity, honesty, impartiality, and objectivity' in their public duties. Whereas formerly civil servants faced with issues of conscience could appeal only to the Permanent Secretary of their Department or, if this failed, to the Cabinet Secretary, the new Code permitted complaints to the Civil Service Commissioners. However, the First Division Association, the top civil servants' trade union which represents 11,000 leading officials, argued that the new Code failed to address two key issues. First, the code reaffirmed the convention that civil servants give evidence to Commons committees on behalf of ministers and subject to ministerial instructions: officials say that this can put them in the position of having to mislead parliament or of going beyond the constraints imposed by civil servants' political neutrality. Second, the Association expressed concern that ministers could make changes to the civil service under prerogative powers without reference to parliament. In the face of the failure of the Code to resolve the important issue of civil servants' duties to parliament and the public, civil service dissatisfaction continued and there were calls for a Civil Service Act which would provide proper democratic and legal protection for civil servants and the public. Nolan had called for a statutory code for the civil service but this was rejected by the Government.

The Scott Report (1996)

Controversy blew up in November 1992 over sales of British arms to Iraq in the late 1980s. The Opposition parties alleged that the government secretly relaxed its own guidelines on the sale of arms to Iraq in 1988, that numerous government ministers over the following years told Parliament that this was not the case, and that leading officials in the Foreign Office and DTI assisted ministers in the misleading of Parliament. The incident had come to light accidentally during the prosecution by Customs and Excise of three businessmen of the

Matrix Churchill Company for illegally exporting arms for Iraq. Denying charges of deception, the Prime Minister, John Major set up an inquiry into the affair under Lord Justice Scott, whose 1,806 page, five-volume report was published in February 1996. The Report provided the most comprehensive examination of the inner workings of British government ever undertaken; in the words of one academic commentator, it was 'the longest, most thorough, most revealing and most damaging public inquiry into the heart of central government ever seen' (Tomkins, 1996, p. 349). Its main findings were as follows:

(1) In 1988, the Conservative Government broke its 1984 guidelines on not approving new orders for defence equipment which would significantly enhance the capability of Iran or Iraq. The claim by the three ministers involved (William Waldegrave, Alan Clark and Lord Trefgarne) that they were not changing policy but merely reinterpreting the guidelines was described by Scott as 'not remotely tenable'.

(2) The policy shift was deliberately concealed from parliament. Ministers thereby failed to comply with their constitutional duty 'to give parliament … and the public as full information as possible about the policies, decisions and actions of the government, and not to deceive or mislead parliament and the public' (paragraph 27, *Questions of Procedure for Ministers*). Answers to parliamentary questions (PQs) on the export of arms to Iraq were described by Scott as 'inaccurate and misleading' and designedly 'uninformative'. 'In circumstances where disclosure might be politically or administratively inconvenient,' the Report says,' the balance struck by the government comes down time and time again against full disclosure.'

(3) The criminal prosecution by HM Customs and Excise of three directors of Matrix Churchill, a weapons manufacturing company, was wrong. First, before bringing the case, HM Customs and Excise should have investigated the possible defence of the directors to the prosecution charge that they had misled the DTI about the nature of the machine tools they were exporting to Iraq. This was that MI5 and MI6, and the government, knew about these exports (one of the company's directors had been an MI6 informer since 1976) and that the DTI had encouraged the company to expand such exports. Second, whilst the government did not intend to

send innocent men to gaol, its use of PII certificates to block the release of government information which would have helped them was wrong both in law (PIIs are normally used in civil cases and there was no precedent for their use in a criminal case) and principle (the release of the information concerned would not have damaged the public interest, as the government maintained).

The Report had serious constitutional implications. It revealed that Ministers had seriously misled parliament over government policy (at the least; many would put it more strongly) and that they had been assisted by civil servants in doing so. However, the government managed to limit the political damage that might have been expected to follow such a critical Report. It did this, first, by manipulation of the Report's reception, gaining access to the Report itself (for six ministers and eighteen civil servants) eight days before it was published but allowing the Opposition spokesman, Robin Cook, a mere three and a half hours and MPs ten minutes to study it before the initial House of Commons debate. This ensured that the initial response to the Report was somewhat muffled. Second, during the following eleven days preceding the full Commons debate, the government marshalled its forces behind the collective defence of the two most vulnerable ministers, William Waldegrave (then Chief Secretary to the Treasury, formerly a Foreign Office minister during the 'Arms to Iraq' affair), and Sir Nicholas Lyell (the Attorney General), ignoring Scott's criticisms of them and fastening on the fact that Scott had cleared Waldegrave (and other ministers) of 'any duplicitous intention' in his claim that there had been no change in policy over arms sales to Iraq. During this period and in the full Commons debate on 26 February 1996, the government was assisted, and critics handicapped, by the sometimes ambiguous language of the Scott Report itself, the absence of a concluding summary of its findings and the unwillingness of Scott himself to provide journalists with a succinct account of his conclusions (beyond advice to 'Read the Report'). Accordingly, the Conservative Government won the Commons vote on the Report by one vote (320–319). No minister resigned and only one civil servant resigned – for reasons of conscience because he could not put up with the deceit and hypocrisy, not because he was pushed into it by his superiors.

Ministerial responsibility

The convention of **individual ministerial responsibility** governs relations between ministers, civil servants and Parliament. It means that ministers – and ministers alone – are responsible to Parliament for the actions of their Departments (Box 15.3). Individual ministerial responsibility is the major form of constitutional accountability, forms the basis of the relationships between ministers, civil service and Parliament and involves ministers in several levels of responsibility. Thus, they are required to inform Parliament about the conduct of their departments, explain their own and their departments' actions, make amends for their own or their departments' errors and ultimately in certain circumstances resign. Resignation may be for personal misconduct, political misjudgment, departmental fault in which the minister is involved, and policy differences with the government. This section examines the contemporary validity of this convention.

Individual ministers certainly remain responsible to Parliament in the first sense (see Box 15.3). They constantly explain and defend departmental policy – at Question Time, during the committee stage of legislation, before select committees and privately to MPs. Ministerial answers to political questions are not always entirely full or satisfactory and sometimes they are downright evasive. None the less, individual ministerial responsibility in its first meaning of 'answerability' or 'explanatory accountability' still applies. But how accountable are ministers, in the second sense of the term, for personal misconduct, political misjudgements and mistakes, and fault within their departments?

Personal misconduct

Ministers still frequently resign for personal misconduct, which was the largest single category of resignations between 1962 and 1997 (Table 15.2). All except three resignations for personal misconduct

> **Individual ministerial responsibility**: the constitutional convention by which each minister is responsible to Parliament for the conduct of his or her department.

The convention of individual ministerial responsibility

The convention denotes:
- Answerability: Ministers have an obligation to explain and defend the work of their Departments in Parliament.
- Accountability: Ministers are responsible for their own and their officials' conduct and for departmental policy and should resign if serious faults are revealed in any of these matters.

The convention implies and assumes that civil servants are anonymous, responsible to their ministers alone and without any wider accountability to Parliament or general public, and that their advice to ministers is secret.

(Nicholls, Stewart, Willetts) in this period fall into the categories of sexual impropriety, mixing with unsavoury or shady associates or financial irregularity. John Major's 1992–7 government suffered a spate of resignations arising out of sexual misconduct and financial impropriety plus several resignations by Parliamentary Private Secretaries to ministers. The background to these resignations was intense media publicity over sexual and financial 'sleaze' in the context of the government's 'Back to Basics' campaign and the increasing public concern over the ethical standards of politicians which led to the appointment of the Nolan Committee. In contrast with the resignations of Parkinson and Mellor, which were protracted affairs in part because both ministers enjoyed prime ministerial support, resignations in the later phase of Major's premiership occurred immediately sexual misconduct had been revealed. Major had instituted a policy of demanding instant resignations from any front-benchers caught compromising their morals.

Political misjudgements and mistakes

Several ministerial resignations in the 1980s (Fairburn, Carrington, Luce, Atkins, Brittan and Currie) fall into this category. Nicholas Fairburn resigned after committing the error of informing the Scottish press about his reasons not to prosecute the suspects in a rape case before answering questions about it in the House of Commons, where his explanations proved unconvincing. He had also suffered

from bad publicity about his private life.

The *Falklands crisis* brought the resignations of the Foreign Office team, Lord Carrington, Richard Luce and Humphrey Atkins. The reason Lord Carrington gave for his resignation was his failure to foresee and to take steps to prevent the Argentinian invasion, which he later called 'a humiliating affront to this country'. However, John Nott, the Defence Secretary, who was criticised for the weakness of the Falkland Islands' defences and, more realistically, for signalling an apparently diminished British commitment to the retention of the Islands by a proposal to withdraw *HMS Endurance,* remained in office.

On this occasion, because of the seriousness of the situation and the intensity of parliamentary and public disquiet, collective responsibility could not save the Foreign Office ministers. In order to minimise damage to the credibility of a government in which blame for misreading the situation and for military unpreparedness spread as far as the Prime Minister, a considerable sacrifice was called for but not so great a one that it rocked the government. So Carrington and his subordinates went, but Nott stayed.

In the *Westland affair* (1986), Leon Brittan, the Trade and Industry Secretary, resigned after severe pressure from Conservative backbenchers over the role of his Department in leaking to the press a select passage in a letter from the Solicitor-General to the Defence Secretary, Michael Heseltine. The letter requested the correction of the 'material inaccuracies' contained in a letter Heseltine had written to the European consortium who were the rivals of the American Sikorsky Company for the take-over of the ailing Westland Helicopters. The leaking of the letter – 'an improper act' in the words of the Commons Select Committee on Defence which investigated the affair – was one episode in the semi-public struggle between the Ministry of Defence and the Department of Trade and Industry over the destiny of the British helicopter firm. The leak was wrong, first because the letter was marked 'Confidential' and second, because, according to convention, advice from the government's Law Officers is never revealed. Brittan apparently authorised the leak but only 'subject to the agreement of No. 10' (Young, 1990, p. 442).

At the time, Bernard Ingham, the PM's Press Officer, and Charles Powell, her Private Secretary,

Table 15.2 Individual ministerial responsibility: resignations, 1962–97

Minister	Post	Date	Reason
Thomas Galbraith	Under-Secretary Scottish Office	1962	Security: consorting with the spy Vassall
John Profumo	Minister of War	1963	Sexual misconduct followed by lying to the House of Commons about it.
James Callaghan	Chancellor of the Exchequer	1967	Devaluation of sterling (Re-shuffled to Home Office).
Reginald Maudling	Home Secretary	1972	Involvement with corrupt architect, Poulson
Lord Lambton	Under-Secretary of State, Defence	1973	Call-girl scandal
Earl Jellicoe	Lord Privy Seal	1973	Call-girl scandal
Lord Brayley	Under-Secretary of State, Defence	1974	Irregularities in business life.
Nicholas Fairburn	Solicitor-General, Scotland	1982	Mixture of personal misconduct and political failings arising out of Glasgow rape case.
Lord Carrington	Foreign Secretary	1982	Misjudgements over Argentine intentions in Falklands.
Humphrey Atkins	Lord Privy Seal	1982	Misjudgements over Argentine intentions in Falklands.
Richard Luce	Minister of State, Foreign Affairs	1982	Misjudgements over Argentine intentions in Falklands.
Cecil Parkinson	Secretary of State, Trade and Industry	1983	Sexual misconduct: Sarah Keays affair.
Leon Brittan	Secretary of State, Trade and Industry	1986	Political misjudgement over leak of letter in Westland affair.
Edwina Currie	Under-Secretary of State, Health	1988	Misleading statement with regard to salmonella in eggs.
Patrick Nicholls	Under-Secretary of State, Environment	1990	Arrest for driving with excess alcohol.
David Mellor	Secretary of State, National Heritage	1992	Errors of judgement in personal conduct.
Norman Lamont	Chancellor of the Exchequer	1993	Economic and political consequences of Britain's forced withdrawal from ERM, September 1992; also personal financial affairs.
Michael Mates	Minister of State, Northern Ireland Office	1993	Links with disgraced businessman, Asil Nadir
Tim Yeo	Minister of State, Environment	1994	Adultery: fathered illegitimate child.
Tim Smith	Minister of State, Northern Ireland Office	1994	Financial misconduct
Neil Hamilton	Minister of Corporate Affairs, Board of Trade	1994	Financial misconduct
Lord Caithness	Minister, Department of Transport	1994	Adultery: wife committed suicide.
Charles Wardle	Minister of State, Board of Trade	1995	Immigration policy.
Allan Stewart	Minister, Scottish Office	1995	Violence in a demonstration.
Robert Hughes	Minister of State, Office of Public Service and Science	1995	Adultery
Jonathan Aitken	Chief Secretary to the Treasury	1995	To fight libel action.
Rod Richards	Under-Secretary of State, Welsh Office	1996	Extra marital affair
David Heathcote-Amery	Paymaster General	1996	European policy
David Willetts	Paymaster General	1996	Conduct before Standards Committee.

sought to distance themselves from the leak but Brittan later (1989) claimed that they both 'approved' it. It was the contention of Colette Bowe, the information officer at the DTI who actually leaked the letter, that she would not have done so without both the authorisation of her minister and the consent of top officials at No. 10. This resignation is similar to the Foreign Office resignations in 1982 in that there was departmental fault both in the Minister and officials, the political outcry from the Conservative backbenches demanded a ministerial sacrifice, and the protective cloak of collective responsibility could not be extended. Therefore, Brittan resigned: it was his misfortune to become embroiled in the political struggle between Thatcher and Heseltine but his political misjudgement to authorise the leak of the letter *in any circumstances*.

Edwina Currie, the Parliamentary Under-Secretary of State for Health, resigned after making the statement that 'most of the egg production of this country, sadly, is now infected with salmonella'. As well as causing considerable public alarm, this 'gaffe' led to several egg producers issuing writs against the government, the need to offer financial support to the egg production industry, and strong criticism of the minister by backbenchers of her own party.

Policy errors

Ministers do not normally resign if associated with a *failed policy*. In such circumstances, the prime minister and Cabinet usually come to the aid of a beleaguered colleague, expressing support in public, whatever may be said privately. In other words, individual ministers in political difficulties are shielded by the convention of *collective responsibility*. There are numerous examples of non-resignation after serious failures of policy, in several of which – Suez, the spy scandals of the early 1960s, *Concorde,* and Britain's departure from the ERM – the close involvement of the prime minister was probably conclusive in 'saving' the minister concerned (Box 15.4).

In 1967, James Callaghan, a Chancellor who, like Norman Lamont in 1992, presided over a devaluation of sterling, did resign. But the political circumstances were rather different in that unlike Lamont, Callaghan had long wanted to move from the

---

> **BOX 15.4**
> ## *Ministerial non-resignation: policy failure*
>
> - The East African groundnuts scheme (1949), a spectacular fiasco which cost the taxpayer £36.5 million and which failed to provide either margarine for Britain or jobs for Africans. The Minister for Food, John Strachey, was closely associated with the scheme, having described it as 'one of the most courageous, imaginative and well-judged acts of this government for the sake of the world'.
> - The Suez affair (1956), a discreditable failure which brought major international humiliation upon Britain.
> - Various spy scandals (early 1960s). The then Prime Minister, Harold Macmillan, rejected the need for resignations on the grounds that it was the reputation of the government as a whole that was in question and this was best left to the judgement of voters at a general election.
> - Large-scale miscalculations of the cost of the *Concorde* programme (early 1960s).
> - The evasion of sanctions against Rhodesia by the major oil companies with covert Government acquiescence (late 1960s).
> - The decision to withdraw *HMS Endurance* from the South Atlantic in June 1981 thereby seeming to indicate British lack of commitment to the Falklands.

Treasury, and Prime Minister Wilson, unlike John Major, had been anxious to have a new Chancellor. But Callaghan was careful not to resign from the Cabinet and his resignation was followed immediately by a discreet reshuffle in which he moved to the Home Office and Roy Jenkins took over as Chancellor. A similar manoeuvre occurred in 1948 when Emanuel Shinwell was moved from Fuel and Power to the War Office eight months after the Fuel Crisis of 1947. The resignation of Norman Lamont (1993) occurred eight months after the British ejection from the ERM, after collective responsibility appeared to have sheltered him from accepting individual blame for the disaster. In the later stages of John Major's premiership, Charles Wardle and David Heathcoat-Amory resigned from the government over policy issues, and John Redwood resigned from the Cabinet in order to contest the leadership. These cases suggest that, while parliamentary criticism over failed policies can certainly damage a minister and can sometimes prompt policy changes, it cannot force resignation if the minister wishes to

---

BOX 15.5
Ministerial non-resignation: official errors

- Alan Lennox-Boyd, the Colonial Secretary, after eleven prisoners died and others received injuries from beatings meted out by colonial wardens at the Hola Camp in Kenya (1959).
- Sir Julian Amery, the Minister for Aviation, after it had been revealed that the Ferranti Company had made excess profits from Defence Ministry contracts to make the Bloodhound missile (1964).
- John Davies, President of the Board of Trade, after a Tribunal of Inquiry had revealed the failure of his Department to deal with the risk of the imminent insolvency of the Vehicle and General Insurance Company (1971).
- Tony Benn, Secretary of State for Industry, after being blamed by the Ombudsman for giving misleading public assurances about the holiday operations of the Court Line travel company (1975).
- William Whitelaw, Home Secretary, after security arrangements at Buckingham Palace were revealed to be deficient and the Queen was confronted by an intruder in her bedroom (1982).
- James Prior and Nicholas Scott, respectively Secretary of State and Parliamentary Under-Secretary of State for Northern Ireland, after 38 Republican prisoners escaped from the Maze Prison in Belfast, killing a prison officer (1983).

- Kenneth Baker, Home Secretary, after two Republican prisoners escaped from Brixton Prison (1991).
- Peter Lilley, Secretary of State for Trade and Industry, after it was revealed that his Department had sanctioned sales of nuclear and chemical material to Iraq until three days after Iraq's invasion of Kuwait (1991).
- Michael Howard, Home Secretary, after the escape of two dangerous prisoners from Parkhurst gaol and the Learmont Report criticising the prison service.
- William Waldegrave, junior Foreign Office minister, and Sir Nicholas Lyell, Attorney General, after criticism by the Scott Inquiry for respectively misleading parliament over a change in the government guidelines over the export of arms to Iraq and mistakes in the prosecution of armaments company Matrix Churchill and over the use of Public Interest Immunity certificates (PIIs) (1996).
- Nicholas Soames, Defence Minister, following the failure of his department to investigate the alleged link between the use of organo-phosphate chemicals in the Gulf War and the subsequent illnesses suffered by many Gulf War veterans (1997).
- Douglas Hogg, Agriculture Minister, following revelations of food safety offences after the BSE and *E coli* outbreaks (1997).

---

remain in office and has the support of prime minister and party.

Official errors

It is even more unusual for ministers to accept vicarious responsibility for their officials and resign after mistakes within their Departments have been brought to light. The assumption by ministers of personal accountability for all that happens in their Departments has been undermined, it is often said, by the sheer size and complexity of modern Whitehall Departments and the consequent impossibility of one person being able to keep informed of all that goes on in them. Numerous cases in the postwar period suggest the reluctance of ministers to shoulder the blame for civil servants when things go wrong (Box 15.5).

Today, it seems, ministers are not normally held responsible for decisions made in their name but of which they could have had no knowledge. As

Reginald Maudling stated after the Vehicle and General debate: 'One must look at this classic doctrine in the light of modern circumstances. In my own department we get one and a half million letters a year, any one of which may lead to disaster. No Home Secretary could be expected to supervise all those one and a half million letters'. Sir John Hunt, then Cabinet Secretary, giving evidence to the Commons Expenditure Committee in 1977, commented that the idea of ministers resigning over the mistakes of someone they had never heard of was 'out of date and rightly so'. Normally, the support of the prime minister is sufficient to shield a minister under parliamentary attack for administrative errors from resignation. No postwar case, Geoffrey Marshall has observed, has involved the assumption that 'a ministerial head must roll for civil service error' (Marshall, 1989, p. 130).

The resignation of Sir Thomas Dugdale in the Crichel Down affair (1954) used to be regarded as an example of a minister resigning for the mistakes of his officials. Dugdale, it was said, accepted full responsibility for the negligence of his civil servants in dealings with a landowner who was anxious to buy back land which had been compulsorily acquired by the government for use as a bombing range in 1938. In fact, the issue was less clear-cut. Dugdale, it seems, was personally involved in the maladministration which led to his downfall. Moreover, hounding by his own backbenchers played a key part in the resignation (Hennessy, 1990, p. 503; Brazier, 1988, p. 139).

Conclusions

Table 15.2 shows that 29 ministers resigned under the convention of individual ministerial responsibility between 1962 and 1997. At face value, these figures suggest that the convention is far from being a myth and neither is it in decline, since resignations averaged over one per year in the eighteen years after 1979. However, no fewer than nineteen resignations were for personal misconduct of one sort or another, four were for political misjudgements, one (Currie) was for a misleading political statement, two (Wardle and Heathcoat-Amory) were for policy disagreements, one (Fairburn) was for a mixture of political failings and personal misconduct, and only two (Callaghan and Lamont) were for a failure of policy (and even here, in the case of Callaghan, it did not involve leaving the government). There were no ministerial resignations for mistakes by officials although arguably mistakes by officials were involved as well as misjudgements by ministers in the three Falklands and the Brittan resignations (Woodhouse, 1994, pp. 101–2, 118–20).

No definitive conclusions can yet be reached about the constitutional consequences of the Next Steps agencies. Supporters of the agencies argue that accountability has been increased by making those responsible for service delivery directly accountable to parliament. After an initial struggle, the Major government agreed to publish replies of agency chief executives to parliamentary questions in *Hansard*. However, critics argue that, although accountability in the sense of *answerability* may have been enhanced, accountability in the fullest sense may have decreased. Thus, although Ibbs wanted chief executives to be personally accountable to parliament, the Conservative Government of John Major

---

BOX 15.6

The politics of individual and collective responsibility

In cases involving governmental failure and criticism:

- A matter of **collective responsibility** may be treated as a matter of **individual responsibility** in order to minimise loss of public confidence in the government; however
- A matter of **individual responsibility** is sometimes transformed into a case of **collective responsibility** in order to shield a particular minister.

---

insisted that ministers retain formal constitutional responsibility and hence chief executives answer on behalf of their ministers. But the difficulty of dividing responsibility neatly between 'policy' for which ministers are responsible and 'operations' (for which chief executives are responsible) was illustrated in the sacking of Derek Lewis, the Director-General of the Prisons Agency, in 1995, following the Parkhurst prison escapes. Lewis took the blame for failures in the prisons service, despite the extent to which policy and operations issues merge and despite the extent to which intervention by the Home Secretary, Michael Howard, compromised Lewis's operational independence in practice. An authoritative study concludes that the ability of ministers to evade their responsibilities stems mainly from executive dominance over parliament but also derives from the lack of precision in the definition of accountability (Woodhouse, 1994, pp. 284–5).

Even when they do resign, ministers rarely do so immediately upon the outbreak of some scandal or crisis, which means that in the following days and weeks the attitudes of the prime minister, the Cabinet, the backbenchers of the governing party, the press and public opinion will all play a part in whether a minister stays or goes. The inter-relatedness of individual and collective responsibility, in particular, should be noticed together with the political considerations underlying their invocation (Box 15.6).

The impact of recent changes on the traditional Civil Service

We conclude by considering the impact of recent changes on the leading features of the traditional civil service: permanence, neutrality and anonymity.

Permanence

Traditionally, the Civil Service Commission organised appointment to a unified career civil service, a single hierarchical organisation characterised by security of tenure and a common system of pay and promotion. The permanence of the civil service underpinned its public service ethos and commitment to impartial service of the government of the day. Ministers came and went but civil servants went on, if not for ever, to honourable pensioned retirement at the end of their forty-year term. This system and its supportive non-material values – in particular, the commitment to openness, fairness and merit in the civil service culture – have been undermined in the last two decades by several developments, notably: the appointment of increasing numbers of outside political advisers to ministers; the hiving off of the majority of civil servants into executive agencies; and the introduction of market testing and contracting out. By 1982, over four-fifths of civil service recruitment had already become a departmental responsibility; in 1991 departments and agencies became responsible for 95 per cent of all recruitment and in 1996 for all pay and grading below the senior staff. The Civil Service Commission retained direct responsibility only for recruitment to the top grades – from 1996 the new Senior Civil Service created following the government's white paper *The Civil Service: Continuity and Change* (1994). The government envisaged that most senior posts would continue to be filled by insiders but opened the door for increased outside recruitment whilst also providing for individual (although not fixed term) contracts for senior civil servants, different rates of pay for permanent secretaries in different departments, and payment according to responsibilities and performance. To summarise: by the mid-1990s, a unified, career civil service no longer existed. In 1996, approximately one-quarter of Agency Chief Executives and some top civil servants were appointed from outside; responsibility for appointment, pay and grading was divided between the Civil Service Commission for the policy core and departments and agencies for the rest; and the job for life concept had disappeared, as civil servants were forced to compete with outsiders for their jobs through market-testing and privatisation.

Neutrality

In traditional theory, the role of a top civil servant is to give to the Minister 'honest and impartial advice, without fear or favour, and whether the advice accords with the Minister's view or not' *(Duties and Responsibilities of Civil Servants in Relation to Ministers, 1987*, para.7). A good civil servant will ask of a policy proposal: 'Will it work? Is it fair? and will it lead to extra work or cost?' (John Ward, former general secretary of the First Division Association, cited Butler, Adonis and Travers, 1994, p. 215). Significant facets of this role are 'hunting for snags' and serving as the departmental 'memory' in the sense of reminding ministers what has been tried unsuccessfully before (Hennessy, 1995, p. 127). A leading criticism of the Thatcher–Major years was that the civil service was 'politicised'. There are three main concerns behind this charge. First, Mrs Thatcher looked for a different kind of civil servant, offering a 'can do' approach rather than 'whingeing, analysis and integrity', and combined this with a close interest in top appointments. The worry was that this would produce an atmosphere in which civil servants told ministers what they wanted to hear rather than what they needed to know (Hennessy, 1995, p.130). In other words, it might appear a preferable option to the senior civil service to settle for a quiet life by not serving up analysis and advice known to be unpalatable to ministers. Indeed, some academics have suggested that this is (in part) how 'policy disasters' such as the poll tax can happen. William Waldegrave exonerated the civil service from any blame for the poll tax in 1993 but historians of the tax consider that civil service failures to advise and warn played a part in the catastrophe. In the case of the Department of the Environment and the poll tax, they argue, 'its warnings were ineffective and its advice poor' (Butler, Adonis and Travers, 1994, p. 223). Some survey evidence points to concern within the service that the new pay and recruitment systems are threatening its neutrality. Thus, a MORI poll for the First Division Association showed that most senior civil servants believed that being open and frank with ministers was a barrier to promotion and that they have to toe the line if they want to get on (*Guardian,* 13 July 1995).

A second worry is the use of the civil service for party political purposes. Some charges relating to 1990s include:

- the use of civil servants to cost the Labour Opposition's policy commitments
- the authorisation by senior Treasury officials of the use of public funds to help pay Chancellor of the Exchequer Norman Lamont's legal fees in a private case in 1993: the government argued that the case was covered by the guideline in *Questions of Procedure for Ministers* which states that 'Ministers occasionally become engaged in legal proceedings primarily in their personal capacities, but in circumstances which also involve their official responsibilities'
- the vigorous public attack on Labour's policy and defence of the Government's policy on the NHS by Duncan Nichol, the NHS Chief Executive, a senior civil servant, in the run up to the 1992 general election
- the use of civil servants to draft party political speeches, prepare briefings for party events, prepare material for manifestos, brief on responses to Opposition speeches and write party political speeches when political advisers were absent
- the employment of civil servants in 1995 to back up the Conservative Government's Committee to coordinate policy presentation (the so-called 'banana skins' committee)
- the failed attempt by the then Deputy Prime Minister Michael Heseltine in late 1996 to use civil servants to assemble a squad of 'robust defenders' of government policy amongst service providers, an attempt that was vetoed by the Cabinet Secretary.

Many of these examples – using civil servants to cost the Opposition's policy commitments or to draft party speeches or overt criticism of Opposition policy by a leading public official – certainly seem to stray over the boundary marking the legitimate use

of the civil service. Many of them too occurred in late 1996 – i.e. in the long run-up to the 1997 general election and well after the recommendations of the Nolan Report on the central executive had been accepted and largely implemented by the government. An indication of the official concern about the possibility of infringement of the political neutrality of civil servants during the campaign itself was the issue of the document 'General Election Advice', a guide to ministers and civil servants designed to prevent the party political use of the machinery of government including the civil service during the election (*Guardian,* 18 March 1997). It was the first time such guidance has been published. However, an earlier Cabinet Office note, leaked to the press, *Guidance on Guidance,* told civil servants that they could not refuse ministers' order to provide factual information on which pre-election campaigning was based; the note, designed for internal Whitehall use only, also authorised civil servants to provide costings of Opposition policies (*Observer,* 14 April 1996).

Thirdly, a more subtle worry is that top level civil servants are necessarily politicised by engaging in 'the devising, promotion, execution and defence of policies and strategies rooted in adversarial partisan politics' (Madgwick and Woodhouse, 1995, p. 148). In many – perhaps the majority of – situations, civil servants expect and can live with this. But serious ethical questions arise where officials are required, for example, to cooperate in concealing the full truth about a policy to save the government's face and to prevent a publicity victory for the Opposition. This was the situation facing Ponting and several officials in the arms to Iraq case. The view of the Armstrong Memorandum promulgated after the Ponting case is that the sole obligation of the official is to serve the government of the day. But critics have argued strongly that as well as possessing a duty to conscience civil servants have a duty to the state or public interest, which can differ from their duty to the government of the day.

Anonymity

The anonymity of civil servants – an important corollary of ministerial responsibility – has been seriously eroded since the war. As ministerial willingness

BOX 15.7
Naming and blaming civil servants: some examples

- *Bloodhound missile contract* (1964): officials in the Ministry of Aviation blamed for excessive profits made by Ferranti Ltd on this contract.
- *Sachsenhausen case* (1968): faults in the conduct of Foreign Office (FO) officials (and the Minister, George Brown) revealed by the Parliamentary Commissioner's investigation into the FO's refusal to pay compensation to British victims of Nazi persecution. During its consideration by the Commons Select Committee, Airey Neave MP named the official whom he considered to have the greatest responsibility for the day-to-day administration of the case.
- *Vehicle and General Insurance Company collapse* (1971): officials in the Board of Trade criticised by the Tribunal of Inquiry for negligent conduct.
- *Westland affair* (1986): leading civil servants in the Prime Minister's Office and the DTI who were involved in the leaking of the Solicitor-General's letter were all identified in Parliament and the press: in addition to Bernard

Ingham, Charles Powell and Colette Bowe, these included John Mogg, Private Secretary to Leon Brittan, and John Mitchell, an Under-Secretary at the DTI.
- *Arms to Iraq: the Scott Report* (1996) criticised a large number of officials over a range of grades,departments and agencies:these included Eric Beston, Head of the DTI's Export Control and Licensing Branch, Rob Young and David Gore-Booth, the successive Heads of the Foreign Office's Middle East Department, Ian McDonald and Alan Barrett of the MoD's Defence Export Services Secretariat, and Stephen Wall, Private Secretary to the Prime Minister. A frequent criticism was involvement in giving 'misleading' answers to parliamentary questions (Young, Wall) or defending the practice of giving incomplete answers to parliament (Gore-Booth); other criticisms included producing memoranda which contradicted intelligence reports (McDonald and Barrett) and lack of frankness in giving evidence to the inquiry (Beston).

to assume responsibility for the mistakes of officials has declined, so the practice has grown of naming and blaming individual bureaucrats (Box 15.7). In the Westland case, in addition to its criticisms of the minister and the other civil servants involved, the House of Commons Select Committee on Defence censured Sir Robert Armstrong, the Cabinet Secretary and Head of the Home Civil Service, for falling 'to give a clear lead'. The government's reply defended its behaviour in terms of the traditional doctrine of ministerial responsibility: 'Constitutionally ministers are responsible and accountable for all actions carried out by civil servants of their departments in pursuit of government policies or in discharge of responsibilities laid upon them by Parliament' (*Civil Servants and Ministers: Duties and Responsibilities.* Government Response, 1986). But this defence was criticised as not entirely satisfactory by the Commons because it left a hole where government accountability should be: thus, not only did ministers not make themselves fully accountable to Parliament during the affair, the Defence Committee was not allowed to question any of the officials. This prompted the Treasury and Civil Service Select Committee to comment that in cases in which ministers deny responsibility for their action, a mechanism must be provided to make officials accountable to Parliament (1985–6). 'Who ought to resign or be penalised if mistakes are made?', it asked. 'If it is not to be Ministers, it can only be officials.' The Scott Inquiry in its exposure of the inner workings of Whitehall brought a far larger number of officials into the public spotlight. Once again, the Cabinet Secretary (Sir Robin Butler) was criticised, on this occasion for refusing to allow two ex-civil servants to appear before the Inquiry, as were several ministers and numerous civil servants for their role in the affair. But there were no ministerial resignations over the affair and, apart from the resignation of Mark Higson, the Foreign Office Iraq desk clerk, none of the officials involved were subject to sanctions of any kind. All had been assured by Sir Robin Butler before giving evidence to the Inquiry that they would not be disciplined for any evidence given (Adams and Pyper, 1997, pp. 173–4).

Summary

- The bulk of governmental decisions are made in the Departments – hence, the importance of establishing (1) an appropriate model to understand how departmental decisions are made; and

(2) of analysing the contemporary validity of the convention which purports to describe ministerial accountability.

- Under (1) it was suggested that the reassertion of political control over the Civil Service by the Conservative Administrations of Margaret Thatcher and John Major (1979-97) has led to the reinstatement of the traditional *liberal democratic* or *public administration* model of minister-civil servant relations, although limited in scope, the *Whitehall village* model is also relevant. However, the far-left *power-bloc* and New Right *bureaucratic over-supply* theories have been undermined (the latter because of the 'correctives' applied by Conservative Governments since 1979). The *liberal bureaucratic* model, although containing valuable insights, is – perhaps temporarily – of reduced significance in practice. But it retains its potential value as a tool of analysis in explaining situations in which departments elude full ministerial control.

- Falling standards of conduct among ministers led to the establishment of the Nolan Committee (1994–5), which made a large number of recommendations aimed at laying down clearer and firmer guidelines for ministers and civil servants, appointments to quangos and MPs. The Government responded more positively to the Nolan recommendations on executive matters than on MPs (see Chapter 16).

- The sweeping managerial reforms of the 1980s and 1990s including the radical 'Next Steps' programme, certain episodes leading to charges of politicisation, and the light shed on the inner workings of government by the Scott Report (1996) led to fears that the key principles of the modern civil service – permanence, political neutrality and anonymity – were being compromised. Some commentators considered that capacity of the civil service to move smoothly from serving a Conservative Government to serving a Labour Government gave the lie at least to charges of politicisation; but other critics believe that the traditional civil service has been undermined, by the management changes, by politicisation and by the growing practice of naming and blaming civil servants.

- With regard to (2), although still normally invoked, the traditional doctrine of ministerial responsibility does not mean that ministers automatically resign after public criticism of their own or their officials' errors and misconduct. They resign mainly for personal misconduct, more rarely for political misjudgements, more rarely still for policy failures and, in recent times, are not expected to resign at all for the errors of their officials. In the later years of John Major's government, mainly for political reasons, the number of resignations increased sharply, although they remained largely for the personal misconduct of ministers.

- But although its working is far from satisfactory, it is difficult to maintain that the principle of ministerial responsibility has been dislodged, so central is it to understanding British constitutional practice. Ministers remain (at least) *answerable* for the conduct of their Departments, and the maximum sanction (resignation) still exists, even if its practice at any given moment is more a function of the political circumstances of the government, of relationships within it, and of relations between the erring politician and his own party, than of the automatic play of ministerial consciences or of enforcement by Parliament.

Questions

1. 'Civil Servants owe their primary duty to the state, not to the government which happens to be in office.' Discuss this statement in the light of developments and cases in the 1980s.

2. 'Apart from personal misconduct, ministerial responsibility is now an outmoded convention.' Discuss.

3. Evaluate the usefulness of the models of minister–civil servant relationships described in this chapter.

4. 'Current controversies – especially those arising from the Scott Inquiry (and the poll tax fiasco) – suggest that the civil service is too obedient, not too recalcitrant' (Barker and Wilson, 1997). Comment critically on this opinion.

Assignments

Assignment (1)
Write a brief account of the managerial reforms of the civil service in the 1980s and early 1990s and examine the benefits and disadvantages occurring as a result of them.

Assignment (2)
Study the discussion of the permanence, neutrality and anonymity of the civil service which concludes this chapter. Then state to what extent these features remain a valid description of the service today.

Further reading

On the civil service generally, see Pyper, R. *The British Civil Service* (London: Harvester Wheatsheaf) and Drewry, G. and Butcher, T. (1991) *The Civil Service Today*, 2nd edn (Oxford: Blackwell). On the postwar history, Hennessy, P. (1990) *Whitehall*, rev. edn (London: Fontana), and Theakston, K. (1995) *The Civil Service since 1945* (Oxford: Blackwell) should be consulted. On relations between minister and civil servants, see Theakston, K. (1995) 'Ministers and Civil Servants', in R. Piper and L. Robins (eds), *Governing the UK in the 1990s* (London: Macmillan) and Smith, M.J., Marsh, D. and Richards, D. (1995) 'Central Government Departments and the Policy Process', in R.A.W. Rhodes and P. Dunleavy, *Prime minister, Cabinet and the Core Executive* (London: Macmillan).

On ministerial responsibility, Woodhouse, D. (1994) *Ministers and Parliament: Accountability in theory and Practice* (Oxford: Clarendon); Marshall, G. (ed.) (1989) *Ministerial Responsibility* (Oxford: Oxford University Press); Marshall, G. (1991) 'The

Evolving Practice of Parliament Accountability', *Parliamentary Affairs* 4:4; Pyper, R. (1991) 'Governments, 1964–90: A Survey', *Contemporary Record* 5:2, autumn; Pyper, R. (1994) 'Individual Ministerial Responsibility. Dissecting the Doctrine', *Politics Review*, 4:1; and Gray, P. (1996/7) 'When the Minister Won't Resign', *Talking Politics*, 9:2, winter, provide authoritative analyses.

On the implications of the Scott Report for ministerial responsibility and departmental decision-making generally, see Tomkins, A. (1996) 'The Scott Report: The Constitutional Implications', *Politics Review*, 6:1, September; and Adams, J. and Pyper, R. (1997) 'Whatever Happened to the Scott Report?', *Talking Politics*, 9:3, spring. On civil service reform since 1979, see Hood, C. and James, O. (1997) 'The Central Executive', in P. Dunleavy, A. Gamble, I. Holliday and G. Peele (eds), *Developments in British Politics 5* (London: Macmillan); and Butcher, T. (1995) 'A New Civil Service? The Next Steps Agencies', in R. Pyper and L. Robins (eds), *Governing the UK in the 1990s* (London: Macmillan).

Websites
Home Office:
http://www.homeoffice.gov.uk/
Foreign Office:
http://www.fco.gov.uk/
Health:
http://www.open.gov.uk/index/../doh/dhhome.htm
Education
http://www.open.gov.uk/index/../dfee/dfeehome.htm
Scotland:
http://www.Scotland.gov.uk/
Wales:
http://www.cymru.gov.uk/
Northern Ireland:
http://www.alexandra14nio.gov.uk/

Parliament

The central concern of this chapter is the role of Parliament in national politics. We examine the importance of party to the working of the House of Commons, the nature of the representativeness of the lower House of Parliament, the functions of Parliament in the political system, party organisation, recent changes in parliamentary behaviour and organisation, the role of the House of Lords and prospects for the future. The theme of **party** is the connecting link between these topics. It is argued that the role of **Parliament** in the political system has to be understood primarily in terms of the working of the party system within the context of a democratic electorate channelled in a particular way by the electoral system (Chapter 8). We begin by exploring this key statement.

The importance of party in the House of Commons

The House of Commons is the country's premier assembly. It consists of 659 MPs returned by that number of single-member constituencies, each elected on a simple majority by about 69,000 electors on average. MPs are elected as representatives of party, and party underpins their activities once in the House.

Table 16.1 shows how party determines the composition of the House of Commons, structuring it decisively into a party of government (Labour) and

Table 16.1 Party allegiance in the House of Commons after the 1997 General Election

Labour	419	Governing party
Conservative	165	Official opposition party
Liberal Democrat	46	
Ulster Unionist	13	
Scottish National Party	6	
Plaid Cymru	4	Combined opposition parties
Social Democratic and Labour Party	3	
Sinn Fein	2	
Independent	1	
Overall Labour majority	179	

BOX 16.1

House of Commons: main functions

- Representation
- Legislation
- Scrutiny
- Forum for national debate
- Recruitment of a government

a party of official opposition (Conservative) flanked by several much smaller opposition parties. Party underlies the activities of government in the House of Commons in four ways – by providing it with a programme based on its election manifesto, which forms the basis of the legislation it puts before the Commons; by supplying a team of leading politicians to fill ministerial posts (Chapter 14); by influencing backbenchers by its ethos, ideology and organisation to vote cohesively in support of the government; and by providing a mass organisation to select parliamentary candidates, campaign on their behalf, and, once they are elected, assist in keeping them up to the mark. Its overall majority taken together with the normally loyal support of its backbenchers ensures that the governing party can govern – that is, gain overall support for its executive activity and legislation from the House of Commons.

Party also underpins the activities of the official opposition, sustaining its two main constitutional functions of providing an alternative programme and team of leaders with which to replace the government and regular criticism of the government of the day. Equally, the minor political groupings are swayed by the imperatives of party to behave and vote cohesively behind a united policy.

Party, then, dominates Parliament, but the reverse is also true. Parliament equally clearly dominates party. Thus virtually all UK parties accept the legitimacy of Parliament, have as their major aim the winning of seats in the House of Commons, and choose their leaders from their MPs, who also have a major influence on their policies. (Adonis, 1993, pp. 40–1) In addition, Parliament provides the main arena for the party battle between elections. Although not well reported in many sections of the press, the consequences of the struggle in the House of Commons between competing teams of party leaders to establish the authority of their respective cases, and of backbenchers to make their mark, gradually filters down to the electorate via television, radio and the quality press.

Functions of the Lower House

The House of Commons has five main functions. (Box 16.1)

The middle three functions are shared with the House of Lords, although the Commons is easily the predominant partner.

The essence of Parliament, its primary role in the political system, is *legitimation*. In other words, it authorises the actions of rulers thereby justifying their acceptance by the ruled. And it can fulfil this purpose because of its historic status, constantly renewed, as a unique forum for national representation, law-making, political criticism, debate and leadership recruitment.

Representation

The representative character of the House of

Party government: In liberal democratic systems, competition between two or more parties for votes and their alternation in power is the method by which popular wishes are translated into public policy. Government and opposition are both by party and much of the behaviour of representatives suggests they owe their first loyalty to party rather than to their consciences, their constituents or the national interest.

Parliamentary government: The British form of constitutional and representative government in which executive and legislative power is fused in and exercised through a two-chamber assembly. Legislation and taxation originated by government are validated by the consent of Parliament whose acceptance signifies and symbolises the consent of the nation. Parliament does not itself govern but the policies and activities of government are criticised in Parliament and, most importantly, all legislation emanates from Parliament.

Table 16.2 Trade union-sponsored MPs, 1945–92

	1945	1950	1951	1955	1959	1964	1966	1970	1974	1974	1979	1983	1987	1992
Total TU MPs	120	111	108	95	92	120	127	112	127	126	134	115	129	143
Total Labour MPs	393	315	295	277	258	317	363	287	301	319	269	209	229	271

Commons underpins its other roles. It is **representative** in three senses: party, pressure group and constituency. These three kinds of representation combine in the member of Parliament, who is a representative of party (almost always), of interest (frequently) and of constituency (invariably).

In the case of *party*, representativeness does not mean that the party composition of the Commons exactly reflects the distribution of party support in the country. The difference between the actual representation of parties in the Commons after the 1997 General Election and the distribution of party support if an alternative system had been in operation is shown in Chapter 8. What 'representativeness' in this context does mean is that MPs are elected to the House and speak and vote there as as representatives of party.

Second, an MP may represent an *interest*. Representation of interests in the Commons can occur in many ways:

- *sponsorship of election candidates through a particular party*, for example, of Labour Party candidates by trade unions. This practice ended in 1995 (Table 16.2). In general, small sums were involved and went towards the candidate's election expenses rather than directly to the candidate. Union money now goes to a central fund to be distributed from Labour HQ (see Chapter 7). Unions could not instruct MPs how to speak or vote as that would be a breach of parliamentary privilege but they have expected MPs to watch over their interests. Union-sponsored MPs were prominent in helping to defeat Labour's Industrial Relations Bill in 1969. When union-sponsored Labour MPs put down an amendment to the the motion on the Queen's Speech in 1995 deploring the diminution in trade union rights, their action was referred to the Standards Commissioner by a Conservative MP as potentially a breach of the new rule banning paid advocacy and of the rule requiring the declaration of an interest.

- *payment of fees to MPs to serve as advisers, consultants or directors*: the Nolan Committee (1995) found that 168 MPs, consisting of 145 Conservatives, 15 Labour and 6 Liberal Democrats, shared 356 consultancies; of the 168, 26 MPs held multi-client consultancies whilst 142 MPs possessed consultancies with specific companies and trade associations. The 1996 Register of Members' Interests revealed that consultancy fees brought MPs up to about £2 million although this is likely to be a significant underestimate.

- *access to the Commons as MPs' research assistants and aides*: the use of House of Commons photo-identity passes by organisations as a cover for commercial lobbying activities in return for services to the MP concerned first became evident in the late 1980s (Adonis, 1993, p. 116).

- *lobbying of MPs by professional consultancy firms*: this kind of lobbying developed into a multi-million pound industry during the 1980s, with the total fee income earned by 50 consultancy firms estimated at over £10 million a year in 1991.

- *direct lobbying of parliament by all types of group*: three-quarters of groups in a Study of Parliament Group survey had regular or frequent contacts with one or more MPs (Rush, 1990, pp. 14,109); a study of the 129 all-party parliamentary groups in 1992 which specialised in subjects rather than

> **Representative government**: a form of democratic rule in which government is by representatives (e.g. MPs or Congressmen) elected by popular votes; the exercise of authority is legitimated ultimately (although not solely, since it must be exercised also according to constitutional rules) by the popular election of power-holders.

BOX 16.2
The Nolan Report, 1995 and its implementation

Nolan recommendation	Implementation
1. MPs should be permitted to have outside employment unrelated to their role as MPs.	None needed: endorsement of existing practice.
2. MPs should be banned from holding consultancies with lobbying companies.	Not accepted.
3. The House of Commons should make its own inquiry into other types of consultancy.	Paid advocacy banned, including tabling questions, motions and amendments for fees on behalf of outside interests. Ban on acting in any delegation on behalf of a paid outside interest. Restrictions on MPs' right to speak in debates for a paid outside interest.
4. House of Commons should restate 1947 resolution barring MPs from entering into contracts which restrict their freedom to act and speak as they wish, or which require them to act in parliament as the representatives of outside bodies.	Commons accepted need for a recommitment to the objectives of the 1947 Resolution, but will review its wording in the context of the draft Code.
5. The nature of MPs' interests should be described more clearly and fully in Register of Members' Interests, with remuneration listed in bands, e.g. £1,000–£5,000, and estimates made of the monetary value of benefits in kind. Contracts relating to provision of services for outside services should be deposited with the Register.	Accepted: first Register under new Nolan rules published in May 1996, but remains an inconsistent and incomplete record of MPs' outside interests, with many MPs finding ways to avoicl full disclosure and not penalised for their evasions. However the second Register (November 1997) under the new rules showed a 66 per cent fall in the number of consultancies registered (from 240 to 80), indicating the severe deterrent effect of exposure under the Nolan rules (as well as the greatly-changed composition of the House of Commons).
6. House of Commons should draw up a new Code of Conduct for MPs, with more detailed rules and guidance on avoiding conflicts of interest.	New Code of Conduct published July 1996. Includes ban on use of confidential information received in course of parliamentary duties for personal gain.
7. An independent Parliamentary Commissioner for Standards should be appointed, with responsibility for maintaining the Register, giving guidance on matters of conduct and investigating misconduct.	New Parliamentary Commissioner on Standards, Sir Gordon Downey, began work in November, 1996; reports to new Commons Committee on Standards and Privileges. In March 1997, Sir Gordon cleared 15 MPs of any impropriety in accepting election expenses in 1987 and 1992 from the lobbyist Ian Greer, but the cases of 10 more MPs accused of misconduct remained under investigation when Parliament was prorogued for the 1997 General Election. The Downey Report (July 1997) cleared a further 4 MPs of any impropriety in accepting election expenses from Greer, but it found 5 MPs, including the former minister, Neil Hamilton and Tim Smith, guilty of not declaring payments from the Harrods owner Mohammed Al-Fayed or Greer, and criticised another MP for behaviour which 'fell well short' of what was expected in the declaration of interests. The Standards and Privileges Committee upheld the Downey Report on Hamilton (November 1997), criticising him for behaviour which fell 'seriously and persistently short' of the standards expected of MPs. But doubts remained over the role of the Standards and Privileges Committee i.e. whether its role is simply to ensure the Parliamentary Commissioner is fulfilling his remit and any misdemeanours he finds are punished or whether it should function as a court of appeal.

international ties revealed that a large number were financed by individual businesses, groups of companies, trade associations, lobbying firms and charities.

- *specialised assistance on an ad hoc unpaid basis*: a wide range of groups provide information and support for MPs' parliamentary activities, e.g. Select Committees, Private Members' bills.
- *MPs' pursuit of outside occupations*: outside interests are represented in the House of Commons through MPs' part-time engagement in outside occupations such as, for example, journalists, lecturers, lawyers, and company directors. Income from such sources does not have to be declared in the Register of Interests, but a 1995 investigation found that 130 MPs, mostly Conservatives, received over £3 million a year from 275 directorships whilst others gained sizeable sums from media work.

Since 1975, Parliament has kept an annual register of interests to strengthen the custom that MPs declare their interests at the beginning of any debate in which they participate. However, although it is difficult to state precisely what benefits economic interests derive from these contacts, doubts remained about the adequacy of existing public information about MPs' financial interests. Public concern about the apparently declining ethical standards of MPs increased in the 1990s. Following the well-publicised cases of Conservative MPs John Browne, Michael Grylls and Michael Mates involving inadequate recording or declarations of interest, the 'cash for questions' (1994–5) affair scandalised public opinion. Two Conservative backbenchers, David Tredinnick and Graham Riddick, were reprimanded by the Commons, and suspended without pay for 20 and 10 days respectively, after allegations in the *Sunday Times* that each had accepted £1,000 for tabling a parliamentary question were upheld. Soon after this affair broke, the Committee on Standards in Public Life under the chairmanship of Lord Nolan was appointed.

The recommendations of the Nolan Committee (May 1995) and the extent to which they were implemented by parliament are shown in Box 16.2. The key moves were the banning of paid advocacy, the adoption of a new Code of Conduct and the appointment of a Parliamentary Commissioner for Standards. However, self-regulation of its own affairs by the House of Commons remained on trial in 1997, with allegations against Conservative MP Neil Hamilton concerning financial improprieties including failing to declare receipt of hospitality and failing to register cash payments finally accepted by the new Parliamentary Commissioner for Standards, Sir Gordon Downey, in a 900-page report published after the General Election in July 1997. Sir Gordon found 'compelling' evidence that Hamilton had taken up to £25,000 in cash from Mohammed Al-Fayed, the owner of Harrods, to ask parliamentary questions, and the Commons Standards and Privileges Committee accepted this report in November 1997, criticising Hamilton for standard that 'fell seriously and persistently below' what was expected of an MP. The Nolan restrictions on paid advocacy led to a 66 per cent drop in the number of consultancies declared by MPs in the 1997 Register of Members' Interests (from 240 to 80). The defeat or retirement of large numbers of Conservative MPs at the 1997 General Election also contributed to this fall (see further, Assignment 1).

Third and finally, the House of Commons is representative of the United Kingdom in a geographical sense – that is, as divided up into territorial units called *constituencies*. Candidates for Parliament may stand as representatives of party but, once elected, each MP is expected to represent the interests of the constituency as a whole and to be at the service of all constituents. In this way, as Members for particular constituencies, MPs collectively may be said to represent the entire country, which would not be true of their roles as party and group representatives. This is the oldest meaning of 'representation' and formed the basis of the individualist liberal concept of parliamentary representation, which prevailed in the nineteenth century but now coexists with the collectivist concept of party representation which came to prominence in the twentieth century. The liberal idea of a representative in this system (also known as the Burkean view) is the prevalent one in Britain. This view holds that the representative, whilst having the duty to consult constituents and take into account their opinions, owes his or her primary duty to the national interest and to conscience. Parliament in this view is 'a deliberative assembly of one nation rather than a congress of ambassadors', i.e it should lead public opinion rather than simply reflect it. But there is also the delegate theory of representation – part of the ideology of radical democracy – in which the elected representatives are considered to be the agents of and directly accountable to their constituents. The national assembly on this view is or should be a direct register or mirror of public opinion rather than a director of it (always suspected as manipulation). This theory became very influential in the Labour Party in the late 1970s and early 1980s.

The idea of the MP as constituency representative and of Parliament as an assembly of constituency representatives is a resilient one. It has undergone a resurgence since the 1960s, primarily because people facing the complexities of local and national welfare bureaucracies have turned to MPs to assist them in understanding and asserting their rights. The burden of constituency work upon MPs is now very considerable, with most MPs receiving on average over 30 letters per day from their constituents and setting aside 2–3 days each week as well as a sizeable part of the weekend to the task (Norton and Wood, 1993, p. 43; Cowley, 1996, pp. 12–15). MPs' constituency work falls into two main categories. First, there is the local welfare officer/social worker role, dealing with a wide variety of problems on behalf of individual constituents. Problems and grievances connected with housing, health and social security predominate but other concerns include education, pensions, local taxation, conservation, animal testing, law and order and Sunday trading. MPs tackle the problems at the appropriate level, conducting a voluminous correspondence with ministers, Departments, local authorities, 'quangos', local Department of Social Security (DSS) offices and so on: when Parliament is sitting, ministers receive about 20,000 letters from MPs per month, up 50 per cent even on the early 1980s. Also MPs can raise constituents' grievances through the medium of parliamentary questions and debate and, if all these means fail, they can refer cases of alleged public maladministration to the Ombudsman.

Second, MPs act as promoters of local interests, working to further the interests of the constituency as a whole by, for example, working to get orders for local industries, to attract new commercial and industrial investment, to get roads built, to find solutions for local industrial disputes, and to prevent local factories, schools and hospitals closing. In a democratic society, this MP–constituency relationship is of profound practical and theoretical importance, serving as a barometer of public opinion for representatives and as both safety-valve and potential mechanism of grievance resolution for citizens.

The House of Commons, then, can be seen as representative in these three distinct but overlapping ways. It is not, however, a *social* microcosm of the nation, MPs being predominantly white, male, middle-aged and middle class. Thus, there were only nine black/Asian MPs in 1997 (five Labour), constituting just over 1 per cent of the House of Commons. However, a record number of women were elected (120, cf. 60 in 1992) and women now constitute 18.2 per cent of the House. The main reason for the larger total was the significant increase in Labour Party women MPs (up by 64 cf. 1992), the party breakdown being: Labour 101, Conservative 13, Liberal Democrat 3, SNP 2, plus the Speaker. A majority (70 per cent) of MPs in 1997 were aged between 40 and 59. Finally, parliament is socially untypical in that over two-thirds of MPs have received higher education and over four-fifths have professional or business backgrounds.

Legislation

Parliament no longer makes policy either in the sense of initiating legislation or strongly influencing it (Figure 16.1). Most legislation originates with government and emerges from its passage through Parliament more or less in the form intended by the government. The government's majority backed by generally cohesive party voting normally ensures that this is so. Nevertheless, in order to become law, government measures must pass through both Houses of Parliament in a series of stages with amendment and, very occasionally, even defeat of a bill a possibility. Table 16.3 details these stages, commenting on the points (column 3) at which amendment is possible. Not only is the parliamentary legislative process a constitutional necessity, politically, owing to the possibility of amendment or even defeat of the government's legislation, it is more than a formality or forgone conclusion. Even if Parliament no longer makes policy, its assent is vital to the establishment of the legitimacy of that legislation.

Table 16.3 Legislative stages in Parliament

Stage	Where taken	Comments
First Reading	Floor of the House of Commons	Formal introduction only, no debate.
Second Reading	Floor of the House of Commons (non-contentious bills may be referred to a second reading committee).	Debate on the general principles of a measure; if these are contested, a bill may be voted on, and even defeated.
Committee	Standing committee (Constitutionally important and certain other measures e.g. finance bills may be taken in committee of the whole House).	Considered in detail, clause by clause; amendments can be made, but normally most successful ones are by ministers since standing committee composition reflects party representation in the House.
Report	Floor of the House of Commons (there is no report stage if the bill reported is unamended from Committee of the whole House).	Reported to the House by the standing committee; amendments can be made.
Third Reading	Floor of the House of Commons (there is no debate unless six members submit a motion beforehand).	Final approval of the bill – generally a formality for all but controversial bills. Debate limited to final text of bill.
House of Lords	Bill passes through similar stages to House of Commons (committee stage of public bills is normally taken on the floor of the Lords not in standing committee).	Lords can propose amendments, which Commons accepts, rejects or substitutes amendments of its own, returning bill to Lords with 'reasons' for its actions. Lords then agrees not to insist on its rejected amendments or accepts Commons amendments; if Lords insists or proposes another amendment, search for agreement between two Houses continues. If no agreement is reached, bill lapses (this happens very rarely). Bill can then be reintroduced in the next session and passed without the Lords' consent.

Source: Adapted from Norton (1981), p. 86.

Scrutiny and influence of the Executive

Serving as an arena for constitutional opposition is another major function of Parliament. It is in Parliament (primarily in the House of Commons) that the government must explain and defend its actions.

Nowadays, the backbenchers of the governing party have more to do with setting the limits of government action than do the opposition parties. Faced by a government with a working majority, there is normally little the opposition can do except resort to delaying tactics. This perhaps is as it should be since the primary function of Parliament is to sustain a government. Nonetheless, the constitutional requirement embodied in specific parliamen-

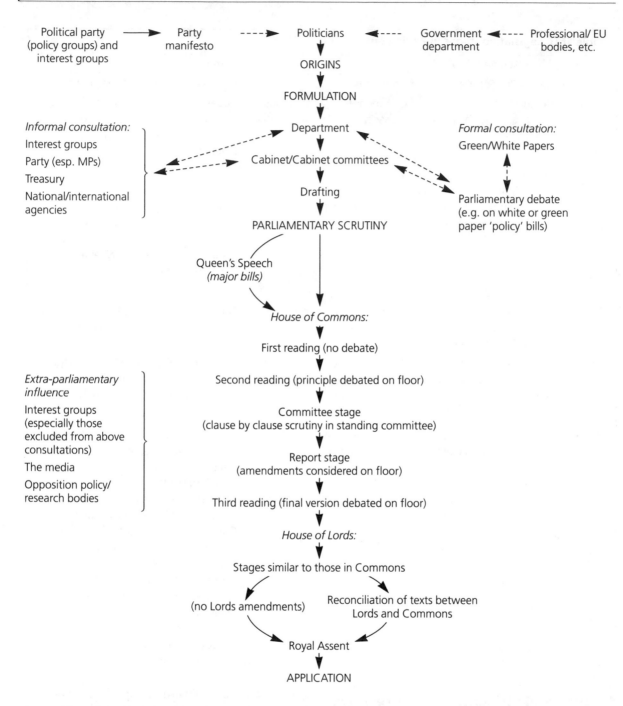

Source: Adapted from tables in Drewry (1988) pp. 124–5, and Adonis (1993) p. 93.

Figure 16.1 Principal stages in the legislative process for government bills

tary procedures that government must publicly subject its activities to appraisal is of paramount importance. Major scrutinising procedures and agencies of the House of Commons are Questions, general, adjournment and emergency debates, early day motions, select committees, and correspondence with ministers (Table 16.4).

Forum for national debate

Parliament commands attention as the focus of national debate on all kinds of occasion in a manner no other institution can match. Such occasions include Prime Minister's Question Time; the beginning and end of major debates in normal circumstances; more heated moments such as the Westland affair (1986) when a government's, a prime minister's or a leading Cabinet minister's reputation are at stake, with even a whiff of resignation in the air; and, lastly, the great historic occasion such as the fall of the Chamberlain Government in May 1940, Suez in 1956 and the Falklands crisis in 1982. On these occasions, the *theatrical* element in Parliament is to the fore as a tense but almost ritualistic rhetorical combat takes place between rival teams of political gladiators urged on by compact stage armies of supporters. The House of Commons, it has been said, provides a forum in which a continuing general election is fought (Brazier, 1988, p. 169).

Recruitment and training of the personnel of government

Parliament no longer selects ministers but it remains 'a school of statesmanship' in the sense that ministers are invariably drawn from Parliament, predominantly from the House of Commons. Thus, whilst the electorate effectively elects the government directly, it is in the Commons that politicians serve as members of 'shadow' teams before receiving office or, as ministers, defend government policy. The skills of parliamentary debate are widely acknowledged to be no real preparation for running a Department nor are the two kinds of ability invariably present in the same person. Nevertheless, it is in the House of Commons that ambitious politicians first attempt to make, and then as ministers try to sustain, their reputations.

Party organisation in the House of Commons

There are three main elements in party organisation in the House of Commons: whips, party meetings and party committees.

Whips

Since government and opposition are by party, it is vital for parties to remain united, especially in their formal activities such as voting in Parliament. It is essential to avoid overt expressions of disagreement by significant numbers, and to minimise and counteract those which do occur. Failure to do so may, at the least, give encouragement to the rival party and, at worst, for a government, may jeopardise the passing of legislation and, for an opposition, destroy any chance to embarrass or defeat a government. The worst eventuality is that a party will split and, and as may happen as a result, suffer electoral defeat – as Labour did in 1983 and 1987 after splitting in 1981.

MPs are subject to three influences conducive to party loyalty before any formal mechanisms might begin to operate. These are, first, their natural sympathy for the causes and purposes their party represents; second, their desire (especially if they are ambitious) not to alienate the leadership; and, third, their concern to keep on good terms with their local parties which tend to dislike rebellions against party policy. MPs, then, vote with their parties for many reasons, other than the formal power of the whips.

Whips none the less play a key part in the management of their parties in parliament. The leaders of the two major parties appoint about a dozen or so whips led by a Chief Whip. The main task of the whips is to ensure that the government's business is carried through successfully or opposed resolutely and to do this they need to ensure that backbenchers support party policy in the House of Commons votes. To this end they keep their own MPs informed by producing and sending to them the documentary whip. This is a weekly outline of parliamentary business which indicates the degree of importance attached by the party to the various items by the number of underlinings. Thus, for items of minor importance, an MP's attendance is merely requested (a one-line whip); for items of

Table 16.4 Main methods of Commons' scrutiny of the executive

Procedure	Function
Questions	• Backbenchers may submit both oral and written questions.
	• Ministers reply to oral questions daily (Mon–Thurs, usually for about 40–50 minutes from 2.35 p.m.).
	• MPs are allowed one further unscripted question (a 'supplementary') after which other MPs may continue the interrogation.
	• On Wednesdays for 30 minutes from 3.00 p.m. the Leader of the Opposition and other MPs can tackle the PM directly at Prime Minister's Question Time.
	• Most questions to ministers (about three-fifths) are written and are recorded – together with the replies – in *Hansard*.
Debates	• *General* – Debate on the government's programme (Queen's Speech) at outset of each parliamentary session; also on 'no confidence' motions (rare except when government majority is very small) and, mainly, on motions tabled by the government to discuss government policy (about 20 days per session) or motions tabled by the opposition (20 days per session, with three allocated to the second largest opposition party).
	• Adjournment debates and private members' motions: adjournment motions enable backbenchers to raise issues relating to government policy or items of constituency interest and get a reply from a junior minister;
	• 11 days per session are allocated for private members' motions and backbenchers may also initiate short debates immediately before each recess, providing about another 7 days.
	• *Emergency* – way for MPs to raise urgent matters for debate which lie within responsibility of the government and cannot be raised rapidly in another way;
	• very rarely granted (one or two per session) but popular with backbenchers because of the media attention even when not granted.
Early day motions	• Much used method of enabling MPs to express their views, although no debate follows on points raised; increasingly popular, with numbers tabled rising significantly since 1960.
Select committees	• Able to scrutinise executive away from the floor of the Commons;
	• have powers to send for 'persons, papers and records' and can interrogate civil servants and on occasion ministers;
	• 16 departmental select committees now exist together with the Public Accounts (examining government expenditure) and Parliamentary Commissioner for Administration ('Ombudsman') Committees.
	• The party balance on select committees reflects that of the House as a whole.
Correspondence with ministers	• Main way in which MPs pursue case-work on behalf of constituents.

greater importance on which a division will take place, an MP's presence is expected (a two-line whip); and for very important items, an MP's attendance is regarded as essential (a three-line whip). Defiance of a three-line whip constitutes a serious breach of political conduct.

An MP wishing to be absent for a vote must find a member of the opposing party who also wishes to stay away. This practice is known as 'pairing' and is arranged through the whips; routinely used on two-line whips, it may even on occasion be permitted on three-line whips.

The written whip also informs members of the forthcoming business of standing, select, party and other committees.

Whips play a central role in linking the party leaderships with the backbenchers. It is the whips who advise leaders on what the party will or will not stand; who offer ideas to leaders on how to head off backbench rebellion; and who indicate to disaffected backbenchers the likely consequences of their actions. Whips are personnel managers rather than disciplinarians. The ultimate sanction against a party rebel – withdrawal of the party whip (i.e. expulsion from the parliamentary party) – almost never happens: it is hardly a realistic threat against 20 or 30 backbenchers. However, the whip was withdrawn from the Conservative MP, Rupert Allason, in July 1993 for abstaining on a confidence motion on the EU Social Chapter, and from a further eight Conservative backbenchers in November 1994 for abstaining on the Second Reading of the European Communities(Finance) Bill, which had once again been made a confidence issue. The way in which such an extreme tactic can rebound against its perpetrators was shown almost immediately when the eight whipless Conservative rebels failed to support the government on the imposition of a second round of VAT on fuel in December 1994, thereby ensuring a government defeat, and further when the Major Government was humiliated by being forced to restore the whip to the rebels with the promise of no reprisals in spring 1995 (Alderman, 1995, pp. 9–10; Ludlam, 1996, pp. 118–19). More realistically, the whips employ cajolery, bribes and threats against potential rebels. The bribes may include recommendations for improved office accommodation, a party-sponsored overseas trip or a place on a partic-ular select committee, a favourable mention for junior ministerial office, and even, for Conservative MPs, a knighthood either for themselves or their constituency party activists. The threats are non-preferment in any of these ways. After a 'rebellion', recalcitrant MPs may suffer at least personal abuse and sharp rebukes, at worst long periods on the backbenches without hope of office. Most of the time, the whips just seek to persuade, often by invoking party loyalty and the desirability of not 'rocking the boat' or giving aid and comfort to the 'other lot', and, if they fail, just resign themselves to failure. There is always a certain number of MPs in both major parties who are beyond the reach of blandishments and threats – for example, the former ministers and backbenchers without ambition to become ministers who formed the overwhelming majority of Conservative cross-voters on the poll tax in 1987–8. But the way in which many threatened rebellions peter out suggests that, whilst the model of their role as disciplinarians is inappropriate, the whips possess an armoury of 'persuasion' which is far from negligible.

Party meetings

The Conservative Party meets weekly in the 1922 Committee when Parliament is sitting. When the party is in government, only backbenchers attend but not ministers; when it is in opposition, the Committee includes all Conservative MPs except the leader. Its chairman, who enjoys direct access to the leader, is an important figure and the '1922' plays a key role in the party especially in times of controversy and crisis.

When in opposition, the Labour Party meets as the PLP (Parliamentary Labour Party), i.e. it is attended by members of the shadow Cabinet. When the party is in government, Labour ministers attend meetings of the PLP when the work of their Departments is under discussion; communication between the government and its backbenchers is maintained by the Parliamentary Committee whose members include the leader and deputy leader, the chief whip, four ministers (three from the Commons) and six backbenchers.

The minor parties also meet weekly and appoint whips.

Party committees

Each major party in opposition forms a Shadow Cabinet. In the Conservative Party, it is chosen by the leader and known formally as the Consultative Committee. In the Labour Party, the Shadow Cabinet or Parliamentary Committee consists of the leader and deputy leader, the chief whip in the Commons, the chairman of the PLP, 15 backbenchers (who like the chief whip and the chairman are elected by the PLP), the leader and chief whip in the House of Lords and an elected Labour peer. The leader allocates Shadow Cabinet portfolios and appoints additional members of 'Shadow' teams.

Each major party also forms a large number of specialist committees. In 1988, the Conservatives had 24 specialist committees, 7 regional groups, a committee on party organisation and one on unpaired members. When the party is in office, the committees elect their own chairpersons; when it is in opposition, the committees are chaired by the appropriate shadow minister who is appointed by the Leader. In 1988, the PLP had 14 subject and 8 regional committees, each appointing its own chair. In opposition, frontbenchers as well as select committee members are expected to attend their appropriate committees; in office, ministers are expected to attend when requested (Griffith and Ryle, 1989, pp. 107–13).

Consideration of party organisation in the House of Commons suggests, first, the extent to which already existing party loyalties are reinforced by party activities within the House, especially those of the Whips but also those of party meetings and committees as parties strive to govern or prepare themselves for government; and second, the considerable amount of important political activity which takes place away from the floor of the House in backstage party gatherings.

Recent changes in House of Commons behaviour and structure

The government controls Parliament but cannot always rely on getting its way. In the following sections, this point is explained first with reference to the behaviour and structure of the House of Commons and then with reference to the House of Lords. We start with the mechanisms of government control before considering the ways in which the will of governments can be flouted.

Government control of the House of Commons rests on four main factors: its possession in normal circumstances of a majority, allied with the habit of loyal voting by its own supporters; its power to determine the parliamentary timetable; its ability to curtail debate; and its control over the drafting of legislation.

Thus, first, over two-thirds of elections since the war have produced governments with majorities ranging from the adequate (17) to the massive (over 100) (Table 7.1) and we have already looked at the forces constraining those majorities to vote cohesively.

Second, although a significant proportion of Commons business is initiated by the opposition and backbenchers, government business has priority on the majority (75 per cent) of the sitting days of the House. (Note: The actual breakdown of Commons time in a particular session will look rather different: more like 55 per cent – 45 per cent in favour of the government; this is because much debate on government business is inspired by the opposition or backbenchers – e.g. by moving amendments to government bills.)

Third, two devices mainly enable the government to restrict debate: the closure and the guillotine. The closure – the request 'that the question be now put', stopping debate if successful – is rarely used now to restrict debate on government business (a mere three times in 1987–8, cf. eleven times, 1961–2). The guillotine – an 'allocation of time' motion regulating the amount of time to be spent on a bill – is normally used when the government considers that progress on a major piece of legislation is unsatisfactory at committee stage. In recent years, guillotine motions have been used more frequently – six times in 1987–8, ten in 1988–9 (a record number), four in 1989–90, and six in the short session of 1991–2. But it is also true that the length of time elapsing before an allocation of time order is moved at standing committee stage is now much greater – over 80 hours for the 19 bills guillotined in standing committee between 1979 and 1988, compared with under 30 hours which was common between 1946 and 1961.

Finally, despite often extensive consultations by

government at the pre-legislative stage (Figure 16.1), policy-making – including legislation down to the final drafting – is dominated, as we have seen in Chapters 14 and 15, by the Cabinet, Cabinet committees and the Departments.

The result of these factors is that it is virtually impossible in normal circumstances (i.e. government possession of a working majority) to bring a government down and, in practice, very difficult to engineer any defeat in the House of Commons. Of course, an opposition can make life awkward for a government in a number of ways, which include harassment of ministers in debates and at Question Time, motions of censure, the frequent use of delaying tactics and the suspension of pairing arrangements. Censure motions ('That this House has no confidence in Her Majesty's Government') are normally rare in periods of sizeable government majorities, but more frequent when the opposite situation prevails: there were three between 1976 and 1979, the final one – in March 1979 – resulting in defeat for the Labour Government. In February 1997, a Labour censure motion on the beef crisis was narrowly defeated (Box 16.3). Oppositions can delay the passage of government measures by stalling ploys at the committee stage of bills and by calls for frequent divisions at the second and third reading stages. Finally, oppositions can harass minority governments or those lacking a majority by breaking off pairing arrangements as Tony Blair did in December 1996, thereby putting pressure to turn up and vote on sick MPs or even those out of the country.

In fact, notwithstanding its adversarial context, much government business is conducted by mutual agreement between government and opposition and the question of opposition obstructiveness does not arise. Indeed, for much of the time, a consensual model is more appropriate to the House of Commons than an adversarial model: it has been calculated that between 1945 and 1983, 79 per cent of government bills were not divided against on second reading; the Opposition forced divisions against a mere 18 per cent of bills, and backbenchers of the other opposition parties forced divisions on the other 3 per cent (Van Mechelen and Rose, 1986, p. 57).

This consensual aspect of the House arises for several reasons. First, much government legislation – notably that of a technical or administrative kind

– is uncontroversial. Second, the Opposition may have its own motives for not pressing resistance too far: in addition to recognising the difficulties of governing, it wants to avoid being stigmatised as merely factious, provoking similar treatment when the roles of government and opposition are reversed, and to avoid opposing legislation which is popular or for which there is a mandate.

Increasing backbench dissent

In practice, governments may be defeated by a combination of their own backbenchers with MPs from the Official Opposition and the smaller parties. Between 1945 and 1970, no government was defeated in the House of Commons as a result of the dissenting votes of its own backbenchers but after 1970 the situation changed and cross-voting and the number of government defeats increased (Tables 16.5 and 16.6).

1970–4: The Conservative Government of Edward Heath (majority 30) was defeated six times, three of these defeats being on three-line whips. Defeats occurred as a result of cross-voting by backbench Conservatives on a range of issues, including immigration, the export of live animals for slaughter and the siting of a third London airport.

1974: The minority Labour Government suffered 17 defeats, all of them as a result of opposition parties combining, rather than cross-voting.

1974–9: The Labour Government (majority 3 to 1976, thereafter in a minority) suffered 42 defeats; 23 occurred as a result of its own backbenchers voting with the Opposition whilst the other 19

Table 16.5 Government defeats in the House of Commons, 1970–97

	Government	Number of defeats
1970–74	Conservative	6
1974	Labour	17
1974–79	Labour	42
1979–83	Conservative	1
1983–87	Conservative	2
1987–92	Conservative	1
1992–97	Conservative	3

Table 16.6 Dissent by government backbenchers, 1945–96

Rank order	Date	Party	% of divisions with dissenting votes
1	1974–9	Labour	20
2	1970–4	Conservative	19
3	1983–7	Conservative	17
4	1992–6	Conservative	14
5	1979–83	Conservative	13
6	1987–92	Conservative	12
7	1959–64	Conservative	12
8	1966–70	Labour	8
9	1974	Labour	7
10	1945–50	Labour	6
11	1950–1	Labour	2
12	1951–5	Conservative	1
13	1955–9	Conservative	1
14	1964–6	Labour	0.25

Source: Cowley, *Talking Politics*, 9:2, winter 1996–7.

defeats were brought about by combinations of opposition parties after it became a minority government in April 1976. Defeats occurred on economic policy and on the devolution bill.

1979–92: Backbench dissent continued but, with the Conservative Governments enjoying large or reasonable majorities (43, 1979–83; 144, 1983–7; 101, 1987–92), brought about government defeats on only four occasions: in 1982, on an amendment tightening the immigration rules; in 1986, on the second reading of the Shops Bill and on MPs' pay; and in 1990, on social security benefits for the elderly. However, the *threat* of cross-voting by its own backbenchers persuaded the 1979–83 government to retreat on several occasions, including student grants, charges for eye tests, reductions in the external services of the BBC, 'hotel' charges for patients in NHS hospitals, and the sale of parts of British Leyland to Americans, and forced concessions on various matters including housing benefits, the Police and Criminal Evidence Bill and the rate support grant from Mrs Thatcher's second adminis-

tration between 1983 and 1987.

1992–7: Conservative backbench rebelliousness intensified against the Major government whose small initial majority of 21 declined steadily as a result of by-election defeats and removal of the whip. Backbench dissent centred on Europe and was triggered by Thatcher's populist anti-Europeanism and by the financial cost and humiliation of Britain's expulsion from the ERM in September 1992. Normally involving between 20 and 30 MPs, backbench dissent was dangerous to the government first because it had the covert backing of several ministers and the open support of the former leader Mrs Thatcher and of three former party chairmen but mainly because of the disciplined stance adopted by the Labour Opposition. Thus, whereas the support of pro-European Labour cross-voters enabled Edward Heath to prevail against his own rebels and to avoid any defeat on Europe between 1970 and 1974, Labour's Euro-sceptics were prepared to support the official Labour pro-European line after 1992 in order to defeat the Major government. This combination of official Opposition and Conservative rebels resulted in 3 defeats for the 1992–7 Conservative Government, two of which were on European legislation (Table 16.6). First, the government was defeated on a Committee of the Regions amendment to the Maastricht Bill and then, despite a pact with the Ulster Unionists, it lost a vote on the Social Chapter in July 1993, only surviving by winning a vote of confidence the following day. Then, having removed the whip from 8 of its backbench rebels, the Major government suffered another defeat over the second stage of its plan to impose VAT on domestic fuel (Ludlam, 1996, pp. 106–20). Earlier, in October 1992, the *threat* that over two dozen of its backbenchers would support a Labour motion calling for a freeze on all pit closures led to the government agreeing to a review which temporarily delayed the closure programme.

A particular combination of circumstances is required for a government to be defeated in the House of Commons, including a small majority, a certain level of rebelliousness among its own backbenchers and a disciplined Opposition. As Philip Norton has argued: 'The larger the government's overall majority, the greater its capacity to absorb cross-voting by its own supporters. . . . The smaller

Table 16.7 Conservative rebellions on Europe, 1990–7

Year	Vote	Cross-voters	Abstainers	Total rebels	Rebels as % of backbench MPs	Notes
1992i	European Communities Amendment ('Maastricht') Bill 2nd Reading	22	4	26	10	
1992ii	European Communities Amendment ('Maastricht') Bill Paving Motion	26	6	32	13	Government maj. 3, with Lib.–Dem. votes
1993i	European Communities Amendment ('Maastricht') Bill Council of the Regions amendment	26	18	44	17	Government defeat by 22 votes
1993ii	European Communities Amendment ('Maastricht') Bill referendum amendment	38	13	51	20	Government win by 239 votes
1993iii	European Communities Amendment ('Maastricht') Bill Third Reading	41	5	46	18	Government majority 180
1993iv	Postponed Social Chapter vote, 22 July	23	1	24	9	Government defeated by 8 votes
1993v	Major's confidence vote, 23 July, on Social Chapter	0	1	1	0	Government maj. 40. Whip removed from abstainer
1994i	Major's confidence vote, 28 November, European Communities (Finance) Bill 2nd Reading	0	8	8	3	Lab. abstain. Govt majority 241. Whip removed from 8 rebels, 9th resigns
1994ii	Vote on Labour amendment to Finance Bill to abandon stage 2 of imposition of VAT on fuel	7	10	17	6	Government defeat by 8 votes. All but one of 'un-whipped' Euro-rebels rebel

Note: 'Abstainers' here refers to MPs known to have abstained on principle, rather than through non-political absence. Approximate percentage figures assume 80 MPs on the 'payroll' vote, (ie frontbenchers in government). A total of 86 Labour MPs defied their government in the 1967 vote, 89 in the 1971 vote, and 178 in the 1975 vote. 71 Labour MPs defied the official line to abstain on the Maastricht Bill Third Reading vote in 1993; 66 voted against the Treaty, 5 voted with the government.

Source: Adapted from Ludlam in Ludlam and Smith (1996) pp. 104–5.

BOX 16.3

Key votes in the final months of the 1992–7 Conservative Government

14 November 1996   The Government won a one-vote victory (303–302) on the BSE crisis:the nine Ulster Unionists voted against the Government.

16 December 1996   The Government defeated a Labour amendment on fishing policy (which claimed that not enough had been done to protect the industry) by 11 votes (316–305): concessions to Northern Irish fishermen led to crucial abstentions by the nine Ulster Unionists.

15 January 1997   After Labour had increased the pressure on the Government by ending the pairing arrangement, the Government won a vote on the Finance Bill by a comfortable majority,322–287: the Ulster Unionists voted with the Government.

21 January 1997   The Government survived an opposition attack on its health policy by 319 votes to 312,with three Ulster Unionists staying at home.

17 February 1997   The Government won a Labour censure motion on the handling of the beef crisis by the Agriculture Minister Douglas Hogg, 320 votes to 307. The nine Ulster Unionists abstained after the government made a last-minute concession of £9 million additional compensation to the Northern Ireland beef industry.

---

it is, the more vulnerable the government is to defeat as a consequence of its own supporters voting with opposition MPs' (Norton, 1995–6, p. 113). The former situation prevailed between 1979 and 1992; the latter situation was the case between 1970 and 1974, between 1992 and 1997 and especially between 1974 and 1979.

Contemporary trends in Commons voting behaviour can now be summarised. The government controls parliament and the bulk of its legislation still goes through without dissent even in the more volatile parliamentary circumstances prevailing after 1970. On the other hand, especially when it has a small or even no majority, it certainly needs to exercise more vigilance to get its way than it did 40 years ago and has become susceptible to occasional embarrassing defeats (Box 16.3 and Table 16.7).

Private members' legislation

Only a small proportion of private members' legislation reaches the statute book but it has become an important method for making laws on controversial social matters with a strong moral dimension. Private members' legislation liberalised the law on capital punishment, homosexuality, divorce and abortion in the 1960s, outlawed video 'nasties', compelled front-seat passengers to wear seat belts, restricted advertising on cigarettes in the 1980s and banned cruelty to wild animals (although not fox-hunting) in the mid-1990s. Normally such legisla-

tion requires government support, including government Commons time, if it is to succeed. For example, it was for lack of such support that private members' bills designed to move Britain on to Central European Time, to protect whistleblowers at work and to force water companies to conserve water failed in the 1995–6 session.

Commons workload

The legislative burden upon parliament has increased massively in recent decades primarily because of the length rather than the number of Bills and Statutory Instruments. The Water Bill (1989) – only one of several very extensive bills – was nearly 350 pages. The 1996 Finance Bill was the longest ever, its 408 pages comparing with an average length for finance bills of 103 pages between 1974 and 1979 and 193 pages between 1979 and 1995. In 1991, the House approved 2,200 pages of legislation and 2,945 pages of Statutory Instruments. Much of the increased workload necessarily has fallen on Standing Committees, sittings of which increased from under 200 to over 300 per session on legislation and from nothing to between 45 and 95 per session on Statutory Instruments between the 1960s and the late 1980s (Norton, 1992, p. 141). Such a huge increase has led to serious concern about the adequacy of parliamentary scrutiny of legislation. The number of Statutory Instruments – regulations issued without reference to MPs – doubled to over

Table 16.8 Departmental select committees as at 7 November 1997

Committee	Chairman	Party
Agriculture	Peter Luff	Conservative
Culture, Media and Sport	Gerald Kaufman	Labour
Defence	Bruce George	Labour
Education and Employment	Rotating amongst members	
Environment, Transport and Regional Affairs	Rotating amongst members	
Foreign Affairs	Donald Anderson	Labour
Health	David Hinchliffe	Labour
Home Affair	Chris Mullin	Labour
International Development	Bowen Wells	Conservative
Northern Ireland Affairs	Peter Brooke	Conservative
Science and Technology	Dr Michael Clark	Conservative
Scottish Affairs	David Marshall	Labour
Social Security	Archy Kirkwood	Liberal Democrat
Trade and Industry	Martin O'Neill	Labour
Treasury	Giles Radice	Labour
Welsh Affairs	Martyn Jones	Labour

Source: House of Commons Information Service.

3,000 per year between 1989 and 1994 compared with 1,900 per year in the early 1980s and a mere 543 in 1979. Some commentators see the increasing use of SIs as a way for governments to evade parliamentary opposition on small but politically sensitive issues.

Select Committees

Parliamentary reformers from the 1960s advocated the greater use of *Departmental Select Committees* (DSCs) to improve scrutiny of the executive and their case was reaffirmed by the Select Committee on Procedure (1978) which recommended the establishment of a new system of select committees to provide regular scrutiny of the work of every government department. These proposals were implemented by Norman St John Stevas as Leader of the House in 1979. Some existing Select Committees were abolished; those retained included Public Accounts, which scrutinises the government's use of public funds, the Parliamentary Commissioner (to

oversee the work of the Ombudsman), Statutory Instruments and European legislation. The new departure was the introduction of fourteen new Departmental Select Committee (DSCs) to scrutinise the work of government departments (although not the Lord Chancellor's Office). The list of DSCs in November 1997 is shown in Table 16.8. Their task is 'to examine the expenditure, administration and policy in the principal government departments . . . and associated bodies' and to make reports with recommendations. In conducting their investigations, they can send for 'persons, papers and records'. With all except one of the DSCs composed of eleven members allocated according to the party balance of the House as a whole, the DSCs gave employment to 176 backbenchers in the 1992 Parliament, the total party composition being 96 Conservative (54 per cent) 70 Labour (40 per cent), 5 Liberal Democrat (3 per cent) and 5 minor parties (3 per cent). In order to increase the authority of their reports, of which they produced over 900 between 1979 and November 1994, they generally seek consensus among their all-party membership.

The Departmental Select Committees (DSCs) have been described by former Cabinet Minister Michael Jopling as: 'The most important development in parliamentary procedure in my thirty years in the House. Select Committees are giving backbenchers teeth with which to tackle the executive'. (the *Guardian,* 22 March 1997). They undoubtedly constitute a marked improvement on the Commons machinery to scrutinise the executive available before 1979. Their reports in the mid-1990s included criticisms of the Bank of England's handling of the collapse of the Barings merchant bank, government complacency over the safety of roll-on roll-off ferries, the failure of health ministers and managers to tackle the chronic underfunding of the London ambulance service and the shortcomings of government proposals on long-term care for the elderly. How effective are the DSCs in scrutinising government and influencing policy? Two possible effects may be noticed. First, they can have a *pre-emptive* – or what Philip Norton has described as a deterrent – effect. Griffith and Ryle point out that there is 'much evidence that Ministers and civil servants are influenced in policy-making by the knowledge that what they propose may well come under the scrutiny of these committees and by the very process of committee inquiries' (Griffith and Ryle, 1989, p. 520). The thought that they may be harshly cross-examined in public on it may deter ministers from pursuing a policy they might be unable to justify in that situation (Norton, 1994b, p. 30). Second, the DSCs may have a *delayed reaction* – or, in Norton's words, a 'delayed drop' – effect, forcing the government slowly, after initial denials and rebuttals, to accept their point of view. A good example is the Defence Select Committee's pressuring of government over the 'Gulf War Syndrome' (Box 16.4). Greater specialisation and openness underlie the impact of the investigative Select Committees. The increased specialisation comes in the forms of greater expertise among MPs, some of whom achieve formidable reputations in particular fields; the specialised assistance available to each DSC; and most of all perhaps in the capacity of the select committees to take evidence from outside pressure groups and academics. As well as increasing the authority of their reports, this last

feature enhances public involvement in the political process. The DSCs have contributed to greater openness in government by conducting their meetings in open session and by publishing their conclusions, normally backed by a wealth of data, in substantial reports.

However, critics of the DSCs point out that, despite the frequent excellence of their reports and the occasional publicity achieved by their investigative sessions, they lack real clout. Thus, their occasional effectiveness is offset by their more frequent lack of impact, their rare displays of toughness by feebleness and deference. They are the product of 'an executive-dominated system and lack the resources or prestige to sustain the kind of inquisatorial role that US congressional committees have long enjoyed' (the *Guardian*, 22 March 1995). Specific criticisms of the DSCs include

- *insufficient resources*: Most DSCs lack the staff and budgets which would enable them to carry out substantial independent research.
- *inadequate personnel*: Although a few of their number make a name for themselves as experts in their fields, many members of DSCs lack the knowledge and skills required for genuine effectiveness. Few backbenchers choose to make such work their career.
- *limited remit*: Although they often try to get round the restriction by considering subjects about to lead to government legislation, the DSCs are not permitted to consider legislation. Some reformers, however, believe that legislation would be improved if DSCs were allowed to examine it.
- *limited powers*: Although normally attending when requested, Ministers are not obliged to answer questions: for example, both Edwina Currie over salmonella in eggs and Leon Brittan on the Westland affair stalled before their respective committees. The government can on occasion prevent civil servants from attending the DSCs – as, for example, over Westland, when the Defence Committee was not allowed to interview five named civil servants (three from the DTI and two from the PM's Office) and was given the Cabinet Secretary and the Permanent Under-Secretary at the DTI to interrogate instead. Also, under the 1980 Memorandum of Guidance

BOX 16.4
Defence Select Committee and Gulf War Syndrome

February 1991	End of Gulf War.
June 1993	First signs of illnesses among veterans.
October 1993	Ministry of Defence (MoD) establishes medical assessment programme but later denies existence of syndrome linked to service in the Gulf.
November 1995	Defence Select Committee report condemns the MoD for its 'hopelessly inadequate' response to the mysterious illnesses suffered by Gulf War veterans,contrasting the 'compassion' shown by the Clinton Administration to US veterans with the 'scepticism, defensiveness and general torpor' of the British response. The Committee calls for more research into the possible causes of the illnesses, especially the 'cocktail' of inoculations and anti-nerve-gas tablets with which British and US, but not French, troops were treated prior to the war.
January 1996	On Medical Research Council advice, the MoD announces an epidemiological survey, but no immediate research into causes.
October 1996	MoD admits Parliament was misled about the use of dangerous pesticides in the Gulf.
February 1997	MoD rejects compensation for victims of 'Gulf War Syndrome'.
March 1997	Defence Select Committee calls for disabled Gulf War veterans exposed to organo-phosphate chemicals to be given immediate compensation by the government. Following the Committee's Report, the Labour Opposition demands the resignation of the armed forces minister, Nicholas Soames.The Defence Select Committee also calls for faster settlement of pension claims and again requests direct research into the causes of Gulf War Syndrome.
May 1997	Blair government announces it is giving 'top priority' to Gulf War Syndrome, is allocating new resources to researching the effects of the combination of pills and vaccines as well as of exposure to organo-phosphate chemicals and chemical weapons and will consider extra financial help to victims.

Sources. Based on articles from *The Guardian,* 21 March 1997; *The Observer,* 11 May 1997.

(Osmotherly Rules) to civil servants appearing before the DSCs, civil servants are told that they may withhold information in the interests of 'good government' or national security, and that they should not disclose advice given to Ministers, inter-departmental exchanges on policy issues, the level at which decisions were taken, the manner in which a Minister has consulted his colleagues, information about Cabinet committees and their discussions,'questions in the field of political controversy' or 'sensitive information of a commercial or economic nature'.

- *no sanctions against government:* The DSCs cannot even ensure their reports are debated on the floor of the House of Commons, and few in fact are debated. Parliamentary procedure provides for the debate of at most six reports per session(two in each of the three Estimates Days allocated): thus, only a quarter of DSC Reports were debated by the House between 1979 and 1988.

- *lack of influence:* Ministers can and habitually do ignore DSC reports. Thus, although the Trade and Industry Select Committee achieved widespread publicity in 1992–3 during the public campaign against pit closures, the President of the Board of Trade Michael Heseltine brushed aside its recommendations once the furore had died down. Most of the 150 DSC recommendations accepted by government in 1985–6 were on minor matters.

- *power of the whips:* Selection of MPs to serve on DSCs should be a matter for the Select Committee on Selection but in practice the party whips have an important role, thereby compromising the Select Committees' independence of the Executive. The whips' influence came to light in July 1992 when a newly-devised rule that a Conservative MP could not serve for more than two successive terms on a Select Committee was the means by which the independent-minded Conservative Nicholas Winterton was ousted from the chairmanship of the Health Select Committee, to be succeeded by the more compliant Marion Roe (Norton, 1994b, pp. 29–33).

A balanced consideration of the influence of the

Departmental Select Committees needs to bear in mind, therefore, that the select committees are 'in the business of scrutiny and exposure, not of government' (Drewry, 1989, p. 426).

The Public Accounts Committee (PAC). Established in 1860, the PAC has a central role in the Commons' scrutiny of government expenditure. A committee of fifteen members, chaired by a senior member of the Opposition, it is particularly concerned to ensure the taxpayer gets value for money from public spending. It has been powerfully assisted in its work since 1983 by the *National Audit Office,* an independent body directed by the *Comptroller and Auditor-General* (CAG) with a staff of 900 which produces 52 Value for Money reports every year. Reports of both the PAC and the CAG are often extremely critical of government departments. In 1995, for example,one PAC report condemned methods used by Ministers in the sale of London's County Hall, including lack of openness, allowing the purchaser over-favourable deferred terms and unfair treatment of one bidder, the London School of Economics, whilst another condemned the 'appalling management' of the British Embassy in Yemen, which admitted it had turned a blind eye to bribery, fraud, corruption and black-market currency dealings worth nearly £1 million among its diplomats. The previous year (1994), the PAC had turned its attention to quangos, highlighting 21 cases of fraud and management by these bodies in its report 'The Proper Conduct of Public Business'. CAG reports in 1995 severely reprimanded the Ministry of Defence for not pursuing vigorously a corruption scandal which led to the payment of at least £1.3 million in bribes to an official for ammunition contracts, censured the Metropolitan Police for failure to observe basic financial procedures which exposed it to massive fraud in which a senior administrator stole over £5 million from his employers; and revealed taxpayers had lost at least £40 million in the sale of the Property Services Agency to private companies. The 'economy, efficiency and effectiveness' audits of the PAC and the CAG have thus produced some hard-hitting reports. However, PAC reports are rarely debated by the House and, when they are, are poorly attended and receive little public attention. Moreover, certain aspects of public expenditure are excluded from the CAG's remit, one being the

Sovereign's expenditure under the Civil List which came to light in 1992. None the less, the scrutiny of government expenditure by parliamentary officers has improved considerably in the last decade; what remains inadequate is parliament's own ability to deploy to maximum effect the information they provide (see further, Liddell, 1994, pp. 46–50).

Scrutiny of European legislation

With an increasing proportion of UK legislation emanating from the European Union, parliamentary surveillance of European directives and regulations is a matter of some importance. The task involves both Houses of Parliament. In the Commons, the system was strengthened in 1991 by the addition of two Standing Committees of thirteen members each to the already-existing Select Committee on European Legislation (the 'Scrutiny Committee'). The Scrutiny Committee refers EU legislation which it sees as requiring further scrutiny and debate to one of the two Standing Committees which have the power (1) to question ministers and officials; (2) debate the merits of the issues at stake on a substantive motion; and (3) refer documents for debate on the floor of the House, subject to the agreement of the Leader of the House. However, debate by the House as a whole can lead not to amendment but only to a 'take note' motion, in the hope that the government will modify its position. The House of Lords also has a scrutiny committee, the Select Committee on the European Communities (1974), whose task is to decide which of the hundreds of EU documents deposited with it each month require scrutiny because they raise important questions of policy or principle or for other reasons. The scrutiny work is then carried out by six sub-committees whose reports are normally debated by the House.

The Maastricht Treaty stipulated that national parliaments should receive Commission legislative proposals in good time for information or possible examination. However, in its highly critical 24th Report (1995), the Commons Scrutiny Committee asserted that this declaration had proved to be 'a sham' and that EU law 'increasingly seemed to be made in a private club', with the Brussels Commission routinely requiring Ministers to endorse laws for which there is no formal or official text. The Select Committee warned that if future practice did not conform to basic democratic procedures, it would consider a boycott.It listed over 40 examples of proposed laws that it had had to consider without being able to read a formal text or *after* a decision had been taken by the Council of Ministers. Two specific examples of the problem appeared in summer 1995: after late French changes, an EU draft directive on pollution prevention became available in English only two days before European Environmental Ministers met to make decisions on it; a month later, the English text of an EU directive on health checks for the trade in cattle and pigs was not available until the day after the directive was adopted. The Committee demanded a minimum 4-week period between an official text being available in each of the national languages and the taking of a decision in the Council but was still pressing for the timely receipt of an English language text of routine EU legislation in 1996. By then ideas for tightening the scrutiny procedure had been broached within the Labour Party: these included first that Departmental Ministers attending monthly meetings with their European counterparts should be required to brief the relevant Commons committee on the agenda before and after their meetings; and second that 10 minutes in every departmental session of Commons question time would be set aside for ministers to be examined on their EU policies (Adonis, 1993, pp. 155–7, 222–4; Kingdom, 1994–5, pp. 126–7; Norton, 1995b, pp. 168–73; *The Observer*, 15 October 1995; the *Guardian,* 8 December 1995; 28 August 1996).

Reform of the House of Commons

For a variety of reasons including parliament's declining public reputation and its weaknesses in relation to the executive and the scrutiny of European legislation, reform of parliament came to the fore in the 1990s. However, by 1997 only minor reforms had been implemented in the House of Commons: the Jopling reforms of procedure (1994) and the Blair reform of Prime Minister's Question Time (1997). The Jopling reforms, based on the recommendations of an inquiry chaired by the former Conservative minister, Michael Jopling, reformed working hours of the Commons,provided for fewer

Friday sittings to make way for constituency work, morning sessions on Wednesdays, early 7 p.m. finishes on some Thursdays, a 10-minute limit on speeches from 6 p.m. to 9 p.m. and a formal timetable for government bills after they have won second reading. Critics of the changes complained that they unduly shortened the working week (by about a quarter) and deprived the opposition of a significant weapon: the ability to exploit late and unpredictable procedures. Tony Blair changed Prime Ministers Question Time from a twice-a-week quarter of an hour event on Tuesdays and Thursdays to one taking place once a week for half an hour on Wednesdays. The aim of the reform was to transform the nature of PMQT from its 'bearpit',conflictual atmosphere to one involving more considered and reflective exchanges between PM and Leader of the Opposition. For most reformers, these two reforms constitute only a modest start to improving the legislative, scrutinising and debating functions of the Commons and Box 16.5 sets out some major reform proposals.

The House of Lords

The powers of the House of Lords have been considerably reduced in the twentieth century, so much so that by the 1950s – according to one commentator – the institution was 'dying in its sleep' (Hennessy, 1987). However, since the failure of the 1968 attempt to reform its composition, the Lords has undergone a resurgence and this section examines the overall significance of this recent revival. Has the Upper House become 'the only constitutional counterweight to elective dictatorship' (Brazier, 1991, p. 73) or has the constitutional impact of its new-found vigour been exaggerated (Adonis, 1993, p. 247)?

Powers and functions

By convention, the House of Lords is part of the legislative sovereign – 'the Queen-in-Parliament'. Constitutionally, therefore, despite its reduced powers, the Upper House remains an essential part of the legislative process. By the Parliament Act of 1911, the Lords completely lost its power to delay or amend money bills: these go for the Royal Assent

---

BOX 16.5

The House of Commons: proposals for reform

Representation

Proportional representation.	To ensure fairer representation of national opinion.
Fixed-term parliaments.	To abolish advantage to governments of control over election date.
Reduce number of MPs by one-third, about 200.	To provide opportunity to enhance quality of Commons by improving MPs' pay and research facilities.

Legislation

Provide for pre-legislative scrutiny of draft bills.	To pre-empt need for last-minute mass revision of bills by civil servants.
Reform Standing Committees on lines of Special Standing Committees (introduced 1980 but little used).	To improve scrutiny of government legislation.
Give Select Committees oversight of legislation in their areas.	
Introduce ability to amend Statutory Instruments which at present must be accepted or rejected as a whole.	To encourage more careful and more serious scrutiny of delegated legislation
Allow more than one session for bills to complete parliamentary scrutiny.	To reduce chance of badly-drafted bills becoming law.
Provide for automatic time-tabling of bills, with each part allocated some time; alternatively, give Speaker control over time-tabling.	To permit balanced scrutiny of legislation and eliminate partisanship of guillotine procedure.
Take Committee stage of bills before, not as at present after, the Second Reading.	To increase influence of the Committees.
Allow constitutional bills to be debated in committee rather than floor of the House.	To prevent sabotage of constitutional legislation by opponents.
Give fixed number of Private Members' Bills guaranteed government time each year.	To prevent government killing Private Members' bills which have majority support.

---

one month after leaving the House of Commons, whether approved by the Lords or not. But it retained other powers which included the power to delay non-money bills for up to two successive sessions (reduced to one session only by the Parliament Act of 1949). The present powers of the House of Lords – as defined by the Parliament Acts of 1911 and 1949 – are as follows:

1. To delay non-money bills for up to one year;
2. To veto (a) bills to prolong the life of parliament beyond the statutory five-year period; (b) private

bills (not to be confused with private members' bills); and (c) delegated legislation.

The bulk of the work of the House of Lords may be conveniently summarised in terms of the following functions:

- *Deliberation*: the provision of a forum for debates on matters of current interest;
- *Legislation*: revision of House of Commons bills, giving Ministers the opportunity for second thoughts; initiation of non-controversial legisla-

---

BOX 16.5 *(continued)*

Scrutiny

More debate of Select Committee reports on the floor of the House.

To foster greater Executive accountability

Require Departmental Select Committees to investigate Departments' expenditure,extend remit of Public Accounts Committee to include all public spending, improve staffing levels of PAC and NAC, and increase Estimates days from present four or so per session.

To strengthen Commons' ability to act as a financial watchdog on the raising and spending of public funds.

Extend scrutiny and debate of European documents and policies beyond present Select Committee on European Legislation and two special (European) Standing Committees (established in 1991).

To improve scrutiny and debate of European legislation and policies.

Require Ministers to answer departmental questions regularly in committees as well as on floor of the House; also monitor questions Ministers have refused to answer through House of Commons Public Service Committee and appoint new senior officer with power to call for government papers to adjudicate when information is being withheld.

To force Ministers to answer questions by MPs: between November 1994 and March 1995 668 questions were refused answers by Ministers(*Guardian*, 24 March 1995).

Forum for debate

Improve resources, research facilities and working conditions of MPs. Improve capability of Opposition by secondment of civil servants to Shadow Front Bench.
Accord minor parties greater role in planning Commons business and greater status by salaries for their leaders.
Clarify Commons documents, language, and procedure.

To modernise the House,improve its sources of information and make the imbalance of facilities between government and opposition parties less pronounced, thereby rendering it a more effective forum for debate.

Ethical standards of MPs

Enforce 1996 Code of Conduct rigorously, including full disclosure of outside interests.

To improve the public standing of parliament.

---

tion, including government bills, private bills (promoted by bodies outside parliament, e.g. local authorities) and bills by individual peers; and consideration of delegated legislation;

- *Scrutiny*: the Lords subjects government policy and administration to scrutiny through questions and through the work of its select committees (e.g. European Communities, Science and Technology);
- *Supreme court of appeal*: the Lords is the ultimate court of appeal in the United Kingdom.

Composition

Membership of the Upper House is determined by birth, creation (by the Crown on the advice of the prime minister) and position. Nearly two-thirds (765) of its 1,207 members are hereditary peers, just under one-third (391) are life peers and there are twenty-six Church of England bishops (including two archbishops) who hold their seats until they retire and nineteen Law Lords (including the Lord Chancellor). Eighty-five (7.0 per cent) of its members are women, 69 of them life peers and 16 hereditary. Its composition has been significantly affected by the Life Peerages Act 1958, which empowered the Crown to create life peers and peeresses, and the Peerages Act 1963, which allowed hereditary peers to disclaim their titles and admitted hereditary peeresses into the House of Lords in their own right. Nominally very large for an Upper House, the Lords is much reduced in practice by non-eligibility and non-attendance: thus, in the 1996–7 session, 137 peers were not eligible (through leave of absence or not obtaining the writ of summons) whilst only 457 of its members attended on a regular basis. Regular attenders compose the 'working House' – defined as those peers who attend at least a third of sittings per session. Life peers – outnumbered roughly 2:1 by hereditary peers in the House as a whole – figure disproportionately in the 'working House', constituting 53 per cent to the hereditary peers' 47 per cent in the 1996–7 session.

Political allegiances

Party functions rather differently in the Upper House compared with the Commons but is still very important. One marked difference is the large number of peers who choose to remain independent of political ties – **the crossbenchers**. However, over two-thirds of peers holding firm political views support one of the major parties, with the Conservatives in an overall majority and the Liberal Democrats better represented and Labour worse represented than in the Commons (Table 16.9). New Labour Prime Minister Tony Blair moved swiftly to reduce the Conservative advantage in the Lords by appointing the largest number of Labour peers for decades (31 compared with 15 new Conservative peers in August 1997). However, the Conservatives retained a very large advantage over Labour of over 300 in the upper house.

Conservative strength in the 'working House' is less pronounced owing to the conscientiousness of Labour and Liberal Democrat peers. In the 1996–7 session, for example, 77 per cent of Labour peers, 74

Crossbenchers: peers who choose to remain independent of party ties. They are called crossbenchers because of the position they occupy in the Upper House between the two seats of facing benches.

Table 16.9 Party strengths in the House of Lords as at 22 May 1997

Conservative	477 (48.9%)
Labour	120 (12.3%)
Liberal Democrat	55 (5.6%)
Crossbenchers	323 (33.2%)
	974 (100%)

Source: House of Lords Information Service.

---

per cent of Liberal Democrats but only 48 per cent of Conservatives attended over one-third of sittings. However, even in the 'working house', the Conservatives are still by far the largest party (Table 16.10).

Recent behaviour

House of Lords activity has increased steadily over recent decades (Table 16.11). The breakdown of its time for the 1996–7 session was as shown in Figure 16.2. As can be seen, the Upper House spends rather over half its time on legislation – government bills, private members' bills and delegated legislation (statutory instruments); between one quarter and one-third on debates – general debates, debates on unstarred questions and debates on the reports of the European Communities and Science and Technology Committees; and under one-tenth on

---

Table 16.10 Party strengths in the 'working House', 1996–7

Peers attending at least 33% of sittings, 1996–7

Conservative	230 (49.7%)
Labour	92 (19.9%)
Liberal Democrat	41 (8.8%)
Crossbenchers	96 (20.7%)
Others	4 (0.9%)
	463 (100%)

Source: Calculated from information supplied by House of Lords Information Service.

Table 16.11 Growth in activity of the House of Lords, 1950–97

	1950–1	1960–1	1970–1	1990–1	1996–7
Average daily attendance	86	142	265	321	381
Total hours sat	292	599	966	1089	526*
Average length of sitting (hrs/mins)	3.03	4.48	6.19	7.10	6.40

* This figure is distorted because the 1996–7 session had only 79 sitting days because of the General Election.
  Figures for previous years are more typical: 935 (1955–6), 904 (1994–5), 971 (1993–4).

Sources: Griffith and Ryle (1989) p. 472; House of Lords Information Office.

oral questions (i.e. starred questions not leading to debate) and ministerial statements. How effective in its major legislative and scrutiny tasks is it?

Legislation

The Lords accepts certain limitations on its own power of delay. The main guiding rule – firmly

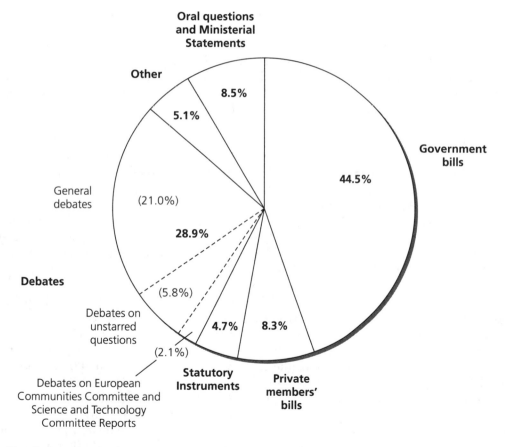

Source: Derived from figures produced by the House of Lords Information Office.

Figure 16.2 How the House of Lords spends its time (percentage of total time for the 1996–97 session)

Table 16.12 Government defeats in the House of Lords, 1964–97

Years	Government	Number of defeats
1964–70	Labour	116
1970–74	Conservative	25
1974	Labour	15
1974–79	Labour	347
1979–83	Conservative	45
1983–87	Conservative	62
1987–92	Conservative	72
1992–97	Conservative	62

established by Conservative Opposition peers in the immediate post-war period – is that the Upper House does not oppose measures included in the governing party's manifesto at the previous election (the Salisbury/Addison doctrine). In addition, the Lords rarely presses an amendment or delays a measure to the point where the Parliament Acts (Parliament Act 1911, S.2, as amended by Parliament Act 1949, S.1) have to be invoked: i.e. the requirement that if the Commons passes a public Bill in two successive sessions and the Lords rejects it in both of them, the Bill receives the Royal Assent after the second rejection. On only four occasions since 1911 has this clause of the Parliament Act been employed – the Government of Ireland Act (1914), the Welsh Church Act (1914), the Parliament Act (1949) and the War Crimes Act (1991). This last Bill – which allowed former Nazi war criminals living in Britain to be tried in British courts – was twice rejected by the Lords but forced through by the Conservative Government using Parliament Act procedures. Of more importance, however, are those cases where the Lords has passed adverse amendments on government legislation, thereby causing delay. A Conservative-dominated Lords often subjected Labour Governments in the 1960s and 1970s to legislative defeats, and this Upper House rebelliousness continued although on a far lesser scale against Conservative Governments after 1979. On average, whereas the Lords inflicted 70 defeats a year on Labour Governments between 1974 and 1979, it defeated Conservative

Administrations only 13 times a year between 1979 and 1997 (Table 16.12).

The constitutional and political significance of the Lords' so-called 'independence' is controversial. One recent commentator regards the Lords as the only constitutional bulwark against dictatorship, as it had proved its capacity to treat the legislation of both parties 'with something approaching impartial rigour', whilst, by contrast, another academic maintains that although it may no longer be a rubber stamp, it still has not provided anything more than 'minor obstructions' to the government's legislative programme (Brazier, 1991, p. 73; Adonis, 1993, p. 247). Where does the truth lie? These observations help place the debate in perspective.

First, government defeats in the Lords still do not occur very often. Between 1979 and 1997, Conservative Administrations suffered 241 adverse votes in 2,859 divisions (8.4 per cent). However, this rate of defeat is greater than that of their Conservative predecessors: 3.7 per cent, 1959–64 and 5.7 per cent, 1970–4. Second, defeats on major legislation are even more rare. Moreover, governments do not invariably react to hostile amendments by 'thinking again': on the contrary, they frequently use their Commons majority to reverse the Lords' vote and then force the Upper House to give way by threatening to use the Parliament Act or since 1979 to call upon their 'reserve army' of peers in the Lords. Thus, the third Thatcher Administration used its Commons majority to reverse hostile Lords' amendments on, for example, charges for eye tests, increases in dental charges, and the preservation of local authority contracts compliance protecting job opportunities for disabled people, and, also in 1988, mobilised large numbers of 'backwoodsmen' peers to vote down an amendment to its poll tax legislation which would have required the government to relate the charge to ability to pay. The amendment was defeated 317–183: on only one another occasion since 1931 had 500 or more peers turned out to vote (1971). In contrast, the first two Thatcher Administrations gave way more often when defeated in the Lords, accepting quite important changes over school transport in rural areas, the sale of council houses built for the elderly, and interim councils for its abolished authorities (1984). Third, Lords' rebelliousness has a relatively narrow focus – issues affecting the Constitution, local government, the old, the disabled, the countryside, and the voluntary services and their users (Adonis, 1993, p. 238; Welfare, 1992).

The truth, therefore, appears to be that the House of Lords can cause political embarrassment to the government of the day, but no more. The Upper House has on numerous occasions impeded government legislation and forced concessions, although generally on minor issues. But it is far from being a severe constitutional obstacle to the party in power. Nor can it be said to treat the legislation of both parties impartially, being much more severe on Labour legislation than on Conservative. Its relatively greater 'independence' dates from the failure of the Parliament (no.2) Bill (1969) which would have reduced its delaying power to six months and eliminated the voting rights of hereditary peers. The failure of this reform attempt boosted its morale by prompting the realisation that it had a valuable role to fulfil after all. The advent of life peers after 1958 enhanced the quality of debates and the televising of the Lords from 1983 increased its prestige. After 1979, when large government majorities and weak oppositions prevailed, the Lords did become one of the main sources of resistance to government, but only in a minor key.

Another significant trend in recent decades has been the greater use made of the Lords by governments to revise and generally tidy up their legislation. The extent of this change may be gauged from the fact that between 1987 and 1990 the Upper House made 7,868 amendments to government bills compared with 2,854 amendments to government legislation between 1970 and 1973. Most of these changes are introduced by Ministers. Because much of this tidying-up process has to be done hurriedly at the end of sessions, one peer has described the Upper Chamber as 'a gilded dustpan and brush'. Suggested causes for this development include inadequate consultation, government indecisiveness and poor drafting in the early stages of legislation, but whatever the reasons, it has made the House of Lords an increasingly attractive target for pressure groups (Shell, 1992a, pp. 165–6).

Deliberation and scrutiny

The House of Lords – which devotes approximately one day per week to general debate – is often praised for the overall quality of its debates but their overall impact is probably not large. Its exercise of its scrutiny functions (through Questions and Select Committees) is of greater consequence. Thus, Conservative Governments after 1979 were embarrassed by *ad hoc* Select Committee Reports on Unemployment (1979–82) and Trade and Industry (1984–5) and by the Science and Industry Select Committee's criticisms of cuts in the government's budget for scientific research (1991). In addition, the House of Lords Select Committee on the European Communities, which considers initiatives proposed by the EC Commission, is well-staffed, able to consider EC proposals on their merits, and expert; it produces over 20 reports a year which, like other Lords Select Committee reports but unlike their equivalents in the Commons, are all debated. Overall, however, the House of Lords has made no attempt to establish through its Select Committees a mechanism for consistent, comprehensive scrutiny of government but has rather used them to fill gaps left by the Commons Select Committee system.

Reform of the House of Lords

Reform of the Lords moved swiftly up the political agenda with the advent of the new Labour Government in May 1997. Labour's election manifesto promised to end the right of hereditary peers to sit and vote in the Upper House and to review the system of appointment of life peers in order to achieve over time a second chamber that more accurately reflected the proportion of votes cast at the last election. It specifically ruled out simply replacing a Conservative-dominated Upper House with a Labour-dominated one. A Cabinet Committee chaired by Lord Irvine began work in January 1998 on the task of deciding the powers and composition of the new Upper House after the rights of hereditary peers had been removed. The Liberal Democrats – and other individuals and groups – also favour reform (Table 16.12). After its heavy electoral defeat, the Conservative Party moved towards a pragmatic acceptance that reform was imminent but was prepared to be critical over its terms. The position of William Hague and Lord Cranborne, the Conservative leader in the Lords, in early 1998 was that they would resist abolition of the

---

BOX 16.6
The House of Lords: proposals for reform

Source	Proposed reforms
Labour	Two-stage process: (1) end right of hereditary peers to sit and vote in the Upper House, leaving present legislative powers unchanged; (2) review system of appointment of life peers to ensure that over time party appointees reflect more accurately the proportion of votes cast at the last election without according a majority to any one political party. Appoint committee of both Houses to undertake wide-ranging review of possible further change and propose reforms.
Liberal Democrat	Move over two parliaments to a predominantly elected second chamber using proportional representation; new Upper House will be able to represent the nations and regions of the UK and play a key role in scrutinising European legislation.
The Economist, 4–10 November 1995	New Second Chamber elected preferably by a different method to the House of Commons and on a different cycle. To possess similar powers of delay and revision to present Upper House plus more explicit powers to act as a constitutional backstop. If devolution succeeds, could also act as a forum for regional interests.
Institute for Public Policy Research (1991)	Replace with Second Chamber elected by proportional representation (Single Transferable Vote) for fixed four-year term; subordinate as now to Commons in relation to financial and general legislation but equal powers concerning constitutional legislation and amendments.
Tony Benn Commonwealth of Britain Bill (1991)	Replace with elected Second Chamber drawn from England, Scotland and Wales in proportion to their populations with powers to delay legislation for one year and Statutory Instruments for one month.

---

hereditary peerage if the government failed to set out acceptable long-term plans for the second chamber.

The main stumbling block to reform in the past has been lack of agreement among reformers. On the last occasion (1968) when broad agreement on reform existed between the parties, Labour left and Conservative right combined to defeat the proposals in the Commons. The Labour legislation then would have phased out hereditary peers and provided for a chamber of appointed members with voting rights dependent upon attending at least 30 per cent of sittings, and with the government guaranteed a 10 per cent majority and the delaying power reduced to six months (see further, Coxall and Robins, 1998, p. 147). The Conservatives themselves were prepared to consider reform in the 1970s, and the Report of the Home Committee (1978) recommended phasing out hereditary peers (with a view to the Upper House becoming one-third appointed and two-thirds elected) and restoring the House's delaying power to two years. But these proposals did not become party policy and after 1979 the party standpoint became retention of the Lords with its existing position and powers. In the late 1970s and 1980s Labour favoured abolition of the Lords but moved away from this stance in 1979 towards the reformist position it shares with the Liberal Democrats. The 1990s saw a variety of other reform schemes which sought to 'mend' the institution rather than simply preserve it as it is or end it.

There is widespread support for the abolition of the political power of the hereditary peerage, but one concern expressed even by supporters of Labour's reform plans is that, in the interim situation pending the complete reform of the Upper House, too much patronage power will reside with the Prime Minister, thereby turning the House of Lords into the 'ultimate quango'. Such critics also fear that full reform may not follow within a reasonable length of time, thereby permitting the 'ermined quango' to become permanent by default. Andrew Adonis has suggested that this problem might be resolved in part by the establishment of an independent appointments body with the task of ensuring an overall balance between the parties and a steady stream of able non-party appointees (*The Observer*, 8 December, 1996). In fact, the second stage of reform, involving decisions about the ultimate composition of the Lords as well as its precise powers, raises the much larger problem for Labour of whether ultimately it wants a more powerful second chamber than the present House or a less powerful one. Some commentators, indeed, have discerned a 'Second Chamber paradox' regarding reform: that, whilst election provides the only appropriate basis for a second chamber in a democracy, reform along such lines – by increasing the legitimacy of the Upper House – might transform it into a dangerous rival of the Commons, thereby precipitating more bitter and more frequent clashes between the two bodies. This fear, however, may be exaggerated as most modern states have elected second chambers without facing this situation.

Retrospect and prospect

Parliament as an institution has changed considerably over recent decades. The increased propensity of MPs to defy the Whips by voting against the party line, the activities of a wide range of Select Committees, the growth in importance of Private Members' legislation especially on 'conscience' but also on other issues, the rising significance of the 'welfare officer' role of MPs, and a modest revival in the position of the House of Lords have all boosted the capacity of parliament to scrutinise government policy, influence legislation and reflect public opinion. MPs are better paid, better equipped, harder-working and more professional than ever before. However, the *Westminster model* of the role of parliament – as outlined in the opening sections of this chapter – retains its validity. Parliament is dominated by party, and party discipline ensures that even in a time of narrow majorities the bulk of government legislation goes through as intended. Reformers' increasing recognition of the unlikelihood of parliament evolving into a policy-making body in its own right (the *revived independent powerhouse* or *transformative* model) prompted them to focus in the early 1990s on strengthening Parliament's functions of representation, scrutiny (of both government legislation and decisions) and public debate. Only very minor mainly procedural reforms had been achieved by 1997 but with the advent of a modernising Labour Adminstration, expectations of reform of both Houses were high.

Comparison

A merely *policy-influencing* legislature such as the Westminster parliament stands in stark contrast to a *policy-making* assembly like the US Congress. The subordinate role of the British parliament stems from the fusion of executive and legislature in the Westminster system whereas the powerful position of Congress flows from the separation of powers in the US constitution. Whereas executive and legislature in Britain are elected at the same time by the same process, the executive being formed by the party that gains a majority in the legislature, executive and legislature in the United States are elected separately and for different terms. Thus, the British parliament is controlled by the government by means of the majority it possesses in the leading house of the legislature. By contrast, the US Congress shares power with the Presidency: legislative power is vested by the constitution in Congress, and both the House of Representatives and the Senate have to agree before legislation can go forward for presidential approval. But congressional legislation is subject to presidential veto which, in turn, may be overridden by a two-thirds majority of both houses of Congress. The system is one of 'checks and balances'. In Britain, most legislation is *government* legislation and the government's majority backed by a disciplined party system normally ensures that it becomes law. In the United States, the President now normally proposes a significant legislative programme but this is often obstructed by Congress which is sometimes controlled by a different party from the one in possession of the executive branch of government. Thus, with regard to legislation, 'the President proposes but Congress disposes' (cited Hague et al., 1992, p. 299). A Democrat president may face a Republican Congress, and vice-versa, which, in a system which sets much store upon cooperation between executive and legislature, can be a recipe for deadlock. Whereas the British parliament possesses only nominal financial control, in the United States funds for the Executive are provided by Congressional appropriations. In only one aspect does the UK parliament possess a comparative advantage. Government in the UK in order to continue governing must retain the confidence of parliament, whereas in the United States, there is no such constitutional requirement upon the president. However, only in the relatively rare circumstances when government lacks a parliamentary majority, as in 1979, is it likely to be overthrown by a Commons vote. And while a British prime minister may be turned out of office by an adverse vote of his or her party, as Margaret Thatcher was in 1990, an American president may be impeached by Congress. The United States Congress is, therefore, a rare example of an active policy-making legislature: it both formulates its own legislation and can modify or reject legislative proposals from the executive. The British parliament falls into a much more common category in western Europe, that of a reactive, policy-influencing assembly that merely modifies or more rarely rejects government measures but cannot initiate legislation of its own (Norton, 1997, pp. 156–7).

Where does the European Parliament (EP) stand in comparison to these two parliaments? Until relatively recently, the EP was perceived as a weak, virtually powerless assembly, an unelected, merely advisory body. It would not have been inappropriate to characterise it as a *marginal* body in the European Community, more akin in its role to the limited functions of third-world assemblies than to the policy-influencing legislatures of western Europe. However, over the last two decades its influence over EU policy-making has increased. Since 1979, it has been directly elected, giving it democratic legitimacy, and it has acquired new powers through such provisions as the cooperation procedure (1987) and the co-decision procedure (1993). Whilst lacking full legislative powers and the ability to overthrow a government, its powers may none the less be said to be 'comparable with the powers exercised by many national parliaments' and indeed it may even exert 'a greater influence over affairs than do the more executive-dominated parliaments of some member states' (Nugent, 1994, p. 206; Norton, 1997, pp. 172–4; see further Chapter 13).

Summary

- Parliament consists of two Houses, the House of Commons and the House of Lords, with the democratically elected Commons as the dominant partner over the semi-feudal Lords, two-thirds of which consists of hereditary peers.

- The House of Commons has five main functions: representation; legislation; scrutiny; serving as a forum for national debate; and recruitment of a government. It shares the legislative, scrutiny and debating functions with the House of Lords, which also forms the highest court of appeal.

- Although backbench rebelliousness increased after 1970 and the government was defeated more frequently, the strength of party discipline means that the Government is normally able to use its majority to enact its legislative programme.

- Parliament remains the major location of political opposition in Britain, with formal recognition of the role of Leader of the Opposition and the official opposition party allocated opportunities to initiate a significant proportion of Commons business. In practice, the government's own backbenchers play a larger role in setting limits to government action than do the opposition parties.

- The main Commons committees are: standing committees to examine and amend legislation; select committees to scrutinise government expenditure and the main government departments; and committees of the whole House to consider (at least in part) finance bills and constitutional legislation. There are also many party committees, including e.g. the Conservative 1922 Committee, the Shadow Cabinet, and numerous specialist committees.

- The most important institutional change occurring in recent decades is the formation of the Departmental Select Committees to scrutinise the main government Departments but, although generally accounted a success, these require strengthening especially with regard to public expenditure.

- The House of Lords has statutorily limited powers of amendment and delay. As a result of the Parliament Acts (1911 and 1949), it possesses no power over money bills and may delay other legislation for one year only. Since 1947 it has also imposed a self-limiting rule (the Salisbury/ Addison doctrine) by which it does not oppose measures contained in the governing party's manifesto at the previous general election. Within these limits, the Lords enjoyed a modest revival as a checking and revising chamber after the failure to reform it in 1969, but its predominantly hereditary character has made it the subject of continuing political controversy.

- Compared with parliaments in other Western democracies, parliament ranks fairly low in powers and influence but remains an important institution in the British political system. It declined in public estimation after the late 1980s as a consequence of 'sleaze'. However, many reform schemes exist which, if implemented, would improve its public standing and increase its legislative and scrutinising capacities.

Questions

1. Discuss the view that Parliament is no longer of central importance in the contemporary British political system.
2. Analyse the effectiveness of the Commons select committees as a system of scrutiny of the executive.

Assignments

Assignment (1)

Following the Nolan Report, MPs may hold outside interests but are required by a House of Commons rule to declare any relevant financial interest or benefit in debate or other proceeding and are banned from paid advocacy. They must enter their interests in the House of Commons Register of MPs Interests in the following ten categories: remunerated directorships; remunerated employment; provision of paid services to a client; receipt of sponsorship e.g. from a trade union, trade association or professional body; gifts, benefits and hospitality; overseas benefits; overseas benefits and gifts; ownership of land and property; shareholdings worth more than £25,000 and greater than 1 per cent of the company's shares; and other relevant interests. The 1996 Register revealed MPs in receipt of gifts of

foreign trips, meals, bottles of wine, tickets for top sporting occasions, free hotel stays, office equipment including word processors and printers, and free cars; of the payment of their election expenses and the cost of research assistants; of (often substantial) payments from lobbying companies for political advice;and of income from directorships, paid jobs outside parliament and of fees for journalism and media appearances.

A MORI State of the Nation public opinion poll printed in the *Guardian*, 31 May 1995 produced the following findings:

Percentage considering that MPs should be allowed to:

	Allowed	Banned
Carry on a trade or profession (e.g. farmer, lawyer, dentist, etc.) while being an MP	45	33
Be paid to write articles for newspapers	35	43
Have any paid job outside parliament	28	48
Be paid to represent a non-commercial interest group, e.g.the Police Federation	21	44
Be sponsored by trade unions	21	48

Who should enforce rules of MPs' conduct?

	Percentage
MPs – as now	8
MPs – but tightened up	19
Law – civil courts and independent commission	38
Law – police and criminal courts	29

Questions

(i) A new tighter Register of MPs Interests supposedly came into force in 1996 but certain gaps and loopholes remained, one being donations to the 'fighting funds' of MPs' constituency associations rather than directly to the MPs themselves by e.g.trade unions and wealthy businessmen such as the Yorkshire millionaire Paul Sykes who gave money to over 200 Conservative Eurosceptics. The Parliamentary Commissioner for Standards therefore proposed in July 1997 to ban MPs from speaking for a year on behalf of individuals, companies and trade unions who donate more than £2,000 to their constituency association. Is such sponsorship by wealthy individuals, companies and trade unions acceptable or should it be banned, with, for example, parties being subsidised by the state on the basis of votes received at the previous general election?

(ii) Should MPs be allowed to accept any gifts from outside interests and individuals? If so, what type of gift is permissible, and why? If not, why not?

(iii) Should MPs be permitted to hold paid jobs outside parliament? If your answer is 'no', do you consider that a parliament entirely composed of professional politicians presents any dangers? How fair is such a ban on MPs who may be rejected by the electors at the next general election?

(iv) Should MPs be allowed to enter into paid contracts with outside organisations even if the contracts are for advice only, not advocacy? Give reasons for your answer.

(v) Since 1689 MPs have been immune from prosecution for bribery and corruption in the courts, but the Labour Home Secretary Jack Straw has published plans (June 1997) to jail corrupt MPs for up to seven years. At the same time the Leader of the House Ann Taylor has set up a joint Lords–Commons Committee to review parliamentary privileges, which as well as ensuring freedom from arrest for MPs also include immunity from prosecution for what they say in the House of Commons. At present, allegations of misconduct against MPs are investigated by the Parliamentary Commissioner for Standards reporting to the Committee of Standards and Privileges and the maximum punishment applicable to an MP found guilty of misconduct is expulsion from the House. Who should enforce the rules of conduct on MPs – MPs themselves through the Committee of Standards and Privileges or the courts? Give reasons for your answers, in particular referring to the cases of Conservative MPs, Tim Smith and Neil Hamilton.

Assignment (2)

It is correct to speak of parliament as a 'policy-influencing' assembly but public concern has arisen about how effectively it legislates and scrutinises government policy. As already noted in Chapter 15, doubts arose about how effectively parliament carries out its scrutiny role from its failure to force any ministerial resignations over the Scott Report into the Arms to Iraq affair. However, criticisms have also been heard about over-hasty, poorly drafted, inadequately scrutinised legislation, involving for example such matters as dangerous dogs, football spectators and the future of broadcasting. We now consider defects in legislative procedure in detail in four short case-studies.

(1) The Education Act (1988). The White Paper outlining this bill was published in July, so that the consultation period took place during the school summer holidays. Consequently, relatively little real consultation took place with those who would be most affected by the legislation (despite the fact that the poll tax was still fresh enough in mind as a warning to Ministers over what can happen when there is little consultation). In addition to this, the sheer complexity of legislation is becoming an issue. The Education Bill began with 225 clauses and 17 schedules, which makes it twice the size of the Act which has become a milestone in educational history – the (Butler) Education Act of 1944. The government then made 278 amendments in the Commons committee stage, 78 more at report stage, 258 more in the Lords committee stage, 296 more on report, and 71 at third reading. Some amendments appeared only hours before they were debated, leaving members very little time in which to consider them. The position has been reached where Parliament enacts more legislation – now running to several thousand pages a year – than it can handle efficiently. Commonsense suggests that this must affect the quality of legislation.

(2) The Child Support Act (1991) provides another example of how the legislative process can fail.

Labour and Conservative MPs supported the Act but, only months after its introduction, they were receiving a massive number of complaints and demands for radical alterations to be made in the legislation. Many of them later wondered how they managed to pass it in the first place without picking up all the problems contained in the Act. The government rushed the bill through Parliament, and Labour failed to operate as an effective opposition. The Child Support Act has its origins in the last days of the Thatcher era. Mrs Thatcher wanted quick action on the problem of absent fathers who refused to pay maintenance to help bring up their children. A White Paper was published and sent to over 90 pressure groups which had six weeks in which to respond. As with the Education bill, this is not long enough for proper consultation. Many pressure groups supported the ideas and principles in the White Paper, but felt that there were many practical faults which needed sorting out. But groups like the National Council for One Parent Families felt that the government was not really interested in what they had to say, since the contents of the bill was almost identical to the White Paper. The lobby felt that the consultation process had failed.

(3) The pensions legislation(1986) was inspired by right wing think tanks such as the Centre for Policy Studies in the early 1980s. Its basic ideas were to encourage private pensions for all and to remove the state from pension provision as far as possible.On the basis of this legislation, many people who possessed sound occupational pension schemes were persuaded to leave them for inferior private schemes. The consequence of this large-scale mis-selling of pensions was that the pensions industry owed millions of pounds of compensation to tens of thousands of nurses, miners, teachers and steel-workers by the early 1990s, many of whom had still not received the sums owed them when Labour took office in 1997. Yet MPs on the standing committee which considered the legislation pointed out its flaws at the time: these included the lack of protection against high pressure salesmen and the failure to make clear how much much of the pension holders' money would be swallowed up by commissions and administrative costs (Andrew Marr, *Ruling Britannia* (1993), pp. 143–53).

(4) The Poll Tax (1988) proved to be a legislative disaster that caused massive dislocation in local government, provoked a huge public outcry, led to non-payment on a large scale, triggered the downfall of a prime minister, and had to be replaced by a new local tax within five years. Yet neither the detailed substance nor the principle of the legislation received adequate scrutiny by Parliament. Parliamentary scrutiny took place only when ministers had decided the policy in all essentials. Consideration by standing committee was 'a futile marathon', in which, as usually happens with controversial measures, a huge amount of time was spent on the early clauses of the bill (35 hours on the first two clauses) and the government applied a guillotine after 70 hours and a mere 17 clauses, allocating only 18 sittings for the consideration of the remaining 112 clauses. Press reporting was minimal and opponents of the bill lacked reliable data on which to build their case. The government lost none of the 173 votes held at the committee stage and, although a significant back-bench rebellion occurred at the report stage,based on an amendment calling for a banded poll tax related to income tax thresholds, the government prevailed with a comfortable majority of 25 votes. A Lords amendment that tried to relate the poll tax to ability to pay was defeated by 317 votes to 183. Furthermore,at no point between 1983 and 1992 did a House of Commons Select Committee consider the question of local government, it being the deliberate policy of the Select Committee on the Environment not to become involved in topics which were the subject of major political controversy or which were likely to be fully debated on the floor of the House in any event (Butler, Adonis and Travers, *Failure in British Government* (1994), pp. 112–25, 224–45).

Questions
(i) Identify the main faults in the legislative process as revealed in the above case-studies.
(ii) Then state how far, in your view, the passage of flawed and unworkable legislation is the consequence of:
  (a) The dominance of the executive in Britain's majoritarian system?
  (b) The lack of qualifications of 'amateur' MPs to scrutinise legislation which is couched in

specialised legal and technical language?

(c) Weaknesses in parliamentary drafting, notably the failure to employ good, adequately remunerated lawyers?

(d) A failure to consult with and to take seriously the advice of outside affected interests and legal experts on the probable consequences of proposed legislation?

(e) Excessive haste in governments which now pass too much legislation?

(f) The failings of the upper house, with its permanent Conservative majority, as a revising chamber?

(g) Inadequate press coverage of parliamentary proceedings, both of legislation as it happens and of the impact of legislation so that ministers involved in bad legislation can be held accountable?

Further reading

Adonis, A. (1993) *Parliament Today,* 2nd edn (Manchester: Manchester University Press) can be recommended as an introduction, whilst Griffith, J.A.G. and Ryle, M. (1989) *Parliament* (London: Sweet & Maxwell) is an authoritative longer study. Ridley, F.F. and Rush, (eds) (1995) *British Government and Politics since 1945* contains valuable essays on aspects of parliament, whilst Rush, M. (ed.) (1990) *Parliament and Pressure Politics* (Oxford:

Clarendon) considers the relationship between parliament and pressure groups. Shell, D. (1992) *The House of Lords*, 2nd edn (London: Harvester Wheatsheaf) should be consulted on the Upper House. Judge, D. (1993) *The Parliamentary State* (London: Sage) is an advanced work locating parliament at the centre of an analysis of the UK state.

On specific aspects of parliament, the following articles can be recommended: Norton, P. (1994) 'Select Committees in the House of Commons', *Politics Review*, 4:1, November; Norton, P. (1995) 'Standing Committees in the House of Commons', *Politics Review*, 4:4, April; Alderman, K. (1995) 'The Government Whips', *Politics Review*, 4:4, April; Norton, P. (1995) 'National Parliaments and European Union', *Talking Politics*, 7:3, Spring; Berrington, H. (1995) 'The Nolan Report', *Government and Opposition,* 30:4, Autumn; Norton, P. (1995–6) 'Parliamentary Behaviour since 1945', *Talking Politics*, 8:2, Winter; Shell, D. (1992) 'The House of Lords', Politics Review, 5:1, September; Borthwick, R. L. (1996) 'Changes in the House of Commons', *Politics Review,* 6:3, February; Cowley, P. (1996–7) 'Men (and Women) Behaving Badly? The Conservative Party since 1992', *Talking Politics,* 9:2, Winter; Wright, A. (1997) 'Does Parliament Work?', *Talking Politics*, 9:3, Spring.

Website
Parliament (links to House of Commons and House of Lords):
http://www.Parliament.uk/

CHAPTER 17

Quasi-government

The number of extra-governmental bodies, or quangos, has increased and continues to increase, leading to public concern over issues of democratic control and public accountability of bodies spending taxpayers' money. Should such bodies be reduced in number, abolished altogether, or reformed in ways which make good the current 'democratic deficit'? The dividing line between the public and private sectors has been transformed in recent years by the disposal of public assets, through privatisation sales, as well as by the public sector adapting many private sector managerial techniques. How successful have these developments proved in terms of reducing costs and improving services? Has the most radical initiative of them all – the Private Finance Initiative- still to establish its reputation in terms of effectiveness, efficiency and economy? Finally, to what extent has the cumulative effect of the expanding quangocracy, the increase in privatisation and deregulation, as well as the adoption of more commercial practices in the civil service, radically altered the nature of the British state?

The world of the quango

The world of quasi-government is inhabited by organisations referred to by political scientists as 'fringe bodies', 'non-departmental organisations', 'governmental bodies', 'public bodies', extra-governmental organisations, 'semi-autonomous authorities' and 'quangos'. Even the latter name has been modified so that it may now refer to organisations which are 'quasi-non-governmental', 'quasi-autonomous-non-governmental' or 'quasi-autonomous-national-government'.

Quasi-government has been described as 'arm's length' or 'indirect' government. It is made up of organisations involved in government which is not done by central government departments such as the Inland Revenue or by local authorities. Is consists of state-related organisations which may or may not have been created by government but which are influential in making or applying government policy.

The *Pliatzky Report on Non-Departmental Public Bodies* (1980) examined the world of quasi-government. It was reported that there were 489 non-departmental bodies which were 'executive' in nature and had a regulatory function; these employed 217,000 staff. Examples of executive-type quangos are the Arts Council, Agricultural Wages Board, Eggs Authority, United Kingdom Atomic Energy Authority, Countryside Commission, British Council, General Nursing Council and Commission for Racial Equality. In addition, there were 1,561 'advisory' bodies which directly employed relatively few staff. Examples include the Food Hygiene Advisory Committee on the Safety of Nuclear Installations, the China Clay Council, the Police Advisory Board and the Parliamentary Boundary Commission for England. Finally, there were 67 systems of tribunals which were often staffed by the department concerned. Examples include the Supplementary Benefits Appeal Tribunals, Pneumoconiosis Medical Panels, Vaccine Damage Tribunals and Rent Tribunals.

The rise of the quango state

A survey conducted by the Democratic Audit in 1996 revealed that both the nature and number of quangos had changed a great deal since the days of the Pliatsky Report. Firstly, quangos no longer oversee rather remote or specialist functions, as in Pliatsky's time, but now implement policies which touched on aspects of most people's lives, such as school, college and university education, vocational training, public housing, health care and hospitals, inner-city regeneration, and environmental protection. Since some quangos have become so involved in the policy process, some political scientists argue that there is very little difference between them and 'Next Step' agencies, such as the Child Support Agency and the Prison Service, which are part of central government. Secondly, there has been a rapid expansion in the number of quangos in existence; in fact 'there is an executive quango for every ten thousand people in the United Kingdom' (Hall and Weir, 1996; p. 4).

Quangos are a controversial issue in British politics. Many Conservative politicians argue that many of the bodies which the Democratic Audit identified as undemocratic quangos were, in fact, the end result of a democratic process. Conservatives argued that power had been seized from bureaucrats and professional bodies, fragmented and distributed to empower local groups of citizens. Such bodies, they argued, were not quangos at all but part of a process which redistributed power from 'producer' groups to 'customers'. Conservatives frequently cited the creation of more powerful school governors as an example of reducing the influence of teacher unions and local authorities (the 'producers of education') and increasing the influence of parents (the 'customers'). Critics disagree with this view and counterargue that appointed local business interests effectively form the major voice on governor bodies, that trade union representation is absent, and that parental power is limited.

Quangos have been criticised for being undemocratic and unaccountable. The point made by Sir Norman Chester in his article in *Public Administration* remains as relevant today as when he wrote it in 1979:

> The growth of fringe bodies is a retreat from the simple democratic principle evolved in the nineteenth century that those who perform a public duty should be fully responsible to an electorate – by way of a minister responsible to Parliament or of a locally elected council. The essence of a fringe body is that it is not so responsible for some or all of its actions. (Chester, 1979, p. 54)

From monitoring the answers to parliamentary questions put in 1996, Democratic Audit found nothing to reduce Sir Norman's concerns over democracy and accountability. For example, only 62 per cent of executive quangos were required to publish annual reports, 74 per cent were required to publish annual accounts, 80 per cent subject to a full public audit, 42 per cent under the jurisdiction of the Ombudsman, 11 per cent allowed the public the right to inspect a register of members' interests, 6 per cent gave the public the right to attend meetings and none gave the public the right to inspect agendas or minutes of meetings. In other words, 'it is extraordinary that a third of the executive quangos which government formally recognises still do not perform the elementary duty of publishing an annual report on their activities and one in five escapes a full public audit'. With the exception of education and police quangos, 'public rights of access to the documents, meetings and business of executive quangos at national and local level are either non-existent or poorly developed' (Hall and Weir, 1996, p. 10).

It can be seen that much of the work of quangos is conducted in near secrecy. This together with the increased number of quangos has intensified problems concerned with openness and accountability. Firstly, the opting-out process in education and health and the loss of other local government functions to quangos (Training and Enterprise Councils, Urban Development Corporations, Housing Action Trusts) has resulted in quangos spending a much larger amount of public money. In 1994–5, quangos spent a fifth of all public spending (£60.4 billion), 45 per cent more in real terms than

BOX 17.1
Britain's emerging quangocracy

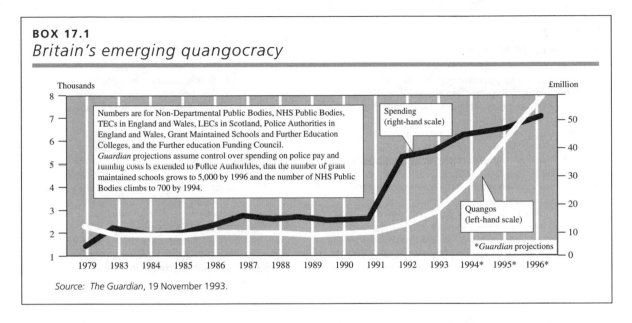

Numbers are for Non-Departmental Public Bodies, NHS Public Bodies, TECs in England and Wales, LECs in Scotland, Police Authorities in England and Wales, Grant Maintained Schools and Further Education Colleges, and the Further education Funding Council.
Guardian projections assume control over spending on police pay and running costs is extended to Police Authorities, that the number of grant maintained schools grows to 5,000 by 1996 and the number of NHS Public Bodies climbs to 700 by 1994.

Source: The Guardian, 19 November 1993.

when Sir Norman Chester first expressed his political anxieties about quangos. The appointed 'quangocrats' responsible for spending this large sum of public money are neither accountable to any electorate for their decisions, nor are they directly responsible to the public for their actions.

Secondly, the secret world in which quangos operate risks corruption and private greed. Lord Nolan's committee on standards in public life examined quangos and called for a return to the principle of public service rather than personal gain for those who wished to serve on quangos. Periodic disclosures in the press of petty corruption within some quangos, large £4,000-a-day salaries paid in other quangos, together with the irresponsible management of some educational institutions, has led to political demands for stricter policing of the quango state.

Thirdly, quangos have been criticised because of their political bias. Anxieties have been expressed over a number of related issues. Firstly, as Prime Minister, Margaret Thatcher initially waged a campaign against quangos because they appeared to her as part-and-parcel of the corporate state. Quangos were non-elected and secretive bodies which provided 'jobs for the boys', by which she meant the appointment of trade unionists by previous Labour governments. As a result of her attack on quangos, some were wound up, some merged, and some disappeared only to reappear with

a new title. As a consequence of the 'hands-off' and 'opting-out' policies pursued by the Thatcher and Major governments, thousands of new posts resulted from the creation of many new quangos. There were accusations that a disproportionate share of these

Table 17.1 The Democratic Audit's 1996 quango count

NHS Bodies	788
Advisory bodies	674
Non-departmental/executive quangos	309
Local executive quangos	4,653
Career Service Companies	91
City Technology Colleges	15
Further Education Corporate bodies	560
Grant-Maintained Schools	1,103
Higher Education Corporations	175
Housing Associations	2,565
Local Enterprise Companies	22
Police authorities	41
Training and Enterprise Councils	81
The Total quango count	6,424

Source: Based on Hall and Weir (1996) p. 5

BOX 17.2
The new magistracy

The recent and rapid growth in quangos has led to concern about the *democratic control* and accountability of these bodies. Sometimes political commentators refer to these problems as the *democratic deficit*. Since members are not elected on to quangos, but appointed by government, the term *the new magistracy* is being used to describe this new elite which is becoming responsible for so many areas of government.

- Since it is the government which appoints members of the new magistracy, some have been worried that there will be a political bias among those who serve on quangos. Ministers are responsible for making nearly 4,000 quango appointments. Recent Conservative governments have been accused of bias in appointing Conservative sympathisers and managers of businesses which make donations to the Conservative Party. Proposals for solving this problem have included creating a Public Appointments Commission, which would advertise vacant posts on quangos. All private interests would be listed on a public register, and a parliamentary select committee would ratify the most important appointments. A more radical proposal involved competitive tendering for the 'contract' of running a quango, opening up the appointments process to businessmen, councillors, charity workers or any other interested group which felt qualified to run a quango. The quango appointments would go to the best of the rival bids.

- Quangos can be created to compensate for the governing party's losses in local government elections. It has been argued that John Major's government by-passed the impact of local government election defeats, particularly in Wales, by doubling the number of quangos to around a hundred to manage Welsh affairs. In opposition, Labour argued that it would abolish many such quangos transferring their powers back to local councils or to new devolved authorities.

- The large number of quangos in existence leads to problems concerning control and scrutiny. At the same time, the greater involvement of businessmen may lead to differing ethics and ways of making decisions than existed previously in public service. Some are concerned about the number of scandals which have already come to light – the House of Common's Public Accounts Committee slammed into the Welsh Development Agency and found it guilty of a long list of misdemeanours. These included making unauthorised payments, running up extravagant expenses and appointing a convicted con-man to a top post. Lord Nolan's investigation into quangos recommended that members should be attracted by the desire to serve the public rather than the prospect of making money.

- Critics argue that corruption and policy failure will occur more in quangos than in local government. This is because in a democratically elected council there will normally be one or more opposition parties which will work hard to expose all the faults of those wielding power. Quangos lack the vital ingredient of critical opposition. Also, councils can ensure that there is a public debate about issues which concern local people, whereas quangos decide vital issues in private. Because of the democratic process, decisions made by councillors are generally seen as legitimate – even if they are unpopular – whereas decisions made by quangos have little legitimacy.

- The Widdicombe inquiry into local government reported

---

new posts went to Conservative sympathisers. It was argued that even when Conservative candidates were routed in local government elections, many important local policies remained under the control of Conservative 'quangocrats'. There were also accusations that too many quangocrats had vested interests in decisions made by the quangos on which they sat; thirteen of the 21 members of the Committee on Safety of Medicines had interests in pharmaceutical companies and 9 of the 15 members of the committee on Toxicity of Chemicals in Food, Consumer Products and the Environment had consultancy interests in companies such as Cadbury-Schweppes, Smithkline Beecham and Proctor and Gamble.

Finally, the political bias exhibited by some quangos results from their role in delivering contro-versial policies. The Funding Agency for Schools is a powerful quango which now dispenses billions of pounds of public money, and which can close 'failing' local schools and convert them into what was then grant-maintained schools. Members of the Funding Agency for Schools are appointed, and can be removed, by the Secretary of State. As a result of these arrangements, many local schools conform to politically controversial and centralised policy, the details of which are made by a locally unaccountable, ministerially appointed quango. Whereas local councillors could be voted out of office if their decisions on school financing were unpopular, FAS quangocrats are immune from local opposition to their policy decisions.

The reduction (and abolition) of the powers of

BOX 17.2 *(continued)*

that many councillors held surgeries and received considerable mail from the public. The report, published in 1986, found that around a third of the electorate knew who one of their councillors was and around a fifth had been in recent contact with a councillor. But even MPs have found it impossible to find out who sits on quangos; the Conservative government informed Labour MP Peter Kilfoyle that 'information on the 42,606 appointments is not held centrally and could only be provided at disproportionate cost' (*The Observer*, 3 July 1994). The public stand even less chance of knowing who sits on quangos or making their views known to them.

- Councils are well placed to have an overview of their area's problems and can coordinate policies and services to maximise on efficiency, effectiveness and economy. Quangos represent a very fragmented, piecemeal approach to government. A survey of 200 local executive quangos found that none of them had ever communicated with quangos having a different concern than their own (Plummer, 1994).

- Important leadership posts and executive quangos are filled through ministerial patronage or on the advice of senior civil servants. This closed process almost ensures that quangos become self-perpetuating elites, as one quango chairman admitted; 'I became chairman as a consequence of sharing a cab with a stranger. Another quango chairman was appointed following a pheasant shoot at which the Secretary of State was a fellow gun; the subsequent chairman of a water authority bumped into a cabinet minister while birding on a Greek Island' (*The Economist*, 6 August 1994).

- A Conservative minister in John Major's government

argued that fears over democracy and accountability were unfounded. He argued that accountability was maintained because the relevant minister remained answerable to Parliament for what quangos do. But, more importantly, he argued that the power of citizens as consumers over public services meant that there was no democratic deficit. William Waldegrave argued that 'the key point is not whether those who run our public services are elected, but whether they are producer-responsive or consumer-responsive. Services are not necessarily made to respond to the public by giving our citizens a democratic voice . . . but by giving them choices, or by instituting mechanisms for publicly approved standards' (Waldegrave, 1993). In other words, just as Marks and Spencer can satisfy its customers without being democratic, so too, it is argued, can quangos. Furthermore, publishing Citizens' Charters for public services can provide an additional measure of accountability and means of redress. Critics argue that all these arguments are unconvincing. Firstly, it is not realistic to expect ministers to be responsible for indirect government. Secondly, not everyone shops at Marks and Spencer. Young people may feel that the stores clothes are unfashionable, and since they are unable to influence corporate purchasing policy, they shop elsewhere. People are unable to influence quango policy but generally they do not have the option of 'shopping' elsewhere for services. Finally, Citizens' Charters have proved inadequate safeguards of service standards and achieved relatively little in increasing accountability.

---

elected local government, as well as the decline in autonomy of bodies like universities, has resulted in the centralising of government power. The increase in the number of quangos is seen by some political scientists as an important means of centralising power.

Some argue that there is nothing sinister about the growth of quangos, and that media-spread stories about Britain being run by an unelected quango state is no more than political myth. Quangos, it is argued, represent no more than an attempt to reform the public sector in order to improve the quality of services provided to people. Quangos are not new, nor are they deliberately Conservative-dominated. It is only natural that people with the skills necessary to provide a public service tend to

come from the business community and, therefore, tend to support Conservative ideas. Finally, whilst quangos are not democratically elected bodies, this does not mean that they are unresponsive to the needs of the public.

Anthony Sampson has taken a different view: 'the re-organisation of the health service, education and regulation created rich new opportunities to reward political friends, while Thatcher was far more ruthless than her predecessors in appointing "one of us" to key positions – all the way to museum chairmanships and archbishops. The long British tradition of patronage was taking new shapes, but it still remained at the heart of political power – more than ever concentrated at Number Ten' (*The Independent*, 14 March 1995).

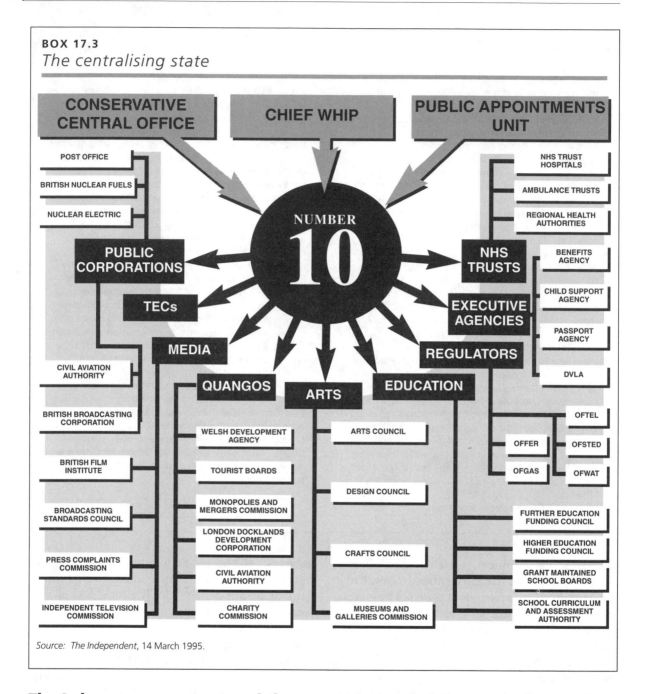

BOX 17.3
The centralising state

Source: *The Independent*, 14 March 1995.

The Labour government and the future of quangos

Quangos were a soft target for Labour MPs when they sat on the opposition benches, quangos were undemocratic, part of a highly centralised state, sometimes corrupt, and Conservative-dominated which was particularly unrepresentative in Scotland and Wales. Labour demanded the abolition of quangos and promised a 'bonfire of quangos' once it formed the government. Yet the party's manifesto promised to 'democratise the quango state' rather than abolish quangos. Political commentators believed that some quangos would surrender their responsibilities to local authorities and devolved assemblies, but the majority would continue to provide much indirect government. Labour's change of attitude towards quangos resulted from the party's emphasis on 'community' policies. Quangos, properly constituted, can serve the community alongside other voluntary bodies, charities and local government. It was announced that individuals nominated to run large quangos would now have to undergo cross-examination by MPs, somewhat in the style of Congressional ratification hearings in the United States. This reform represents the first step in opening up the secret world of the quango state.

Rolling back the state

The Labour Government elected in 1945 embarked on a programme of nationalising the basic industries in order to help rebuild the British economy (see Coxall and Robins, 1998, ch. 9). The nationalised industries and other public sector enterprises came under increasing political attack and, during the 1970s, the government began small-scale sales of public assets in order to finance public spending. Policies of selling-off state assets, of denationalising and of privatising became central to the Thatcherite programme of the 1980s. Policies were designed to enlarge the role played by the free market in society, necessitating a reduced role for government. It was intended that attitudes would change – creating the so-called 'Thatcher revolution' – in which the dependency culture associated with state intervention would be eclipsed by an enterprise culture associated with the entrepreneurialism of the free market. Privatisation was to play a crucial role in the process of economic and social transformation.

What is privatisation?

Privatisation covers a variety of techniques which reduce or eliminate the role of the state in owning, managing and providing services in favour of the private sector. Privatisation policy includes:

> **Privatisation** is a general term to cover a variety of policies which concern the sale of public sector assets to the private sector.

- Denationalisation – of public enterprises, such as the government's disposal of British Coal, and of public assets, such as Labour's sale of BP shares in the 1970s.
- Liberalisation and deregulation – in order to encourage greater competition in the provision of services, such as with bus transport.
- Contracting out of public sector services – health authorities and local authorities put many of their services out to tender. A private company may provide the best value for money and replace the service previously provided by public sector employees. Market testing is a similar method of comparing civil service with private sector costs in performing specific functions.
- Reduction of the public sector control – in areas such as urban redevelopment and youth training – through increasing the responsibility of the private sector.
- Introduction of market forces into public sector welfare areas such as health care and education. 'Realistic' charges or 'competing for customers' result in welfare departments being run more like commercial businesses than traditional public services.

Privatisation under the first Thatcher Government began as a piecemeal process but quickened in pace after the 1983 general election. Some sales of state assets, as in the case of British Telecom, British Gas, British Airways, British Steel, the water companies, electricity companies, and the railways – and also the biggest public-to-private transfer, that of council houses – were to the public. Other state assets, such as Sealink, Fairey Engineering, the Rover Group and the National Bus Company, were sold to private concerns or to the existing management. In 1979, before these privatisations, state-owned industries accounted for 11 per cent of Britain's national output; by 1997 it was less than 2 per cent. During the same period around a million jobs have been transferred from the public to the private sector. Although, in retrospect, some public assets were sold too cheaply, the Treasury has raised a massive total of £80 billion at 1997 prices from all the privatisation sales.

During the 1980s the Conservative Government's privatisation policies were generally popular with the electorate. Selling the public utilities and nationalised industries promised improved services at a lower cost. It was argued that once such bodies were in the private sector, competition would increase efficiency and keep prices down. However, during the 1990s privatisation policies became increasingly unpopular with the electorate. Anxiety was expressed over privatising water, alarm over privatising the railways, and effective opposition to privatising the Royal Mail.

Has privatisation been successful?

The verdict on privatisation is a mixed one. Whilst 'bad news' stories about privatised industries make interesting newspaper headlines, 'good news' stories tend not to get reported. Some privatised industries have experienced problems which has little to do with the fact that they are privatised, others have enjoyed success which also have little to do with them being privatised. The public utilities have made gains in economic efficiency, but this had been paid for in part by shedding 180,000 jobs. Using an interesting example, Will Hutton describes how the 'gains' of the private bus operator are at the expense of other motorists, the wider society:

> The bus operator, after all, by stripping out two-man crews is making his buses more efficient. Why pay a wage to a conductor when the driver can take the money for tickets? But the efficiency for the bus operator has inefficient consequences for the rest of us. It slows up the bus, and that makes the traffic slower. The sacked bus conductor is added to the pool of the unemployed, and so social security payments are increased, crowding out a little bit of public expenditure that might otherwise have been allocated to improving the road or rail network. The next job he will obtain will, as is typical for most of the employed, be lower paid and have fewer employment rights. His life and that of his family will have been blighted. And so, in a similar way, have the lives of the people on the bus . . . he offers a reassurance to travellers that if, for example, some teenagers on the bus act threateningly, he is on hand . . . His very presence acts as a prior sanction . . . here is the representative not just of authority but of wider society (Hutton, 1997 pp. 23–5).

Since privatisation, consumers have paid less for gas, electricity and telephones in real terms. Was this because of privatisation, or the result of falling oil, coal and natural gas prices and advances in technology? Since privatisation, water bills have risen by a third in real terms. Was this because of privatisation, or the result of an already inefficient and ageing system prior to privatisation? Answering these questions involves making complex judgements; sometimes members of the public rushed to simpler judgements, the issues which occupied their thinking included:

• The poor management of some privatised companies. The ten privatised water companies had failed to tackle the problems of damaged pipes which they inherited from the public sector. Many companies lost over 30 per cent of their water through leaks, some over 40 per cent. Yet they were spending less on repairs since they were privatised and consequently losing more water than ever. It struck many people that the water companies were looking after their shareholders more carefully than they were looking after their customers, who were expected to endure water shortages.

British Gas withdrew from the government's charter mark scheme after complaints reached record levels.

The poor reliability of some rail services caused a public scandal. South West Trains and Regional Railways North East were fined for cancelling trains. The former company, owned by Stagecoach, was said by a Conservative Transport Minister to be excellent news for passengers when it successfully outbid its rivals and promised to run services for less subsidy than British Rail had received. However, South West Trains cancelled services, produced a chaotic timetable, and was described by the same Minister as 'inept' (the *Guardian*, 4 March 1997). The head of South West Trains, rather tactlessly, claimed that passengers only complained because they have nothing to do when they get into the office in the morning: 'They sit down and write to SWT. I feel like writing to their bosses and saying, do you know this guy spends two hours a week writing to a train company' (*Sunday Telegraph*, 23 March 1997).

- The so-called 'snouts in the trough' or 'fat cats' issue. The very large pay rises for the chief executives of some privatised industries were thought to be excessive and undeserved. Also huge profits were made from selling on privatised companies: for example, Eversholt Leasing, a privatised rolling stock company, was sold after only two years for twice its original price.
- The merger of utility companies. There are fears that water, gas and electricity companies might merge into one multi-functional utility which could then 'gang up' on consumers. The creation of United Utilities concerned many, particularly on the political right, that all the anticipated benefits of competition would be lost if such mergers became commonplace.
- The impact of privatisation on public finances. Some, particularly on the political left, argued that privatisation had resulted in increasing the tax burden paid by the electorate. This is because the surpluses, or profits, made by the old nationalised industries were paid to the Treasury and used to finance the welfare state and defence. In contrast, the profits of privatised industries go to shareholders. The taxes paid by privatised industries is less than the surpluses of the old nationalised industries. For example, in the four years before privatisation, the electricity industry provided £6 billion of surpluses to the Treasury but in the four years since privatisation only £3.1 million in taxes went to the Treasury. The difference between these two sums equates to £139 for every household, which has to be found from another source such as raising taxation.

Others argued that privatisation was a good deal for taxpayers. One calculation suggested that in 1979 the nationalised industries cost each taxpayer approximately £300 a year in real terms, whereas today the privatised industries pay a total tax bill equivalent to £100 for each taxpayer.

Old Labour, emotionally faithful to the original Clause Four, opposed privatisation in principle. New Labour has displayed a much more pragmatic

The Chancellor's claw-back

and positive attitude towards privatisation. It has accepted that privatisation cannot be reversed. Where old Labour demanded the renationalisation of the railways, New Labour emphasised the need for more effective regulation of the railways in order to improve services to the public. During the 1997 election campaign Tony Blair announced that small-scale privatisations might continue under a Labour Government 'where they are in the public interest' (the *Guardian*, 8 April 1997).

Labour intends to levy a one-off windfall tax on what are seen as the excess profits of the privatised utilities in order to fund the training of young unemployed people. Labour spokesmen argued that such a windfall was morally justified, whilst many businesses take commercial risks in order to make profits, the privatised utilities inherited highly prof-itable concerns which were virtually risk free.

The PFI: a policy more radical than privatisation?

The Channel Tunnel is a massive private enterprise venture: it is privately financed, privately owned and privately run. It is effectively bankrupt, with its debts accelerating faster than its income. Clearly it would have been a more secure speculation for the original investors if the public sector had been involved either to share the risks or provide certain guarantees. The Private Finance Initiative (PFI) is an arrangement which aims to get the public and the private sectors to work together more closely in pro-viding services to the public. Basically, under the PFI the private sector funds the design, construction, maintenance and management of public projects, such as hospitals, motorways or other civil engi-neering projects such as the Skye Bridge.

The PFI involves a new way of funding the public sector. The traditional method would involve the government borrowing to pay for the construction of a large capital project. Under PFI the private sector invests in the project which is then leased back to the public sector. The PFI was announced in 1992, and it was envisaged that private sector firms would compete to become government partners, and that in partnership with government, private sector companies should assume some commercial risk.

The advantage of PFI financing for government is that there is public investment without public sector borrowing. Leasing is cheaper than borrowing and it has been estimated that PFI will save around 15 per cent of traditional costs over a thirty-year period. The advantage of PFI for private companies is that they benefit from the building involved and from the financial leasing arrangements.

The record of PFI is, however, somewhat disap-pointing and is to be reviewed by the Labour Government. Private companies have complained that the tendering process involved in making a bid for a PFI contract is very complex, lengthy and expensive. Small and medium sized companies do not have the resources necessary to tender, and large firms are increasingly reluctant to spend a large sum of money preparing a bid which is then unsuccess-ful. If Labour is able to streamline the tendering process, then PFI is likely to play a bigger role in financing public investment.

The regulatory state

Margaret Thatcher's mission to 'roll back the state' has changed radically the nature of public adminis-tration in Britain. The combined effect of:

- the privatisation programme, market testing and compulsory competitive tendering
- the reduction in the role of local government resulting from the transfer of services to quangos (such as education), to the private sector (such as nursing homes) and the disposal of assets (council house sales)
- a reduction in the scope of the welfare state with greater reliance placed on private provision
- the creation of semi-autonomous agencies within the civil service, as well as
- the loss of some functions through EU harmoni-sation measures

has resulted in a restructuring of the state. Some political scientists have argued that the type of state which developed from the mid-1940s to the mid-1980s has been 'broken up' or 'hollowed out' as tra-ditional state activities have been transferred to either quasi-government or the private sector. In other words, rather than being a direct provider of

BOX 17.4
A new super-regulatory body

In 1997 Labour announced that a new body would be set up, the Financial Services Authority (FSA), to regulate investment, assurance and possibly mortgage business conducted by solicitors, accountants and actuaries. Previously these activities were regulated by professional bodies such as the Law Society and the Institute of Chartered Accountants.

services as in the past, the state now enables such services to be provided by other agencies such as quangos or private sector companies. But the change in emphasis from role of provider to enabler does not mean that government has given up its interest in the quality of services delivered to the public. The enabling state needs a framework of rules and guide-lines – regulations – to ensure that agencies act in a proper manner. Regulations provide the means by which government is able to influence the behaviour of individuals providing services in the public utili-ties, telecommunications and education. The state has a long tradition of regulating various profes-sional activities – medicine, law and education – but the change from providing to enabling has seen a considerable increase in regulation.

Regulation has become a complex and controver-sial issue. Critics argue that state regulation has a poor record in preventing fraud and scandal. For example, the Bank of England failed to prevent people losing money when the Bank of Credit and Commerce International (BCCI) collapsed in 1991, and again in 1995 when Britain's oldest merchant bank, Barings, collapsed with huge debts. The regu-latory body, the Investment Management Regulatory Organisation (IMRO) failed to prevent Robert Maxwell from plundering his employees' pension fund; the Financial Intermediaries, Managers and Brokers Regulatory Association (FIMBRA) could not prevent Knight Williams from going under; and nor could the Security and Investments Board (SIB) prevent one and a half million people being mis-sold unsuitable private pensions during the 1980s.

Regulating bodies established to oversee the public utilities, such as Oftel (1984), Ofgas (1986), Offer (1989) and Ofwat (1990) have also been criticised for their ineffectual performance. Too often they have appeared unable to either enforce compliance or punish with other than derisory fines. They have also been criticised for having 'tunnel vision' when it comes to deciding what is in the public's interest. In particular, the insistence of the regulators on the promotion of competition has resulted in short-term advantage (the 'dash for gas' in energy) over longer-term benefits (Britain's coal resources).

Deregulation

Some Conservatives believed that much of British industry was restricted by 'red tape', which resulted in increasing costs and reducing competitiveness. As

President of the Board of Trade, Michael Heseltine encouraged the removal of what was seen as unnecessary regulations. It was thought that this would enable entrepreneurs to respond freely to market opportunities and expand their businesses rather than remain restricted by bureaucratic rules and regulations. But in many ways the public mood has moved against deregulation and self-regulation in favour of tighter regulation.

The experience of deregulation has raised questions about the wisdom of giving private bodies greater freedom over deciding their own conduct. The full scientific account of the causes and means of transmitting BSE ('mad cow disease') are not yet known, but many commentators feel that rule changes played a part in this crisis. From the outset, in 1980, the government was warned of the dangers of deregulating hygiene rules governing feeding animal protein to cattle. The Ministry of Agriculture ignored such warnings and scrapped the tighter regulations which were drawn up in 1978. At the same time, the public was generally unaware of factory farming methods which allowed feeding infected sheep carcasses to cattle as a cheap form of protein. The subsequent crises resulted in risking the public's health, souring relations with our European partners, damage to the farming industry, and an estimated cost of £8 billion to the taxpayer.

Bus deregulation was an example where many restrictions to trade were removed and the market was opened up to new players. Bus deregulation frequently resulted in 'bus wars' between established operators and their 'cowboy' rivals for passengers on the most profitable routes. Deregulation has resulted in less areas being served and a decline in passengers. A 1997 report found that outside of London, the number of passenger journeys had fallen by 29 per cent between 1986 and 1996. Deregulation of buses had the unintended effects of concentrating services on fewer routes, rather than opening up new routes through competition.

Finally, the issue of self-regulation was publicly debated as a result of the brewing industry marketing 'alcopops' in 1995. Alcopops are sweet, fruit-based alcoholic drinks which now account for 10 per cent of all alcohol sales. Originally alcopops were brightly labelled and had names designed to appeal to young people. Much criticism was voiced about these drinks since it was suspected that brewers were aiming sales at under-age drinkers. The church argued that far from acting responsibly, brewers were cynically targeting the under-age drinker and that alcopops represented the unacceptable face of a deregulated market. In light of this and similar criticism in Parliament and the press, some breweries and supermarkets assumed a more responsible attitude in changing packaging and prices and also in restricting access to the under-aged. A survey, *Young People and Alcohol* (Schools Health Education Unit, Exeter University 1997) found that alcopops did not introduce young people to alcohol as much as encourage them into habits of heavy drinking. In light of the response of brewers and supermarkets in making alcopops less accessible to the young, some argued that self-regulation clearly worked successfully in controlling the behaviour of the brewing industry. Others disagreed, and argued that if self-regulation had worked successfully, alcopops would never have been produced in the first place.

Summary

- Indirect government is a politically useful, if undemocratic, way of making decisions and providing services. Although there have been attempts in the past to reduce the size of quasi-government and the number of quangos in existence, government policies have led to a proliferation of quangos and quango-like bodies. Those who campaigned for devolution argued that their policies would increase democracy and reduce quangocracy; their opponents argued that this promise was easier to make than it will be to keep.

- Privatisation also promised to deliver greater choice to the public, at a lower cost and with improved performance, but the record has been extremely variable. At its worst, privatisation has resulted in less choice, higher costs and poorer quality of service despite elaborate regulatory frameworks and Citizens' Charters. This has resulted in demands to tighten up on regulation by giving the various regulatory bodies greater powers in controlling the privatised utilities and other concerns which deal with the public.

- The PFI seems likely to play a larger role in financing and managing public sector facilities.

Questions

1. 'Quasi-government is undemocratic and therefore cannot be justified.' Discuss this view.
2. 'Since Britain's private sector has performed so poorly against international competitors, it is hard to understand why it has become a model for the public sector to emulate.' Critically analyse this statement.
3. 'As with nationalisation, strict regulation can place business executives in a straitjacket which prevents them from responding to customers' needs and market forces.' What is the political case for and against complete deregulation of business?

Assignments

Assignment (1) Charities run along business lines

Public sector institutions – from local government to the universities – are now run much more on business lines than used to be the case. Even charities in the voluntary sector have had to adjust to the Thatcherite rigours of a more competitive market place. The Women's Royal Voluntary Service (WRVS for short) is Britain's biggest voluntary organisation and is an excellent example of a charity becoming a more commercialised, professional and management-conscious organisation. Founded in 1938 by Lady Reading to help with Britain's war effort at home, the WRVS is now experiencing the pains of transforming itself from an old-fashioned charity to a modern voluntary organisation.

- Many of the volunteers – typically middle-class and middle-aged women – are very disgruntled over the changes that are taking place within the WRVS. In particular, the organisation used to be run by women who had worked their way up in the voluntary hierarchy, and many are upset that it is now run by a new breed of business managers recruited from the private sector who have no direct experience of voluntary community service. One volunteer who quit the WRVS after more than 15 years of voluntary service said 'the Lady Reading spirit has gone. A lot of the older members are saying that it is not the organisation they joined. They feel the volunteers are no longer appreciated.' Another member was furious that the new highly-paid executives were wearing WRVS badges yet had never done 'voluntary' work.

- Predictably, the new WRVS has adopted a new logo and attempted to widen its appeal by casting off its 'twinset and pearls' image. The new executive sees the WRVS as 'big business', with its hospital outlets alone generating an annual income in excess of £21 million. The new executive was also ruthless in sacking some its permanent staff who were appointed under the old regime. This led to a number of resignations amongst other of the established staff who were shocked over the way in which the WRVS – a so-called 'caring' organisation – had treated its own long-serving staff.

- Like many other firms which have 'rationalised, de-layered and down-sized' during the Thatcher years, the WRVS is now undergoing changes which are resulting in the closure of its smaller offices. This means that its 'customers' seeking second-hand clothes, hearing-aid batteries and its other services, will have to travel further to get 'served'. One ex-member commented that the whole philosophy of the WRVS has changed very quickly from that of a voluntary organisation which put people first, to a commercial organisation where profits mattered most.

Questions

(i) What are 'the Thatcherite rigours of a more competitive market place'?

(ii) Describe the differing values of the new WRVS and the old WRVS of 'Lady Reading'.

(iii) What distinguishes commercial values from the 'public service ethos'? Is it simply a matter of emphasis in deciding which ways are best in meeting the needs of the public or are there fundamental differences which include contrasting definitions of 'the public' as well as different ways of recognising what constitutes 'a need'?

Assignment (2) School governors

School governing bodies are a combination of appointed, elected and co-opted governors. The way a governing body is made up (its composition) is set out in the school's instrument of government. The membership of the governing bodies of county schools and controlled schools must be as follows:

Schools with up to 99 registered pupils
2 parents
2 people appointed by the LEA
1 teacher
3 co-optees*
 (in controlled schools two of the co-optee posts are filled by the foundation instead)
1 head (unless he or she chooses not to be a governor)
Total of 9 (including the head)

100–299 Registered Pupils
3 parents
3 people appointed by the LEA
1 teacher
4 co-optees*
 (in controlled schools three of the co-optee posts are filled by the foundation instead)
1 head (unless he or she chooses not to be a governor)
Total of 12 (including the head)

300–599 Registered pupils
4 parents
4 people appointed by the LEA
2 teachers
5 co-optees*
 (in controlled schools four of the co-optee posts are filled by people appointed by the foundation instead)
1 head (unless he or she chooses not to be a governor)
Total of 16 (including the head)

600+ Registered pupils
These can either have the same as schools with 300–599 pupils or:
5 parents
5 people appointed by the LEA

2 teachers
6 co-optees*
 (in controlled schools four of the co-optee posts are filled by people appointed by the foundation instead)
1 head (unless he or she chooses not to be a governor)
Total of 19 (including the head)

*In primary schools, one co-optee post is filled by a person appointed by a minor authority (a district or parish council) instead if there is one in the area.

The different types of governor
- *Parent* governors are elected by the parents of pupils at the school, and must be parents of children on the school-roll at the time of the election. They do not have to stand down if their child leaves the school during the period they serve, though they may do so if they wish. Parent governors may stand for re-election at the end of their term of office if they still qualify. If not enough parents stand for election, parent governors may be appointed by the governing body.
- *Governors appointed by the LEA* can be re-appointed. They can also be removed by the LEA in certain circumstances.
- *The head* is a member of the governing body unless he or she chooses not to be. In either case the head has the right to attend all meeting of the governing body.
- *Teacher governors* are elected by, and from among, the teachers at the school. They can stand for re-election. If they leave the school, they have to stand down form the governing body.
- *Co-opted governors* are chosen by at least two-thirds of other governors who have not been co-opted. When deciding who to co-opt, governors should make sure that their governing body reflects a balance of interests. They must make sure that the local business community is represented on the governing body. They can be reappointed, but they cannot be removed from office by those who selected them.
  At some primary schools another authority besides the LEA may have a right to appoint governors, and the number of co-opted governors

has to be reduced. A primary school will be affected if it serves an area where there is a *minor authority* such as a district or parish council. In such a case, one governor must be appointed by the minor authority, and the number of co-opted governors is reduced by one. It may be that the instrument of government allows two or more minor authorities to appoint a governor jointly. If the minor authorities cannot agree on their representative, the Secretary of State can be asked for a decision.

- *Foundation governors* are appointed to voluntary school governing bodies to represent the interests of the church authority or voluntary organisation which provides the school. They can be reappointed and they can be removed from office in certain circumstances by the people who appointed them. The instrument of government may allow for an office holder (such as a Minister of the Parish) to be a foundation governor ex-officio.

Source: *School Governors: A Guide to the Law*, DFEE, 1997.

Questions

(i) Identify one factor which influences the composition of school governing bodies.

(ii) Assess the extent of 'parent power' in the governing of schools.

(iii) In what ways do local businessman and businesswomen enjoy a special position on school governing bodies? What reasons might account for this?

Further reading

Burch, M. and Wood B. (1997) 'From Provider to "Enabler": The Changing Role of the State', in Robins, L. and Jones B. (eds), *Half a Century of British Politics* (Manchester: MUP) pp. 29–45: an historical survey of how the modern state has changed since 1945. Hall, W. and Weir, S. (1996) *The Untouchables: Power and Accountability in the Quango State* (London: The Democratic Audit/ Scarman Trust): a survey which plots the growth and extent of the quango state.

Territorial government and politics: the Disunited Kingdom

The British state is under stress as various political processes challenge, even erode, its structures, competences and territorial boundaries. At one level it is being absorbed into a larger unit, the European Union. An increasingly wide range of national regulations, standards and practices are being harmonised with or displaced by their European equivalents. The 'Europeanisation' of the British state was accelerated with the implementation of the Single European Act (see Chapter 13) and will be further accelerated at such time as Britain participates in the single currency of an inevitably more federal EU.

At another level, the British state is under pressure to fragment into smaller units, as with Wales and especially Scotland, or to develop closer cross-border links with its foreign neighbour, as in the case of Northern Ireland. This chapter explores the implication of such processes from above and below on the stability and persistence into the future of the United Kingdom of Great Britain and Northern Ireland.

A confused national identity?

Political geography, in its widest sense, is subject to constant change and frequent upheaval. For example, a map of Europe drawn at the end of the First World War bears little resemblance to the Europe which emerged from the Second World War, and even this map has changed dramatically within the last decade by the break-up of the Soviet Union and fragmentation of Czechoslovakia and Yugoslavia. Britain has not escaped from change. Withdrawal from empire reduced territorial responsibilities overseas, bringing change to both the structure and functions of the 'Imperial' Parliament at Westminster. Even internally Britain has experienced territorial change and persistent border tensions. Britain's boundaries changed in 1922 with the partition of Ireland; twenty-six counties succeeded to form the Irish Free State (now the Republic of Ireland) whilst Northern Ireland remained British. The border between the North and the South has remained contested; whilst the Republic's constitution claimed that its national territory consists of the whole island of Ireland, British legislation has recognised Northern Ireland as part of the United Kingdom.

The links between Britain's territorial boundaries and the various cultural identities of the population living within these boundaries is complex. How many Scottish and Welsh people identify primarily with being 'British' or even 'European'? What proportion of the Catholic community in Northern Ireland identifies in ways similar to most Protestants and look to the United Kingdom rather than to the Republic of Ireland? What, if anything, does Irish, Welsh and Scottish nationalism have in common? What are the implications of smaller cultural communities, such as the Afro-Caribbean and Asian communities in many of Britain's large cities or the British citizens of the Channel Islands and Isle of Man who are not part of the United Kingdom? Finally, what position does the dominant country, England, occupy in this complex mosaic?

Before these points can be addressed, the fundamental questions have to be asked about the nature of the United Kingdom. Basically, is the United Kingdom

- a unitary state, containing a socially integrated population who share a common culture, or
- a multinational federal body where power has moved from a central political authority to the various peripheral communities and to the EU?

It is useful to consider a brief explanation of the evolution of the United Kingdom in order to assess its contemporary nature.

Core and periphery

Some political scientists have attempted to explain the history of Britain's political culture and institutions in terms of a core-periphery theory. In other words, much can be explained in terms of the relations between the country's core, or 'centre of gravity', and its outlaying areas which comprise the periphery. It can be thought of as based on the idea of Britain as a multinational state, with its 'core' in South East Britain, an 'outer core' comprising East Anglia, the Midlands and Wessex, its 'inner periphery' made up of the North of England, Wales and the South West, and its 'outer periphery' being Scotland. These areas correspond with arcs drawn around London at 80, 200 and 300 miles. Michael Steed argued

> The 17th-century civil war can be seen as a victory of the inner core over the inner periphery; most of the battles were fought in the outer core. From the mid-18th century onwards there came the fundamental shift from lowland Britain to upland Britain. The repeal of the Corn Laws in 1846, a turning point in British politics, reflected that shift; not only did the Anti-Corn Law League start in the periphery, in Manchester, and capture the core; it represented the interests of those parts of Britain trading westwards and wishing to import cheap food as opposed to those parts of Britain more able to produce food. By the end of the 19th-century peripheral Britain had been mobilized solidly (except Western Lancashire) for Gladstonian Liberalism, and core Britain for Unionism. In the 20th-century Labour and Conservative have reflected the same dichotomy

> . . . Even the split in 1985 in the miners' strike could be seen as reflecting 'the division between north and south with its roots deep in the nation's history'. (Steed, 1986, pp. 591–5)

The core–periphery idea has been developed in terms of the colonial domination of the Celtic periphery by the English core. Michael Hechter has advanced a persuasive theory of internal colonialism whereby the advanced areas dominate and exploit the less advanced peripheral areas. In other words, by much the same process as Britain colonised much of the wider world, so the area making up Britain's core colonised the areas on its periphery. Historically this process was marked by the statutes of 1536, 1707 and 1800 which brought Wales, Scotland and Ireland respectively into the English-dominated Union. Relations between the core and periphery are complex and will vary over time, but in terms of modern history, as Bulpitt commented, the Second World War had an integrative affect on the whole of the United Kingdom and even the communities in Northern Ireland were drawn closer together in the face of the common German enemy (Bulpitt, 1983 p. 136).

At other times the relations between core and periphery might be tense, and, as Hechter has argued, despite domination by the core the political culture of the periphery survives until eventually there is a reaction against core domination. The first major protest came from Irish nationalists. For Ireland was always the least integrated part of the periphery; in the 1840s Irish agriculture failed resulting in widespread poverty and famine within the United Kingdom which was tolerated by the core. Concern for Ireland was not helped by dominant English attitudes towards the Irish which comprised racist caricatures of slow, simple-minded peasants. Irish assertion against the English core began in earnest during the 1880s with demands from the Irish for self-government, or as it was known at the time, 'Home Rule'. Irish nationalists convinced the Liberal leader, William Gladstone, that Home Rule was the only solution to 'the Irish problem'. This led to a crisis in British politics and caused deep divisions within the Liberal Party. The defeat of Home Rule in Westminster was a crucial factor in the general election victory of the Conservatives who supported the Union. As Denis

Judd has argued, 'the Irish Home Rule crisis was a dress rehearsal for later confrontations with a variety of colonial nationalist movements' (Judd, 1996, p. 47).

The solution to the Irish problem, as already mentioned, was partition in 1922. But was the 'Irish problem' really an 'Ulster' or 'British problem' resulting from 'the English, and their self-serving strategies of plantation and subordination begun in the seventeenth century'? (Judd, 1996, 49). Concern for the issue rose and subsided, but never disappeared altogether. Irish nationalist sentiments resurged in the 1960s and 1970s alongside Welsh and Scottish nationalism.

Welsh cultural linguistic nationalism

In the 1945 general election Plaid Cymru won 1.1 per cent of the Welsh vote. Domination by the English 'core' had resulted in the decline of Welsh culture, particularly the Welsh language. As Madgwick and Rawkins commented, by the beginning of the twentieth century the Welsh language had become 'the language of the hearth, and not a public language, except in the chapels. In the new Board schools of the late nineteenth century, English was taught as the language of advancement, and the use of Welsh was actively discouraged' (Madgwick and Rawkins, 1982, p. 67). Reaction to 'core domination' came during the 1960s and 1970s in the form of a determined campaign to save the Welsh language from extinction. In this sense Welsh nationalism focused more on the political arrangements necessary to preserve the Welsh culture than on political demands for comprehensive Home Rule.

The cultural linguistic flavour of Welsh nationalism has been reflected in the results of the two devolution referendums. In the 1979 referendum only 11.8 per cent of the Welsh electorate voted 'yes' to devolution, heavily crushed by the 46.5 per cent who voted 'no' and the complacent 41.7 per cent who did not bother to vote one way or the other. An even lower turnout marked the 1997 devolution referendum (see Chapter 8) and although the percentage voting 'yes' more than doubled, it still only represented one in four of the Welsh electorate.

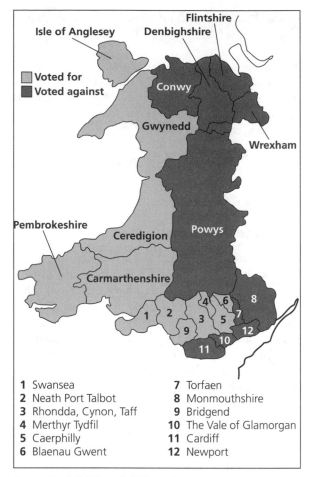

1	Swansea	**7**	Torfaen
2	Neath Port Talbot	**8**	Monmouthshire
3	Rhondda, Cynon, Taff	**9**	Bridgend
4	Merthyr Tydfil	**10**	The Vale of Glamorgan
5	Caerphilly	**11**	Cardiff
6	Blaenau Gwent	**12**	Newport

Source: The Daily Telegraph, 20 September 1997.

Figure 18.1 How the referendum vote divided Wales

Figure 18.1 shows the political geography of the 1997 Welsh devolution vote, which gave a wafer-thin 0.6 of a percent majority to pro-devolutionists. Predictably, the strongest 'yes' vote was in the Welsh-speaking heartlands and Labour strongholds. The 'no' vote was in areas of South Wales – the Vale of Glamorgan, Cardiff, Newport, Monmouthshire and Pembrokeshire – along with the border regions of Powys, Denbighshire, Flintshire, Wrexham, and Colwyn to the North. Some anti-devolution voices contested the legitimacy of the narrow 6,700 majority of the 'yes' vote, particularly when procedural irregularities were revealed in the Caerphilly area which delivered a 6,000 majority to the 'yes' campaign.

Finally, the limited demands from the Welsh 'periphery' for autonomy from the 'core' are reflected in the relatively weak powers of the new Welsh *assembly*, especially when compared with those of the new Scottish *parliament*. The Welsh assembly will comprise 60 members; having a ten member executive with a leader elected by the assembly; jurisdiction over economic development, planning, transport, health and education; no tax-raising powers; and no right to pass primary legislation.

Scottish nationalism

Scotland provides a second interesting example of the failure of the United Kingdom to meet perfectly the nation-state ideal. The expansion of the English core absorbed Scotland in 1707 with two separate parliaments becoming one. However Scotland retained its distinctive national identity which, in the twentieth century, was reflected in a separate legal system, education system and established church. Scottish affairs were handled by the oldest and largest of the multi-functional ministries, the Scottish Office, with a 'mini-parliament' of Scottish MPs meeting in the form of the Scottish Grand Committee.

Scots shared a wider British nationalism in so far as it facilitated participation in Britain's imperial glory and two victories over expansionist Germany. Scots peopled the empire, including settlement of Scottish Presbyterians in Northern Ireland in the early years of the seventeenth century. Even as late as the 1945 general election, nationalist sentiment was weakly expressed with the Scottish National Party winning only 1.3 per cent of the Scottish vote. The decline of Britain's world role, and with it the prestige of being associated with the Empire, gave renewed significance to Scottish nationalism.

Because the 1979 devolution referendum had a requirement that at least 40 per cent of the Scottish electorate must support devolution in order for it to proceed, and not just a simple majority of voters, the pro-devolution campaign lost. Some 32.5 per cent of the Scottish electorate voted 'yes', 30.7 per cent voted 'no', with 37.1 per cent abstaining. Nationalist feelings, however, were to become aroused by Margaret Thatcher's strident expression of English

nationalism, with the number of Conservative MPs returned to Scottish seats declining with each successive election until none at all were elected in 1997.

The increasing number of SNP MPs elected from the 1960s led to anxiety within the Labour Party that it could be displaced from the position it now occupied as the main party representing the Scottish electorate. Gradually devolution became accepted as a solution which would satisfy nationalist ambitions whilst protecting Labour's position. Labour supported the Scottish Constitutional Convention, a cross-party body also embracing Liberal Democrats, Scottish trade unions, local authorities and a number of other small bodies. The Constitutional Convention was pledged to devolution, which resulted in the SNP being ambivalent towards its existence and recommendations. For some Scottish Nationalists feared that devolution was a compromise which would satisfy many of their supporters' demands making full independence an unobtainable goal; others supported devolution which they saw as a 'half-way house' on the road to a fully independent Scotland.

The diversity of opinion which existed prior to the 1997 devolution included the following positions:

- The SNP wanted full independence for Scotland, with Scottish membership of the EU, NATO and the Commonwealth. (According to opinion polls, a fully independent Scotland was supported by two-thirds of SNP supporters.) The SNP proposed a single-chamber parliament for Scotland with full legislative powers, comprising 200 members (two MPs elected by proportional representation from each of the existing 72 constituencies and 56 from party lists.) The Queen would remain head of state, but the parliament's Chancellor would act on her behalf. A written constitution would contain a bill of rights, and the Gaelic language would be given official status.
- The Scottish Constitutional Convention proposed setting up a parliament with 129 members; 73 Scottish MPs would be elected by first-past-the-post and 56 elected from the Euro-constituencies by proportional representation. Parliaments would be fixed-term, and have the power to vary income tax by plus or minus three pence. The parliament would legislate on

Scotland's 'home affairs' policies of education, health, housing, local government, transport, planning, industry, the environment, arts and the media, heritage and sport. Scotland would remain part of the United Kingdom, with Westminster responsible for policies on the economy, defence foreign affairs, immigration, nationality, and social security.

The Scottish Labour Party's position of supporting the Constitutional Convention was thrown into disarray when Tony Blair announced that there would be a referendum prior to any devolution in which Scottish voters would be asked, firstly, whether they wanted a Scottish parliament and, secondly, whether it should have tax-varying powers. Blair's imposition of what was seen as an unnecessary referendum by Scottish Labour represented a move to defend Labour from Conservative attack. Some Conservative critics had argued that the only evidence that the Scots wanted their own parliament was found in changing opinion poll data and the proclamations of an appointed semi-official Convention. Also the referendum question about tax-varying powers defended Labour from the accusation that it was straining at the leash to impose a 'Tartan tax' on an unsuspecting Scottish electorate.

- The Conservatives remained true to their historic mission of defending the Union. Where Labour believed that devolution was a safety valve which would take the pressure out off Scottish nationalism and thereby protect the Union, Conservatives saw devolution as weakening the Union. They argued that Labour had been duped by SNP propaganda which had successfully obscured the fact that Scots were concerned about the same issues as the English, namely the economy, health and education. When pollsters enquired, the constitution was the tenth most important issue in the Scottish electorate's mind at the recent general election. Most Conservatives are convinced that once Scots experienced the reality of devolution they would oppose it fiercely. This belief is borne out by the fact that Scots benefit from public spending, receiving considerably more than is raised in Scotland through taxation. The 'Tartan tax', if levied at the maximum 3 pence, would raise only £450 million, far less than Scotland might lose through possible changes in funding

arrangements by central government after devolution. The Conservative answer to Scottish aspirations was the transfer of some powers from the Scottish Office to local authorities as well as increasing the powers of the Scottish Grand Committee regarding the scrutiny of Scottish legislation.

- A variety of other views existed including the quarter of Scottish public opinion which opposed both independence for Scotland and devolution. Based on the results of the 1979 referendum, it was suspected that much of this opposition was located in the Highlands and islands. Here the electorate had expressed fears that a devolved or independent Scotland would be dominated by the heavily populated central urban belt, resulting in the disregard of the very different needs of more remote areas.

The 1997 referendum

The referendum asked the Scottish electorate two questions in line with the Tony Blair's wishes for Labour to 'democratically anchor the Scottish parliament by a specific vote by the Scottish people' rather than on the recommendations of the Constitutional Convention. Labour supported the multi-party campaign, Scotland Forward, which urged Scots to answer the questions with a double 'yes'. The referendum was not held under ideal circumstances, with campaigning delayed until after the funeral of Diana, Princess of Wales and in the middle of a Scottish Labour sleaze dispute. Nevertheless, the electorate voted decisively for both the parliament and the limited tax-varying powers (see Chapter 8) with around three-quarters of voters supporting the parliament and two-thirds the taxation powers. It was a result which would have easily met the 40 per cent requirement of the 1979 referendum (such a condition was not set for the 1997 referendum).

Figure 18.2 shows that in 1997 the traditional opponents of devolution, the Highlands and islands, swung around to support the setting up of a Scottish parliament. The largest 'yes-yes' vote came from the Labour strongholds of Glasgow (although turnout was low) and Dumbartonshire. The least enthusiastic areas about the tax-varying powers were those areas which rejected devolution in

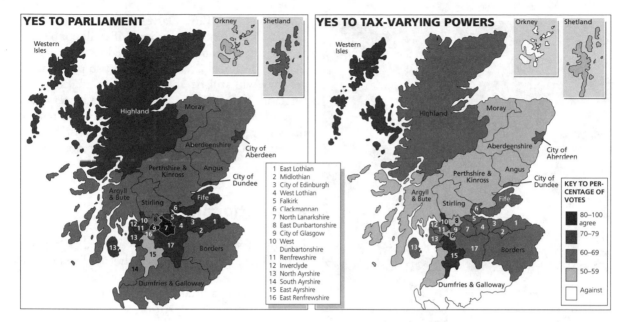

YES TO PARLIAMENT

YES TO TAX-VARYING POWERS

1 East Lothian
2 Midlothian
3 City of Edinburgh
4 West Lothian
5 Falkirk
6 Clackmannan
7 North Lanarkshire
8 East Dunbartonshire
9 City of Glasgow
10 West Dunbartonshire
11 Renfrewshire
12 Inverclyde
13 North Ayrshire
14 South Ayrshire
15 East Ayrshire
16 East Renfrewshire

KEY TO PER-CENTAGE OF VOTES

- 80–100 agree
- 70–79
- 60–69
- 50–59
- Against

ABERDEEN
Q1 Scottish parliament:
For 65,035 (71.77%) Against 25,580 (28.23%)
Q2 Tax varying powers:
For 54,320 (60.34%) Against 35,709 (39 66%)
Electorate 169,683; Turnout 90,615 (53.40%)

ABERDEENSHIRE
Q1: For 61,621 (63.86%) Against 34,878 (36.14%)
Q2: For 50,295 (52.27%) Against 45,929 (47.73%)
Electorate 170,310; Turnout 96,499 (56.66%)

ANGUS
Q1: For 33,571 (64.66%) Against 18,350 (35.34%)
Q2: For 27,641 (53.43%) Against 24,089 (46.57%)
Electorate 86,582; Turnout 51,921 (59.97%)

ARGYLL AND BUTE
Q1: For 30,452 (67.30%) Against 14,796 (32.70%)
Q2: For 25,746 (56.99%) Against 19,429 (43.01%)
Electorate 69,995; Turnout 45,248 (64.64%)

CLACKMANNANSHIRE
Q1: For 18,790 (79.97%) Against 4,706 (20.03%)
Q2: For 18,112 (88.66%) Against 7,355 (31.34%)
Electorate 35,725; Turnout 23,498 (85.77%)

DUMFRIES AND GALLOWAY
Q1: For 44,819 (80.72%) Against 28,883 (39.28%)
Q2: For 35,737 (48.80%) Against 37,499 (51.20%)
Electorate 115,204; Turnout 73,482 (63.78%)

DUNDEE
Q1: For 49,252 (76.00%) Against 15,553 (24.00%)
Q2: For 42,304 (65.50%) Against 22,280 (34.50%)
Electorate 117,101; Turnout 64,805 (55.34%)

EAST AYRSHIRE
Q1: For 49,131 (81.13%) Against11,426 (18.87%)
Q2: For 42,559 (70.48%) Against 17,824 (29.52%)
Electorate 93,958; Turnout 60,557 (64.45%)

EAST DUNBARTONSHIRE
Q1: For40,917 (69.77%) Against 17,725 (30.23%)
Q2: For34,576 (59.11%) Against 23,914 (40.89%)
Electorate 81,025; Turnout 58,642 (72.38%)

EAST LOTHIAN
Q1: For 33,525 (74.19%) Against 11,865 (25.81%)
Q2: For 28,152 (62.68%) Against 16,765 (37.32%)
Electorate 69,615; Turnout 45,190 (64.91%)

EAST RENFREWSHIRE
Q1: For 28,253 (61.65%) Against 17,573 (38.35%)
Q2. For 23,580 (51.56%) Against 22,153 (48.44%)
Electorate 67,363; Turnout 45,826 (68.03%)

EDINBURGH
Q1: For 155,900 (71.93%) Against 60,832 (28.07%)
Q2: For 133,843 (61.96%) Against 82,188 (38.04%)
Electorate 362,245; Turnout 216,732 (59.83%)

FALKIRK
Q1: For 55,642 (79.95%) Against 13,953 (20.05%)
Q2: For 48,064 (69.19%) Against 21,403 (30.81%)
Electorate 109,723; Turnout 69.595 (63.43%)

FIFE
Q1: For 125,668 (76.08%) Against 39,517 (23.92%)
Q2: For 108,021 (64 68%) Against 58,987 (35.32%)
Electorate 274,384; Turnout 167,008 (60.87%)

GLASGOW
Q1: For 204,269 (83.59%) Against 40,106 (16.41%)
Q2: For 61,359 (62.05%) Against 37,525 (37.95%)
Electorate 165,751; Turnout 99,982 (60.32%)

INVERCLYDE
Q1: For 31,680 (77.98%) Against 8,945 (22.02%)
Q2: For 27,194 (67.19%) Against 13,277 (32.81%)
Electorate 67,660; Turnout 40,625 (60.04%)

MIDLOTHIAN
Q1: For 31,681 (79.88%) Against 7,979 (20.12%)
Q2: For 26,776 (67.72%) Against 12,762 (32.28%)
Electorate 61,135; Turnout 39,660 (64.87%)

MORAY
Q1: For 24,822 (67.19%) Against 12,122 (32.81%)
Q2: For 19,326 (52.70%) Against 17,344 (47.30%)
Electorate 64,235; Turnout 36,944 (57.51%)

NORTH AYRSHIRE
Q1: For 51,304 (76.31%) Against 15,931 (23.69%)
Q2: For 43,990 (65.68%) Against 22,991 (34.32%)
Electorate 106,511; Turnout 67,235 (63.12%)

NORTH LANARKSHIRE
Q1: For 123,063 (82.55%) Against 26,010 (17.45%)
Q2: For 107,288 (72.17%) Against 41,372 (27.83%)
Electorate 246,704; Turnout 149,073 (60.43%)

ORKNEY
Q1: For 4,749 (57.29%) Against 3,541 (42.71%)

Q2: For 3,917 (47.42%) Against 4,344 (52.58%)
Electorate 15,579; Turnout 8,290 (53.21%)

PERTHSHIRE AND KINROSS
Q1: For 40,344 (61.74%) Against 24,998 (38.26%)
Q2: For 33,398 (51.30%) Against 31,709 (48.70%)
Electorate 104,138; Turnout 65,342 (62.75%)

RENFREWSHIRE
Q1: For 63,711 (79.05%) Against 18,213 (20.95%)
Q2: For 55,075 (63.59%) Against 31,537 (36.41%)
Electorate 139,269; Turnout 86,924 (62.41%)

SCOTTISH BORDERS
Q1: For 33,855 (62.79%) Against 20,060 (37.21%)
Q2: For 27,284 (50.73%) Against 26,497 (49.27%)
Electorate 83,674; Turnout 53,915 (64.43%)

SHETLAND
Q1: For 5,430 (62.38%) Against 3,275 (37.62%)
Q2: For 4,478 (51.61%) Against 4,198 (48.39%)
Electorate 16,561; Turnout 8,705 (52.56%)

SOUTH AYRSHIRE
Q1: For 40,161 (66.86%) Against 19,909 (33.14%)
Q2. For 33,679 (56.23%) Against 26,217 (43.77%)
Electorate 90,433; Turnout 60,070 (66.42%)

SOUTH LANARKSHIRE
Q1: For 114,908 (77.81%) Against 32,762 (22.19%)
Q2: For 99,587 (67.61 %) Against 47,708 (32.39%)
Electorate 235,108; Turnout 147,670 (62.81%)

STIRLING
Q1: For 29,190 (68.47%) Against 13,440 (31.53%)
Q2: For 25,044 (58.88%) Against 17,487 (41.12%)
Electorate 65,075; Turnout 42,630 (65.51%)

WEST DUNBARTONSHIRE
Q1: For 39,051 (84.69%) Against 7,058 (15.31%)
Q2: For 34,408 (74.74%) Against 11,628 (25.26%)
Electorate 72,744; Turnout 46,109 (63.39%)

WESTERN ISLES
Q1: For 9,977 (79.40%) Against 2,589 (20.60%)
Q2: For 8,557 (68.43%) Against 3,947 (31.57%)
Electorate 22,733; Turnout 12,566 (55.28%)

WEST LOTHIAN
Q1: For 56,923 (79.57%) Against 14,614 (20.43%)
Q2: For 47,990 (67.27%) Against 23,354 (32.73%)
Electorate 114,836; Turnout 71,537 (62.29%)

Source: The Times, 13 September 1997.

Figure 18.2 The 1997 referendum vote in Scotland

Source: *The Guardian* 13th September, 1997 p. 4.

Figure 18.3 The Yes – Yes campaign's victory party

1979, the Borders, Perth and Kinross, and the Shetlands.

The new parliament is planned to be set up by 2000, and generally in line with the recommendations of the Constitutional Convention. Around two-thirds of its 129 MPs will be elected by first-past-the-post, with the remainder being additional members elected from party lists. The Chief Minister, likely to become known as 'Scotland's prime minister', will select a cabinet; the parliament will have tax-varying powers; it will have the right to pass primary legislation; and will have wide jurisdiction over 'home affairs'.

An intriguing point yet to be fully answered is the so-called 'West Lothian' question, which concerns the number and role of Scottish MPs in the Commons. As Tam Dalyell, the MP for West Lothian, has pointed out, these MPs will not be able to vote on, for example, Scottish education because that has been devolved to the Scottish parliament, yet they will still be able to vote on education in England. Some believe that a future Conservative government will accept devolution but will reduce the number of Scottish MPs at Westminster, over-represented in terms of size of the electorate, from the current 72 to around 60.

Irish nationalism

It is often said that Northern Ireland is 'a place apart'. The people of Northern Ireland live in a distinctive political culture, support different political parties, and face a unique constitutional problem yet to be resolved. The partition of Ireland in 1922, creating what was initially known as the Irish Free State to the south, did not solve the 'Irish problem', since a sizeable Catholic minority, now amounting to 40 per cent of the population, lived in the North (see Figure 18.3). In a sense, two minorities live side by side in Northern Ireland; the Catholic minority in Northern Ireland which feels threatened by the Protestant majority, and the Protestant minority which feels threatened by the Catholic majority should the North reunite with the South.

This chapter has already mentioned some of the historical events which have been reflected in relations between 'core' and 'periphery', such as William Gladstone's support for *Home Rule*, which would have given Ireland its independence. As Bulpitt mentioned, the years following the end of the Second World War were relatively peaceful ones in Northern Ireland. It was commonly assumed that conflict between Protestants and Catholics was being diluted by their shared interest in increasing affluence. Although Catholics remained discriminated against in terms of employment, welfare and political rights, they were better off than their counterparts to the South. The Irish Republican Army (IRA) waged an unsuccessful campaign in the late 1950s and this too was taken as evidence that Catholics now accepted the political status quo in return for improved living standards.

The appointment of Captain Terence O'Neill as Prime Minister in March 1963 would, it was assumed, lead to continued tranquility in the politics of Northern Ireland. For O'Neill was a 'liberal conservative' committed to reforms which would modernise the political system and break down further the ancient hatreds between the rival communities.

O'Neill's brand of progressive Unionism was opposed by many Ulster loyalists who were worried about the direction in which his reforms were leading. Conservative Loyalists became determined to resist change and a more militant attitude was taken towards the Catholic minority.

The position of Prime Minister O'Neill weakened, but nevertheless he pushed ahead with his reforms and, long overdue, provided for universal adult suffrage in local government elections. Soon afterwards his position became untenable and he resigned, to be replaced by Major James Chichester-Clark. Fire-bombings and street rioting continued to the point where Westminster sent in troops to end sectarian violence and protect Catholics from militant Unionists. Initially British troops were welcomed by Catholics, but inevitably their strong-arm role was to become identified with supporting the Protestant state rather than defending the Catholic minority. The political condition of Northern Ireland moved close to a state of revolution. Chichester-Clark resigned in 1971 to be replaced by Brian Faulkner, an old hard-line opponent of O'Neill.

Violence against Catholics led them into accepting the IRA as their defence force, particularly true regarding the newly formed more militant provisional wing of the IRA. The position of the IRA was strengthened by the policy of *internment*, a practice sometimes referred to as the 'recruiting officer for the IRA', since it involved the inprisonment of suspected terrorists which included many innocent Catholics. The troubles were to become yet more intense in January 1972 when, in controversial circumstances, British paratroopers appeared to over-react on the streets and killed 13 unarmed individuals in a tragedy come to be known as 'Bloody Sunday'. British Prime Minister Edward Heath announced that Stormont was to be suspended and from April 1972 Northern Ireland would come under *Direct Rule* from Westminster. A referendum on core–periphery relations held in 1973 did little to clarify the position because of Catholic abstention. Some 57.5 per cent of Northern Ireland's elec-

Source: Arthur (1984)

Figure 18.4 Ireland, showing the boundary between Northern Ireland and the Republic

torate wanted to remain part of the United Kingdom, 0.6 per cent wanted Northern Ireland to unite with the Republic of Ireland outside the United Kingdom, and 41.9 per cent abstained.

The roots of conflict

The sources of contemporary conflict in Northern Ireland are complex and they change in nature from time to time. Nevertheless, some progress towards understanding can be made by exploring three basic propositions.

BOX 18.1

The vocabulary of conflict in Northern Ireland

The majority of the Protestant community supports **Unionist** or **Loyalist** political parties. This is an expression of their loyalty to the Union between Northern Ireland and the British monarch who is at the head of the Protestant Church. Most Protestants oppose the idea of Northern Ireland being reunited with the South and being governed from Dublin under a Catholic-influenced constitution. There are and have been numerous groups and organisations which reinforce general Unionist beliefs amongst Protestants; some of these groups are permanent, others come and go whilst some are set up as rivals to existing groups which may be seen as either too moderate or too extreme. Examples include the influential **Orange Order** and the **Ulster Volunteer Force** (UVF) whose motto was 'For God and Ulster' and which was absorbed into the para-military **Ulster Defence Association.** The leader of the **Loyalist Volunteer Force**, **Billy Wright**, who set up the paramilitary force in 1996, was killed in the Maze prison by armed INLA prisoners.

Although there are political divisions within the Protestant community it is assumed that if faced with a crisis of survival these divisions would disappear and Protestant leaders would be able to resist change by 'playing the Orange card' which would involve organising mass civil unrest. The **Reverend Ian Paisley** emerged as a Protestant leader during the era of O'Neill's liberal reforms and was originally associated with the UVF. Paisley, the 'big man', is a remarkable figure in the politics of Northern Ireland, having founded both his own **Free Presbyterian Church of Ulster** in 1951 and his populist **Democratic Unionist Party** in 1971 which commands the support of half of Unionist voters. The other main Unionist party is the more middle-class **Official Unionist Party** which is led by **David Trimble.**

Security and law and order have long been important and sensitive issues. Many Catholics see the **Royal Ulster Constabulary** (RUC) as a Protestant force despite the fact that it is open to Catholic recruits. A part-time arm of the RUC, the **B Specials**, were exclusively Protestant but these were disbanded and replaced by the Ulster Defence Regiment.

Irish Nationalists support the reunification of Ireland, which would involve the withdrawal of Britain and the dissolution of Northern Ireland. The Nationalist cause is expressed by a variety of organisations all of which receive Catholic support. Moderate constitutional nationalism is pursued by the **Social Democratic and Labour Party** (SDLP), which has an open membership but is supported mainly by Catholics. The SDLP was formed in 1970 to pursue the goal of reunification but based on majority consensus. SDLP's **John Hume** has played a major role in inaugurating the peace process. More militant nationalism is expressed in the shape of Republicanism and is symbolised by the Tricolour rather than the Union Jack of the Unionists. **Sinn Fein**, led by **Gerry Adams**, represents Republicanism in Northern Ireland. Many believe that Sinn Fein has direct links with the IRA, although this is denied by its members. Sinn Fein has put candidates forward in local and parliamentary elections, the most dramatic being the success in a Fermanagh and South Tyrone by-election of **Bobby Sands** who eventually died on hunger strike in an **H-Block** prison.

The **Irish Republican Army** is the paramilitary wing of Republicanism which has committed terrorist acts in Northern Ireland and mainland Britain. The IRA has experienced internal divisions which have resulted in break-away factions such as the **Provisional IRA** (the 'Provos') and the **Irish National Liberation Army** (INLA).

Finally, there have been political initiatives which have attempted to end the polarisation of politics in Northern Ireland. In 1976 the **Peace People**, a peace movement organised by women after three children were killed in an incident, organised successfully and for a time their message found echoes of support on both sides of the divide. Women were again the focus for action in the **Northern Ireland Women's Coalition** which successfully contested the Forum elections. Another attempt to integrate the two communities has been made by the **Campaign for Equal Citizenship**, which wanted the electorate to have the opportunity to support Labour, Conservative and Liberal Democratic parties rather than the parties of Northern Ireland which, it was argued, contributed to Northern Ireland's problems rather than solved them.

Firstly, how far is the conflict between Protestants and Catholics a religious struggle? Steve Bruce has argued that Protestantism and Roman Catholicism 'were not *any two* different religions. They stood in opposition to each other. The former began as a "protest" against features of the latter and, after they separated, each developed elements which most

clearly distinguished it from the other' (Bruce, 1986, p. 6). He continued by speculating how different the history of Ireland would have been had the original settlers from England and Scotland also been Catholic: 'Differences of power, status, and wealth between settler and native would have remained, of course, but a common religious culture would have encouraged intermarriage and eroded ethnic boundaries' (ibid.). In the 1990s religious differences still keep the two communities apart and, unlike on mainland Britain, church attendance is high and there are other institutions working to maintain the link between religion and politics. For example, on the Protestant side the 'link between religion and politics within the Unionist Party continued to be provided and maintained by the Orange Order' (Wichert, 1991, p. 69). The Orange Order remains a semi-secret fraternal organisation having the support of around two-thirds of Protestant males. On the Catholic side religious and political links are sustained through segregated schooling which provides the children of the Catholic community with an Irish identity.

Secondly, the conflict in Northern Ireland might be understood as an internal colonial struggle between periphery and core. The argument runs as follows. Although the native populations enjoyed rising living standards under minority colonial rule, they still demanded the return of land taken by the settlers as well as majority rule. The beleaguered settler population includes fundamentalists who are not willing to compromise. There is a struggle, often bloody, between the native majority which have discovered nationalism and who want independence and a settler minority who want to maintain the power and privileges enjoyed under the colonial system of exploitation.

Finally, is the conflict in Northern Ireland no more than a class struggle distorted by the labels of Ulster Protestantism and Irish Catholicism? In other words, has the ruling class maintained its position of power by manipulating members of the working class into fighting each other? According to this analysis the Protestant working class 'have been duped into thinking they enjoy (economic) advantage' over Catholics (Bruce, 1986, p. 254). Because they believed that they were better off than Catholics, the Protestant working class remained loyal to the state and were unwilling to unite with the Catholic working class in order to advance their common class interests. The usefulness of this sort of explanation has been eroded by recent events. For example, the economic gap between members of the Protestant and Catholic working class in employment has diminished, and a common culture of poverty afflicts Protestants and

Catholics alike who are without work and rely on welfare.

The search for a solution

Direct Rule from Westminster was not seen by the British government as a long-term future for Northern Ireland. The ultimate goal of the Conservative administration led by Edward Heath was the re-establishment of some form of devolved government in Northern Ireland in the hope that this would find widespread acceptance in both communities. The Secretary of State, William Whitelaw, proposed the setting up of an assembly elected by proportional representation which would gradually assume greater policy responsibilities. The assembly would have a power-sharing executive with Unionist and SDLP representatives. Also a Council of Ireland would be established with its membership drawn from the assembly as well as from the parliaments in Westminster and Dublin. The elections to the assembly fragmented the Unionist vote with ten representatives elected on an anti-power-sharing platform. This experiment was ended in 1974 by a general strike organised by the Ulster Workers Council which brought the province to a standstill. The 'Orange Card' had been played to great effect, and left some commentators asking whether Ulster militants or the British state now governed Northern Ireland.

A later Conservative Secretary of State, James Prior, conducted a rather similar experiment with 'rolling devolution'. Once again an assembly was to be elected which would in time gain greater and greater responsibility for policy-making. As before there was relatively little support for the idea, which was made unworkable in practice, and the assembly was dissolved after four years. Yet again the devolution experiment ended in failure.

The New Ireland Forum, a conference made up from nationalist parties north and south of the border published its conclusions on future possibilities for the province. The first option was that of a unitary Irish state with special protection for the Protestant minority. Secondly, there could be a federal or confederal state which would allow for a degree of self-government for 'Northern Ireland' within a United Ireland. Thirdly, there could be arrangements for joint authority in which the governments of London and Dublin would have equal responsibility for administering Northern Ireland.

Despite Prime Minister Thatcher's rejection of the New Ireland Forum, the Anglo-Irish Agreement signed by her and Charles Haughey, the Irish Taoiseach, bore some similarities to the third option in the Forum report. The agreement (or 'accord' as it was sometimes described) involved provision for much cooperation between Britain and Ireland, including greater cross-border cooperation to defeat terrorism, with Dublin consulted routinely on Northern Ireland affairs. Unionists were outraged by this provision which they saw as constitutionally unique – that is, a foreign government given the power to influence domestic policy in a part of the United Kingdom. 'Ulster Says No' was the slogan of the Unionist parties. Sinn Fein also, but for different reasons, opposed the agreement. The SDLP was in favour, as were the front benches of all Britain's major parties.

The talks process

Initially two sets of talks raised hopes of peace in Northern Ireland – firstly, the *Hume–Adams* talks and, secondly, the *Anglo-Irish Declaration*, based on talks between British Prime Minister John Major and Albert Reynolds (the Irish Taoiseach). Much secret diplomacy prepared the ground for the Anglo-Irish Declaration, which stated:

> The British Government agree that it is for the people of the island of Ireland alone, by agreement between the two parts respectively, to exercise their right of self-determination on the basis of consent, freely and concurrently given, North and South, to bring about a united Ireland if that is their wish.

For some time Britain has acknowledged that the IRA could not be beaten militarily, and it appeared that the IRA accepted that it cannot win by the use of terrorism. Also Sinn Fein has developed into an electoral party which would be able to represent Republicanism at any future negotiating table once it had become clear that terrorism had ended. The Official Unionists, then led by James Molyneaux, responded to the Declaration in a cautious but positive way. In contrast, Ian Paisley condemned it as a 'sell-out'.

Dramatic progress was made in August 1994 when the IRA announced a ceasefire, which was subsequently broken and later restored. A team led by former US senator *George Mitchell* had the task of pushing the peace process forwards. The British Government claimed that it was impossible to negotiate peace sharing the table with a party which could resume armed violence at any time. Yet there seemed little chance of the IRA decommissioning its weapons as a precondition for Republican participation in the forthcoming peace talks. The Mitchell Report called for gradual decommissioning as the talks proceeded, but bombings in London's Docklands and Manchester signalled the IRA's response to that suggestion. In the end, the British Government softened its preconditions for Sinn Fein's participation and demanded a 'lasting' ceasefire rather than a 'permanent' ceasefire.

John Major picked out a suggestion in the Mitchell Report that there might be an alternative route for getting paramilitary representatives to the conference table through holding pre-talks elections. In April 1996 elections were held to a Northern Ireland Forum in order to produce candidates for all-party discussions on Northern Ireland's future. It was intended that the Forum would meet as a 'talking shop' as well as provide members to attend the all-party talks. Thirty-three parties contested the elections; the results are shown in Table 18.1. The Unionists were pleased with the election results, since initially they feared that their support would

Table 18.1 Results of elections to the Northern Ireland Forum

Party	Seats won
Ulster Unionists	30
Democratic Unionists	24
SDLP	21
Sinn Fein	17
Alliance	7
UK Unionist	3
Progressive Unionist	2
Ulster Democratic	2
NI Women's Coalition	2
Labour	2

be spread too thinly amongst the various Unionist parties. Sinn Fein, too, returned more candidates than initially anticipated.

Labour and the peace talks

The IRA announced a restoration of a ceasefire in July 1997, and after six weeks of non-violence the Northern Ireland Secretary, Mo Mowlam, announced that Sinn Fein would be invited to participate in the peace talks. Unionists were disappointed that no pledge was obtained from the Republicans regarding disarming as a precondition for joining the talks. Ian Paisley's Democratic Unionists had already pulled out of the talks, but David Trimble's Ulster Unionists continued to participate (see Box 18.2).

Mo Mowlam's policy included 'confidence building' to win the trust of the Republicans; more prisoners were released from the Maze for longer periods at home, and Sinn Fein's leader, Gerry Adams, had a meeting with the Prime Minister at Number Ten. The Westminster view is that both communities in Northern Ireland can gain from the peace process – political scientists refer to this as a **non-zero-sum** situation. Unfortunately, however, many Loyalists began seeing the peace process in terms of a **zero-sum** situation in which the gains made by the Republicans represented losses to themselves. In other words, Mo Mowlam's confidence-

---

In a **zero-sum** situation, the gains or advantages enjoyed by one side are matched by the losses or disadvantages of the other. In a **non-zero-sum** situation, both sides can either lose or win advantages.

---

building measures were seen as appeasing Republican demands. Despite having being reassured that there would be no constitutional changes without the consent of the people of Northern Ireland, many Loyalists felt that the peace talks had little to offer them.

The peace process was put at further risk in December 1997 by the action of the hardline INLA and UVF splinter groups. Republican INLA did not declare a ceasefire along with the IRA but had a policy not to use violence first. Nevertheless INLA gunmen killed Loyalist Billy Wright, leader of the LVF, in the Maze. Sectarian tension increased and resulted in a number of tit-for-tat killings, with Mo Mowlam taking a calculated gamble by visiting Loyalists in the Maze in order to persuade them to stick with the peace process.

In order to help the peace process meet the summer 1998 deadline, Tony Blair and Bertie Ahern, the Taoiseach, unveiled a blueprint for progress which would form the agenda for the talks. Much of what they proposed was fairly familiar. Firstly, there should be a devolved assembly in Northern Ireland, elected by proportional representation, with legislative and executive functions; secondly, the Anglo-Irish Agreement should be replaced by an inter-governmental 'Council of the Isles', representing England, Wales, Scotland, the Republic of Ireland and Northern Ireland; finally, cross-border authorities, with as yet undefined powers.

As the deadline approached political commentators were asking whether the peace talks were attempting the impossible. Was it possible to forge agreement between hardline Republicans who wanted a united Ireland outside of the United

---

BOX 18.2
The peace process moves on

The Good Friday Agreement reached in the multi-party talks was based around three strands; first, a 108 member *Northern Ireland Assembly* elected by STV; second, a *North–South Ministerial Council* to provide an 'all-Ireland' dimension; third, a *British–Irish Council* to meet twice a year with representatives from the devolved assemblies, Westminster and Dublin. The Agreement was endorsed in a referendum by a majority of both the Catholic and Protestant communities. In a turnout of 81%, 71% voted 'yes' and 29% voted 'no'. Closely following the referendum were elections to the new Northern Ireland Assembly. The results were:

Ulster Unionists	28	Sinn Fein	18	Independent Unionists	3
SDLP	24	Alliance	6	Progressive Unioists	2
Democratic Unionists	20	United Kingdom Unionists	5	Women's Coalition	2

Kingdom, and absolute Loyalists who wanted the border to remain in place, so keeping them within the United Kingdom? Or was there sufficient goodwill in each community which would settle for less than total victory and accept a compromise as represented by the Blair–Ahern blueprint in order to end the years of violence?

English nationalism

English nationalism rested comfortably within the wider British nationalism associated with the glories of empire and the defeat of Germany in the Second World War. From this position, as well as being the political expression of the 'core', the assumptions and values of English nationalism dominated the way in which Westminster viewed the world without being frequently or stridently voiced. In other words, whilst Scottish and Welsh nationalism became increasingly articulated as an ideology from the 1960s, English nationalism remained relatively silent although its goals could be seen in the actions of 'nationalist' politicians such as Mrs Thatcher.

Some commentators have expressed fears that devolution will encourage the growth of negative and illiberal forces which in part underlie Welsh and Scottish nationalism, and this in turn will stir up English nationalism as a political force. For example, some have argued that the Welsh Language Society and other Welsh nationalists are in part the heirs of an anti-semitic and anti-English form of Welsh fascism (see the *Guardian*, 26 July 1997). If a more fervent or extreme form of nationalism returned to Wales (or Scotland) what sort of response will it provoke in England? Commentators have asked whether English nationalism would develop as a popular sentiment like its Scottish and Welsh counterparts leading, if it did so, to the inevitable break-up of the United Kingdom into its constituent parts.

George Orwell made a distinction between patriotism (a positive feeling towards one's country) and nationalism (negative, insular and xenophobic attitudes towards other countries) in *England Your England*. If this distinction is accepted then it is possible to identify English nationalism as a continual response to Britain's involvement in Europe, from the days of the Common Market, and European Economic Community, to today's European Union. It can be argued that 'English nationalists' have been and still are members of all the major parties, being found within the left wing, right wing and centre of each of them.

During the 1960s both Labour and Conservative parties were nationalist, although Labour acted more vigorously in the role of the 'English Nationalist Party'. Despite Labour's internationalist rhetoric, its leader identified the party with the nation, describing Britain's membership of the Common Market as risking 'a thousand years of history'. Although some Labour MPs on the left and right wings of the party supported entry, the mood of the party was set firmly against closer relations with Europe, especially Germany, in favour of the status quo. Later, when Labour opposed membership in principle, some Europhile MPs defected to form the Social Democratic Party.

Labour reappraised the European Union since other members opposed the free-market anti-trade union policies pursued by the Thatcher governments. The Social Chapter looked attractive to Labour, and prospects of pooling sovereignty with other like-minded Social Democrats was far less daunting than the prospect of sharing with Christian Democrats and Gaullists who had been in power a generation earlier. Labour was now willing to participate in principle with the single European currency, and no longer opposed close cooperation with Europe for nationalistic reasons.

For Conservatives the 'nation' is an important symbol which demands their loyalty. Edmund Burke described it as a 'partnership not only between those who are living but between those who are living, those who are dead and those who are to be born', showing how Conservatives see the nation as a force for continuity (Sabine, 1949, p. 517). It is this reverence for national continuity which is reflected in habitual Conservative support for traditional institutions such as the church, monarchy, ancient universities and public schools. It has also been reflected in anti-immigration sentiments, since immigrants are seen as unable to share the nation's history, and anti-Europeanism, since that too breaks with the nation's history of parliamentary sovereignty.

The first application to join Europe was made by a Conservative prime minister, but in order to gain the support of his party he portrayed the Common

Market as a trading organisation and he played down the political implications of membership. Conservatives were relatively content to join the Common Market as long as it was an organisation of nation-states. Their enthusiasm for Europe increased under the leadership of Edward Heath, who saw in membership of the European Economic Community the means to manage Britain's economy more successfully. Also, with empire gone, Conservatives believed that Europe would provide an alternative arena for them to exercise world influence.

From the late 1980s, however, Conservatives have donned the mantle of the English Nationalist Party. Europe was not developing as many had expected, and many were alarmed by the prediction of the Commission President that within a decade 80 per cent of economic and social legislation would come from Brussels. The British Prime Minister, Margaret Thatcher, responded with her Bruges address in which she stressed the need to defend national sovereignty. John Major's leadership of the party was dogged by rebellions on Europe, provoking a leadership contest, and defection of some Conservatives to the highly Eurosceptic Referendum Party. In opposition, William Hague has distanced his party from participation in a single currency for at least ten years.

Towards federal Britain?

In constitutional terms Britain is a unitary state, but it is sometimes argued that in practice it has already operated with limited federalism. It seems likely to operate with greater federalism in the future. What are the arguments?

Some political commentators have identified the relations between the devolved Stormont Parliament and Westminster between 1921 and 1972 as essentially federal in character. Whatever the precise outcome of the peace talks, should responsibility for the government of Northern Ireland move from Westminster to a devolved assembly and joint authorities then a federal link will have been re-established. In the new millennium, relations between the Scottish Parliament and Westminster will represent another federal link. The same cannot be said for the Welsh Assembly which is more akin to a revitalised form of local government.

England is likely to experience greater regional and sub-regional government; by 1999 nine Regional Development Agencies will have been created, primarily to oversee economic development. In the short term each agency will be accountable to a forum of appointed local councillors, but in the long term it is possible that they each will be answerable to a directly elected regional assembly. At sub-regional level directly elected mayors for London, Manchester, Birmingham and other large towns will possibly rejuvenate and reflect municipal pride.

The power structure of the United Kingdom seems likely to develop from a unitary state to a mosaic of federal, devolved and joint authority relationships between core and periphery, with the English core becoming more decentralised as regional and urban identities find political expression.

Summary

- The United Kingdom is undergoing radical constitutional change with devolution in Scotland and Wales.
- Negotiations between rival parties in Northern Ireland to find a constitutional settlement which will end the years of violence. Once one of these constitutional steps has been taken, it is likely that others will follow quickly.
- For England, that change might come in the form of regional government.

Questions

1. 'Devolution has done little more for the Scots and Welsh than create a new level of glorified local government.' Discuss.
2. To what extent, if any, is the 'Irish Problem' a result of British colonialism?
3. 'For the last thirty years the history of parliamentary politics has been that of a struggle between two opposed forces, not the Conservative Party and the Labour Party but the Eurosceptic party and the Europhile party.' Critically evaluate this statement.

Assignment

Why the nation state is now out of date

Commentary

Roy Hattersley

THE real case for devolution will be neither conclusively won nor comprehensively defeated. It will be largely ignored. The most important arguments have been obscured by all the talk of Scottish nationhood. Scotland is a nation. with a distinct culture and history as well as clearly defined boundaries, and devolution will be the administrative acceptance of that obvious fact. But the basic reason for passing out power from Westminster and Whitehall has nothing to do with the Saltire and the Wallace Monument. The Scottish National Party will be offended by the idea. but the arguments for setting up a parliament in Edinburgh and an elected police authority or London are identical in a democracy, decisions are best taken by those whose lives they directly affect.

All over the United Kingdom the myth of accountability is daily acted out in an essentially British way. Ministers take their spending estimates through the House of Commons and then – according to the parliamentary fiction – are answerable for the way in which the money is distributed. In fact, the allocation within regions and between local authorities is usually taken by civil servants who believe that responding to public opinion is the sacrifice of objectivity. Devolution offers a chance to move away from government by a paternalistic bureaucracy. That must be right for a grown-up people – south as well as north of the border.

Replacing Scottish Office civil servants with an Edinburgh parliament is only the beginning. The impetus that comes from autonomy will promote all sorts of material benefits as Scotland speaks for itself in the arguments about the distribution of European funds, the location of inward investment and improvement of the infrastructure. That will make the enthusiasm for devolution infectious.

Scotland was the obvious place to start because the demand for devolved powers was already vocal and persistent. But soon the North East will begin to insist that the region is penalised by the advantages enjoyed a few miles north. Campaigns for regional assemblies have already begun. Sooner or later, their demands will become irresistible.

If the English regions and Wales (devolution's poor relation) were gradually provided with the powers which Scotland will enjoy, the West Lothian Question would be automatically answered. It is easy to brush Tam Dalyell aside as a zealot who is obsessed with the inconsistency which has made him famous. And for the 40 years between the creation of Stormont and its dissolution, there was no great constitutional outcry against the Northern Ireland members of the Westminster parliament voting on questions which concerned English housing, Scottish education or the Welsh police – even though, in the Six Counties, each one of those powers was the controversial responsibility of a devolved parliament.

Extract from the *Guardian*, 4 September 1997.

Questions

(i)   What does the author define as 'the real case for devolution'?

(ii) Outline the nature of the 'West Lothian Question'. Under what circumstances does the author believe that the West Lothian Question will become irrelevant?

(iii) Is the nation-state out of date?

Further reading

Bulpitt, J. (1983) *Territory and Power in the United Kingdom. An Interpretation* (Manchester: Manchester University Press is an interesting academic examination of various propositions regarding the British state. Hechter, M. (1975) *Internal Colonialism: The Celtic Fringe in British National Development 1536-1966* (London: Routledge & Kegan Paul) gives a detailed account of some arguments explored in this chapter. Williams, T. and Abse, D. 'Birth of a nation', the *Guardian*, 26 July, 1997: this exchange of letters between those holding differing views on the future of Wales provides some interesting insights into the passions of those involved.

CHAPTER 19

Local governance

The world of local government has experienced much radical change in terms of its structure, functions and personnel. During the 1980s political scientists described Conservative legislation as producing a 'policy mess' in local government, which included the administrative chaos of the soon abandoned 'poll tax'. From the point of view of citizens, old-style local government has been replaced by community-based local governance in which their council is simply one of many organisations which meets their local needs. However, there is a tendency to exaggerate the decline of local government since local authorities still have many important responsibilities which are likely to increase under Labour. Nevertheless there are still many arguments about the future of local government. Some are concerned over the declining democratic element in local government; others disagree over the role of local government as 'provider' or 'enabler'. To some, local government means local democracy, with voters deciding priorities; to others, local government is about responding to customers' needs efficiently and economically through greater reliance on market forces. At the same time others are more concerned over issues such as the impact of devolution on local government, electoral reform and the desirability of elected mayors running the large towns of Britain.

The enabling authority

Many on the political right felt for some time that councils were out of touch with local communities By the mid-1980s some had got involved in 'silly politics' such as the setting up of 'nuclear-free zones'; they were wasting too much public money through inefficiency, and too often they were challenging the authority of democratically elected central government. It was argued that this sorry situation should be remedied by stripping local government of some responsibilities and getting them run in ways which would offer greater consumer choice, and by the introduction of more competition generally. The biggest 'overspenders', in the eyes of the right, were the Metropolitan Counties (the 'mets') and the Greater London Council (GLC), and these were abolished in 1986. New bodies which had local responsibilities, such as the Urban Development Corporations (UDCs), Training and Enterprise Councils (TECs) and City Technology Colleges, were set up beyond the remit of local government. Even the 'core services' of local government, education and housing, were eroded as the public were given in appropriate ways the right to opt out from local government control.

During the 1980s radical right-wing think-tanks, such as the Adam Smith Institute, prepared blueprints setting out their vision of councils in the future. It was argued that councils should not be run *like* businesses, but *as* businesses. It was proposed that councils should be replaced by private companies run by elected directors. Local people would have the responsibility of shareholders rather than that of voters. A company like Marks & Spencer would provide the model for radically reformed councils. None of the goods on sale in Marks & Spencer are manufactured by the company, but are made by private contractors and sold as 'St. Michael' products. Marks & Spencer keep a very careful eye on the quality of the products supplied to them, and if a company fails to meet the standards set by Marks & Spencer then it will either have to improve or be replaced by another firm. In the same way, it was argued, a council would be responsible for getting the best quality services at the best price through competitive tendering. The council's principal role would be to monitor the quality of services provided by private firms and renew or cancel contracts accordingly.

This radical vision of local government influenced the thinking of the Conservative minister, Nicholas Ridley, who argued the case that councils should provide an enabling framework for the provision of services without necessarily providing those services themselves. The 'enabling council' was seen

> as only one of a number of suppliers, contracting out to other agencies and the private sector to produce and deliver services. It will be customer centred, seeking to understand its 'customers and clients', responding to the electorate and identifying and serving the community needs. The image underlying the Ridley model is that of a marketing agency identifying markets and devising strategies to meet consumer demands. (Horton, 1990, p. 185)

Part of the reforms also included the replacement of the domestic rates by the community charge, or 'poll tax', which was intended to make the entire local electorate more cost-conscious. It was thought that when the whole electorate, and not just ratepayers, were responsible for providing local government revenue they would vote for 'prudent' candidates for the council who promised 'value for money' rather than for 'profligate' candidates who would be 'high-spenders'. But as we shall see, this unpopular tax was replaced with the council tax early in John Major's first term as Prime Minister.

The enabling model involved the entry of new organisations into local government; as either successful private sector bidders to provide services;

as quangos with responsibilities which had previously rested with local authorities; or as quangos which worked as partners with local authorities in areas where local authorities once worked alone. A new fragmented pattern – a mosaic – of service delivery which characterises local governance includes:

- private sector companies providing services such as school meals, street cleaning and rubbish collection
- opted out schools; new schools (City Technology Colleges) set up outside local authority control; also removal of colleges and polytechnics (the 'new' universities) from local authority control
- Housing Action Trusts which have taken over temporary ownership of old council estates before disposing of them to public or private sector landlords; tenants once housed by councils now housed by Housing Associations; tenants who took advantage of 'right-to-buy' legislation and are now owners of what were council houses
- loss of local authority influence in District Health Authorities, local hospitals and local police committees
- local authorities working in partnership with private sector dominated quangos set up to develop the local economy: with Training and Enterprise Councils (TECs) to increase the skills of both the employed and unemployed to meet local needs; with Urban Development Corporations (UDCs) to regenerate local economies
- joint arrangements whereby authorities which are too small to provide some services, such as fire or police, cooperate with other authorities through joint boards to provide these services.

It cannot be denied that the role of local government has been reduced but, as David Wilson pointed out, it would be 'a mistake to underestimate the continued importance of elected authorities as service provider' (Wilson, forthcoming). Even within the provision of education, where local authorities have lost considerable control of the service, what they are left with comprises large areas of responsibility which are likely to expand under Labour. Local authorities spend over a quarter of all

Table 19.1 Who does what? English county and district councils, 1997

Activity	County Council	District Councils
County farms	All services	
Education	All services	
Highways and transportation	Transportation planning Constructing new county roads Maintenance of county roads* Public transport infrastructure and co-ordination Highways and street lighting Public rights of way	Street cleansing Street lighting
Housing		All services
Leisure and Amenities	Libraries Archaeology Archives County parks and picnic sites Grants to village halls, sports, arts, countryside and community projects	Allotments Museums/art galleries County parks, local parks and open spaces Playing fields, other than schools Swimming pools and sports centres
Planning	Structure plans Minerals control Environment and conservation Economic and tourism development	Local plans Development control Local land charges Environment and conservation Economic development
Public Protection	Waste disposal control Waste regulation and disposal, waste recycling centres Trading standards Registration of births, deaths and marriages Coroners courts Fire and rescue	Refuse collection Food safety and hygiene Markets Control of pollution Cemeteries/crematoria
Social Services	All services	
Council tax		Collection of own tax, plus precepts for county and parishes

*Some highways functions are undertaken by District Councils on an agency basis.

Source: Wilson and Game, 1997, p. 85.

public spending on services such as education, community care and personal social services, housing, fire and rescue services, environmental health services, refuse disposal, consumer protection, roads, planning, parks and open spaces, libraries, museums, leisure centres, cemeteries and crematoria (see Table 19.1).

Local government structure

Providing a system of local government that matches the demographic structure is a complex affair. Most of the population live in one of the great conurbations, but some live in small market towns, and others in remote rural areas such as Dartmoor or

---

BOX 19.1
The four primary roles of elected local government

1. **Service provision**: the planning, resourcing and provision, directly or indirectly, of individual local services.
2. **Regulation**: the regulation of the economic behaviour of individuals or other agencies in the public interest by insisting on their compliance with standards, rules and procedures of various kinds for exchange or provision of goods and services. This is where the licensing, inspection, monitoring, registration and certification come in.
3. **Strategic planning**: the provision of a longer-term

planning framework to influence the activities of internal departments and external organisations in relation to individual service areas or authority-wide issues.
4. **Promotion and advocacy**: the persuasion of one or more other organisations (e.g. private industry, voluntary bodies) to carry out activities which are likely to benefit the local community (e.g. by loans to small businesses, by grants to voluntary organisations). (Leach and Stewart, 1992, cited in Wilson and Game, 1997, p. 83)

East Anglia. Some areas are much more prosperous than others: unemployment is relatively low in the South and higher in the North. Some populations have a different age-structure from others: for example the 'dependency ratio' – calculated as the number of young children under 15 and people of pensionable age per 100 people of working age – is 0.99 in Worthing, 0.87 in Eastbourne but only 0.45 in Oxford and 0.20 in the City of London. Finally, some areas have relatively large ethnic communities which may have special needs. Thus, in terms of the diversity found amongst the population alone,

organising one single pattern of local government that can be applied across the country seems an impossibility.

Additionally if local people's needs are being met in new ways, including having services provided by enabling councils, then it follows that changes might be necessary in the internal and external structures of local government. The Conservative Secretary of State at the Department of the Environment, Michael Heseltine, set up a review of (1) local government finance, which resulted in the replacement of the poll tax by the council tax, (2) the internal

Source: Local Government Chronicle 14 March 1997

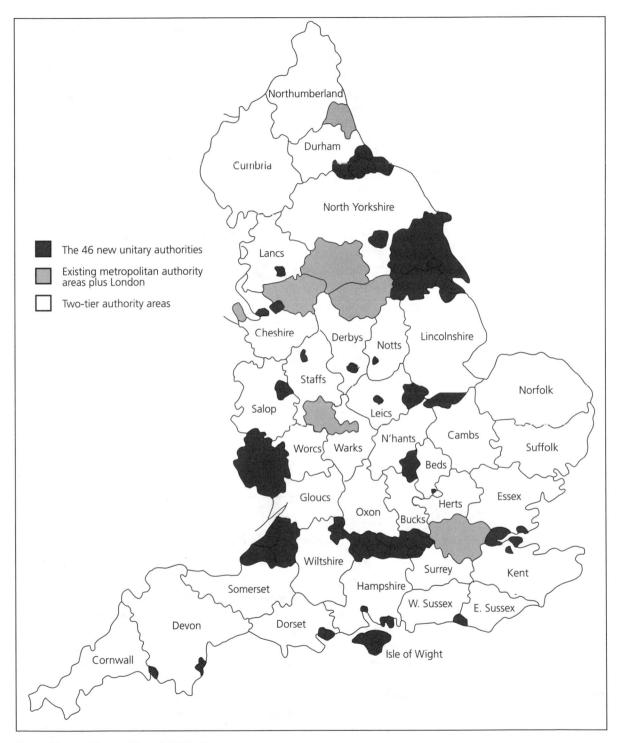

The 46 new unitary authorities

Existing metropolitan authority areas plus London

Two-tier authority areas

Northumberland

Durham

Cumbria

North Yorkshire

Lancs

Cheshire

Derbys

Notts

Lincolnshire

Staffs

Salop

Leics

Norfolk

Worcs

Warks

N'hants

Cambs

Suffolk

Beds

Gloucs

Oxon

Herts

Essex

Bucks

Wiltshire

Surrey

Kent

Somerset

Hampshire

W. Sussex

E. Sussex

Devon

Dorset

Cornwall

Isle of Wight

Source: Based on Wilson and Game (1997) p. 62.

Figure 19.1 The new local authority map in England

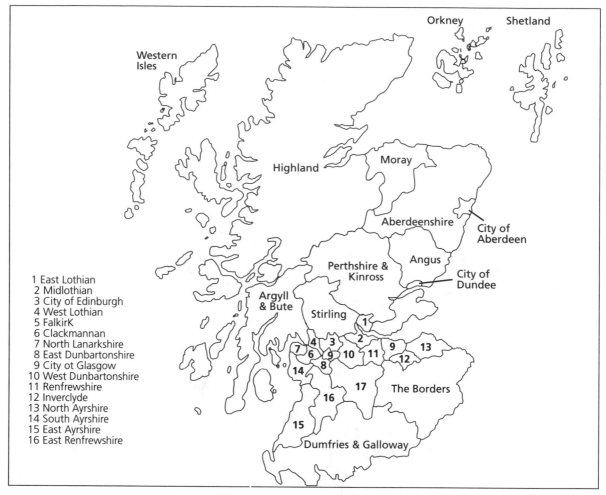

Source: Based on Wilson and Game (1997) p. 64.

Figure 19.2 Scotland's 32 new unitary authorities, operational from April 1996

management of local government, and (3) the structure of local authorities.

The two-tier system which applied to most of Britain was seen by some as too complicated, because local citizens were never sure which tier was responsible for what. At the same time, there were political tensions between the two tiers which resulted in more confusion and inefficiency. Not everyone agreed that these weaknesses amounted to reasons serious enough to warrant abolishing one tier; indeed, it was argued that two tiers in local government bring certain advantages. Above all, two-tier structures combine economy with maximum local responsiveness. For example,

the top tier can obtain economics of scale in providing appropriate services to large populations (such as policing), whilst the lower tier can provide services which require closer contact with the public (such as housing). A Local Government Commission, chaired by Sir John Banham, was set up in 1992 to consult interested parties before advising the government on what shape the reforms should take. From the outset, the government made it clear that unitary (single-tier) authorities were its preferred alternative for local government reorganisation. As part of its review, the Local Government Commission consulted the public for its opinion, which would be taken into

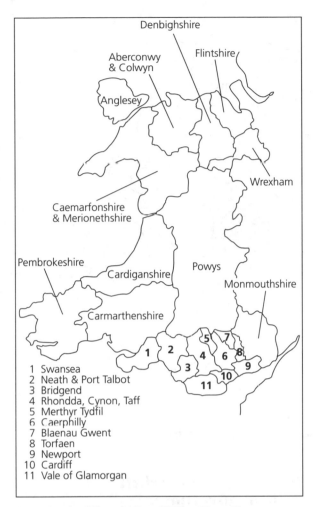

Denbighshire

Aberconwy
& Colwyn

Flintshire

Anglesey

Wrexham

Caemarfonshire
& Merionethshire

Pembrokeshire

Cardiganshire

Powys

Monmouthshire

Carmarthenshire

5
7
1　2
4　6
8
3　10
9
11

1 Swansea
2 Neath & Port Talbot
3 Bridgend
4 Rhondda, Cynon, Taff
5 Merthyr Tydfil
6 Caerphilly
7 Blaenau Gwent
8 Torfaen
9 Newport
10 Cardiff
11 Vale of Glamorgan

Source: Based on Wilson and Game (1997) p. 66.

Figure 19.3 The 22 new unitary authority in Wales, operational from April 1996

account alongside the preferences of other interested bodies.

Sir John Banham was a controversial chairman and relations between the Commission and the Government deteriorated as the Commission made 'hybrid' or 'no change' recommendations. Leicestershire provided an interesting example of the Commission's exercise since the county included Rutland, with only 33,000 inhabitants, which was England's smallest county until 1974. Many of Rutland's residents (the cartoon on p. 366 makes fun of its small population) remained unhappy about their county being absorbed into Leicestershire and

conveyed this feeling to the Commission. The Commission's draft recommendation was for the creation of five new unitary councils, including one which embraced Rutland. Other options were (1) Leicester City becoming a unitary authority with a two-tier structure being retained for the remainder of the county, and with Rutland becoming restored to its historic county status; (2) Leicester City and Rutland becoming unitary councils with the existing two-tier structure being retained for the remainder of the county. In the event, Leicestershire's structure was 'hybrid' with two unitary authorities, Leicester City and Rutland, with a two-tier structure of county and seven district councils for the remainder of the county. Some queried whether the time and cost of this structural reform, not to mention the turmoil and uncertainty it had created, had been worthwhile. Leicestershire had changed from county and nine districts (including Rutland DC) to two unitary authorities, county and seven districts. What some asked locally, others were asking nationally.

The reformed local government system, which will be fully in place by 1998, will see the creation of 46 new unitary authorities, far fewer than the originally anticipated hundred or more (see Figure 19.1). Some 'unloved' counties, such as Avon, Humberside and Cleveland, have been abolished and each replaced by four unitary authorities. Cornwall, Gloucestershire, Hertfordshire, Lincolnshire and ten others remained unchanged. The remainder, some 19 counties, shared Leicestershire's outcome of a 'hybrid' structure combining unitary and two-tier structures.

The local government systems of Scotland and Wales have also been reformed, but the respective Secretaries of State assumed responsibilities for consultation and recommendation. In Scotland the reforms eventually materialised in creating 29 new unitary authorities, giving 32 in all (see Figure 19.2). But the creation of single-tier structures does not necessarily result in simplification in Scotland or elsewhere. As Wilson and Game observed, in the Strathclyde region 'there are now more bodies responsible for fewer services than there were previously' (1997, p. 63). A consultation paper from the Welsh Office contained the options of 13, 20 or 24 unitary authorities; in the event 22 were set up (see Figure 19.3).

Until the devolved assemblies in Scotland and

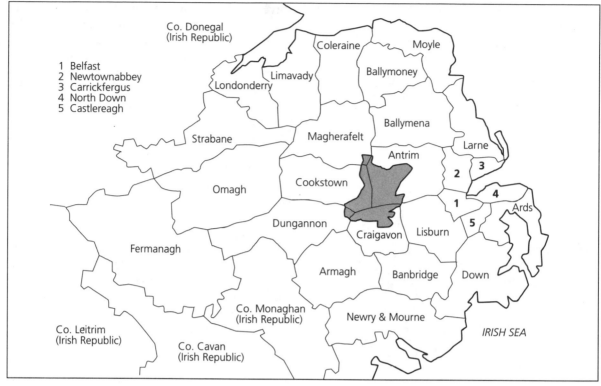

Source: Based on Wilson and Game (1997) p. 67.

Figure 19.4 Northern Ireland's 26 district councils, operational from April 1996

Wales are established, local authorities relate to central government which is represented by the respective Secretary of State at the Scottish and Welsh offices. The precise relationships between the Scottish parliament, the Welsh assembly and their respective local governments have yet to be fully resolved.

Local government in Northern Ireland was not part of the restructuring exercise which took place in the United Kingdom. At present, local government is a 'pale imitation' of that elsewhere in the United Kingdom: 'Elected local government is confined to 26 district councils, relatively small in British terms [see Figure 19.4] and responsible for far fewer services than their counterparts elsewhere . . . Most services affecting people's daily lives – housing, education, libraries, health, community relations – are administered on behalf of the Northern Ireland Office by appointed quangos and other public bodies' (Wilson and Game, 1997, p. 66).

The democratic deficit in local government

Local government democracy is under twin attack. Firstly, many quangos have taken over local government responsibilities, but unlike local government, they are unelected and unaccountable (see Chapter 17). Secondly, after reorganisation there are fewer councils and fewer councillors. In England there will be seventeen fewer authorities after reorganisation and 1,085 fewer councillors. The extent of Britain's democratic deficit is demonstrated when like-with-like comparisons are made with other EU neighbours:

- France has one elected local member for every 116 citizens
- Germany has one elected local member for every 250 citizens
- Denmark has one elected local member for every 1,084 citizens

- The UK has one elected local member for every 2,605 citizens

Scotland and Wales each emerged from reorganisation with half the number of elected councils. The Scottish local electorate would be voting in 450 fewer councillors; the Welsh, 704 fewer councillors.

Some argue that the loss in the total number of councillors need not be so damaging for local democracy as the figures suggest. This is because other reforms and experiments have increased local participation, such as parent governors and citizens' juries.

Central-local government relations

The relationship between central and local government is an extremely complex one to which political scientists have devoted considerable resources in analysing. There is agreement on the general trends but it is often the case that the complex detail uncovered in one particular case-study cannot be applied to all other cases. The relationship between central and local government is diverse, subject to changes in circumstance between one authority and another, and within one authority over time.

There has been a general trend in which central government has assumed more and more control over local government. Of course, in a democracy such as Britain where Parliament is sovereign, local government has never been autonomous. If an authority acts beyond the powers granted to it by Parliament, the doctrine of *ultra vires* will be invoked; the action of a local authority may be declared unlawful by the courts. Sometimes Acts of Parliament give ministers great powers over local authorities. Indeed, many Acts give ministers strong reserve powers over local authorities that fail to carry out their duties.

It has been argued that increased centralised powers over local authorities had become necessary because local democracy was not working. Local mandates were often extremely weak because of the low turnouts in local government elections. And surveys suggested that local issues did not feature in influencing the way people voted in local elections since they voted on national considerations.

Counter-arguments to these points have been made with some vehemence. For example, although local government elections attract a lower turnout than general elections, the former are held far more frequently. To this extent, it is argued, local authorities are much more subject to electoral pressure than is Parliament. Also, the fact that in some areas people tend to vote the same way in both local and general elections should not be surprising. The argument does not invalidate the local mandate; it just means that the local mandate favours one party because that party is strongest locally.

The general view, however, is that if local government is to have substance within the democratic system it needs to be invigorated in terms of becoming seen as more important in the eyes of local people. The Commission for Local Democracy reported on ways in which local government could be revived in order to justify a more substantial role (see Assignment 1) including the proposal for electoral reform, which has been accepted in principle by Labour. Also the Local Government Commission is continuing its rolling review with an authority-by-authority examination of local electoral geography, representation and the desirability of having professional councillors.

Some political scientists have explored ways in which central–local relationships might be understood in more theoretical terms. Basically, four models have been fashioned, each based upon a different type of relationship.

- The first portrays local government as an *agency* for central government. In this model, local government is simply the servant of central government, implementing the policies which central government lays down. In terms of power, local government is subordinate to central power.
- The second model portrays the central–local relationship in terms of a *partnership* with both sides working together for common ends. The two partners might not be equal in terms of power, but local government is not totally subordinate to central government.
- The third describes the central–local relationship in terms of a stewardship model. Here the 'master', central government, delegates considerable authority to its subordinates, the local authorities.

- The fourth model sees central–local links in terms of a *power-dependence* relationship. It is argued that both central government departments and local authorities have a number of resources which each can use against the other. According to this model, central and local government are independent of each other with neither having total control; their relationship is one of bargaining, exchange and negotiation. How might the 'power-dependence' relationship work in practice? Central government might supply (or refuse) financial resources to get a local authority to do (or not to do) something over which central government has no authority. R.A.W. Rhodes, who first applied this model to central–local relations, states that for both parties concerned 'their relative power potential is a product of their resources, the rules of the game and the process of exchange . . . the process of exchange is influenced by the resources of the participants, strategies, personalities' (Rhodes, 1981, pp. 97–108).

There is no one relationship which is typical of all central–local relations. Even though there has been a trend towards greater centralisation, different authorities have developed different relationships with central government, which may also vary in nature over time.

Local government finance

More than a quarter of all public spending is done by local authorities. Any government determined to control public spending has therefore to control local authority spending (see projected figures in Table 19.2). The Conservative government experimented with spending targets for local authorities to adhere to, with clawback penalties for authorities which overspent their targets.

Since most of the 'overspending' was in 'high-spending' Labour-controlled authorities, there was a demand for specific controls to contain their spending and not general controls which sometimes penalised 'low-spending' Conservative authorities. Overspending was calculated by how much an authority spent over and above what the government assessed it needed to spend, the Grant-Related Expenditure Assessment (GREA). Some low-spending Tory shires had been penalised for spending less than their GREA but more than their target. Also some authorities, mostly Labour-controlled, compensated for what they saw as inadequate funding from central government by the simple remedy of increasing rates to make up the shortfall.

In 1986, however, spending targets for local authorities were scrapped, with the new system of central government control known as 'rate-capping' replacing them. Rate-capping enabled central government to control the budgets of overspending councils through setting upper limits on the amounts they could spend and the amounts they could raise in rates. An authority which ran into financial difficulties would no longer be able to get the money it needed to fund its spending from demanding higher rates because asking the public to pay 'excess' rates would be illegal.

Local government finance had become a 'policy mess' by the mid-1980s. On the one hand, 11 significant changes in local government finance had been introduced during the first two Thatcher governments which had the effect of increasing uncertainty and making it very difficult for town halls to plan their budgets for the year ahead. Although councils lost £713 million in penalties by 1984, the penalty system was not preventing large rate increases. Local government spending continued to rise faster than government had planned. On the other hand, some local authorities had got themselves into a mess in trying to dodge central controls on spending. In 1985, for example, Liverpool City Council was left with enough resources to run its services for nine months but not for a full year. Councillors from the 'hard left' wanted to 'shut up shop' for three months and make council employees redundant. The Council avoided bankruptcy on this occasion by borrowing from Swiss banks.

Some right-wing Conservatives were persuaded by the Adam Smith Institute that the 'problem' of local government finance could be solved in large part by reforming local taxation. Also the Prime Minister felt that the time was right for radical change. However, events which followed resulted in what was arguably Britain's biggest postwar domestic policy disaster: the community charge, or as it soon became known, the 'poll tax'. Although the events in question occurred a decade ago, they are worth

Table 19.2 Local authority spending and taxes, 1996–9

	1996–7	1997–8	1998–9	1999–2000
Total spending (£ billion)	44	45	46	47
Central grant (%)	79	78	77	75
Council tax revenue (%)	21	22	23	24
Tax increase on 1996–7 (%)		6	14	24

Source: Association of Metropolitan Authorities, cited by John (1997) p. 258.

recounting in outline since the episode stands as an unrivalled case-study in disastrous policy-making.

Reforming the rates

Since the time when Margaret Thatcher was a shadow Environment Minister in the mid-1970s, she championed the idea of abolishing the rating system and replacing it with a new method of raising local revenue. Rates were an ancient tax on property and were unpopular for a variety of reasons. They were a highly visible form of taxation, unlike, for example, value-added tax (VAT) which is 'hidden' within the price of goods. Rates are not directly related to the use made of local authority services. Individuals in the 18–30 age group, for example, who made great use of services, paid disproportionately little in rates. Improvements made to a property led to an increase in rates on that property. Rates tended to hit poorer households hardest in the sense that they paid a higher proportion of their incomes in rates than more affluent households. And finally, rates were often based on the assumption that urban areas were wealthier than they actually were.

The advantages of rates tended to be procedural – they were easy to collect; they were cheap to administer; they were a form of tax which people understood and which it was difficult to avoid paying; and finally, there was great certainty about the amount of money rates would produce and they could be easily adjusted.

After intense deliberations during 1985–6, the government came down in favour of a 'community charge' to replace the rates. It was very similar to a poll tax, although it was based on residence rather than on the electoral register. Critics, including many Tories, argued that the community charge was regressive. In other words, individuals would pay the same despite differences in income. The community charge would be a 'bureaucratic nightmare' according to some Tories, who pointed out that it would cost £400 million a year to collect – twice as much as the old rating system.

The Thatcher Government's rejoinder to these criticisms included the point that no taxation system was popular or perfect. The regressive nature of the community charge was no different from VAT where individuals pay the same rate regardless of whether they are rich or poor. The Conservative Government believed that a flat rate was appropriate for the consumption of local authority services. It admitted that the community charge would be more costly to administer but pointed out that many more people would be paying it. A total of 35 million individuals would pay the new community charge including 17 million who had never previously paid rates. This was seen as the great advantage of the community charge, since it is likely to make all people who use local authority services take an interest in the affairs of local government. Under the old rating system, many people who used local authority services voted in the local elections yet did not pay rates. The community charge, argued the government, would restore the link between taxation and representation which had been absent in local government.

It had been argued that whatever system replaced the rates, it should have the following characteristics:

- It should be seen as a fair system of raising revenue from citizens.
- It should be easy to collect from those who paid it.

- It should be hard for dishonest citizens to evade payment.

The 'poll tax', it was argued, failed on all three counts, and the government was thrown into a crisis entirely of its own making. When things began to go wrong at a very early stage in implementation, Margaret Thatcher acknowledged that 'adjustments' had to be made in the way the community charge worked. A six-month review took place which resulted in some amendments being made to 'transitional relief' and to some of the issues raised by worried Tory backbenchers, such as second-home ownership and the plight of businessmen who 'lived above the shop'. Critics argued that this review changed little – the community charge remained a deeply flawed tax. What were the problems associated with the poll tax?

It was seen by many as even more unfair than the rates, because people living under the same council would be paying the same amount, no matter how wealthy they were. Many of the poorest in the community receiving income support, and who had not previously paid rates, now found that they had to pay at least 20 per cent of the 'poll tax'.

Margaret Thatcher's stubborn refusal to acknowledge widespread hostility towards the poll tax, as well as her hostility towards Europe, were amongst the main causes behind her departure from Number Ten. The new Conservative Prime Minister, John Major, was anxious to replace the unpopular poll tax as soon as possible, although the uniform business rate would remain. In the short term the Chancellor announced a £140 a head rebate in the March 1991 budget, which threw many councils into turmoil since they had already sent out poll tax bills which now had to be replaced by new and lower demands. Back in the DoE, Michael Heseltine undertook a quick review of what should replace the poll tax and, in many ways, he re-invented the rating system which Mrs Thatcher had abolished.

The council tax

A government consultation document on local finance argued that the poll tax's replacement should be fashioned by five principles. Firstly, there should

be clear lines of accountability in terms of local people seeing a link between their level of payments and council spending. People should agree generally that the new tax is fair. It should be easy to collect. There should be a fair sharing of the tax burden, with more people, rather than fewer, contributing towards paying for council services. Finally, central government should be able to control local authority spending through means of 'strong and effective capping powers'. With these principles in mind, government policy retained the uniform business rate but replaced the community charge with a new 'council tax', of which the main features are:

- *Single bill for each household.*
- *There will be no register of adults.* The bill falls on the occupier of the house – normally the 'head of the household'.
- *It will reflect the value of property.* Each domestic property – house, flat, bungalow, etc. – will be allocated to a *valuation band.* The scheme first suggested by the government included seven bands:

Band	Property value band	Ratio of tax bill
A	Up to £40,000	0.67
B	£40,000–£52,000	0.78
C	£52,000–£68,000	0.89
D	£68,000–£88,000	1.00
E	£88,000–£120,000	1.22
F	£120,000–£160,000	1.44
G	Over £160,000	1.67

Later a new value band 'H' was added at the top end, for properties over £320,000. The ratio of tax bill shown in the final column refers to the proportion of the council tax paid; for example, a household living in a Band A home would pay two-thirds of the council tax; a Band D household would pay all of it; and a Band G household would pay one-and-two-thirds. A different scale of property band values will be used in Scotland and Wales.

- *It will allow rebates to 'the poorest section of the community'.* Even the poorest people in society had to pay 20 per cent of their 'poll tax'. People on very low incomes will receive full rebates of their council tax bill. Where only one person lives in a

BOX 19.2
Rate reform: the alternatives for the Thatcher government

Local sales tax: This method of raising local revenue was opposed by many Conservatives because it was not consistent with the notion of the Tories being a tax-cutting party. The Treasury also disliked the idea of a local sales tax since it might limit the chancellor's freedom to raise VAT. Also, concern was expressed about the distorting effects this form of local tax would have if neighbouring authorities levied it at differing rates.

Local income tax: This option was recommended by the Layfield Committee, 1976, and a decade later was supported strongly by the Alliance parties. But, as with local sales tax, it is contrary to the Tory party's tax-cutting image. Again the Treasury is opposed to this alternative because it would weaken the Department's control over income tax in general.

Poll tax: This alternative was opposed by a former Environment Secretary, Michael Heseltine, as well as by many others who did not want a tax based on the electoral register. Apart from problems of collecting this tax from poor and highly mobile inner-city populations – later summed up in the anti-poll-tax slogan 'can't pay, won't pay' – the idea that 'the duke and the dustman' would be paying the same amount of poll tax struck many as being grossly unfair.

A combination of two or more of these alternatives or a hybrid fashioned from a compromise between two or more: An example of the former would be a combination of a local sales tax together with a modified rating system; an example of the latter would be a 'variable poll tax' graduated according to income or the rateable value of the area lived in.

As critics had predicted, collecting the 'poll tax' proved to be a bureaucratic nightmare for many councils. Generally speaking, it was twice as costly to collect as the rates. Often the cost of collection from the poorest in the community was greater than the amounts collected. Whereas the 'poll tax' proved easy to collect from rural and suburban areas, non-payment was a major problem with the mobile and shifting populations of the big inner cities.

Finally, the unfairness of the 'poll tax' provided a moral justification for some people who were seeking any excuse not to pay. For them, 'can't pay, won't pay' broke the habit of paying taxes. The 'poll tax' may have had the unintended effect of producing a 'culture of non-payment' which could result in greater evasion of any new tax introduced in the future.

house, he or she will get a 25 per cent discount on the council tax bill.

- *It will relate the size of the council tax bills to the spending of each local authority.* As at present, the government grant to each council is based on a Standard Spending Assessment of what is needed for each council to provide a standard level of services. In future this will be adjusted for each council according to the spread of properties within each band. So, in theory, all households in the same value band across the country will pay the same council tax for the same level of service. If a council decides to spend more in order to provide a higher standard of service then, subject to capping, the council tax would go up accordingly. In other words, there will still be a strong link between what an authority spends and the level of the council tax locally.

In many ways the council tax is a hybrid tax (see Box 19.2) which is based on principles found in a variety of other taxes. For example, it contains many elements of a *property tax*, since it reflects the value of property, a *poll tax*, since there is a personal element with two or more adults paying the full tax, and a *tax based on income*, since the least well-off will receive rebates. Whether in practice the council tax represents a happy blend of elements or 'the worst of all worlds' remains to be seen. Some critics of the council tax predict that it will not prove as 'efficient' as the rates since it still involves 'counting heads', and that councils will receive many appeals from people about their property having been put into the wrong band.

Responding to customers and voters

Political scientists have noted that the democratic link between local authorities and the populace can range from 'authentic participation', where the electorate shares power in making decisions, to 'bogus participation', where the public may be given the feeling that they are participating whilst not actually being allowed to influence any decisions. In a recent

Table 19.3 Three models of change

1 Traditional passive roles	2 New active roles	3 Character of active roles	4 Mode of provision	5 Nature of related initiatives
Ratepayer	Shareholder	Protective	Market-based and privatised	Municipal pluralism with a private sector leading edge
Client	Consumer	Instrumental	Individual consumer responsive	Informative and consultative
Voter	Citizen	Developmental	Democratic and collectivist	Participative and consultative.

Source: Gyford (1991) p. 181.

study, John Gyford has redefined these links in terms of three broad relationships. Firstly, there is the *participative* relationship in which the electorate take a real part in local government through sharing in decision-making and service provision. Non-elected individuals may be co-opted on to council committees, tenants may participate in running their estates, and parents may participate in the local management of schools.

The link between a local authority and its public may be *consultative* in nature – as in the case of citizens juries – with the electorate having the right to be heard even if no direct part is taken in decision-making. For example:

Some councils have established consultative and liaison committees with social service user groups and voluntary organisations in line with the recommendations of the Seebohm Report in 1968. Housing departments have set up consultative committees and councillor–tenant meetings. Leisure and recreation departments have devised ways of consulting users of their facilities in the sporting and artistic fields. Planning departments have employed a variety of means to consult public opinion on planning proposals since the publication of the Skeffington Report in 1969. (Gyford, 1991, p. 82)

Finally, there is the *informative* relationship. It has to be acknowledged that most people do not wish to become actively involved in the local decision-

making process and are happy to leave it to others in local government to supply them with the services they want. But even those not wishing to participate in local government require information from local government about the services provided. Some councils have made it easier for the public to gain such information through setting up 'one-stop information shops' in the town hall or library. Rather than members of the public having to traipse from one department to another in search of information, some councils provide 'a contact point for all council services, together with information on local organisations and their activities, free "hot-lines" to all council departments, space for displays and promotions by both the council and outside bodies and a tourist information centre' (ibid., p. 109).

How far have the radical changes which have taken place in local government affected the relationship between citizens and their elected representatives? Possible ways in which the relationship may be redefined are set out in Table 19.3. The debate then focuses on which set of roles and relationships brings councils 'closer to the public'. Would the enabling authority, responding to market forces, provide exactly the right services at the right quality which local consumers demand? Or would it provide too narrow a range of services, ignoring those demands not backed by cash from the less well-off amongst the public? Or, finally, would the citizen role draw the public and councils closer through giving influence to all members of the public in decisions about what services should be provided? The development of local government in the years ahead will be influenced by the outcome of this debate.

The political dimension

In what ways might party politics influence the links between councils and the public? One researcher, Gerry Stoker, concluded that the willingness of councils to respond to various types of pressure groups depended closely on their prevailing politics. In broad terms, in urban left-wing authorities

> Voluntary sector, cause and community groups are highly active and the local authorities have responded to and supported this development . . . tenants', women's, ethnic minority and single-issue cause groups will be amongst those that are active. Good relations with local authority trade unions and other trade unions are also prized by councillors. Relationships with other producer interests notably business organisations may, however, be antagonistic and even hostile. (Stoker, 1991, p. 133)

Soft-left Labour councils 'are less likely to support radical cause groups and more willing to work with business interests' (ibid.). In centre-right Labour authorities, and those where Liberal Democrats have influence, pressure-group activity appears actively encouraged. There is, however, preferential treatment of groups representing the voluntary sector and professional groups over and above the treatment of some community groups. For example, councils may be cool towards tenants' associations because they are seen as being led by extremists, and hostile towards residents' associations which are viewed as selfish or simply a front for the Conservative Party.

Suburban and rural authorities when dominated by Conservative and Liberal Democrat councils produced a different pattern of pressure-group activity. What might be described as 'respectable' voluntary sector groups, along with farming, landowning and environmental interests, play an active role. But in such areas 'some interests may never find a voice, for example, agricultural workers or those who require housing for rent' as well as other politically unacceptable cause groups (ibid.,

p. 134). In authorities led by radical New Right Conservatives 'there is likely to be a willingness to work closely with a select group of middle-class residents' associations, amenity groups and business interests' but a hostility towards any groups considered to be left-wing, such as CND, Shelter and feminist organisations.

The electoral dimension

Much of the debate about electoral reform is concerned with the undesirability of any system which encourages coalition governments because of their inherent instability and the risk that they do not represent what the electorate thought that they were voting for. Yet minority rule and coalition formation are commonplace features in the world of local government.

Where local elections produced a hung – or 'balanced' – council with no one party having overall control, local parties had to bargain with each other in order to produce a working arrangement. In some cases, the largest of the parties governed with the support of another party in a coalition; in other cases, the smallest party was left holding the balance of power and able to exert the most influence on policy-making.

Some political commentators argued that hung councils were more democratic than councils ruled by one party. This was because in many hung councils the chairpersons of both the council and its committees rotated between two or even three parties, and council officers were now responsive to all parties and not just the ruling party. Local government appeared far more open under hung councils, since meetings were no longer 'rubber stamps' of policy previously decided in private. Councils were reflecting all the opinions within the local electorate, since no policy options were ruled out because they were politically unacceptable to the ruling party.

In contrast, councils firmly under the control of one party seemed undemocratic by comparison, with the ruling party meeting in secret to decide policy prior to the council meeting. Also there are fears that 'one-party' states at local level risk all the problems of one-party states at national level. Without effective opposition, there is a tendency for the governing party to become inefficient with some members feeling that it is safe to indulge in sleaze and petty corruption. Soon after coming into office, Labour focused its attention on Glasgow City Council where it was rumoured that some Labour councillors were swapping their votes in council for trips abroad. West Scotland has long had a reputation for New York style 'Tammany Hall' politics, where local politics is lubricated with bribes in the form of jobs, housing or some other benefit for electoral support. It is envisaged that electoral reform in local government will give opposition parties more effective representation in future and eliminate the possibility of one-party councils.

How strong is the link between local government elections and national politics? Political journalists have encouraged the view that local government elections results can be converted, through calculation of the 'equivalent popular vote' (see p. 140), into predicting which party would have won a general election had one been called. The assumption underlying this approach is that local factors play little or no role in local government elections. As Patrick Dunleavy has argued, 'local election results overwhelmingly reflect national swings of opinion for or against the incumbent government, as they are modified by the different social bases in different areas' (Dunleavy, 1980, p. 136).

This view, however, has been modified by researchers for the Widdicombe Committee (1986) on local government. They found that local events can, 'in a small but not insignificant number of cases, . . . have a decisive impact on individual ward-level elections, and occasionally, as a consequence, on the overall election outcome within an authority' (Research Volume 1, 1986, p. 44). Others giving evidence to Widdicombe thought that '80 per cent of local voters vote exactly in accordance with their national party choice. The remainder it could be claimed are making a local choice' (Stoker, 1991, p. 53). If this estimate is accurate, then for at least a fifth of the electorate voting under typical circumstances, local factors are important. Whilst defenders of local government might wish that the proportion voting this way was greater, it represents for them a welcome departure from the pessimistic view that council elections are no more than a local reflection of national politics.

The EU dimension

Local authorities are now amongst the most vigorous lobbyists in Brussels. This is largely because financial resources from both central government and local taxes are restricted, and in response many authorities began looking to the EU as an additional source of funding. The European Regional Development Fund had provided financial support for local economic regeneration; the Social Fund has alleviated the local impact of unemployment; as well as specific funding for problems such as the decline of coal mining.

Local authorities are also responsible for implementing much EU-wide legislation on the environment, waste-management, transport and planning.

Local government personnel

Councillors

Councillors are not typical of the population at large in terms of social class. For example, only a quarter of councillors have working-class jobs. Councillors tend to be better educated and to earn more than the average person in Britain. Councillors also come from the older sections of the population: only 8.5 per cent of councillors are aged between 21 and 34 years, yet 28.5 per cent of the total population is in this age group. In contrast, people between the ages of 55 and 74 years form 29.5 per cent of the total population, yet 47.5 per cent of councillors are in this age group. A significant difference of another kind is found in the 17 per cent of councillors that are female; far below the percentage of women in the general population.

It has been argued that paying a salary to councillors would attract more women to come forward as candidates, as well as more working-class and young candidates. This was considered by the Robinson Committee (1977) which recommended an annual payment of £1,000 a year for councillors in addition to travelling and subsistence expenses. But Robinson fell well short of proposing that councillors should be paid a full-time salary. Some felt that paying councillors would attract the 'wrong sort of person' who would be encouraged to stand for office by thoughts of the salary rather than the idea of public service.

A survey of councillors carried out by Tony Wood and Gerald Crawley reported some interesting findings regarding gender and party differences in the attitudes and conduct of councillors. They found that on average councillors spent more than 30 hours a week on council business, but also that this average was made up from widely varying amounts of time. Firstly, women councillors work longer each week on council work than their male colleagues. In general women spend 22 per cent more time each week on council matters.

Women appeared to be more committed towards their council work than men since they 'expressed a more community centred view of their duties and were much readier to define their council work as a full time job than were male councillors' (Wood and Crawley, 1987). Younger women councillors with children could only manage if they lived in what the researchers called a 'political household'. Typically in such a household 'both adult members have strong ideologically based beliefs which makes their exceptional efforts worthwhile. In such cases, the husband's support for his wife in terms of housework and childcare is not only given for personal reasons, but because he believes equally strongly in the political work she is doing.'

The researchers also found that there was a difference in the time spent on council work between Labour and Liberal councillors on the one hand, and Conservative councillors on the other. Labour councillors spent 30 per cent more time on council work than Tories, Liberals 20 per cent more. In contrast to Labour and Liberal councillors, most Conservative councillors 'defined their role in more limited terms. It was seen as one of a number of leisure interests, but certainly nothing more than a voluntary activity requiring only limited commitment.'

Councillors at work

Where does power lie in local government policy-making? What influence do elected members have in making the decisions which affect their local communities? There are no simple answers to these questions, because different patterns of power exist in different authorities. Generally speaking, however, the prevailing situation is that there is a 'joint élite' comprising 'committee chairs and vice-chairs together with chief officers and their deputies' (Stoker, 1991, p. 92). But it has been stressed that this is not the situation to be found in every authority, and even where it does exist, the joint élite is not necessarily a unified and cohesive group. What might appear to be a joint élite may be, in fact, made up of two or more élites competing with each other for influence. In many cases, the new management structures introduced into local government have opened up the policy-making process, enabling less-senior officers and councillors to take policy initiatives.

Thus the picture of leading councillors, together with senior officers, dominating the policy-making process is an exaggeration. There are cases where the ruling party group exerts as much, or more, influence than the leading councillors. Although it is not commonplace, it is possible for inexperienced yet assertive councillors to initiate policy and play a 'crucial role in developing a whole range of new planning and industrial policies. They persuaded party leaders and the party group to adopt the initiatives and subsequently took an important role in the process of implementation' (Stoker, 1991, p. 96). It is also possible, as we shall see below, for unelected local party members to pressurise a reluctant party group into adopting policies it would have otherwise decided against.

The roles of the 'party caucus' and non-elected constituency party members became a matter of political controversy during the 1980s. Some argued that the role of the party caucus distorted the working of the council system. In authorities where one political party had a ruling majority, the party caucus may have become the dominant decision-making body. Although there may have been nothing intrinsically wrong in this since it represented the reality of power, some voices became alarmed by irregularities which had increased in custom and practice. In a number of authorities, including some London boroughs, those permitted at group meetings included not only the elected councillors but also members of constituency committees. Decisions arrived at by both elected and non-elected members of the party caucus would then be rubber-stamped in council meetings.

The Widdicombe Committee examined practices and procedures in local government and made a number of important recommendations. One

Table 19.4 Councillors, by political party membership, age, gender, activity status, socio-economic group and income, 1990

	Con (%)	Lab (%)	Lib (%)	Ind (%)	Other (%)	All councillors (%)
Age 60+	37	32	22	52	30	36
45–49	42	33	30	36	33	37
18–44	19	33	49	11	33	26
Gender: Male	78	83	79	81	81	81
Female	21	17	21	19	19	19
Activity Status						
Employed (full or part time)	64	59	74	47	67	60
Unemployed	2	8	3	3	2	4
Retired	24	22	13	40	30	25
Permanently sick/disabled	–	2	–	1	–	1
Looking after a home	9	6	9	9	7	8
Other	–	1	–	–	–	1
Socio-economic group:						
Professional	11	6	15	8	5	9
Employer/manager	42	20	28	37	26	32
Intermediate non-manual	14	22	23	11	30	18
Junior non-manual	8	11	15	6	2	10
Skilled manual/own account						
non-professional	10	25	8	14	14	16
Semi-skilled manual	1	8	4	5	–	4
Unskilled manual	–	2	–	1	–	1
Armed forces/NA	12	8	8	16	5	11
Income						
15,000+	25	7	18	14	33	16
£10,000-£14,999	22	23	29	17	2	22
£6,000-£9,000	23	28	23	27	25	26
Up to £5,999	22	38	23	29	23	28
None	1	1	2	2	–	1
Refused/NA	8	4	3	10	12	7
BASE	(595)	(496)	(133)	(224)	(43)	(1557)

Sources: Widdicombe (39, 1986c) table 4.5, p. 39; Stoker (1991) p. 36.

proposal was that committees which take decisions for the council as a whole should reflect the political make-up of the whole council. It was felt that such committees take decisions on behalf of the whole council, not just part of it. Where a party group existed, this should be made clear to the public. Widdicombe recommended that decisions should be taken only by elected members.

Local government officers

Local authorities employ administrators to assist them in carrying out their duties and in implementing their policies. The relationship between officers and councillors is frequently the focus of academic attention because it contains a number of inherent tensions. In the crudest sense, these tensions spring from the differences between professional adminis-

---

Table 19.5 Pressures on Councillors

Externally imposed ◄───────────────────────────────► Self-generated

Structural changes to local government
  e.g. Larger authorities and larger wards

    Electoral pressures
      e.g. increasing electoral volatility, more hung councils

      Socio-demographic changes
        e.g. increasing number of old people

        Economic pressures
          e.g. scarcer resources, unemployment

          Central government pressures
            e.g. more complicated legislation, more central intervention

            Community pressures
              e.g. from local parties and interest groups

              Councillor's own interests
                e.g. implementing the manifesto, distrust of senior officers

Sources: Adapted from Widdicombe Report (1986, p. 63) by Barron, Crawley and Wood (1991) p. 74.

---

trators and amateur politicians. The former are selected for their qualities of expert knowledge, experience and professionalism. The latter are elected as candidates of political parties, often in elections with low turnouts. Frequently, the electorate will have little personal knowledge of the candidates and vote for them solely on party political lines.

There may be occasions when officers recommend a policy which is rejected by members. Typically, the officers will feel that the policy formed on the basis of their professional expertise is superior. It will develop out of their specialised knowledge of the problems concerned and, in this sense, is politically neutral. Councillors may not perceive professional values as being politically neutral and will prefer policies which are consistent with their own party's political philosophy. Also, councillors will be concerned with the political impact of policies on the electorate and may reject the 'best' policy if it is unattractive to local voters.

Some commentators have been concerned that officers wield too much influence in local government. This situation arises in part from the fact that the officers are permanent whereas councillors are essentially temporary, coming and going on the tides of electoral fortune. They feel that the contest between the permanent full-time professionals and the temporary part-time councillors is not evenly matched. This is why some support the case for full-time salaried councillors in the belief that this reform would allow councillors to build up their expertise and thereby become a match for the professionals.

In most authorities the senior officer is known as the chief executive, and the most important officer–member relationship is that between the chief executive and the leader of the council. It was sometimes alleged that this officer–member link could develop into a powerful, cosy but essentially private relationship in which deals were 'sewn up', sometimes with scant regard for the wishes of other elected members. But as we have seen, recent changes in the world of local government, including greater politicisation, more assertive councillors and even the election of hung councils, have challenged this 'behind closed doors' view of decision-making.

Internal structure

Whilst at the DoE in John Major's Conservative Government, Michael Heseltine also produced a consultation paper on the internal management of

BOX 19.3
Does the committee system work?

BLOWER

Both Conservative Michael Heseltine and Labour Tony Blair seem to prefer other forms of executive structures to the existing system of committees and sub-committees. A recent report from the Audit Commission, *Representing the People: The Role of Councillors*, found that councillors spent an average of 50 per cent of their time on committee work.

Some argue that the committee system works well, especially if the influence of 'backbench' councillors is compared with that of backbench MPs. In other words, and unlike their parliamentary counterparts, councillors have an impact on decisions through the committee system. For this reason many councillors support the committee system, are very familiar with how committees work, and are reluctant to contemplate reform.

Others believe that the committee system is inefficient and undemocratic insofar as it effectively excludes councillors from decision-making. It is argued that many committees are little more than 'talking shops' and vulnerable to manipulation by officers. Apart from Policy and Resources Committees, many other committees have declined in importance. It is argued that if councillors spent much less time on even fewer committees they would have more time to devote to surgery work, to monitoring the quality of local services, and to rigorously holding professional officers to account.

local authorities. It was recognised that different structures would suit the needs of different authorities, and that no single management structure should be recommended universally. Where changes took place, they should (1) promote more effective and business-like decision making, (2) enhance the scrutiny of decisions, (3) increase the interest taken by the public in local government, and (4) provide scope for councillors to devote more time to their constituency role. The paper includes various options 'as an aid to the consultation process', which are summarised below:

- *Retention of the present system*: It is acknowledged that in some local authorities the present system

works satisfactorily, and where this happens the government do not wish to impose changes. Elsewhere, however, as the government points out, councils have sought to streamline arrangements: for example, by establishing joint member/officer working parties to deal with specific projects, or by delegating urgent decision-taking to small representative sub-committees or to officers. The government expresses the view that because of the existing legislative framework there are limits to the new systems and streamlining that can be adopted. If the present system is retained, consideration, it suggests, might be given to allowing councils to delegate decision-making to committee chairmen (at present prohibited by law). More controversially, consideration might be given to removing the requirement, given legislative force only as recently as 1989, for minority representation on committees. A theme running through the consultation paper is that the present arrangements – which vest decision-taking in the full council – blur the executive and constituency roles of councillors, and involve minority party members in time-consuming activity out of all proportion to their influence. In future, it is suggested, committees *might* consist primarily or exclusively of those members of the majority party with executive responsibilities, although as a safeguard minorities could be given more opportunity to demand debates in council on specific issues and to question 'the executive'.

- *Cabinet system*: This option, essentially, envisages the introduction of the existing central government model into local government. An executive of elected councillors (or 'ministers') would be chosen from the council as a whole, possibly on the nomination of the leader of the majority party. The majority of council members, whether in the party forming the executive or in opposition parties, would not take part in day-to-day decision making. They would scrutinise the work of the executive, and concentrate on constituency cases. The whole council, however, would be responsible for approving the budget.

- *Council managers*: In this option the council would appoint an officer to run authorities on a day-to-day basis. The council would retain *overall* policy responsibilities, and could scrutinise the managers' work but would have little involvement in day-to-day decision-making.

- *Directly elected executives*: Under this arrangement the executive (or Cabinet) would be directly elected by the local electorate. This would involve separate elections to the council and to the executive, but in other respects the executive would operate in the same way as the cabinet model.

- *Directly elected mayor*: A variation of the previous option which Mr Heseltine was widely known to have supported whilst on the back benches. A directly elected single individual would take over the council's executive responsibilities. In an arrangement similar to that found in many cities in the USA, the 'mayor' would be elected separately from the council. The Consultation Paper leaves open the question of whether the directly elected mayor should be able to make political appointments ('ministers') to support him.

Source: Greenwood (1991–2).

The future of local government

A House of Lords Select Committee chaired by Lord Hunt called for improved relations between central and local government to ensure that local government did not 'wither away through sheer neglect'. The early signs from Blair's Labour government are fairly optimistic regarding the future of local government (see cartoon). Although the role of local authorities will not be restored to their position in the 1960s and 1970s it is, to use Blair's words, to be 'modernised . . . re-invigorated . . . reborn and energised' during his premiership (the *Guardian*, 3 November 1997). As a sign of Labour's commitment to local government, Britain has now signed the Council of Europe's Charter of Local Self-Government which recognises that local government should have discretion and initiative in deciding how to meet local needs. The previous Conservative Government was not prepared to recognise the autonomy that signing the Charter implied.

UNDER TORY RULE   UNDER LABOUR RULE

The transition from Conservative to Labour administrations will be marked by both continuity and change in the world of local government. Some Conservative policies, such as CCT and capping, are to be phased out or eased. New responsibilities, such as a greater role in regulating school standards, are to be introduced. However, other Conservative policies, such as local authorities forging partnership

---

BOX 19.4

In contrast to Britain: California's 'bottom-up' approach to local government

In California the pattern of local government is determined to a great extent by whether neighbouring citizens wish to incorporate to form a city, or wish to remain living totally under the county. Local residents living in an unincorporated area of the county may wish to incorporate for a wide variety of reasons. They may wish to maintain the distinctive character of their neighbourhood and form a city in order to keep out developments which the county might allow. On the other hand, they might feel that as a city they could encourage business development and thereby increase local revenue. Or they might simply feel that as a city they could provide better value for money than the county in providing services. Typically this might occur when residents living in an affluent high income area, which produces a high tax revenue, incorporate so that their new city boundary excludes the poorer neighbouring areas which otherwise would 'consume' their taxes. For this reason, incorporated cities frequently have oddly shaped boundaries which include 'desirable' areas and exclude the 'undesirable'.

Sometimes residents living in an unincorporated area may wish to be annexed by a neighbouring city. Occasionally an unincorporated area might play off neighbouring cities in order to see which will promise the best services. This can sometimes lead to unforeseen circumstances. For example, a businessman owning some unincorporated land wanted to develop a mall complex, and he approached the neighbouring City of Placentia with a view to his land being incorporated and permission granted to develop the mall. He assumed that Placentia would agree to his proposal because of the extra tax revenue the mall would provide. In fact Placentia turned down the proposal because of the heavy traffic congestion that the development would likely cause. The businessman then approached the neighbouring City of Fullerton with the proposal, and Fullerton agreed to annex the area and permit the mall complex. The result was that Fullerton received the tax revenue whilst Placentia suffered most from the consequences of the traffic congestion.

How does an area get incorporated? The process varies, but is essentially based on citizens' initiative and two-thirds support in a ballot for incorporation to take place. The incorporation process also involves a feasibility study being undertaken by a Formation Committee which is appointed by the State. In the southern California area discussed above, LAFCO would undertake that study. Occasionally residents will sponsor an independent feasibility study in order to challenge any negative decision by LAFCO. Finally, it is worth noting that the process can work in the opposite direction – that is, disincorporation – whereby the area of an old incorporated city is returned to the county. Disincorporations are very rare.

---

links with the private sector, are to be further developed.

Labour's sweeping programme of constitutional reform will have great impact on the world of local government, including adjustments to devolution and electoral reform. In England new Regional Development Agencies will be set up to co-ordinate regional economic development by promoting inward investment and helping small firms. These agencies will liaise closely with the regional bodies which represent local government (such as the West Midlands Regional Forum).

Labour is committed to increasing participation in local government, particularly by women and young people, and is in favour of extending citizens' juries and other similar means of consulting the local electorate. The Government intends establishing watchdog committees in order to rid local government of sleaze.

Finally, Labour is implementing some of the ideas contained in the Heseltine reviews regarding encouraging innovations with cabinet-style leadership and elected mayors. In particular, much interest was shown in Labour's proposal for London having a directly elected mayor and a small assembly of some 24–32 members. The Greater London Council (GLC) was abolished in 1986, leaving London as the only western capital without a 'single voice'. These proposals will remedy this situation, although it is not without risks. For whilst the American example illustrates that dynamic mayors can provide a civic identity to residents of Chicago or New York, they can also be an embarrassment as in the case of Washington DC. Much detail has still to be decided regarding the relationship between London's future mayor and the 32 London boroughs, but he or she will have the power to appoint chiefs and boards for London Transport, police, fire and ambulance services as well as have some responsibility regarding strategic planning. The mayor will not be responsible for either education or housing. It is likely that other large British towns will follow London's example and directly elect executive mayors.

Summary

- Commentators have observed that since the 1950s local government has become increasingly political in nature. During the 1980s ideas from the New Right began to redefine the very purpose of local government, from being a direct provider of services to an indirect enabling role in service provision.
- Labour is much more favourably disposed towards local government than was its Conservative predecessor. Although the pattern of governance will remain with services delivered by a variety of providers, many in the private sector or unelected public sector, Labour's constitutional reforms promise to revive public interest and participation in local government.

Questions

1. Is there a case for local government in Britain?
2. To what extent can it be said that local government is 'alive and kicking' in Britain?
3. 'An elected mayor in every town'. To what extent would this innovation increase public interest in local government?
4. 'The community charge was a moral tax, despite its unpopularity with the public.' Examine the case for and against the introduction of the community charge (or 'poll tax'). In what ways is the council tax an improvement on the community charge?
5. Explain the philosophy behind the case for enabling local authorities.
6. 'Councillors must remember they cannot, and must not, do everything themselves: there can be no monopoly of service delivery by councils' (Tony Blair). Explain how local governance differs from local government.

Assignments

Assignment (1) The Commission for Local Democracy

The Commission for Local Democracy, not to be confused with the Local Government Commission, has published its report, *Taking Charge: The Rebirth of Local Democracy*. The Commission was set up outside of government because of a fear that local democracy is in decline and that 'British politics has become too exclusively national'. The authors felt that democracy in Britain could not thrive if it was contained to a single national tier of government. With the growth of *quangos* and *enabling authorities* in mind the report argued:

> Democracy implies a commitment to collective decision-making. Local government is not just a matter of delivering services to the public, it is about making choices for a locality. These choices have a collective character and cannot be reduced to the individualised preferences of consumers. Deciding priorities between services, expressing the concerns of a community and meeting the social and economic challenges of modern society require collective debate, deliberation and decision. These political processes are enriched and made more valid by the varied practices of democracy, both representative and participatory. The legitimacy of local government should rest on the health of its democratic activity not on the status of its leaders or the expertise of its paid officials.

The Commission's report made a number of radical recommendations to improve local democracy, including:

- local government elections should be conducted on a system of proportional representation using the single transferable vote in multi-member wards
- universal postal balloting should be introduced in local elections
- the age of candidature for election to a local authority should be lowered to 18
- both the leader/mayor and the council should have powers to conduct an advisory referendum of citizen opinion at any time
- preparation for citizenship should become part of the core curriculum in schools.

Questions
(i) Distinguish between the Local Government Commission and the Commission for Local Democracy.

(ii) Do the findings of the Commission for Local Democracy fully support the concept of enabling authorities?

(iii) Evaluate the measures recommended to increase local democracy.

(iv) Do you agree that political education should be introduced for all school students? How might this enhance local democracy over a period of time?

Assignment (2) Why Do They Do It?

The following extract is based on Barron et al. (1991, pp. 42–3).

We decided to ask political activists (councillors, candidates and non-candidates) a series of deliberately open-ended questions regarding their decision to stand – or not – for their local council. We received a wide variety of responses, of which the following are examples:

'I'm not the sort of person to be able to sit back if I don't agree with what's going on. I can't just sit back and do nothing, I have to become involved.' (Daphne Herriott, Conservative candidate and town councillor)

'Mrs Carlisle asked me if I would stand for selection. I didn't think I was ready. There may come a time . . . But I didn't feel I was ready then. I hadn't thought about it enough.' (Audrey Lightfoot, Conservative Party member and non-candidate)

'At the time, my branch was rather small and it took me three months to decide whether I'd do it or not – with very little confidence, I might add . . . I know what I wanted to do, and what I wanted to change, but I didn't really know that [the council] was the avenue I wanted to do it through.' (Pauline Smith, Labour backbencher)

How can we make sense of these various reactions? In our view, these responses suggest a subtle interplay between the resources available to them, the opportunities open to them and personal motivations and intentions. Our general conclusion was that candidature was not necessarily a deliberate or consciously worked-for objective, as the classic model would lead us to expect, but nor was it strictly an 'accidental' outcome.

. . . we see this as a process of drift, 'a gradual process of movement, largely unperceived by the actor', the outcome of which may at any stage be accidental or unpredictable.

Some individuals who eventually become councillors engage initially in sporadic community activity, may become party members, hold party office and stand for an unwinnable seat before successfully contesting a local election. For these people, the final decision to stand for election may be seen as the culmination of an extended process which commences long before the formal selection stage.

. . . Some candidates – having been persuaded merely to fly the flag for their party – had no real intention of becoming councillors and felt it would be personally disastrous if they were elected.

Questions

(i) 'People stand for election as councillors for a variety of reasons.' Explain at least two different sets of reasons and motives behind individuals' willingness to stand for office.

(ii) Explain the sort of pressures that councillors may have to cope with in office. Which councillors are likely to be subject to the greatest pressures? How might the pressures experienced by many councillors have been greater in the 1980s and 1990s than in the 1960s and 1970s?

(iii) Evaluate the case for councillors being full-time paid representatives.

(iv) The extract mentions some individuals who might be described as 'reluctant councillors'. Explain how these people ended up in this role.

Further reading

Gyford, J. (1991) *Citizens, Consumers and Councils: Local Government and the Public* (London: Macmillan): the 'new' consumer friendly vision of local government. Stoker, G. (1991) *The Politics of Local Government* (London: Macmillan): a comprehensive account of the world of local government. Wilson, D. and Game, C. (1997) *Local Government in the United Kingdom* 2nd edn (London: Macmillan): a thorough account of contemporary local government

Politics, the courts and redress

This chapter is concerned with the broad question of the relationship between law and politics. After a brief description of the general functions of law in our society, including types of law and the courts system, it focuses on the very important issue of citizens' rights and redress, first outlining the main civil liberties in Britain and then examining the procedures and institutions through which traditionally these rights have been protected. Finally, it considers some leading criticisms of the 'British way of protecting constitutional rights' which surfaced in the mid-1990s and examines the case for a British Bill of Rights before considering the main provisions of Labour's Human Rights Bill.

The law and politics

Law and politics are closely related. Three key connections exist:

- at the level of *principle,* the 'language of the law' and its accompanying norms and practices inform political discourse in virtually all its guises;
- at the level of *personnel,* lawyers are to be found occupying important positions in politics and government;
- at the level of *practice,* the courts system provides an orderly method of setting disputes between individuals and between citizens and government.

Principle

First, politics is consistently discussed in terms of law, notably in terms of *rights, obligations and remedies* – for example, of the right of the citizen to a fair trial, of the obligation of the government to provide an education service under a particular Act of Parliament, and of the remedies available to citizens in cases where their rights are infringed. Above all, politics is constantly discussed in terms of the *principle* of the rule of law (Chapter 12; and below, pp. 394–5).

Personnel

Legal personnel are strongly represented in politics. Lawyers formed one-tenth of the House of Commons in the 1997 Parliament, and one-third of the 1997 Labour Cabinet had legal qualifications. More significantly, the Lord Chancellor, Attorney-General, Solicitor-General and the Scottish law officers possess both political and legal roles. The *Lord Chancellor* is a Cabinet minister; heads an important office of state; presides over the House of Lords in its legislative and deliberative capacities; can sit as a judge; and appoints other judges. In other words, he is a practising politician as well as being the nation's senior judge and head of the legal profession. His Department has a £500 million budget. The *Attorney-General* and the *Solicitor-General* as well as the Scottish law officers are also members of the government. There are other important instances of overlap between political and legal personnel. In addition, judges – generally considered to be politically impartial – are often used to head inquiries into politically sensitive events, e.g. the inquiry headed by Lord Justice Woolf into the prison system in 1991 and Lord Justice Scott into the Arms to Iraq affair (1992–6). Finally, politics and the law mingle in the institution of the House of Lords, which draws a number of its members from the law (the Law Lords) and which combines the major constitutional roles of upper House of Parliament and supreme court of appeal. The *Law Lords* act both as judges and legislators.

Practice

The role of the legal system is to provide an orderly method of settling disputes between citizens and between citizens and the state. Broadly speaking, the *criminal law* provides standards of conduct as well as machinery (police, courts system) for dealing with those who commit crimes. Crimes are normally classified as (1) against the state (treason, public order), (2) against the person (murder, assault, rape), and (3) against property (robbery, malicious damage). *Civil law* is concerned with the legal relations between persons. Normally, proceedings in a civil court depend upon a plaintiff pursuing an action against a defendant and they generally result in some 'remedy', such as damages, specific performance (where the defendant has to keep his side of the bargain), or a 'declaration' of the plaintiff's legal rights. Cases in criminal law have to be proved 'beyond reasonable doubt'; actions in civil law are decided on the 'balance of probabilities'. In general, and for the most part, a clear-cut distinction exists between civil and criminal law, but they may on occasion overlap, as, for example, where a private person initiates criminal proceedings, or the state takes action in the civil courts, or where someone is sued privately for damages and also prosecuted in the criminal courts, or, where a court has jurisdiction (as magistrates' courts have) in both civil and criminal matters.

Administrative law is 'the body of general principles which govern the exercise of powers and duties by public authorities' (Wade, 1988). This sphere of law has undergone prodigious expansion in the twentieth century as the state through legislation has intervened in aspects of social life hitherto untouched. Administrative law is concerned with the legal restraints which surround the activities of those who apply policy decisions. It is a key example of the interconnectedness of politics and law, with a variety of judicial and quasi-judicial institutions (the ordinary courts, tribunals, the ombudsman) supplying and applying a framework of rules within which public authorities act. It is centrally involved in the question of citizen rights and redress of grievances.

Civil rights and the redress of grievances

The hallmark of a liberal democratic state, it is often said, is the effectiveness with which a range of basic citizen rights or civil liberties is guaranteed. These rights or liberties have long been enthusiastically extolled by British people, and it is vital, therefore, to examine to what extent this confidence in the security of such rights is justified. Three points provide a context for this discussion:

- Virtually all British civil liberties stem from a fundamental principle: that people may do what they like so long as no law prevents them.
- Legal protections against infringements of this fundamental freedom in specific instances (e.g. freedom of expression, meeting, association and so on) have been established gradually throughout history and are not enshrined in any particular statute (whether they *should be* is considered later in the chapter).
- The question of citizen rights or liberties has both a positive and negative aspect: the right to do certain things *and* the right *not* to have certain things done to you.

Box 20.1 is concerned with the **civil rights** enshrined in the principle of classical liberal theory, rights which achieved gradual realisation in Britain, largely over the past two centuries.

How are the rights and freedoms set out in Box 20.1 protected? Six distinct areas of judicial and political support may be identified:

- An **independent judiciary**;
- Judicial review of executive actions;
- A political culture and a public opinion in which

Citizenship: In its most basic meaning, citizenship refers to membership of a state but beyond this it normally suggests possession of certain fundamental political and civil rights such as the right to vote and the right to a wide range of freedoms together with reciprocal responsibilities to the community.

BOX 20.1
Civil liberties in the United Kingdom

- **Political rights**
Include right to vote in periodic elections, at local and national level (peers, prisoners, aliens and mental patients excluded). Guaranteed by *Representation of the People Acts* (1918, 1928, 1948 and 1969).

- **Freedom of movement**
Includes right to move freely within one's own country, to leave it; and not to be deprived of one's nationality. But Home Secretary has power to detain suspected terrorists under *Prevention of Terrorism Temporary Provisions Act* (1989); police have powers to stop and search without first establishing 'reasonable suspicion' that an offence has been committed under the *Criminal Justice and Public Order Act* (1994)

- **Personal freedom**
Includes freedom from police detention without charge, i.e. right to be brought promptly before a judge or court; freedom from police searches of home without warrant; right to a fair trial including assumption of innocence until proved guilty; freedom from torture or coercion by the state. Protection against wrongful detention first enshrined in Magna Carta (thirteenth century) and Habeas Corpus legislation (seventeenth century). No person may be detained for more than 24 hours without charge or, if a 'serious arrestable offence', for more than 36 hours without charge (*Police and Criminal Evidence Act,* 1984). Exceptions in Northern Ireland, where police abuse of emergency powers has led to unlawful detention and local security forces have committed abuses against detained terrorists; also, in wartime when Defence Secretary (under Defence Regulation 18B) could detain any person he believed hostile to the state. Freedom from police searches of house without a warrant *not* applicable if arrested at one's premises or arrested elsewhere for an arrestable offence. Accused's 'right to silence' in criminal trials infringed by *Criminal Justice and Public Order Act* (1994)

- **Freedom of conscience**
Includes right to practise any religion (freedom of worship); to marry a person of another religion; to withdraw one's children from an Established religion in school; and not to be compelled to undergo military service. Religious assemblies enjoy legal protection from disturbance.

- **Freedom of expression**
Includes individual freedom to seek information and communicate ideas; freedom of the press, publishing houses and the broadcasting media from political censorship; and the absence of state policy and machinery to direct artistic work (theatre, cinema, literature) in accordance with a particular ideology. Free expression limited by law on treason, sedition, blasphemy, obscenity, libel, insulting words or behaviour, incitement to racial hatred, defamation, contempt of court and parliament and Official Secrets Act;

'D Notice' system imposes constraints on press. No censorship of theatre (since 1968) but some of TV, cinema and videos.

- **Freedom of association and meeting**
Includes the right to meet, process and protest freely; and to associate for political and other purposes. Again no absolute freedom exists; public meetings are limited by laws on trespass, nuisance, obstruction, and local authority bye-laws; also, by discretion of police (who can re-route or ban a march they consider likely to provoke disorder) and of home secretary (who imposed a temporary ban on all marches in 1980). Whilst there are few restrictions on setting up or joining a trade union, picketing in furtherance of a trade dispute is that of 'first customers' / 'first suppliers' (*Employment Act,* 1980).

- **Right to property**
Includes right to hold property, to use it as one will and not to be deprived of it without due process. Frequently invaded by Parliament in twentieth century in name of nationalisation, compulsory purchase for slum clearance and safeguarding of public health. Right to use as one will also qualified by, e.g., legislation preventing certain forms of transfer or imposing taxation.

- **Right to privacy**
This 'right' is not recognised in British law although as a moral norm it is invoked with increasing frequency against what are taken to be state intrusions on the individual by political surveillance, 'bugging', telephone tapping, and so on; also, on behalf of public figures (e.g. royalty) against harassment by the media. Since no general right exists, privacy has to be protected in practice by specific laws, e.g. against trespass, nuisance, and breach of trust and confidence.

- **Rights at work**
These include protection from unfair dismissal, the right to a satisfactory environment at work and freedom from racial and sexual discrimination in employment. These rights have been the subject of legislation, e.g. the *Employment Protection Act* (1978), which lays down the criteria for fair dismissal; workers may appeal to tribunals against unfair dismissal. The *Race Relations Act* (1976), the *Equal Pay Act* (1970) and the *Sex Discrimination Act* (1975) legislate against various kinds of racial and sexual discrimination, including at work.

- **Social freedoms**
These include the rights to marry and divorce (for men and women equally), to use contraceptive methods, to early abortion and to practise homosexual relations between consenting adults. Divorce (1969), early abortion on broad social and medical grounds (1967) and homosexuality (1967) have all been the subject of post-war legislation.

the principle of the rule of law is widely understood and zealously guarded;

- The vigilance of members of Parliament in defence of civil liberties;
- The effectiveness of administrative law, and, in particular, the system of administrative tribunals and inquiries;
- The capacity of the ombudsman to investigate and provide remedies for cases of administrative injustice;
- The role of the European Court of Human Rights in assisting British citizens to obtain their rights
- The European Convention on Human Rights

The independence of the judiciary

The independence of the judiciary from political control or influence is a fundamental safeguard of civil freedoms. In the United States, judicial independence is assisted by the constitutional separation of powers – that is, by the separation in functions and personnel of the legislative, executive and judicial agencies. It is achieved in the UK by a combination of statute, common law, parliamentary rules, conventions, and judicial and governmental restraint. In the UK, whilst judges are largely separate from the other two branches of government, there are some exceptions to the strict separation of powers, the main ones being that the Lord Chancellor has a key role in all three branches of the state whilst senior judges belong both to the judiciary and, as members of the Upper House sitting as the Law Lords, the legislature (see Chapter 16).

The practice of senior judges holding office

Civil rights are the legal rights which underpin individual freedom such as the freedoms of speech, assembly, movement, conscience and equality before the law. Unlike human rights which are universally applicable moral principles attaching to people by virtue of their humanity, civil rights attach to individuals as members of particular societies.

Judicial independence: the constitutional principle that in order to protect individual freedom the judiciary should be independent from the other branches of government, the executive and the legislature.

'during good behaviour' dates back to the Act of Settlement, 1701. Since then their conduct has been the subject of complaint in Parliament on less than a score of occasions and only one judge has been dismissed (in 1830). From 1981 (*Supreme Court Act*), judges have been removable by an address presented to the Queen by both Houses of Parliament, but the political difficulties inherent in such a move render its success improbable. Judges' salaries are fixed by statute so that annual parliamentary debate is avoided; since 1971 their salaries have been kept under review by the Top Salaries Review Body. Parliamentary rules prevent parliament debating matters which are *sub judice* (in the process of being decided in the courts) and, unless the judge's behaviour is the subject of a motion, individual judges may not be criticised in parliament. Motions criticising judges are rarely debated. For example, the handling of the appeal of the Birmingham Six by the Lord Chief Justice, Lord Lane, in 1988 led after their acquittal to a Commons motion for his dismissal signed by 102 MPs because of his failure to apologise to the Six for the miscarriage of justice they had suffered, but the motion only earned its signatories a rebuke from the Lord Chancellor. By convention, the law lords and judges avoid commenting on political matters, although on occasion recently there have been some departures from this convention. In 1989, Lords Lane and Donaldson criticised proposals in the Courts and Legal Services Bill because, in their opinion, it gave the government greater control over the legal profession, thereby threatening its independence, whilst in 1993 several judges objected to the legislation extending the 'bugging' powers of the police as an infringement of fundamental rights and the proposals to increase the use of imprisonment as undesirable because contrary to research and comparative experience. The government riposted that the judges were 'soft on crime'. Further tension between the Conservative Government and the judges occurred in 1995–6 over sentencing policy, with the judges up in arms over the Government's decision to increase the use of mandatory sentences. In the past, governments have accepted the rule-of-law principle that they should not interfere with the conduct of the courts. How far these episodes will form exceptions to this self-restraint remains to be seen.

The highest judges are appointed by the Queen on

the advice of the prime minister (normally after consultation with the lord chancellor); judges at High Court level and below are appointed by the lord chancellor. Although they are appointed and promoted by or on the advice of politicians, professional rather than political grounds are paramount in their appointment. Judges have a statutory retiring age of 75. They enjoy immunity from civil proceedings for anything said or done while acting in a judicial capacity. It is sometimes said that because judicial independence in the UK is in large part secured by statute, it is illusory. What Parliament has given, Parliament can with equal ease take away. But this is almost certainly to go too far. Whilst the independence – from political pressures – of politically appointed judges sounds paradoxical and is not enshrined in a single written constitutional settlement, it nonetheless possesses a certain validity. Considerable political difficulties would follow any attempt to tamper with judicial independence.

Judicial review

In the last 30 years, the political role of the courts in scrutinising the actions of government and public officials has become steadily more important. In the opinion of one recent academic observer: 'the great success story of the past thirty years has been the remorseless march of administrative law calling governments to account in court' (Lee, 1994, p. 137). Before the scope of **judicial review** is examined, however, it is worth noting its limits. First, judges work within the framework of parliamentary sovereignty. Because Parliament is sovereign, judges cannot strike down legislation as unconstitutional. Thus, in the UK judicial review means preventing public authorities from doing anything which the ordinary law forbids or for which they have no statutory authority. By contrast, in codified constitutions such as the United States, the Supreme Court from the early days of the Republic assumed the role of striking down legislation deemed unconstitutional.

> **Judicial review**: the constitutional function exercised by the courts to review the legislation, regulations and acts of the legislative and executive branches.

Second, judges in Britain cannot pronounce on the *merits* of legislation – that is, they are not justified in substituting what they would have done for what parliament enacted on a given occasion. Judges distinguish clearly between matters of *policy* on which parliament is the only authority and matters concerning *lawfulness* on which the courts may legitimately intervene. Third, judicial review can be subject to statutory exclusion by some such wording as 'The decision of X shall not be called into question in any court of law'. This type of exclusion is less common today, however, than the restriction of judicial review to *a limited period of time*. Finally, the courts themselves in particular types of case have imposed strict limitations on their own power to scrutinise executive action. These types of case relate to executive decisions made under the royal prerogative and were defined by Lord Roskill in the GCHQ case (1985) to include the making of treaties, the defence of the realm, the prerogative of mercy, the grant of honours, the dissolution of parliament and the appointment of ministers (Madgwick and Woodhouse, 1995, p.88). However, even in this area, judicial self-limitation is not total. This was revealed in the Divisional Court's decision in the Bentley case (1994) that the Home Secretary's action in not granting a full pardon to Dereck Bentley (executed in 1953 for his part in the murder of a policeman) was unlawful since he had failed to comprehend the full nature of his discretion, which included the power to grant less than a full pardon (Carroll, 1994, p. 56).

A range of remedies exists in the courts for individuals who feel aggrieved by the behaviour of a public authority and a remedy may be sought by means of an application to the High Court for *judicial review*. Specific legal remedies are available. Thus, it is possible for a court to quash (*certiorari*) or prevent (*prohibition*) an order or decision; to compel the performance of a public duty (*mandamus*); to restrain the commission or continuance of unlawful conduct (an *injunction*); and simply to clarify the legal position (a *declaration*).

The grounds on which an application for review can be made were summarised by Lord Diplock in the GCHQ case as *illegality, procedural impropriety* and *irrationality*, to which *proportionality* can now be added.

Illegality The principle here is that exercises of

power by public authorities must have specific legal authority. The fundamental doctrine invoked by the courts is *ultra vires* (beyond their powers), which prevents public servants taking actions for which they have no statutory authority, i.e. from acting illegally. When courts consider an administrative action under an enabling statute, they have a regard to whether the power in question was directly authorised by the statute or whether it may be construed as reasonably incidental to it. They can also consider whether a minister or other public authority abused his power by using them for a purpose not intended by statute or whether, in exercising power, a decision-maker took irrelevant factors into account or ignored relevant factors. The Laker case (Box 20.2) provides an example of the striking down of a minister's decision as *ultra vires* because he had abused his power as laid down by Act of Parliament, thereby acting illegally. In the Padfield case (Box 20.2), the Minister was held to have misused his discretion by having regard to irrelevant considerations.

In the 1990s, with judges becoming even more active in exercising their powers of review of executive decisions, the House of Lords held in 1993 that the Home Secretary was in contempt of court for failing to comply with its order that an asylum seeker, whom the Home Secretary had deported, should be brought back to England pending his application for judicial review. In 1995, the Court of Appeal ruled that the Home Secretary had acted unlawfully in introducing a new Criminal Injuries Compensation Scheme contrary to the one approved by parliament, whilst the High Court held that the Foreign Secretary had acted unlawfully in seeking to pay money to the Pergau Dam project in Malaysia from the Overseas Development Fund, thereby forcing the government to use Treasury money to fund the project. The Court considered that an earlier promise by the Thatcher Government of aid for the Pergau project in return for arms contracts meant that the aid was for political purposes rather than economic development. Finally, in a series of judicial decisions culminating in 1997, the courts ruled that regulations made by the Secretary of State for Social Security removing the right of many asylum seekers to income-related benefits were unlawful, the Appeal Court declaring the policy 'so uncompromisingly draconian' that ' no civilised

nation can contemplate it' (Woodhouse, 1997, pp. 32–3; the *Guardian*, 18 February 1997).

Procedural impropriety The courts also allow executive decisions to be challenged on the grounds that the procedures laid down by statute have not been followed. There have been several cases involving procedural improprieties in the 1990s. In 1993, a court quashed the Home Secretary's attempt to exclude the Reverend Sun II Moon from the UK under powers granted by the Immigration Acts because he had not given Moon an opportunity to argue that he should be admitted; he had failed to behave with procedural fairness. Again in 1993, a court ruled that the Home Secretary's failure to grant asylum to a Saudi Arabian dissident, Professor Al Mas'ari, was unlawful because he had regard more to irrelevant considerations – the fear that the Saudi Arabian government would be less inclined to buy arms and other goods from Britain if the dissident was allowed to stay – than relevant ones such as the likelihood that the refugee would suffer harm if returned to his homeland. Further in 1993, a court ruled that in closing pits to make the coal industry more attractive for privatisation the Coal Board had failed to observe the required consultative procedures, whilst in 1995 a court ruled that the withdrawal of the London–Fort William sleeper in a governmental move to make the line more profitable was unlawful, also because of lack of consultation.

In reviewing administrative actions, the courts may invoke the common law principles of *natural justice*. These are twofold: first, the rule against bias (no one to be a judge in his own cause); and second, the right to a fair hearing (hear the other side). Under the first rule, administrators must not have any direct (including financial) interest in the outcome of proceedings; nor must they be reasonably suspected of being biased or of being likely to be biased. Justice must not only be done but manifestly must be seen to be done. The right to a fair hearing requires that no one should be penalised in any way without receiving notice of the case to be met and being given a fair chance to answer that case and put one's own case. The action of Brighton Watch Committee in 1964 in dismissing its Chief Constable was struck down because the Committee had not notified him or given him an opportunity to answer the charge, thereby contravening the rules

BOX 20.2
Review of administrative action by the courts

Laker Airways Ltd v. Department of Trade (1977)
At issue: Freddie Laker obtained a licence from the Civil Aviation Authority (CAA) in 1972 to operate his Skytrain on the transatlantic route. However, in 1975 the Secretary of State for Trade directed the CAA that British Airways were to retain a monopoly on scheduled transatlantic routes and Skytrain's licence was withdrawn. Laker appealed.

The decision: The High Court found that the Secretary of State's action was *ultra vires* (a) because he was statutorily authorised (by the Civil Aviation Act, 1971) only to guide and not to direct the Civil Aviation Authority; and (b) because his advice was contrary to the criteria laid down in the Act for the licensing of air services by the CAA, which included the principle that British Airways should not have a monopoly on any route.

Result: The court held that the Secretary of State had acted unlawfully. Laker Airways accordingly won their action and hence their right to compete on the transatlantic route.

Padfield v. Minister of Agriculture (1968)
At issue: South-east milk producers complained to the Minister of Agriculture that the prices paid by the Milk Marketing Board were too low and requested him to refer the question to a committee of investigation. The Minister refused to do so, giving his reasons, which included the political difficulties which would ensue if the committee found against him and he were forced to implement its report.

The decision: The House of Lords held that the Minister had allowed irrelevant considerations to weigh with him and had failed to promote the purposes of the Act establishing the milk marketing scheme. An order of *mandamus* was issued directing the Minister to consider the complainants' case. The Minister was held to have *misused his discretion*.

Result: The Minister appointed a committee, whose report in favour of the south-east milk producers was subsequently rejected by the Minister.

However, the important principle established was the subjection of executive discretion to review by the courts and their identification and remedy of misuse of administrative power.

Ridge v. Baldwin (1964)
At issue: The Chief Constable of Brighton, who by statute could only be removed on the grounds of neglect of duty or inability, was dismissed by the Watch Committee without a hearing.

The decision: The House of Lords held that the Watch Committee's act was invalid. In dismissing the Chief Constable (a) without prior notification of the charge and (b) without giving him the opportunity to put his case, it had failed to observe *natural justice* (hear the other side). It had not given the Chief Constable a fair hearing.

Results: A very important decision: hitherto, the courts had limited the application of the rules of natural justice to authorities acting in a *judicial* or *quasi-judicial* capacity; thereafter, the courts were prepared to extend the application of the rules of natural justice to any *administrative* authority whose decisions affected people's rights or legitimate expectations.

of natural justice (Box 20.2). Similarly, the decision of the Secretary of State for the Environment to rate cap Brent Council was quashed as unfair (1982) because he had not given the council the opportunity to make representations against the capping.

Irrationality This ground for review dates back to a case in 1948 when the judge held that a decision made by an authority would be unreasonable if 'it were so unreasonable that no reasonable authority could have come to it'. Although the test of unreasonableness has been used since then to strike down local authority actions, its use is rare.

Proportionality The use of proportionality as a ground for judicial review in the 1990s reflects the increasing influence of European Union law on British judges, especially the European Court of Justice and the Treaty of Maastricht which contains within it the statement that 'Any action by the Community shall not go beyond what is necessary to achieve the objectives of the Treaty'. In 1993, the Court of Appeal found that prison rules authorising the screening of prisoners' correspondence did not apply to communications between prisoners and their legal advisers other than to the extent necessary to decide they were genuinely legal correspondence. In other words, the degree of screening of prisoners' letters to their legal advisers must be proportionate to the mischief it was designed to prevent – using such correspondence to circumvent the general screening process.

Judicial review has undergone considerable expansion in recent years. In 1974, there were 160 applications for review of administrative decisions by the courts, in 1980, 525, in 1984, 918, in 1991, 2,089 and in 1996, about 3,800. Leave to apply can be refused and was granted in only a quarter of cases in 1996. There has also been an extension of the legal criteria judges are prepared to consider in helping them decide the legality of a particular decision. Before *Pepper* v. *Hart* (1992), the courts – for whatever reason – had observed a self-limiting rule not to refer to the records of parliamentary debates in *Hansard* in order to clarify the meaning of an ambiguous statute, but in this case reference was made to a parliamentary debate to establish the meaning of legislation (Loveland, 1993).

Support for the rule of law in political culture and public opinion

A second main support for civil liberties is well-established public support for **the rule of law**. It is important as a norm constraining the behaviour of authorities and guiding the expectations of citizens. In broad terms, it means the framework of rules guiding political behaviour in a liberal-democratic society, especially with regard to the exercise of political power (no power to be held over citizens unless authorised by law and exercised according to law) and redress of grievances (remedies available to all citizens). To a considerable extent, these principles are institutionalised in the procedures and practices of the legal, political and constitutional systems.

The modern principle of the rule of law owes much to the nineteenth-century lawyer, A. V. Dicey, who remains important because he stated well two of its cardinal principles (indicated below). A modern definition, however, needs to go further than Dicey for a number of reasons. First, Dicey saw the judge-made common law as the foundation of individual liberties: the twentieth century has revealed the extent to which these can be undermined by a sovereign Parliament which has conferred arbitrary powers on governments in wartime

and in emergencies. Second, Dicey distrusted what he called 'administrative law' as savouring of Continental systems of law which gave a privileged position to state officials; however, under the aegis of the welfare state, vast new empires of administrative power have been established. The modern problem is neither to dismiss, ignore nor keep administrative law at arm's length but, rather, to infuse into 'the administrative powers of the state . . . the legal ideals of fair procedure and just decision' (Wade, 1977). Even though the rule-of-law guidelines need to be more extensive than in Dicey's day, however, and their coverage wider, the *point* of producing such a list remains the same: to provide a constant witness of legal ideals for both public and practitioners.

These are the main principles, then (Dicey's formulations indicated):

- *All persons are equal before the law*: In more detail, people of any class, race or gender are universally subject to one law administered in the ordinary courts and there is no distinction in law between ordinary citizens and servants of the state (Dicey).
- *No one is punishable except for a breach of the law*: The laws are published and publicly accessible – that is, they are known or can be discovered (Dicey); and they are enforced through independent courts.
- *The powers held by the authorities must be conferred by law (i.e. by Parliament) and exercised according to authorised procedures*: In particular, powers conferred by Parliament must be defined and exercised within strict limits – by a combination of administrators' self-restraint and the vigilance of the courts.
- *Certain basic standards of justice should permeate the law*: Natural justice (the right to a fair hearing, the rule against bias) should inform procedures wherever people's rights and legitimate expectations are under consideration; since rights depend upon remedies, remedies should be available against those who exceed and abuse discretionary authority.
- *Redress – i.e. legal remedies for wrongs – should be available to all citizens against any other citizen no matter how powerful and against officers of the state.*

As the *British Social Attitudes* survey has shown,

The rule of law: the framework of legal rules guiding and restraining political behaviour in a liberal democratic society.

there is widespread support in Britain both for the rule of law and for individual rights. Society, it has been argued, is becoming more 'rights-conscious' in the two senses of increasing awareness of rights and greater willingness to protect them through the political system (Norton, 1993, p. 150). Having noted strong support for freedom of speech and assembly in British political culture, Anthony Heath and Richard Topf conclude: 'Protecting freedom of speech and assembly can be seen as part of that 'sturdy independence' . . . which makes up the 'active' component of the civic culture. Such evidence as we have suggests that this sturdy independence is increasing' (Heath and Topf, 1987, p. 58). The UN Human Rights Committee considered that Britain's possession of a wide range of pressure groups and associations concerned in varying ways with political and civil rights played 'an essential role in furthering protection of human rights in the country' (cited Klug et al., 1996, ch. 4). These include, for example, Charter 88, Justice and Liberty, and their efforts on behalf of civil liberties are further reinforced by sections of the legal profession, trade unions and the media.

Members of Parliament as defenders of civil liberties

According to traditional constitutional theory, both in their collective and individual capacity, MPs occupy a prominent role in the defence of civil liberties. The rights of citizens, so the theory goes, are protected in two ways: first, by means of ministerial accountability to Parliament; second, through the case-work of members on behalf of their constituents. Few now consider this theory to be valid. For whilst Parliament remains the central forum for scrutiny of the actions of the executive, it is no longer a particularly effective mechanism for doing so (Chapter 16). Indeed, civil libertarians have argued that parliamentary sovereignty, which in effect means executive sovereignty, is 'a double-edged sword' so far as the protection of civil liberties is concerned. This is because 'the government, through Parliament, has the same powers to pass laws, or even to issue statutory instruments, which restrict and violate civil rights, as it has to make laws which improve and protect them' (Klug et al., 1996, ch. 3). Thus, whilst parliament has enhanced rights

by passing laws against race and sex discrimination, it has also diminished rights by its legislation on closed shops, corporal punishment, prisoners' rights, immigration rules and other matters. The Democratic Audit for the United Kingdom, a University of Essex-based study of the compliance of British law and practice with its international human rights obligations, found that 24 of the 37 British violations of the European Convention as determined by the European Court of Human Rights between 1975 and 1995 were the work of parliament, either by primary legislation (15) or secondary legislation (9). Second, parliament is equally clearly no longer an effective mechanism (if indeed it ever was) through which aggrieved individuals can pursue remedies for perceived injustices. Basically, this is because the limit of an MP's influence on behalf of a constituent is the limit of the power of public opinion – or the threat of it – to compel. Whilst effective on occasion, this system is unsound as a *general* enforcer of executive respect for civil rights simply because, faced by an obstinate minister, an MP lacks the capacity either to insist on a revelation of the facts or to compel any form of restitution if it can be shown that a constituent has suffered an injustice. The system is arbitrary in its dependence on the investigative skill and persistence of MPs and on the voluntary willingness of Departments or other executive agencies to make amends where faults have occurred. In short, even though parliamentarians may play a valuable role in first airing an individual problem or grievance, this method of defending civil liberties lacks both universal reliability and certain remedies.

Administrative law

Administrative tribunals

Tribunals are a very important part of the British system of administrative justice. They are normally established by legislation and cover a wide range of functions, many of them in the field of welfare. Thus, there are tribunals for national insurance, pensions, housing, education, the National Health Service (NHS) and immigration. Claims arising out of injuries at work, industrial disputes, unfair dismissal and redundancy are dealt with by industrial tribunals. Tribunals are usually composed of a chairman with legal qualifications (often a solicitor) and two lay-members representing interests related to the concerns of the particular tribunal. They are independent and not subject to political or administrative interference from the Departments under whose aegis they usually work. Their functions may be described as quasi-judicial: to hear appeals against initial decisions of government agencies or, sometimes, disputes between individuals and organisations. Their role is to establish the facts of each case and then apply the relevant legal rules to it, i.e. in the majority of instances to decide what the statutory rights and entitlements of the aggrieved actually are. Except where the parties request privacy, tribunals hear cases in public. They provide simpler, cheaper, speedier, more expert and more accessible justice than the ordinary courts in their specific sphere of responsibility. It is possible to appeal against their decisions – normally to a superior court, tribunal or a minister. For a small number of tribunals, however, including the National Health Service Tribunal, the Social Security Commissioners and the Immigration Appeal Tribunal, no appeal is available.

The mode of operation of tribunals is determined by the Tribunals and Inquiries Act, 1971. Under this Act, a Council on Tribunals has the functions of reporting on the tribunals under its supervision (to the lord chancellor and secretary of state for Scotland, and ultimately to Parliament); of hearing and investigating complaints against tribunals for members of the public; and of being consulted by the responsible minister before procedural rules for tribunals and inquiries are made. A second important provision of the Act concerns the giving of reasons for tribunals' decisions, another matter supervised by the Council on Tribunals. Most of the tribunals listed in the first schedule of the Act are required to supply oral or written reasons for their decisions (unless exempted by order of the chancellor after consultation with the Council). But tribunals are only required to give reasons if requested and are not obliged to inform the parties of their right to request them.

The general trend of the last quarter of a century has been towards making the procedure of tribunals more judicial, but without forfeiting the advantages of tribunals over ordinary courts. These are greater informality, specialisation, capacity to conduct their own investigations and flexibility in terms of the formulation of reasonable standards in their own spheres. The Franks Committee on Administrative Tribunals and Inquiries, 1957 recommended that tribunals move towards 'greater openness, fairness and impartiality'. Proceedings should be held in public and reasons for decisions should be given; the parties before tribunals should know in advance the case they had to meet, should have the chance to put their own case either personally or through representatives, and should be able to appeal against decisions; finally, proceedings should not only be impartial, through stronger safeguards regulating their composition, but also be seen to be impartial by no longer being held on the premises of government departments. Under the supervision (since 1958) of the Council of Tribunals, the procedures of administrative tribunals have become both more uniform and more fair in many of the ways recommended by Franks, such as proper notice of hearings and of the case to be answered, rights to appeal and legal representation at hearings. Outstanding problems in the system relate primarily, although not solely, to the lack of appeal from certain tribunals (already noted); its limited extension (not all tribunals are included); and the particular condition (on request only) of the obligation to give reasons even if, in practice, tribunals do provide reasons.

Statutory inquiries

The standard method for giving a hearing to objectors to a government proposal is the *statutory inquiry*. Virtually all legislation concerned with planning and land use makes provision for holding an inquiry. Most often, inquiries arise about new towns, housing, town and country planning, road, aviation and other transport developments, agriculture and health. Inquiries are usually held, then, within the context of government policy: notable examples are individual appeals against a compulsory purchase order for the acquisition of land for a specific purpose or against the refusal of planning permission by a local authority. Procedure before, during and after the inquiry is regulated by rules laid down by the Tribunals and Inquiries Act, 1971. Decisions of inquiries may be challenged either on the grounds of procedure or the substance of the decision in the High Court within six weeks of the decision. Whilst affected third parties in land-use cases do not have legally enforceable rights, legislation governing planning usually protects their interests to a certain degree. Proposals have to be adequately publicised, for instance, and third parties have to be afforded the opportunity to state their cases before decisions are taken.

Whilst realising the need not to impose unnecessary delays on inquiry procedure, the courts in hearing appeals from inquiry decisions have sought to safeguard the rights of the public. For example, they have ruled that objectors at an inquiry should be able to take 'an active, intelligent and informed part in the decision-making process' (1977) and that they must be given 'a fair crack of the whip' (1976) in putting their case. The courts have received important support in this regard from the Council on Tribunals which not only raises specific questions relating to inquiries with the chancellor but also (as with tribunals) reports on their working, has the right to be consulted before procedural rules are made for them, and receives public complaints about them. How successful the courts and Council had been in bolstering the inquiry system as a bastion of democracy became a matter of increasing controversy, however, during the 1980s mainly as a result of disquiet about government handling of issues arising out of its proposals for the management of nuclear waste. Keen to avoid the delays and furore surrounding the 340-day Inquiry into the Sizewell-B Nuclear Reactor (1985), the government in late 1985 proposed to limit the terms of reference to the Inquiry relating to the Dounreay Fast-Breeder Reactor to the question of where to dump the waste rather than to allow the Inquiry to enter the debate about whether to dump or, as its critics preferred, store it. In 1994, after the government had given the go-ahead to the Thorp nuclear re-processing plant, the High Court rejected an attempt by environmentalists to force a public inquiry.

The ombudsman

As well as legal rights, citizens have a more general right to a good standard of administration. Despite difficulties of precise definition, this right is still a significant element in administrative justice. In 1967, after rising public concern that traditional parliamentary channels were inadequate to protect the citizen against administrative abuse by government departments and agencies, the Parliamentary Commissioner for Administration (ombudsman)

was established by Act of Parliament. His brief is to investigate and, if possible, remedy complaints by individuals and corporate bodies who feel that they have experienced 'injustice in consequence of maladministration' at the hands of central government.

Appointed by the Crown on the advice of the lord chancellor, the ombudsman enjoys an independent status similar to that of a high court judge. His salary is fixed by statute and charged on the Consolidated Fund; he holds office 'during good behaviour' and can be removed on addresses from both Houses of Parliament. He has a staff of about fifty-five, largely drawn from the civil service. During his investigations, which are conducted in private, he can call for the relevant files of the Department concerned; as a matter of course, he informs the head of Department, and any civil servant involved, of his investigation. He possesses the powers to investigate a matter thoroughly: he can administer oaths and compel the attendance of witnesses as well as the presence of documents. His brief covers maladministration which can embrace a wide range of faults. As de Smith and Brazier put it:

corruption, bias, unfair discrimination, harshness, misleading a member of the public as to his rights, failing to notify him properly of his rights or to explain the reasons for a decision, general high-handedness, using powers for a wrong purpose, failing to consider relevant materials, taking irrelevant material into account, losing or failing to reply to correspondence, delaying unreasonably before making a tax refund or presenting a tax demand or dealing with an application for a grant or license, and so on. (de Smith and Brazier, 1990, p. 649).

Complainants have no right of direct access to the Parliamentary Commissioner for Administration (PCA) but must approach him through an MP. He received 1,920 new referrals through MPs in 1996 but only a small proportion were accepted for investigation – 15 per cent, a smaller proportion than in previous years. Figure 20.1 shows the growing caseload of the Parliamentary Commissioner over the decade to 1996. Complaints were rejected for investigation mainly because they did not concern administrative actions or because there was a right to appeal to a tribunal. The departments generating

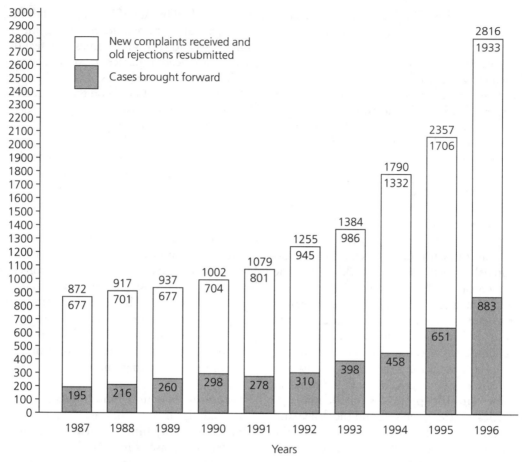

Source: *Parliamentary Commissioner for Administration*, Annual Report, for 1996 (1997) p. 37.

Figure 20.1 The growing caseload of the Parliamentary Commissioner, 1987–96

the most complaints are the Department of Social Security and its agencies (47 per cent of all referrals) and the Inland Revenue (12 per cent). In 1996, the PCA completed 260 investigations, finding that complaints were justified (73 per cent) or partly justified (22 per cent) in the vast majority of cases.

The PCA issues a report on each investigation to the referring MP, with a copy to the Department involved. Where maladministration is found, a Department will be expected to correct it – e.g. by issuing an apology or financial recompense to the aggrieved person – but the ombudsman has no power to compel it to do so. Where, as occasionally happens, the Department refuses to correct an injustice, the PCA may first bring pressure to bear on it by means of the Commons Select Committee on the PCA, and if this fails, he can lay a Special Report

pointing out the unresolved injustice before both Houses of Parliament.

Initially limited to the investigation of maladministration in central government, the ombudsman system was later enlarged by the addition of ombudsmen for Northern Ireland (1969), the National Health Service (1973), and Local Government in England and Wales (1974) and Scotland (1976). No ombudsman was established for the police. Unlike the position with regard to the

Redress of grievances: the legitimate expectation by a citizen in a democratic society that complaints against public officials will be considered fairly and impartially and that legal remedies for wrongs will be available should malpractice be revealed.

Table 20.1 Number of complaints received by ombudsmen, 1981–93

	1981	1991	1993
Police Complaints Authority[1]	–	18,065	17,991
Commissioners for Local Administration	3,295	14,060	16,507
Banking Ombudsman	–	6,327	10,231
Building Societies Ombudsmen	–	8,264	9,142
Insurance Ombudsman	1,517	4,334	8,133
Independent Commission for Police Complaints for Northern Ireland	–	2,530	2,419
Corporate Estate Agents Ombudsman	–	1,236	2,340
Pensions Ombudsman	–	2,186	2,179
Health Service Commissioners	686	990	1,384
Legal Service Ombudsman	–	1,248	1,235
Broadcasting Complaints Commission	114	1,048	1,049
Parliamentary Commissioner for Administration	917	801	986
Northern Ireland Parliamentary Commissioner and Commissioner for Complaints	654	547	605
Scottish Legal Services Ombudsman	41	303	295
Investment Ombudsman	–	67	103

[1] England and Wales only.

Source: Social Trends (1995) p. 169.

PCA, direct access to these ombudsmen is allowed (in the case of local government, only since 1988), and both the health and the local government commissioners receive a much larger volume of complaints than the PCA (Table 20.1). As with the PCA, however, neither local nor health commissioners have any enforcement powers, although in Northern Ireland, a complainant does have legal redress where a legitimate grievance is found, being able to apply to the county court for an appropriate remedy. If a local authority in mainland Britain chooses not to comply with an adverse report by a local ombudsman after various efforts (report, informal meeting with senior officers and councillors, further report) have been made to persuade it, the Ombudsman can require it to publicise the reasons for non-compliance. (Thompson, 1993, pp. 19–20).

The ombudsmen have made a less dramatic impact on British public administration than their early advocates hoped. There are many areas excluded from the jurisdiction of the PCA – government contractual and commercial transactions, for example. The public have no direct access to the PCA, and for this and other reasons such as lack of public awareness of his existence, rather a small number of complaints actually reach him. The only powers of the ombudsmen against a recalcitrant public authority are those of publicity. Even where cases of maladministration leading to injustice are found, the complainant has no legal remedy available (except in Northern Ireland).

On the other hand, the ombudsmen *have* been more – sometimes much more – than 'ombudsmice'. Most of their recommendations, in fact, are accepted and implemented by the Departments and authorities concerned.

On occasion even, the PCA has achieved considerable success. One of the best-known successes

Table 20.2 European Court of Human Rights, judgements, 1959–95

State	Ratification	Individual petition[1]	Total judgements	Adverse judgements[2]
UK	1951	1966	60	35
Austria	1958	1958	51	34
Italy	1955	1973	45	32
France	1974	1981	54	28
Netherlands	1954	1960	31	23
Sweden	1952	1952 (1966)	30	21
Belgium	1955	1955	32	20
Switzerland	1974	1974	24	14
Germany	1952	1955	28	12
Greece	1974	1985	9	7
Ireland	1953	1953	8	6
Portugal	1978	1978	10	6
Spain	1979	1981	11	6
Denmark	1953	1953	6	2
Finland	1990	1990	3	2
Iceland	1953	1955 (1958)	3	2
Turkey	1954	1987 (1990)	3	2
Cyprus	1962	1989	1	1
Luxembourg	1953	1958	1	1
Malta	1967	1987	1	1
Norway	1952	1955 (1964)	1	1

[1] Date upon which the right of individual petition to the European Commission of Human Rights was accepted (Article 25). Where a state has recognised the compulsory jurisdiction of the European Court of Human Rights at a later date (Article 46), this date is given in brackets

[2] Cases which give rise to a finding of *at least one* violation

Source: Klug, Starmer and Weir (1996) p. 55.

occurred over the famous *Sachsenhausen* case (1967) when the PCA found that the Foreign Office (FO) was responsible for procedural maladministration in its handling of an application by former prisoners-of-war for compensation for their sufferings in a Nazi prisoner-of-war camp, and the FO paid compensation.

A more recent case was the PCA's discovery of significant maladministration leading to injustice in five areas of the Department of Trade and Industry's handling of the Barlow Clowes investment group when the government, without accepting the finding of maladministration, agreed to pay huge compensation to aggrieved investors (1989). But these are exceptional cases. More usually, small-scale payments in compensation follow a PCA report: in 1996, for instance, 65 per cent of those whose complaints were found to be wholly or partially justified received a financial remedy, 13 per cent led to a change of procedure or practice but no financial remedy, and the remaining 22 per cent received just an apology (*Parliamentary Commissioner for*

BOX 20.3

European Court decisions bearing on the rights of British citizens

---

The European Court:

- has criticised treatment of suspected terrorists interned in Northern Ireland by the UK government;
- allowed prisoners their right to correspond with their lawyers, MPs and the newspapers;
- condemned corporal punishment in schools;
- ruled against inhuman conditions in solitary confinement;
- criticised undue interference with a free press in the *Sunday Times* thalidomide case against Distillers;
- upheld the rights of workers against closed shops;
- condemned as inadequate the review procedure for life-sentence prisoners recalled after release;
- declared British immigration rules to be unlawful because they discriminated against women; the rules allowed foreign men with full residency rights in the UK to bring in

their wives or fiancees, but did not allow women with residency rights to bring in their husbands;
- criticised the ineffective judicial protection of a detained mental patient; it ruled that *habeas corpus* provided inadequate redress against wrongful confinement in this instance;
- condemned the legal ban obtained by the government on press disclosure of documents used in evidence in court;
- ruled that a group of shareholders in shipbuilding and aircraft companies nationalised in 1977 had been inadequately compensated;
- ruled that the UK government's ban on three British newspapers for disclosing evidence of MI5 wrong-doing contained in *Spycatcher* was invalid because the book had already been published in the USA;
- ruled that the British government had used excessive force in shooting three IRA suspects in Gibraltar.

Administration. Annual Report for 1996 (1997), p. 40).

The European Court of Human Rights

The European Court of Human Rights has played an important part in upholding and enlarging civil liberties in Britain although between 1966 and 1997 it did so in a somewhat roundabout way. The United Kingdom ratified the European Convention on Human Rights in 1951 and allowed individuals to petition it from 1966 (Box 20.4). Although these were not legal rights in Britain and therefore not enforceable in British law, they turned out to be an important influence on civil rights. British Courts could take note of the convention and presume Parliament did not intend to legislate inconsistently with it. Moreover, the UK government normally complied with judgements of the European Court. However, these rights were not enforceable in British law because, although Britain renewed its ratification of the Convention every year, unlike the other countries who have signed the document, it did not, until 1998, incorporate the Convention into British law. Hence, British citizens were not able to use the Convention to appeal to British courts when their rights were infringed. They were able to appeal to the European Court, but only after they had tried and failed to find remedies in the British courts.

Complaints went to the *European Commission* at Strasbourg in the first instance. The Commission then decided whether the case was 'admissible' to the European Court; normally cases went before the Court only after the Commission had first failed to achieve a friendly settlement between the parties concerned. Every year the Commission opened about 800 provisional files on complaints by British citizens – more than from any other country. Of these, a small number were declared 'admissible'. If 'admissible', cases were registered. In all, down to 1997, the Court pronounced on 98 British cases and found violations of human rights in 50 of them. Box 20.3 gives some major examples of cases in which the 'rights' of British citizens have been upheld by the European Court. The United Kingdom has lost more cases before the European Court than any other signatory state (Table 20.2). The decisions of the European Court were not, strictly speaking, enforceable in the United Kingdom. But the UK government agreed to respect the decisions made by the Court and, in practice, its verdicts were observed, normally by changing British law accordingly. Box 20.4 lists the rights available under the European Convention on Human Rights and its Protocols.

The situation was by no means ideal. The Strasbourg Court would hear a case only if domestic attempts to find a settlement are exhausted; no legal

---

BOX 20.4

Rights under the European Convention on Human Rights and its Protocols

Convention

Article 2 Right to life
         3 Freedom from torture or inhuman or degrading treatment or punishment
         4 Freedom from slavery or forced labour
         5 Right to liberty and security of person
         6 Right to a fair trial by an impartial tribunal
         7 Freedom from retroactive criminal laws
         8 Right to respect for private and family life, home and correspondence
         9 Freedom of thought, conscience and religion
     10 Freedom of expression
     11 Freedom of peaceful assembly and association, including the right to join a trade union
     12 Right to marry and found a family
     13 Right to an effective remedy before a national authority
     14 Freedom from discrimination

Protocol No. 1

Article 1 Right to peaceful enjoyment of possessions
         2 Right to education. Parental right to the education of their children in conformity with their religious and philosophical convictions must be respected.
         3 Right to take part in free elections by secret ballot.

Protocol No. 4

Article 1 Freedom from imprisonment for debt
         2 Freedom of movement of persons
         3 Right to enter and remain in one's own country
         4 Freedom from collective expulsion

---

aid was available; and the Court took a long time to reach its judgements – an average of five years for a case to move through the entire process. Nonetheless, the Court did bolster the rights of prisoners, immigrants, women, mental patients, journalists, expropriated shareholders and workers who may not want to join a union in as effective a way as circumstances allowed. Box 20.5 summarises the strengths and weaknesses of contemporary means of redress of grievances in Britain.

The case for a British Bill of Rights

British civil rights and the way they are secured – in general by a mixture of common and statute law – are set out in Box 20.1. However, during the 1980s and 1990s many political commentators came to doubt whether civil liberties in Britain were sufficiently secure. These doubts surfaced for a number of reasons. The primary reason was the growth of concern about the capacity of *Parliament* to protect individual liberties either positively by espousing the causes of aggrieved citizens or negatively by not actually invading individual rights. How many MPs see one of their major roles as that of serving as a one-person ombudsman or, assuming they do, have

the time, energy, capacity and resources for such a role? Again, as already noted, Parliament – by means of legislation pushed through by the governing party with the aid of its majority – may invade civil liberties as much as protect them. Two authors writing in 1990 of extensions of state power by parliament and the executive in the 1980s concluded that civil liberties in Britain were in a state of crisis.

> We have charted the unprecedented extension of police powers; a far-reaching statute for the interception of communications by the state; wide-ranging restrictions on the freedom of assembly and public protest; the growth of a national security consciousness used to justify major limitations on press freedom in particular; the extension of the powers of the security service and the lack of any effective accountability for the way these powers are exercised; and, finally, the assumption of quite extraordinary powers to deal with the north of Ireland, admittedly an issue of immense complexity (Ewing and Gearty, 1990, p. 255).

Other critics such as Lord Scarman remarked upon the inability of the courts to guarantee rights and liberties relating to welfare, the environment, industrial

BOX 20.5

Contemporary means of redress of grievances in Britain: strengths and weaknesses

Means of redress/ Protection of rights	Strengths	Weaknesses
Independent judiciary	Long established statutory guarantee of judicial security of tenure.	No constitutional guarantees. Depends on statute law. Recent government interference with courts over sentencing policy.
Judicial review of executive	Courts can strike down executive acts on a variety of grounds. Seven fold expansion in judicial review, 1980–1996.	Parliamentary sovereignty: judges can pronounce only on legality not on merits. Parliament can exclude or set time limits to judicial review.
Pro-rights political culture and public opinion	Widespread support for rule of law in political culture and public opinion strongly backed by constitutional and legal pressure groups.	*British Social Attitudes* (14th Report, 1997) suggests some reduction in public support for accused's 'right to silence' in 1990s.
MPs	Have access to powerful: can contact ministers on behalf of constituents, raise grievances in Commons adjournment debates and refer cases of alleged maladministration to Ombudsman.	Parliament can reduce as well as enhance rights by legislation. MPs lack power to compel public authorities to respect individual rights.
Parliamentary Commissioner for Administration (Ombudsman)	Independent investigator of wide field of maladministration by central government. Departments accept and implement most of ombudsman's recommendations.	Access to Ombudsman is through MPs, not directly. No power of compulsion. Exclusion of some areas of government activity. No Ombudsman for complaints against police.
Administrative law	*Administrative tribunals*: provide an independent, speedy, expert, cheap and accessible form of redress. *Statutory inquiries*: provide for objectors to e.g. land use decisions to be given a say and for decisions to be challenged on grounds of procedure or substance.	Cover relatively limited field – mainly welfare and industrial. Limits on rights of appeal and on obligation to give reasons for decision. Held within framework of government policy. Government can restrict scope.
European Court of Human Rights	Judgements have enhanced rights in Britain e.g. children, prisoners, immigrants. Governments usually complied with judgements.	Judgements not enforceable in British law until 1998. Very lengthy procedure pre-1998 with cases having to be heard by European Court of Human Rights, not British courts.
European Convention on Human Rights	Proposed legislation by Labour Government (White Paper 1997) making it illegal for public authorities to contravene European Convention on Human Rights. Will constitute considerable advance on present situation.	Certain exemptions, including death penalty and detention without trial in Northern Ireland.

BOX 20.6

Concerns about political rights in the United Kingdom: the United Nations Human Rights Committee, 1995

The UN's verdict on the UK

1 GOVERNMENT powers under statutory provisions allowing infringements in civil liberties— 'such as extended periods of detention without charge or access to legal advisers, entry into private property without judicial warrant, imposition of exclusion orders within the UK'—are excessive.

2 'NOTE is taken of the Government's own admission that conditions at the Castlereagh detention centre are unacceptable.'

3 WHILE prison conditions have improved, the Committee is disturbed 'by the high number of suicides of prisoners, especially among juveniles.'

4 THE Committee is disturbed by reports of the continuing practice of 'strip-searching male and female prisoners' in the light of the low security risk and the existence of sound alternative search techniques.

5 EXTERNAL investigations by the police of incidents involving the police or military, 'especially incidents that result in death or wounding', lack sufficient credibility.

6 'MEMBERS of some ethnic minorities, including Africans and Afro-Caribbeans, are often disproportionately subjected to "stop and search" practices'.

7 THE extension under the Criminal Justice and Public order Act 1994 of the legislation in Northern Ireland, whereby inferences may be drawn from the silence of persons accused of crimes, violates various provisions in Article 14 of the Covenant, despite the range of safe guards built into the legislation . . .'

8 '. . . MANY persons belonging to minorities frequently feel that acts of racial harassment are not pursued by the competent authorities with sufficient rigour and efficiency . . .'

9 '. . . THE incarceration of persons ordered to be deported and particularly the length of their detention may not be necessary in every case . . . [the Committee) is gravely concerned at incidents of the use of excessive force in the execution of deportation orders'.

10 THE privatisation of core state activities 'which involve the use of force and the detention of persons' weakens the protection of Covenant rights. The Committee stresses that the UK government remains responsible in all circumstances for the observance of those rights.

Source: The Guardian, 4 October 1995.

relations and Britain's obligations under the European Convention.

Several reports in the mid-1990s seemed to confirm that civil liberties were not well protected in Britain. The UN Human Rights Committee (1995) criticised Britain for failing to protect political and civil rights adequately and for not fully providing for an effective remedy for all violations of the rights contained in the UN Covenant (Box 20.6). The 'Democratic Audit' of the UK identified 42 separate violations of international human rights in Britain (Klug et al., 1996, ch. 3). Its authors argued that the failure to protect political rights and freedoms in the UK was 'systemic': neither separately nor in combination were the 'three pillars of liberty' – parliamentary sovereignty, a political culture of liberty and the rule of law – capable of effective protection of civil liberties, as tradition, the government of the day and some judges all claimed. Rather, these three pillars of liberty had need of the additional support of a consistent set of civil and political rights to strengthen parliament against the executive, reinforce public opinion and give the courts constitutional legitimacy and establish standards and tests for the interpretation of statute, judicial review and the development of the common law.

The clamour for a **Bill of Rights** first surfaced in the 1970s, but by the 1990s many individuals and groups were advocating one, including the Liberal Democrats, some Labour and Conservative MPs, Charter 88, Liberty, the Institute for Public Policy Research, and several leading judges. Arguments for and against a Bill of Rights are set out in Box 20.7.

There are three ways of enacting a Bill of Rights:

1. By drawing up a list of individual rights and providing for their constitutional entrenchment by an Act of Parliament. The courts would have the authority to strike down any subsequent Act of Parliament or administrative action which conflicted with it. This way of proceeding would destroy parliamentary sovereignty since, once enacted, the Bill of Rights would take precedence over all subsequent legislation and would in all cases have to be upheld by the courts.
2. (A modified form of 1, preserving parliamentary sovereignty.) Legislation could enact a Bill of Rights which the courts would uphold unless otherwise directed by parliament, and which would remain in place until amended or even superseded by subsequent rights legislation.

The first has the merit of greater security for rights at the expense of parliamentary sovereignty as well as a certain rigidity; with the second, rights are rather less secure but parliamentary sovereignty as well as a greater flexibility remains.

3. By incorporating the European Convention on Human Rights into British law. This would give Britons the right to seek redress in British courts against infringements of their liberties as set out in that code. This is the weakest form of enactment of a Bill of Rights but justifiable as a 'first step' (see below).

In their 1997 manifestos, the Liberal Democrats promised to incorporate the European Convention

---

> **Bill of Rights**: a constitutional document which lays down the legal rights and freedoms of individual citizens.

---

on Human Rights as 'a first step' to a Bill of Rights, a Human Rights Commission to strengthen the protection of human rights and a Ministry of Justice while Labour promised the incorporation of the European Convention to establish 'a floor, not a ceiling, for human rights' which parliament could enhance by, for example, a Freedom of Information Act.

The incorporation of the European Convention on Human Rights

Following its manifesto promise to incorporate the European Convention on Human Rights into British law and the confirmation in the Queen's Speech that it intended to 'repatriate British rights to British courts' and to 'protect the individual against the misuse of power by the state', the Labour Government published a White Paper outlining its legislative proposals, *Rights Brought Home: The Human Rights Bill*, in October 1997. Incorporation of the Convention into British law will mean that British citizens who consider that their rights have been infringed will be able to take their cases to British courts rather than to the European Court of Human Rights in Strasbourg. The proposed Human Rights legislation will make it illegal for public authorities, including the government, the courts and public bodies discharging public functions to act in a way incompatible with the European Convention on Human Rights (Box 20.4). Judges will not have the power to strike down Acts of Parliament (as they do in Canada, for example) because that would be inconsistent with parliamentary sovereignty. Instead, they will be able to declare a law 'incompatible with the Convention', which, in the words of the White Paper, 'will almost certainly prompt the Government and Parliament to change the law'. The legislation will take effect once the judiciary has completed its training. A Committee of both Houses of Parliament will report on whether there should be a Human Rights Commission, whose role would need to be reconciled with that of existing bodies such as the Commission on Racial Equality and the Equal Opportunities Commission. There will be no Human Rights Minister. There will be certain exemptions from the Convention: thus, parliament will retain the right to consider a return to the death penalty and the government will retain

---

BOX 20.7
A British Bill of Rights: for and against

For Greater clarity: A code would make clear governmental responsibilities, enable citizens to know their rights more easily and provide courts with a well-defined set of freedoms to protect.

Against Difficulty of defining rights: (a) Socialists and most liberals would include social and economic rights, Conservatives seek to limit civil and political rights. (b) If social and economic rights are included, these are likely to fluctuate: e.g. Labour in 1970s legislated in favour of closed shop, Conservatives in 1980s against it.

For Courts are superior to parliament at protecting civil rights: (a) Courts are independent of the government, not aspiring to be part of it, like MPs. (b) A Bill of Rights would make available to British citizens civil rights which at present have to be sought at the European Court, but more speedily and cheaply.(c) A code of rights would have a moral force lacking in present law, and thereby be harder to flout – by, for example, government or big interest groups.

Against Courts are *not* better than parliament at protecting civil rights: (a) Unlike MPs, judges are unelected and unaccountable, and have undeclared rather than explicit political biases. (b) Certain issues – e.g. race relations, industrial relations, press freedoms, privacy, police powers and national security – are inherently political and therefore need to be decided openly by politicians, not covertly by judges. (c) Judges might interpret rights narrowly, whittle them down

rather than guarantee them; anyway, its unwise to *politicise* judges.

For Bill of Rights backed by courts works well in other countries: e.g. USA, where Supreme Court judgement against racial segregation (1954) played key part in eventually gaining civil rights for the black minority.

Against Institutions do not necessarily transplant well: US Bill of Rights works in context of very different separation of powers system. British system is based on parliamentary sovereignty. Better to reform rather than transform it, e.g. by extending powers of Ombudsman, restricting coverage of Official Secrets Act, increasing investigative powers of MPs, introducing freedom of information. Under parliamentary sovereignty, a Bill of Rights (or part of it) could be overturned by a later parliament.

For Educational value of Bill of Rights: Great need in Britain is for understanding of rights to be well-grounded in political culture, and this would be facilitated by a specific code.

Against Nothing in present situation regarding rights to prevent spread of understanding of them. Rights well supported in political culture.

For Bill of Rights can be *extended* according to changing circumstances by addition of Protocols, e.g. European Convention on Human Rights.

Against Bill of Rights inflexible because contain social values at the time of their enactment.

---

detention without trial for seven days in Northern Ireland. Finally, by December 1997 the government was having second thoughts on the consequences of incorporation for privacy. Initial opinion had been that incorporation would not affect press self-regulation through the Press Complaints Commission, but later advice suggested it would and that there could be appeals to the courts from individuals dissatisfied with its findings. Hence, the government was reported to be considering whether to amend the Bill to prevent it becoming a 'back-door' privacy law by mistake.

Human rights campaigners welcomed the Human Rights Bill whilst also expressing disappointment that it did not go further. It was welcomed first and above all because it enshrined positive rights for the first time in British constitutional history. As well as

providing better protection for existing rights, the Bill would incorporate into Britain rights inadequately covered by existing law, such as freedom of expression (Box 20.7). Second, human rights advocates welcomed the proposals to protect the individual against abuse of power by the state as a huge advance on the current situation in which 'public officials could only be challenged in court if they defy procedures, act contrary to statute' or behave with extreme irrationality (Francesca Klug, the *Guardian*, 24 October 1997*)*. Third, the 'fast-track procedure' to amend the law to comply with judges' rulings was also endorsed. Campaigners expected that human rights values would gradually infuse British political and public life, changing the practices of all public officials from immigration officers to care workers.

Disappointments included, first, the failure to allow the courts to strike down legislation contrary to the Convention and, second, the failure to establish immediately a Human Rights Commission (HRC) to police the Convention. As well as helping individuals to assert their rights, the HRC could promote a culture of rights and responsibilities through education and the media. Third, even if Britain did incorporate the Convention's article on privacy, some critics felt this was too weak. The article permits interference with privacy where it is necessary 'in the interests of national security, public safety or the economic wellbeing of the country, for the prevention of disorder or crime, for the protection of health or morals, or for the protection of the rights and freedom of others'. Fourth, the Convention was drafted nearly fifty years ago and contains weaknesses such as the right to be free from discrimination and gaps such as the rights of children which, in the view of critics, would need to be remedied later by a full-scale human rights bill. Finally, critics considered that the legislation should have included provision for a senior Cabinet minister responsible for Human Rights.

Summary

- Law underpins democratic politics in various ways, two very important ones being the provision of guiding principles such as the rule of law and of a courts system for the orderly settlement of disputes, including disputes between the citizen and the state. Administrative law regulates the behaviour of public authorities and is of central concern in considering citizen rights and redress of grievances.
- Civil liberties are extensive in Britain and include a wide range of political and civil rights such as the right to vote, freedom of speech, assembly, conscience and movement, and the right to hold property. They derive from, and are limited by, a complex variety of procedures and laws largely emanating from statute and common law, but not from a single written document.
- Civil liberties are protected by a number of political and judicial methods with varying degrees of adequacy. These include judicial review, support for the rule of law in political culture and public opinion, MPs in their collective and individual

capacities, administrative tribunals and statutory inquiries, the parliamentary commissioner for administration and the European Court on Human Rights.
- Civil rights in Britain came to seem less secure in recent decades than formerly and in the mid-1990s both the 'Democratic Audit' and the United Nations Human Rights Committee criticised the UK for violations of its international human rights obligations.
- In circumstances in which British citizens often and successfully appealed to the European Court of Human Rights, civil libertarians advocated a Bill of Rights for Britain, and in the 1997 General Election both Labour and the Liberal Democrats advocated the incorporation of the European Convention on Human Rights into British law as a preliminary step towards further extensions of rights.
- Labour's Human Rights Bill will make it illegal in Britain for public authorities to act in a way which is incompatible with the European Convention on Human Rights. However, whilst welcoming the measure, critics expressed disappointment that the Bill did not permit UK judges to strike down legislation which contravened the Convention.

Questions

1. How far will the protection of individual rights in Britain be enhanced by the incorporation into British law of the European Convention on Human Rights?
2. What do you understand by the 'rule of law'?

Assignment

Examine the criticisms by the UN Human Rights Committee of civil rights in Britain in Box 20.6.

(i) What rights and liberties does the Committee consider are being infringed?
(ii) What social groups are particularly affected by these infringements?
(iii) Evaluate the overall significance of the Committee's findings for the state of civil liberties in Britain.

Further reading

On key themes covered by this chapter, including the rule of law, the executive and the courts and redress of grievances, see Madgwick, P. and Woodhouse, D. (1995) *The Law and Politics of the Constitution* (London: Harvester Wheatsheaf), and de Smith, S. and Brazier, R. (1994) *Constitutional and Administrative Law*, 7th edn (London: Penguin). On specific aspects, there are Davis, H. (1993) 'The Political Role of the Courts', *Talking Politics*, 6:1, autumn; Thompson, K. (1993) 'Redressing Grievances: The Role of the Ombudsman', *Talking Politics*, 6:1, autumn; Grant, M. (1994) 'The Rule of Law – Theory and Practice', *Talking Politics*, 7:1, autumn; Carroll, A. (1994) 'Judicial Control of Prerogative Power', *Talking Politics*, 7:1, autumn; Watts, D. (1994) 'Europe's Bill of Rights', *Politics Review*, 3:4, April; Oliver, D. (1993) 'Citizenship in the 1990s', *Politics Review*, 3:1, September; and Freeman, M. (1997) 'Why Rights Matter', *Politics Review*, 7:1, September.

On developments in the 1980s and 1990s: Ewing, K.D. and Gearty, C. (1990) *Freedom under Thatcher: Civil Liberties in Modern Britain* (Oxford: Clarendon); Lee, S. (1994) 'Law and the Constitution', in Kavanagh, D. and Seldon, A. (eds) (1994) *The Major Effect* (London: Macmillan); Woodhouse, D. (1995) 'Politicians and the Judiciary', *Parliamentary Affairs*, 48:3; Woodhouse, D. (1997) 'Judicial/Executive Relations in the 1990s', *Talking Politics*, 10:1, autumn; and Loveland, I. (1997) 'The War Against the Judges', *Political Quarterly*, April–June.

Finally, the British system of civil rights and their protection and the issues involved in adopting a Bill of Rights are covered clearly and incisively in Klug, F., Starmer, K. and Weir, S. (1996) *The Three Pillars of Liberty* (London: Routledge), and the special issue of *Political Quarterly* (1997), 68:2, April–June.

The secret state

In recent decades, issues of national security and defence have attained considerable prominence in British politics. This chapter deals with some central questions arising out of these issues, focusing particularly upon the character of state secrets, the nature and accountability of the **intelligence agencies** and the controversy generated by government reforms in these spheres after 1988. In broad terms, it is concerned both with the 'secret state' – the non-elected institutions which exercise considerable power in substantial freedom from democratic control together with the legislation and practices by which governments preclude public discussion of purportedly secret matters – and with pressures for greater 'openness'. These pressures emanate from the values and norms of liberal constitutionalism, in particular, those of political accountability (executive responsibility to Parliament), civil liberties and the freedom of the press.

The security services

Britain has four main security and intelligence-gath-

> **Intelligence services**: secret services such as MI5, MI6 in the UK, Central Intelligence Agency (CIA) in the US, with the task of obtaining information vital to the security of the state.

ering agencies. These are MI5, the domestic security service; Special Branch, the internal political police; MI6, the overseas intelligence service; and GCHQ, the Government Communications Headquarters, responsible for international surveillance. Basically, these services have two main tasks: at home, to gather information on individuals, groups and organisations considered to be a threat to the state, and to counter those threats; abroad, to gather intelligence of all kinds, e.g. economic, political, military, about potential enemies and competitors, with a special focus on threats to political stability (terrorism, weapons developments) (Box 21.1).

Issues of control and accountability, competence and scope

In the 1990s, the changing role of the security and intelligence services, continuing revelations about their role in domestic **surveillance** and further government legislation affecting them led to intense public debate about their control and accountability, competence and scope (breadth of surveillance).

Key roles in the control and coordination of the security services are played by the prime minister, the home secretary and the Cabinet Office. The precise constitutional position is by no means clearcut. The home secretary holds overall responsibility for MI5 and Special Branch whilst MI6 is formally answerable to the foreign secretary (Box 21.1). However, ultimate responsibility for national

> **State surveillance**: the watch kept by the security services over persons and groups whose activities are suspected of endangering the safety of the realm.

BOX 21.1
Britain's security services

MI5 (Security Service)
Director-General: Sir Stephen Lander
Headquarters: Thames House
Established: 1909 (to counter German spies)
Staff: 2,000, over half of them women
Budget: £170 million
Functions: Formerly mainly counter-terrorism but also counter-espionage and counter political subversion; from 1996 involved in countering 'serious crime'. Also concerned with political 'vetting'.

Police Special Branch
Senior officer: Deputy Assistant Commissioner, Metropolitan Police; chief constables, local forces
Headquarters: Top Floor, New Scotland Yard; provincial police HQs
Established: 1883 (to counter the Irish Republican Brotherhood – successors to the Fenians)
Staff: 1,800 (1988)
Budget: £19.5 million (Met SB – 1988)
Functions: Assisting MI5 to combat terrorism, espionage, sabotage and subversion (in addition to intelligence-gathering, makes arrests for MI5) Also concerned with protecting VIPs, watching ports and airports, vetting naturalisation applicants and enforcing Official Secrets and Prevention of Terrorism Acts.

MI6 (Secret Intelligence Service)
Chief: David Spedding
Headquarters: Vauxhall Cross

Established: 1909 (also to counter German spies) 'MI' stood for Military Intelligence
Staff: 2,000
Budget: £150 million (estimated)
Functions: Gathering political, military and economic intelligence in foreign countries through agents attached to British embassies and high commissions. Works closely with the Defence Intelligence Staff (DIS) – established 1965, current staff over 600 – whose main role is to provide world-wide military threat analyses and assessments. Role from 1994 in combating serious crime such as money-laundering, drug-smuggling, nuclear proliferation, illicit dealing in conventional weapons and organised illegal immigration.

Government Communications Headquarters (GCHQ)
Director: David Omand
Headquarters: Cheltenham
Established: Developed out of Government Code and Cypher School at Bletchley in Second World War. Operates under secret UK–USA treaty (1947) by which UK and USA, assisted by Canada, Australia and New Zealand, share responsibility for monitoring international communications.
Staff: 6,000 (at GCHQ, set to fall to 5,000 in 1999); 3,000 military personnel throughout Britain.
Budget: Over £500 million
Functions: Interception and decoding of international communications – diplomatic, military, commercial and private – by means of spy satellites and listening posts. Responsible for signals intelligence–SIGINT. Cooperates closely with the US National Security Agency at Fort Meade, Maryland.

---

security is held by the prime minister as is clear from occasional statements by prime ministers in the House of Commons; the PM chairs the Cabinet Committee on the Security and Intelligence Services (IS) and the heads of MI5, MI6 and GCHQ along with the chairman of the Joint Intelligence Committee have direct access to the PM. Only the prime minister sees the true security services budget. The security services have been placed on a statutory basis only recently – MI5 in 1989 and MI6 and GCHQ in 1994.

An important role in the day-to-day coordination of the security and intelligence services operations and budgets is played by the *Cabinet Office*: one of its six secretariats is specifically concerned with security and intelligence (*Joint Intelligence Organisation*); it contains a key official, the *Co-ordinator of Intelligence and Security*, who reports directly

to the PM; and the Cabinet secretary chairs a range of important committees concerned not only with internal Whitehall security but also with general oversight of security services budgets (the *Permanent Secretaries Committee on Intelligence Services* (PSIS)). The central roles in the processing of intelligence information are shown in Figure 21.1. As can be seen, the *Joint Intelligence Committee* (JIC) serves as the 'central filter' (Norton-Taylor, 1990) between the expert assessors in the Cabinet Office – themselves drawing upon information provided by the main intelligence-gathering agencies – and key ministers on the Cabinet Overseas Policy and Defence Committee (OPD). The *Security Commission*, set up in 1964, investigates security lapses and advises on vetting procedures at the request of the PM. The overall picture with regard to roles and responsibilities in the control,

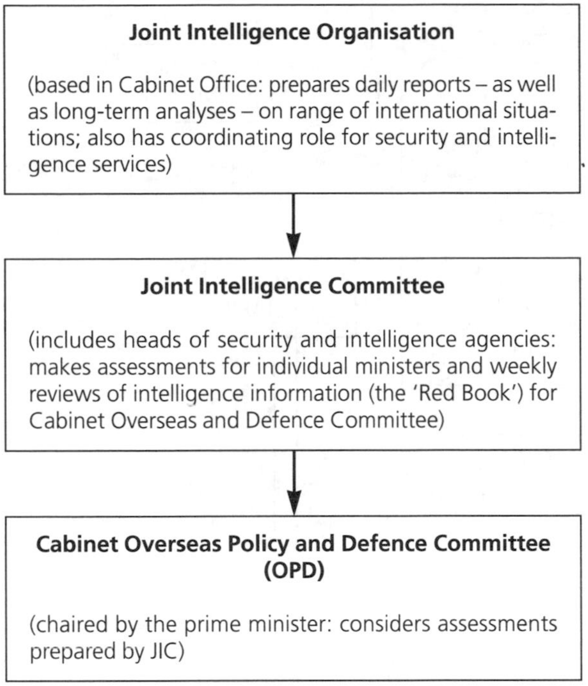

Joint Intelligence Organisation

(based in Cabinet Office: prepares daily reports – as well as long-term analyses – on range of international situations; also has coordinating role for security and intelligence services)

↓

Joint Intelligence Committee

(includes heads of security and intelligence agencies: makes assessments for individual ministers and weekly reviews of intelligence information (the 'Red Book') for Cabinet Overseas and Defence Committee)

↓

Cabinet Overseas Policy and Defence Committee (OPD)

(chaired by the prime minister: considers assessments prepared by JIC)

Figure 21.1 The processing of intelligence information in Britain

processing and gathering of intelligence is shown in Figure 21.2.

Three main questions arise about Britain's security and intelligence services:

- How much are ministers told about their operations? The main point at issue here is the adequacy of *political control* over national security.
- Should the security services be accountable to parliament, and if so in what ways?
- How far are security operations a threat to civil liberties? This raises issues of the extent and methods of surveillance of the security services as well as of their legal and political control.

We look at each of these questions in turn.

Political control

A key document here is the 1952 government directive to the director-general of MI5. This stated that there was a well-established convention whereby ministers *'do not concern themselves with the detailed information which may be obtained by the Security Service in particular cases but are furnished with such information as may be necessary for the determination of any issue on which guidance is sought'*. This has usually been taken to indicate considerable ministerial – including prime ministerial – ignorance of the day-today operations of the security services. However, on occasion there has been considerable ministerial intervention, as in the early 1980s when the Ministry of Defence used MI5 for partisan purposes (Lustgarten and Leigh, 1994, p. 364). On the other hand, there have been periods when MI5 has been out of control: for example, the situation in the 1970s described by the former MI5 officer Peter Wright in *Spycatcher* (1987) when MI5 became an independent power centre uncontrolled by ministers and even built up a file on the then Prime Minister Harold Wilson, attempting to undermine and 'de-stabilise' his government (Tomkins,1997, p. 122).

Political accountability

Britain's security services are not democratically accountable. The prime minister and other ministers do from time to time answer questions in Parliament about the services but seek to give away as little as possible – to be in fact 'uniformly uninformative'. The government argues that what can be said publicly about security is very limited – for good security reasons. The then Home Secretary Kenneth Clarke forbade the Head of MI5 to appear before the Home Affairs Select Committee in 1993. However, in its report *Accountability of the Security Services* (1993), this Committee demanded the right to scrutinise the role of the Security Service (MI5), arguing that such scrutiny would 'meet an important public interest and help to protect against any possible abuse of power'. Pointing out that the security services are democratically accountable in Canada, Australia and the United States, the Home Affairs Committee called for parliamentary oversight of the policy and effectiveness of MI5, not of operational matters. It also considered that MI5 should be accountable to a parliamentary committee for its £185 million annual budget.

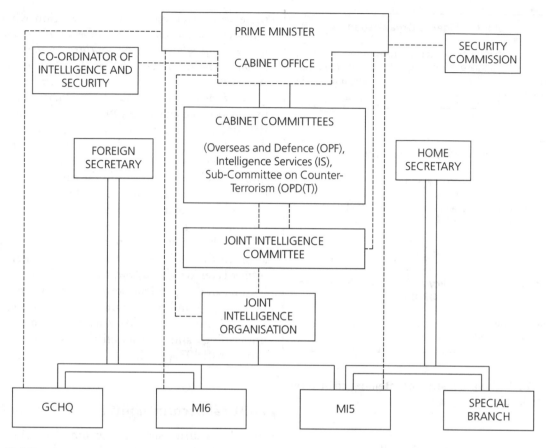

Figure 21.2 The security services: responsibility, coordination and control

However, the new Intelligence and Security Committee established by the Major Government under the *Intelligence Services Act* (1994) went much less far than parliament requested. The new Committee, composed of nine members drawn from both Houses, was charged with examining 'the expenditure, administration and policy' of MI5, MI6 and GCHQ. It meets weekly in Whitehall when parliament is sitting, under the chairmanship of Tom King, who retained this role after the 1997 general election. It operates under 'the ring of security', its members being bound by the lifelong duty of confidentiality under the Official Secrets Act (1989). Its first report (1995) criticised the heads of MI5 and MI6 for failing to investigate the potentially serious damage done to British interests by the CIA agent Aldrich Ames and for failing to warn ministers about the implications of his eight years spying for Moscow. King has subsequently (1997) urged MI5 and MI6 chiefs to demand more information from the US on the recent spate of espionage scandals in the CIA and FBI and also expressed concern about the lack of uniform security procedures in MI5, MI6 and GCHQ.

Critics argue that the new committee is too weak for the following reasons:

- Heads of the security agencies and ministers decide what information the committee is given and can prevent it from seeing any material deemed sensitive.
- The committee is appointed by, and reports to, the prime minister, who can veto sections of its reports.
- The committee has no power to require the attendance of witnesses or to compel the handing over of documents; moreover, witnesses are not compelled to give evidence on oath.

- The committee has no staff of its own but is dependent on Cabinet Office staff.

For these reasons, according to Conservative MP Richard Shepherd and other critics, the committee is incapable of demonstrating to parliament that the security and intelligence agencies are properly accountable and operating ethically.

Political surveillance and civil liberties

Britain's security services gather information 'by the interception of communications'. Authorisation for these practices is by means of warrants obtained from the home secretary, foreign secretary or the secretaries of state for Scotland or Northern Ireland. Before 1985, the criteria for the issue of warrants were defined by the executive (*Birkett Report*, 1957; *White Paper on Interceptions*, 1980). These were:

- *National security*: There had to be major subversive or espionage activity likely to injure the national interest and, second, the material likely to be obtained by the interception had to be of direct use to the security service in carrying out its specific tasks.
- *Serious crime*: A warrant would be granted only where the crime was really serious, normal methods of investigation had been tried and failed, and there was good reason to believe that the interception would obtain information liable to result in a conviction.

In 1985, however, the issue of warrants for interceptions was given a statutory basis. The *Interception of Communications Act* (1985) had three major provisions. First, it broadened the criteria upon which warrants could be issued to include: (1) national security; (2) preventing or detecting a serious crime; and (3) protecting the economic well-being of the UK. The broadening of the criteria was reflected both in item (3) and in a vaguer notion of 'national security' (Item (1)), which was no longer equated as previously with 'major subversion or espionage'.

Second, the Act made unauthorised interception of a postal communication or telephone message a criminal offence for the first time. Third, it established a remedy for those aggrieved by what they considered to be improper interception of communications in the form of a right to complain to a tribunal of legally qualified members.

The tribunal has power to quash improperly issued warrants, to order the destruction of material obtained in an improper manner and to require the secretary of state to pay compensation. However, none of the first 68 complaints to the tribunal was upheld. Critics argue that the powers of the tribunal are *too limited* and, in particular, that it has no power to investigate whether unauthorised interceptions are taking place. They also criticise *the exclusion of the courts* from any role in the scrutiny of illegal or improper behaviour by the security services (Ewing and Gearty, 1990, pp. 72–7). Supervision of the powers exercised by the home secretary and tribunal under the Act is carried out by a security service commissioner.

Intelligence-gathering is done in three main ways: listening in to telephone conversations and opening letters; employing spy satellites to photograph military installations and intercept communication signals; and through human agents using concealed radios to pass back information. The concern of civil libertarians focuses on the first two methods.

Official figures greatly underestimate the extent of telephone-tapping This is for two main reasons. First, the published figures do not include warrants issued by the foreign secretary (usually about one-third of the number issued by the home secretary) or those issued by the secretary of state for Northern Ireland. Second, a single warrant can cover a target organisation with thousands of members and may include their friends and relatives.

Even on official figures, telephone-tapping has increased in recent decades. Whereas the home secretary and Scottish secretary issued 464 warrants in 1980, they approved over 1,000 warrants in 1995, a record number. The number of warrants obtained by the surveillance agencies to bug and burgle private property was not disclosed.

The sheer size of the net cast by the surveillance agencies has led to periodic public outbursts of alarm and controversy. The attention of civil libertarians has focused on the 'broad' interpretation of the rules governing the operation of the security services. Some of the main allegations about improper conduct by these services are:

- faking and forging of documents, smear campaigns and illicit 'bugging' and burglaries of political parties and trade unions by MI5 in the 1970s (Peter Wright, *Spycatcher*, 1987)

- subversion of the Wilson Government by attempts to discredit ministers by MI5 in 1974: campaign codename 'Clockwork Orange' (Wright, *ibid.*; Colin Wallace, former Army Information Officer; Lord Hunt, former cabinet secretary, 1996)
- tapping phones of trade union leaders by MI5 in late 1970s both during industrial disputes and routinely – for example, on one occasion to discover 'the Ford union's bottom line in pay negotiations' – and also targeting civil rights activists and members of CND (Cathy Massiter, former MI5 agent, 1985)
- routine spying by security services on EC countries to discover the bottom line on Community deals, and large-scale commercial spying on car, chemical and oil companies and finance houses (Robin Robison, former civil servant on Joint Intelligence Committee, 1991)
- MI5 targeting of the National Union of Mineworkers during the 1984–5 Miners' Strike by infiltration of an undercover agent at a high level and systematic phone tapping of the NUM's Sheffield Headquarters (Milne, 1994; Labour backbench motion, 1993; the *Guardian,* 19 November, 1994))
- tapping the phone of Peter Mandelson, currently Labour Minister without Portfolio, in the late 1970s, monitoring the activities of Jack Straw, currently Home Secretary, and tapping the private phone of the *Guardian's* deputy foreign editor, Victoria Brittain, and planning to break into her home between late 1993 and 1995 (David Shayler, former MI5 agent, 1997)

The government's response to criticisms of the security services

The government responded to the Massiter allegations by ordering an inquiry by the Chairman of the Security Commission but annoyed the opposition and other critics by restricting its terms of reference to whether ministers since 1979 had operated under official guidelines in authorising telephone-tapping. *Lord Bridge's Report* – produced in five days – cleared the Thatcher governments up to that date of issuing

warrants for interceptions outside accepted procedures and criteria but did little to allay disquiet. Opposition leaders remained concerned about surveillance without ministerial knowledge or warrant; about blanket surveillance of a whole organisation under a single warrant; about the unauthorised interception of transatlantic communications; and about the possibility that the security services were gathering information on the members of non-subversive organisations.

In 1985, however, the government was forced to create a statutory framework for the operation of the security services by an adverse judgement in the European Court of Human Rights. The judgement arose in the case of Roger Malone, an antiques dealer whose phone had been tapped – in fact with the authority of a warrant – by the police. The Court ruled that British law was insufficiently clear about the circumstances and conditions under which the authorities would resort to this intrusion into privacy. However, the *Interception of Communications Act* (1985), for the reasons already outlined, did little to allay public concern, and controversy about the operation of the security services continued. By the late 1980s, following the *Spycatcher* affair, it would probably not be an exaggeration to say that there was 'a true crisis of confidence in the security services of this country' (Ewing and Gearty, 1990, p. 170).

The government responded with further legislation, the first being the *Security Services Act* (1989). This Act placed MI5 on a statutory footing for the first time; provided for the appointment of a security services commissioner to review the powers of the home secretary to issue warrants for telephone-tapping and other forms of surveillance; and created a tribunal (of 3–5 legally qualified members) to investigate complaints by persons aggrieved about any action of MI5 in relation to their property. But critics pointed out once more the weakness of these provisions: the wide definition of the powers of MI5 (see Box 21.2); the authorisation of burglary in the form of burglar warrants; and the inadequacy of the review procedures, with the powers of both commissioner and tribunal being strictly limited. The commissioner, for example, has no power to order the cessation of improper practices, whilst the tribunal lacks the power to decide whether the service acted reasonably in exercising surveillance

---

BOX 21.2
The functions of MI5

The **Security Service Act (1989)** defined the functions of MI5 as being 'the protection of national security and, in particular, its protection against threats from espionage, terrorism and sabotage, from the activities of agents of foreign powers and from actions intended to overthrow or undermine parliamentary democracy by political, industrial or violent means'; and, also 'to safeguard the economic well-being of the United Kingdom against threats posed by the actions or intentions of persons outside the British Isles'. **The Security Service Act (1996)** gave MI5 a 'supporting role' behind the police and Customs in the fight against 'serious crime'. 'Serious crime' is defined as any offence for which a person might face three years in prison; any offence involving violence or the prospect of 'substantial gain'; and 'conduct by a large number of persons in pursuit of a common purpose'.

---

over a particular category of persons, e.g. trade unions or the Labour Party. Above all, the security and intelligence services remained unaccountable to Parliament.

The second piece of legislation was the *Intelligence Services Act* (1994), which placed GCHQ and MI6 on a statutory basis;established the Intelligence and Security Committee (see above); and, following the 1989 *Security Service Act,* set up an Intelligence Services Commissioner and a complaints tribunal whose decisions cannot be subject to appeal or questioned in any court. Warrants for surveillance, burglary and entering property are issued by ministers. This Act also protected security and intelligence agents abroad from acts which would be illegal if committed in Britain, including lethal force. Finally, following substantial lobbying by the head of MI5, Stella Rimington, for a new role for the organisation after the post-Cold War reduction in its counter-espionage role and the post-IRA truce reduction in its counter IRA terrorism functions, the *Security Service Act* (1996) gave MI5 a new role in countering 'serious crime' (Box 21.2). Once MI5 decides that a target fits into one of the criminal categories, it may seek a 'property warrant' from the home secretary allowing 'any entry on to property', 'interference with property' (e.g. by opening a letter or planting a bug) and 'interference with wireless telegraphy'. Critics believed that it was unnecessary to extend MI5's role into policing and that to give an additional role in countering crime to a self-tasking, secret, largely unaccountable organisation creates a potential threat to civil liberties. Whilst engaged in a similar role now to the police, MI5 officers who bent or broke the rules were not subject to a complaints procedure like the police. Moreover, the broad interpretation of crime, permitting investigation into 'conduct by a large number of persons in pursuit of a common purpose', could enable MI5 surveillance of road protesters, for example, or animal rights activists. By 1997, some critics even pondered whether rather than extending its role MI5 should be shut down and its counter-domestic terrorism role transferred to the police.

In the continuing absence of proper parliamentary accountability of the security services, questions continued to be raised in the 1990s about the legitimacy of some of their activities, the adequacy of the complaints procedure and their effectiveness. First, the *Diaries* (1993) of Alan Clark, a former minister under Thatcher, suggested that ministers are subject to MI5 surveillance despite the widespread understanding – based on an assurance by Harold Wilson in 1966 – that MPs (and peers) are generally exempt from 'bugging' by the security service. Where such surveillance does occur, it needs the express authorisation of the prime minister and is reported to the House of Commons later. The *Clark Diaries* appeared to confirm earlier statements by MPs Jonathan Aitken and Sir Richard Body (in 1990) that MPs are under MI5 surveillance. Second, no complaint to the security services commissioner and tribunals between 1985 and 1995 was upheld; there were 187 unsuccessful complaints between 1990 and 1995. Third, with regard to the effectiveness of the security and intelligence agencies, critics point, for example, to intelligence service failures over the Argentinian invasion of the Falklands, the US invasion of the Commonwealth island of Grenada and the Iraqi invasion of Kuwait. Further – and related – questions are how much intelligence information actually finds its way to ministers and the use which is made of that which is received. These questions arose in relation to the collapse of the Bank of Credit and Commerce International (BCCI) about which it was reported that MI5 and MI6 were aware that the bank was being used by drug-money launderers and terrorists like Abu Nidal at least two years before the Bank ended; and the collapse of the financial empire of Robert Maxwell, over which the Prime Minister, John Major, in 1992 denied that ministers had received security service information on Maxwell's business dealings in 1989 two years before the tycoon's death.

Finally, three major conclusions of the *Scott Inquiry* (1996) had implications for the functioning of the security services and their relations with government:

- In 1988, MI5 and MI6 provided information that Iraq was using British machinery exports to make armaments but pressured the government not to revoke firms' export licences in order to protect their sources.
- In 1989, ministers granted Matrix Churchill export licences for high-speed lathes and machining centres despite the plentiful evidence that they were being used in Iraqi arms production.
- The lack (before July 1990) of coordination of intelligence relating to British involvement in Iraqi arms procurement represents a serious failure of the Joint Intelligence Committee (Tomkins, 1997, pp. 114–22).

Political vetting

Political vetting – as well as control and accountability – has also been a matter of public concern. One aspect is internal vetting within the security services themselves. In 1984, Michael Bettaney, a middle-ranking MI5 officer, was sentenced to 23 years' imprisonment on spying charges. His heavy drinking suggested that he was a high security risk and indeed that he ought to have lost his security clearance at an earlier date. Three years later internal vetting procedures once again became the subject of a furore when the Prime Minister disclosed to the House of Commons that Sir Maurice Oldfield, the head of MI6 between 1972 and 1978, had in 1980 admitted to concealing his homosexuality during vetting and as a result had had his internal security clearance withdrawn. At the time of his confession, he had been recalled from retirement to oversee security in Northern Ireland because of severe problems in the relationship between the police, the army and the undercover forces. In 1995, the Security Commission criticised MI5 and the Ministry of Defence for a series of astonishing mistakes, unwarranted delays and unnecessary secrecy which allowed an electronics engineer, Michael Smith, jailed in 1993 for selling military secrets, to spy for the Soviet Union for 16 years.

Another aspect of political vetting raises the issue of civil liberties. This issue arose in the case of a journalist, Isobel Hilton, who was prevented from joining the BBC because she had been blacklisted by MI5. She had been blacklisted because, as a student, she had been secretary of the Scotland–China Association. The Association, whose members included churchmen, academics and a former governor of Stirling Castle, was regarded as a subversive organisation by MI5, whose negative vetting continued after her resignation from the Association in March 1977. Isobel Hilton's case was turned down by the European Court of Human Rights because she could not provide incontrovertible proof (she was unable to do this because her lawyers did not have access to MI5 files).

State secrecy in Britain

A state secret is government information which for reasons of national security is not revealed in the public domain. In Britain, information kept secret by the government generally goes beyond information vital to public safety and often includes information whose publication would merely be political embarrassing. Thus, secrecy is a central characteristic of British government and there exists a variety of constitutional, political, bureaucratic, military, cultural and historical factors which help to explain the obsession with it (Box 21.3). As Patrick Birkinshaw has observed 'very few comparably developed states allow government such complete protection against claims for information by citizens or legislatures' (Birkinshaw, 1997, p. 167). Its major legislative bulwarks down to the late 1980s were the Official Secrets Acts of 1911, 1920 and 1939. Secrecy laws were reformed in 1989 by a new

---

BOX 21.3
Secrecy and the UK political system

There are several features of the UK political system which tend to promote government secrecy.

- The lack of a written, codified, constitution, or a Bill of Rights, which outlines the duties of government and the rights of citizens means the public has no 'right to know' laid down in writing. The lack of a Freedom of Information Act is also a factor, although this is as much a result of the predominance of secrecy as its cause.
- A unitary form of government which concentrates political power at Westminster and increases the centralisation of administrative information tends to favour secrecy in the centre.
- For the most part, a two-party system, given its adversarial nature and the wish to keep information from 'the other side', encourages secrecy.
- The doctrine of ministerial responsibility which holds that ministers, not civil servants, are answerable for government decisions promotes secrecy among public officials.

The secrecy of the civil service is a mark of its subservience to ministers.

- The civil service also tends to be secretive because of the sheer administrative burdens. In addition, the rivalry for Treasury resources encourages secrecy between the various departments.
- A political culture deferential to strong leadership and pragmatic government, which traditionally has not placed accountability as a priority, has provided a climate for secrecy. The inward-looking administrative culture in the 'Whitehall village' also promotes secrecy.
- Military secrecy, during threats of war and invasion, has led to general government secrecy.
- Historically, government by an elite which regarded openness as unnecessary and undesirable favoured secrecy, as did a lack of commitment to democratic values inside and outside Parliament.

Source: Hunt (1992b).

Official Secrets Act, which repealed section 2 of the 1911 Official Secrets Act. Our discussion leads inevitably to a consideration of the campaign for freedom of information and to the prospects for greater openness in Britain.

The main problem relating to the *Official Secrets Act* (1911) was its very widely drawn Section 2. This clause made it a criminal offence for public servants to retain without permission or to communicate without authorisation any information obtained in the course of their employment or for a person to receive such information knowing or having reasonable cause to believe that it had been disclosed in breach of the Act. The *catch-all* nature of Section 2 meant that it was unable to distinguish between sensitive information such as intelligence and certain kinds of defence matters which in the national interest must be kept secret, and more trivial, harmless information. According to one authoritative estimate, Section 2 created no fewer than 2,324 offences (de Smith and Brazier, 1990, p. 494). Under this section, the government could if it wished prosecute someone for revealing such a trivial matter as the number of cups of tea drunk in a particular government department. The clause also provided government with an essentially *arbitrary* weapon making it impossible for public servants and journalists to predict when a prosecution would be

launched. Prosecutions could be launched for *political* reasons, to suit the convenience or to spare the embarrassment of the government of the day.

The key consideration is *authorisation*. Government as a matter of course routinely divulges large quantities of information through ministers who are self-authorising in the matter and through civil servants whose authorisation, more vaguely, is implied. Security classifications – in ascending scale of sensitivity, 'restricted', 'confidential', 'secret' and 'top secret' – play in government terms 'an essential administrative role in handling information' (Box 21.4). But the point is that no matter how information is classified and no matter how much 'leaks' of classified information have become part of the system by which the media acquire news, government could make the disclosure of any item of *unauthorised* information an offence. The very wide coverage of the Act meant that civil servants and journalists could be in technical breach of the law frequently. The Defence, Press and Broadcasting ('D' Notice) Committee currently advises media editors on what they may not publish (Box 21.5).

The excessive secrecy of British government has long been the object of criticism. The Fulton Committee (1968) concluded that the administrative process was surrounded by 'too much secrecy' and recommended 'a greater amount of openness'.

BOX 21.4
Whitehall's security classifications

Category	Consequences of disclosure
Top secret	Exceptionally grave damage to the state.
Secret	Serious injury to the interests of the state.
Confidential	Prejudicial to the interests of the state.
Restricted	Undesirable in the interests of the state.

BOX 21.5
The 'D' Notice system

A 'D' Notice is a confidential letter sent by the government to media editors and sometimes to publishers requesting that information be not published because publication would damage national defence or security. The system, which functions on a voluntary basis, constitutes a further inhibition on the publication of 'sensitive' information on defence and security matters: it was used, for example, to block news stories on the spies George Blake (1961) and Kim Philby (1963). The system is managed by the Defence, Press and Broadcasting Committee (comprising senior officials and representatives of the media) which in October 1992 announced a thorough review of 'the purpose scope and operation' of the 'D' Notice system in the light of the end of the Cold War and of 'government policy on greater openness'.

The Franks Committee (1972) criticised Section 2 of the Official Secrets Act as a 'catch-all' and 'a mess'. But attempts at reform of the Official Secrets Acts undertaken by Labour (1978) and the Conservatives (1979) came to nothing, and after 1978, governments had increasing recourse to the Official Secrets Acts to inhibit publication of materials which in their view endangered the national interest, and certain of these widely publicised prosecutions had the effect of intensifying pressures for reform.

Trials under the Official Secrets Acts in the 1980s

Prosecutions under the Official Secrets Acts proceeded at a relatively modest level in the postwar decades, fell away in the 1970s but increased dramatically after 1978. Thus, there were 23 prosecutions involving 34 defendants between 1945 and 1971 but no fewer than 29 people were prosecuted between 1978 and 1986. The following are some leading trials from the 1980s.

The Tisdall case (1984): Sarah Tisdall, a Junior official in the Foreign Office, was prosecuted and sentenced to six months imprisonment for leaking secret Ministry of Defence documents to the *Guardian* newspaper in October 1983. One of the documents, marked 'Secret–UK eyes only', outlined plans by the Defence Secretary to handle the parliamentary and public response to the arrival of Cruise missiles at RAF Greenham Common, whilst the second document related to security preparations for the Greenham base. Tisdall was annoyed by the evidence contained in the first document of political calculation by the government in its handling of the Cruise issue: it intended to make a statement to Parliament after and not before the arrival of the

nuclear missiles. Even though it published only the first document which did not relate to national security, the *Guardian* lost its case to protect its sources of information and was forced to return the document, possession of which enabled the government to trace the leak back to Tisdall.

The Ponting case (1985): Clive Ponting, a senior official in the Ministry of Defence, was prosecuted for leaking two official documents (one unclassified, the second marked confidential but later declassified) concerning the sinking of the Argentinian ship, the *General Belgrano,* during the Falklands conflict. Ponting believed that ministers were deliberately misleading the House of Commons over the circumstances of the sinking. Ponting's defence was that he had acted in accordance with the national interest, which was to know the truth about this particular event; his broader duty as a citizen overrode his narrower duty as a public official. He believed that the government had been concerned only with saving itself from political embarrassment. The prosecution case, upheld by the judge in his instruction to the jury, was that the national interest was the same as the policy of the government of the day. Ponting's duty as a civil servant, therefore, was simply and solely to support the government's decision to withhold *Belgrano* information. To general surprise, and government consternation, Ponting was acquitted.

The 'Zircon affair' (1987): This episode involved a film made for the BBC's 'Secret Society' series about

Britain's proposed spy satellite, Zircon, by the journalist Duncan Campbell. The film was withdrawn by the BBC, possibly after government pressure, but Campbell then proposed to show the film to MPs (to demonstrate that there was no risk to national security). This, however, was blocked by the Speaker, after a briefing from the Attorney-General. The government then attempted by legal injunction, but failed, to prevent Campbell speaking or writing about his film and the contents of the programme appeared in the *New Statesman*. On the authority of a warrant issued under the Official Secrets Act, Special Branch then raided the BBC's Glasgow office and seized the Zircon film. The government maintained that the proposed disclosures would alert the USSR to the existence of the satellite and would endanger cooperation with the USA in gathering intelligence. But critics argued that the government wanted to stifle the programme because of its political embarrassment, that the project was likely to be delayed and that national security was not threatened by the film since the existence of the proposed satellite was more widely known than the government alleged and, once launched, its position would be easily detected by the Soviet Union. The affair died down: the injunctions against Campbell were lifted and the BBC showed the Zircon film two years later. But the episode had raised worrying questions about government infringements of media freedom.

Spycatcher (1986-8): In this drawn-out case, the government obtained injunctions against newspapers in Britain reporting or repeating what they had already reported of the revelations about the security services contained in the book *Spycatcher* by a retired MI5 agent, Peter Wright. The government based its legal case not on the Official Secrets Acts but on breach of confidence by a servant of the Crown. At the same time, the government sought through injunctions to prevent the publication of the book in Australia. It was during the trial in New South Wales that the Cabinet Secretary, Sir Robert Armstrong, caused a considerable public stir by confessing that he had been 'economical with the truth'. The government argued that publication would damage the confidence of other members of the security service in each other and of other countries in the British security services. But it lost its case both in Britain and in Australia, a decisive point in its defeat being the publication of *Spycatcher* in the United States in July 1987.

Critics pointed out both the illogicality of the government's position in continuing to ban a book the substance of which from late July 1987 was already in the public domain in Britain or readily obtainable in the US, and its inconsistency since no action had been taken in the early 1980s against books by Chapman Pincher and Nigel West which contained revelations about the security services. Critics also argued that the seriousness of Wright's allegations – notably, that the British security services had been involved in an attempt to assassinate President Nasser and a plot to destabilise the Wilson Government and that a former head of MI5, Sir Roger Hollis, was a Soviet double-agent – warranted an immediate inquiry, but the government refused this on the grounds that an administration does not investigate the conduct of previous governments.

Reform of the Official Secrets Acts

In the aftermath of the Ponting and *Spycatcher* cases, political pressures for reform of the Official Secrets Acts became irresistible.

The Official Secrets Act (1989)

First, the Act reduces the categories of information protected against disclosure by the criminal law to six, as follows:

- Security and intelligence
- Defence
- International relations
- Information relating to crime and its investigation
- Information about or obtained by activities under warrants issued under the Interception of Communications Act (1985) and the Security Services Act (1989)
- Information provided in confidence by another state or international agency.

Second, it defines the circumstances for each category in which disclosure of information will be considered 'harmful' to the public interest. For example, the disclosure of *defence* information is harmful if it 'endangers the interests of the United

Kingdom abroad, seriously obstructs the promotion or protection by the United Kingdom of those interests or endangers the safety of British citizens abroad'. It is also harmful if it damages the capability of the armed forces, results in loss of life or injury to any of their members, or leads to 'serious damage' to military equipment or installations. A jury decides whether any disclosure is sufficiently harmful to justify the application of criminal sanctions.

Third, in the categories of 'security and intelligence' and the interception of communications, the mere disclosure of information is regarded as harmful in itself, and actual or probable harm need not be proved. These are 'absolute offences' under the Act. For example, any unauthorised disclosure of information by a member or former member of the security services is a criminal offence.

Fourth, criminal liability for the disclosure of unauthorised information is not confined to Crown servants and government contractors but extends to e.g. newspaper editors who will be liable to prosecution for printing unlawfully disclosed information.

Fifth, no defence of 'public interest' or 'prior publication' is available to those accused under the Act.

The Act during its passage and afterwards was subjected to strong criticisms. Critics discounted the government's claim to have 'liberalised' the law on official secrets as misleading. Certainly, the reform of Section 2 of the 1911 Official Secrets Act (the counter-espionage provisions of Section 1 remained intact) did exclude large quantities of harmless information from the scope of the secrecy law.

But in narrowing the law of secrecy, the 1989 Act also tightened it. For opponents of the Act, this was the government's real intention: to close up loopholes in the law revealed by the Ponting and *Spycatcher* cases, to eliminate 'whistle-blowers' and further inhibit newspaper editors. More specific criticisms of the Act included its creation of 'absolute offences' with regard to disclosures by members of the security services and those involved in 'authorised bugging'; the extreme vagueness of the test of 'harm' to the public interest; and the absence of the defences of 'prior publication' and 'public interest'. The ethos of secrecy, critics concluded, had been strengthened rather than eroded.

Freedom of information

The Official Secrets Act (1989), therefore, was seen by many critics as strengthening – rather than weakening – the case for a **Freedom of Information Act** argued by the Freedom of Information Campaign. The proposed legislation would give individuals the right of access to all official information except for that in certain exempt categories (security, defence, etc). Limited progress had been made towards this goal before the advent in 1997 of a Labour Government with a manifesto commitment to freedom of information. Thus, the Data Protection Act (1984) provides access to *computerised* personal files; the Local Government (Access to Information) Act (1986) allows access to background papers used in preparing council reports; and the Access to Health Records Act (1990) permits access to manual health records.

Measures of greater **openness** taken by the Major Government included:

- the publication of details of Cabinet committees, the document *Questions of Procedure for Ministers* on ministerial rules of conduct, the names of the heads of MI5 and MI6 and the opening of some previously closed Public Record Office files.
- a legal right of access to non-computerised personal files and to information on health and safety.
- a new 'Open Government Code of Practice' (1994) laying down the information government departments and agencies should make available: namely, the facts and analysis of facts considered by government to be relevant and important in framing major policies and materials concerning

---

Freedom of Information Act: legislation allowing individuals a legally enforceable right of access to government information and documents with certain clearly defined exemption regarding matters of genuine national security.

Open government: this entails the publication of official information about the internal workings of government and government policy to the press and public.

departments' dealings with the public such as rules, regulations and internal guidance affecting the public and reasons for decisions. There were 1,353 requests for information under the Code in 1995, with 114 refusals.

Whilst welcoming the Code as an advance, critics pointed out its limitations, the main ones being:

- the code is merely administrative, not legal, and therefore lacks means of enforcement through the courts or tribunals.
- the serious exceptions with regard both to the *type* and *areas* of information which can be made available. Information relating to departmental policies, actions and decisions is not released automatically but only on request and subject to exemptions, and a large number of areas are exempted including defence and security, internal discussion and advice, law enforcement and legal proceedings and effective management of the economy and public relations.
- the code does not provide direct access to documents but only to information filtered through officials.

The Scott Report (1996) gave a further impetus to freedom of information legislation with its testimony that 'in circumstances where disclosure might be politically and administratively inconvenient, the balance struck by the Government comes down, time and time again, against full disclosure'. Tony Blair responded in September 1996 that 'If the case was not unanswerable before, Scott has made the case for a Freedom of Information Act unanswerable now.'

The Labour Government published a white paper on a Freedom of Information Act in late 1997. The proposed legislation would enshrine a statutory 'right to know' in Britain for the first time and give individuals the right to appeal to an independent Information Commissioner with the power to order public authorities to disclose documents on a wide range of issues. However, there would be certain exemptions, including the activities of the security and intelligence services and the law enforcement agencies; information relating to 'national security, defence and international relations' which will not be disclosed if it would cause 'substantial harm'; and,

in the interests of maintaining collective Cabinet responsibility, civil servants' advice to ministers and correspondence between Whitehall departments. Freedom of Information legislation was scheduled for the 1998–9 parliamentary session.

However, reformers have suggested that freedom of information legislation is just one of a range of measures required if open government is to become a reality. These include:

- 'a **whistleblower**'s charter', i.e. legal protection for conscientious employees who leak information about wrongdoing by their employers in the public interest.
- a statutory basis and legal means of enforcement for the Code of Practice (1994) together with its extension to include release of internal government discussions after decisions have been made
- repeal of the 1989 Official Secrets Act and provision of a public interest defence to prosecutions where information was leaked against a legal prohibition but in the public interest.
- EU treaty revisions to allow a right of access by national parliaments to EU Commission and EU Council information and that of their subordinate institutions.

Reformers give high priority to the EU dimension of open government. A joint code (1993) already allows public access, albeit with some public interest exemptions to documents of the EU Commission and Council but fails to cover access to the documents of important lower-level EU institutions. In addition, EU Council proceedings are protected by confidentiality and national parliaments continue to face difficulties in extracting timely and complete information from the Commission (Birkinshaw, 1997, pp. 174–80).

It seemed likely in late 1997 that the proposed Freedom of Information Act would be backed up by a Public Interest Disclosure Bill which would give legal protection to whistleblowers. Introduced by Richard Shepherd, the Conservative backbencher, this Bill had broad government support.

Whistleblower: an employee who leaks to the media or others information about the purported malpractices of his or her employer.

Summary

- The activities, control and accountability of Britain's security and intelligence services became a matter of acute public concern during the 1980s and 1990s. The revelations of former MI5 officers raised serious questions about the scope and methods of the surveillance agencies, the extent of ministerial knowledge of – and control over – their activities, and the lack of accountability of the security services to Parliament. Other cases revealed a serious failure of internal vetting in MI5.

- Government legislation on the interception of communications (1985) and the Security Services (1989, 1994 and 1996) failed to allay public disquiet. This was largely because the legislation broadened the criteria upon which warrants to intercept communications could be issued, extended rather than curtailed the functions of MI5 and failed to provide adequate procedures for parliamentary supervision or review.

- The extent of official secrecy in Britain and in particular Governments' use of the very widely drawn Section 2 of the Official Secrets Act (1911) to protect it also became a matter of intense political controversy. The new Official Secrets Act (1989) both reduced the categories of information protected against disclosure by the criminal law and defined the circumstances in which disclosure might be considered 'damaging' to the national interest. But critics maintained that the government had tightened rather than 'liberalised' secrecy law, especially by failing to provide a prior publication or public interest defence to disclosure.

- Some concessions, especially the Open Government Code of Practice (1994), improved public access to official information in the 1990s. However, the Code was criticised for wide exemptions and lack of enforceability and campaigners continued to demand a Freedom of Information Act, a case reinforced by the lack of government openness revealed by the Scott Inquiry (1996) into arms to Iraq.

- The 1997 Labour general election manifesto included a commitment to freedom of information legislation and a white paper on a Freedom of Information Act was published in late 1997. A private member's bill giving legal protection to whistleblowers is also under consideration and has broad government support. Other reforms called for include repeal of the 1989 Official Secrets Act and extensions of the EU 1993 code on access to EU Commission and EU Council documents to include EU subordinate institutions and improved access by national parliaments to EU Commission and Council information.

Questions

1. How far do you agree that secrecy remains a hallmark of British government?
2. State the case for and against greater freedom of information in the UK.

Assignment

A whistleblower's charter?

It was reported in late 1997 that the Labour Government may support legislation granting legal protection to individuals who disclose crime, fraud or serious malpractice at work. The failed private member's 'Public Interest Disclosure Bill' (1996) would have protected employees only if the disclosure was in the public interest, had been raised with the management internally, and the disclosure was not made for spite or financial gain. It would have protected the identity of sources of information and enabled whistleblowers to obtain injunctions against reprisal threats and claim compensation through the courts for loss of earnings and stress. Its supporters argued that the bill would save companies millions of pounds and help to prevent scandals such as the BCCI bank collapse and the Maxwell pension fund affair as well as catastrophes like the Zeebrugge Ferry disaster and the Piper Alpha platform explosion, where employees had kept quiet about working malpractices. It was argued that the Scott Report had shown the value of 'whistleblowers'. But the government maintained that the bill would impose a considerable burden on business and talked it out.

At present, 'whistleblowers' usually face considerable psychological pressure, personal anguish, dismissal, financial loss and difficulties in finding new employment. They are often deemed 'tale-tellers' and 'troublemakers' and suffer social ostracism,too. Although some employers currently encourage employees to report problems over safety and their working environment, many others are embarrassed by such reports and take a harsh attitude. Yet the charity *Public Concern at Work* has argued that in reality 'whistleblowers' are unsung heroes and heroines who save companies millions of pounds by uncovering fraud, protecting jobs and exposing poor safety standards. This argument can be applied to the public sector also where political embarrassment can be an additional reason for cover-ups and secrecy. In recent decades, Clive Ponting, Sarah Tisdall, the Manchester nurse Graham Pink, sacked in 1990 after campaigning for more staff on the acute geriatric wards at his hospital, and Mike Arnold, the Ministry of Defence computer scientist, dismissed in 1996 after revealing millions of pounds of waste and false accounting within the MoD, all fall into this category. The Civil Service Appeal Board later concluded that Arnold's dismissal was unfair, criticising the procedural failings and the inadequacy of the investigations into his allegations as so serious as to involve a denial of natural justice.

Questions

(i) Examine a case involving a 'whistleblower' in detail (e.g. Mike Arnold, the *Guardian*, 1 October 1997). In so far as you can judge, where do you think the rights and wrongs of the case lie?

(ii) Should 'whistleblowers' be regarded as model employees/good, loyal public servants or self-aggrandising 'troublemakers' out for personal reasons to aggravate their employers?

(iii) What are the main arguments for and against parliamentary legislation introducing 'a whistle-blower's charter'?

Further reading

On state secrecy, see Hunt, S. (1992) 'State Secrecy in the UK' *Politics Review*, 1:4, April; Griffith, J.A.G. (1989) 'The Official Secrets Act 1989', *Journal of Law and Society,* 16:2, autumn; and Palmer, S. (1990) 'Tightening Secrecy Law: The Official Secrets Act 1989', *Public Law*, summer. On the secret state intelligence and security services, Dorril, S. (1992) *The Silent Conspiracy. Inside the Intelligence Services in the 1990s* (London: Heinemann); Lustgarten L. and Leigh, I. (1994) *National Security and Parliamentary Democracy* (Oxford: Clarendon); and, on their history, Porter, B. (1989) *Plots and Paranoia: A History of Political Espionage in Britain 1790–1988* (London: Unwin Hyman) can be recommended.

On particular episodes involving the intelligence services, see Milne, S. (1994) *The Enemy Within – MI5, Maxwell and the Scargill Affair* (London: Verso, 1994); Norton-Taylor, R. (1995) *Truth is a Difficult Concept: Inside the Scott Inquiry* (London: Fourth Estate); and Tomkins, A. (1997) 'Intelligence and Government', in 'Under the Scott-Light: British Government Seen Through the Scott Report', *Parliamentary Affairs*, 50:1, January.

On the impact of state security and secrecy on civil liberties, see Ewing, K.D. and Gearty, C. (1990) *Freedom under Thatcher: Civil Liberties in Modern Britain* (Oxford: Clarendon); and on reform, Birkenshaw, P. (1991) *Reforming the Secret State* (Milton Keynes: Open University Press); and Norton-Taylor, R. (1990) *In Defence of the Realm? The Case for Accountable Security Services* (London: Civil Liberties Trust).

On freedom of information and open government, there are Birkinshaw, P. (1997) *Freedom of Information*, 2nd edn (London: Butterworths) and, for a review of 1990s developments, Birkenshaw, P. (1997) 'Freedom of Information', *Parliamentary Affairs,* 50:1, January.

PART 4

DECISION-MAKING, ISSUES AND POLICIES

| # The policy process

Earlier chapters in this book have examined the machinery of government and the wider political, social and economic environment within which government operates. Part Three examines how government works in terms of how political issues are processed and the nature of public policy which emerges. How does government make policy? Who participates in policy-making? Why do policy-makers tackle certain political issues whilst ignoring others? How important is leadership? This chapter explores some theoretical approaches which will help in answering these questions.

The political agenda

At any one time there is a vast number of issues and problems facing people in Britain, yet the government will attempt to solve only some of them. Some issues will get on to the political agenda and be debated publicly, whilst others, which might be just as urgent for those concerned, fail to do so. Why is this? It is because there are factors which both help certain issues emerge whilst suppressing and restricting debate on others.

Firstly, some issues have more *salience* than others as far as the government is concerned. Salience 'can be regarded as roughly equivalent to the *immediate importance* attributed to an issue or element . . . salience can be equated with the *prominence* of the issue' (Frankel, 1970, p. 61). Joseph Frankel has sug-

gested, for example, that one reason why Britain failed to seize the leadership of Western Europe in the postwar years (see Chapter 13) was because the Attlee Government saw other issues as much more salient. During the late 1940s and 1950s the Labour Government was preoccupied with what it saw as the more important policies of establishing the welfare state (Chapters 24 and 25) and nationalisation. In his study of environmental politics, Anthony Downs devised a somewhat similar model of the political process in terms of a five-stage issue-attention cycle with green issues gaining salience, moving up the political agenda, only to fade away in importance. Downs's model is examined in Chapter 29.

Governments may attempt to reshape the political agenda in order to refocus public attention away from areas of policy failure. For example, the Conservatives used their 1993 Conference to swing public debate away from economic management issues to aspects of public policy such as law and order (Chapter 31) and the future of the welfare state (Chapters 24–25). Deliberately controversial arguments were injected into the debate which were bound to attract and engage the media. A new hard line was taken on crime, with ministers appearing to argue that longer prison sentences would curb increasing lawlessness and that single-parent families were a cause of indiscipline as well as sources of a dependency culture which was a burden on the welfare state. Although the government cannot normally control the political agenda, it was on this occasion successful in manipulating public debate away from issues concerning the recession, unemployment and poverty on to issues concerning the family and the responsibility of parents, schools and churches in developing social awareness and morality.

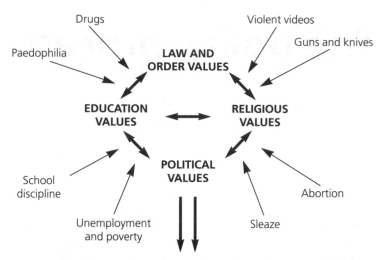

Figure 22.1 The morality agenda of the mid-1990s

Whilst successful in the short term, agenda manipulation backfired on John Major's Government in the years which followed. From his agenda of increasing lawlessness, single parenting, and declining public morality emerged a new framework for organising public debate. A number of barbaric crimes, each of which may have been a unique incident, were linked by many people who saw them as part of an alarming trend. At the same time, publicity about unruly school pupils led many people to link together indiscipline in schools and lawlessness in society.

The new morality agenda worked to the disadvantage of the Conservatives. Right-wing Conservatives converted their party's 'Back to Basics' platform into a moral campaign, which collapsed under the weight of sleaze scandals involving numerous Conservative politicians (Figure 22.1). The morality crisis, exaggerated by the media, worked to the advantage of the Labour Party. Issue after issue – from poor school discipline, increasing violence in society to political corruption at Westminster – were linked by a set of values which portrayed Britain sinking ever deeper into a crisis of poor leadership, increasing immorality and uncontrollable lawlessness (see Figure 22.1).

Where Conservative 'Back to Basics' policies had failed to solve salient issues – indeed, appeared to be the cause of some – Labour's policies based on Community and Stakeholding promised to restore order to society by giving individuals greater security in both employment and welfare. Also, the morality framework against which issues now emerged and were evaluated extended to the churches. The Church of England's *Faith in the Cities* report, which was critical of many Thatcherite policies, was re-publicised in the church's renewed attempt to remoralise society, and a Roman Catholic report, *The Common Good*, informally endorsed Labour's pre-election programme. At the same time, and well-suited to the morality crisis, prominent Labour politicians were known to be devout Christians. In reshaping the political agenda successfully in 1993, Conservatives had lost their advantage only to become political victims of their own agenda in the two years running up to the general election.

An issue may be deliberately kept off the political agenda resulting in the absence or sabotage of policy. Peter Bachrach and Morton Baratz have argued that power has 'two faces': one where policy decisions are made and another where non-decisions are made because issues are deliberately suppressed. They have argued that

> non decision-making is a means by which demands for change in the existing allocation of benefits and privileges in the community can be suffocated before they are even voiced; or kept covert; or killed before they gain access to the relevant decision-making arena; or, failing all these things, maimed or destroyed in the decision-implementing state of the policy process. (Bachrach and Baratz, 1971, p. 44)

The hidden face of power is explored in Chapter 26 in relation to the political agenda and myths concerning poverty in Britain.

Finally, when governments find that particular policies are failing to attract public support they may argue that the fault lies in the media rather than with ministers. In such cases it will be argued that there is nothing wrong with the *policy* in question, but there are problems with the way in which it is being *presented*. This argument was made by the Thatcher Government during the introduction of the unpopular 'poll tax' (Chapter 19). Ministers argued that there was a sound logic behind the poll tax, but this was not being put across by the media and understood by the public. It was argued that once the public understood the poll tax, they would support it. The Major Government accepted that presentation of the poll tax was negative because the policy was flawed and that the public fully understood this.

Policy-making and decision-making

Whilst it is important to define terms in the study of government and politics, this is particularly difficult when it comes to **policy-making** and **decision-making**. For example, is it valid to refer to 'opposition party policy' using the same term to describe 'government policy'? There is an important difference between the two in so far as opposition policy

> **Decision-making** involves selecting what is considered to be the best plan of action from alternative plans.

is no more than a set of *aspirations* about what the party thinks it might do if in office, whereas government policy is *operational* since it is generally implemented. Also there are definitional problems with Bachrach and Baratz's concept of a 'non-decision' since deliberately keeping an issue off the political agenda involves making a choice, so a 'non-decision' is also a 'decision'. And finally, what is the difference between a **policy** and a *decision*? The replacement of rates with the community charge, the privatisation of prisons, or putting VAT (value-added tax) on domestic fuel: were these measures, policies or decisions? A basic distinction is that 'what to do' answers policy-making questions, and 'how to do it' answers decision-making questions.

Decision-making theory

How are decisions actually arrived at? There has been a great deal of research by American political scientists into the process of decision-making. The pioneers in this area of research include Herbert Simon, David Braybrooke, Charles Lindblom, Graham Allison and Amitai Etzioni. Between them, they have devised a number of 'models' or theories to help explain how decisions are made in the real world of politics and government.

Rational decision-making

Most individuals want others to see them as 'rational'. The term 'rational' is used in a slightly different sense when it comes to decision-making theory. A rational decision is one where decision-makers consider all the possible courses of action, then work out the consequences which would follow each one and finally evaluate all the consequences before selecting the 'best' choice, which is the one most likely to achieve their goals.

Herbert Simon, who first defined the rational decision, was criticised because in real-life situations politicians rarely have all the information necessary to make rational decisions. Would Margaret Thatcher

> A **policy** involves adopting a position on an issue or problem; it may remain as a set of recommendations or it may be put into practice.

have pressed ahead with the 'poll tax', rejecting all compromises, had she known all its future political consequences? Even when governments make great efforts to collect all relevant information, rational decisions need not follow. For example, in the 1960s Britain was developing a sophisticated multi-role combat aircraft, the TSR-2, whilst the Americans were developing the rather similar swing-wing F-111 aircraft. A new Labour Government reviewed the TSR-2 project, taking into account all information available at the time concerning the costs of the TSR-2 compared with the F-111, the defence needs of Britain's changing external role, and the likely decline in importance of manned aircraft in the 'age of the missile'. Labour Defence Secretary, Denis Healey, considered all options and took the *rational* decision in 1965 to cancel the TSR-2 and buy the much cheaper F-111, but was it the *right* decision? Subsequent events showed that the F-111 performed poorly, that manned aircraft were to remain important, and that TSR-2 costs were artificially high because they included development costs of the Phantom and Harrier aircraft.

Simon accepted the criticism that decision-makers rarely have total information, and he modified his theory to one of *bounded rationality*. He acknowledged that real-life decision-making is bounded by constraints and that usually a choice has to be made between poorly defined and ambiguous options each with incomplete information. Under these circumstances, decision-makers agree on what is an 'acceptable' decision. This is referred to as *satisficing*; in other words, decision-makers do not select the 'best' rational decision, but one which is satisfactory in terms of being 'good enough'. Given the imperfect information about the TSR-2 and F-111 available to Denis Healey in 1965, his decision to cancel the project seems, then, a better example of satisficing than of rational decision-making.

Incrementalism

David Braybrooke and Charles Lindblom argued that decision-making could be best understood in terms of what they termed *disjointed incrementalism*. This can be described as 'decision-making through small or incremental moves on particular problems rather than through a comprehensive reform programme. It is also endless, it takes the form of an indefinite sequence of policy moves' (Braybrooke and Lindblom, 1963 p. 71). In a later article, Braybrooke was to describe his theory as 'the science of muddling through'.

Basically, it was argued that when a particular policy began failing and producing an unsatisfactory or undesirable situation, small changes in policy are made as decision-makers move cautiously towards what they hope will be an improved situation. It is important to note that incremental decision-making tends to move away from an undesirable situation rather than be directed towards predefined policy goals.

Mixed scanning

Amitai Etzioni has devised a decision-making model which is basically a compromise between the rational approach and incrementalism. Mixed scanning involves decision-making being done in two distinct phases. In considering a problem, decision-makers first make a broad sweep, or scan, of all the policy options available and assess them in terms of how far each would go toward meeting their objectives. Then decision-making becomes more narrowly focused and incremental in nature as details are agreed on the selected policy option.

How might mixed scanning operate? A chancellor faced with a problem such as a budget deficit may consider a wide range of measures which are available to him. He may decide to do nothing, or to raise taxes, or to cut public spending. Having decided which option or option mix best matches his goals, then attention will focus on the detail of, say, which tax should be raised, by what percentage, and starting from what date, etc.

The organisation model

In his study of the Cuban missile crisis of 1962 Graham Allison analysed events in terms of alternatives to the rational model. The first of these was the organisation process model in which decisions are seen as the outputs of large organisations functioning according to regular patterns of behaviour. Decisions emerge as the result of negotiation and bargaining between organisations. In the past, political scientists have pointed out how the organisation of government in Britain affected decisions concerning Northern Ireland (see Chapter 29). Until 1972 Northern Ireland was governed from Stormont, and Westminster took relatively little interest in the Province's affairs until the 'Troubles' began. Unlike Scotland, there had been no separate government department concerned with its affairs. It is interesting to speculate how different the recent history of Northern Ireland might have been had there been greater Westminster involvement during the 1950s and 1960s.

The bureaucratic politics model

Graham Allison also analysed the Kennedy Administration's decisions in terms of what he called the government politics model, but which in the context of British politics is better understood as a bureaucratic politics model. Allison argued that what happened in 1962 was characterised as the result of various negotiations between those in government with top civil servants playing a key role. Policy emerges from bargains and compromises made by ministers and their civil servants representing different departmental interests and priorities (see Chapter 9). In other words, decisions which emerge are not in the *national interest* but in the interests of particular bureaucracies. For example, Chapter 30 gives details of the large cuts made in Britain's armed forces during the early 1990s. Were these cuts in defence calculated by the Ministry of Defence in response to the reduced international threat resulting from the ending of the Cold War? Or, as some Conservative MPs suspected, were the defence cuts insisted on by the Treasury which was determined to reduce spending on defence under the guise of the 'peace dividend'? They suspected that bureaucratic politics resulted in defence cuts providing public spending savings which suited the needs of the Treasury rather than the defence needs of the country.

The policy-making process

Having considered decision-making theory, it is timely to examine how and where policies are made in Britain's political system. Figure 22.2 shows a basic representation of the political system, and it should be noted that all the institutions shown have been discussed in earlier chapters.

At the heart of the system lies the Cabinet and Cabinet committee system. Chapter 14 examined power and decision-making within the executive in terms of defining the role of the Prime Minister in the policy process and identifying the constraints on prime ministerial power. Chapter 15 explored the revolution which has taken place within the civil service as well as the power relationship between ministers and their civil servants. What is particularly notable about the British decision-making process is the power of the Treasury to influence the policy proposed in every other ministry through its control over departmental spending.

It is possible to argue that when dealing with technical issues in which the public has little interest, these small and powerful élites make decisions in a rational manner. This is based on the big assumption, of course, that all members of the elite concerned are highly informed and share similar policy goals. In reality, this would be unlikely. It is normal for political tensions to exist between government departments and between ministers and their civil servants, in which case the organisation model and bureaucratic politics model will be more useful in explaining decision-making than the rational model.

However, once an issue is placed on the political agenda by the mass media (Chapter 11), is discussed in Parliament (Chapter 16), considered by political parties (Chapter 17) and concerns public opinion (Chapter 9), so the issue will become increasingly politicised. Under these circumstances it is very unlikely that those involved in the policy debate will share similar political goals. Even members of the same political party will be divided into competing factions or tendencies, and it is commonplace for members of the same pressure group (Chapter 10) to have different political aspirations. Where policy emerges through the close involvement of sectional interest groups with government departments in a client or corporate relationship, or where policy emerges through a central–local dependency relationship (Chapter 19), then it is likely to have the characteristics of 'muddling through'.

Decisions will be the result of the interaction of participants in a power network. In order to reach agreement on issues they are likely to avoid setting out their political goals in detail, since this would be the cause of conflict. Policies and decisions which are

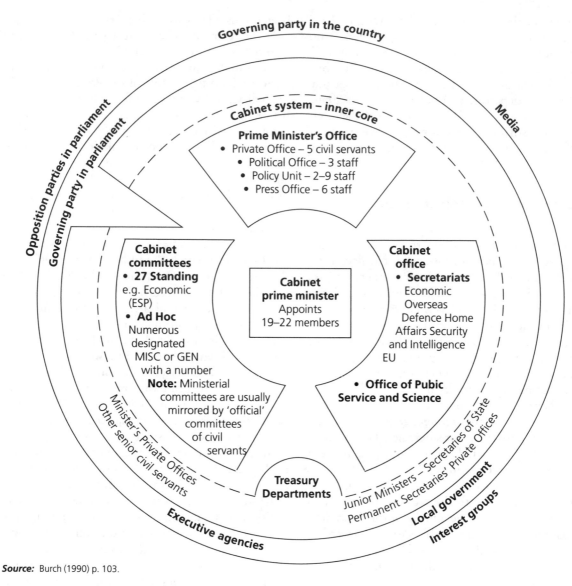

Source: Burch (1990) p. 103.

Figure 22.2 The policy-making process

ambiguous and understood differently by participants in the policy process generally contribute towards building a consensus and enabling progress to be made on an issue. In contrast, conviction politics based on explicit political goals generates conflict and maximises opposition. It is for this reason that incrementalism in policy-making has been the general hallmark of contemporary British politics.

Political leadership

Political scientists have paid considerable attention to the significance of leadership style in policy-making. In particular there has been lengthy debate about the development of the office of prime minister into a presidential role. A recent contribution to this debate from Michael Foley considered issues such as the changing ways in which prime ministers and modern presidents communicate with the electorate and relate with other elements of government. A feature of the American political system is the political distance presidents put between themselves and Washington politics, a strategy which

> allows a president to remain an integral and even central part of government, whilst at the same time affording him the opportunity of detaching himself from government and, thereby, relinquishing responsibility for much of what it does. Paradoxically, it might even be said that this sort of spatial detachment has become one of the most effective ways for a president to maintain his central position in government. (Foley, 1993, pp. 24–5)

In British politics, Prime Minister Margaret Thatcher frequently acted like an outsider in Number Ten, becoming engaged in a struggle against her Cabinet and Whitchall over the direction and content of policy. The outsider role enabled Thatcher to campaign against her own government ministers, implying that they lacked her vision and generally were not up to the job, whilst at the same time detaching herself from their policy failures and allowing her to dominate the machinery of government. The media attention given to the Labour leader, and the portrayal of new Labour as a Blairite party which rejected old Labour, gave the 1997 general election many features of a presidential contest.

Leadership involves qualities in the exercise of power which are over and above prime ministerial and presidential styles. Within a given power structure, leadership can be exercised in a number of qualitatively different ways. For example, some prime ministers have played a 'hands-off' role regarding policy-making and issues of government, intervening only when a major problem arose or if a specific policy was failing consistently. As prime minister, Sir Alec Douglas-Home adopted a *laissez-faire* or 'hands off' form of leadership. He explained his leadership style in an interview, stating that 'a good prime minister, once he had selected his ministers and made it plain to them he was always accessible for comment or advice, should interfere with their departmental business as little as possible'.

Other prime ministers have played a more positive

role in leading the government, making sure that policy kept the backbenchers relatively content. Sometimes this might involve the prime minister acting as broker to make compromises in policy; other times it might involve the prime minister as a wheeler-dealer satisfying one party faction in one policy area and another faction in another policy area. Sometimes this type of leadership is referred to as *transactional*, and Harold Wilson as prime minister provides an example of power being exercised in this manner.

Finally, some prime ministers have led in ways which were initially at odds with the wishes of their followers but which won their support in the course of time. Charismatic personality and inspiration have frequently been important factors in gaining the support of others in the party who come to share the leader's vision of what sort of society should be created. This type of leadership is referred to as *transformational*. Margaret Thatcher's dislike of lengthy cabinet discussions, which she saw as a waste of time, her distaste for consensus politics, which were at odds with her strong political convictions, together with her personal domination of the cabinet and wider party, were preconditions for the *Thatcher revolution*, a contemporary example of transformational leadership in practice. Similarly Tony Blair accelerated the transformation of the Labour Party in opposition, changing its constitution, and in government has embarked on a radical programme of modernising the British Constitution.

The way in which leadership is exercised has a considerable impact on the policy-making process. The *laissez-faire* approach tends to result in strong continuity in policies which are made at departmental level. The prime minister's thinking is guided by the 'if it ain't broke, don't fix it' rule. Only when one Department's policy works against other Departments' policies or is failing in some other way, will the prime minister intervene in order to find a solution. Such a government's policies will reflect different departmental views, tend to be pragmatic in nature and, although coordinated at cabinet level, are unlikely to be unified through being based on the same ideological beliefs.

Prime ministers leading in a transactional way will play a much greater 'hands on' role in managing policy-making. Harold Wilson once described the role of prime minister as being like the conductor of an orchestra; talented and ambitious players, many of whom will want to star as soloists, have to be brought together to play the same tune in harmony. In political terms, this means rewarding some people, disappointing others, whilst still keeping the support of as many as possible. Policy emerges heavily influenced by patronage and compromise. For example, prime minister Harold Wilson created a new ministry, the Department of Economic Affairs (DEA), as a long-term-thinking counterweight to the short-term-thinking Treasury. Clearly this initiative had the potential for making a considerable impact on Labour's economic policy-making as well as challenging the Treasury's influence on other departments' policy-making. But many suspected that Wilson created the DEA simply to provide his troublesome deputy, George Brown, with an apparently important role whilst preventing him from being Foreign Secretary, which was the job George Brown really wanted. If this suspicion was true, then policy-making was influenced by the way in which personal political ambitions in cabinet were satisfied and rewarded. It had little to do with counter-balancing the Treasury.

Transformational leadership is very much a 'hands on' approach to government, with the political vision of the inspirational leader providing the basis of all policy-making. Departmental policies should be unified since they are all derived from the same ideological source. For example, Margaret Thatcher's convictions about the enterprise economy and competition, and her strong preference for free-market solutions, provided the basis not only for economic policy, but also for education reforms, health service reforms, civil service reforms and local government reforms. The main danger for the transformational leader is policy which deviates from the vision. This happened for Thatcher when her Chancellor took Britain into the ERM (see Chapter 23), a policy she believed doomed to failure since 'you can't buck the market' by having strict foreign currency controls. The main danger for others is that the ideology is flawed. If markets fail, if they produce too many losers who rebel against government, if people are not motivated by the profit motive, or if market forces result in corruption, then there would be massive policy failure. Policy would be characterised by what political sci-entists refer to as 'unintended consequences' which beyond a certain point result in a 'policy mess' at the level of implementation.

Sources of policy advice

Parties competing for office have wanted to win support on the basis of what has become known as the 'Big Idea'. In many ways, Thatcherism was the Big Idea which inspired a number of policy initiatives which prevented Conservative administrations from looking exhausted at successive general elections. Labour has conducted a policy review which has eliminated its traditional big idea – socialism – from its manifesto in favour of more centrist policies. In its place have emerged two Big Ideas which unite Labour policies; Community and Stakeholder Society. These ideas, or themes, enabled the party to present the electorate with fresh policies which put 'clear red water' between Labour and Conservative programmes.

The Conservatives have been assisted in policy formulation by a constant stream of proposals from right-wing think-tanks such as the Institute of Economic Affairs, the Centre for Policy Studies, the Adam Smith Institute, Policy Search and the Social Affairs Unit. The importance of these groups was that they were able to 'think the unthinkable' since their activities were conducted outside the party. If one of the think-tanks floated a policy proposal which was widely criticised, it did not damage the reputation of the Conservative Government. Damage was done, however, if a flawed think-tank policy was adopted and implemented by government. The latter occurred when the Adam Smith Institute's idea of financing local government with a 'poll tax' was adopted by Mrs Thatcher.

In the past Labour had the reputation of being a 'thinking party' capable of producing radical policies, but during the 1980s Labour's policy-making was criticised for lacking fresh ideas. The Fabians did not play a very vigorous role in generating new ideas, nor were there individuals able to do this as Anthony Crosland did in the past. However, during the 1990s it restored its reputation as a 'thinking party', drawing ideas from a newly formed Commission on Social Justice as well as devising policies around theories and concepts discussed by

Amitai Etzioni, J.K. Galbraith, John Kay and Will Hutton.

It has been argued that civil servants, unlike their partisan counterparts in the United States, are poor sources of policy ideas. British civil servants are frequently portrayed as amateurs and generalists, living in a Whitehall village which is cut off from the real world of industry, commerce and those at the delivery end of the public sector (see Chapter 15). What civil servants are able to do skilfully, it is argued, is take on board policy advice from specialists – scientists, professional specialists and others with specific expertise – and blend it with what is politically feasible as the basis of advice for their ministers.

Many pressure groups have established networks which include Whitehall contacts. Groups with insider status frequently have the opportunity of influencing policy at the formulation stage, whilst less favoured outsider groups have to rely on influencing public opinion in their attempts to shape policy (Chapter 10). The involvement of pressure groups in Whitehall can be seen as a feature of consensus politics, and it is therefore not a surprise that pressure groups played a smaller role in policy-making during the Thatcher years. Indeed, one of her ministers attacked pressure groups, describing them as 'strangling serpents' which increased the workload of ministers and got in the way of good government. In contrast, Labour is likely to be more receptive to pressure group proposals.

Finally, Britain's membership of the European Union (see Chapter 13) is an increasingly important source of policy. However, although Labour is not as divided as the Conservatives on the prospects of greater federalism and policy harmonisation, European policies are likely to present the new government with some problems. Indeed, as with Conservative predecessors such policies may be approached in terms of a damage limitation exercise; much emphasis will be put on presentation, subsidiarity will be emphasised, with the comforting knowledge that there is little that backbenchers can do to change such policies.

Summary

- Decision-making is a complex process.
- In politics, decision-making can be understood more clearly by applying a number of theoretical perspectives such as rational decision-making and incrementalism.
- All the theories have some use in explaining how decisions are made but it is not easy to make generalisations. Nevertheless, given the institutional context within which policy is made in Britain, there is a strong case for arguing that incrementalism most typifies the policy process.

Questions

1. Herbert Simon argued that the task of decision-makers was 'to select that one of the strategies which is followed by the preferred set of consequences'. To what extent is the government made up of rational decision-makers?
2. Explain the nature of incremental decision-making. Evaluate its usefulness in explaining how policy is made in Britain.
3. How would you assess whether or not a particular issue was on the 'political agenda'?

4. In what ways might different styles of political leadership affect the policy-making process?

Assignments

Assignment (1)
Interpretations of Thatcherism

- Thatcherism and policy change
  There is no doubt that 1979 was a watershed in British politics since the old policies of the postwar consensus began being replaced by radical Thatcherite policies. New thinking by the Thatcher governments resulted in policies which no previous postwar government had followed with any vigour. The old policies of the 1970s had failed and were swept aside. Corporatism was replaced by monetarism. Large tracts of the nationalised industries were privatised. Millions of council tenants were given the chance to become home-owners, and many seized the opportunity. The old debilitating 'dependency' culture was replaced by an energetic 'enterprise culture'.

- Thatcherism and policy continuity
  Margaret Thatcher's policies appeared different because of her robust personality and clever rhetoric when presenting them. Essentially her policies were based on those pursued by previous governments. Thatcherism was no more than a recycling and repackaging of old, mostly Labour, policies. For example, monetarism was not new since the Labour Chancellor had been applying monetary controls since 1976. Thatcher's key policy of privatisation was not new: the previous Labour Government had sold part of its shareholding in British Petroleum. Nor was the sale of council houses new – it had been taking place on a small scale since the 1920s. Finally, there was no 'enterprise culture'. Poll after poll showed that the electorate favoured greater public spending on health, education and social benefits.

Questions
Consider the contrasting accounts of Thatcherite policies;
(i) How could each version be explained in terms of decision-making models?

(ii) Which version and which model appear to be most useful in explaining Thatcherite policy-making?
(iii) To what extent would additional information on the role of trade unions and local government provide support for the choices you have made?

Assignment (2)
Replacing the Army's Ambulances

The *Guardian* carried a report on a policy dilemma facing the new Defence Secretary. The British army has soon to replace its fleet of 700 ambulances, and his predecessor has been advised by MoD officials to purchase Austrian made vehicles. The current fleet of ambulances are based on modified Land Rovers. But the Austrian vehicles, made by Steyr Daimler Puch, have a radical new design, with no conventional chassis and a revolutionary suspension system. In trials, they performed better than Land Rovers. The main disadvantages of the Austrian vehicles were cost; they will cost nearly twice as much as Land Rovers to purchase, they are dearer to run in fuel terms, and more expensive to maintain. Some found the Austrian vehicles more difficult to drive.

However, if the Defence Secretary pulls out of the deal with Steyr Daimler Puch he risks Austrian retaliation and the cancellation of a deal for £30 million British defence exports. On the other hand, if he does not reorder British-made Land Rovers, this will be seen as a vote of no confidence and a £100 million export deal of Land Rovers to the Czech Republic is likely to be lost. Land Rover offered the MoD a bargain deal under PFI for servicing the fleet of Land Rovers world-wide, saving the MoD a large sum in maintenance costs.

Questions
(i) Devise a matrix which shows the pros and cons of buying Land Rovers and Steyr Daimler Puch vehicles.
(ii) In reaching his final decision, how important will vehicle specifications be to the Minister and how important will wider considerations be?
(iii) What other considerations, not mentioned in the article above, might the Defence Secretary take into account when reaching his final decision?

Further reading

Burns, B. (1978) *Leadership* (New York: Harper & Row). A classic text exploring the concept of effective leadership. Foley, M. (1993) *The Rise of the British Presidency* (Manchester University Press): an interesting interpretation of the changing role of Prime Minister. Greenaway, J., Smith, S. and Street, J. (1992) *Deciding Factors in British Politics: A Case-Studies Approach* (London: Routledge): an analysis of recent governmental decisions.

Management of the economy

Britain was the first country to have an industrial revolution and to develop a capitalist economy. Over 40 per cent of the world's trade once involved British goods. Two hundred years later Britain had an ailing economy and a 6 per cent share of world trade. For many years the British economy has been in relative decline with Britain seeming unable to shake off the reputation of being the 'sick man of Europe'. Successive governments seemed content to manage Britain's decline so as to soften the blows and mitigate its worst effects. Some were critical of this fatalistic attitude and argued that there was nothing inevitable about Britain's decline. They believed that Thatcherite economics would reverse Britain's fortunes. Were they justified in thinking this? When the economy began recovering during John Major's Conservative administration, why did the electorate refuse to reward his party by supporting it in the 1997 general election? Have the Conservatives lost their traditional reputation for economic competence to Labour?

The tools of economic management

The state of the economy and how it affects them personally is an important issue in influencing the way people vote. Because of this, political factors play a central role in the way that government manages the economy. Past governments have been criticised for 'stop–go' **Keynesian economic policies** which 'go' for growth during the period in the run-up to a general election, winning the approval of the electorate, but then 'stop' once the election has been held in order for the economy to cool down. In political terms it may represent a successful economic strategy, but businessmen are critical of the damage done to the economy through the instability and uncertainty that 'stop–go' creates (Figure 23.1). What, then, are the major tools available to government for managing the economy?

Intervention

Governments can manage the economy through direct controls and intervention. In directing the wartime economy, the government led by Winston Churchill assumed massive powers of intervention in controlling the labour force, deciding on the location of industry, requisitioning economic assets, rationing the supply of raw materials to factories, and so on. These controls largely disappeared during the 1950s but nevertheless peacetime governments have attempted since to control aspects of the economy through intervention. For example, in the fight against inflation Labour and Conservative governments have implemented prices and incomes policies. In 1961 a Conservative Chancellor, Selwyn-Lloyd, introduced the 'pay pause', a nine-month-long incomes policy designed to hold down pay awards. Between 1965 and 1969 Labour pursued a prices and incomes policy, and the Conservative government which followed converted an informal incomes policy into a statutory policy

> **Keynesian economics** is based on the idea that government can control the economy and so reduce unemployment through increasing public expenditure.

438

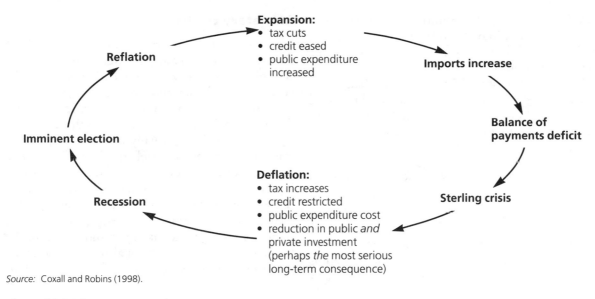

Source: Coxall and Robins (1998).

Figure 23.1 The stop–go cycle

which controlled all incomes between 1972 and 1974. The Labour government returned to office in 1974 developed a voluntary incomes policy – known as the 'social contract' – which, under the leadership of James Callaghan finally broke down in the 'Winter of Discontent' of 1978–79. The industrial disputes during Labour's winter of discontent were an important factor in the Conservative election victory which saw Margaret Thatcher enter Number Ten promising economic management which would rely much more on market forces and far less on government intervention. For further details, see chapter 9 of Coxall and Robins's *British Politics Since the War* (1998).

During Thatcher's years in office her governments gained a reputation for thinking that 'industry doesn't matter' within the context of Britain having a successful economy. Previous governments, Labour and Conservative, had taken a different view and had implemented industrial policies designed to achieve growth and improve productivity.

Impressed by the success of economic planning in France, a Conservative government set up the National Economic Development Council (NEDC) – also known as 'Neddy' – in 1962 as a forum in which governments and both sides of industry discussed plans to improve Britain's industrial efficiency and international competitiveness. Later Labour

governments set up other interventionist bodies – the Industrial Reorganisation Corporation (IRC) in 1966 and the National Enterprise Board (NEB) in 1975 – with a view to restructuring and strengthening Britain's industrial base. By the 1990s all of these interventionist bodies had been abolished.

Economically depressed areas of Britain can be stimulated and improved through an interventionist regional policy which attempts to attract new investment though grants and other financial incentives. Britain's industrial base would have been in an even worse state had it not been for the foreign investment – some £40 billion between 1988 and 1993 – which has created new manufacturing jobs. Some believe that by the year 2000 one in five of Britain's manufacturing jobs will be in a foreign-owned factory.

Fiscal policy

Fiscal policy involves the government managing the economy through taxation and public spending. If the economy is depressed with high levels of unemployment, the government may (1) reduce taxes in order to stimulate the economy – income tax may be reduced so that employees will have more money to spend, or other taxes such as VAT or car tax may be reduced in order to make goods cheaper and thereby encourage more people to buy them; (2) increase public spending on, for example, new roads, hospitals and schools, in order to create new jobs which, as these new workers start spending more, will create yet more new jobs.

Other economic problems, such as a balance of payments deficit or a budget deficit, may be tackled by the government raising taxes and attempting to reduce public spending. Government may pursue other policies through taxation, such as promoting good health through taxing cigarettes or improving the environment through lower taxation of lead-free petrol.

Until 1992 governments announced taxation and spending plans as two separate but related exercises, but from thereon the budget and autumn statements were merged. In 1992, in the depths of a recession, the government was borrowing a massive £50 billion a year. Governments frequently spend more than they raise in taxes, and so have to borrow to fill this gap. The sum borrowed is known as the Public Sector Borrowing Requirement (PSBR).

Monetary controls

Monetary policy is carried out by the Bank of England and the Treasury in attempting to control the volume of money and purchasing power in the economy, and thereby influencing movements in the inflation rate and the level of consumer spending. The main tool of monetary control is the minimum lending rate (MLR), usually referred to by politicians and the public as simply the 'interest rate'. The level of interest rate determines the cost of borrowing money – a high interest rate will make borrowing expensive and so will lower the demand for credit. It will also mean that mortgages will become more expensive and so take more money out of the home-buyers' pockets, which also means that they in turn will have less money available to spend on goods. A low interest rate will mean that money will be cheap to borrow, encouraging consumers to purchase goods on credit. Lower mortgage payments will also mean that home-buyers will have more money available for consumer goods.

Interest rates gained a greater significance when Britain joined the Exchange Rate Mechanism

Figure 23.2 Unemployment through the Tory years

(ERM) of the European Monetary System (EMS). Some believe that the EMS is the first step towards the economic and monetary union which would be necessary for a federal European Union, whilst others see it as simply providing the currency stability necessary for the single market to operate successfully. The ERM involved fixing the exchange rates of Community members so that they could move only marginally against each other. If sterling's international value slipped, then interest rates would be raised in order to make the pound more attractive and thereby increase its value on the foreign exchanges. Should demand for sterling push its value towards the upper limit of its ERM band, then the interest rate would be lowered in order to depress demand.

Margaret Thatcher was persuaded in 1990 that Britain should enter the ERM, although she did not believe in fixed exchange rates since 'you can't buck the market'. Her scepticism was justified to some extent on Wednesday 16 September 1992 when, within hours, interest rates were raised from 10 to 15 per cent to defend the falling pound, then reduced again to 10 per cent with the pound being

withdrawn from the ERM. Furthermore, almost all Britain's foreign reserves had been spent in this unsuccessful defence of sterling.

Managing the economy

Some have argued that the most distinctive features of Conservative economic management were to be found in the policies followed during the 1980s. In basic terms, previous postwar governments had identified *unemployment* as the biggest economic evil to be tackled, and thus they gave high priority to policies which reduced the number of people out of work. The Thatcher governments identified *inflation* as the biggest economic evil, and so governments followed policies which were designed to 'squeeze' inflation out of the economy. These policies were referred to as 'monetarism', and involved measures to reduce the levels of public spending, placing greater reliance on free market forces, and tighter control on the money supply. Under the leadership of John Major, and with the ERM policy in tatters, the Thatcher prior-

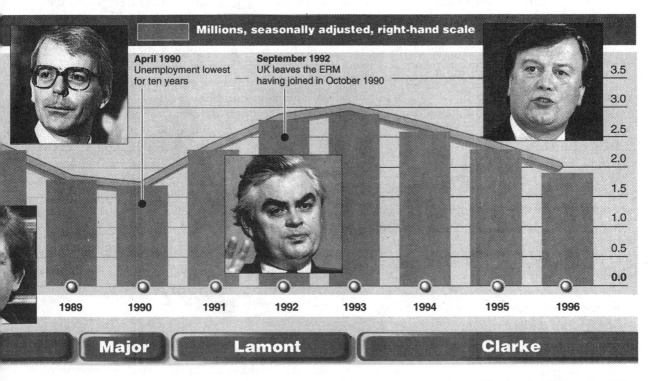

Source: The Guardian, 19 December 1996.

ities were abandoned and the creation of jobs became the central, if elusive, goal of economic policy.

The monetarist experiment

Monetarist policies were implemented during the period 1979–82. The Chancellor lowered the rate of income tax, doubled the level of VAT, and used high interest rates to limit the growth in the money supply. Inflation eventually began to fall but the high interest rate crippled many firms and caused a massive rise in unemployment. By 1982, one in five jobs in manufacturing had disappeared.

Some believed that mass unemployment was being used as a political weapon to curb trade union power. Previous governments which had used interventionist tools of economic management frequently relied on the cooperation of trade unions. But trade unions were not in a strong position to 'deliver' on deals made with the government. For what often seemed an acceptable agreement to trade union leaders was rejected by the rank and file. The attraction of monetarist policies to the government was that they could be implemented without the cooperation or consent of the trade unions. Since the goodwill of the trade unions was no longer necessary to implement economic policy, the government felt able to erode the power and privileges until then enjoyed by unions. Unemployment weakened trade unions, particularly in the old traditional industries of the North most noted for their union militancy.

In the spring of 1988 the Chancellor, Nigel Lawson, was being described as 'the greatest chancellor of the century', but interest rates were to rise nine times before the end of the year and there was speculation that the Chancellor was in danger of being sacked. The economy was overheating; the Chancellor wished to slow down economic activity and bring an end to the consumer boom without causing a recession. Britain's economy now faced a massive balance of payments crisis accompanied by rising inflation and rising interest rates.

After a bitter row with Mrs Thatcher, Nigel Lawson resigned from the Cabinet and was replaced, briefly, by John Major. His task was to bring about what was referred to as a 'soft landing' in which the economy slowed down without sliding into recession. Sterling entered the ERM and it was recognised that this would cause some economic hardship in the short term, particularly if inflation made British goods uncompetitive abroad, but longer-term benefits of ERM membership would be low inflation and low interest rates. The government was taken by surprise by the depth and length of the recession which began in the late 1980s. At first it was described as a 'blip' in the economy; later it was clear that Britain was in the middle of the deepest recession since the 1930s. From December 1990 Chancellor Lamont began observing the 'green shoots of recovery' and reassured the public that the recession would be 'relatively short-lived and relatively shallow'.

By 1993 some economists were worried that Britain's recession was turning into a slump which was bankrupting or closing a firm every six minutes. The government argued that Britain's recession was not unique since the economics of all European countries were undergoing a prolonged period of recession. But critics argued that Britain's economy was experiencing both a longer and a deeper recession than our European partners.

After the dramatic events of September 1992, referred to above, some economists believed that Britain's withdrawal from the ERM and subsequent devalued pound would stimulate the economy and bring about a recovery. The failure of free-market Thatcherism, and the collapse of the ERM policy left the government with no substantive economic policy.

Labour inherits an improving economy

Until Black Wednesday, the Conservatives were seen by the electorate as more competent in managing the economy than Labour. In reality the economy was in poor shape as a result of sterling being at too high a level in the ERM, which pushed up interest

> **Monetarism** is based on the belief that Keynesian policies cause inflation and unemployment. Monetarist policies are based on restricting the amount of money in circulation, including government spending.

BOX 23.1
The political decline of trade unions

The monetarist policies pursued by the early Thatcher governments left no role for the trade unions to play. Unlike previous Labour and Conservative governments, cooperation from trade unions was not required to implement economic policies. Weakened by high unemployment and loss of members, particularly in traditional industries such as coal and steel where unionism was strong, as well as restricted by strict new legislation, trade unions were pushed to the margins of British politics. Resulting from successive privatisations during the 1980s, the government had become much less involved in industrial relations since it was no longer such a large-scale employer. Unlike previous occupants of Number Ten, particularly Harold Wilson and James Callaghan, neither Margaret Thatcher nor John Major invited trade union leaders for 'beer and sandwiches' whilst they resolved industrial problems.

Given their declining membership and weakened political position, many trade unionists came to accept that the old militant attitudes were no longer appropriate. For many, the defeat of the miners after a year-long strike had shown that the 'old ways' of conducting industrial relations had come to an end. A 'new realism' emerged as an increasing number of trade unionists realised that they had to adapt to working in a free-market economy, and with governments now having low inflation as their top economic priority, not unemployment as in the past.

Trade union leaders welcomed the election of a Labour government in 1997 but none expected that this would mean 'winding the clock' back to the 1970s with militancy on the factory floor and corporatism in government. The TUC, now much more influenced by white-collar trade unions, seeks 'social partnership' in Britain. Unthinkable in the past, the TUC has established strong links with the CBI. Relations between Labour and affiliated unions have also changed, with the unions playing a less influential role in Labour party politics than during the 1960s, 1970s and 1980s. Also changed are relations between unions and the Labour government; whilst union leaders may make occasional visits to Number Ten, the days of 'beer and sandwiches' have not returned. In making important public appointments, old Labour would have instinctively selected a union leader whereas new Labour is just as likely to appoint a top businessman from the private sector.

Trade Union membership as a percentage of the civilian workforce in employment

United Kingdom
Percentages

Source: *Social Trends* 27 (1997) p. 80

---

rates to keep sterling attractive thereby encouraging low growth, high inflation and high unemployment. It was, however, the political panic surrounding Britain's withdrawal from the ERM which cost John Major's Government its reputation for economic competence; David Sanders' research revealed that after Black Wednesday 'the competence graph plunges downwards and continues to trend downwards thereafter' (Sanders, 1995, p. 161). In many ways, John Major's Conservative Government experienced the same political fate as Harold Wilson's Labour Government, which never recovered its popularity after devaluation in 1967.

All the economic benefits of devaluation stimulated the economy after Black Wednesday: cheaper sterling led to a surge in export profits and Britain's worrying trade deficit narrowed; the economy grew, wages rose steadily but without risking the return of high inflation; and by autumn 1997 unemployment was below 1.5 million for the first time in 17 years. Polls recorded a return of economic optimism to the business community and signs of the 'feel good' factor returned to the electorate. Yet the Conservative Government was not rewarded for these improvements, and its popularity ratings fell still further behind Labour.

Source: The *Guardian*, 16 July 1997.

Conservative reputations also suffered from promoting themselves as the 'party of low taxation.' Whilst income tax had fallen, other indirect taxes had risen to the point where it was calculated that a typical family was paying £630 more tax a year in 1996 than in 1992. The main election promise of 1992 was broken. At the same time, New Labour was shedding its electorally damaging 'tax and spend' image which had dogged 'old' Labour. Labour neutralised potential Conservative attack by accepting Conservative public spending limits for two years and no income tax rises for five years. Labour also worked hard on what journalists called the 'prawn cocktail circuit', attending business lunches and other meetings, in order to convince the business community that New Labour was both 'business-friendly' and more competent than the Conservatives.

For the first time on entering office, in 1997 Labour inherited an economy which was performing relatively well. Compared with, for example, 1974, trends in inflation, growth, exports and unemployment were all moving in a favourable direction in 1997. Some of the strength in the economy resulted from Conservative policies which old Labour instincts had opposed. The position of trade unions had changed considerably; whilst they brought dis-

ruption to Labour in the mid-1970s, culminating in the 'winter of discontent', by 1997 they were much weaker and posed little threat to the economy. Many restrictive practices and labour protection of the 1970s had also been swept away by Conservative governments, leaving Labour with a 'flexible labour force' much better able to compete for trade. Of course some problems remained, such as the decline in manufacturing, a relatively under-skilled working population, low levels of investment and an attitude of 'short-termism' towards business development.

The latter problems were addressed in part by the Labour Chancellor's bold move in separating 'politics' from 'economics' when he granted the Bank of England independence from government in setting the level of interest rates. The impact of Gordon Brown's decision was to remove the temptation from government to manage the 'boom and bust' economic cycle to coincide with the 'electoral' cycle (see Coxall and Robins, 1997, ch. 9). The Bank of England is now free to set interest rates as a weapon to combat inflation rather than the Chancellor setting interest rates to help create an economic boom in the run-up to a general election. In taking this measure, the Chancellor has improved the prospects of long-term stability and growth to the economy.

BOX 23.2
Labour's Comprehensive Spending Review

After a two-year freeze on public spending the Labour Chancellor, Gordon Brown, announced the Government's three-year 'Comprehensive Spending Review'. A total increase of nearly £50 billion in public spending was promised, with departments knowing three years in advance how their budgets would be affected. Public spending on health and education will get big increases while other areas, such as agriculture and defence, will get less in real terms.

Labour's increases in public spending

	billion
Health	£21.0
Education	£19.0
Housing	£3.6
Pensions	£2.5
Transport	£1.7
Science	£1.1
Training	£0.8
Total	£49.7

While Labour backbenchers welcomed the spending review as evidence that the spirit of 'old' Labour was still alive, others were more cautious and noted that many conditions had to be met before the increases took place. Some were suspicious about the increases being 'end-loaded'; for example, on education there will be a £3 billion increase in 1999–2000, £6 billion in 2000–01 and a £10 billion increase in 2001–02. Finally other critics challenged the Chancellor's method of calculating the increases so that, for example, the promised £21 billion increase in health spending amounted to just £1.5 billion in real terms. In real terms, it was argued, Labour's planned 3.6% a year increase in health spending compared poorly with the previous government's record of 4.1% a year.

Summary

- What voters believe is happening to the economy is more important electorally for a government than what is actually happening to the economy. The Conservative Government of John Major lost its reputation for economic competence when Britain withdrew from the ERM. Despite the improvements in the economy which followed this devaluation, the electorate failed to return its confidence in Conservative economic management.
- New Labour has accepted market economics and

intends to work within Conservative spending targets for its first two years as well as not raising income tax for five years. Pressure on health and education spending may make this a difficult task for the Labour Chancellor.

Questions

1. In what ways did the Thatcher governments' approach to trade unions differ from that of previous governments?
2. Explain how John Major's Conservative government lost its reputation for economic competence.
3. 'Governments no longer have the freedom to manage their countries' economies.' How valid is this statement with regard to management of the British economy?
4. 'There will be stop-go economic policies as long as governments want to be re-elected.' How accurate is this statement in light of Labour policy regarding the Bank of England?

Assignments

Assignment (1) Conservatives lose support of business

In the months leading up to the 1997 general election newspapers carried reports of increasing disillusionment in the business community regarding the performance of the Conservative government. The image of new Labour was no longer seen as a threat by businessmen who, a decade earlier, would have feared the election of a Labour government. The chairmen of top companies, such as Granada and Great Universal Stores, have openly declared their support for Tony Blair. A poll of businessmen revealed that 80 per cent were not at all worried by the prospects of a Labour government being elected, whilst 15 per cent actually believed that their businesses would do better under Labour. Another poll of business managers found that support for the Conservatives had dropped from 62 to 40 per cent over a five-year period.

It is not just the positive image of New Labour which has won the support of many businessmen, but also the poor performance of John Major's Conservative government. In many ways the old businessmen's political nightmare of a nationalising Labour government has been replaced by the new nightmare of a right-wing Conservative government hostile towards the European Union. European markets are important for British businessmen, and the prospects of a Cabinet containing some ministers who would like Britain to withdraw from the EU is their main fear if the Conservatives are re-elected.

Questions

(i)   To what extent had support for the Conservatives declined amongst businessmen prior to the 1997 general election?

(ii)   Apart from the Conservative government's Euroscepticism, what other issues might have led to businessmen deserting the Conservative party?

(iii) To what extent does the above report support the notion that class-based politics no longer exists in Britain?

Assignment (2) 'If Blair and Brown repeat the US experience, they will be odds-on for the next election'

But the most fascinating political aspect is the Budget's intellectual genesis. Ask any Clintonite to describe what lies behind the American recovery and they will cite the deficit reduction programme, flexible labour markets, earned income tax credits that make low-wage jobs more attractive, new pension arrangements that have raised contributions and saving – and the hard 'workfare' approach to welfare, time-limiting benefits and insisting that the poor work for a living.

In these terms the Brown Budget was an exercise in classic Clintonism – from the stage-management of the media to the announcement of a five-year deficit reduction programme and the 'New Deal' on welfare-to-work.

The US economy has had a remarkable few years, with investment climbing to new heights, sustained growth and little inflation. If Britain under New Labour repeated that experience, Mr Blair and Mr Brown would be odds-on at the next election. In this respect, the Budget is a remarkable bet that what has worked in one Anglo-Saxon economy will work in another.

The American political influence on New Labour

has been well documented – less so the economic influence. Ever since Harvard-educated Ed Balls joined Mr Brown's team as economic adviser, the Chancellor has regularly crossed the Atlantic to talk to the best economic brains around Mr Clinton. Larry Summers, Deputy Secretary to the Treasury, and Robert Reich, the outgoing Secretary at the Department of Labour, are particular influences. It was during one trip early last year that Mr Brown finally determined to give the Bank of England operational independence while building up the statutory competence of a new City regulator – both modelled on creating UK versions of the Federal Reserve and the Securities and Exchange Commission. The thinking behind the Budget is no less influenced by Mr Clinton. The commitment to a five-year deficit reduction programme is a straight lift from Mr Clinton's approach to macro-economic management – even the term is borrowed.
(*The Observer*, 7 July 1997)

Questions

(i)   In what ways was the first budget of Labour Chancellor, Gordon Brown, inspired by the American experience?

(ii)   According to the above report, what Labour policy may have been influenced by the Chancellor's visit to the United States?

(iii) To what extent is 'New' Labour really 'Clintonised Labour'?

Further reading

Gamble, A. (1994) *The Free Economy and the Strong State,* 2nd edn (London: Macmillan), examines the political context of Thatcherism. Maynard, G. (1988) *The Economy under Mrs Thatcher* (Oxford: Blackwell) is an early assessment of the impact of Thatcherism on the economy. Thain, C. (1992) 'Government and the Economy', in B. Jones and L. Robins (eds), *Two Decades in British Politics* (Manchester University Press): a useful overview of economic management and mismanagement. Thomas G. P. (1992) *Government and the Economy Today* (Manchester University Press): a comprehensive explanation of the relationship between government and the economy.

Education

Education is a highly political issue. This chapter explores the past ideological struggle between left and right which took place throughout the education system from the corridors of Whitehall to the school classroom. For it was believed that the shape of society in the future, be it egalitarian or inegalitarian, was determined by today's education system. More recently the emphasis has been on the link between educational standards and the performance of the economy.

The current crisis in education

A recent survey conducted by the Organisation for Economic Co-operation and Development compared education systems in the OECD's 24 member countries. It found that the UK spends less of its gross domestic product (GDP) on education than other members, with other findings reflecting this financial fact, such as Britain having one of the highest teacher-pupil ratios, being one of the poorest providers of nursery education, and having one of the lowest proportions of young people going on to full-time tertiary education.

Britain's poor performance in providing education

> **Education** is the process by which the knowledge and culture of one generation is passed to the next.

for its young people is not a recent development. Britain has a long history of spending less, providing less and getting less from education than other industrialised countries. In an article lamenting this situation, Corelli Barnett quoted from a Schools Inquiry Royal Commission which reported in 1868:

> We are bound to add that our evidence appears to show that our industrial classes have not even the basis of a sound general education on which alone technical education can rest. In fact our deficiency is not merely a deficiency in technical education but in general intelligence. (*The Sunday Times*, 26 May 1991)

The style of language used in the Royal Commission of 1868 and the recent OECD report may differ, but the message remains much the same over a century and a quarter – namely, that Britain lags behind its industrial competitors in providing an effective education system. The problems which were present in the last century are still present today, although they have become more acute in recent years as Britain's economic performance has teetered towards disaster. Clearly, then, one of the central goals of any government, whether Labour or Conservative, has been to raise the standard of education in Britain. Whilst there may be consensus on this general goal, the political Left and Right have disagreed very much on the means by which it might be achieved.

The politics of progressive education

The Education Act of 1944 – the 'Butler Act' – was a milestone in the history of education in Britain in so far as it introduced a universal education system, but by the 1960s its implementation was recognised as being both flawed and damaging to the interests of most children. Essentially the Act led to selective education – a bipartite division in most parts of the country – where the results of an 'eleven plus' examination sealed the fate of the pupils who sat it. The 20 per cent who 'passed' the eleven plus continued their secondary education in prestigious grammar schools, whilst the 80 per cent who 'failed' mainly went on to secondary modern schools.

The solution to the deficiencies of the 1944 Act, promoted in the Department of Education and Science (DES) circular 10/65, was an invitation to local education authorities (LEAs) to submit plans to reorganise secondary schools into a comprehensive system. Since it was a Labour Minister at the DES, and since it was Conservative-controlled LEAs which resisted pressures to go comprehensive, education began to become much more of a party political issue. Ironically, the original initiative for comprehensive schooling came from a liberal-minded Conservative Education Minister, Edward Boyle, and some Conservative-controlled LEAs such as Leicestershire. By the mid-1960s, however, comprehensive education was seen as a Labour policy. This was in many ways inevitable since comprehensive education was more consistent as a concept with Labour's egalitarian ideals than with the values of one-nation Toryism.

The educational left developed a radical philosophy of education, together with the necessary principles for implementation, which went far beyond the original concept of comprehensive schools. Egalitarian methods, which were expected to increase educational opportunity and thereby raise standards, had a place in the classroom. The left argued, for example, that selection in any form was undesirable. Thus streaming within a school was seen as just as iniquitous as the practice of the eleven plus in dividing pupils between schools. Mixed-ability teaching was the method advocated as consistent with the comprehensive ideal.

Traditional methods were based on an essentially élitist power structure in which reward and progress depended upon the individual effort of pupils, whilst progressive methods were more democratic with the skills of participation and cooperation as important as individual effort.

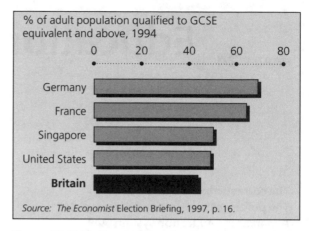

% of adult population qualified to GCSE equivalent and above, 1994

Source: *The Economist* Election Briefing, 1997, p. 16.

Figure 24.1 'Bottom of the class'

In terms of equalising educational opportunity, comprehensive schools were probably the most effective reform to date. But in terms of educational standards, comprehensive schools and progressive methods seemed to lag behind traditional schooling. The decline in standards comprised one of the central themes of the *Black Papers,* written by right-wing academics who had become disenchanted with modern educational reforms.

The attack on education mounted by the Right struck a chord with many parents and employers, and by the mid-1970s there was widespread anxiety and dissatisfaction with state education in Britain. In 1976 Labour Prime Minister James Callaghan delivered a speech at Ruskin College, Oxford, which opened what is sometimes referred to as the 'great education debate'. The Prime Minister raised questions about levels of literacy and numeracy, the purpose of the school curriculum and the needs of industry, and expressed unease about certain teaching methods:

there is the unease felt by parents and teachers about the new informal methods of teaching which seem to produce excellent results when they are in well qualified hands but are much more dubious in their effects when they are not . . . There is no virtue in producing socially well adjusted members of society who are unemployed because they do not have the skills. (Quoted in Bash and Coulby, 1989)

Thus education standards were now a major political issue, and the political right and centre were challenging the effectiveness of the 1960s reforms. By chance, the educational left which had promoted many progressive reforms, were caught unguarded and produced no real defence for the changes which had taken place. This was because the left was somewhat disillusioned by the relative lack of impact that comprehensives and progressive methods had had in terms of social engineering. Pupils left comprehensives to take their predestined roles in what was still a class-based society; in short, 'open schools' did not produce an 'open society'. Egalitarian education, it seemed, was failing in this respect. Disenchantment on the left enabled the right to take the initiative on education and largely take control of shaping the political agenda. Radical right-wing groups such as the Hillgate Group, the Adam Smith Institute, and the Institute for Economic Affairs, took charge of the 'great debate' and in so doing redefined the purpose and means of schooling in Britain.

A market-led education system

The political right argued that education had been subverted to the cause of social engineering rather than the pursuit of high academic standards. To repair the situation, the right argued that the influence of those responsible for causing the damage, those with professional vested interests, must be reduced. At the same time the influence of those with the greatest interest in raising educational standards, parents and employers, must be increased. This, it was argued, could be best accomplished by making education more responsive to market forces. As Stewart Ranson stated, the

> failures of education, it is argued, derive from professionals and (local) politicians appropriating control of the service from its proper source – the parents. The 'producers' have taken over and pursue their own purposes at the expense of the needs of the 'consumers' of the service . . . The professionals create a technical language which serves only to bamboozle ordinary people and they organize the system for their convenience rather than to respond to the demands of consumers . . . For consumers to fulfil their allotted role as quality

controllers in the market place they require some diversity of product, information about the scope of choice and the quality of performance, as well as the opportunity to choose. (Ranson, 1990)

The radical right argued that a market-led system in education would mean that schools would have to compete with each other for 'customers', and that this competition would lead to a general rise in standards. The creation of a market, however, meant that the 'producer' monopoly must be curtailed. Firstly, it was argued, the influence of teachers must be reduced. Secondly, the influence of local education authorities must reduced. In the event this occurred through delegating more financial and managerial responsibilities to individual schools and through providing opportunities for schools to 'opt out' from local authority control. Having reduced the influence of the 'producers', the right argued that the creation of a market in education rested only on increasing the role of 'consumers' in terms of providing greater choice and control. Parental influence was increased through open enrolment, the provision of more information by schools, and a bigger role in the management of individual schools.

Having acknowledged the considerable influence over education policy exerted by the right, the Education Acts of the 1980s were not simply legislative expressions of right-wing thinking. The Acts contained contradictions, ambiguities, and even measures which won support from the educational Left. The main legislation included:

- *The 1980 Education (no. 2) Act*
  This Act introduced the Assisted Places Scheme which was designed to allow a relatively small number of parents on modest incomes to send their children to private schools. This policy was in line with the goal of increasing parental choice, although its critics saw it as simply a way of subsidising private schools with government money.
- *The 1986 Education (no. 2) Act*
  The Act provided for the secret postal ballot of all eligible parents for the election of parent governors. To be eligible, a parent must have a child attending the school at the time of the election. The period of office is four years, but a parent governor can continue to serve if his or her child leaves before the term ends.

- *The 1988 Education Reform Act*
The 1986 Act enlarged the responsibilities of school governors, and the 1988 Act built further on this through introducing Local Management of Schools (LMS). The central purpose of LMS, with greater parental and community involvement, was to ensure that individual schools were effectively managed and responsive to 'customer' needs.

The Act also specified that a national curriculum be taught to pupils until they reached the age of 16. A core curriculum would include English, maths and science, together with seven foundation subjects covering history, geography, technology, art, music, physical education and a foreign language. Religious education would also be taught as well as certain cross-curricular themes such as citizenship. The Act also introduced the national testing of pupils at four key stages of 7, 11, 14 and 16 years old.

In line with increasing parental choice, the Act introduced open enrolment and the possibility of schools opting out of LEA control and assuming grant maintained status. In line with reducing the influence of progressive forces in education, including an emphasis on multiculturalism and equal opportunities, the Act abolished the Inner London Education Authority (ILEA).

Source: *The Guardian*, 5 February 1997.

Developments in the 1990s

During the 1990s Conservative education policy developed further along lines set in the 1980s; the market was extended into primary schools with the publication of league tables for eleven-year-olds and the introduction of a voucher scheme for nursery-school places. The education market place was made more efficient by reducing the volume of the national curriculum and improvements in pupil testing. Further measures were taken to encourage schools to opt out from local authority control.

Schools were now policed by the Office for Standards in Education (OFSTED) which adopted a more confrontational style when inspecting schools than the HMI system which it replaced. The Chief Inspector of OFSTED, Chris Woodhead, upset many teachers by his apparently hostile and critical approach towards their profession. He was accused of selective interpretation of OFSTED data, always to the disadvantage of teachers' reputation, but most hurtful to them was his claim that 15,000 of them were incompetent.

As the 1997 general election approached, differences between Conservative and Labour education policies were confined to subtlety, nuance and detail rather than extending to principle. Both parties were committed to raising standards without the provision of additional resources. Only the Liberal Democrats were prepared to raise income tax and spend more on schools. Labour pledged that it would end the newly introduced nursery voucher scheme, and would reduce class sizes from resources released from phasing out the Assisted Places Scheme. Apart from these rather minor differences, Labour's approach was sometimes a diluted version, other times a concentrated version, of Conservative policy.

The Conservative government was moving towards greater selection in education. Possibly calculated to embarrass Labour's frontbenchers Tony

Blair and Harriet Harman, whose children were attending selective schools, John Major called for the creation of 'a grammar school in every town'. Primary school selection was also emerging as Conservative policy. Whilst Labour remained opposed to 'eleven plus' type of selection, Labour accepted 'specialisation' whereby pupils with certain abilities or aptitudes would be taught in distinctive schools. Although Labour envisaged a somewhat greater role for local authorities, there was to be no return of schools which had opted out during the Conservative's period in office. Grant maintained status would be replaced by basically similar 'foundation' school status.

As with the Conservative approach, Labour now rejected progressive teaching methods in favour of traditional classroom methods. Under Labour, pupil tests and league tables would continue.

Higher and further education

In the past, the purpose of further and higher education was seen in terms of enabling individuals to realise their academic potential, whichever directions that led in. More recently the emphasis has been on equipping students with the key vocational skills which will enable them to find employment. In order to increase the chances of finding work, recent governments have encouraged more and more young people into further and higher education so that by the mid-1990s nearly a third of all school-leavers proceeded to degree and diploma courses.

In order to finance the expansion of higher education, an enquiry chaired by Sir Ron (now Lord) Dearing proposed introducing tuition fees. This proposal was accepted by the Labour Government which also abolished the means-tested maintenance grant in favour of an all-loans system.

Many anticipated a restructuring of higher and further education in which two-year diplomas, with the possibility of an extra year's 'top-up' to a degree, would become more important. The long-awaited White Paper was demoted to a Green Paper, *The Learning Age*, the centrepiece of which were 'individual learning accounts' to finance retraining, a 'University for Industry' based on learning packages on the web and a freephone helpline. It was sus-

pected by political commentators that the Treasury refused to finance the more ambitious policy originally formulated; hence the downgraded Green Paper containing its modest, low-cost proposals.

Labour in office

Labour's pledge to the electorate was to make education its 'number one priority' with 'zero tolerance of underperformance' in schools (Labour manifesto, 1997). These aspirations were reflected in the contents of the new Labour Government's white paper, *Excellence in Schools*, which proposed more pupil testing with a baseline assessment for all children when they started school and new English and maths tests for nine-year-olds; targets for all schools, to be monitored by local authorities; more parent governors, and OFSTED inspections every six years rather than every four.

Labour's version of a 'back to basics' approach in education was reflected in the white paper's proposal for an hour a day in primary schools being devoted to raising standards in literacy and numeracy and in compulsory home/school contracts in which parents undertake responsibility for their children's behaviour in school, good attendance and ensuring that children complete their homework. Somewhat reminiscent of Conservative plans to send 'hit squads' into failing local education authorities to take control of schools, Labour proposed to set up Education Action Zones in twenty-five of Britain's most deprived urban areas with elite teachers 'parachuted in' to raise standards (Figure 24.2).

The morale of the teaching profession is not high. Many teachers feel that they have been denigrated by politicians and have become the scapegoats blamed for society's problems, from increasing crime and violence to Britain's poor position in international education league tables. Few of the measures announced by Labour's Secretary of State, David Blunkett, seem likely to raise teachers' morale. The pressure is on them to raise the academic performance of their larger classes, accept a greater administrative burden, with only small additional sums of money found for improving dilapidated buildings and providing elementary classroom resources such as books. Unlike the legal or medical profession, teachers are graded on a 1 to 7 scale with quick and

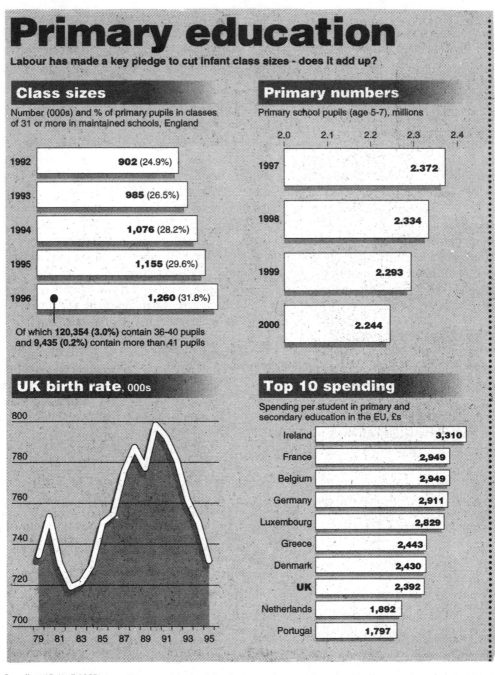

Primary education

Labour has made a key pledge to cut infant class sizes - does it add up?

Class sizes

Number (000s) and % of primary pupils in classes of 31 or more in maintained schools, England

1992	**902** (24.9%)
1993	**985** (26.5%)
1994	**1,076** (28.2%)
1995	**1,155** (29.6%)
1996	**1,260** (31.8%)

Of which **120,354 (3.0%)** contain 36-40 pupils and **9,435 (0.2%)** contain more than 41 pupils

Primary numbers

Primary school pupils (age 5-7), millions

	2.0	2.1	2.2	2.3	2.4
1997				**2.372**	
1998				**2.334**	
1999			**2.293**		
2000			**2.244**		

UK birth rate, 000s

800
780
760
740
720
700

79 81 83 85 87 89 91 93 95

Top 10 spending

Spending per student in primary and secondary education in the EU, £s

Ireland	**3,310**
France	**2,949**
Belgium	**2,949**
Germany	**2,911**
Luxembourg	**2,829**
Greece	**2,443**
Denmark	**2,430**
UK	**2,392**
Netherlands	**1,892**
Portugal	**1,797**

Source: *The Guardian*, 15 April 1997.

Figure 24.2 Primary education, 1992–2000

simple procedures for dismissing the incompetent. It is, then, little wonder that recruitment to teacher training is in sharp decline among young people and that pension restrictions had to be imposed to stem the flood of early retirements among middle-aged teachers who felt that they had had enough.

Summary

• Harold Laswell once defined politics as 'who gets what, when and how'. In many ways education could be defined in a similar way. The 'great education debate' was dominated by the political right, with arguments about standards given priority over concern about social engineering. The 1980s was a period in which many market mechanisms were proposed and introduced in order to raise standards. The Labour government elected in 1997 accepted the Conservatives' education agenda in large part.

Questions

1. To what extent is it possible to 'keep politics out of education'?
2. 'A highly educated young workforce will improve Britain's economic performance.' How valid is this statement?
3. To what extent have educational reform measures been shaped by political philosophies?
4. A distinctive Labour approach to education.' To what extent does such an approach exist?

Assignments

Assignment (1) Education boss 'too political'?

The Chief Inspector of Schools, Chris Woodhead, has become a politically controversial figure, sometimes appearing to contradict the views of the Secretary of State as well as his own colleagues. For example, he accused his own staff of treating teachers too softly when OFSTED inspectors reported an improvement in teaching quality compared with the year before. When asked about this in the Commons, the Secretary of State, Gillian Shepherd, confirmed that OFSTED data based on many school inspections had revealed a small improvement in teaching standards. This finding seemed at odds with the Chief Inspector's controversial claim that 3,000 heads and 15,000 teachers were incompetent.

The Liberal Democrat education spokesman, Don Foster, also challenged Chris Woodhead's views on incompetent teachers. After examining much data on school inspections, Foster said that only 1 per cent of lessons were judged to be poor. Union leaders added their voices to the debate arguing that the Chief Inspector's consistently gloomy view about teaching standards was sapping the morale of their members. They wanted him to focus his remarks on the shortage of classroom resources, from computers to books, which was holding back many pupils' learning.

Some political journalists felt that in terms of education philosophy the Chief Inspector had associated himself too closely with Conservative 'back to basics' policy. For this reason they were surprised when the Opposition Leader, Tony Blair, announced that Chris Woodhead would remain in his job should Labour win the forthcoming general election.

Questions

(i) What was Labour's attitude towards the Chief Inspector?

(ii) Identify critics of the Chief Inspector, stating reasons for their criticism.

(iii) Give possible reasons why the Secretary of State might want to publicise positive news about education, and why the Chief Inspector might want to emphasise negative news.

Assignment (2) The standards debate

There is much contradictory news about education standards in Britain; for example, within months newspapers reported the following:

• More students had taken 'A' levels, and more were passing them. Compared with the previous year, there was a 5.2 per cent rise in the number of entries in 1997, with the overall pass rate up by 1.3 per cent.

• A 41-nation survey of maths and science standards among 13-year-olds showed that on maths England was ranked 25th (Scotland 29th) and on science England was 10th (Scotland 26th). The top four on maths were the Asian 'tigers': Singapore, South Korea, Japan and Hong Kong. The top four on science were Singapore, the Czech Republic, Japan and South Korea. The United States ranked 28th on maths and 17th on science.

- An employer's report on standards of literacy and numeracy among young job applicants showed a sharp decline over a ten-year period. Many graduates and school-leavers were reported to have both a poor vocabulary and difficulties with simple mental arithmetic. General knowledge was also shown to be poor, with one in five unable to identify a photograph of President Clinton.

Questions

(i) Outline possible ways in which politicians from different parties might use the contents of the three reports above in public debate.

(ii) 'In order to compete successfully in a global market means that Britain's workforce must be better educated and better skilled than our competitors.' How far do you agree with this statement? How relevant is the content of each of the reports above to this statement?

(iii) 'Around 7 per cent of pupils attend private schools, they are taught in smaller classes with better resources. As long as the political elite can send their children to these privileged schools, the state system will remain under-funded and mediocre.' Is this argument still relevant in the late 1990s?

Further reading

Bash, L. and Coulby, D. (1989) *The Education Reform Act: Competition and Control* (London: Cassell): a comprehensive account of the Act. Education Group II (1991) *Education Limited: Schooling, Training and the New Right in England since 1979* (London: Unwin Hyman): a radical critique of traditional education. Flude, M. and Hammer, M. (eds) (1990) *The Education Reform Act 1988: Its Origins and Implications* (London: Falmer): this book traces the political and educational origins of the Act. McVicar, M. (1990) 'Education Policy: Education as a Business?', in S. Savage, and L. Robins (eds), *Public Policy Under Thatcher* (London: Macmillan): places education in the context of other policies.

Health and welfare

This chapter considers aspects of welfare provision concerned with health care and housing. The National Health Service (NHS) came into existence in 1948 as the only universal national health service where treatment was free at the point of access. The medical profession had to be persuaded by the Labour Minister, Nye Bevan, to accept the NHS but it was an immediate success with the public and has remained popular ever since. Nevertheless, successive governments have been concerned about the expense of the NHS and a number of reforms have aimed to improve management, constrain costs and hopefully, improve services. The last reform, introduced in 1991, which organised health care around an internal market, was the most controversial.

Housing is different from other social policies such as health or education which make up the **welfare state**. For whilst the overwhelming majority of the population rely on the services of the NHS and state education, an overwhelming majority rely on private owner-occupation for housing. Whilst a

> The **welfare state**, funded through taxation, is the means by which individuals and their families are protected from the excesses of free market forces.

failure in health policy or education policy would threaten the well-being of many of the electorate, a failure in housing policy would affect only a minority.

CHAPTER 25

The health service reforms: rhetoric and reality

After much initial opposition from the medical profession, the postwar Labour Government set up the NHS in 1948 (see Coxall and Robins, 1998). Governments which followed became increasingly concerned over the rising costs of the NHS. In 1991 the biggest reform of the NHS took place since its foundation. Labour argued that the new-style self-governing hospital trusts and fund-holding general practices designed by the Conservative Government to work in a marketplace represented the creeping privatisation of health care in Britain. Looking back, Labour probably overstated the case against the Conservative reforms. Central to Labour's objections were, firstly, that opting out would represent the first step by hospital trusts to becoming private hospitals. Indeed, to the annoyance of the Conservative Government, this view was shared by some of the radical right of the Conservative Party (for example, in the pamphlet *All Private Patients Now*). Secondly, Labour argued that the Conservative reforms would break up the NHS; hospital trusts were opting out of the NHS and a two-tier system of health care would emerge as fund-holding general practitioners (GPs) bought immediate treatment for their patients whilst others faced long waits. The introduction of a 'market mentality', with doctors forces to consider commercial criteria and think like accountants before deciding on recommending treatment or not, would destroy the ethos of compassion and care associated with the NHS. Thirdly, the new freedom granted to hospital trusts would allow them, if they so wished, to end the provision of 'unprofitable' operations or treatments even if it was needed. Hospital trusts would be free to offer 'profitable' treatment, even if there was no local need, and sell such treatment to private patients.

The then Prime Minister, John Major, attacked Labour for what he called 'the big lie' on NHS reforms. He argued that 'NHS trust hospitals are and will remain part of the NHS. They will be run by NHS staff and will treat NHS patients just as they have done before – only better' (*Observer*, 19 May 1991). The government argued that the NHS reforms were simply an attempt to modernise the management of the NHS. But it is probably true to say that the Conservatives misled the public about the nature of those reforms in the White Paper *Working for Patients* which promised that patients and doctors would enjoy greater freedom of choice. Expectations were created by ministers and their civil servants that the market reforms would result in patients being referred to the specialists and hospitals of their choice. It was argued that the new-style contracts made between the purchasers and providers of health care would mean that 'money followed patients'.

In the event, however, the reforms gave very limited choice to patients and doctors since health authorities made contracts which bought health care 'in bulk' from a limited number of hospitals, resulting in 'patients following money'. Like buying any other product, it is cheaper and more efficient to buy health care in bulk, which health authorities do in order to make their money go further. But it is not possible to reconcile greater efficiency and savings with increased patient choice as did Conservative Government rhetoric in *Working for Patients*.

The market reforms

In the White Paper, *Working for Patients,* the Conservative Government argued that although the NHS was a monolithic organisation which provided health care to the public, it played two distinctive roles. In the same way as a market is made up of people who are buying products (the purchasers)

from people who are selling them (the providers), the NHS could also be organised into a market of purchasers and providers. On the one hand it '*provided*' health care, but this health care had to be paid for, so on the other hand the NHS was also a '*purchaser*' of health care. Being both a provider and a purchaser of health care would not have become a problem for the NHS, it was argued, had it not been for the fact that the NHS had become 'producer orientated'. In much the same way as state education had been seen by the government to have fallen into the hands of producers (LEAs, teachers' unions) rather than serving the interests of consumers (pupils, parents) so too the NHS was seen as working to serve the needs of the producers (the medical profession) rather than the needs of the consumers (the patients).

The government believed that the grip of the professionals, be they teachers or doctors, could be broken by the introduction of market forces which would operate in ways which would mean that the respective service would become shaped by the needs of the 'consumer'. At the same time, the increased competition resulting from the working of the market would increase efficiency in education and health at a time when costs were rising fast.

Before April 1991 District Health Authorities (DHAs) were responsible for channelling resources for the provision of health care and they served both the '*provider*' and '*purchaser*' functions. However, after April 1991 there was a split between these functions and under the new system

District Health Authorities, together with budget-holding GP practices, have become purchasers of health services from suppliers such as hospitals, community services and ambulance services (the providers). The new purchasing units are able to draw up contracts with any hospitals and other provider units both within and outside their own district. Their stated objective will be to achieve the best value for money available within the constrains of the budget handed down to them from the Regional Health Authority to which they belong. (Bartlett, 1991, p. 56)

Figure 25.1 outlines the provider market of Trusts, Directly Managed Units (DMUs) including those in other DHAs as well as private institutions compet-

Table 25.1 Welfare services: the market and the state

Public sector	Semi-autonomous public sector	Private sector
Health care		
• Directly Managed Units under the control of District Health Authorities	• Trust status hospitals accountable directly to the Secretary of State	• Private hospitals
• Non fundholding GPs	• Fundholding GPs	• Private health insurance, such as BUPA
Housing		
• Municipal or council housing	• Housing Association provision	• Owner-occupation
	• Housing Action Trusts	• Privately rented
Education		
• Schools maintained by local authorities	• Opted-out Grant Maintained Schools	• Private schools
	• City Technology Colleges	• Conservative Assisted Places Scheme

ing for patients. A provider which successfully bids for business will draw up a service contract with the purchaser. It is this system of decentralised contracts which replaced the bureaucratic method of organising health care which existed up until 1991. There are three types of contracts which can be drawn up between provider and purchaser: block contracts, cost-as-volume contracts and cost-per-case contracts. Under the block contract 'the purchaser pays the provider an annual fee in return for access to a defined range of services' (Bartlett, 1991, p. 57). This block contract can involve considerable risks for the provider since there will always be much uncertainty about what resources are needed overall. For example, as the BMA argued, admittance to hospital of a number of young adults with a hernia condition would require much less overall treatment than an equivalent number of elderly, unstable diabetics with the same condition.

Cost-per-case contracts, which can be set on an 'average' cost, can place a greater risk on the purchaser because of the uncertainty involved in forecasting the upper limit on the number of cases to be treated. This type of contract will be used to treat referrals which are not covered in any block contract. Finally, cost-and-volume contracts will be made

between purchaser and provider which are essentially a mixture of the block contracts and the cost-per-case contracts; they will fund 'a baseline of activity to be undertaken by the provider beyond which all funding is at a cost-per-case basis' (Bartlett, 1991, p. 59).

The internal market of the NHS will comprise thousands of purchasers and hundreds of providers which, in the main, will conduct business in terms of block contracts. But is this internal market a 'real' market? Bartlett refers to the internal market of the NHS as a 'quasi-market' since 'this is not a normal market in which consumer choice is reflected directly by individuals' decisions to purchase varying levels of service, but rather a quasi-market in which consumers' decisions are mediated through a variety of intervening specialised agents (the DHA and the budget-holding GP practice) who purchase services on their behalf' (Bartlett, 1991, p. 56). It is assumed that the forces of the quasi-market will lead to keener competition and mergers of DHAs and Family Health Services Authorities (FHSAs) in an effort to increase their power in the purchasing of services. This argument underlines the original criticism of *Working for Patients:* namely that the market-like reform mechanisms were always likely

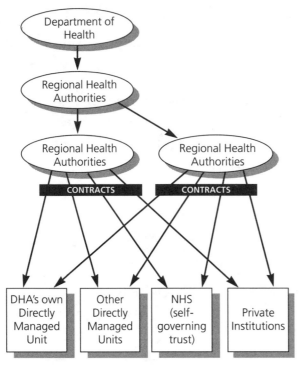

Source: Adapted from S. Harrison, D. J. Hunter and C. Pollit, *The Dynamics of British Health Policy* (London: Hyman, 1990).

Figure 25.1 The purchaser/provider split

to lead to some improvement in efficiency, although some academics doubt this, but to no increase in patient choice.

The politics of health

In basic terms, the Conservative record on health care spending was impressive; spending on the NHS rose by 72 per cent in real terms between 1979 and 1996. Despite this large increase in health care spending under the Conservatives, Labour was the party most trusted by the public. It entered the 1997 general election with a 38 per cent lead over the Conservatives on the health issue. What went wrong for the Conservatives?

Labour's attack on health service reforms as preparation for the privatisation of the NHS had some credibility despite John Major's firm denials. Also the reforms had created a bloated bureaucracy inside the NHS to administer the internal market, and

press stories of sacked nurses to pay for more clerks needed to process a mountain of invoices fed public anxiety. Finally, it was feared that the new reforms had created a two-tier service with, for instance, GP fundholders able to purchase better care for their patients than non-fundholding GPs.

Labour entered the 1997 general election accepting that it could not recreate the integrated NHS that it had established forty years earlier. The party was committed to retaining the basic structure, separating the purchasing from the providing of health care, but also operating it in a more cooperative and democratic manner. For example, GPs will continue to purchase health care but formal fundholding status will be abolished; contracts will be replaced by 'health care agreements'; and elected local authority representatives will sit on trust hospital boards.

On assuming office, Labour's Health Secretary, Frank Dobson, found that the NHS was facing a financial crisis. Over 30,000 patients had been on waiting lists for longer than the 18 months promised in the Patient's Charter. The crisis, he was told, would worsen during the winter of 1997–8. In response, the first budget allocated an additional £1.2 billion to health spending to tide the service over until Labour's anticipated savings on management costs materialised.

Care in the community

Many people, particularly the elderly, with illnesses such as dementia, depression, anxiety or physical disabilities, are not cared for entirely within the NHS but through local authority managed Care in the Community. Although local GPs and hospitals do provide care for these people, other support services are involved such as home-helps, meals on wheels, visiting district nurses and facilities at day-care centres. Many argue that Care in the Community is currently under-funded and will face severe economic difficulties as a consequence of Britain's ageing population and the resulting increased demand which will be made on already stretched resources.

Critics argue that 'care in the community' is a flawed concept since there are insufficient resources to provide adequate care and, in reality, 'community' does not exist. The result is that many vulnerable people have been shunted into seedy bed-and-break-fast accommodation which is more repressive and fearful for them than the old asylum institutions in which they were once housed but which are now closed down.

Care in the community was attractive to liberal-minded decision-makers and professionals since it promised to give the most vulnerable a more digni-fied life. It was also attractive to the New Right since it reduced the activity of the state and held the promise of reducing public expenditure. In reality successful policies have been too rare. Much public-ity has focused on the miserable lives of those receiv-ing 'care in the community', their high suicide rate and the estimated murder rate of one per fortnight committed by care in the community patients.

The housing crisis

Providing sufficient good quality housing for the population of Britain would appear to be a simple goal to achieve in a relatively rich, technologically advanced society. Indeed, much progress was made in tackling the housing problem in the postwar years. Mistakes were made, such as the popularity of building high-rise flats in the 1960s, but generally speaking slums were cleared and replaced by improved housing. The growth of owner-occupa-tion was supported by both Labour and Conservative governments and encouraged through subsidising mortgage payments with tax relief. Local authorities provided accommodation with sub-sidised rents for the less affluent people in society.

The Thatcher governments of the 1980s adopted a more ideological approach to the housing problem which was based on free-market principles and the wish to limit local authority involvement. Owner-occupation was boosted by the biggest of all privati-sation measures, the 'right to buy', which enabled council tenants to buy their own homes. Efforts were made to revive the once-important role of the private landlord in providing accommodation. Finally, the government preferred housing associa-tions to local authorities in providing 'social housing' for the less well-off. How successful have these reforms been in tackling the housing problem?

During the 1980s Britain's housing problem developed into the proportions of a housing crisis.

Groups of homeless people and cardboard cities are now commonplace sights in British towns. Shelter has estimated that 1.7 million individuals are now squatting or staying with friends, with young people being the fastest growing group amongst the homeless. On top of this, many families endure a bleak bed-and-breakfast existence, whilst many vul-nerable people with histories of mental illness wander the streets each night in search of hostel accommodation. Others, in their own homes, become unemployed, default on their mortgages, and have their homes repossessed by the building societies. Others simply live in very poor accommo-dation. Together, these are the victims of policy failure which make up Britain's army of the homeless and poorly housed.

Table 25.2 shows changes in housing tenure in England and Wales, with private landlords playing a decreasing role and owner-occupiers playing an increasing role. The impact of the 'Right to Buy' leg-islation can be traced in the changing trend in the role of local authority housing. The decline of private renting has reduced the amount of cheap accommodation which is available. Obtaining a council house can be a lengthy process, and virtually impossible for people deemed to have a low housing priority need. Owner-occupation has grown in pop-ularity, since it generally offers greater security as well as better housing conditions.

Part of Britain's housing problem results from the old age of many houses. Over six million homes, which is almost a third of all homes, were built before the end of the First World War. Many of these homes are in need of modernisation and major repair work. More than a million council homes were built between the wars – these are now fifty or sixty years old – and so are approaching an age when major refurbishing and repair will be necessary.

A change of direction in housing policy

Conservative legislation on housing was based on a number of principles found in legislation on, for example, education or health. Reforms aimed to reduce the role of local authorities, encourage the growth of private sector involvement, increase com-petition and choice, whilst containing public

Table 25.2 Housing tenure in England and Wales, 1971 and 1995

	Owner-occupied (%)	Rented from local authorities and housing associations (%)	Rented from private landlords (%)
1971	52	29	19
1995	67	22	10

spending. There has been much legislation on housing policy. The most important Acts are:

The Housing Act 1980

In 1979 Parliament was informed that the new Thatcher Government intended to fulfil an old political ambition held by many Tories:

> Thousands of people in council houses and new towns came out in support of us for the first time because they wanted a chance to buy their own homes. We will give every council tenant the right to purchase his own home at a substantial discount on the market price and with 100% mortgages for those who need them. This will be a giant stride towards making a reality of Anthony Eden's dream of a property owning democracy.

The most significant part of the Act which was to accomplish this gave council tenants the 'right to buy' their homes. This measure was very popular with voters who lived in council houses. The Act ensured that councils would provide mortgages where necessary with tenants able to buy their homes at a discount. For those tenants who had lived in council houses for a long time, the discount was 50 per cent, later rising to 60 per cent. For long-term flat tenants the discount was 70 per cent. For many council tenants, then, the purchase of their homes from the council represented a bargain. By 1989 a million council homes had been sold to sitting tenants, with some local authorities having sold over a third of their council houses.

From the government's perspective the sale of council homes represented its largest privatisation policy. In fact, 43 per cent of all privatisation proceeds from the first decade of Thatcherism came from council house sales. Opponents saw the sale of council houses as 'asset-stripping' in order to buy votes from the working-class electorate. It was argued that council houses were provided for families in greatest need but under the 'right to buy' council houses were being bought by better-off tenants at bargain discount prices. Critics argued that once a council house became privately owned, it would never again be used to house the poorest members of society. Labour critics were particularly annoyed that councils could only spend a proportion of the money they received from house sales in building new homes to let.

The Housing Act 1988

This Act introduced the 'Tenants' Choice' which involved the possibility of transferring council houses to other landlords such as private landlords, housing associations or tenants' cooperatives. Private landlords would be able to bid for council properties, with over 50 per cent of tenants having to vote against to prevent such a transfer (abstentions by tenants would be counted as a vote in favour of a transfer).

The 1988 Act also established Housing Action Trusts (HATs) which were designed to take over running the most deprived council estates with dilapidated houses, high unemployment and high crime rates. It was intended that HATs, more efficiently than local authorities, would tackle all the problems of urban blight, improve council estates, then pass them back to the local authorities or on to another, possibly private, landlord. The minister responsible saw HATs as the 'cutting edge of government's inner city regeneration' and they were to be based on the model of Urban Development Corporations (see Chapter 19).

BOX 25.1
Communitarian and stakeholder approaches to welfare

It has been argued that neither government intervention through a massive welfare state nor private enterprise based on free-market policies have shaped a society which is free from poverty, crime and violence. A new approach to welfare has been discussed by the political parties, particularly Labour, which involves placing a new value on community and the shaping of society in ways which include every body.

Labour believes that communities which have declined and disintegrated should be restored in order to create a new moral, social and political order. The importance of the family and schools is seen as crucial in building up a sense of citizenship and social responsibility. All disadvantaged groups would be integrated into strong communities and not excluded, as many were during the 1980s and 1990s, to form a dispossessed and threatening underclass. Although not without its critics on the left, communitarian ideas were seen by many as consistent with old Labour values of solidarity and collectivism.

In addition, stakeholder policies would both reinforce and work through strong communities. The stakeholder economy acknowledges that companies do have a responsibility to their shareholders, but also to many others who have a stake in their success such as workers, customers, suppliers and the wider community. A stakeholder welfare system would also be based on inclusivity, with no group or class excluded from society – the temporarily poor, unemployed or homeless would remain full citizens during hard times. Their welfare would not be provided solely by the state, but through a framework which stressed community. The co-ordinated efforts of local authorities, families, neighbours, voluntary bodies and charities would provide much important welfare. If implemented more successfully, Care in the Community could provide a model for such a system. Individuals would also be expected to play a greater role in providing for their own welfare through a stakeholder system. Labour showed considerable interest in Singapore's Central Provident Fund, a compulsory savings scheme for benefits and pensions. Unlike the British system where an individual's national insurance payments simply disappear into the Treasury, the Singapore system enables people to keep track of their contributions (their 'stake').

Some feminists are suspicious of communitarian and stakeholder ideas, since the burden of responsibility falls unfairly on women. As with Care in the Community policies, it is mainly women who are the unpaid or low-paid carers of the elderly and handicapped.

The politics of housing

Any surviving political cleavage with owner-occupiers supporting the Conservatives and social housing tenants supporting Labour was shattered during 1997 by Tony Blair's appeal to Middle England. He promised greater economic security which attracted home-owners trapped by negative equity or in fear of repossession. Housing did not feature particularly strongly as an election issue in 1997; of the 22 per cent who thought it was an important issue, 48 per cent judged Labour the best party on housing and only 11 per cent judged Conservatives best (*The Times*, 10 April 1997).

Labour's housing policies were cautious and there were no promises to bring a speedy end to the crisis; in fact, Labour argued that it would need two full parliaments in order to solve the problems besetting the private and social housing sectors. An immediate measure, however, was to commence phasing in new spending on housing from the proceeds of earlier council house sales.

Summary

- During the 1980s and into the 1990s many social problems were tackled by governments which were committed to simple market reforms. The failure of this approach became increasingly acute in housing and to a lesser extent in health care. Reliance on home-ownership and private health care is an option for those who are relatively well-off. The less well-off will need to be housed in rented accommodation and treated by the NHS or through Care in the Community. They lack power as customers and consequently are treated poorly in any market or quasi-market system.

- Labour has accepted the purchaser–provider split in the NHS and will not undertake any organisational reforms designed to re-establish the NHS as a monolithic, centralised and state-provided institution. Likewise, Labour accepts the importance of owner-occupation in its housing policy. There will be no return to large municipal housing projects although local authorities will play a somewhat larger role than during the 1980s and early 1990s.

- Care in the Community policies are in a crisis.

Questions

1. Explain why 68 per cent of electors in 1997 believed that health was an important issue, but only 22 per cent said the same about housing.
2. Assess the political impact of Conservative NHS reforms.
3. Assess the impact of privatisation policies on housing.
4. The 'right to buy' policy was a political success but a failure in terms of solving the housing crisis. Evaluate this statement.
5. 'Competition and the working of the free market produces winners and losers'. How valid is this comment with reference to recent reforms in health care and housing?

Assignments

Assignment (1) Controversy over the NHS

Strengths of the NHS

Access
- equal access, based on medical need for treatment
- a public service with a lot of public accountability
- organised systems for investigating complaints

Quality
- doctors have no incentive to overtreat patients (as they receive annual salaries rather than fees for each little piece of activity they undertake)
- clinical autonomy of doctors is not interfered with by managers or politicians

Costs
- cheap system to administer (USA spends four times as much on overheads, for example)
- fixed public expenditure budgets has kept the total costs of the NHS under control
- most services, and all hospital services, are free to the patient and met from public funds
- very high public support for the NHS ensures its future

Weaknesses of the NHS

Access
- long waiting lists, particularly for hospital treatment (in Germany and the USA access is virtually instant)
- the health gap between the classes has not narrowed

Quality
- low capital investment in new technologies and treatments
- poor amenities and inconsiderate treatment of patients
- only a limited emphasis on health education, health promotion and illness prevention

Costs
- staff are poorly paid
- history of tense industrial relations at all levels – doctors to porters
- no stability due to constant political uncertainty

Source: B. Wood (1992, pp. 33–7).

Draft a brief speech for either the Minister for Health or the Opposition's Shadow Health Minister. Select appropriate points listed in the boxes as well as material in the rest of the chapter when constructing your arguments for or against current changes. Exchange your speech with a class member who has written for the opposite side of the debate. Discuss the politics of health care mentioning how easy or difficult you found it to attack or defend the government's record.

Assignment (2) An anti-housing policy?

Since 1979 the Conservative Government of Margaret Thatcher has, in one sense, pursued a coherent and politically successful housing policy, based on cuts in public expenditure on the housing programme and the expansion of home ownership. However it has been suggested that this is merely a tenure policy, not a housing policy, although it is possible to go further and to argue that the government has been pursuing an anti-housing policy. The charge that the government has merely a tenure policy is based on the centrality of the council tenants' right to buy, which is about transferring the ownership for existing dwellings, having little or nothing to do with the key housing policy issues of quantity and quality. Moreover, the sale of council houses is a policy aimed at providing benefits for people who are already well housed, doing nothing for those in greatest need. A key feature of current tenure policy is its unfairness, best illustrated by the imposition of a strictly means tested housing benefit scheme for tenants (a scheme which has been a target for spending cuts), while the inverted means test of tax relief on mortgage interest is defended despite escalating cost. In addition the tenure policy accusation rests on the observation that for the individual household the achievement of home ownership is assumed to represent the end of their housing problem.

The idea that the Thatcher government has pursued an anti-housing policy goes beyond the attack on council housing to recognise the contradictions between housing and economic policy objectives. First, it is clear that the housing programme bore the brunt of the cuts in public expenditure in the early 1980s, not for any carefully argued housing reasons but for political and economic reasons. Second, the use of high interest rates and high unemployment as tools of economic policy, at the same time as relying on further growth of home ownership, is highly contradictory. Economic policy has frustrated the achievement of housing policy objectives by raising the cost of mortgages.

Extract from Malpass (ed.) (1990b), pp. 232–3.

Questions

(i) To what extent did the Thatcher governments pursue a 'tenure' policy rather than a 'housing' policy?

(ii) Explain the author's opinion on the 'Right to Buy' legislation.

(iii) Outline reasons why some critics have accused the Thatcher governments of pursuing an 'anti-housing' policy.

(iv) Construct a brief argument which challenges the criticisms made in the extract and which supports the Thatcher government's housing policy.

Further reading

Atkinson, R. and Durden, P. (1990) 'Housing Policy in the Thatcher Years', in S. Savage and L. Robins (eds), *Public Policy Under Thatcher* (London: Macmillan) places housing policy within the framework of other policies. Klein, R. (1989) *The Politics of the NHS* (London: Longman) is an authoritative study. Malpass, P. (1990) *Reshaping Housing Policy* (London, Routledge) puts housing policy into an historical context. Malpass, P. (ed) (1990) *The Housing Crisis* (London: Croom Helm) is a very useful guide to the current debate. Wood, B. (1992) *The Politics of Health* (Manchester: Politics Association) is a useful introduction to the topic.

CHAPTER 26

Inequality in Britain

In the 1940s Sir William Beveridge set out a blue-print for the government to follow which would banish the 'giant evils' of Want, Disease, Squalor, Ignorance and Idleness from Britain. Half a century later, and despite the creation of a welfare state, Britain remains a society plagued by social and economic problems. Why is Britain a 'one-third/two-thirds' society in which the majority enjoy lifestyles based on a decent standard of living but alongside a significant minority who are materially poor and disadvantaged in terms of having poorer health, poorer education, and less chance of employment than the rest? The arguments of the 'poverty lobby', that poverty is an issue for government to tackle, are contrasted with the New Right critique of welfare, which is blamed for creating a 'dependency culture'. The development of poverty in contemporary Britain is considered along with the implications for society of the emerging underclass and Labour's policies to end social exclusion. The chapter concludes with an exploration of political myths and realities which have influenced government policy concerning the poor.

Rich Britain: poor Britain

Britain is a society characterised by great inequalities in terms of wealth and income. The most wealthy 5 per cent of the population own 37 per cent of the country's wealth. The most wealthy 50 per cent own

93 per cent of the country's wealth or, to put it another way, the poorest half of the population own 7 per cent of the country's wealth. This pattern of inequality is reflected in the incomes households receive. For example, the poorest 20 per cent receive 7.6 per cent of all incomes, whilst the wealthiest 20 per cent receive 40.1 per cent of all incomes.

According to official statistics the situation of the poorest section of society has deteriorated since 1979: whilst average real income rose by 40 per cent from 1979 to 1994, the poorest tenth of the population became 13 per cent worse off and the richest tenth became 65 per cent better off. Around 13 million people were living on an income below half of the national average in 1995; in 1979 the equivalent number was 5 million. What do these poverty statistics mean in human terms? Paul Wilding has described the plight of the poorest:

Six and a half million people lacked household goods which the mass of the population saw as essential – a fridge, a telephone, or carpets in the living area of their homes. Twenty-one million people could not afford hobbies, holidays or celebrations at times like birthdays or Christmas. Thirty-one million – more than half the population – live without what might reasonably be regarded as minimal financial security [such as the ability to save £10 per month or insure the contents of their home]. (Wilding, 1993)

The purpose of the Beveridge Report was to combat poverty and the social ills which accompanied it. Postwar governments of the 1950s, 1960s and 1970s accepted in general terms that a redistribution of resources in society from the better-off to the poor should be the principle that underlay social policy. Although governments, and the electorate,

BOX 26.1
Changing patterns of inequality

Complex changes have taken place in the structure of British society during the 1980s and 1990s. Although the rich have become richer and the poor have got poorer, even the better off members of society are experiencing increased insecurity. Two classifications below attempt to illustrate the changing nature of inequality.

Pupils in comprehensive schools in the poorest urban areas achieve half the success rate at GCSE of those in the better-off urban areas

Poor people are one and a half times as likely to have a long-standing illness and twice as likely to have a disability

24% of the population lives in poverty

17% of the population receives income support

7.5% of all dwellings are 'unfit for human habitation'

19.1% of households have no working adults

Source: The Observer, 13 April 1997.

Alexandra Frean reporting on survey of lifestyles by City University, London (*The Times*, 25 June 1997)

Getting on
This group comprises high-flyers with a degree and middle-class parents. They tend to live alone or with friends and have postponed marriage and parenthood until later in life. Well-qualified, able 26-year-old women are as likely to be in high-powered jobs as their peers.

Getting by
These people are the barometer of the boom and bust economy. They have few qualifications and tend to be in jobs with limited prospects, working long hours for modest wages.

   They do well if the labour market is expanding and have gained from the expansion in the service sector, but lose out during recession.

   Most are in committed, long-term relationships. Those with children are likely to be struggling financially.

Getting nowhere
This significant minority includes people who left school with no qualifications and went on training schemes followed by temporary jobs and periods of unemployment. Most are on benefits and many became parents at a very young age. The women are doubly disadvantaged as they are unlikely to be able to find work and have often been deserted to bring up children on their own.

Will Hutton's 30/30/40 analysis of society (*Talking Politics*, 8:3, 1996)

The advantaged 40 per cent
This group includes individuals in permanent full-time jobs with above-average incomes. But some in the advantaged 40 per cent will be working to fixed contracts or be self-employed. Changes such as **market-testing** and **contracting out** is threatening some members of the advantaged 40 per cent of society. Even this privileged group is not totally secure. Each year this group is reduced in size by about 1 per cent as a result of increasing insecurity.

The newly insecure 30 per cent
This group includes individuals who are in work but are insecure and poorly paid. Many will be part-timers. The newly insecure have much less trade union protection than in the past. The recently publicised Burger King practice of requiring workers to sign on when customers appeared and sign off once they had been served, therefore getting paid for the minutes they actually worked, is an example of the conditions of the newly insecure.

The disadvantaged 30 per cent
This group includes the unemployed and those experiencing poverty. Those individuals who become socially and economically excluded are in danger of falling into the underclass.

accepted that there would inevitably be rich people and poor people in society, it was also accepted that reducing these inequalities was politically and socially beneficial. Taxation was progressive, with the better-off paying much greater percentages of their incomes in tax than the less well-off. Tax revenues were used by governments to provide a welfare state – the equivalent of 'social wages' – to provide free education, free health care and other benefits to those who would not otherwise have been able to afford these basic needs. Local authorities provided subsidised housing. Although the redistributive principle did not always operate in the way intended, it was assumed that welfare benefits would be financed disproportionately by the better-off members of society but drawn disproportionately by the less well-off. Through such a redistribution of resources, it was intended that the worst impact of poverty would be softened and that even the poorest members of society would be able to lead dignified lives in which they or their children would enjoy some equality of opportunity despite their relative poverty.

New Right thinking increasingly influenced Conservative policy-making from the 1970s onwards. The result was that the assumptions shared by earlier Conservative and Labour governments – that poverty was an evil which should be tackled by government – were no longer held with such certainty. Indeed it was argued that the high levels of taxation which were needed to finance the welfare state actually reduced people's incentive to be enterprising and to work hard. Furthermore, it was argued that a high level of welfare had a negative impact on the poor. For it produced a 'dependency culture' which sapped their determination and ability to lead independent lives. Cutting taxes and reducing welfare would, it was argued, release enterprise and energy which would result in the creation of more wealth. The fear of poverty, no longer cushioned by generous welfare benefits, would encourage many poor people to reassess their lot and see them move back into the job market. Once in employment, the opportunity to keep more of their income by paying less tax would encourage them to work harder. In this way, it was argued, the existence of poverty has a beneficial effect on society through eventually creating more wealth. Even those in poverty who, for whatever reason, could not redirect their lives, would benefit from the 'trickle down' of prosperity from the richest to the poorest. In other words, the New Right argued that the creation of wealth was more socially beneficial than the redistribution of wealth.

Government policies have not always resulted in their intended impact and reduced poverty. For example, it was frequently middle-class people who benefited disproportionately from the welfare state and not the poorest section of society. Chapter 24 illustrated how middle-class parents could ensure that their children went to well-equipped comprehensives in the leafy suburbs whilst inner-city pupils were destined to attend 'sink' schools. Nor did the poor benefit from the trickle-down of wealth in Mrs Thatcher's enterprise culture. Indeed, the poorest 10 per cent of the population were 6 per cent worse off in real terms in 1989 than they were a decade earlier. The poor, in other words, had become poorer.

Inner-city deprivation

Has a new social class emerged in contemporary Britain? Whilst some academics and politicians claim that it is not so, others argue that in Britain, as in the United States, a sub-working-class stratum of individuals disconnected from mainstream society now forms a distinct 'underclass'. This underclass is characterised by poverty, crime, poor education, drug abuse, ill health, and alienation from the political system. Serious crimes committed by young teenagers in deprived areas of Manchester, Liverpool, Newcastle and other large cities, have generated a public debate about the links between underclass poverty, mental illness, suicide and crime.

An example will help to illuminate the issues.

Meadow Well has been described as a 'sink estate' located in Tyneside in one of Britain's most deprived areas. Poverty is the norm. In 1991 the Meadow Well estate had an unemployment rate of 40 per cent, but this rose to 80 per cent in some streets. Every one of the 252 children attending the Meadow Well primary school received a clothing allowance. Visitors to the estate have reported that its fabric is in a poor condition, with houses which look drab and neglected. Most gardens are overgrown and some houses have windows which are boarded over. In September 1991 the Meadow Well

BOX 26.2
The myth of the work-shy

The crudest form of this is Norman Tebbit's 'on your bike' statement, which is a good example of the popular confusion between 'All . . .' and 'Some . . .'. The most tough-minded and fast-talking politician could not sustain for ten seconds the proposition that *all* unemployed people are able-bodied and mentally fit bicycle-owners, and this is probably not what Mr Tebbit intended to say. But it was crude, for all that, and in less crude forms the philosophy is enduring and pervasive: a form of tunnel vision which ignores the realities of mass unemployment – the lack of jobs, the waste of skills, the dashed hopes, and the pathetically restricted horizons – and leads to the conclusion that 'the poor' could perfectly well help themselves if they wanted to; all they need is to 'get up and go'.

It was the spirit of the 1834 Poor Law. The threat of the workhouse seared the minds of successive generations. Anyone who is over 70 today (and that means more than six million people in England and Wales alone) was approaching 30 when the Poor Law was finally abolished in 1948. It was the spirit of the Majority Report of the Royal Commission on the Poor Laws of 1905–9; and yet the Commission's own research staff provided overwhelming evidence that most poverty was not due to the failure of able-bodied males to support themselves. A statistical survey in Part II of the report demonstrates beyond argument that only a quarter of paupers were male – the rest were women and children. The age breakdown was even more telling. In the 15–25 age-group, only 3.3 per thousand were unemployed. The figure rose steadily, with a quantum leap around the edge of retirement, to 353 per thousand (more than one in three) over the age of 85.

This statistical picture of the increasing proportion in successive age-groups unable to work (whether through disability or through inability to find a job) should have been enough to kill the myth of the 'work-shy' for all time.

But the myth survives, rippling along at some subliminal level in the public consciousness until it is needed, and then surfacing again. It disappears in times of full employment, when it is not needed (though those are the periods in which any physically and mentally fit person of either sex who is available for work and refuses to work might well be called a layabout); and it surfaces in times of high unemployment, when it is least true. The women, the children, the old people, and the disabled or handicapped are forgotten. The jobs are assumed to be there for the taking (though everybody knows that they are not).
From K. Jones (1991) pp. 36–7.

---

estate erupted into violence with firebomb attacks, rioting, looting and ram-raiding. What are the causes of this and similar urban unrest?

Theories from the liberal left recognise an inextricable link between an environment of poverty and lawlessness. It is not argued that all poor people are potential criminals, but that poverty increases the vulnerability of some people to committing crime. It has been argued, for example, that the increase in poverty during the 1980s went hand-in-hand with the increase in reported crime from 2.2 million offences in 1979 to 5 million in 1991. Robert Reiner argued that the pattern of crime reflected the state of local economics, and that 'the 1980s were the first time when the government held out no hope for the poor' (*Observer*, 15 September 1991).

The political right tends to dismiss explanations which link poverty with crime. There may be agreement with the left on the existence of a new underclass, but no agreement that the criminality of the underclass is caused by its poverty. The right argues that poverty was more severe earlier in this century than it is now, yet it was not accompanied by lawlessness. Hence poverty in itself does not result in criminality. The principal cause of criminality is immorality. Christie Davies has argued that an

> earlier generation of Britons succeeded in changing the character of their people and reducing the many forms of deviance that have reappeared and flourished in our own time, because they saw them as constituting not a social but a moral problem whose solution lay in the reform of personal conduct. (Davies, 1993)

To support this view – that poverty is not a direct cause of crime – the right is able to point out that the Meadow Well estate, then known as the Ridges estate, experienced riots in the 'affluent' 1960s. The lack of moral guidance rather than material poverty is recognised to be the main cause of lawlessness, and the right tends to attribute the decline in moral guidance to the increase in one-parent families.

The controversy surrounding the question 'what impact does poverty have on society?' is unlikely to be settled. The attention of the left is focused on improving employment opportunities, improving education and providing more and better housing as the immediate solutions to urban poverty. The left has faith in believing that less poverty will result in less crime. The right is concerned with a decline in morality which is generally recognised to be a consequence of changing family structures, particularly those which result from illegitimacy or broken marriages in which there is no 'authority' from a father. Many on the right believe that the increase in one-parent families is linked with increased anti-social behaviour, and it is argued that social policies should discourage the break-up of the traditional family structure and thereby reduce crime.

Poverty: political myths and the political agenda

It might be expected that the increase in poverty, the emergence of an underclass, the growth of 'cardboard cities' in many towns, together with an associated culture of crime and drug abuse, would be issues at the top of any government's political agenda. Yet in Britain this is not so. How can this be?

Firstly there has been a political debate on the meaning of 'poverty' in contemporary Britain. What the left recognises as 'poverty' the right sees as 'inequality'. The right argues that the least well-off are not poor; they are just not as well off as the rest of society. It is argued that no one in Britain experiences genuine absolute poverty as do many people living in Ethiopia, Somalia or Bangladesh. In Britain those who are relatively poor never go hungry and may own many possessions associated with affluence such as cars, videos, fridges and telephones. John Moore, once Secretary of State for Health and Social Security, attacked the left's claim that poverty existed in Britain, since according to the left's definition of poverty, there would be 'poverty in paradise'. Paul Wilding has argued that this New Right argument which redefines 'poverty' as no more than 'inequal-

ity' is no more than a political convenience: 'since it lifts responsibility for action from the shoulders of government since inequality is not a matter for government . . . responsibility for this so-called poverty is personal' (Wilding, 1993).

Wilding further contends that there are additional beliefs about the nature and causes of poverty which block poverty from being a priority issue. One of these is encouraging people to believe that the unemployed were really work-shy and that job vacancies existed if only they would get 'on their bikes' in search of them (Box 26.1). Another is that the welfare state actually encouraged people to get into the position of needing help – the 'perverse incentive' – by which it was argued by the Right, for example, that young single females chose to become pregnant in order to obtain a council house. Wilding commented that 'blaming the victim' is an approach adopted by all governments when they are either unable or unwilling to tackle poverty, and the 'perverse incentive' argument is used to support the belief that any government policies to tackle poverty will be ineffective.

There is also the belief that inequality stimulates people into working harder and that low wages for some workers help keep Britain competitive in international trade. It is argued that high wages for all, together with the costs of a large welfare state, would make Britain uncompetitive.

Finally, the government does little to tackle poverty because it believes that 'it can get away with inaction. The so-called poor are unorganised and powerless. They don't matter much as voters and, more importantly, poverty does not matter much to other voters' (Wilding, 1993).

Labour's anti-poverty programme

The Labour government elected in 1997 adopted a 'stick-and-carrot' approach to reducing poverty, which was more coordinated than the policies of the previous Conservative administration but not ideologically distinct from them. In other words, Labour believed that policies from education and training to employment, taxation and welfare would have a greater impact on relieving poverty if they all worked

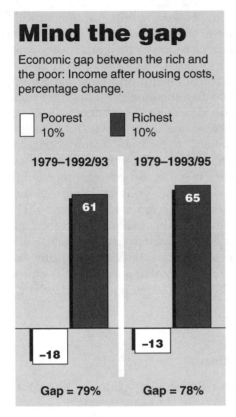

Mind the gap

Economic gap between the rich and the poor: Income after housing costs, percentage change.

☐ Poorest 10%   ■ Richest 10%

1979–1992/93   **1979–1993/95**

61   65

–18   –13

Gap = 79%   **Gap = 78%**

Source: *The Guardian*, 15 November 1996.

Figure 26.1 'Mind the gap'

in harmony. But traditional Conservative aims to reduce welfare-dependency were also reflected in Labour policies, and there was no intention from Labour to solve poverty through raising welfare benefits.

At local level this approach was implemented in Labour's measures to tackle the problems of the permanently excluded underclass. Around 3 million of Britain's poorest people live in the worst thousand inner-city sink estates, and they are the first target of Labour policy to end 'social exclusion'. Labour intends setting up units to better coordinate existing policies in order to have greater impact on raising the quality of life on these estates and, in time, build up a sense of community so that residents can start tackling problems themselves.

At national level Labour policies are pursuing the Conservative goal of breaking the dependency culture with its welfare-to-work policies for single parents and longer-term unemployed young people. In each case the 'stick' to move people into work takes the form of sanctions and benefit cuts, with the 'carrot' being the training of more child carers and subsidies for employers who take on young people respectively.

Labour's anti-poverty programme includes establishing a minimum wage, as well as higher-quality education and training, in order to help people lift themselves and their children out of poverty. This approach has generated political tension between old and new Labour. Roy Hattersley, a previous deputy leader, expressed the views of old Labour; he saw Labour as the party of the poor, which would

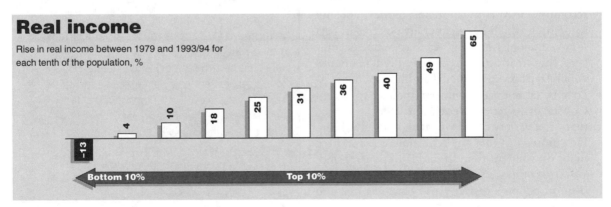

Real income

Rise in real income between 1979 and 1993/94 for each tenth of the population, %

–13   4   10   18   25   31   36   40   49   65

Bottom 10%   **Top 10%**

Source: The *Guardian*, 28 April 1997.

Figure 26.2 Real income, 1979–1993/4

tackle poverty through government intervention and policies which would redistribute wealth from the rich to the poor. He argued that 'the good society is the equal society' (*Guardian*, 26 July 1997).

Gordon Brown, Labour's Chancellor, representing the voice of new Labour, argued that Hattersley's approach tackled the *consequences* of poverty, not the *causes* (unemployment, low skills and low wages). He argued in favour of equality of opportunity, 'not equality of outcome because it is neither desirable nor feasible'. He continued to argue against Hattersley's 'equal society', saying that

Predetermined results imposed, as they would have to be, by a central authority and decided irrespective of work, effort or contribution to the community, is not a socialist dream but other people's nightmare of socialism. It denies humanity, rather than liberates it. It is to make people something they are not, rather than helping them to make the most of what they can be. (*Guardian*, 2 August 1997)

Summary

- Politicians and academics from the political left and right do not agree on whether a condition called 'poverty' exists in Britain or not. The left recognises 'poverty' as a state which debilitates people and reduces their equality of opportunity to lead full and decent lives. A comprehensive welfare state is seen as the means by which the evil effects of poverty can be overcome. The right recognises 'inequality' in society as inevitable but something which has a generally positive impact on society. The right believes that welfare encourages the creation of a culture of dependency which traps people rather than liberates them.
- Poverty has not been an important issue for recent Conservative governments, but Wilding argued that for a variety of reasons it should have been. He pointed out that any government committed to maximising freedom should fight poverty since 'poverty is the great unfreedom, the great limitation on people's capacity to behave as free and autonomous beings' (Wilding, 1993). Quoting Beveridge 'Misery generates hate', Wilding adds that 'hate is a very dangerous feeling to have

around'. Following this, government will find it easier to maintain order in a society based on greater social justice than in a society containing much poverty which has created an alienated underclass. Finally, he argues that governments should do something about poverty because they *can* do something. Government allowed poverty to increase during the 1980s, and although it may not be able to eradicate it from society, it could lessen it. The new Labour government has begun to implement an anti-poverty programme which included some policies inherited from the previous Conservative administration. There are tensions within Labour between traditional socialists who want to create an egalitarian society, and modernisers who accept inequality but want greater equality of opportunity so that people can lift themselves out of poverty and welfare dependency.

Questions

1. 'The poor are always with us.' Can politics and government eliminate poverty?
2. What was the possible impact of a '30/30/40' society on voting behaviour? Why has poverty failed to become an election issue?
3. Explain how the political left and right differ in their views on the effects of the welfare state.

Assignments

Assignment (1) Labour must stop ducking issue of inequality

Britain has become a shockingly unequal society: the top 10 per cent enjoy an income equal to the whole of the bottom 50 per cent. As a country we have the highest proportion of children living in poverty in Western Europe. The link between poverty and poor health, family breakdown and indifferent life chances is inescapable. Poverty – grinding, unavoidable, debasing – is the daily reality for a growing number of Britons.

Yet, so far at least, this has had little impact on the political debate. The Conservatives are largely indifferent: the poor don't vote and, if they do, don't vote Tory. In their lexicon, poverty is the down-payment a society makes for its success; to attempt any systematic programme of poverty alleviation is by definition self-defeating. It creates dependency, undermines the work ethic, and places an insupportable and unfair tax burden on the better-off. In any case, the notion of a poverty trap is illusory because those in poverty do not stay there long. Those who do are the feckless who refuse to help themselves.

It is telling that, despite its majority, the Labour Party has assumed a similar position. Its manifesto does not talk of redistribution of income, nor of significantly improving the welfare state as a commonly held system of social insurance. Indeed there are pledges on not raising income tax rates and on meeting the Conservatives' tight targets for public spending for the first two years. The only two instruments the government has permitted itself to attack inequality – at least early in its administration – are the minimum wage and the welfare-to-work programme.

The Observer, 3 August 1997

Questions

(i) According to the author, what is the Conservative attitude to the poor?

(ii) To what extent is the author critical of Labour's policies towards combatting poverty?

(iii) Should governments be concerned about poverty in society? Discuss what sort of policies would be most effective in reducing poverty.

Assignment (2) Workfare or welfare?

When he was prime minister John Major toyed with the idea of workfare in a speech he made to the Carlton Club; he said 'I increasingly wonder whether paying unemployment benefit, without offering or requiring any activity in return, serves unemployed people or society well.' Workfare – the idea of forcing the jobless to work for benefits – is not new and has been put into practice in countries such as Sweden and the USA.

In the United States President Clinton had promised 'to end welfare as we know it'. There are 15 million American poor on welfare programmes, with one in five children living in poverty. The mood of the American public supported his policy of reducing massive federal funding of welfare by ensuring that increasingly the poor received 'pay checks instead of welfare checks'. Clinton's welfare bill ended 60 years of block grants to states to fund the Aid to Families with Dependent Children (AFDC) with what his critics saw as a 'work or starve' policy. Single mothers are eligible for AFDC, but under Clinton's measures a family will lose welfare benefits if the head of the family does not find work within two years. In addition, states will not be able to use federal funds to provide welfare to individuals for more than five years over the course of a lifetime.

Labour politicians borrow American terminology when defending their new approach to the welfare state. But Labour's election pledge to provide a 'hand-up rather than a hand-out', reflected by 'welfare-to-work' policies in office, fall short of American-style workfare. Some Labour politicians anticipate that eventually Tony Blair will be thinking along the same lines as Clinton because of the reality of the global environment. He will be faced with a dilemma which workfare could help to solve; because of competition from cheap labour in the Far East, Britain's market economy can no longer provide full employment. But in order to compete with countries which are not burdened by large welfare spending, Britain will have to make deep cuts into the welfare state. Workfare measures would reduce the numbers supported by welfare, undermine the dependency culture, and encourage people to make themselves qualified for vacancies which do occur.

Questions

(i) Identify at least two political leaders who have advocated workfare policies.

(ii) What are the similarities and differences between Democrat and Labour positions on workfare?

(iii) In what ways might workfare policies end the dependency culture?

Further reading

Hutton, J. et al. (eds) (1991) *Dependency to Enterprise* (London: Routledge)is a wide-ranging set of contributions based on an academic conference.

Oppenheim, C. (1990) *Poverty: The Facts* (London: CPAG) provides the detailed statistics of poverty in Britain.

CHAPTER 27

Ethnic minority politics

Black people tend to be portrayed as a 'problem' in British politics – the problems of controlling immigration numbers, and of maintaining law and order in the black populated inner cities, and the problems posed by the disadvantages of black people in areas such as housing, education and employment. How justified is this problem image of Britain's black population? Could the real problem be white racism, explicitly and implicitly present in the mainstream culture, rather than in black shortcomings? And how have politics and the political system worked to resolve or exacerbate the situation? This chapter explores these questions.

Black and British

Britain has experienced considerable demographic change in terms of immigration and emigration. Numerous groups have settled in Britain – Irish, Jewish, Polish, Chinese, among others – whilst British-born people have set up new homes in countries such as Canada, Australia, New Zealand, South Africa and the former Rhodesia. Britain has a long history of immigration and emigration but a new pattern of immigration was established after the Second World War. The British Nationality Act 1948 allowed citizens of the Commonwealth to settle in Britain and this facilitated a new era in which most of those people who made new homes in Britain were black.

New Commonwealth immigrants formed numerous ethnic communities based on common language, religion and race. But, unlike previous immigrants from countries such as Ireland or Poland who could 'blend in' with the way of life, immigrants from Pakistan, India and the West Indies remained visibly distinctive through skin colour. In other words, they were visible as 'strangers' and because of this many British people formed hostile attitudes towards them which, in turn, made it more difficult still for the new black immigrants to adapt to Britain's traditional culture. It was hoped that in the course of time, British-born blacks would not experience the isolation of their immigrant parents but a survey conducted by the Runnymede Trust in 1986 found this was not the case. It was reported that fewer than 5 per cent of black schoolchildren had been invited into a white home and, although over 40 per cent said they had white friends at school, most felt that British society at large did not like them.

The use of 'black' as a shorthand term in both everyday language and the social sciences can be misleading. At the immediate level, it is obvious that 'blacks' are no more black than 'whites' are white. But just as the term 'white' can embrace widely differing cultures, so the term black disguises the diversity that exists amongst people from a relatively small number of countries in the new Commonwealth. Although general distinctions are made between the Afro-Caribbean and Asian communities, far greater diversity exists than is implied by this simple twofold categorisation, with some ethnic communities having surprisingly little in common. In Leicester, for example, one resident in five is a member of what is popularly known as the 'Asian community'. Yet this community is actually made up of numerous groups based on seven main languages further divided into numerous dialects.

BOX 27.1
The Ugandan Asians

In 1972 the leader of Uganda, Idi Amin, began expelling the 50,000 Asians who had settled in his country. He gave them only 90 days notice to leave. Most belongings had to be left behind and many Asians who had built up profitable businesses lost everything.

Conservative Prime Minister Edward Heath, backed by liberal opinion, argued that Britain had a moral duty as well as a legal obligation to admit the majority of fleeing Asian families who held British passports. He was opposed by the right-wing of his party, particularly by Enoch Powell (see p. 477).

Many Ugandan Asian families settled in the East Midlands city of Leicester, where today nearly a quarter of the population is drawn from the ethnic minorities. In addition to setting up many Asian restaurants which are highly visible on the high street, businessmen invested in building up Leicester's then-declining hosiery industry creating around 30,000 jobs.

Some groups have to resort to a second language, such as English, in order to communicate at anything more than the most basic level with other groups. The Asian community is further fragmented by different religions, values, cultural practices and castes, as well as by the political tensions found in the politics of the Indian subcontinent. For our purposes, then, 'black' is a general label or political colour which covers members of all ethnic communities who are located in a broadly similar position in society (Figure 27.1).

Race relations

It is a sad fact that many individuals have negative attitudes towards others purely on the grounds of racial difference. Racial prejudice can be expressed by whites against blacks, blacks against whites or, indeed, between ethnic groups, as in the case of Asian prejudice against West Indians. Clearly, the most politically significant prejudice is that expressed by the white majority against the black minority. On occasions in the past that prejudice could be activated lawfully into racial discrimination for example, with lodging houses displaying 'No Blacks' signs in their front windows. There is little doubt that deliberate acts of racial discrimination still take place in British society which are beyond the remit of law. Sometimes, however, racial discrimination has been unintentionally practised by organisations in the public and private sectors which have operated policies which contain a hidden bias against black people. Many bodies now practise race-monitoring in specific areas as a check against unintentional discrimination.

In the late 1950s Britain experienced its only major race riots – as opposed to gang skirmishes – when whites attacked blacks in Notting Hill and Nottingham. These riots came as an unexpected shock and the government adopted both a tough and tender response. The former represented a response to public anxiety about black immigration to Britain whilst the latter was an attempt to promote racial harmony within Britain.

The Commonwealth Immigrants Act 1962 was the first of a number of Acts which restricted the entry of black first-time immigrants and their families to Britain. A second Commonwealth Immigrants Act was rushed through Parliament in 1968 to tighten up the 1962 Act, which did not apply to East African Asians. The Immigration Act 1971 tightened controls still further, although its restrictions were waived on humanitarian grounds to allow Asians expelled from Uganda to enter Britain freely. A new Nationality Act in 1981 represented even tighter restrictions. All this legislation, passed by both Conservative and Labour governments, has been criticised for being founded on racist principles. The prime goal has been not the restriction of immigrants who have claims to be British, but the restriction of *black* immigrants who have claims to British status.

Illiberal immigration policies towards blacks living outside Britain have been accompanied by liberal policies towards those already resident within Britain. The Race Relations Acts of 1965, 1968 and 1976 outlawed direct and indirect discrimination in widening areas of public life and provision such as housing, employment and education. What is sometimes called the 'race relations industry' was established, with complaints taken to the Race Relations Board, later replaced by the Commission for Racial Equality, with Community Relations Councils operating at local level. The view expressed by many liberal-minded individuals of the time was that the 'race' problem would eventually wither away. It was felt that the children of immigrants would not suffer from the cultural problems and disadvantages of being newcomers and, given time, economic growth would provide benefits to all Britain's citizens. The blacks, at the end of the queue for prosperity, would be served in due course. How far have these early beliefs been justified by subsequent developments and trends?

Racism and discrimination

A recent NOP poll revealed that a majority of the white, Afro-Caribbean and Asian individuals sampled agreed that Britain is a 'fairly' or 'very' **racist** society. Whilst most Britons saw themselves as being 'fair minded', they recognised that a minority of the white population was deeply racist and agreed that many institutions of the state, such as the courts and the police, as well as many employers, discriminate against black people. In what ways can such discrimination be reduced and eventually eliminated so that a 'fair minded' society develops in Britain?

Some on the left have argued that Britain should follow the American practice of 'affirmative action'. They cite Northern Ireland as an example of using positive action in order to penalise employers who discriminate on religious grounds by refusing to employ Catholics. It is argued that in much the same way, positive action could be used on the mainland to combat racial discrimination in the job market. The Commission for Racial Equality supports the idea that employers in the public and private sectors should be obliged by law to monitor the ethnic com-

> **Racism** is the belief held by people of the same culture that they are superior to those of other cultures. Frequently skin colour has been used to denote cultural membership.

position of their various workforces in order to strengthen the working of the 1976 Race Relations Act. The political right tends to dislike affirmative action on the grounds that it lowers the self-esteem of the ethnic minority communities; a minister recently argued against positive action because it had not worked well in the United States, and added 'People dislike it intensely. It doesn't do much for your morale if you think that you have been chosen for a job because you are black rather than because you are good. What people want is fair treatment' (*Independent on Sunday,* 7 July 1991).

These contrasting attitudes towards positive action reflect two distinct philosophies towards equal opportunities in Britain. The minister's viewpoint places the emphasis on equal treatment for all people so that no one is discriminated against. In the example of individuals applying for a job, no person should be discriminated against, with the job being offered to the 'best' candidate. As Dave Russell has stated, this liberal approach 'insists that equal opportunity laws and policies require people to be judged *as individuals* without regard to racial/ethnic group membership but only on his or her own qualities and performance. All individuals should be treated equally in a meritocratic, "colour-blind", non-discriminatory manner.' In other words, fair treatment is seen as the absence of racial discrimination.

In contrast to the liberal approach is what Russell refers to as the 'radical' approach to equal opportunities, which is more concerned with a fair distribution of resources than with fair procedures. The radical approach is more concerned with 'who gets what' in terms of different ethnic groups getting their fair proportional share of society's resources (jobs, houses, education, etc.) As Russell stated:

> This perspective puts the case for racial explicitness, arguing that people should be treated with regard to *group membership,* therefore directly going against the liberal principle of 'blind justice' whereby everyone is treated as an individual . . . It also understands fairness to exist where members of different racial/ethnic groups are distributed in *proportion* to their presence in the wider population and in order to provoke a yardstick by which to measure the success for such a *redistributive* approach, equality *'targets'* or *'quotas'* are often established. This might involve some deliberate

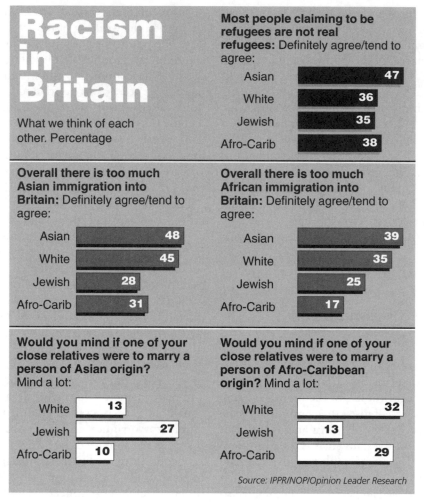

Source: The Guardian, 5 February 1997.

Figure 27.1 Racism in Britain

manipulation of selection procedures and standards in pursuit of proportionality whereby individuals can be selected for a job partly on the basis of group membership rather than because they are the best qualified candidate. (Russell, 1990, p. 11; see Box 26.1)

Legislation concerning equal opportunities and anti-discrimination has embraced both the liberal and radical approaches. How effective has it been? The 1976 Race Relations Act included two important developments. The first was the introduction of the concept of *indirect discrimination*, based on the American model of affirmative action. This made

unlawful actions which had an unintended adverse effect on members of ethnic minority communities even when formally they were being treated the same as everyone else. The second development was the setting up of the Commission for Racial Equality with its wide powers to impose sanctions against unlawful discrimination. It is fair to say that these two measures looked far more promising on paper than they have turned out to be in practice. Removing indirect discrimination has proved to be very difficult, and consequently this part of the 1976 Act has done little in removing racial inequalities from society. The Commission for Racial Equality has been attacked from a number of different direc-

BOX 27.2
Liberal and radical approaches to equal opportunities

	Equal What?	Principles	Approach
Liberal	Equal TREATMENT of individuals from different groups.	People should be treated as individuals WITHOUT regard to group membership.	Regulatory and procedural, e.g. all job applications subject to same rules.
		Fairness – absence of racial discrimination.	Prohibition of discriminatory forms of behaviour, e.g. insistence on minimal height for a job which may disadvantage certain minorities.
		Free competition between individuals. Blind justice.	Concern for processes favouring whoever is the best qualified.
Radical	Equal SHARES of scarce goods (jobs, housing).	People should be treated WITH regard to group membership.	Positive discrimination in terms of making allowances for the disadvantages experienced by some minorities.
		Fairness = proportionality in employment. If 10 per cent of local community is Asian, then 10 per cent of all firms' employees should be Asian.	Targeting particular groups who will benefit – setting quotas.
		Social justice.	Concern for outcomes.

Source: Based on Russell (1990) p. 11.

tions. In practical terms its success rate in combating discrimination has been low. Also right-wing critics have argued that the Commission follows *multicultural policies* which stress the differences between various groups rather than the similarities.

The political response

The most controversial contribution from the Conservative right came in a speech made by Enoch Powell in 1968 when he called for a halt to black immigration and for moves to repatriate blacks already settled in Britain. In a widely publicised section of his speech he stated: 'As I look ahead I am filled with foreboding. Like the Roman I seem to see the River Tiber foaming with much blood.' He was immediately sacked from his post in the Shadow Cabinet by the Tory leader, Edward Heath. Conservative nationalism, such as that expressed by Powell, stressed the continuity of Britain's institutions and culture. The nation is seen as being founded on the race, so, by definition, black newcomers to Britain who are excluded from its history cannot be included in its present or future. There is an unwillingness to accept Britain as a multiracial society since that is seen as breaking with the past and Britain's strengths lie in its continuity with the past. Only once in public did Margaret Thatcher appeared to be influenced by this sort of nationalism when in 1978 as new Conservative leader she told a radio audience that she understood fears that the British character might be 'swamped' by people of a different culture. As Prime Minister, Thatcher distanced herself from those on the Tory right who supported repatriation and called for the dismantling of the 'race relations industry'.

A well-publicised deplorable incident, condemned by senior Tories, concerned the selection of a black candidate, John Taylor, to fight the Cheltenham seat in the 1992 General Election. Taylor was the subject of outright racial abuse from some local Tories as well as the thinly coded message that he was unacceptable in Cheltenham because 'he was not a local man'. However, in the run-up to the 1997 general election the Conservative leader, John Major, made a high profile tour of India in what some commentators saw as a bid to win over the ethnic vote in Britain.

Labour's political image is one of being 'soft' on immigration but this does not conform to Labour's tough policy when in government. For example, Labour severely restricted new Commonwealth immigrants in the 1968 Act, and its alternative to the Conservative Nationality Act 1981, whilst sounding more liberal, would have worked in much the same way.

Labour in the 1980s and 1990s has been posed the politically interesting problem of how to accommodate increasing demands for black influence within the party. Whilst recent general elections have revealed that Labour has been losing working-class support, the black vote has remained largely loyal. A Labour subcommittee investigated the issue of black participation and recommended the establishment of black sections, but the NEC and conference rejected this proposal. The leadership argued that black sections were unnecessary because black candidates had been selected as parliamentary candidates and returned to Westminster. Also, it was argued that having black sections was unacceptable because it would segregate people according to their racial origin, an action which had more in common with apartheid than with socialism. Members from the unofficial black sections that already existed at constituency level argued that the establishment of black sections was vital because they provided a way in which the ethnic minority communities could participate in the Labour Party.

The debate concerning black sections subsided somewhat as the overall number of parliamentary representatives drawn from the ethnic minority communities increased. Although the total number remained relatively small, four MPs from ethnic minorities were elected in 1992 and seven in 1997. The latter included Britain's first Muslim MP, Mohammed Sarwar, but who was unfortunately to become involved in allegations of sleaze.

'Race' politics

The rise of the far right in Europe – in France and Germany in particular – has been accompanied by displays of considerable violence towards foreigners and refugees. Naturally there were fears in Britain of a fascist revival with a new wave of racist hostility being directed towards the ethnic minorities. Although fascist parties have done poorly in general elections since the war, there have been occasions when support soared in local elections.

The new British National Party won 27 per cent of the vote in Southall in 1963 and in 1976 the combined vote of the National Party and the National Front reached the 44.5 per cent level in Deptford. In September 1993 the British National Party (BNP) candidate won a local government by-election victory in Millwall. Although parties such as the National Front published a manifesto which included policies on a variety of issues, race relations and immigration were the issues they campaigned on. As Steve Hunt argued,

> The NF [National Front] also maintained that it represented the 'majority view' on the issues of black immigration and race relations. To this end the party took full advantage of Enoch Powell's infamous 'River of Blood Speech' in 1968 in which he forewarned that future immigration would result in widespread racial conflict. The NF's opposition to immigration was clearly racist – highlighting a negative prejudice against blacks on the basis of perceived racial and cultural differences. But the party were prepared to go further and in doing so displayed a clear Nazi ideological orientation. The influx of 'non-whites' was regarded as a threat to the 'authentic British community' which was designated 'superior' by a pseudo-scientific logic. (Hunt, 1992a, p. 24)

Far-right-wing and fascist groups which campaigned on the 'race' issue, then, have failed to make significant electoral impact except in a limited number of areas where 'race' was at the top of the local agenda. There is a fear that because these groups have failed in the area of conventional politics, they are now becoming increasingly involved in organising racial violence of one type or another. Why did their 'race' manifestos generally fail to win support? There is no simple answer to this question but the following points are important in helping to explain the political failure of British fascism.

Firstly, whilst it can be recognised that there is much racism and discrimination at large in British society, there are limits to how far these attitudes and behaviours extend. In other words, whilst there may be many in Britain who are not 'fair minded' regarding race relations, they are not the race bigots of the type which joins fascist organisations. Secondly, the far right remains weak because of constant internal disputes and factionalism. Thirdly, the first-past-the-post electoral system discriminates against minority and fringe parties. Finally, the rise in influence of the radical Right inside the Conservative Party, with its anti-multi-cultural platform, weaned some support away from the periphery of British politics into the fringe of the Conservative Party. Dr Roger Eatwell has put this point more strongly:

> The BNP and NF are now desperately short of people who are experienced local campaigners so in electoral terms they are non-starters. But when one looks at the NF you have to look at other things that indicate they are active. Under Thatcher, there was no political space for the NF and she hijacked a lot of their policies. In 1979, there was a clear play for the NF vote by adopting policies on law and order and strict immigration controls. (*Guardian,* 27 April 1991)

Other groups have formed to promote good race relations and to defend the position of the ethnic minorities in Britain. One of the most notable was the Anti-Nazi League (ANL), relaunched in 1992 in response to the rise in fascism in continental Europe. Originally the ANL was organised to mobilise young people to 'rock against racism' during a time when the National Front had done better than expected in a few local elections. The talented rock guitarist, Eric Clapton, made a long rambling speech

in which he seemed to encourage support for Enoch Powell on the race issue. The ANL was launched to counter any influence that Clapton and any other like-minded musicians might have with young people, and represented a political alliance of various groupings in which the Socialist Workers Party (SWP) played the leading role. A rival anti-racist group, the Anti-Racist Alliance (ARA), co-chaired by Labour MP Ken Livingstone, was set up to involve greater representation from the black community as well as to exclude the risk of manipulation by the SWP. Ironically, then, disputes within the anti-racist left have resulted in the factionalism typical of the racist far right.

During the last 150 years different ethnic groups have been the target of racial intolerance; first the Irish, then Jews and more recently, black and Asian communities. However, a recent report from the Runnymede Trust suggests that racist attitudes are increasingly directed at Muslims. There is a long history of bloody religious conflict between Christians and Muslims that stretches back to the crusades, but contemporary tension is more cultural and political in nature between the values of liberal democracy and the values of Islam. Islamophobia in Britain and other western countries has been fed regularly by 'bad news' stories such as the fatwa against Salman Rushdie, the mass slaughter of children and women by Islamic fundamentalists in Algeria, and the trial for murder of two British nurses in Saudi Arabia. In the latter case, the trial was grotesque and unfair, but tabloid news coverage tended to depict everything Islam as cruel and barbaric. Whilst it is legitimate for newspapers to criticise unfair aspects of Islamic practice, it is misleading to portray Islam as monolithic and fundamentalist perhaps leaving the impression that Britain's Muslims are no different from those abroad who have abused human rights.

The political tensions within Britain's Muslim community surfaced during the late Dr Kalim Siddiqui's campaign to establish the Muslim Institute. He described this as a Muslim parliament to represent a 'non-territorial Islamic state' in Britain. Essentially the non-elected parliament became a forum in which Muslim views could be expressed and get reported to a wider public. Proponents of the parliament argued that Muslim views, particularly on race issues, were not well represented by the national parliamentary parties nor reflected in national political debate. Therefore a separate Muslim organisation was needed to put forward in a robust way the distinctive Muslim viewpoint on issues, otherwise Muslims would be ignored. It can be argued that all Siddiqui was arguing for was recognition that Britain was a pluralist society, and that attempts to portray him as a militant were unfounded. Certainly the Muslim parliament was controversial, and raised fears in other sections of the Muslim community that fascist groups would make political capital from the publicity it received. Dr Hesham el-Esawy, President of the Islamic Society for the Promotion of Religious Tolerance, voiced this anxiety when he opposed the Muslim parliament on the grounds that it 'will give ammunition to people who hate Islam'.

Summary

- Many white British people have found it hard to accommodate to the reality that new black ethnic communities now exist in Britain. Governments have found it necessary to pass legislation outlawing racial discrimination internally whilst operating racially biased immigration policies towards people external to the United Kingdom.
- There is disagreement amongst social researchers about both the scope and nature of such disadvantages. There is, however, a commonly accepted stereotype existing amongst the population at large which associates ethnicity with criminality. Unfortunately, the way in which the tabloid press sometimes presents news reinforces this misleading impression.
- Although there are now eleven black MPs, the role of the political parties is not particularly successful in terms of channelling and responding to black aspirations. Generally speaking, racist political parties in Britain have been unsuccessful. This is in contrast to the French National Front which, campaigning on a platform of 'immigrants out', won over 50 per cent of the vote in elections in Provence in 1997.

Questions

1. In what ways are some ethnic minorities disadvantaged in Britain?
2. Consider the case for and against major political parties having constitutions which guarantee black representation on policy-making committees.
3. To what extent is the failure of fascist groups to make a political impact proof that Britain is a fair and tolerant society?

Assignments

Assignment (1) Ethnic minority action compared: the Million Man March

The Nation of Islam, founded in 1930s America, is led today by Louis Farrakhan. The controversial black leader, Malcolm X, was expelled from the Nation of Islam before he was killed in 1964. Hoping to repeat the impact of Martin Luther King's 'I have a dream' rally, the Nation of Islam organised a Million Man March in Washington, but women and sympathetic whites were not invited to participate. Over 200 black organisations supported the March but in the event the main civil rights organisation, the National Association for the Advancement of Colored People, stayed away.

Louis Farrakhan called the March a 'day of atonement' and asked blacks who did not march to stay at home from work, avoid shopping, and to register to vote as independents. He hoped that this voter registration drive would drum up a million new black voters. His message was one of racial pride and self-respect, and the March was organised to display black men's moral and political strength. Louis Farrakhan argues that the typical image of American black men is one of 'thieves, criminals and savages', and that the March could help change this by giving black men a vision of success. The Nation of Islam holds a conservative philosophy; it is authoritarian and patriarchal, believing in family values, with women playing domestic roles; it is opposed to gay/lesbian rights; it is anti-black feminists and anti-abortion; it is pro-private enterprise. The Nation of

Islam believes that black men can succeed only through their own efforts.

Many feminists oppose the Nation of Islam because of its sexist politics, and many whites see Louis Farrakhan and the Nation of Islam as expressions of racist politics. Indeed, Farrakhan caused an outcry when he described the Jewish community as 'bloodsuckers'. The Nation of Islam represents separatist black nationalism and a rejection of King's integrationist politics and the multiracial politics of Jesse Jackson's Rainbow Coalition. Dr Manning Marable, the black academic, argues that Farrakhan has emerged because of the absence of other moderate civil rights leaders. Those that do exist, such as Jesse Jackson, have failed to communicate with young urban males. In the absence of other leaders to represent them, Farrakhan's racial militancy has attracted them. It is felt that if Farrakhan is to be taken seriously, he will have to mellow his militant image and become moderate.

Questions

(i) Outline similarities and differences between the Muslim Institute in Britain (see p. 480) and the Nation of Islam.
(ii) Identify possible political leaders of Britain's ethnic minorities.
(iii) Discuss the differences in political significance of the Notting Hill Carnival in London and the Million Man March in Washington.

Assignment (2) Equal opportunities in the civil service

The report is the third under the Civil Service Programme for Action to Achieve Equality of Opportunity for People of Ethnic Minority Origin, which was launched in 1990. The Programme was adopted and implemented in the belief that an effective equal opportunities policy is essential in terms of social justice and the benefits to be gained for organisational effectiveness as well as in terms of legal obligations. It was launched against a background of very low ethnic minority representation within all management grades of the Civil Service and, in par-

ticular, within the administrative stream of management grades. Ethnic minority staff were employed in the Civil Service in proportion to their representation in the economically active population in Great Britain overall but were concentrated in the most junior grades.

Service-wide representative of ethnic minority respondents as a percentage of total respondents at each grade level in 1989, 1992 and 1993

Grade level	1989 (%)	1992 (%)	1993 (%)	1993 (Number)
Administrative				
Class 1–2	–	–	–	–
3	–	0.2	0.2	1
4	0.7	0.0	0.0	0
5	1.8	1.8	2.2	55
6	2.2	2.2	2.6	114
7	1.2	1.8	2.0	318
Senior Executive Officer	1.2	1.7	1.8	383
Higher Executive Officer	1.7	2.1	2.4	1,530
Executive Officer	2.9	3.6	3.9	4,105
Administrative Officer	5.6	7.0	7.1	10,468
Administrative Assistant	6.5	7.3	7.4	5,576
Others	1.2	1.1	6.4	7
Total, G7 and above	1.5	1.8	2.1	488
Total, EO and above	2.3	2.8	3.0	6,506
Total, AO and AA	5.9	7.1	7.2	16,044
TOTAL	4.2	5.0	5.2	22,557

Questions

(i) Comment on the pattern of ethnic minority employment in the Civil Service. How has this pattern changed during recent years?
(ii) Why might the Civil Service and other public sector bodies believe that it is important to monitor equal opportunities?
(iii) What other minority groups in society have argued that they too have been discriminated

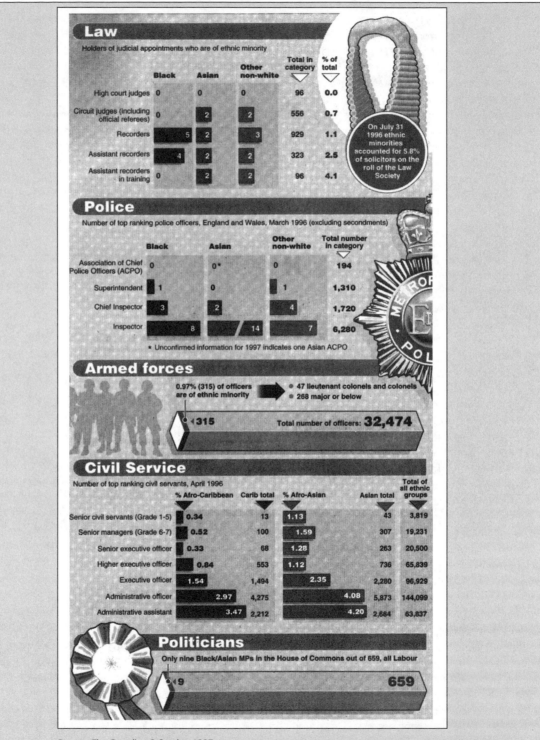

Source: The *Guardian*, 2 October 1997.

Figure 27.2 Equal opportunities in the public sector

against by employers? Should equal opportunities monitoring involve all such groups?

(iv) What percentage of officers in the armed forces are drawn from the ethnic minorities?

(v) Describe the patterns of ethnic minority presence in the police force and legal profession. Should government pursue 'affirmative action' policies to ensure a 'fair' level of employment at senior levels?

(vi) To what extent is the civil service a success in terms of ethnic minority employment?

Further reading

Coxall, B. (1992) 'The Social Context of British Politics: Class, Gender and Race in the Two Major Parties, 1970–1990', in B. Jones and L. Robins (eds), *Two Decades in British Politics* (Manchester University Press) is a useful account of recent trends. Layton-Henry, Z. (1992) *Immigration and 'Race' Politics in Post-War Britain* (Oxford: Blackwell) is a comprehensive account of 'race' in British politics. Lupton. C. and Russell, D. (1990) 'Equal Opportunities in a Cold Climate', in S. Savage and L. Robins (eds), *Public Policy Under Thatcher* (London: Macmillan) examines technical aspects of implementing EO policies. McIlroy, J. (1989) 'The Politics of Racism' in B. Jones (ed.), *Political Issues in Britain Today* (Manchester University Press) is a useful overview of the area.

CHAPTER **28** | # Gender and sexuality

In the past, an understanding of women's role in political life was gained from the research of male political scientists. Recently female political scientists have challenged the familiar portrayal of women and successfully modified the way in which women are seen to act politically. This chapter examines the new portrayal of 'political woman', explores the feminist perspective and considers the women's movement as a force for change in society. We shall see that women do occupy many political roles but despite claims of 'girl power' and the 'feminisation of society' the pattern remains uneven. The chapter concludes by considering the politics of sexuality in terms of gay and lesbian rights.

The women's movement

All contemporary societies are to varying degrees male-dominated. In Britain, as in other Western countries, prestige is attached to 'men's work', be it the glamour of a professional career or the *machismo* of manual labour, whilst women's place of work is seen as in the home. The difference is reflected in rewards; men's work earns a salary or wage whilst women's domestic labour is unpaid. When women enter paid employment, their average incomes are lower than men's. Part-time, unskilled and low-paid jobs are filled overwhelmingly by women. Despite the fact that women account for approximately half of Britain's total labour force, women receive far less

promotion and career advancement than men. Also, the very nature of women's jobs makes them most vulnerable to automation, and it is women's jobs that are most likely to be lost first as a direct result of the introduction of new technologies.

The women's movement is not a formal political organisation in the sense that it has a national, regional and local structure which recruits members who, in turn, elect officials. It is informally organised and highly factionalised. The women's movement is made up of a network of small localised groups, some of which work within established organisations such as trade unions or political parties. At the beginning of the century, the first wave of the movement exhibited 'moderate' and 'radical' wings and these survive today. The struggle to obtain the vote was waged by the 'respectable' suffragists and the 'militant' suffragettes. The Housewives' League, led by Irene Lovelock, was an example of a 'moderate' postwar protest against 'women's lot', which was made up of rationing, queueing and austerity.

The contemporary women's movement has been studied by Vicky Randall and in *Women and Politics* (1987) she has identified at least three major strands or factions:

1. *Radical feminists* are the most militant within the women's movement and include extremists such as the political lesbians. Generally speaking, radical feminists emphasise the extent to which women are physically oppressed and dominated by men. They point to wife-battering, rape and pornography as manifestations of male oppression.
2. *Marxist feminists* also have a conflict view of society, but believe that the struggle of the working class and the struggle of women are not

484

BOX 28.1
Women's 'invisible' political activity

It has been argued that women make a contribution to political life through informal, less conventional means and, furthermore, that this contribution goes largely unrecorded by political scientists and journalists. For example, women have campaigned on numerous moral issues which have failed to attract sustained media attention. In the past, women were highly influential in the Temperance movement; during the 1970s, the 'Mothers of Peace' movement lit a brief glimmer of hope in Northern Ireland, and in the 1980s women played a large role in the Peace Movement.

What all these campaigns have in common is a loosely structured organisation. Their activities are only 'newsworthy' when dramatic newsreel can be filmed; otherwise, their activities go unnoticed. Frequently, women organise 'protest politics' at local or community level regarding the provision of facilities, and this too tends to be ignored by the media. Women are prominent in tenants' groups, childcare campaigns, health campaigns, and anti-poverty lobbies. Women combine self-help projects – such as meeting the needs of the single-parent family – with pressure-group activity.

Furthermore, some women's groups which are often defined as apolitical in nature do, in fact, attempt to influence government policies. Women's Institutes, Townswomen's Guilds, the Mothers' Union and the Women's Royal Voluntary Service (WRVS) have an estimated membership of 3 million. They have participated in campaigns and lobbying on issues such as the payment of Child Benefit, taxation policy, local planning decisions, closure of local schools and the provision of public transport in rural areas.

necessarily one and the same. The class struggle is recognised as the more significant of the two, but it is also believed that female inequality will still exist after the overthrow of the capitalist system and that a separate struggle will still lie ahead for female emancipation. Marxist feminists do not shun collaboration with men, as does the radical element, and they work with left-wing and trade union organisations in order to improve the lot of women. The second-wave radical and Marxist feminists are often lumped together by the mass media and described as 'Women's Lib'.

3. *Reformist feminists*, the heirs of the constitutionally minded suffragists, form the third strand. It is probably true to say that most people, male and female, would accept the arguments of reformist feminists as constituting the 'reasonable face of feminism'. Reformists argue that generally speaking women suffer from a series of handicaps and disadvantages in society, and that all of these can be eliminated over time by equal rights legislation.

Reformist feminists argue that much of the battle against female inequality has been won. The Equal Pay Act 1970 stipulated equal pay for equal work and the Sex Discrimination Act 1975 ended discrimination against women in employment, education, housing, as well as in other service areas. The Act also established the *Equal Opportunities Commission*, a body to investigate infringements of the Equal Pay and Sex Discrimination Acts. Residual inequalities – in areas such as retirement and taxation – are being eliminated by successive legislation.

The women's movement has also made legislative advances in the area of abortion reform. The abortion issue is of great importance to feminists since it symbolises a woman's reproductive self-determination. As a result, some feminists have taken an extremely hard line on abortion and have been accused of displaying a fascist disregard for human life. On the other hand, many women, including Roman Catholics, put the 'right to life' above 'the woman's right to choose'.

The women's movement is not without its critics. Some of them point out that, despite feminist claims that sex is the fundamental division in society and causes inequalities above and beyond those caused by social class or race, the women's movement itself *is* a very middle-class political phenomenon. It has failed to appeal to or to mobilise those women who suffer greatest social disadvantage, namely those found in the working class. It is argued that this proves that social class is a greater cause of inequality in society than is sex. In addition, critics contend that the women's movement has failed to win the support of all middle-class women.

Some critics of the women's movement argue that feminists undervalue the traditional role of women in society and underestimate the political influence already wielded by women. For example, it is argued that feminists neither recognise the responsibilities involved in child-rearing nor do they understand the extent to which mothers shape the personalities and views of their children be they boys or girls.

The politics of feminism

Some feminists now argue that the 'women's lib' thinking of the 1960s was flawed. Basically, what feminists then demanded was that women should achieve equality through being treated in exactly the same ways as men were treated. In other words, some feminists who once argued that men and women should be treated equally now believe that this was a political mistake.

The main reason for that change of mind has been the experience of areas where men and women have been treated equally; for it has inevitably been on male terms. For example, when women entered the world of business to pursue careers as executives, success generally depended on them acting like men. Feminists are now arguing that women are not like men; they have different needs, behave in different ways, and prefer to work in different environments. The early feminist goal of getting women treated in an equal way to men ignores all these differences. Some feel that the feminists of the 1960s fought hard but for the wrong things. They should have fought for the recognition of 'gender differences' as well as demanding 'gender equality'.

The 'feminisation' of poverty

In 1952 Ferdynand Zweig, a sociologist, wrote a study titled *The British Worker* which was entirely about men and, similarly, *The Affluent Worker*, pub-

> **Feminism** is a political ideology which explains women's role in the family, the workplace and wider society in terms of power held by men.

BOX 28.2
Affirmative action for women in the public sector?

In what might prove to be a landmark ruling for women's employment rights, the European Court of Justice dismissed a German male teacher's case that he lost promotion because of his gender. The Court ruled, in November 1997, in favour of affirmative action for women where male and female candidates were equally qualified. Lissy Groener, of the European Parliament's women's rights committee, welcomed the ruling whilst a German minister for sexual equality declared the judgement as 'an historic day for women in Europe'.

---

lished in 1968 by Goldthorpe and his colleagues, was focused on men and their world at work. The male bias reflected the reality of the time, with men dominating the work force. By the late 1990s a revolution had taken place in the jobs market with more women at work than men. The recessions of the 1980s and 1990s saw the permanent loss of many full-time, well-paid men's jobs. The demands of a more 'flexible' labour market favoured the employment of women over men. Furthermore, because of the large number of women available for work the laws of supply and demand ensure that wage levels for both women and men are kept low.

Whilst men cannot command the relatively high wages of the past when they dominated the labour market, the jobs frequently filled by women are part-time, casual, repetitive, boring, low-paid and insecure. In this sense, many women are not getting a 'good deal' from being at work. In fact the labour market has led to much exploitation of women and resulted in what is referred to as the 'feminisation' of poverty. Many women now have to find employment at a time when market forces have reduced the economic power of women (see cartoon on p. 487). In this sense the political campaign for women's right to work has not emancipated all women as anticipated, but resulted in many women having no more control over their lives than before.

In both the United States and Britain, women, particularly working-class and black, have been the implicit target of 'family values' crusades. Resulting from complex social factors, including the reduced ability of men to provide for families financially, new family structures such as single-parenting have

Source: The *Guardian*, 11 November 1997.

Women in political office

It has been argued by political scientists that if women had voted Labour in the same proportion as men, Labour would have been in government continuously from 1945 to 1979. In the 1992 general election if women had voted in the same pattern as men, the result would have been a hung parliament rather than an outright Conservative victory. The 'gender gap' in voting behaviour is examined in Chapter 9 but it is important to note here that support of the 'women's vote' was seen by the principal political parties as the key part of the electorate which would decide the 1997 general election.

The 1997 general election resulted in a record 120 women entering the Commons. Of these, 101 sat on the Labour benches (compared with 37 in 1992) which meant that around a quarter of the PLP were now women (Figure 28.1). The mass entry of women to parliament resulted mainly from Labour's use of all-women shortlists which, ironically, was declared unlawful in 1996 because it was in breach of the Sex Discrimination Act. The first Labour Cabinet of 22 ministers contained five women, which compared only marginally unfavourably with the five women in Lionel Jospin's 15-member cabinet following the socialist advance in the 1997 French general election. As important as the number of women promoted to senior positions in both Britain and France is the subject of their departmental responsibilities. In neither country were these restricted to 'women's issues' such as welfare, where Harriet Harman is in fact Secretary of State, but included briefs such as overseas responsibilities (UK), Northern Ireland (UK), trade and economy (UK and France) and the environment (France).

It remains to be seen whether or not the increased number of women in the party of government will result in a less confrontational, more partnership-minded style of politics. However, the content of Labour's policies are likely to reflect women's concerns more than in the past. The Social Security Secretary has set up machinery inside government, an 'equality task force', which will promote, coordinate and monitor policies across Whitehall in order to influence the elimination of any unintended bias against women as well as the promotion of women's interests.

become more common. It has been estimated that by the end of the century 70 per cent of working-class births and 15 per cent of middle-class births will be outside of traditional marriage. This 'breakdown' of the two-parent family has been linked to rising crime-rates, educational underachievement and unacceptably high welfare support needs by radicals from the New Right. John Major's 'Back to Basics' campaign on policy issues concerning the economy, education and law and order was converted by the Conservative radical right into a moral crusade against single-parent families.

Figure 28.1 Blair's women MPs

Lesbian and gay rights

Until 1967 homosexuality between consenting men was illegal. Since then there has been a near revolution in attitudes towards sexuality with the social climate of the late 1990s being one in which many people with gay or lesbian preferences feel secure enough to 'come out'. Television has done much to promote changing attitudes, with gay people given positive rather than 'pansy' characters in soap operas and drama. An increasing number of MPs have 'come out', and other institutions, such as the Church of England and armed forces, are redefining their traditional attitudes. For example, the Archbishop of Canterbury has argued that whilst God loves homosexuals, homosexuality remains a sin. Other bishops have argued a more liberal position and reconciled homosexuality with their religious beliefs.

The lesbian and gay lobby, Stonewall, has traditionally looked to the Labour Party in order to promote their political rights. Sometimes they have been disappointed as when, in opposition, Labour supported the right of the armed forces not to enlist gay recruits. An ICM opinion poll (*Guardian*, 14 December 1995) found that Labour was not necessarily the natural ally of the gay community. Surprisingly, the poll found that Conservative supporters were often more tolerant of gay relationships than Labour supporters; that women were more tolerant than men; and that the skilled working class was often more tolerant than the middle classes.

Unlike other minorities, gays and lesbians feel that they are the only groups whose rights are outlawed. It is argued that Section 28 of the Local Government Act (1988) prevents schools and local authorities 'intentionally promoting homosexuality'. However, an interesting case which might result in promoting gay and lesbian rights has been considered by the European Court of Justice. The issue at the heart of the case was whether or not an employer (South West Trains) could discriminate on grounds of sexuality. The husbands, wives and opposite-sex partners of employees enjoyed free travel perks and pension entitlements. These perks were not available to same-sex partners. The preliminary opinion of the court was that by denying perks to same-sex partners South West Trains were breaking equal pay legislation. However, in the event, the judgement was in favour of South West Trains. This dismayed the lesbian and gay communities since it was felt that they could be discriminated against legally.

Summary

- The social, economic and political roles of women have changed a great deal during recent decades. The 1997 general election was a watershed in terms of returning women MPs to the Commons. However, political gains made by women risk being eroded by market forces which, having destroyed many traditional men's jobs, consign women to low-paid, insecure and boring employment.
- The 1990s have also seen greater gay and lesbian political activity, which has resulted in the acceptance of gay rights by an increasing number of both the political elite and general public.

Questions

1. 'Where power is, woman is not.' Is this an accurate reflection of women's role in British politics?
2. Comment upon the successes and failures of the women's movement.
3. 'Women approach politics in ways which differ from men.' Assess the validity of this statement.
4. 'Women's rights and gay rights are simply human rights.' How valid is this view?

Assignments

Assignment (1) The 300 Group

THE 300 GROUP is an all-party campaign for more women into Parliament, European Parliament, Local Government and Public Life.
We are a campaigning organisation which:

- works towards equal representation of women in Parliament
- encourages women to seek and hold public office
- encourages women to participate in decision making processes at all levels.

Since 1980, the Group has helped countless women achieve their political ambitions.
We have seen:

- the first woman Prime Minister
- the first woman Speaker
- the number of women increasing at the '87 and '92 elections, but still to less than 10%
- 26% of public appointments going to women

Whether you have ambitions yourself, or just want to see more women elected, join us today.

Questions

(i) Summarise the aims of the 300 Group in one sentence.
(ii) Discuss how members of the 300 Group might have reacted to the election of 120 women MPs in the 1997 general election.
(iii) What factors might account for the under-representation of women in political life?
(iv) Discuss what distinctive qualities women might

bring to the conduct of politics at national and local levels.

Assignment (2) Ben Bradshaw tells his gay Labour colleagues that at last they can come out and reveal themselves, thanks to a revolution in British Politics.
The voters of Exeter did not elect me because of, or despite, my being gay but because I was the Labour Party candidate. Being gay did not matter. It was not raised by anyone during the General Election campaign except my Conservative and Lib-Dem opponents. They both received record swings against them. It was as supremely irrelevant to the electorate as being left-handed or having red hair.

Nobody can ever again say that being gay is a bar to success in public life. It still is, of course, an obstacle in practical terms for many. Most minorities suffer social discrimination, but gays and lesbians are the only adults in Britain discriminated against in law.

We have no protection at the workplace. The loved ones with whom we share our lives have no rights of inheritance, no rights to our pensions, life insurance pay-outs and tenancies. There is a hypocritical ban on gays and lesbians fighting for their country when thousands died in both world wars, and many continue to serve in the armed forces – in the closet – with distinction.

State-sanctioned injustice against gay and lesbian people goes deep. This is wicked (in the pre-eighties meaning of the word) and right-minded people will not tire until such discrimination is eradicated. But

we must ask ourselves if the mindset and tactics of the past are still appropriate in Blair's Britain.
(*Guardian*, 30 September 1997)

Questions
(i)   Did Ben Bradshaw's sexuality become an election issue in Exeter?
(ii) In what ways does Bradshaw argue that gays are discriminated against in Britain?
(iii) Bradshaw argues that discrimination against gays serving in the armed forces is hypocritical. What arguments might be made on retaining the ban on gays serving in the armed services? Evaluate such arguments.
(iv) Explain why the social climate of the 1990s is more tolerant than that of the liberal 1960s. To what extent have the actions of successful government contributed to changing attitudes?

Further reading

Hunt, K. (1997) 'Women and Politics', in B. Jones (ed.) *Political Issues in Britain Today* (Manchester: Manchester University Press): a useful overview. Maclean, M. and D. Groves (eds) (1991) *Women's Issues in Social Policy* (London: Routledge): a feminist perspective on a wide range of issues. Oakley, A. (1972) *Sex, Gender and Society* (Hounslow: Temple Smith): an influential text. Randall, V. (1987) *Women and Politics*, 2nd edn (London: Macmillan): a concise analysis of feminism.

Politics and the environment

What is meant by the term 'green politics'? How is it possible for the environment to have emerged as an important issue with the public, yet for the Green Party to have failed to win a single parliamentary seat? The major political parties now claim to have policies for the environment; how valid is this claim? The chapter concludes with an assessment of the EU's impact on Britain's environmental policy-making.

The environment debate

In his book *The Closing Circle*, Barry Commoner spelt out the 'laws of ecology': everything is connected to everything else; everything must go somewhere; Nature knows best; and, finally, there is no such thing as a free lunch. We tend to see the simple acts which fill our everyday lives as inconsequential, even trivial, without realising how the laws of ecology operate and draw them together with what can be awesome impact. A simple example of changing the battery of a transistor radio makes the point. The old battery is thrown into the dustbin, is collected along with other domestic rubbish and taken to the council incinerator. 'But,' asked Professor Commoner, 'where does it really go?' The battery contains a heavy metal element, mercury, which cannot be destroyed but can only be combined with other elements. As the battery is heated in the incinerator it

produces mercury vapour which is emitted by the incinerator stack, and mercury vapour is toxic. Mercury vapour is carried by the wind, eventually brought down to earth in rain or snow. Entering a mountain lake, let us say, the mercury condenses and sinks to the bottom. Here it is acted on by bacteria which convert it to methyl mercury. This is soluble and taken up by fish; since it is not metabolised, the mercury accumulates in the organs and flesh of the fish. The fish is caught and eaten by a man and the mercury becomes deposited in his organs. (Commoner, 1971, pp. 33–46)

The interconnection of seemingly unrelated yet commonplace acts – changing a battery and eating a fish; the fact that the mercury did not disappear but simply moved from one place to another; that man-made changes were detrimental to the environment; and that the benefits of a battery-operated radio are gained at the cost of pollution and possible ill-health – together illustrate the working of ecological laws. These laws are working across such a wide range of behaviours with such adverse effects that some scientists talk of there being an 'ecological crisis'. They believe that great damage has already been done to the thin skin of earth, water and air that clothes 'Planet Earth' with yet greater damage in store. The air is polluted by carbon dioxide resulting from the burning of coal and oil, and this is producing the 'greenhouse effect' as the atmosphere slowly heats up because excessive carbon dioxide absorbs heat that previously would have radiated away. Some believe that this will result in climatic changes which will melt the polar ice-caps and transform the world's most fertile areas into deserts. Burning coal and oil also produces large quantities of sulphur dioxide in the atmosphere resulting in acid rain which kills forests and water life. Nitrogen fertilisers used in increasing quantities by farmers have now been washed from the land and have found their way into drinking water causing a major health hazard for young children. Nuclear testing has put radioactive substances into the bones of children for the first time in human history. Exposure to another heavy metal – lead – put into the atmosphere by car exhausts has resulted in the impaired mental development of many urban children. Cancers have been caused through exposure to asbestos. The thinning in the ozone layer which surrounds the Earth has concerned the scientific community. This layer of gas acts as a vital filter which protects animals and plants from the sun's ultraviolet rays and it has almost disappeared altogether over Antarctica. This list of potential disasters seems endless, so why is global society not in a state of panic?

Environmentalists argue that many of the major ecological threats are recent, and their effects have not yet been fully understood or felt. They sometimes use the analogy of a pond which is gradually being covered by a weed. The area covered by the weed doubles each day, so that by the twelfth day half the pond is covered. Suddenly, on the thirteenth day, the pond will be totally covered by weed. Environmentalists see a crisis creeping up on mankind and taking governments by surprise in a similar way. How has the political system responded to the relatively new environmental lobby and with what results?

The political agenda and the political process

Much of the postwar consensus was built on the assumption common to both Labour and Conservative that it would be economic growth which would provide the extra resources needed to provide an expanding welfare state. Economic growth would improve the lives of the less well-off in society without having to tax and redistribute wealth from the better-off. The major parties competed with each other principally in terms of which would be the most competent in managing the economy and maximising its growth. Many commentators look back at the period from the mid-1950s onwards as the 'age of affluence', with newspapers capturing the feeling of the times when they reported Conservative Prime Minister Harold Macmillan as having told an election rally, 'You've never had it so good'.

It was at the very time Macmillan's words were being spoken that the modern environmental debate began, in a modest, undramatic way, with the publication of Rachel Carson's book *Silent Spring* in 1962. However, it was not until the 1970s that the 'first wave' of environmental concern challenged the assumptions which underlay the consensus about economic growth providing a politically painless way of meeting the rising expectations of the electorate. A report by the Massachusetts Institute of Technology for the Club of Rome, *The Limits to Growth,* examined patterns of growth for various elements, including industrialism and the consumption of non-renewable natural resources. The investigation concluded that (like the surface of the pond discussed earlier) within a short time-period a situation of great abundance can turn into one of scarcity.

The 'second wave' of environmental concern emerged during the 1980s as a response to a number of issues including Britain's greater dependence on military and civil nuclear power (the latter being a response to the energy crisis) with the risk of accidents demonstrated by the near-miss at Three Mile Island and the Chernobyl disaster; pollution and acid rain damage; the depletion of the ozone layer through CFC (chlorofluorocarbons) damage and the risks of global warming through increased carbon dioxide in the atmosphere.

The first and second wave of environmental concern differed in one important way. As McCulloch has argued, the debate over the environment was transformed in two respects between the 1970s and 1980s: 'First, a broadening of the way in which the concept of "the environment" has been used, and second, a tendency for the environment to become rather less an issue and rather more the basis for an ideology' (McCulloch, 1988, p. 15). However, in another way, the first and second wave of environmentalism shared a similar political fate.

BOX 29.1
Political concern about the environment: the five-stage cycle

- **Stage 1: The pre-problem stage.** The problem exists and may be severe but the public is unaware, the media uninterested and only interest groups are alarmed.
- **Stage 2: Alarmed discovery and euphoric enthusiasm.** The problem is suddenly discovered as a result of some particular event; the public call for solutions and the politicians promise action.
- **Stage 3: Realising the cost of significant progress.** This comes slowly and follows disclosure about the sacrifices necessary and the uncertainty of successful techno-

logical solutions.
- **Stage 4: Gradual decline of public interest.** Public concern falls either through boredom or rejection of the scale of the changes necessary or the costs involved.
- **Stage 5: Post-problem stage.** The public forgets about the issue but most original problems remain; a few institutions devoted to the problem may survive but on severely reduced funding.

Source: Bradbeer (1990).

After a period of intense debate, the issue slipped down the political agenda in terms of public concern.

In the United States Anthony Downs argued that political concern about the environment would pass through a five-stage process (Box 29.1) Downs's model has proved to be generally accurate in so far as public concern for environmental issues and governmental response has passed through the five-stage cycle twice; once with the first wave of environmental concern in the 1970s and again with the second wave in the 1980s. No doubt there will be a third wave of public concern in the future with every chance that it too will pass through five stages.

Green ideology

Green politics has been described as 'new politics' in so far as it does not fit into the framework of conventional parliamentary politics. Yet many aspects of green politics connect with aspects of pre-existing belief systems. In this sense, green politics is not really new. As Robinson has stated: 'Environmentalist rhetoric has drawn inspiration from such diverse ideological wells as Christian, Buddhist, Hindu, Taoist and Pagan religious belief systems, Anarchist, Marxist and Conservative political ideologies, the critical rationalist tradition in science from ecology to quantum physics, and the romantic reactions to post-Enlightenment social changes from Keats to Kerouac' (Robinson, 1992, p. 34).

Environmentalism is, then, an eclectic ideology which is drawn from numerous and diverse sources. It rejects 'industrialisation' and policies of economic

growth which remain at the heart of both Conservative and Labour programmes. Environmentalists argue that the economy should produce no more than is necessary to meet people's essential needs, and in a society where people live simpler lives such needs will be met by local production

Figure 29.1 An officer on points duty attempts to breathe less polluted air

(rather than by multinational companies). Seven basic principles underlie contemporary environmentalism:

- **A world approach.** All human activity should reflect appreciation of the world's finite resources and easily damaged ecology.
- **Respect for the rights of our descendants.** Our children have the right to inherit a beautiful and bountiful planet rather than an exhausted and polluted one.
- **Sufficiency.** We should be satisfied with 'enough' rather than constantly seeking 'more'.
- **A conserver economy.** We must conserve what we have rather than squandering it through pursuit of high growth strategies.
- **Care and share.** Given that resources are limited we must shift our energies to sharing what we have and looking after all sections of society properly.
- **Self-reliance.** We should learn to provide for ourselves rather than surrendering responsibility to experts and specialised agencies.
- **Decentralise and democratise.** We must form smaller units of production, encourage cooperative enterprises and give people local power over their own affairs. At the same time international integration must move forward rapidly. (B. Jones, 1989–90 p. 51)

Finally, some commentators have pointed to the strong links between environmentalism and the women's movement. They have argued that there is a parallel between the domination of nature by men and the domination of women by men. Environmentalism, they claim, cannot be based on traditional masculine values such as economic rationality, competitiveness and individualism. Rather it must be based on traditional female values such as caring, cooperation and intuition. Because of this relationship there is an overlap between many environmentalist and feminist goals.

Environmentalism is a broad approach to life on the planet which is concerned primarily with the impact of humans on the environment of themselves and other species.

The Green Party

Britain's Green Party has not enjoyed the electoral success of its European counterparts. For example in Germany the Green Party has won seats with only 5.6 per cent of the vote. Yet with nearly 15 per cent in 1989, the British Greens failed to win a single seat in the European Parliament. The Greens are a party opposed to conventional politics, yet their failure to win representation in traditional parliaments has resulted in resignations and divisions within the party. Even at the height of its electoral success in 1989 the Green Party was suffering an internal crisis.

Greens are divided on both the strategy and goals of their party. Was the Green Party an orthodox political party interested in winning political power or not? Some Greens saw the European election results as evidence that their party had 'taken off' and they believed that they could gradually build up and improve upon their 15 per cent level of support until they began winning seats. When this failed to happen and their support tailed off, 'Green 2000' was set up to relaunch the party as a real contender for power. But not all Greens agreed with this initiative, since they did not believe that the Green Party could operate within the conventional party political system. Dark-green fundamentalist party members saw Green 2000 as a sell-out to what they saw as the already failed system of power politics. By the time of the 1997 general election, the Greens operated more in the nature of a pressure group than a political party with parliamentary aspirations.

The greening of political parties

How far have green ideas influenced policy-making in the major parties? All of them claim to have coherent environmental policies, but some critics argue that their policies are designed merely to reassure public opinion that problems are being tackled rather than offering real solutions. In his study of green politics, Robinson concludes that the

main political parties are still chained to the idea that the natural ecosystem exists primarily as a resource for man's exploitation. Although, as a review of environmental policy documents of recent years show, the parties have begun to

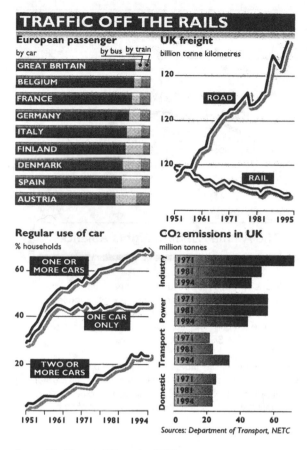

Source: The Observer, 9 November 1997.

Figure 29.2 Traffic off the rails

address issues of resource planning, future energy policy, recycling and the nascent concept of sustainability, the sacred cow of economic growth has not been sacrificed, nor is it likely to be in the near future. (Robinson, 1992, p. 217)

Hence, the 'greenness' of the major parties is very different from that of the Green Party. The gulf between Labour's greenness and environmentalism was revealed by the Deputy Prime Minister, John Prescott, in his review of transport policy. Britain's road system is nearing crisis; it coped with 2 million vehicles in 1950, 9 million in 1963, 27 million in 1997 and will have to cope with an estimated 40 million within 20 years unless political action is taken (see Figure 29.2). The previous Conservative government learnt the lesson that more and wider roads do not solve traffic congestion. Some town

centres have kept cars at bay through pedestrianisation, but the real solution rests in getting people out of the habit of using their cars and into the habit of using public transport. Environmentalists have argued that a 'stick and carrot' approach would be required to achieve such change. The 'stick' might include road pricing (drivers pay to use certain roads); charges for motorists who enter town centres; lower speed limits on all urban and rural roads; much higher car tax, based on engine size; taxing companies on their car parks so that they begin to charge employees for parking at work, and much higher fuel prices. At the same time, government must continue to discourage out-of-town shopping centres, which generates car usage.

The 'carrot' would have to include alternative means of public transport which was reliable, frequent, convenient, clean and cheap. It might offer the possibility of making one journey with one ticket, even if a train and a bus trip were both involved. John Prescott rules out such an approach becoming part of Labour's transport policy, and he acknowledged that for the foreseeable future the car would remain an 'integral part of modern society' (*Guardian*, 21 August 1997). He faced the reality that motorists are attached to using their cars, would continue to use them even if it became more expensive, and that they frequently lack any public transport alternative to car use. Prescott's 'greenness' fell short of the 'stick and carrot' approach and rested on limited measures to change the balance between car and public transport usage. The 'integrated transport system' remained a political goal, albeit a distant one.

Legislating for the environment

Much legislation contains elements which concern aspects of the environment. However, there have also been a number of Acts centrally concerned with the environment. In 1956 the Clean Air Act was passed in order to solve the problem of choking urban smog (smog = SMoke + fOG) particularly in London. Also concerned with cleaning up the environment was the 1974 Control of Pollution Act. In 1981 the Wildlife and Countryside Act was overwhelmingly concerned with environmental issues. More recently the 1990 Environment Protection Act, containing 120 clauses, covered a wider range

BOX 29.2
The New Age politics of animal rights

Has the parliamentary system failed?

Some feel that the animal welfare lobby and the anti-motorway lobby represent a new style of political participation. The new politics has emerged because the old style of politics, parliamentary democracy, has failed to represent widespread public concern for these issues. It is argued that many people have become frustrated, even disillusioned, with party politics, seeing parties as unresponsive to their demands. For example, Conservative protesters on the moderate wing of animal welfare felt that *their MPs* and *their Government* were not listening to them. Labour protesters felt much the same way about their party. This has resulted in new alignments; individuals of very different political persuasions have come together to form new alliances outside the structure of the political parties.

The politics of protest

Public order has been threatened by a new type of political protest. At Brightlingsea it was estimated that a third of this small town's population joined a demonstration against the export of veal calves. The use of the *Criminal Justice Act* in Essex had not prevented 'respectable' people, who would normally consider themselves as 'friends of the police', from participating in direct action against what they saw as cruelty to animals. In much the same way, anti-motorway protesters – particularly at Twyford Down near Winchester – have included many people who had never before taken direct action. As *The Economist* observed: 'Middle-aged Britons have taken to the streets . . . To the surprise of the country's political elites, animal rights has emerged as Britain's closest thing to a mass social movement' (19 August 1995). Indeed, amongst protesters at Brightlingsea, Shoreham, Dover, Coventry and other locations, have been sober, Tory-voting members of Middle England.

Concern for animal welfare has a long history in Britain. The RSPCA, with half a million supporters, was set up in 1824, the world's first society of its kind. Whilst members of the RSPCA represent the 'moderate' wing of those concerned with animal rights, animal liberation activists represent the 'radical' wing which emerged in Britain during the 1970s. Another moderate group, *Compassion in World Farming*, has organised much protest activity and publicised the poor

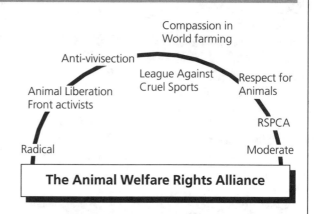

The Animal Welfare Rights Alliance

conditions in which many exported animals were slaughtered. Responding to increasing public anxiety about exporting live animals, some ferry companies have ended transporting live animals. This led to animals being exported from smaller ports like Brightlingsea.

Newspaper journalists differed greatly in the balance of reporting events concerning direct action. Whilst all journalists supported the actions of 'moderate' organisations concerned with animal welfare, radical groups provoked contrasting responses:

> Animal-rights protests are the latest cause to have come under the influence of the hard-core agitators . . . 'These people are committed soldiers' said one intelligence source. 'An animal rights activist is probably as dedicated as the vast majority of Irish terrorists.'
> *The Sunday Times* (5 February 1995)

> Something is stirring in the heart of Middle England . . . a new generation has grown up concerned more about the way animals have been boxed up and injected with drugs to produce cheap supermarket produce than with the food shortages of their parents' childhood memories.
> *The Observer* (22 January 1995)

---

of environmental issues than any prior Act.

Has recent legislation shown that, at last, the government is responding positively to environmental issues? The reaction from the green lobby to recent legislation has been mixed. On the one hand there has been satisfaction, even relief, that the environment is recognised as a complex issue which is now receiving legislative attention. On the other hand, the green lobby has been disappointed in individual Acts which frequently contain delays in implementation, loopholes of one kind or another, often address the more superficial issues, and are marked by a timid approach containing all the hallmarks of retreat and compromise. In this sense environmental legislation has played a symbolic role which reassures the electorate that 'something is being done about the environment' whilst avoiding the radical and unpopular policies that promise to bring real solutions.

The European Union

Britain's membership of the European Union (EU) has been an important influence on environmental policy. EU Directives have been designed to harmonise environmental policies throughout member states, especially important in equalising commercial costs in the single market. Although EU Directives are binding on member governments, their impact can in effect be avoided through blocking and delaying tactics. Nevertheless, the government has responded positively to many Directives, and where it has not, it has been embarrassed by the publicity which results. Directives on the quality of drinking water and bathing water around Britain's coasts received much publicity in the media. The Commission can bring pressure on national governments if it believes that Directives are being ignored. But some commentators believe that the EU's influence on environmental policy will decline in the future. This is because of the principle of subsidiarity, much favoured by the British government, which will return responsibility for much environmental policy back to national governments.

Summary

- Green ideology has been described as a cocktail of beliefs because of its diverse origins. This diversity, as well as lack of electoral success, has led to a crisis in the Green Party. The Greens have also been undermined by the major parties which have convinced many voters that they too are green.
- Although the influence of the EU on environmental policy is likely to decline, it can be anticipated that environmental issues will get on to the agenda of future governments.

Questions

1. What is meant by the term 'green politics'?

2. To what extent can it be argued that environmental concern is 'non-political' and above party politics since everyone suffers from the consequences of environmental deterioration?
3. Assess the impact of the Green Party on British politics.
4. Explain how the public can be anxious about green issues one year, yet be unconcerned about them in another.

Assignments

Assignment (1) Earth Summit II

Thirty-six national leaders attended the second Earth Summit held in New York in 1997 in order to keep alive the spirit of the first Earth Summit held in Rio. Labour Prime Minister Tony Blair took a leading role in arguing for binding global targets to reduce fossil fuel consumption. He pledged that Britain would cut its gas emissions by 20 per cent over a period of thirteen years. He argued that all developed countries should accept similar targets.

Australian Prime Minister John Howard disagreed with Blair and said that implementing Britain's target would shrink the Australian economy by 2 per cent and result in large wage cuts in some industries. He argued that 'an approach to reducing greenhouse gases which requires every developed country to make the same arbitrary cut ... strikes us as irrational and ultimately unworkable' (*Southern Cross*, 25 June 1997). The American President, with an eye on voters at home delivered a strong-sounding speech which actually committed the US to doing very little for environmental improvement. Former Conservative Environment Secretary, John Gummer, was a member of the British delegation and he attacked Bill Clinton's empty words: 'He admitted that America was the biggest culprit. He asserted that action was imperative. He pledged that the US would do something. The trouble was he wouldn't say what and he couldn't say when' (*Sunday Telegraph*, 29 June 1997). He continued to attack Tony Blair for failing to criticise Clinton's 'do-nothing' approach to the environment, asking 'is the Bill and Tony show so important to this Government that it is frightened of straight talk between friends'?

Questions
(i) Outline the different approaches of Blair, Howard and Clinton towards universal targets for greenhouse gas reductions.
(ii) Explain why the former Conservative Environment Minister criticised Bill Clinton and Tony Blair. What did he mean by his reference to the 'Bill and Tony show'?
(iii) Discuss whether or not environmentalists have exaggerated the dangers of global disaster.

Assignment (2) The third Battle of Newbury
The first Battle of Newbury was between the Roundheads and Cavaliers in 1643, the second was during the 1980s at Greenham Common, only a few miles away, when a women's peace camp protested against nuclear missiles being sited at the US air base. The third battle involved the £100 million nine-mile bypass planned to run around the east of Newbury and ease traffic congestion in the town centre.
Newbury has an inner bypass built in the 1960s which funnels all traffic between the Midlands and the South through Newbury.

As in the struggle against veal exports (see p. 496) 'respectable' citizens of middle England protested alongside more radical individuals. The 'tribe' which protested at the M3 construction at Twyford Down (near Winchester) in 1992 – the *Dongas* – occupied many of the trees near Newbury which were due to be felled to make way for the new road. They built tree houses, connected by rope walkways, and planned to cause as much delay to the road-building as possible. The Dongas did not believe that they could prevent the bypass being built, but they could cause delay, which would increase costs, and so reduce the amount of money available for future road-building projects.

Although the radical Dongas received most publicity in the media, the new bypass was also opposed by many local people including the local business community *Newbury Business Against the Bypass*. One newspaper reporter noted the wide social base of the protest movement in Newbury: 'You can see products of the public school system alongside products of the sink estate system.' Much the same

comments were being made about the composition of the animal rights protesters.

The Newbury protesters see the political parties represented in local government and at Westminster as irrelevant as far as their struggle against the bypass is concerned. As with the veal export protesters, direct action took the place of local authority and parliamentary politics.

The Newbury protesters believed that Conservatives were mainly motivated and driven by money, although there was a rumour that a private party deal secured the bypass. Some were convinced that the local Conservative MP, Sir David Mitchell, who was in favour of the bypass, gave unexpected support to John Major in the Conservative leadership contest (see p. 127). This was very quickly followed by the Newbury bypass scheme getting the go-ahead when many other new road building schemes were halted. Protesters saw New Labour as too timid to oppose the bypass, and they wrote off the Liberal Democrats as potential allies. Liberal Democrats, who controlled the local authority, argued that the new bypass was environmentally friendly and should be built.

The arguments in favour of building the new bypass were not overpowering. Firstly, the environmental costs did appear high; the route of the bypass involves the destruction of much woodland, 3 SSIs (sites of special scientific interest), some rare heathland, ancient bogland, and wildflower meadows. It also threatens stretches of the River Kennett as well as destroying a number of archaeological sites, including a Roman villa. Secondly, the Highway Agency has conceded that during off-peak periods the new bypass will save only two minutes on journeys past Newbury. It will save fifteen minutes during rush-hours. Although the bypass will take many vehicles out of Newbury, *Friends of the Earth* have calculated that Newbury's town traffic will be back to current levels by the year 2002.

The protesters feel that they won the argument against the ideology of road-building, although they lost the battle to stop the bypass being built. The public now accepts that more roads will not solve traffic problems. For example, those who believed that building the M25 would solve outer London's traffic problems now concede that congestion is worse than ever. Even the government now accepts that new roads do not end traffic congestion, but simply encourage more traffic. The A34 Newbury bypass was particularly controversial because it was the only major new road project to get the go-ahead in 1996.

Did green arguments or financial costs win the day?

New-road-building has come to a halt; does this mean that environmentalists have won the argument? Has the government accepted that the 'true' cost of more roads is environmental damage, increased pollution and poor health, as well as increased deaths and injuries? Are these the reasons why the Salisbury bypass scheme has been dropped and why local authority road-building has been reduced? The answer to this question is probably 'no'. It seems more likely that the government is spending less on new roads because of a squeeze on public spending. Increasing amounts spent on health, education and social security mean that savings have to be made elsewhere, and the budget for roads is an obvious target for making financial cuts.

The British Roads Federation still argues that current traffic problems will not be solved unless new roads are built. Others disagree with this and argue that traffic has to be 'managed' so that existing roads can carry more. Again, these arguments tend to be 'technical' rather than 'green'. In other words, what might look like political victory for environmentalists in terms of far less new roads being built could be the result of other factors such as public spending cutbacks as well as new approaches to controlling traffic.

Questions

(i) Identify 'radical' and 'moderate' groups involved in the politics of transport and road-building.

(ii) What is meant by the 'ideology of road building'? In what ways has this ideology been challenged? What factors might have contributed to the slow-down in major new road construction in Britain?

(iii) Outline the similarities and differences between the animal rights lobby and the anti-motorway protesters

Further reading

Bradbeer, J. (1990) 'Environmental Policy', in S. Savage and L. Robins (eds), *Public Policy under Thatcher* (London: Macmillan): a useful summary of developments in policy-making. Dobson, A. (1993) 'Ecologism', in R. Eatwell and A. Wright (eds), *Contemporary Political Ideologies* (London: Pinter): a more theoretical approach to environmentalism, or ecologism, as an ideology. Robinson, M. (1992) *The Greening of British Party Politics* (Manchester University Press): a useful account of how British parties came to terms with environmental concern.

Foreign and defence policy

Within the memory span of many middle-aged adults, Britain has moved from being a major world power to being a middle-sized regional power. What factors led to this decline? How has Britain adapted in international politics to its new, reduced circumstances? This chapter examines how Britain's policy-makers adapted to change and moved, falteringly, their focus from an Atlanticist to a European outlook. The conclusion considers the opportunities for British influence in the 'New World Order'.

The differing nature of external policy

External policy, such as foreign and defence policy, differs from internal or domestic policies in three important areas. Firstly, foreign policy tends to be *reactive* rather than *pro-active*. The government has far greater control over areas such as education or health, where it can direct policy through legislation and financial support. The day-to-day conduct of foreign policy tends to be in reaction to international politics made up of the actions of other governments and international organisations. As one diplomat stated, 'most important decisions are often made, not as part of a concerted and far-sighted policy, but under the urgent pressure of some immediate crisis' (quoted in Sampson, 1962, p. 311).

Secondly, public opinion tends to divide less on foreign policy issues than on domestic issues. On issues such as the economy, education or health, government policy tends to create 'winners' and 'losers'. A situation of zero-sum politics may exist in which the gains made by one section of society are at the direct expense of the losses incurred by another section. This is rarely the situation when government faces a foreign crisis or threat from abroad, when all sections of society feel the need to support their own government against the common foe. If armed conflict arises, as between British and Argentinian troops in 1982 over control of the Falklands, even to question the wisdom of one's own government may appear treacherous in the eyes of others.

Thirdly, foreign and defence policy issues tend to interest only a small minority of the population. As a consequence, pressure groups, parties and the media play a minor role compared with their influence in shaping domestic policy. Even Parliament's role, despite the energetic work of various party groups and select committees in scrutinising policy, is limited. William Wallace argued that in Britain 'as in other democratic countries, there is a long-established parliamentary tradition that foreign policy ought to be insulated from the rough-and-tumble of domestic debate' (Wallace, 1975, p. 1).

This situation can be explained in part by the fact that much foreign policy is concerned with the security of the country and it is crucial that many issues remain secret. David Vital has confirmed how few participate in the foreign policy community: 'the making of foreign policy . . . is the business of the Executive, and for almost all practical purposes the Executive is unfettered in its exercise of this function'

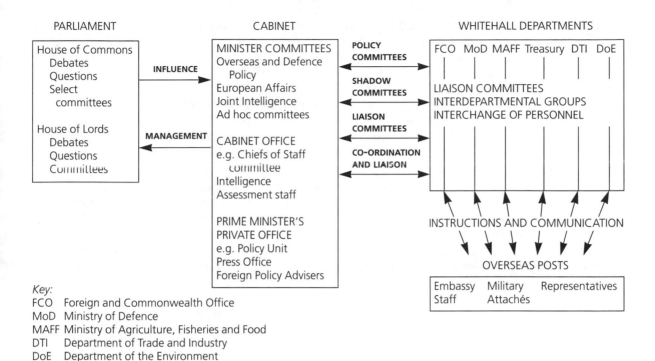

PARLIAMENT

| House of Commons
Debates
Questions
Select
   committees |
| House of Lords
Debates
Questions
Committees |

CABINET

MINISTER COMMITTEES
Overseas and Defence
   Policy
European Affairs
Joint Intelligence
Ad hoc committees

CABINET OFFICE
e.g. Chiefs of Staff
   committee
Intelligence
Assessment staff

PRIME MINISTER'S
PRIVATE OFFICE
e.g. Policy Unit
Press Office
Foreign Policy Advisers

INFLUENCE

MANAGEMENT

POLICY
COMMITTEES

SHADOW
COMMITTEES

LIAISON
COMMITTEES

CO-ORDINATION
AND LIAISON

WHITEHALL DEPARTMENTS

FCO MoD MAFF Treasury DTI DoE

LIAISON COMMITTEES
INTERDEPARTMENTAL GROUPS
INTERCHANGE OF PERSONNEL

INSTRUCTIONS AND COMMUNICATION

OVERSEAS POSTS

| Embassy Military   Representatives
Staff   Attachés |

Key:
FCO   Foreign and Commonwealth Office
MoD Ministry of Defence
MAFF Ministry of Agriculture, Fisheries and Food
DTI   Department of Trade and Industry
DoE Department of the Environment

Source: Sanders, 1990 (Macmillan), based on the original in M. Clarke, 'The Policy-Making Process', in M. Smith, S. Smith and B. White (eds) (1988) *British Foreign Policy* (London: Unwin Hyman) p. 86.

Figure 30.1 The British foreign policy-making process

(Vital, 1968, p. 49). Generally speaking, then, the making of foreign policy is dealt with as a technical matter by a small élite of decision-makers. Foreign-policy-making is not an open process characterised by pluralism.

The making of foreign policy

Figure 30.1 shows the institutional framework of contemporary foreign policy-making. It is useful to compare it with Figure 22.2, which refers to the general policy-making process which is bedded much more firmly in the wider context of parties, media, pressure groups and various other agencies such as local government. In constitutional terms, responsibility for the conduct of foreign policy lies with the Secretary of State for Foreign Affairs. Normally there is close liaison between his Department, the Foreign and Commonwealth Office (FCO) and the Ministry of Defence, the

FCO's 'closest cousin in Whitehall' (M. Clarke, 1992, p. 84). The FCO also works with other Departments on issues of common interest, in which case 'the Foreign Secretary or his officials formulate policy in consultation with those Departments. These policies are implemented by the FCO, either directly or through the agency of British embassies and missions abroad'. (Wallace, 1975, p. 21)

Most academics have recognised the close political relationship between the foreign secretary and the prime minister. Of course, in many cases the prime minister has previously held the post of foreign secretary, such as James Callaghan and John Major, and this may explain why in the past so many prime ministers intervened in the work of the FCO. But perhaps the main reason for intervention lies in the fact that the prime minister is expected to be a statesman on the international stage and so has to have a command of foreign policy issues. As Prime Minister, Margaret Thatcher was noted for her long-running hostility towards the FCO and occasional bitter battles with the Foreign Secretary. There were complex reasons for this antagonism, but of central importance amongst them was the clash between Thatcher's *Atlanticist* foreign policy outlook and the *Europeanism* of the FCO.

Whatever foreign policy is pursued by ministers or their civil servants, it will inevitably be accompanied by claims that this decision or that treaty is 'in the national interest'. Yet as we have seen in Chapter 13, some Labour and Tory MPs supported the Maastricht Treaty because closer involvement in a potentially federal structure was in Britain's 'national interest'. Yet other Labour and Tory MPs opposed Maastricht because they believed that it threatened Britain's sovereignty and therefore was against 'the national interest'. What, then, is meant by the term 'national interest'? As Joseph Frankel has stated, '"National interest" is a singularly vague concept. It assumes a variety of meanings in the various contexts in which it is used and, despite its fundamental importance, these meanings often cannot be reconciled' (Frankel, 1970, p. 15).

The basis of Britain's foreign policy

Looking back, it is remarkable that until the 1960s this small country was one of the leading world powers. Britain was an independent nuclear power, held a permanent seat on the Security Council of the United Nations, and was responsible for policing much of the world. Britain, it was argued, had a unique contribution to make to world politics since it wielded influence in three distinct areas. Winston Churchill described Britain's role in terms of being at the intersection of 'three majestic circles'. The first was the Commonwealth circle which, being the legacy of Britain's imperial power, embraced much of Africa and Asia as well as the dominions of Canada, New Zealand and Australia. The second was Britain's 'special relationship' with the United States, and the third was Britain's close relationship with Western Europe, where armed forces were based as part of the defence against the Soviet threat. But changes abroad such as the rise of nationalism in developing countries, as well as changes at home resulting from Britain's declining economic strength,

have meant that Britain has had to adapt and make far-reaching changes in each of its 'foreign policy circles'.

The Commonwealth

The process of decolonisation, the transformation of the British Empire into the Commonwealth of Nations, began in the 1940s with India, Pakistan and Ceylon (Sri Lanka) gaining independence. In the 1960s what Prime Minister Harold Macmillan described as the 'wind of change' was to sweep through Britain's African colonies. Country after country became *self-determining*, with the exception of Rhodesia, which emerged as a problem when an experiment in multiracial government (the Central African Federation) failed, and South Africa, which left the Commonwealth in 1961. Britain retained its global military presence in its former colonies in order to (1) deter the Soviets from intervening, as in the Gulf, (2) defend countries against insurgency, as in Malaya, and (3) defend Western trade routes, from bases such as Simonstown in South Africa. But the international role encapsulated by the Commonwealth 'circle' was to decline, and many historians see the Suez fiasco of 1956 as critical in eventually changing the direction of British foreign and defence policies (see Coxall and Robins (1998), ch. 11).

Labour Prime Minister Harold Wilson faced the familiar political problem of having to reduce public expenditure and in 1968 his Cabinet decided that big savings must be made in the defence budget. Britain had 220,000 soldiers, 125,000 airmen and 95,000 sailors. Substantial costs would be saved, it was decided, by withdrawing British forces which were garrisoned *East of Suez*. This involved Britain pulling out of Singapore, Malaysia and the Gulf. Along with this the Defence Secretary, Denis Healey, emphasised the growing importance of Europe in strategic thinking: 'our army is well trained and superbly equipped, and has more recent and varied fighting experience than any other European army . . . We shall thus be able to contribute to the security of NATO on a scale corresponding with our efforts to forge closer political and economic links in Europe.'

The reduction in Britain's involvement in the

Commonwealth circle continued during the 1970s and 1980s as rebellious white Rhodesia found independence as black-majority-ruled Zimbabwe. Britain's responsibilities now involved only a handful of commitments: after the handback of Hong Kong to China in 1997, the most important are the Falklands, Gibraltar and Bermuda. Ten additional 'colonial outposts', such as Montserrat, the Pitcairn Islands, and Turks and Caicos Islands, are either too small or too poor to survive as independent states. The Commonwealth has long ceased to be a viable basis for Britain's foreign and defence policy, yet it has grown in importance for some other countries. It provides a useful diplomatic network for developing countries; South Africa has rejoined the Commonwealth, and Mozambique, which was a Portuguese colony and has no colonial links with Britain, has applied to join.

The special relationship with the United States

The history, institutions and culture of Britain and the United States (US) are intertwined, and out of the close cooperation during the Second World War developed the **special relationship**. Labour Foreign Secretary Ernest Bevin drew the US into a post-war European defence commitment with the establishment of the North Atlantic Treaty Organisation (NATO). America continued to contribute directly to British defence forces when, after the failure of Britain's own nuclear weapons system, the US provided Britain with the most modern systems in the shape of *Polaris* and *Trident*.

The special relationship was strained during the Suez crisis and weakened considerably during the 1960s and 1970s. Withdrawal of forces East of Suez meant that Britain was unable to play its traditional role of junior world policeman alongside the US. Britain refused to provide troops to fight alongside Americans in Vietnam and Atlantic ties appeared less important as Prime Ministers Wilson, Callaghan

> Britain's **'special relationship'** with the United States involved the leaders of both countries working together closely as well as the opinions of both the American and British public favouring close ties.

and Heath looked increasingly towards Europe.

Margaret Thatcher did not share the deep Europeanism of her predecessor and re-established the special relationship on a personal level with President Reagan. Both leaders held similar New Right views; both saw the Soviet Union, to use Reagan's words, as the 'evil Empire'; and both got along well together in personal terms. There were disagreements, of course, particularly over trade issues, but Britain resumed patrolling the Gulf and facilitated US strikes against Libya, and the US lent support to Britain during the Falklands War. Allied action in the Gulf War against Iraq was led by the US with Britain playing a major supporting role.

The special relationship was damaged at a personal level by the revelation that British government resources were used to support George Bush's presidential campaign against Bill Clinton. The defeat of the Conservatives in 1997, the removal of John Major from Number Ten and his replacement by Tony Blair, restored improved personal relations. As Peter Jones comments, the future of the Anglo-American relationship in the hands of Clinton and Blair 'could once again become as special as it has been in the past . . . The fact that the new [Labour] government should be able to act more positively towards Europe than its Conservative predecessor may, perhaps surprisingly, help rather than hinder this process.' As an American adviser recalled after Blair's visit to Washington in 1996, he 'was left in no doubt that Britain's influence in Washington is greater if Britain is a full player in Europe' (Jones, 1997, p. 236).

Britain in Europe

As the Commonwealth circle declined and the special relationship was redefined more faintly, so Britain adapted by giving greater prominence to the European circle. Britain's reluctant acceptance that its future lay in Europe generally and in the EU in particular has been examined in Chapter 13. Britain first attempted without success to negotiate a wide free trade area in Europe, then established EFTA (the European Free Trade Association), before eventually deciding to apply for membership of the EEC.

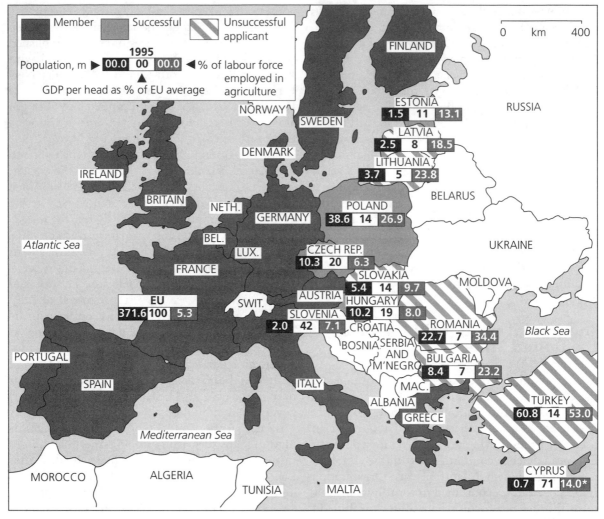

Source: *The Economist*, 19 July 1997.

Figure 30.2 NATO's expanding European membership

The new world (dis)order

The democratic revolutions which swept through Eastern Europe ended the ideological division of Europe which had existed since 1917. The old bipolar certainties of the Cold War disappeared very rapidly; Germany was reunited, the communist Warsaw Pact dissolved, and President Yeltsin announced that he wanted Russia to join NATO. History was moving fast and seemed to be leading to a New World Order. But the Iraqi invasion of Kuwait, civil conflict in former Yugoslavia, the potential for ethnic turmoil within the Commonwealth of Independent States as well as bloodshed in Central Africa meant that aggression, instability and suffering remained the familiar ingredients of international politics. In many ways the stability of the Cold War gave way to a New World Disorder.

NATO could have been seen as a redundant military alliance in the 1990s since its enemy, the communist Warsaw Pact countries, had collapsed. However, NATO is developing a new political and military purpose, and remains important in European affairs. It has transformed from a defen-

---

BOX 30.1
The campaign against landmines

Millions of landmines, which are cheap to purchase, have been laid in many parts of the world. It has been calculated that an innocent victim is injured or killed by a landmine every twenty minutes. Many are children. During the last months of her life Diana, Princess of Wales, drew attention to the international campaign to ban landmines. In August 1997 she visited landmine victims in Bosnia. There was unease in some political circles because it was felt that Diana was becoming 'party political' through identifying herself too closely with Labour's ethical foreign policy aspirations.

---

sive military organisation into a crisis management organisation, which may prevent NATO taking military action which is not defensive in nature. In what ways might reformed NATO bring increased political stability to Europe? Firstly, NATO has enlarged its membership – to include Hungary, Poland and the Czech Republic – to help suppress nationalisms and bring both security and stability to Eastern Europe (see Figure 30.2). Secondly, NATO has avoided isolating Russia from European affairs. Although President Yeltsin's request for formal membership of NATO was not granted, Russia's importance has been recognised by a 'special relationship' – 'Partnership in Peace' – which amounts to an informal 'associate' membership of NATO. Thirdly, NATO has developed military task forces to tackle incidents outside NATO countries. For example, serving alongside Russian troops, NATO troops have attempted to reduce conflict in Bosnia. Finally, a consequence of these developments is that NATO is becoming more European and less American in orientation. As a superpower the US remains the most important individual member of NATO. Yet the end of the Cold War, continuing disarmament and subsequent decline in the importance of military might, as well as the new European members and the special relationship with Russia, have moved the alliance's 'centre of gravity' away from America towards Europe. As a consequence, the Anglo-American special relationship is likely to become more important in Washington as a means of exerting diplomatic influence on the development of NATO.

Potential for world disorder lies in ethnic rivalries, guerrilla warfare and the international behaviour of so-called irresponsible regimes such as Iran, Iraq, Libya, Syria and North Korea which are developing their military capabilities. It has been estimated that 35 non-NATO countries now have ballistic missiles and that 18 of these have the capability of installing nuclear, biological or chemical warheads. The dispersed surplus arsenal of the old Soviet Union is a major source of the military hardware which ends up in the hands of irresponsible regimes. Western arms sales is another major source.

An ethical foreign policy for Britain?

Can political values help to shape Britain's relations with other countries? In the past Labour governments found that socialist values were a poor guide to international politics (see Coxall and Robins (1988), ch. 11). New Labour's Foreign Secretary, Robin Cook, has declared that he wants to put an ethical dimension into international politics by 'putting human rights at the heart of Britain's foreign policy.' The centrepiece of this approach is the promise not to sell arms to repressive regimes; in the hands of irresponsible governments imported arms have been used frequently to suppress the civilian population or aggressively against neighbouring countries.

Previous British ministers have been much less concerned over the moral arguments involved in selling arms abroad. Indeed, one minister was forthright in stating that he had few scruples about the consequences of arms sales when he declared his indifference: 'I don't really fill my mind much with what one set of foreigners is doing to another' (*Observer*, 18 May 1997). Other critics believe that Robin Cook's ethical foreign policy is merely political rhetoric and when he is faced with the choice of promoting human rights abroad or saving thousands of jobs at home in the defence industry, he will choose the latter (see cartoon on p. 506). This, it is argued, will be the case when Britain loses orders for

Source: The Economist, 2 August 1997

defence equipment to other countries such as France or Italy. Labour's ethical foreign policy will have then had no impact on human rights of those living under repressive regimes, and have given British workers' jobs away to workers in other countries. Like previous Labour governments, it is argued, the Foreign Secretary's attempt to base policy on socialist values will prove unworkable, eventually be discarded, and replaced by foreign policy based on the 'realities' of what is in Britain's national interest.

Summary

- Britain has moved from world power status to regional power status and this has forced policymakers into sometimes taking painful decisions. Europe has become the most important focus of Britain's external policy, and here new opportunities and threats have resulted from the end of the Cold War.
- Because of its very nature, foreign and defence policies absorb the interest of small élites rather than the wider public.
- The end of the Cold War has not resulted in a 'New World Order' as some politicians expected,

but to a new disorder with conflict in the former Yugoslavia, North Africa and the Middle East as well as in West and Central Africa.

Questions

1. 'Domestic policy-making is a pluralist process: foreign policy-making is an élitist process.' Discuss.
2. How valid is it to argue that having lost its Empire, Britain has not yet found a role in international politics?
3. Should Britain retain its nuclear deterrent? What security threats does Britain face in the late 1990s?
4. What, if any, are the disadvantages of the 'peace dividend'?

Assignments

Assignment (1) Ethical foreign policy put to the test
Some British journalists have compared the government in Indonesia with the Nazi government in

Table 30.1 How Britain arms the world

How Britain arms the world

UK rank	Company	World rank	Arms sales*	Products	Major contracts	
1	**British Aerospace**	3	64	Aircraft, missiles, artillery shells, small arms, electronics	Saudi Arabia, Indonesia, Sri Lanka, Oman, South Korea, Brazil, Egypt	*These companies could not be ranked given the information available*
2	**GEC** (inc Marconi, VSEL & Ferranti)	10	25–30	Radar, missiles, ships, torpedoes	Brazil, India, Indonesia, Oman, Jordan, Malaysia, Turkey, Nigeria	**Vickers** **Products:** Artillery, tanks
3	**Rolls Royce**	30	8	Aero engines	Saudi Arabia, Indonesia	**Major contracts:** Malaysia, South Korea Zimbabwe, Turkey, Nigeria
4	**GKN** (inc Westland)	42	13	Helicopters, armoured cars	Kuwait, Brazil, Pakistan	
5	**Hunting**	51	39	Small arms/ordnance	N/A	**Shorts** **Products:** Missiles
6	**Lucas-Varity**	65	12	Aerospace	Mostly USA	**Major contracts:** Botswana, Kuwait, Dubai, Jordan, Oman, Pakistan
7	**Smiths Industries**	69	40	Electronics	China	
8	**Racal Electronics**	1 71	31	Electronics communications	Saudi Arabia, Oman, Kuwait	**Alvis** **Products:** Armoured cars
9	**Devonport Management**	84	91	Ships	N/A	**Major contracts:** Indonesia, Malaysia, Turkey
10	**Vosper Thorneycroft**	88	89	Ships, military construction	Kuwait, Qatar	

* percentage of total sales

Source: *The Observer*, 31 August 1997

Germany. They point to the Indonesian occupation of East Timor and the subsequent genocide as evidence in support of their accusation. The population of East Timor has been treated cruelly by Indonesian military forces, which have operated like death squads, and which have tortured and killed an estimated third of the population of East Timor. Amnesty International has accused the Indonesian government as being 'casual with mass murder'. The uncomfortable reality for Britons to contemplate is that the Indonesian forces which operate in East Timor are armed by British companies, which have supplied military hardware from firearms and armoured cars to water cannon and electronic equipment. Arms exports to Indonesia have been sanctioned by both a Labour government in the 1970s and subsequent Conservative governments in the 1980s and 1990s. The Major administration granted export licences for the £160 million sale of Hawk jets to Indonesia in 1996.

The Labour government elected in 1997 argued that Britain would no longer permit the sale of arms to regimes that might use them for internal repression or external aggression. Attention focused on the reaction of Labour's Foreign Secretary to the Conservative sanctioned export of Hawk jets. This was seen as the first test of Labour's ethical foreign policy because Hawk jets have a dual use; they can be used to train fighter pilots and also as low-level ground attack aircraft on lightly and unarmed targets. Some journalists suspected that the Foreign Office and Department of Trade and Industry officials knew that it was highly likely that Hawk jets would be used against civilians in East Timor. The Liberal Democrat defence spokesperson, Menzies Campbell, urged Labour to put its ethical policy into practice, and argued that 'there is absolutely no justification for the UK to be supplying arms to a regime whose suppression of internal dissent and its aggression towards the people of East Timor is so well documented.' Despite such pressure, export licences for the sale of Hawk jets were not revoked.

Questions

(i)   Referring to the information contained in Table 30.1 and the text, outlined the advantages to Britain of exporting arms.

(ii) Briefly describe the position of the three major political parties on having an 'ethical' foreign policy.

(iii) 'We will make the protection and promotion of human rights a central part of our foreign policy' (Labour Party Manifesto 1997, p. 39). Write a paragraph which supports this goal, and a paragraph which argues that it lacks realism.

Assignment (2) Britain's changing defence needs

Britain's spending on defence rose during the 1980s reaching 5.3 per cent of GDP. But once the Soviet threat disappeared, a large army was no longer necessary for defence. It was anticipated that defence spending could be reduced, resulting in a 'peace dividend' which could be spent on other causes, such as education, health and pensions. The defence review of 1990, *Options for Change*, resulted in large cuts in military manpower and a 12 per cent cut in overall defence spending. It was argued that political change in the old Soviet Union and Eastern Europe meant that Britain no longer needed to station a large army in Europe, but the Gulf War in 1991 actually showed that Britain still needed a flexible military force. The new British military machine would be smaller than that needed during the Cold War, but better equipped in order to operate in any military theatre, from desert wars to conflicts in the tundra. Additionally, improved management techniques were introduced to the armed forces in order to cut waste and improve efficiency.

During the 1997 general election campaign Labour argued that many defence reductions were 'Treasury-driven' rather than being rational cuts in response to changing defence needs. As a consequence, Labour argued, Britain's defence forces had become over-committed. Labour promised to solve this on entering government with a new defence review which would first establish Britain's commitments, then match military forces to these commitments.

Questions

(i)   Identify at least one reason why Britain was able to reduce military manpower during the 1990s.

(ii) In previous general elections, defence was a significant issue in may voters' minds. Discuss why defence played such a small role in the 1997 general election campaign.

(iii) 'The Treasury determines all policies, from the shape of Britain's armed forces to the type of higher education on offer in British universities.' How valid is this viewpoint?

Further reading

Berridge, G.R. (1992) *International Politics: States, Power and Conflict Since 1945* (London: Harvester Wheatsheaf): a useful account of the most important developments. Jones, P. (1997) *America and the British Labour Party: The Special Relationship at Work* (London: Tauris Academic Studies): a detailed examination of the importance of the United States in British politics. Sanders, D. (1990) *Losing an Empire, Finding a Role: British Foreign Policy Since 1945* (London: Macmillan): a comprehensive account of Britain's changing foreign policy.

The politics of law and order

The issue of law and order rose to the forefront of British politics in the 1980s and public concern about it intensified in the 1990s. A consideration of the issue involves looking at police operations, accountability and control and at the working of the criminal justice system. It also involves examining the policies the major parties have proposed on law and order, and their effectiveness to date.

The role of the police

The broader context for the discussion which follows is twofold: first, the monopoly of the legitimate use of violence held by the state, and second, its obligation in a liberal democracy to control the law-enforcement agencies and ensure that they operate according to certain rules. Two public needs have to be balanced – (1) the need to protect society from the activities of criminals, especially violent criminals; and (2) the need to ensure that the process of bringing suspects to justice takes place within the law, with the officers of the law fully accountable to elected representatives.

There is also a delicate balancing act required by the second proposition. Police impartiality is a central element in the rule of law yet the police must be ultimately accountable to democratic representatives themselves subject to political pressures. How to ensure that the police service is both independent *and* politically accountable is a recurring theme in discussions of policing.

Police organisation, accountability and control

Most European countries have a national police force under the control of the central government. Traditionally, Britain has been an exception. The 1964 Police Act established a tripartite structure in England and Wales, with responsibility divided between police authorities, chief constables and the home secretary. Police authorities, on which elected councillors were in a majority, were responsible for the maintenance of their forces and the appointment of chief constables; chief constables were operationally independent, although could be dismissed by the police authority; and the home secretary exercised influence on policing through his responsibility for pay and conditions, his approval of police authorities' decisions over resources, his provision of an annual grant equal to about half of each police force's budget, and his supervision of the efficiency of the police service through Her Majesty's Inspectors of Constabulary (HMIC). Only in London (the Metropolitan Police Force) and Northern Ireland (the Royal Ulster Constabulary) does the home secretary have direct responsibility for the police. However, trends in policing from the 1980s and legislation in the 1990s have created a more national, centralised force in England and Wales.

First, in order to combat modern crime, the police have had to develop national data storage and retrieval systems such as the Police National Computers (PNC), on which is recorded national information such as missing persons, stolen vehicles, vehicle owners, names of criminals, fingerprints, and so on; have had to develop specialised units – most of them run by the Metropolitan Police – to deal with e.g. drugs, serious crime, terrorism, and disturbances; and have been required to coordinate large-scale policing activities across county boundaries as done by the National Reporting Centre at Scotland Yard during the miners' strike. National coordination of police forces also comes about through the work of ACPO – the Association of Chief Police Officers. In addition, legislation in 1994 established a national DNA database and the 1997 Police Act promised to set up a National Crime Squad and a Criminal Records Agency. The National Crime Squad, along with the National Criminal Intelligence Service, have been seen as prefiguring the future setting up of a national police institution (Beynon and Edwards, 1997, p. 338).

Second, legislation by the Conservative Government in the 1990s, notably the Police and Magistrates Act (PMCA, 1994), centralised the police service by

- empowering the home secretary to lay down national policing objectives, call for reports from new police authorities and ensure that the plans drawn up by local police authorities with chief constables are consistent with national objectives;
- requiring HMIC to produce national league tables of the performances of police forces;
- abolishing the old police authorities and establishing new police authorities with reduced representation of local councillors and nearly half of their members nominated rather than elected;
- empowering the home secretary to appoint members to serve on police authorities.

Although the tripartite structure established in 1964 is retained in name, in practice local autonomy is much reduced, and with it the likelihood of the kind of public clashes between police authorities and their chief constables which took place in the 1980s. In effect, the PMCA makes the police authority 'an intermediary of central government and the direct agent of the Home Office' (Loveday, 1994, cited Cope, Starie and Leishman, 1996, p. 21). The legislation shifts the balance of power in policing from local to central government. It confirms and extends the extensive powers of the home secretary, which already embraced all law enforcement activities,

including policing practice (notwithstanding the autonomy of chief constables), inspection and, should a force be refused a certificate of efficiency, the options of amalgamating the force with another, sacking the chief constable or imposing a commissioner. Even in the 1980s, the power of the home secretary 'dwarfed' that of the local police authorities (de Smith and Brazier, 1990, p. 392).

Political accountability

In recent decades, very important issues have surfaced with regard to the control and **accountability** of Britain's system of policing. These relate to two main areas – political and legal, including the handling of complaints and internal discipline.

The home secretary has very extensive powers over the police force, but a dilemma over political accountability arises precisely because these seem not to be matched by any corresponding obligation (except in the case of London) to answer to parliament for the police. As de Smith and Brazier point out: 'Home Secretaries still take a very restricted view of their obligations to answer parliamentary questions about law enforcement outside the Metropolis' (ibid., p. 393). It remains unclear to what extent the home secretary is politically answerable for decisions taken by chief constables outside the Metropolis (ibid., p. 389). How far 1990s legislation affected this position remains to be seen.

Legal accountability, the handling of complaints and internal discipline

The police have to keep within the law of the land (although this – as in the case of powers of arrest – is not always easily ascertainable). The police can be prosecuted in the criminal courts for offences such as assault and can be made the subject of civil actions for damages or wrongful arrest.

The main issue here is how far people from outside the force should be involved in investigating

---

Police accountability: the political accountability of the police means their answerability to parliament for their actions and their legal accountability refers to the requirement that they act within the law in carrying out their duties.

complaints against the police. The system since the *Police and Criminal Evidence Act 1984* has been as follows. Any complaint against the police by a member of the public goes to the chief constable who decides whether it should be formally investigated; in pursuing his investigation, he may if he wishes seek the assistance of a police officer from another area. All serious complaints must be referred to the *Police Complaints Authority* (PCA), a completely independent institution none of whose members is or has been a police officer. The PCA then supervises the investigation at the end of which it reports to the chief constable, who must then decide what action to take.

The decision usually amounts to a choice between (a) a recommendation that the case go forward to the Director of Public Prosecutions (DPP), who initiates all prosecutions of particular officers; (b) internal disciplinary procedure; or (c) no further action. The PCA can direct the chief constable to refer a matter to the DPP if he decides not to do so, or to commence internal disciplinary measures, if he decides against that. In the event of internal disciplinary proceedings, two members of the PCA sit with the chief constable on a tribunal to decide whether the charge is proved. The PCA also has general powers of supervision of police disciplinary procedure. It may require the submission to it of any complaint not referred by a chief constable. It presents an annual report to the home secretary.

Although an improvement on the preceding situation, the Police Complaints Authority has been the subject of criticism. Some critics have wondered why the decisions of chief constables themselves were excluded from its remit by the 1984 Act. Others have worried that the PCA itself is insufficiently independent and lacks 'teeth'. Between 1985 and 1995–6, the number of complaints against the police in England and Wales increased by a quarter to nearly 36,000 (*Social Trends*, 1997, pp. 166–7). However, under a third of complaints are considered by the PCA. In 1996–7, it considered 10,243 cases, 1,018 police officers were subjected to disciplinary action and criminal charges were brought against 16 officers. Racially discriminatory behaviour was the subject of 444 complaints and four officers found guilty were dismissed or required to resign whilst a fifth resigned before a disciplinary hearing. The chairman, Peter Moorhouse, reported the PCA's concern that investigations into police misbehaviour were being thwarted by 'soft' inquiries by fellow officers and the use of the right to silence, despite the Police Federation policy that officers should cooperate with investigations. There was also concern about sexual and racial harassment within forces and over deaths in police care or custody (48 in 1996–7).

Critics argue that an ombudsman for the police would have greater independence, be more effective and enjoy higher public confidence. They point to the way in which certain cases involving serious charges against the police almost failed on account of lack of sufficient police cooperation, e.g. the alleged assaults on youths in Holloway Road by officers from a police patrol van. This case culminated in the gaoling of three officers for assault and two for conspiracy to pervert the course of justice, but only after a public outcry after an initial police cover-up (1986). Prosecutions of constables arising out of the disorders during the Wapping printing dispute collapsed on account of delay (1987). The PCA should have its own staff, say critics, in order to enable it to conduct properly independent investigation into allegations of police misdemeanours. In its 1996–7 report, the PCA itself called for the power in exceptional cases to appoint investigators from outside the police. Moreover, in surveys conducted between 1990 and 1996, around 90 per cent of respondents agreed that serious complaints against the police should be investigated by a new independent body (Tarling and Dowds, 1997, p. 206).

Crime, policing and the criminal justice system

The 1990s have seen rising public concern about:

- Continuing large increases in recorded crime despite steadily rising expenditure on the police.
- An apparent deterioration in police–community relations: concerns here involved police relations with black people, police interrogation procedures and treatment of people in custody, and cases involving police corruption.
- Conditions in prisons following serious prison disturbances in 1990 and the rapid rise in the prison population in the mid-1990s.
- The operation of the criminal justice system after

Table 31.1 Notifiable offences recorded by the police in England and Wales, 1981–95 (000s)

	England and Wales	
	1981	1995
Theft and handling stolen goods,	1,603	2,452
of which: theft of vehicles	333	508
theft from vehicles	380	813
Burglary	718	1,239
Criminal damage	387	914
Violence against the person	100	213
Fraud and forgery	107	133
Robbery	20	68
Sexual offences,	19	30
of which: rape	1	5
Drug trafficking	–	21
Other notifiable offences	9	29
All notifiable offences	2,964	5,100

Source: Social Trends 1997 p. 155.

Table 31.2 Reported and recorded crime in England and Wales, 1981–95 (percentages of crime committed)

	1981	1991	1993	1995
Reported	36	49	47	46
Recorded	22	30	26	23

Source: Social Trends 1997 p. 154.

The figures need to be taken seriously but also handled with caution. First, there is a difference between all crime and recorded crime i.e. the crime recorded by the police. Many offences are not reported to the police and many offences which are reported are not – for a variety of reasons – recorded. In 1995, for example, it was estimated that only 46 per cent of all crimes against individuals and their property was reported to the police and only 23 per cent recorded by them (Table 31.2). Second, the proportion of crime reported to the police varies over time. The proportion of crime reported increased in the 1980s but fell in the 1990s, fluctuations which may be to some extent linked to insurance factors (*Social Trends,* 1997, p. 154*)*.

The *British Crime Survey (BCS),* which is pro-

several cases involving serious miscarriages of justice.

Rising crime figures

The postwar crime figures showed a constantly upward trend to the early 1990s with the number of recorded offences rising from 0.5 million in 1950 to 1.6 million in 1971, 2.5 million in 1980 and 5.6 million in 1992, after which the figure declined slightly to 5.1 million in 1995. Over 90 per cent of crime is against property, the two largest categories being theft and burglary (Table 31.1). The average clear-up rate continued to fall – it was 26 per cent in 1995. Within this average, clear-up rates varied considerably according to the offence: it was much higher for violent crimes against the person (77 per cent) and sexual offences (76 per cent) than for burglary (21 per cent) robbery (23 per cent) and criminal damage (19 per cent). Almost two-fifths (39 per cent) of all indictable offences in 1995 were committed by young offenders (aged 14–20).

Source: *The Guardian*, 23 April 1997.

Figure 31.1 Changes in recorded crime and all crime, 1981–95

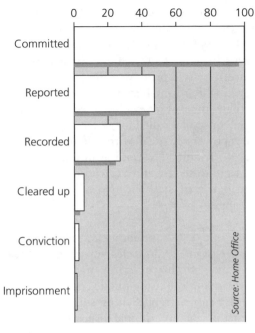

Source: Home Office

Source: The Guardian, 23 April 1997.

Figure 31.2 Crime and the criminal justice system

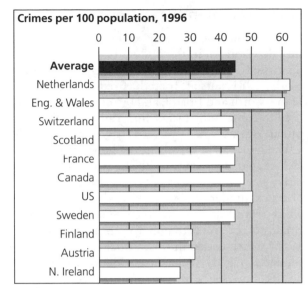

Source: The Guardian, 26 May 1997.

Figure 31.3 Crime: some international comparisons

duced every other year by the Home Office, gives a fuller account of crime. It deals with a narrower range of offences (offences against individuals and their property) than police records but does provide an indication of crime unrecorded by the police. It is based on interviews with the victims of crime. Results from the BSC enabled critics to suggest that the fall in crime claimed by the police and the government between 1991 and 1995 did not occur. Against the police records showing a 10 per cent fall, the BSC indicated a 23 per cent rise in crime (Figure 31.1). One explanation is that police recording practices changed in the first half of the 1990s so that a smaller proportion of reported crime was recorded, the reason for this being the pressure the police came under by the introduction of new performance indicators for each force. With under one half of all crime reported,a little over a quarter recorded by the police and only one fiftieth of offences leading to a conviction, it is clear that only a small proportion of all crime is dealt with by the criminal justice system (Figure 31.2).

As well as being handled with caution, the crime statistics need to be seen in perspective. Crime has increased considerably worldwide since the 1950s. However, according to the International Crime Victimisation Survey (1996) prepared by the Dutch Ministry of Justice and the British Home Office, the crime record of England and Wales was worse than nine other industrialised countries and superior only to the Netherlands in 1995 (Figure 31.3). But confidence in the police remained relatively high in England and Wales with 68 per cent thinking the police did a good job in controlling crime in their area, the fourth highest out of eleven countries.

The crime rate rose continuously in the 1980s and 1990s despite the large sums expended on policing. From 1979, expenditure on the criminal justice system (police, courts and prisons) rose steadily to £9.8 billion by 1995–6; of this money, £6.6 billion was spent on the police. Real terms expenditure on the police in 1995–6 was over one third higher than in 1986–7.

Police–community relations

Police relations with certain sections of the community deteriorated in the 1980s. The police became distrusted by blacks in the inner cities, as evidenced by the 1981 riots at Toxteth, Brixton, Moss Side, Handsworth and Bristol, and by miners, after being used to contain the picket-lines during the 1984–5 miners' strike.

The police were already facing heavy criticism for lack of sympathy towards blacks as a result of their heavy-handed treatment of black suspects, detention of blacks under the 'sus' law and predominantly white recruitment, when the riot occurred on the Broadwater Farm estate in Tottenham (6 October 1985) which ended in the murder of a police constable, a tragedy which itself followed the tragic deaths of two black women during police searches of their homes.

In the mid-1990s, problems still existed. On the one hand, the police pointed out that responsibility for the urban deprivation and racial prejudice that underlay much inner-city crime was not at root theirs. Racial incidents reported to the police almost tripled between 1988 and 1996 to over 12,000. The police felt that they were making serious efforts to improve relations with the black community. On the other hand, critics pointed to the small numbers of black policemen – only 2.9 per cent of Metropolitan Police officers in 1996 – and to the inadequacy of police efforts to investigate racial attacks. In 1997, the Labour Home Secretary Jack Straw ordered an independent judicial inquiry into the handling by the police and Crown Prosecution Service of racist attacks in the context of the 1993 murder of a black youth, Stephen Lawrence, in south London.

Other public concerns about police conduct in the 1980s and 1990s focused on:

- apparent malpractices in interrogation of suspects and in care of people whilst in custody. This is also an issue of the adequacy with which such cases are investigated and, if necessary, prosecuted. In July 1997, for example, the Director of Public Prosecutions admitted that two decisions not to prosecute police officers following deaths in custody were flawed.
- police corruption. Corruption in the Metro-politan Police and the CID (Criminal Investigation Department) was largely eradicated by the 1980s but emerged again in the Met in the 1990s. In late 1997, after the expression of concern by two prominent policemen about the way in which a small minority of corrupt officers in their forces were evading disciplinary action, chief constables called for sweeping new disciplinary powers to deal with corruption in their forces, including fast-track dismissals, abolition of the right to silence and a crackdown on the widespread use of sick leave to avoid disciplinary hearings.

By the mid-1990s, public anxiety about the rising incidence of crime, low clear-up rates and fear of becoming a victim of crime had all increased. Accompanying the rising public concern about law and order came strengthening support for drastic police action against criminal suspects including surveillance, overnight detention and telephone-tapping without police warrant (*British Social Attitudes*, the 14th Report, 1997).

Prison disturbances

A series of major disturbances flared through Britain's prisons in early 1990, leaving two prisoners dead (at Strangeways and Dartmoor), many more prisoners and prison officers injured and much damage to prison buildings and property.

An inquiry by Lord Justice Woolf found the Strangeways riot to be largely the consequence of poor prison conditions. The main goal set out in his report was the progressive improvement of prison conditions leading before the end of the century to a statutory establishment of national standards. The government accepted the main proposals in his Report in a White Paper (1991), which involved among other things seeking improvements in relations between prisoners and prison officers and providing constructive programmes for prisoners to improve their chances of employment on release. At the same time, the Criminal Justice Act (1991) sought to shift the emphasis of penal policy away from custodial sentences towards 'punishment in the community'. However, this policy was soon reversed. There had already been a move back to custodial sentencing under home secretary Kenneth

Clarke before the new home secretary in 1993, Michael Howard, proposed a 27-point policy for criminal justice at the heart of which was the notion that 'prison works'. He announced plans for six more privately built prisons and called for a more 'austere' prison regime. Overall, Howard's policies contributed to a swift rise in the prison population from 47,000 in late 1993 to 62,000 in August 1997. Conservative legislation in 1997 toughened sentences and led to the announcement of the building of 12 new 'super-prisons' together with 'high impact incarceration programmes' ('boot camps') for young offenders (Benyon and Edwards, 1997, p. 334).

However, critics argued that British penal policy made too much of imprisonment, imprisoning for example a larger proportion of its population than other EC countries. They also argued that for lesser crimes greater use could be made of alternatives to prison, such as community service, and that for minor crimes sentences were too long. An inquiry into women's jails by the Chief Inspector of Prisons (1997) suggested that up to 70 per cent of women prisoners did not represent a danger to the public and that open prisons, probation or community service would be more appropriate for them (the *Guardian*, 18 July 1997). In July 1997, alarmed by the rapid rise in the prison population, the Labour home secretary Jack Straw moved away from his pre-election hardline rhetoric on imprisonment and hinted that community sentences might be more appropriate for some offenders, especially if such sentences could be made more effective, thereby restoring public confidence in them.

Miscarriages of justice

Beginning in 1989, there occurred a series of astonishing releases of prisoners from British gaols, as verdicts were overturned in cases involving, it became clear, serious miscarriages of justice. In quick succession, the verdicts in the three largest IRA terrorist trials ever staged in Britain – the convictions of the Guildford Four, Maguire Seven and Birmingham Six – were all quashed between 1989 and 1991. The Birmingham Six had, it appeared, been wrongfully imprisoned for 16 years. Other cases involving the release of prisoners after the quashing of verdicts followed, including the Tottenham Three, the Cardiff Three, Judith Ward –

imprisoned in 1974 for a terrorist offence – Stefan Kiszko, and, in 1997, the Bridgewater Four.

The government responded to the grave crisis facing the British criminal justice system by setting up a *Royal Commission on Criminal Justice* under Lord Runciman (1991) following the release of the Birmingham Six. The Royal Commission's Report (July 1993) proved immediately controversial. Most controversial of all was the Commission's recommendation that the right to jury trial should be removed for a wide range of offences, including theft, burglary and criminal damage.

Among the Commission's 352 other proposals were: an independent authority to look into miscarriages of justice; defendants to be expected to disclose the basis of their defence before trial (their right to silence would remain); uncorroborated confessions to be allowed as evidence although judges should direct juries about how to interpret them; a new forensic science council to keep a watch on standards; and a requirement that cell corridors and police custody offices should be videoed. The government accepted its recommendation of a national DNA database but little else.

Some critics felt that a Commission originally established to offer radical proposals for the reform of criminal justice had been overtaken by a public mood less concerned with a long list of miscarriages of justice caused by 'faulty, fabricated or withheld evidence, uncorroborated confessions, biased comments by judges, police misbehaviour and the reluctance of the Court of Appeal to overturn jury verdicts' than with anxieties about the climbing crime rate (*The Economist*, 10 July 1993). In 1985, 67 per cent thought convicting an innocent person was worse than freeing a guilty one whilst 20 per cent thought the reverse. But in 1996, the proportion thinking it worse to convict the innocent had fallen to 56 per cent and the proportion considering it worse to free the guilty had increased to 27 per cent (*British Social Attitudes*, 1997, p. 207).

Parties' approaches and policies towards 'law and order'

Broadly speaking, there have been two main phases of postwar policy towards crime and punishment. (1) 1950s–1970s, characterised by the social democratic or 'welfarist' approach. In this period, a broad consensus on questions of law and order existed between the two main parties, policy towards crime was not a political issue, and differences between the parties were limited to matters of detail rather than substance. (2) 1980s to the present, characterised by the 'tough on crime' approach associated first with the Conservatives, then, in the 1990s, with Labour. Down to the early 1990s, however, Labour and the Liberal Democrats continued to support the social democratic approach to crime and punishment (Benyon and Edwards, 1997; Tarling and Dowds, 1997). The social democratic approach emphasised the relationship between poor social conditions and anti-social behaviour (crime) and, whilst accepting the need to punish those found guilty of crimes by imprisonment, stressed rehabilitation and reform of criminals more than punishment. Policing policy under this approach stressed crime prevention whilst penal policy explored alternatives to imprisonment. Based on the expectation that crime rates should fall as living standards rose, the welfarist approach was undermined in the 1970s when postwar crime rates were seen to have increased continuously despite the improvement of living standards. This paved the way for the Conservatives to call for the need to be tougher on crime in the 1979 election campaign, an approach which chimed with the changing public mood and gave them a 30-point lead on the law and order issue in the polls. Their approach was less interested in explaining crime or reforming criminals than in protecting society and sympathising with victims. They thought crime was more likely to be reduced by changes in moral attitudes produced by more care and discipline in the home than by improvements in the physical environment. The Conservatives emphasise individual responsibility: the criminal could have chosen otherwise; nothing is inevitable or predetermined. They believe in deterrence; and their policing and penal policy focuses on enhancing the likelihood of capturing wrongdoers by raising police pay and numbers; on deterring wrongdoers by tougher sentences; and on safeguarding society by using imprisonment as the predominant form of punishment.

Three main phases of Conservative policy have been identified between 1979 and 1997: restoring the rule of law, 1979–87; enlisting the community, 1987–93; and back to basic law enforcement (Benyon and Edwards, 1997). As well as rapidly rising spending on the police and the advent of new technology and equipment in policing, the first phase included the introduction of 'short sharp shock' sentences for juvenile offenders, increased police powers of stop-and-search and detention of suspects, and new public order offences and restrictions on marches and demos. The second phase saw a swing back towards crime prevention through the encouragement of Neighbourhood Watch schemes, a Safer Cities Programme and the creation of Crime Concern, towards the rehabilitation of prisoners and towards greater use of alternatives to prison such as community service orders. Finally, in addition to continuing the application of new public management to policing and the prison service, the third phase brought a return to a punitive and social protection priority, with the abolition of the defendant's right to silence in criminal trials without adverse court comment; new laws against squatting, hunt saboteurs, new age travellers and 'rave' parties; tougher sentences for a range of offenders, including automatic life sentences for those convicted of a second violent or sexual offence; and plans for more prisons.

The thirty-four pieces of law and order legislation by the Conservatives failed to halt the seemingly-remorseless upwards rise in the crime figures, which left an opening to be exploited by Labour with Blair's new 'tough on crime, tough on the causes of crime' approach after 1993. Labour's proposals sought to blend the traditional tough approach to crime and stress on individual responsibility associated with the Conservatives with a greater emphasis on crime prevention, the protection of vulnerable minorities, long-term action on poor social conditions, more constructive prison regimes, and alternatives to prison (Box 31.1). Before the 1997 general election, Labour's rhetoric tended to underline its toughness on crime at the expense of its communitarian approach; in particular, it vied with the Conservatives in its enthusiasm for an import from the US, a 'zero-tolerance' policing strategy, which aimed to stop the deterioration of city neighbourhoods by strong action against anti-social behaviour such as begging and drunkenness.

BOX 31.1

The Labour and Conservative manifestos on law and order in the 1997 General Election

Labour

Youth crime

Tougher action against young offenders, including new parental responsibility orders and faster sentencing of young offenders

'Zero tolerance' of anti-social behaviour to ensure that young offender petty criminality is seriously addressed

Protection of society

More police on the beat, not pushing paper

More consistent, stricter punishment for serious repeat offenders

Community safety orders to deal with threatening and disruptive criminal neighbours

New responsibilities for local authorities in crime prevention, including setting targets for crime reduction in their areas

Protection of vulnerable individuals and minorities

Action on stalking and domestic violence

Child protection orders to deal with young children neglected by their parents and left out late at night

New offence of racial harassment and new crime of racially motivated violence

The battle against drugs and drug-related crime

New 'drugs czar' to coordinate battle against drugs

Pilot use of compulsory drug testing and treatment orders for offenders to break link between drug addiction and crime

Prisons

More constructive prisons regime with inmates required to face up to the consequences of their behaviour

Take proper ministerial responsibility for the prison service

Protection for victims and court witnesses

Greater protection for victims in rape and serious offence trials and for victims of intimidation, including witnesses

Gun control

Free vote on a complete ban on handguns

Reform of system of justice

Reform of Crown Prosecution Service in order to prosecute criminals more effectively. At present CPS is too centralised, bureaucratic and inefficient and too many cases are dropped, delayed or downgraded to lesser offences

Attack on causes of crime

By measures to relieve social deprivation

Conservative

Youth crime

Faster sanctions on young offenders, involving where possible an element of reparation to the victim

Parental Control Orders on parents refusing to keep control of their children

Early identification and correction of children at risk of turning to crime

Tough new regimes in young offenders' institutions

Detention of 12–14 year-old offenders in secure training centres

Protection of society

Backing for chief constables who develop local schemes to crack down on petty crime and improve public order

Install 10,000 CCTC cameras in town centres and public places by 1999 plus £75 million to continue installing CCTV to town centres, villages and housing estates over the next parliament

Voluntary identity card scheme to enable retailers to identify under-age purchasers of alcohol or cigarettes or renters of classified videos

National crime squad to provide a nationally coordinated approach to organised crime

Extend electronically monitored curfew orders from adult offenders to those aged over 16

Tougher sentences including minimum sentences for violent and persistent criminals and abolition of automatic early release

Battle against drugs

Mandatory minimum sentence of 7 years for dealers in hard drugs

Continue comprehensive, coordinated strategy against drugs which involves being tough on pushers, reducing demand by educating young people, tackling drug abuse at local level through Drug Action Teams, refusing to legalise drugs, and cooperating internationally to prevent the menace spreading

Prisons

'Prison works' as a deterrent and in keeping criminals off the street – hence, 8,500 more prison places by the year 2000.

Protection of victims and witnesses

Continue strong backing for Victim Support

Discretion to courts to allow witnesses to give evidence anonymously if considered in danger from reprisal

Allow judges to stop a defendant from personally questioning the victim in rape and other cases where victim is particularly vulnerable

Reform of system of justice

Package of measures against City fraud

Action against delays in the criminal justice system

Continue reforms of civil justice system

Change structure of legal aid to ensure it functions within defined cash limits

The Labour government

Early decisions and policies of the new Labour government included measures designed to break what the home secretary Jack Straw termed the 'excuse culture' surrounding juvenile crime and the 'adjournment culture' in sentencing young offenders; to reform legal aid; and to alleviate pressure on the prisons. Policies on youth crime involved legal steps to force parents to control their delinquent children and to speed up justice for young offenders by, for example, imposing financial penalties on professionals who cause delay and setting performance targets for youth courts. Plans for legal aid entailed a virtual dismantling of the postwar civil legal aid scheme; a 'no win, no fee' system would be introduced in all civil proceedings but family cases and legal aid would be available only for criminal cases, family cases and social welfare matters. On prisons, problems of overcrowding forced the home secretary to depart from his pre-election pledge of 'no more private prisons' by inviting security companies to open two new jails, prompted a £43 million cash injection into prisons and lay behind plans to release up to 6,000 prisoners early and place them under 'home detention curfews' by electronic tagging. Labour also proposed measures to protect witnesses from intimidation and to permit judges to increase by up to two years the prison sentences of those convicted of racially motivated violence or harassment.

Summary

- The police force in Britain, traditionally and nominally still organised on a local basis (except in London and Northern Ireland), became much more centralised in the 1980s and 1990s, partly as a result of the need to organise nationally in order to combat crime more effectively and partly as a result of legislation designed to reduce local and enhance central power such as the Police and Magistrates Act, 1994.
- Problems have arisen in police accountability and complaints procedure and these remain unresolved. Critics argue that political accountability for the police needs to be strengthened and that the procedure for investigation complaints against the police has too many loopholes.
- Steady increases in the recorded crime figures postwar accompanied by decreases in the clear-up rate, deteriorations in police–community relations, serious miscarriages of justice, and the emergence of grave problems in the prisons have led to mounting public anxiety over 'law and order'.
- Down to the 1970s, the social democratic or welfarist approach to crime and punishment prevailed but in the 1980s and 1990s a 'tough on crime' approach has determined policy. However, a large amount of Conservative legislation on law and order between 1979 and 1997 failed to stem the rise in crime or public anxiety on the issue.
- Traditionally, the Conservative stress has been upon capture, detention, deterrence and punishment, whilst Labour have emphasised prevention and rehabilitation. However, after 1993, Labour has combined a new tough approach with its traditional stress on removing the causes of crime, and the parties' policies have moved closer together.

Questions

1. Critically review the present system of police accountability and complaints procedure.
2. Why has 'law and order' become such an important political issue? (You need to consider especially such topics as the growth in public concern about crime and the breakdown of the party consensus on law and order in the late 1970s and the reasons for these developments.)

Assignment

Compare the Conservative and Labour proposals on 'law and order' in their 1997 manifestos (Box 31.1).

(i) How far do you find 'convergence' in Labour and Conservative policies and in what areas? Discuss the reasons for this convergence.

(ii) What are the major differences between the two major parties' policies on law and order?

Account for the differences you find, e.g. in terms of underlying philosophy, electoral strategy or other reasons.

(iii) Why does the Labour manifesto include a promise to 'take proper ministerial responsibility' for the prison service ?

Further reading

On the constitutional framework, there is de Smith, S. and Brazier, R. (1994) *Constitutional and Administrative Law*, 7th edn (London: Penguin). On the postwar history: Morris, T. (1989) *Crime and Criminal Justice since 1945* (Oxford: Blackwell); Morris, T. (1994) 'Crime and Penal Policy', in D. Kavanagh and A. Seldon (eds), *The Major Effect* (London: Macmillan); Nash. M. and Savage, S.P. (1994) 'Law, Order and Conservative Policy', in S.P. Savage, R. Atkinson and L. Robins (eds), *Public Policy in Britain* (London: Macmillan); and Nash, M. (1994/5) 'Explaining or Excusing Criminal Behaviour – the Michael Howard Solution'. *Talking Politics*, 7:2, winter.

On the police and policing, Reiner, R. (1992) *The Politics of the Police* (London: Harvester Wheatsheaf); Leishman, F., Loveday, B. and Savage, S. (eds) (1996) *Core Issues in Policing* (London: Longman); Joyce, P. (1994/5) 'Police Reform – a Threat to Democracy?', *Talking Politics*, 7:2, winter; and Cope, S., Starie, P. and Leishman, F. (1996) 'The Politics of Police Reform', *Politics Review*, 5:4, April, can be recommended.

For the statistical background, *British Social Attitudes*, the 14th Report (1997) (Aldershot: Gower) should be consulted.

Bibliography

Adams, J. and Pyper, R. (1997) 'Whatever happened to the Scott Report?', *Talking Politics*, 9:3, spring.

Adonis, A. (1993) *Parliament Today*, 2nd edn (Manchester: Manchester University Press).

Adonis, A. and Pollard, S. (1997) *A Class Act: The Myth of Britain's Classless Society* (London: Hamish Hamilton).

Alderman, K. (1995) 'The Government Whips', *Politics Review*, 4,4, April.

Allison, G.T. (1971) *Essence of Decision* (Boston: Little Brown).

Almond, G. and Verba, S. (1965) *The Civic Culture* (Boston and Toronto: Little, Brown).

Almond, G. and Verba, S. (eds) (1980) *The Civic Culture Revisited* (Boston: Little, Brown).

Anderson, B. (1985) *Imagined Communities* (London: Verso).

Anderson, J. (1989) 'Nationalisms in a Disunited Kingdom', in J. Mohan (ed.), *The Political Geography of Contemporary Britain* (London: Macmillan).

Annual Abstract of Statistics (London: HMSO).

Arthur, P. (1984) *Government and Politics of Northern Ireland* (London: Longman).

Atkinson, R. and Durden, P. (1990) 'Housing Policy in the Thatcher Years' in S. Savage and L. Robins (eds), *Public Policy under Thatcher* (London: Macmillan).

Bachrach, P. and Baratz, M. (1971) *Power and Poverty: Theory and Practice* (London: Oxford University Press).

Baggott, R. (1990–1) 'The Policy-Making Process in British Central Government', *Talking Politics*, 3:2, winter.

Baggott, R. (1992) 'The Measurement of Change in Pressure Group Politics', *Talking Politics*, 5:1, autumn.

Baggott, R. (1995) *Pressure Groups Today* (Manchester: Manchester University Press).

Baker, D., Gamble, A. and Ludlam, S. (1992) 'More "Classless" and Less "Thatcherite"? Conservative Ministers and New Conservative MPs after the 1992 General Election', *Parliamentary Affairs*, October.

Barker, A. and Wilson, G.K. (1997) 'Whitehall's Disobedient Servants? Senior Officials' Potential Resistance to Ministers in British Government Departments', *British Journal of Political Science*, 27:2, April.

Barker, M. (1981) *The New Racism* (London: Junction Books).

Barker, R. (1997) *Political Ideas in Modern Britain* 2nd edn (London: Routledge).

Barnett, A., Eltis, C. and Hirst, P. (eds) (1993) *Debating the Constitution* (Oxford: Polity Press).

Barnett, C. (1991) 'The Education Battle begins, 120 years too late', *Sunday Times*, April 26.

Barr, G. (1992) 'The Anti-Poll Tax Movement: An Insider's View of an Outsider Group', *Talking Politics*, 4:3, summer.

Barron, J., Crawley, G. and Wood, T. (1991) *Councillors in Crisis* (London: Macmillan).

Bartlett, W. (1991) 'Quasi-Markets and Contracts: A Markets and Hierarchies Perspective on NHS Reforms', *Public Money and Management*, autumn.

Bash, L. and Coulby, D. (1989) *The Education Reform Act: Competition and Control* (London: Cassell).

Batley, R. and Stoker, G. (eds) (1991) *Local Government in Europe: Trends and Developments* (London: Macmillan).

Beer, S. (1965) *Modern British Politics* (London: Faber & Faber).

Beer, S. (1982) *Britain Against Itself: The Political Contradictions of Collectivism* (London: Faber & Faber).

Beetham, D. and Boyle, K. (1995) *Introducing Democracy 80 Questions and Answers* (London and Paris: Polity Press and Unesco Publishing).

Bell, A. (1991) *The Language of News Media* (Oxford: Blackwell).

Bell, D. (1960) *The End of Ideology* (New York: Free Press).

Benn, T. (1980) 'The Case for a Constitutional Premiership', *Parliamentary Affairs*, XXXIII: 1, winter.

Benn, T. (1982) *Parliament, Power and People* (London: Verso).

Benyon, J. and Edwards, A. (1997) 'Crime and Public Order' in P. Dunleavy, A. Gamble, I. Holliday, and G. Peele (eds), *Developments in British Politics 5* (London: Macmillan).

Berridge, G. R. (1992) *International Politics: States, Power and Conflict since 1945* (London: Harvester Wheatsheaf).

Berrington, H. (1995) 'The Nolan Report', *Government and Opposition*, 30:4, autumn.

Birch, A. H. (1979) *Political Integration and Disintegration in the British Isles* (London: Allen & Unwin).

Birch, A.H. (1993) *The Concepts and Theories of Modern Democracy* (London: Routledge).

Birkinshaw, P. (1991) *Reforming the Secret State* (Milton Keynes: Open University Press).

Birkinshaw, P. (1996) *Freedom of Information*, 2nd edn (London: Butterworth).

Birkinshaw, P. (1997) 'Freedom of Information', *Parliamentary Affairs*, 50:1, January.

Bogdanor, V. (1984) *What is Proportional Representation?* (Oxford: Martin Robertson).

Bogdanor, V. (ed.) (1988) *Constitutions in Democratic Politics* (Aldershot: Gower).

Bogdanor, V. (1997) 'The Politics of Power', The *Guardian*, June 4.

Bolton, R. (1990) *Death on the Rock and Other Stories* (London: W.H. Allen).

Borchardt, K-D. (1990) *European Unification: The Origins and Growth of the European Community* (Luxembourg: Office for Official Publications of the European Communities).

Borthwick, R. L. (1997) 'Changes in the House of Commons', *Politics Review*, 6:3, February.

Bradbeer, J. (1990) 'Environmental Policy', in S. Savage and L. Robins (eds), *Public Policy under Thatcher* (London: Macmillan).

Braybrooke, D. and Lindblom, C. (1963) *A Strategy of Decision* (New York: Free Press).

Brazier, R. (1988) *Constitutional Practice* (Oxford: Clarendon).

Brazier, R. (1991) *Constitutional Reform* (Oxford: Clarendon).

Bruce, S. (1986) *God Save Ulster: The Religion and Politics of Paisleyism* (Oxford: Oxford University Press).

Bryson, V. (1992) *Feminist Political Thought: An Introduction* (London: Macmillan).

Bulpitt, J. (1983) *Territory and Power in the United Kingdom. An Interpretation* (Manchester: Manchester University Press).

Burch, M. (1990) 'Power in the Cabinet System', *Talking Politics*, 2:3, spring.

Burch, M. (1995a) 'Prime Minister and Whitehall', in D. Shell and R. Hodder-Williams (eds), *Churchill to Major: The British Prime Ministership since 1945* (London: Hurst).

Burch, M. (1995b) ' Prime Minister and Cabinet: An Executive in Transition?', in R. Pyper and L. Robins (eds), *Governing the UK in the 1990s* (London: Macmillan).

Burch, M. and Holliday, I. (1996) *The British Cabinet System* (London: Harvester Wheatsheaf).

Burch, M. and Moran, M. (1985) 'The Changing British Political Elite', *Parliamentary Affairs*, 38, winter.

Burch, M. and Wood, B. (1997) 'From Provider to "Enabler": The Changing Role of the State', in L. Robins and B. Jones (eds), *Half a Century of British Politics* (Manchester: Manchester University Press).

Burch, M., Holliday, I. and Wood, B. (1994–5) 'The Transformation of the State', *Talking Politics,* 7:2, winter.

Burnham, J. and Jones, G.W. with Elgie, R. (1995) 'The Parliamentary Activity of John Major, 1990–1994', *British Journal of Political Science*, 25.

Burns, B. (1978) *Leadership* (New York: Harper Row).

Butcher, T. (1991–2) 'Rolling Back the State: The Conservative Governments and Privatisation, 1979–91', *Talking Politics,* 4:2, winter.

Butcher, T. (1995) 'A New Civil Service. The Next Steps Agencies,' in R. Pyper and L. Robins (eds), *Governing the UK in the 1990s* (London: Macmillan).

Butler, D. and Kavanagh, D. (1997) *The British General Election of 1997* (London: Macmillan).

Butler, D., Adonis, A. and Travers, T. (1994) *Failure in British Government.The Politics of the Poll Tax* (Oxford: Oxford University Press).

Byrd, P. (ed.) (1991) *British Defence Policy: Thatcher and Beyond* (London: Philip Allan).

Cairncross, A. (1981) 'The Post War Years 1945–1977' in R. Floud and D. McCloskey (eds) *The Economic History of Britain since 1700*, vol. 2 (Cambridge: Cambridge University Press).

Cairncross, A. K. (1992) *The British Economy since 1945* (Oxford: Blackwell).

Callaghan, J. (1987) *Time and Chance* (London: Collins).

Campbell, A., Converse, P., Miller, W. and Stokes, D. (1960) *The American Voter* (New York: Wiley).

Carroll, A. (1994) 'Judicial Control of Prerogative Power', *Talking Politics*, 7:1, autumn.

Castle, B. (1980) *The Castle Diaries, 1974–1976* (London: Weidenfeld & Nicolson).

Chalmers, M. (1985) *Paying for Defence* (London: Pluto Press).

Chester, Sir N. (1979) 'Fringe Bodies, Quangos and All That', *Public Administration*, 57:1.

Clarke, M. (1992) *British External Policy-Making in the 1990s* (London: Macmillan/RIIA).

Coates, D. (1984) *The Context of British Politics* (London: Hutchinson).

Commission of the European Communities (1991) *The European Community 1991 and Beyond* (Brussels: ECSC/EEC/EAEC)

Commoner, B. (1971) *The Closing Circle* (London: Jonathan Cape).

Cooper, M-P. (1995) 'Understanding Subsidiarity as a Political Issue in the European Community', *Talking Politics*, 7:3, spring.

Cope, S., Starie, P. and Leishman, F. (1996) 'The Politics of Police Reform', *Politics Review*, 4:4, April.

Cowley, P. (1996) 'Good Value for 19p? The Consequences of Constituent-MP Post', *Politics Review*, 5:4, April.

Cowley, P. (1996–7) 'Men (and Women) Behaving Badly? The Conservative Party since 1992', *Talking Politics,* 9:2, winter.

Cowling, D. (1997) 'A Landslide Without Illusions', *New Statesman,* May Special Edition.

Coxall, B. (1992) 'The Social Context of British Politics: Class, Gender and Race in the Two Major Parties, 1970–1990', in B. Jones and L. Robins (eds), *Two Decades in British Politics* (Manchester: Manchester University Press).

Coxall, B. and Robins, L. (1998) *British Politics since the War* (London: Macmillan).

Crafts, N. (1997) *Britain's Relative Economic Decline* (London: Social Market Foundation).

Crewe, I. (1992) 'Why did Labour Lose (Yet Again)?', *Politics Review*, 2:1, September.

Crewe, I. (1996) '1979–1996', in A. Seldon (ed.), *How Tory Governments Fall* (London: Harper Collins).

Crewe, I. and King, A. (1996) *SDP The Birth, Life and Death of the Social Democratic Party* (Oxford: Oxford University Press).

Crick, B. (ed.) (1991) *National Identity* (Oxford: Blackwell).

Crick, B. (1993) *In Defence of Politics*, 4th edn (Harmondswoth: Penguin).

Crossman, R. (1964) 'Introduction' to W. Bagehot, *The English Constitution* (London: Fontana).

Crossman, R. (1979) *The Crossman Diaries*, ed. A. Howard, condensed version (London: Methuen).

Crouch, C. and Marquand,D. (eds) (1992) *Towards Greater Europe? A Continent without an Iron Curtain* (Oxford: Blackwell).

Culley, L. (1985) *Women and Power* (Leicester: Hyperion).

Curran, J. and Seaton, J. (1990) *Power without Responsibility The Press and Broadcasting in Britain* (London: Routledge).

Curtice, J. (1997) 'Anatomy of a Non-Landslide', *Politics Review,* 7:1, September.

Curtice, J. and Jowell, R. (1995) 'The Sceptical Electorate', in R. Jowell, J. Curtice, A. Park, L. Brook and D. Ahrendt (eds), *British Social Attitudes: The 12th Report* (Aldershot: Dartmouth).

Curtice, J. and Jowell, R. (1997) 'Trust in the Political System', in R. Jowell, J. Curtice, A. Park, L. Brook, K. Thomson and C. Bryson (eds), *British Social Attitudes: The 14th Report* (Aldershot: Ashgate).

Davies, C. (1993) 'The Loss of Virtue', Social Affairs Unit, reproduced in *The Sunday Times,* 21 February.

Davis, H. (1993) 'The Political Role of the Courts', *Talking Politics,* 6:1, autumn.

Denver, D. (1989) *Elections and Voting behaviour in Britain* (Hemel Hempstead: Harvester Wheatsheaf).

Denver, D. (1997) 'The 1997 General Election Results: Lessons for Teachers', *Talking Politics,* 10:1, autumn.

Denver, D. and Hands, G. (1992) 'The Political Socialisation of Young People', in B. Jones and L. Robins (eds) *Two Decades in British Politics* (Machester: Manchester University Press).

de Smith, S.A. and Brazier, R. (1990) *Constitutional and Administrative Law,* 6th edn (Harmondsworth: Penguin).

de Smith, S.A. and Brazier, R. (1994) *Constitutional and Administrative Law* (Harmondsworth: Penguin).

Digby, A. (1989) *British Welfare Policy* (London: Faber & Faber).

Dobson, A. (1993) 'Ecologism', in R. Eatwell and A. Wright (eds), *Contemporary Political Ideologies* (London: Pinter).

Donoughue, B. (1987) *Prime Minister* (London: Jonathan Cape).

Donoughue, B. (1988) 'The Prime Minister's Diary', *Contemporary Review,* 2:2.

Dorey, P. (1994–5) 'Widened Yet Weakened: The Changing Character of Collective Responsibility', *Talking Politics,* 7:2, winter.

Dorey, P. (1995) *British Politics since 1945* (Oxford: Blackwell).

Dorril, S. (1992) *The Silent Conspiracy Inside the Intelligence Services in the 1990s* (London: Heinemann).

Dowds, L. and Young, K. (1996) 'National Identity', in R. Jowell, J. Curtice, A. Park, L. Brook, and K. Thomson (eds), *British Social Attitudes: The 13th. Report* (Aldershot: Dartmouth).

Downing, J., Momammadi, A. and Sreberny-Momammadi, A. (1991) *Questioning the Media; A Critical Introduction* (Newbury Park, California: Sage).

Drewry, G. (1988) 'Legislation' in M. Ryle and P. Richards (eds) *The Commons Under Scrutiny* London: Routledge).

Drewry, G. (1989) *The New Select Committees,* 2nd edn (Oxford: Clarendon).

Drewry, G. and Butcher, T. (1991) *The Civil Service Today,* 2nd edn (Oxford: Blackwell).

Dunleavy, P. (1980) *Urban Political Analysis* (London: Macmillan).

Dunleavy, P. (1995) 'Estimating the Distribution of Positional Influence in Cabinet Committees under Major', in R.A.W. Rhodes and P. Dunleavy (eds), *Prime Minister, Cabinet and Core Executive* (London: Macmillan).

Dunleavy, P. (1997) 'The Constitution', in P. Dunleavy, A. Gamble, I. Holliday and G. Peele (eds), *Developments in British Politics 5* (London: Macmillan).

Dunleavy, P. and Jones, G.W. (1993) 'Leaders, Politics and Institutional Change: The Decline of Prime Ministerial Accountability to the House of Commons, 1868–1990', *British Journal of Political Science,* 23.

Dunleavy, P. and Margetts, H. (1997) 'The Electoral System', *Parliamentary Affairs,* 50:4, October.

Dunleavy, P. and Weir, S. (1995) 'Media, Opinion and the Constitution', in F. F.Ridley and A. Doig (eds), *Sleaze: Politicians, Private Interests and Public Reaction* (Oxford: Oxford University Press).

Dunleavy, P., Jones, G.W. and O'Leary, B. (1990) 'Prime Ministers and the Commons: Patterns of Behaviour, 1868–1967', *Public Administration,* 68, spring.

Dunleavy, P., Gamble, A., Holliday, I. and G. Peele (eds) (1997) *Developments in British Politics 5* (London: Macmillan).

Dunn, J. (ed.) (1992) *Democracy: The Unfinished Journey 508 BC to AD 1993* (Oxford: Oxford University Press).

Dutton, D. (1991) *British Politics since 1945: The Rise and Fall of Consensus* (Oxford: Blackwell).

Economic and Social Research Council (1997) 'Constructing Classes', ESRC Research Centre, University of Essex.

The Economist, (1997) Election Briefing, 1997 (Economist Publications).

Eatwell, R. (1997) 'Britain', in R. Eatwell (ed.), *European Political Culture* (London: Routledge).

Eatwell, R. and Wright, A. (1993) *Contemporary Political Ideologies* (London: Pinter).

Eccleshall, R. (1986) *British Liberalism: Liberal Thought from the 1640s to the 1980s* (London: Longman).

Eccleshall, R., Geoghegan, V., Jay, R. and Wilford, R. (1984) *Political Ideologies* (London: Routledge).

Eccleshall, R., Geoghegan, V., Jay, R., Kenny, M., MacKenzie, I. and Wilford, R. (1994) *Political Ideologies,* 2nd edn (London: Routledge).

Education Group II (1991) *Education Limited: Schooling, Training and the New Right in England since 1979* (London: Unwin Hyman).

Evans, D. J. (1993) *Sexual Citizenship* (London: Routledge).

Evans, M. (1997) 'Political Participation', in P. Dunleavy, A. Gamble, I. Holliday and G. Peele (eds), *Developments in British Politics 5* (London: Macmillan).

Ewing, K. D. and Gearty, C. (1990) *Freedom under Thatcher: Civil Liberties in Modern Britain* (Oxford: Clarendon).

Farrell, D. (1997) *Comparing Electoral Systems* (London: Macmillan).

Finer, C. J. (1997) 'Social Policy' in P. Dunleavy, A. Gamble, I. Holliday and G. Peele (eds), *Developments in British Politics 5* (London: Macmillan).

Finer, S. E. (1979) *Five Constitutions* (Harmondsworth: Penguin).

Finer, S.E., Bogdanor, V. and Rudden, B. (1995) *Comparing Constitutions* (Oxford: Clarendon).

Fisher, J. (1996) *British Political Parties* (Hemel Hempstead: Prentice Hall/Harvester Wheatsheaf).

Flude, M. and Hammer, M. (eds) (1990) *The Education Reform Act, 1988. Its Origins and Implications* (London: Falmer Press).

Foley, M. (1993) *The Rise of the British Presidency* (Manchester: Manchester University Press).

Foote, G. (1996) *The Labour Party's Political Thought* (London: Croom Helm).

Foster, S. and Kelly, R. (1992) 'Understanding Thatcherism: Economics Over Politics?', *Talking Politics*, 5:1, autumn.

Frankel, J. (1970) *National Interest* (London: Pall Mall).

Franklin, M. (1985) *The Decline of Class Voting* (Oxford: Oxford University Press).

Freedman, L. (1994) 'Defence Policy', in A. Seldon and D. Kavanagh (eds), *The Major Effect* (London: Macmillan).

Freeman, M. (1997) 'Why Rights Matter', *Politics Review*, 7:1, September.

Fukuyama, F. (1992) *The End of History and the Last Man* (London: Hamish Hamilton).

Gamble, A. (1997) 'Conclusion: Politics 2000' in P. Dunleavy, A. Gamble I. Holliday and G Peele (eds), *Devlopments in British Politics 5* (London: Macmillan).

Gamble, A. (1994) *The Free Economy and the Strong State: The Politics of Thatcherism* (London: Macmillan).

Garner, R. (1996) *Environmental Politics* (Hemel Hempstead: Prentice Hall/Harvester Wheatsheaf).

Garner, R. and Kelly, R. (1993) *British Political Parties Today* (Manchester: Manchester University Press).

Garnett, M. (1996) *Principles and Policies in Modern Britain* (London: Longman).

Gavin, N. and Sanders, D. (1997) 'The Economy and Voting', *Parliamentary Affairs*, 50:4, October.

Glasgow Media Group (1980) *More Bad News* (London: Routledge).

Glennerster, H., Power, A. and Travers, T. (1991) 'A New Era for Social Policy: A New Enlightenment or a New Leviathan?', *Journal of Social Policy*, 20:3.

Glennerster, H. (1995) *British Social Policy since 1945* (Oxford: Blackwell).

Golding, P. (1974) *The Mass Media* (London: Longman).

Grant, M. (1994) 'The Rule of Law – Theory and Practice', *Talking Politics*, 7:1, autumn.

Grant, W. (1995) *Pressure Groups, Politics and Democracy*, 2nd edn (Hemel Hempstead: Prentice Hall/Harvester Wheatsheaf).

Greenaway, J.R., Smith, S. and Street, J. (1992) *Deciding Factors in British Politics: A Case-Studies Approach* (London: Routledge).

Greenleaf, W. H. (1983) *The British Political Tradition, vol.2 The Ideological Heritage* (London: Methuen).

Greenwood, J. (1991–2) 'Local Government in the 1990s: The Consultation Papers on Structure, Finance and Internal Management', *Talking Politics*, 4:2, winter.

Griffith, J.A.G. (1989) 'The Official Secrets Act 1989', *Journal of Law and Society*, 16:2, autumn.

Griffith, J.A.G. and Ryle, M. (1989) *Parliament* (London: Sweet & Maxwell).

Gyford, J. (1991) *Citizens, Consumers and Councils: Local Government and the Public* (London: Macmillan).

Hague, R., Harrop, M. and Breslin, S. (1998) *Comparative Government and Politics*, 4th edn (London: Macmillan).

Hague, R., Harrop, M. and Breslin, S. (1998) *Comparative Government and Politics*, 4th edn (London: Macmillan).

Hall, W. and Weir, S. (1996) *The Untouchables: Power and Accountability in the Quango State* (London: The Democratic Audit/Scarman Trust).

Halsey, A. H. (ed.) (1988) *Trends in British Society Since 1900* (London: Macmillan).

Ham, C. (1991) *The New National Health Service Organisation and Management* (Oxford: Radcliffe Medical).

Harrison, M. (1985) *TV News: Whose Bias?* (Hermitage: Policy Journals).

Heath, A. and Park, A. (1997) 'Thatcher's Children', in R. Jowell, J. Curtice, A. Park, L. Brook, K. Thomson and L. Bryson (eds), *British Social Attitudes: The 14th Report* (Aldershot: Ashgate).

Heath, A. and Topf, R. (1987) 'Political Culture', in R. Jowell, S. Witherspoon and L. Brook (eds), *British Social Attitudes: The 5th Report* (Aldershot: Gower).

Heath, A., Jowell, R. and Curtice, J. (1985) *How Britain Votes* (Oxford: Pergamon).

Hechter, M. (1975) *Internal Colonialism: The Celtic Fringe in British Colonial Development, 1536–1966* (London: Routledge & Kegan Paul).

Heclo, H. and Wildavsky, A. (1974) *The Private Government of Public Money* (London: Macmillan).

Hennessy, P. (1987) *Cabinet* (Oxford: Blackwell).

Hennessy, P. (1990) *Whitehall*, 2nd edn (London: Fontana).

Hennessy, P. (1995) *The Hidden Wiring Unearthing the British Constitution* (London: Gollancz).

Hennessy, P. (1998) 'The Blair Style of Government: An Historical Perspective and an Interim Audit', *Government and Opposition*, 33:1, winter.

Heywood, A. (1998) *Political Ideologies An Introduction*, 2nd edn (London: Macmillan).

Heywood, A. (1997) *Politics* (London: Macmillan).

Himmelweit, H., Humphries, P. and Jaeger, M. (1984) *How Voters Decide* (Milton Keynes: Open University Press).

Holland, R. (1991) *The Pursuit of Greatness: Britain and the World Role, 1900–1970* (London: Fontana).

Holsti, K.J. (1967) *International Politics* (Englewood Cliffs, NJ: Prentice Hall).

Hood, C. and James, D. (1997) 'The Core Executive' in P. Dunleavy, A. Gamble, I. Holliday and G. Peele (eds), *Developments in British Politics 5* (London: Macmillan).

Horton, S. (1990) 'Local Government 1979–89: A Decade of Change', in S. Savage and L. Robins (eds), *Public Policy under Thatcher* (London: Macmillan).

Hunt, K. (1987) 'Women and Politics', in B. Jones (ed.), *Political Issues in Britain Today* (Manchester: Manchester University Press).

Hunt, S. (1992a) 'Fascism and the "Race Issue" in Britain'. *Talking Politics*, 5:1, autumn.

Hunt, S. (1992b) 'State Secrecy in the UK', *Politics Review*, 1:4, April.

Hutchinson, J. (1994) *Modern Nationalism* (London: Fontana).

Hutton, J. et al., (eds) (1991) *Dependency to Enterprise* (London: Routledge).

Hutton, W. (1996a) 'High Risk Strategy', *Talking Politics*, 8:3, spring.

Hutton, W. (1996b) *The State We're In*, new and revised edn (London: Vintage).

Hutton, W. (1997) *The State to Come* (London: Vintage).

James, S. (1992) *British Cabinet Government* (London: Routledge).

James, S. (1995) 'Relations between Prime Minister and Cabinet: From Wilson to Thatcher', in R.A.W. Rhodes and P. Dunleavy (eds), *Prime Minister, Cabinet and Core Executive* (London: Macmillan).

Jenkins, J. and Klandermans, B. (eds) (1995) *The Politics of Social Protest* (London: University College, London Press).

John, P. (1997) 'Local Governance', in P. Dunleavy, A. Gamble, I. Holliday and G. Peele (eds), *Developments in British Politics 5* (London: Macmillan).

Johnson, P. (ed.) (1994) *Twentieth Century Britain* (London: Longman).

Jones, A. (1994) 'European Union Electoral Systems – An Overview of the Electoral Systems of the European Parliament and the National Legislatures', *Talking Politics*, 6:3, winter.

Jones, B. (ed.) (1987) *Political Issues in Britain Today* (Manchester: Manchester University Press).

Jones, B. (1989–90) 'Green Thinking', *Talking Politics*, 2:2, winter.

Jones, B. and Robins, L. (eds) (1992) *Two Decades in British Politics* (Manchester: Manchester University Press).

Jones, G.W. (1990) 'Mrs Thatcher and the Power of the Prime Minister', *Contemporary Record*, 3:4.

Jones, G.W. (1995) 'The Downfall of Margaret Thatcher' in R.A.W. Rhodes and P. Dunleavy (eds) *Prime Minister, Cabinet and Core Executive* (London: Macmillan).

Jones, K. (1991) 'Mythology and Social Policy' in J. Hutton et al. (eds), *Dependency to Enterprise* (London: Routledge).

Jones, P. (1997) *America and the British Labour Party: The Special Relationship at Work* (London: Tauris Academic Studies).

Jordan, A.G. and Richardson, J.J. (1987) *Government and Pressure Groups in Britain* (Oxford: Clarendon).

Jowell, R. and Airey, C. (eds) (1984) *British Social Attitudes: The 1984 Report* (Aldershot: Gower).

Jowell, R. and Topf, R. (1988) 'Trust in the Establishment', in R. Jowell, S. Witherspoon and L. Brook (eds), *British Social Attitudes: The 6th Report* (Aldershot: Gower)

Jowell, R., Witherspoon, S. and Brook, L. (eds) (1987) *British Social Attitudes: The 5th Report* (Aldershot: Gower).

Jowell, R., Witherspoon, S. and Brook, L. (eds) (1988) *British Social Attitudes: The Sixth Report* (Aldershot: Gower).

Jowell, R., Witherspoon, S. and Brook, L. (eds) (1990) *British Social Attitudes: The 7th Report* (Aldershot: Gower).

Jowell, R., Curtice, J., Park, A., Brook, L. and Ahrendt, D. (eds) (1995) *British Social Attitudes: The 12th Report* (Aldershot: Dartmouth).

Jowell, R., Curtice, J., Park, A., Brook, L. and Thomson, K. (eds) (1996) *British Social Attitudes: The 13th Report* (Aldershot: Dartmouth).

Jowell, R., Curtice, J., Park, A., Brook, L., Thomson, K. and Bryson, C. (eds) (1997) *British Social Attitudes: The 14th Report* (Aldershot: Ashgate).

Joyce, P. (1994–5) 'Police Reform – a Threat to Democracy?', *Talking Politics*, 7:2, winter.

Judd, D. (1996) *Empire: The British Imperial Experience from 1765 to the Present* (London: Fontana).

Judge, D. (1993) *The Parliamentary State* (London: Sage).

Kavanagh, D. (1971) 'The Deferential English: A Comparative Critique' in D. Kavanagh (1990) *Politics and Personalities* (London: Macmillan).

Kavanagh, D. (1980) 'Political Culture in Great Britain: The Decline of the Civic Culture', in G. Almond and S. Verba (eds), *The Civic Culture Revisited* (Boston: Little, Brown).

Kavanagh, D. (1990) *Politics and Personalities* (London: Macmillan).

Kavanagh, D. (1990) *Thatcherism and British Politics*, 2nd edn (Oxford: Oxford University Press).

Kavanagh, D. (1991) 'Prime Ministerial Power Revisited', *Social Studies Review*, 6:4, March.

Kavanagh, D. (1997) 'The Labour Campaign', *Parliamentary Affairs*, 50:4, October.

Kavanagh, D. and Morris, P. (1994) *Consensus Politics from Attlee to Thatcher*, 2nd edn (Oxford: Blackwell).

Kavanagh, D. and Seldon, A. (eds) (1994) *The Major Effect* (London: Macmillan).

Kellner, P. (1997a) 'PR paradox puts Paddy in a quandary', *The Observer*, September 21.

Kellner, P. (1997b) 'Why the Tories were Trounced', *Parliamentary Affairs*, 50:4, October.

Kellner, P. and Crowther-Hunt, Lord (1980) *The Civil Servants* (London: Macdonald).

Kelly, G. (1997) 'Economic Policy' in P. Dunleavy, A. Gamble, I. Holliday and G. Peele (eds), *Developments in British Politics 5* (London: Macmillan).

Kelly, R. (1989) 'Party Conferences: Do They Matter?', *Talking Politics*, 2:1, autumn.

Kelly, R. (1992) 'Power in the Conservative Party', *Politics Review*, 1:4, April.

Kelly, R. (1995) 'The Left, the Right and the Whipless: Conservative Divisions since 1992', *Talking Politics*, 8:1, autumn.

Kemp, P. (1992) 'Housing' in D. Marsh and R.A.W. Rhodes (eds), *Implementing Thatcherite Policies* (Buckingham: Open University Press).

Kemp, P. (1996) 'Handling the Machine: A Memo to Labour', *Political Quarterly*, 67:14, October–December.

Kendall, I. and Moon, G. (1990) 'Health Policy' in S. Savage and L. Robins (eds), *Public Policy under Thatcher* (London: Macmillan).

King, A. (ed.) (1985) *The British Prime Minister: A Reader*, 2nd edn (London: Macmillan).

Kingdom, J. (1994–5) 'Impact of the European Union upon UK Government and Politics', *Talking Politics*, 7:2, winter.

Kingdom, J. (1995) 'The European Context', in M. Mullard (ed.) *Policy-Making in Britain* (London: Routledge).

Klein, R. (1989) *The Politics of the NHS* (London: Longman).

Klug, F., Starmer, K. and Weir, S. (1996) *The Three Pillars of Liberty* (London: Routledge).

Laffan, B. (1992) *Integration and Cooperation in Europe* (London: Routledge).

Layton-Henry, Z. (1992) *Immigration and 'Race' Politics in Post-War Britain* (Oxford: Blackwell).

Leach, R. (1996) *British Political Ideologies*, 2nd edn (Hemel Hempstead: Prentice Hall/Harvester Wheatsheaf).

Leach, S. and Stewart, M. (1992) *Local Government: Its Role and Function* (York: Joseph Rowntree Foundation).

Lee, J. M. (1995) 'The Prime Minister and International Relations', in D. Shell and R. Hodder-Williams (eds), *Churchill to Major: The British Prime Ministership since 1945* (London: Hurst).

Lee, S. (1994) 'Law and the Constitution', in A. Seldon and D. Kavanagh (eds), *The Major Effect* (London: Macmillan).

Leftwich, A. (ed.) (1984) *What is Politics?* (Oxford: Blackwell).

Leishman, F., Loveday, B. and Savage, S. (1996) *Core Issues in Policing* (London: Longman).

Liddell, P.H. (1994) 'The Public Accounts Committee and the Audit of Public Expenditure', *Talking Politics,* 7:1, autumn.

Lijphart, A. and Grofman, B. (1984) *Choosing an Electoral System* (New York: Praeger).

Loughlin, M. and Scott, C. (1997) 'The Regulatory State' in P. Dunleavy, A. Gamble, I. Holliday and G. Peele (eds), *Developments in British Politics 5* (London: Macmillan).

Loveday, B. (1994) 'The Police and Magistrates' Court Act', *Policing,* vol. 10.

Loveland, I. (1993) 'Redefining Parliamentary Sovereignty? A New Perspective on the Search for the Meaning of Law', *Parliamentary Affairs,* 46:3, July.

Loveland, I. (1997) 'The War against the Judges', *Political Quarterly,* April–June.

Lovenduski, J. (1997) 'Gender Politics: A Breakthrough for Women?', *Parliamentary Affairs,* 50:4, October.

Lowe, R. (1993) *The Welfare State in Britain since 1945* (London: Macmillan).

Lucas, J.R. (1985) *The Principles of Politics,* paperback edn (Oxford: Oxford University Press).

Ludlam, S. (1996) 'The Spectre Haunting Conservatism: Europe and Backbench Rebellion', in S. Ludlam and M.J. Smith (eds), *Contemporary British Conservatism* (London: Macmillan).

Ludlam, S. and Smith, M.J. (eds) (1996) *Contemporary British Conservatism* (London: Macmillan).

Lupton, C. and Russell, D. (1990) 'Equal Opportunities in a Cold Climate' in S. Savage and L. Robins (eds) *Public Policy under Thatcher* (London: Macmillan).

Lustgarten, L. and Leigh, I. (1994) *National Security and Parliamentary Democracy* (Oxford: Clarendon).

Lynch, P. (1996) 'Labour, Devolution and the West Lothian Question', *Talking Politics,* 9:1, autumn.

McCulloch, A. (1988) 'Politics and the Environment' *Talking Politics,* 1:1, autumn.

McDowell, L. Sarre, P. and Hamnett, C. (eds) (1989) *Divided Nation: Social and Cultural Change in Britain* (London: Hodder and Stoughton).

Maclean, M. and Groves, D. (eds) (1991) *Women's Issues in Social Policy* (London: Routledge).

McAllister, I. (1997) 'Regional Voting', *Parliamentary Affairs,* 50:4, October.

McGrew, A. and Wilson, M. (eds) (1982) *Decision-Making: Approaches and Analysis* (Manchester: Manchester University Press).

McIlroy, J. (1989) 'The Politics of Racism', in B. Jones (ed.), *Political Issues in Britain Today* (Manchester: Manchester University Press).

McKee, V. (1996) 'Factions and Tendencies in the Conservative Party since 1945', *Politics Review* 5:4, April.

McLellan, D. (1980) *The Political Thought of Karl Marx* (London: Macmillan).

McQuail, D. (1987) *Mass Communications Theory* (Beverley Hills: Sage).

McVicar, M. (1990) 'Education Policy: Education as a Business?' in S. Savage and L. Robins (eds), *Public Policy under Thatcher* (London: Macmillan).

Madgwick, P. (1991) *British Government: The Central Executive Territory* (London: Philip Allan).

Madgwick, P. and Rawkins, P. (1982) 'The Welsh Language in the Policy Process', in P. Madgwick and R. Rose (eds), *The Territorial Dimension in United Kingdom Politics* (London: Macmillan).

Madgwick, P. and Rose, R. (eds) (1982) *The Territorial Dimension in United Kingdom Politics* (London: Macmillan).

Madgwick, P. and Woodhouse, D. (1995) *The Law and Politics of the Constitution* (Hemel Hempstead: Harvester Wheatsheaf).

Malpass, P. (1990a) *Reshaping Housing Politics* (London: Routledge).

Malpass, P. (ed.) (1990b) *The Housing Crisis* (London: Croom Helm).

Marquand, D. and Seldon, A. (eds) (1996) *The Ideas that Shaped Post-War Britain* (London: Fontana).

Marsh, D. (1992) *The New Politics of British Trade Unionism* (London: Macmillan).

Marsh, D. (1995) 'The Convergence between Theories of the State', in D. Marsh and G. Stoker (eds), *Theory and Methods in Political Science* (London: Macmillan).

Marsh, D. and Rhodes, R.A.W. (eds) (1992a) *Policy Networks in British Government* (Oxford: Oxford University Press).

Marsh, D. and Rhodes, R.A.W. (eds) (1992b) *Implementing Thatcherite Policies* (Milton Keynes: Open University Press).

Marsh, D. and Rhodes, R.A.W. (1996) 'The Concept of Policy Networks in British Political Science: Its Development and Utility', *Talking Politics,* 8:3, spring.

Marsh, D. and Stoker, G.(eds) (1995) *Theory and Methods in Political Science* (London: Macmillan).

Marshall, G. (1984) *Constitutional Conventions* (Oxford: Clarendon).

Marshall, G. (ed.) (1989) *Ministerial Responsibility* (Oxford: Oxford University Press).

Marshall, G. (1991) 'The Evolving Practice of Parliamentary Accountability', *Parliamentary Affairs,* 4:4.

Marshall, G. and Moodie, G. (1967) *Some Problems of the Constitution* (London: Hutchinson).

Marshall, G. Swift, A. and Roberts, S. (1997) *Against the Odds? Social Class and Social Justice in Industrial Societies* (Oxford: Clarendon Press).

Maynard, G. (1988) *The Economy under Mrs Thatcher* (Oxford: Blackwell).

Mazey, S. and Richardson, J.J. (eds) (1993) *Lobbying in the European Community* (Oxford: Oxford University Press).

Miliband, R. (1973) *The State in Capitalist Society* (London: Quartet).

Miliband, R. (1984) *Capitalist Democracy in Britain* (Oxford: Oxford University Press).

Miliband, D. (ed.) (1994) *Reinventing the Left* (Cambridge: Polity).

Miller, W. et al. (1990) *How Voters Change* (Oxford: Clarendon).

Mills, C. Wright (1956) *The Power Elite* (New York: Oxford University Press).

Milne, S. (1994) *The Enemy Within: MI5, Maxwell and the Scargill Affair* (London: Verso).

Minogue, K. (1995) *Politics: A Very Short Introduction* (Oxford: Oxford University Press).

Mitchell, J. (1971) *Women's Estate* (Harmondsworth: Penguin).

Moran, M. (1989) *Politics and Society in Britain*, 2nd edn (London: Macmillan).

Morgan, K. (1990) *The People's Peace: British History, 1945–1989* (Oxford: Oxford University Press).

Morris, T. (1989) *Crime and Criminal Justice since 1945* (Oxford: Blackwell).

Morris, T. (1994) 'Crime and Penal Policy', in A. Seldon and D. Kavanagh (eds), *The Major Effect* (London: Macmillan).

Mosley, Sir Oswald (1932) *The Greater Britain* (London: BUF Publications).

Mount, F. (1992) *The British Constitution Now* (London: Heinemann).

Murdoch, G. and Golding P. (1977) 'Beyond Monopoly – Mass Communications in an Age of Conglomerates', in P. Beharell and G. Philo (eds) *Trade Unions and the Mass Media* (London: Macmillan).

Nash, M. (1994–5) 'Explaining or Excusing Criminal Behaviour – the Michael Howard Solution', *Talking Politics,* 7:2, winter.

Nash, M. and Savage, S. P. (1994) 'Law, Order and Conservative Policy' in S.P. Savage, R.A. Atkinson and L. Robins (eds), *Public Policy in Britain* (London: Macmillan).

Neunreither, K. (1993) 'Subsidiarity as a Guiding Principle for European Community', *Government and Opposition*, 28:2.

Norris, P. (1991) 'Gender Differences in Political Participation in Britain: Traditional, Radical and Revisionist Models', *Government and Opposition,* 26:1.

Norris, P. (1997) 'Anatomy of a Landslide', *Parliamentary Affairs,* 50:4, October.

Norris, P. and Lovenduski, J. (1995) *Political Recruitment: Gender, Race and Class in the British Parliament* (Cambridge: Cambridge University Press).

Norton, P. (1981) *The Commons in Perspective* (London: Longman).

Norton, P. (1990) 'Public Legislation' in M. Rush (ed.), *Parliament and Pressure Politics* (Oxford: Oxford University Press).

Norton, P. (1992) 'The House of Commons: From Overlooked to Overworked', in B. Jones and L. Robins (eds), *Two Decades in British Politics* (Manchester: Manchester University Press).

Norton, P. (1993) 'A Bill of Rights: The Case Against', *Talking Politics,* 5:3, summer.

Norton, P. (1994a) 'The Constitution in Question', *Politics Review,* 3:4, April.

Norton, P. (1994b) 'Select Committees in the House of Commons: Watchdogs or Poodles?', *Politics Review,* 4:2, November.

Norton, P. (1995a) 'Standing Committees in the House of Commons', *Politics Review,* 4:4, April.

Norton, P. (1995b) 'National Parliaments and the European Union', *Talking Politics,* 7:3, spring.

Norton, P. (1995–6) 'Parliamentary Behaviour since 1945', *Talking Politics,* 8:2, winter.

Norton, P. (1997) 'The United Kingdom: Restoring Confidence?', *Parliamentary Affairs,* 50:3, July.

Norton, P. and Wood, D.M. (1993) *Back from Westminster: British Members of Parliament and their Constituents* (Lexington, Kentucky: Kentucky University Press of Kentucky).

Norton-Taylor, R. (1990) *In Defence of the Realm? The Case for Accountable Security Services* (London: Civil Liberties Trust).

Norton-Taylor, R. (1995) *Truth is a Difficult Concept: Inside the Scott Inquiry* (London: Fourth Estate).

Nugent, N. (1994) *The Government and Politics of the European Union*, 3rd edn (2nd edn 1991) (London: Macmillan).

Oakley, A. (1972) *Sex, Gender and Society* (Hounslow: Temple Smith).

Office for Official Publications of the European Communities (1986), *The Court of Justice of the EC* (Luxembourg: OPEC).

O'Gorman, F. (1986) *British Conservatism* (London: Longman).

Oliver, D. (1993) 'Citizenship in the 1990s', *Politics Review*, 3:1, September.

Oppenheim, C. (1990) *Poverty: The Facts* (London: CPAG).

Orwell, G. and Angus, I. (1968) *The Collected Essays, Journalism and Letters of George Orwell*, vol. II (London: Secker & Warburg).

Palmer, S. (1990) 'Tightening Secrecy Law: The Official Secrets Act 1989', *Public Law,* summer.

Parry, G. and Moyser, G. (1990) 'A Map of Political Participation in Britain', *Government and Opposition*, 25:2.

Parry, G. and Moyser, G. (1993) 'Political Participation in Britain', *Politics Review*, 3:2, November.

Parry, G., Moyser,G. and Day, N. (1992) *Political Participation and Democracy in Britain* (Cambridge: Cambridge University Press).

Peele, G. (1993) 'The Constitution', in P. Dunleavy, A. Gamble, I. Holliday and G. Peele (eds), *Developments in British Politics 4* (London: Macmillan).

Peele, G. (1997) 'Political Parties', in P. Dunleavy, A. Gamble, I. Holliday and G. Peele (eds), *Developments in British Politics 5* (London: Macmillan).

Pentland, C. (1973) *International Theory and European Integration* (London: Faber & Faber).

Peterson, J. (1997) 'Britain, Europe and the World', in P. Dunleavy, A. Gamble, I. Holliday and G. Peele (eds), *Developments in British Politics 5* (London: Macmillan).

Pilkington, C. (1995) *Britain in the European Union Today* (Manchester: Manchester University Press).

Pimlott, B. (1994) 'The Myth of Consensus', in B. Pimlott, *Frustrate Their Knavish Tricks* (London: Harper Collins).

Pliatzky, L. (1982) *Getting and Spending* (Oxford: Blackwell).

Plummer, J. (1994) *The Governance Gap: Quangos and Accountability* (London: Demos/Joseph Rowntree Foundation).

Porritt, J. (1984) *Seeing Green* (Oxford: Blackwell).

Porter, B. (1989) *Plots and Paranoia: A History of Political Espionage in Britain, 1790–1988* (London: Unwin Hyman).

Pugh, M. (1994) *State and Society: British Political and Social History 1870–1992* (London: Edward Arnold).

Pulzer, P. (1967) *Representation and Elections in Britain* (London: Allen & Unwin).

Pyper, R. (1991) 'Governments, 1964–1990: A Survey', *Contemporary Record*, 5:2, autumn.

Pyper, R. (1994) 'Individual Ministerial Responsibility: Dissecting the Doctrine', *Politics Review*, 4:1, September.

Pyper, R. (1995) *The British Civil Service* (London: Harvester Wheatsheaf).

Pyper, R. and Robins, L. (1995) (eds) *Governing the UK in the 1990s* (London: Macmillan).

Rallings, C. and Thresher, M. (1997) 'The Local Elections', *Parliamentary Affairs*, 50:4, October.

Randall, V. (1987) *Women and Politics,* 2nd edn (London: Macmillan).

Ranson, S. (1990) 'From 1945 to 1988: Education, Citizenship and Democracy' in M. Flude and M. Hammer (eds), *The Education Reform Act 1988: Its Origins and Implications* (London: Falmer).

Reiner, R. (1992) *The Politics of the Police* (London: Harvester Wheatsheaf).

Reward Group Cost of Living Report (1988) (London).

Reynolds, D. (1991) *Britannia Overruled: British Policy and World Power in the Twentieth Century* (London: Longman).

Rhodes, R.A.W. (1981) *Control and Power in Central–Local Relations* (Farnborough: Gower)

Rhodes, R.A.W. (1992a) 'Local Government', in B. Jones and L. Robins (eds), *Two Decades in British Politics* (Manchester: Manchester University Press).

Rhodes, R.A.W. (1992b) 'Local Government Finance', in D. Marsh and R.A.W. Rhodes (eds), *Implementing Thatcherite Policies* (Buckingham: Open University Press).

Richards, S. (1996) 'New Labour – New Civil Service?', *Political Quarterly,* 67:4, October–December.

Richardson, J.J. (ed.) (1993) *Pressure Groups* (Oxford: Oxford University Press).

Ridley, F.F. (1988) 'There is No British Constitution: A Dangerous Case of the Emperor's Clothes', *Parliamentary Affairs,* 41:3, July.

Ridley, F.F. (1991) 'Using Power to Keep Power: The Need for Constitutional Checks', *Parliamentary Affairs,* 44:4, October.

Ridley, F.F. and Rush, M. (eds) (1995) *British Government and Politics since 1945* (Oxford: Oxford University Press).

Ridley, F.F. and Wilson, D. (1995) *The Quango Debate* (Oxford: Oxford University Press).

Robins, L. (1982) *Topics in British Politics* (London: The Politics Association).

Robins, L., Blackmore, H. and Pyper, R. (eds) (1994) *Britain's Changing Party System* (London: Leicester University Press).

Robinson, M. (1992) *The Greening of British Party Politics* (Manchester: Manchester University Press).

Rose, R. (1982) 'Is the United Kingdom a State? Northern Ireland as a Test Case' in P. Madgwick and R. Rose (eds), *Understanding the United Kingdom: The Territorial Dimension in United Kingdom Politics* (London: Macmillan).

Rose, R. and McAllister, I. (1990) *The Loyalties of Voters* (London: Sage).

Rudig, W., Bennie, L. and Franklin, M. (1992) 'Flash Party Dynamics – The Rise and fall of the British Green Party' (Chicago: American Political Science Association paper).

Rush, M. (ed.) (1990) *Parliament and Pressure Politics* (Oxford: Clarendon).

Russell, D. (1990) 'Equal Opportunities and the Politics of Race', *Talking Politics* 3:1, autumn.

Sabine, G. (1949) *A History of Political Thought* (London: Harrop).

Saggar, S. (1997) 'Racial Politics', *Parliamentary Affairs*, 50:4, October.

Sampson, A. (1962) *Anatomy of Britain* (New York: Harper and Row).

Sanders, D. (1990) *Losing an Empire, Finding a Role* (London: Macmillan).

Sanders, D. (1995) '"It's the Economy, Stupid": The Economy and Support for the Conservative Party, 1979–1994', *Talking Politics,* 7:3, spring.

Sanderson, M. (1994) 'Education and Social Mobility', in P. Johnson (ed.) *Twentieth Century Britain* (London: Longman).

Sartori, G. (1994) *Comparative Constitutional Engineering* (London: Macmillan).

Sedgemore, B. (1980) *The Secret Constitution* (London: Hodder and Stoughton).

Seldon, A. (1990) 'The Cabinet Office and Coordination', *Public Administration,* 68:1, spring.

Seldon, A. (1994) 'Policy Making and Cabinet', in D. Kavanagh and A. Seldon (eds), *The Major Effect* (London: Macmillan).

Seldon, A. (ed.) (1996) *How Tory Governments Fall* (London: Harper Collins).

Semetko, H.A., Scammell, M. and Goddard, P. (1997) 'Television', *Parliamentary Affairs,* 50:4, October.

Seyd, P. and Whiteley, P. (1992) *Labour's Grass Roots: The Politics of Party Membership* (Oxford: Clarendon).

Seymour-Ure, C. (1974) *The Political Impact of the Mass Media* (London: Constable).

Seymour-Ure, C. (1995) 'Prime Minister and the Public: Managing Media Relations', in D. Shell and R. Hodder-Williams (eds), *Churchill to Major: The British Prime Ministership since 1945* (London: Hurst)

Seymour-Ure, C. (1997) 'Editorial Opinion in the National Press', *Parliamentary Affairs,* 50:4, October.

Shaw, E. (1996) *The Labour Party since 1945* (Oxford: Blackwell).

Shell, D. (1992a) 'The House of Lords: The Best Second Chamber We Have Got?', in B. Jones and L. Robins (eds), *Two Decades in British Politics* (Manchester: Manchester University Press).

Shell, D. (1992b) *The House of Lords,* 2nd edn (London: Philip Allan).

Shell, D. (1995) 'The House of Lords', *Politics Review,* 6:3, February.

Smith, A.D. (1979) *Nationalism in the Twentieth Century* (Oxford: Martin Robertson).

Smith, A.D. (1991) *National Identity* (Harmondsworth: Penguin).

Smith, D. (1994) *North and South: Britain's Economic, Social and Political Divide*, 2nd edn (Harmondsworth: Penguin).

Smith, M., Smith, S. and White, B. (eds) (1988) *British Foreign Policy* (London: Unwin Hyman).

Smith, Martin J. (1992) 'CAP and Agricultural Policy', in D. Marsh and R.A.W. Rhodes (eds), *Implementing Thatcherite Policies* (Milton Keynes: Open University Press).

Smith, M.J. (1995) *Pressure Politics* (Manchester: Baseline Books).

Smith, M.J. and Ludlam, S. (eds) (1996) *Contemporary British Conservatism* (London: Macmillan).

Smith, M.J., Marsh, D. and Richards, D. (1995) 'Central Government Departments and the Policy Process', in R.A.W. Rhodes and P. Dunleavy (eds), *Prime Minister, Cabinet and Core Executive* (London: Macmillan).

Snyder, R.C., Bruck, H.W. and Sapin, B. (1960) 'Decision-Making as an Approach to the Study of International Politics', in S. Hoffman (ed.), *Contemporary Theory in International Relations* (Englewood Cliffs, NJ: Prentice-Hall).

Stanworth, P and Giddens, A. (1974) *Elites and Power in British Society* (Cambridge: Cambridge University Press).

Steed, M. (1986) 'The Core-Periphery Dimension of British Politics', *Political Geography Quarterly,* supplement to 5:4, October.

Stoker, G. (1991) *The Politics of Local Government* (London: Macmillan).

Stott, T. (1995–6) 'Evaluating the Quango Debate', *Talking Politics,* 8:2, winter.

Tapper, T. and Bowles, N. (1982) 'Working Class Tories: The Search for Theory', in L. Robins (ed.), *Topics in British Politics* (London: The Politics Association).

Tarling, R. and Dowds, L. (1997) 'Crime and Punishment', in R. Jowell, J. Curtice, A. Park, L .Brook, K. Thomson and C. Bryson (eds), *British Social Attitudes: The 14th Report* (Aldershot: Ashgate).

Taylor, G. (1995) 'Marxism', in D. Marsh and G. Stoker (eds), *Theory and Methods in Political Science* (London: Macmillan).

Thain, C. (1992) 'Government and the Economy' in B. Jones and L. Robins (eds), *Two Decades in British Politics* (Manchester: Manchester University Press).

Theakston, K. (1991–2) 'Ministers and Mandarins', *Talking Politics,* 4:2, winter.

Theakston, K. (1995a) 'Ministers and Civil Servants', in R. Pyper and L. Robins (eds), *Governing the UK in the 1990s* (London: Macmillan).

Theakston, K. (1995b) *The Civil Service since 1945* (Oxford: Blackwell).

Thomas, G. (1992) *Government and the Economy* (Manchester: Manchester University Press).

Thompson, K. (1993) 'Redressing Grievances: The role of the Ombudsman', *Talking Politics,* 6:1, autumn.

Tivey, L. and Wright, A. (eds) (1989) *Party Ideology in Britain* (London: Routledge).

Tomkins, A. (1996) 'The Scott Report: The Constitutional Implications', *Politics Review,* 6:1, September.

Tomkins, A. (1997) 'Intelligence and Government', *Parliamentary Affairs,* 50:1, January.

Tonge, J. and Geddes, A. (1997) 'Labour's Landslide? The British General Election of 1997', *ECPRN News,* 8:3.

Topf, R. (1989) 'Political Change and Political Culture in Britain, 1959–1987', in J.R. Giddens (ed.), *Contemporary Political Culture* (London: Sage Publications).

Townsend, P., Davidson, N. and Whitehead, M. (1990) *The Health Divide* (Harmondsworth: Penguin).

Troyna, B. and Williams, J. (1986) *Racism, Education and the State* (London: Croom Helm).

Van Mechelen, D. and Rose, R. (1986) *Patterns of Parliamentary Legislation* (Aldershot: Gower).

Vital, D. (1968) *The Making of British Foreign Policy* (Oxford: Oxford University Press).

Wade, H.W.R. (1977) (1988) *Administrative Law,* 6th edn (Oxford: Clarendon).

Waldegrave, W. (1993) *The Reality of Reform and Accountability in Today's Public Service* (London: Public Finance Foundation).

Wallace, M. and Jenkins, J.C. (1995) 'The New Class, Post-Industrialism and Neo-Corporatism: Three Images of Social Protest in the Western Democracies', in J. Jenkins and B. Klandermans (eds), *The Politics of Social Protest* (London: University College London Press).

Wallace, W. (1975) *The Foreign Policy Process in Britain* (London: RIIA/George Allen & Unwin).

Wallace, W. (1994) 'Foreign Policy', in D. Kavanagh and A. Seldon (eds), *The Major Effect* (London: Macmillan).

Wass, D. (1983) *Government and the Governed* (London: Routledge and Kegan Paul).

Watts, D. (1994) 'Europe's Bill of Rights', *Politics Review,* 3:4, April.

Watts, D. (1996) *Introducing the European Union* (Sheffield Hallam University, Davic Publications).

Watts, D. (1997) 'The Growing Attractions of Direct Democracy', *Talking Politics,* 10:1, autumn.

Weir, S. (1995) 'Quangos: Questions of Democratic Accountability', in F.F. Ridley and D. Wilson (eds), *The Quango Debate* (Oxford: Oxford University Press).

Welfare, D. (1992) 'An Anachronism with Relevance: The Revival of the House of Lords in the 1980s and its Defence of Local Government', *Parliamentary Affairs,* April.

Westlake, M. (1996–7) 'A Unique Constitutional Experiment', *Talking Politics,* 9:2, winter.

Whale, J. (1977) *The Politics of the Media* (London: Fontana).

Whiteley, P. and Winyard, S. (1987) *Pressure for the Poor* (London: Methuen).

Whiteley, P., Seyd, P. and Richardson, J. (1994) *True Blues: The Politics of Conservative Party Membership* (Oxford: Clarendon).

Widdicombe Report (1986) *The Conduct of Local Athority Business*: Report of the Committee of Inquiry into the Conduct of Local Authority Business, Cmnd. 9797 (London: HMSO).

Wilding, P. (1989–90) 'Equality in British Social Policy since the War', *Talking Politics*, 2:2, winter.

Wilding, P. (1993) 'Poverty and Government in Britain in the 1980s', *Talking Politics,* 5:3, summer.

Williams, T. and Abse, D. (1997) 'Birth of a Nation', The *Guardian,* July 26.

Wilson, D. (1990) 'More Power to the Centre? The Changing Nature of Central Government/Local Authority Relationships', *Talking Politics,* 3:1, summer.

Wilson, D. (1996) 'Quangos in British Politics', *Politics Review,* 6:1, September.

Wilson, D. (1997) *Local Government in the United Kingdom,* 2nd edn (London: Macmillan).

Wilson, D. and Game, C. (1997) *Local Government in the United Kingdom* (London: Macmillan).

Wilson, G.K. (1991) 'Prospects for the Public Service in Britain: Major to the Rescue?', *International Review of Administrative Sciences,* 57.

Witchert, S. (1991) *Northern Ireland since 1945* (London: Longman).

Wollstonecraft, M. (1792) (1982) *Vindication of the Rights of Woman,* ed. M. Kramnick (Harmondsworth: Penguin).

Wood, B. (1992) *The Politics of Health* (Manchester: Politics Association).

Wood, T. and Crawley, G. (1987) 'Equal Access to Political Power – A Principle in Danger', *Local Government Chronicle,* 21 August.

Woodhouse, D. (1994) *Ministers and Parliament: Accountability in Theory and Practice* (Oxford: Clarendon).

Woodhouse, D. (1997) 'Judicial/Executive Relations in the 1990s', *Talking Politics,* 10:1, autumn.

Wragg, T. (1992) 'Seeds of Destruction Being Sown in a Three-Class System', *The Observer,* May 17.

Wright, A. (1986) *British Socialism* (London: Longman).

Wright, A. (1993) *Citizens and Subjects* (London: Routledge).

Wright, A. (1997) 'Does Parliament Work?', *Talking Politics,* 9:3, spring.

Young, H. (1990) *One of Us,* expanded edn with new epilogue (London: Pan in association with Macmillan).

Index